Society and Government at Toulouse in the Age of the Cathars

John Hine Mundy

This monograph is designed to continue earlier explorations of the social, economic, political and religious history of Toulouse in the earliest period for which the archives house adequate documentary materials. A second and more interesting intention is to show that there was more to the successful spread of heresy or divergent thought, especially Catharism, than can be attributed to the purported intellectual or moral weaknesses of the Catholic communion or to the theological or mental attractiveness of Catharism and other dissident cults or religions present in the town and its region. The present book and several previous ones (two published by the Pontifical Institute) have noted that religious divergence expanded and flourished when the town's well-to-do were building a semi-popular oligarchy at the expense of local princely power, a movement reaching its apogee shortly before the end of the Albigensian Crusade in 1229. This epoch of political and religious freedom was brief because, immediately after that date, a combination of a newly introduced or expanded ecclesiastical repression and a revival of princely power both enriched Toulouse with new educational and charitable agencies and converted it into a community wedded to political monarchism and orthodox Catholicism.

The present monograph is divided into an introductory chapter, four parts and a conclusion. The introduction concerns the cycles of demographic, commercial and physical growth and retraction of the town. The subject of Part One is society or the evolution of classes and social orders — nobility, burghers, domestics and rural dependents — from the eleventh into the thirteenth century. Part Two describes the family in all the town's social classes, and the definition and progress of its institutions and nomenclature. Part Three deals with the introduction of the law against usury, the regulation of the credit system and the elaboration of corporate economic and social structures. Part Four examines the degree of self-government attained by 1229, its subsequent decline and the relationship of the orthodox and heterodox churches to this transformation. A concluding chapter advances analytical conjectures about the relationship of these manifestations. Thereafter follow nine appendices that provide evidence about family history, both Christian and Jewish, economic, political and religious configurations, ending with two calendars of archival documents used as proofs for the history of Toulousan society in the age when Catharism rose and fell.

STUDIES AND TEXTS 129

SOCIETY AND GOVERNMENT
AT TOULOUSE
IN THE AGE OF THE CATHARS

by

JOHN HINE MUNDY

Columbia University

PONTIFICAL INSTITUTE OF MEDIAEVAL STUDIES

DC
801
.T726
M85
1997

CANADIAN CATALOGUING IN PUBLICATION DATA

Mundy, John H. (John Hine), 1917-
   Society and government at Toulouse in the age of the Cathars

(Studies and texts, ISSN 0082-5328 ; 129)
Includes bibliographical references and index.
ISBN 0-88844-129-0

1. Toulouse (France) - History.   2. Toulouse (France) - Social
conditions.   3. Albigenses - France - Toulouse.
I. Pontifical Institute of Mediaeval Studies.   II. Title.
III. Series: Studies and texts (Pontifical Institute of Mediaeval
Studies) ; 129.

DC801.T726M85 1997   944'.862021   C97-931975-7

© 1997
Pontifical Institute of Mediaeval Studies
59 Queen's Park Crescent East
Toronto, Ontario, Canada M5S 2C4

Printed by
Edwards Brothers Incorporated, Michigan, USA

Contents

↓

Abbreviations

AADML	Angers, Archives départementales de Maine-et-Loire
Canso	*Chanson de la croisade albigeoise.* Eugène Martin-Chabot, ed. 3 vols. Paris, 1931-1973.
HGL	Devic and Vaissete, *Histoire générale de Languedoc.* 15 vols. Toulouse, 1872-1893.
MADTG	Montauban, Archives départementales de Tarn-et-Garonne aris, Archives nationales
PAN	Paris, Archives nationales
PBN	Paris, Bibliothèque nationale
Rolls Series	*Rerum Britannicarum medii aevi scriptores*
TAM	Toulouse, Archives municipales
TBM	Toulouse, Bibliothèque municipale

Maps

Preface

This book is designed to complete my attempt to show the social, economic and political context of religious divergence during the twelfth and thirteenth centuries in the town of Toulouse. Begun long ago at Columbia University, the study was inspired by Austin P. Evans, who together with Lynn Thorndike sponsored my graduate study. Having written a military history of the Albigensian Crusade for the master's degree, I was urged to work on a doctoral topic related to the social history of the Cathars. This subject was one of Evans' lifelong projects, but, having spent a busy life teaching, editing many volumes of the *Records of Civilization* and frequently serving as departmental chairman and university administrative officer, he died before getting to it, although he and Walter Wakefield, another of his students, together prepared an excellent volume of translated materials about heresy for the *Records*. It is to be noted in passing that Wakefield has done much work on the social aspect of this subject, especially in regard to the rural families involved in Catharism.

After defending and publishing my doctoral dissertation, my interest in this topic languished until the nineteen-sixties when Austin Evans died not long after his retirement. It was then that I discerned the full range of the work he had tried to accomplish, work in which he had been aided by a coadjutor named Merriam Sherwood (Mantz). A handsome woman, as I recall, Sherwood was a learned friend of Evans, knowledgeable about the archives in southern France and a good photographer who continued the work he had begun in the Midi. An active career as a translator in government service, however, long prevented her from doing much writing. Evans once told me that she eventually took early retirement with great joy and went to live in France, but sadly died shortly after setting up a new home somewhere in the Midi. The materials withdrawn by mutual agreement from their trove which she took to France to work on in retirement, it appears, have been lost. Before his death, Evans gave most of their remaining work to me. An example is the photographic copy (some of which I had myself made in 1947 to replace an earlier loss) of Manuscript 609 in the Municipal Library of Toulouse together with a transcription (part of which was also lost) made by the students in Evans' seminar. Other resources given me were the brief notes taken by him during his sabbaticals in France in the nineteen-twenties and thirties on the Collection Doat housed in the National Library in Paris. These notes also told me about a nearly complete, although disorderly, photographic copy of the pertinent volumes of the Col-

lection Doat as well as several other pieces of value acquired on his instructions and now housed in the Columbia University Library. Adding
these materials to those I had myself photographed in the archives of Montauban and Toulouse as well as much of the *Layettes du Trésor des chartes*
in the National Archives I had had photographed at Paris in 1947, I began
to see the possibility of undertaking the work these predecessors had thought
about so long before. To add to this, a trip to Toulouse in 1970 enabled me
to acquire good photographic copies (replacing spoiled ones done in 1947)
of an important document used only, to my knowledge, by Philippe Wolff.
Drafted in 1279, this royal diploma amnestied the inheritances of persons
whose property had been confiscated for heresy from the twelve-twenties
on. Since it contained the names of both women and men, the amnesty,
when linked to all the other material collected by Sherwood, Evans and me,
seemed to offer a way of examining the specific social groups involved in
Catharism and the balance of the sexes in this religion.

My first ventures into European and especially French archives and
libraries came after demobilization. A modest grant from Columbia University and a small supplemental one from the Social Science Research Council
permitted a visit to Catalonia, England and especially France in the fall of
1946 and the spring and summer of 1947 to look for documents illuminating
the economic and social history of the town of Toulouse in the age of the
Cathars. At Toulouse and even Paris, research conditions were ideal for a
student whose means barely sufficed to support him abroad for less than a
year. With a Leica camera and stand borrowed from Austin Evans, a black
bag, two developing cans, and several large canisters of war-surplus film,
I was able to offer the archives at Toulouse photographic services in exchange for easy access to the documents, something I then enjoyed on a
scale never again experienced. Even if facilities were rudimentary in the
attics of the Palais de Justice where the Departmental Archives were then
housed, there was usually electricity for illumination and, being allowed to
work among the shelved documents, I was able to photograph as much as
I wanted. A microfilm reader was needed to check the developed film and
a good one was available at the University, a machine to which I had access through the kindness of a dean and professor in the Faculty of Law,
Georges Boyer and Paul Ourliac. The situation at the Town Archives was
less happy because this repository was moved during the winter of 1947
from its handsome installation in the Donjon behind the Town Hall to the
basement of the Municipal Library where it now resides. What's more, the
running water needed for washing developing film was sometimes so short
in the spring of 1947 that roll after roll of film was spoiled. Some of the
work done then had to be repeated in later years (starting over a decade

later in 1958 in my first sabbatical), but at that later time I at least knew
what I was looking for. In the late spring and summer of 1947, access was
not quite so easy for researchers in the National Library and Archives at
Paris. Still, even there, large quantities of documents were more easily
available than has ever afterward been the case, because my remaining
rolls of undeveloped film were treasures to exchange for prompt examination and photography.

Things were changing rapidly even during 1946 and 1947 while I
worked in France. As archives and libraries recovered from wartime desue-
tude, preservation became more central than it had been before. At the
start, once convinced of one's bona fides, archival attendants sometimes
suggested taking documents home over the holidays, a practice I never
profited from because of the weight of my photographic equipment. Toward
the end, such permissiveness had vanished and, in view of the crowds that
nowadays engage in research, it is surely just as well that it has gone. It
was in those earlier years that I noted, photographed and had photographed
the bulk of what I have used ever since.

Parenthetically, however, the loss of this easy access cannot be much
lamented because another revolution was even then beginning or was visible
in the offing. Improved photographic and duplication services were being
rapidly introduced in French archives. By now, indeed, ever better forms
of duplication have resulted in the availability of relatively inexpensive
copies, ones whose clarity sometimes even surpasses that of the original
documents. An effect may be seen in teaching. Before the last great war,
I took a course in Latin paleography with Elias Lowe at the Morgan Library
in New York City. It was decidedly worthwhile, but the exercise a pupil
had in reading hands was pitifully limited by the fact that books containing
duplications were few and valuable and could be studied only in libraries.
Nowadays when that subject or diplomatics is taught, it costs little to give
students good, clear xerox copies of as many documents as can be read in
a semester's work, not to speak of exemplars of particular hands or periods
(with typed transcriptions) for their own later work and teaching.

I published my first book on Toulouse, *Liberty and Political Power*, in
1952. This was a standard "Verfassungsgeschichte" and barely touched on
the social history of the community. I was thus limited by the fact that the
materials for social history involved more microfilm reading than I had time
for during the early years of full-time teaching, which initially required
twelve hours a week in the classroom at Columbia University, not to speak
of frequent moonlighting at other institutions to make ends meet. Only now,
forty-odd years later, has time allowed me to assemble and partly publish

the requisite family histories and much else on this topic, although there are still rolls of film made in 1946 and 1947 I have barely looked at.

Quite apart from its lack of a foundation in social history, this early constitutional history needs rewriting, but my seventy-nine years and desire to work on other projects make it unlikely that I will do this. Some subjects treated earlier, however, have been rehearsed and improved in this volume. Chapter One below contains an expanded version of the layout and geography of Toulouse only touched on in the old book's first chapter. The history of the vicarage of Toulouse, a subject on which the older study was in error because of a lack of material, has been reworked in Chapters Three and Thirteen below. An improved discussion of the election of the consuls – Toulouse's board of magistrates – is found in Chapter Thirteen, and it and Chapters Fourteen and Fifteen and the Conclusion replace and expand the brief Conclusion and Epilogue of the earlier study. Lastly, the consular lists issued in my earlier book have been extended from 1229 to 1280, and the ones before 1229 are occasionally enlarged.

* * *

As a teacher, I have had students who went abroad to do research, and not a few, however good their work, were lonely and unhappy. My reinforcement in Toulouse and Paris in 1946 and 1947 was my wife. An outgoing person forever being stopped on the street by strangers seeking help, she straightway volunteered to help the Unitarian Service Committee and there met and became close to Persis Miller and Dolores Bellido, the latter one of our few friends from Toulouse still alive. She also struck up close and invaluable relationships in Toulouse with Suzanne and Pierre Baroussel, Odette and André de Bercegol, Suzanne and Jacques de Lamaze and, in Paris, with Lotte and Max Brandel and an admirable landlord, Jean de Nomazy, most of whom are now gone.

The staffs of the archives and libraries visited for this study are to be thanked. Most of those in office in 1946-1947 have died. The only one of that original cadre with whom I am still in touch is a friend, Odon de Saint-Blanquat, retired archivist of the town of Toulouse. About a decade ago, when I still traveled to work in Toulouse, the other most hospitable such officer was Pierre Gérard, now the general director of the regional archives of the Midi and the Pyrenees, who is remembered with gratitude. So also is Philippe Wolff, a longtime friend and retired professor in the faculty of letters of the University of Toulouse who is now perched in Andorra midway between two of his favorite cities, Barcelona and Toulouse.

Finally, those who produced this book were both generous and obviously indispensable. First among these are the reverend fathers and secular professors of the Pontifical Institute of Mediaeval Studies. The book is the third issued by the Pontifical Institute's press directed by Dr. Ron B. Thomson. Lastly, because publication requires money, I should not only thank the Institute for its support of this and my other books but also name friends who have contributed sizeable sums for this volume. Half of the required subsidy was provided by Catherine Brown and Harris Snyder Choate of Tucson, Arizona, one of whom I knew when in the U.S. Army in the last great war. The other half was kindly granted by a distinguished colleague here at Columbia University, Paul Oskar Kristeller, Woodbridge Professor Emeritus of Philosophy. Lastly, thanks are owed to Rachel Hermann, a perceptive friend from Chautauqua, New York, and to Jean Hoff, the editor assigned by the Pontifical Institute.

Mary MacKay MacDonald
and
William Henry Hine

Introduction

This is the fourth book I have written about the town of Toulouse in the twelfth and thirteenth centuries. Published in 1954, 1985 and 1990, the first three were a constitutional history of the town, a study of the individuals and classes involved in Catharism and other deviant religion, and an examination of the relations between men and women in that community.[1] Among other things, what I wanted to prove was that there was more to the implanting and repression of Catharism, the prime alternate religion to Catholicism in this area, and other divergent beliefs than can be explained purely in terms of the intellectual aspects of religion.

Although religion is sometimes thought to be divorced from the material side of human life, most agree that it is interwoven with society and politics. Specific classes ranging all the way from rich women to adventurous merchants have been fingered as those most attracted to critical or divergent religious thought by thinkers of almost every ideology. Célestin Douais, a professor at the Catholic Institute at Toulouse and eventually bishop of Beauvais, correctly showed that many rural baronial and knightly families leaned toward Catharism. Others including myself pursued the lead of this scholar to graft motives onto the minds of these long departed gentlefolk. Twelfth century landed aristocrats, it was felt, suffered both from the rising economic power of the urban bourgeoisie and also from their own retrograde behavior, their indifference to estate economy, for example, or their excessive divisions of family property generation after generation. Some have conjectured that landed families, incapable of handling their resources, favored Catharism and seceded from Catholicism, motivated by a desire to escape clerical taxation, notably the tithe.

---

[1]*Liberty and Political Power in Toulouse 1050-1230, The Repression of Catharism at Toulouse: The Royal Diploma of 1279* and *Men and Women at Toulouse in the Age of the Cathars*. A correction of an egregious error in the latter book is recorded in Chapter Three, note 81 below.

Subsequent work on urban participation in heresy and hostility to tithes, however, convinced me that, before the formalization of social relationships in the thirteenth century, upper class townsfolk shared economic attitudes and behavior (although not interests) with rural notables, and that urban persons of all classes did not materially differ from those of the countryside regarding either the tithe or religion.[2] In spite of downturns, furthermore, one of which took place during the twenty year Albigensian Crusade (1209-1229), it is sure that this two hundred year period witnessed great economic growth everywhere in Toulouse and its region. Although rapid growth always harms those wedded to old ways of investment and production, and especially those beyond their economic prime, and although contemporary polemic bewailed change and new wealth, no evidence is available to show that any one class, high or low, rural or urban, was disproportionately damaged or advantaged. To conclude, the durable liberal and Marxian vision of the power of the rising bourgeoisie and the feckless incapacity of the nobility is surely overstated if not wholly mistaken.

Another equally persistent view is that, although religious beliefs influence society (have not Cathars been decried as antisocial by many polemicists, both Christian and secular?), they themselves have little direct relationship to the societies from which they draw their sustenance. One may well agree that religion, being an individual's attempts to define his or her relation to the deity or nature, is like other ideologies initially free and not bound by any particular social structure. When transmitted from one to another person, however, religious ideas immediately become embedded in social contexts that limit or forward them. Such being a reasonable understanding, I began to search for the social contexts surrounding both the increase of Catharism during the twelfth century and the repression of this belief during the next hundred years. What I think I found was that the rise and fall of divergent religious thought was paralleled or accompanied by radical changes in the economy, politics and society at Toulouse.[3] These were:

1) An initially open and flexible society centered on male-headed (agnatic) families evolved into a formalized structure of social classes and orders by which the family was protected but to which it was also subordinated.[4]

---

[2]Tithes were discussed in my *Repression of Catharism*, pp. 54-61, and are touched on several times in this book, especially in Chapter Eleven and the Conclusion.

[3]This argument reformulates the statement in my *Men and Women at Toulouse*, pp. 2-3.

[4]The relationship between the sexes in and out of the family is treated in ibid.

2) An individualist economic structure became a regulated and corporate one characterized by the prohibition of usury, economic casuistry, the multiplication of economic police and the growth of craft and trade gilds.

3) Small and often private and secular charitable institutions and actions gave way to ecclesiastically regulated charity on a large scale directed especially toward the needs of the poorer classes, to the indigent, sick, aged and orphaned.[5]

4) Private education, scribal culture and lay poetry were supplemented and outclassed by the expansion of mendicant preaching, the development of parish schools and university professional schooling, especially in law.[6]

5) On the way to becoming an oligarchic republic, Toulouse became increasingly self-governing from 1189 up to the Peace of Meaux-Paris in 1229 (hereafter simply Peace of Paris) wherein the defeat of the Midi was recorded at the end of the Albigensian Crusade. Renewed princely authority thereafter gradually eroded town liberty, especially under its first Capetian prince from 1249 to 1271, at which date the town became directly subject to France's kings.[7]

Designed to examine the program sketched above, the present book begins with an introductory chapter sketching the geographic, economic and demographic "mise en scène" for this history. Thereafter the large divisions of the book rehearse material about the propositions listed above in the following order:

Part One on society treats subjects found in all five propositions. Propositions 1, 2 and 5 are dealt with in Part Two on the family, Part Three on the economy and Part Four on government. As stated above, I have treated propositions 3 and 4 in published articles.

---

[5]In my "Charity and Social Work in Toulouse 1100-1250," *Traditio* 22 (1966) 203-288.

[6]Parts of this history are sketched in my "Village, Town, and City in the Region of Toulouse," in *Pathways to Medieval Peasants*, ed. J.A. Raftis, pp. 142-190, "Urban Society and Culture: Toulouse and Its Region," in *Renaissance and Renewal in the Twelfth Century*, ed. Robert L. Benson and Giles Constable with Carol D. Lanham, pp. 229-247, "The Parishes of Toulouse," *Traditio* 46 (1991) 171-204, and my "The Origins of the College of Saint-Raymond at the University of Toulouse," in *Philosophy and Humanism*, ed. Edward P. Mahoney, pp. 454-461. Unknown to me at the time, an excellent article on the same topic and publishing some of the same document was issued in 1975, the year before mine was printed, by Dossat, "L'Université et inquisition à Toulouse: La fondation du Collège Saint-Raymond (1250)," in *Eglise et hérésie en France au XIIIe siècle*, pp. 227-238.

[7]This topic was touched on in my *Liberty and Political Power*.

I have adopted two views based on the available sources and past scholarship. The first is that the Cathar religion had no defined charitable, economic, political or social theory. Of all the religions of its period, of which
the major ones were Catholicism and the Waldensian sects, Catharism was
the one most devoid of social doctrine, an absence that made it into the
most purely spiritual of all available cults and religions. Putting aside its
dualism, a gnostic vision about the conflict between good, evil and human
free will that has enjoyed a perennial appeal, Catharism's attraction differed
from Catholicism's because it demanded no repeated penitential obedience
or service during a believer's lifetime: it required simply – a flimsy adverb
given the context – a pledge by a dying person to forgive all enemies and
sin no more. In this regard, Catharism was retrograde, turned, that is,
against the direction in which the penitential discipline of Europe's Catholic
church was evolving. In brief, although requiring severe deprivation and
self-mortification from its clergy or leaders ("perfecti" or "perfecte" who
were, as the Catholic inquisitors said, *the* "heretici"), this divergent cult
rested rather lightly on the social conscience of its believers ("credentes").
In this way, it differed radically from Catholicism's police-like intervention
into private lives and the austere apostolic morality of the Waldensians.

The second view is that the characteristics of, and the changes in, the
economic, political and social life of Toulousans listed above cannot be
proved to have caused either the adoption of Catharism or the triumph over
that faith by what churchfolk called orthodoxy. Catharism did not favor political republicanism and had no conflict with monarchy. Its leaders never
uttered a syllable in favor of an unregulated economy, said nothing about
usury, nor advanced any special teaching about charity. Although, like several dissident sects or religions of the time, they allowed women a somewhat more active role than did Catholics, Cathars did not protest the mascu-
line definition of the family. Such being the case, my intention is to show
that Catharism's emergence as an alternate religion in Toulouse was consonant with the social patterns listed or sketched above, and its extirpation
consonant with their disappearance or transformation.

This limits what may be said about the social background of divergent
religious thought. All it permits is an assertion that the relative lack of police and regulation by ecclesiastical and secular government characteristic
of the late twelfth century allowed substantial groups in society to believe
that they could choose between religious expressions and hence permitted
Catharism and other less radically secessionist divergent groups to live side
by side with Catholicism. This relative freedom was paralleled by a similar
lack of control and regulatory apparatus in economic and political spheres.
One may therefore conclude that in an age when, in spite of difficulties,

society generally expanded and was ruled relatively pacifically by patrician and landed oligarchs, an alternate religion could flourish for a time. Many, it seems, were attracted to thought diverging from the orthodoxy of the majority and, blessed by relatively happy circumstances, may well have imagined that they could indulge their fancy and even secede from the established church.

Such a suggestion flies in the face of a common view that heresy grew because of clerical luxury and wealth and dereliction of duty. As I have elsewhere several times argued, this opinion seems wide of the mark. Undoubtedly, ammunition for criticism by laymen and radical clergy was provided by the incapacity of the clerical order to reach the demanding level of clerical moral legislation and exclusive devotion to duty urged by reform propaganda from the time of the Gregorians. In their attempt to destroy Europe's state churches, Gregorian ideologues used high ideals of liberty and reform in order to condemn resisters, conjuring up imagined worlds of the virtuous seeking no recompense, of brotherhood, humility, poverty and of spiritual freedom from the flesh (family) and from usury (the power of wealth). Rhetorical aggression of this kind worked its usual magic because ordinary churchmen, both Gregorian and anti-Gregorian, were forced to subscribe to ideals they were incapable of achieving by layfolk excited by what they were not themselves obliged to try.

So deeply imprinted in the minds of post-Gregorian clergy and laity were these grand objectives that, although largely beyond the reach both of those who preached and those who listened, future generations employed this vocabulary when speaking of religion and the church. Sincere critics and secessionist heretics picked up these strained convictions and used them to castigate the orthodox clergy. As significantly, many who were relatively indifferent to religion or prescribed morality were also armed with foolproof weapons with which to subvert ecclesiastical authority. Lastly, these exaggerated standards were everywhere useful to ecclesiastical authorities, including the popes, because they helped subordinate and browbeat other clergy, not to speak of the laity, in the name of reform. One wonders, indeed, if moralization demanding the impossible will ever be shunned: it is surely the only unanswerable ideology.

As everybody knows, the Cathar religion failed and, of the first great wave of medieval dissent of which it was part, only the durably popular movement of the Waldensians persisted into modern times. What the orthodox called heresy nevertheless grew apace in later ages to split the institutional church apart a little over two centuries after the events treated here. Aside from the natural and economic events that helped precipitate this huge change, the continued expansion of learning and law in the later middle ages meant that divergent thought became not only more subtle, but also more camouflaged. Unlike Catharism that, significant exceptions apart, was a religion limited to, and defined by, nonprofessional layfolk, these later dissenters remained in the "cursus honorum" of the church and peopled the newly founded legal, medical and theological faculties of the expanding universities. Whereas Cathars (although convinced of being truly Christian) were determined to secede from the orthodox communion, these later sectaries or critics cleaved to the institutional church and to the increasingly powerful secular professions, where they were able to gain a firm grip on the minds of powerful contemporaries before the disruptive qualities of their teaching became evident. Radical reformers were usually aided, also, by the fact that the clerical order had summoned, indeed, had had to summon, laymen to advance its cause from Gregorian days to the repression of the later heresies. And those called on to use their pens, swords or tongues usually want to decide why they should. As many have noted, the enhancement of the lay role in religion empowered the secular professions and governments to redefine Latin Christianity at the beginning of modern times.

However likely they may be, these conjectures clearly transcend the limits of what can be proved in this book. Instead I shall try to prove the reality of the changes sketched in the five programmatic paragraphs recited above which are, one hopes, more amenable to scientific treatment. Before launching that enterprise, however, the reader will be given a brief description of the area in which the town of Toulouse lies and also a sketch of its geography.

B. TOULOUSE AND THE TOULOUSAIN

Men and women, however spirited and however exquisite their arts and intellects, are bound by the specific geography in which they live. Toulousans inhabit a wide plain located on either side of the fast-flowing Garonne river. This broad amphitheater is bounded by the hills of Gascony to the west, the gradients and canyons of Quercy and the Albigeois leading to the Massif Central to the north and east; to the south, after the ample plains of the Lauragais and Comminges, by the sub-Pyrenean depression and behind it the Pyrenees themselves, whose snow-capped curtain can be seen in winter from the town itself. Maps are in order, and will be simple sketches.

Map 1: The Region of Toulouse
The inner dotted line around the town roughly delineates the area administered by the consuls, the board of magistrates elected by the town, called in this period the "dex" and afterward the "gardiage"; the outer dotted line,

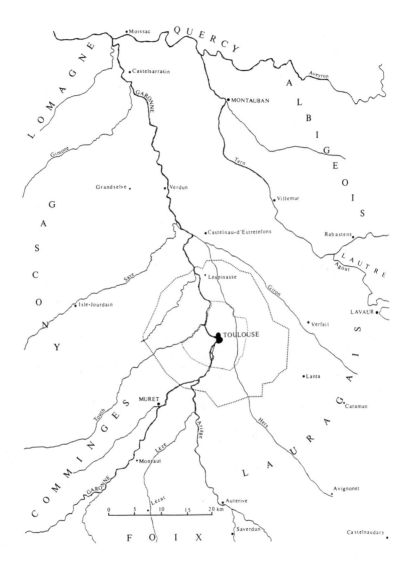

MAP 1 THE REGION OF TOULOUSE

MAP 2 THE TOWN OF TOULOUSE

the vicarage administered by the count of Toulouse's vicar, an officer briefly and partly subject to the consuls before 1229.

Map 2: The Town of Toulouse
This map is a tracing taken from the Plan Saguet of 1750. It is roughly
aligned on a north-south axis, the most northerly gates of the Bourg being
those of Lascrosses and Arnaud-Bernard. The town in 1750 differed from
that of the twelfth and thirteenth centuries in many respects, of which the
following are the most notable:

> Saint-Cyprien was not fortified until the Hundred Years War and hence
> in the time treated here was an open suburb or "barrium" like that of the
> Château Narbonnais or Saint-Michel south of town.
>
> The broad bridge across the Garonne river marked on the map (now
> called the Pont Neuf and still extant) is an early modern construction. The
> history of the medieval bridges will be sketched in Chapter One.

Notable locations and monuments of the town are identified on this
sketch map by numbers, and the numbers read from west to east and north
to south:

1　Lascrosses Gate
2　Arnaud-Bernard Gate
3　Saint-Julien church in the parish of Saint-Sernin
4　The Bazacle, site of the famous mills, a small castle and probably the
　　head of the Bazacle Bridge
5　Saint-Sernin, the basilica of the canons-regular and a parish church
6　Pousonville Gate
7　Saint-Pierre-des-Cuisines, a parish church and priory of the Benedic-
　　tines of Saint-Pierre of Moissac
8　Matabiau Gate
9　The Franciscans
10　The Taur, a parish church under the patronage of Saint-Sernin
11　Saint-Nicholas, a parish church under the patronage of the Daurade
12　The Dominicans
13　The Portaria, having, to its east on the next block, the "Palatium" or
　　Town Hall (the later Capitole), and, on its west, the church of Saint-
　　Quentin under the patronage of Saint-Sernin. The Portaria was named
　　after a Roman gate that stood in this place during the middle ages. The
　　gate was part of a dismantled wall that divided the City from the Bourg
　　called the Saracen Wall, remnants of which are marked on the Saguet
　　map and this sketch map
14　The New or Daurade Bridge constructed in the twelfth century
15　The Bourguet-Nau

16 Saint-Pierre-Saint-Martin in the parish of the Daurade
17 The Villeneuve Gate in the quarter of the same name in the Bourg
18 The Daurade, a parish church, monastery and priory of the Benedictines of Saint-Pierre of Moissac
19 Saint-Roman or Saint-Rome, a church in the parish of Saint-Étienne given to the Dominicans in 1216
20 The Montardy Square
21 The Old Bridge
22 The square and market of La Pierre and the church of Saint-Pierre-Saint-Géraud in the parish of Saint-Étienne
23 The square and market of Montaygon and the church of Saint-Georges in the parish of Saint-Étienne
24 The Neuve Gate
25 The Dalbade parish church under the patronage of the Daurade
26 The street of Joutx-Aigues on which the synagogue was located
27 The church of Saint-Victor in the parish of Saint-Étienne and the square called Rouaix
28 The Baragnon Cross
29 The Hospital of Saint John of Jerusalem and church of Saint-Remésy or Saint-Rémésy
30 The cathedral and parish church of Saint-Étienne and, across the cloister to the south, the church of Saint-Jacques
31 The Templars
32 The Carmelites
33 Saint-Barthélemy church of the parish of Saint-Étienne, once called Sainte-Marie of the Palace
34 The Narbonne Castle (Château Narbonnais) or "Palatium"
35 Montgaillard Gate
36 Montoulieu Gate
37 Saint-Michel, a church in the parish of Saint-Étienne that derived its dedication from the chapel of the Château Narbonnais and eventually gave its name to the "barrium" or quarter in which it was located. Saint-Michel's church was not built until 1331, and, before that time, the quarter was called that of the Château Narbonnais or of Sainte-Catherine.

For these and other details about the town and its region, see Chapter One below.

1

Population, Economy and Geography

A. DEMOGRAPHY AND TRADE

The small section in the Introduction of this book called Intentions repeats what everybody knows, namely that Toulouse, already expanding in the eleventh century, grew throughout the twelfth and thirteenth centuries. The normal proofs for assertions of this kind are population statistics, evidence of physical enlargement and the construction of facilities for cult, charity, commerce, education and traffic.

Philippe Wolff, basing his count on tax figures for the Bourg for the year 1332, estimated the population of the City and Bourg of Toulouse, the two parts of the town, at about 32,000.[1] A later calculation, that of Jean-Noël Biraben, was based on Wolff's statistics but argued that the town was larger, having 45,000 to 50,000 inhabitants.[2] Whatever the true figure, these numbers represent the peak of Toulouse's population after nearly three centuries of growth. Growth, however, as modern experience has informed historians, is not continuous and, although figures are lacking, a disruptive twenty year period like that of the Albigensian Crusade from 1209 to 1229 must have seen a sharp, if temporary, drop in population.

For this period, the extent of Toulouse's trade and industry is hard to estimate. Looking at the relatively rich materials available for the fourteenth and fifteenth centuries, Wolff evaluated the balance between urban industrial production and that done in the countryside. Itself limited by a necessarily non-statistical quality, work of his kind cannot be done for the twelfth and

---

[1] *Les "estimes" Toulousaines des XIVe et XVe siècles*, pp. 54-55. Taxpayer lists of this kind are usually said to under-represent non-payers or "nichils" and these ones may also not have included the inhabitants in the suburbs or "barria" around the walls. For the division of the town into the City and Burg, see pp. 17 and 20 below.

[2] "La population de Toulouse au xive et xve siècles," *Journal des Savants* (1964) 300.

thirteenth because of the nature of the sources. As sketched in an earlier work, notarial registers have not been preserved until the fourteenth century. The documentation for the two hundred previous years therefore depends largely on rare and succinct law books, a few fragmentary investigations dated to the late twelve-hundreds and especially on acts emanating from private persons that transferred real property into ecclesiastical hands. Rich though these charters are in regard to family history and conceptions of property, they constitute an extremely limited base for economic history.[3] About the best that can be done with such exiguous material is to assert what is obvious, namely that the craft and trades were growing throughout the period discussed in this book. Ever larger lists of the names of trades and crafts become available as well as, starting in 1229, the first evidence of craft organization.[4] Substantial evidence of industrial production and exportation, however, awaits the next century.

That being said, it is obvious from the physical growth of the town (to be explored below) that Toulouse's economy generally expanded during much of the twelfth and thirteenth centuries. Profits were usually to be made in both town and countryside. A local millionaire like Pons de Capitedenario, for example, invested in agriculture, animal husbandry and urban real estate and was also a moneylender for both individuals and institutions, though how large a part of his activity that constituted cannot now be discerned. In later life, he seems to have pulled in his horns. Behaving then almost like an ecclesiastical institution, he seems to have preferred the solid but modest income acquired from urban rental property, construction materials and animal husbandry.[5]

Many Toulousans were more adventurous than Pons late was in life. In the early fourteenth century, Toulousan moneylenders and merchants are seen working the region around Foix, and people from that region are known to have banked in Toulouse.[6] Even earlier many had gone further afield in search of wealth, some to the Champagne fairs. In May 1216, a public notary at Toulouse wrote up an act that had been dictated to another Toulousan notary named Arnold Barravus six years or more previously in the town of Troyes. The act recorded the gift of family property as an inheritance to Peter Raymond de Tauro by his father of the same name and

[3]The sources are described in my *Men and Women*, pp. 8-17.

[4]A list of early trade and craft titles is found in my *Liberty and Political Power*, pp. 273-275, notes 22 and 23, and see Chapter Twelve below.

[5]His history is in my *Repression of Catharism*, pp. 155-167.

[6]See Chapter Eleven, p. 202 below.

his mother Ademara.[7] In the years of the Albigensian Crusade, the count of the Champagne also took under his protection the wife of a Peter Raymond "de Tolosa" (probably the one called "de Tauro" above) and a Rainaldus Signarius. Toulousans were undoubtedly well known there: a letter from Pope Gregory IX to Thibault IV in 1227 asked the count to deny people from that rebellious city entry into, and residence in, his territories, but a year later an A. Aimeri[cus] from Toulouse is listed as one of his creditors.[8] To turn far to the south, in 1231 a William Hugh de Tolosa tried to found a consulate or "fondaco" in Lérida in Catalonia to be headed by four Toulousans, who were eventually to be replaced by nominees proposed by the consuls of Toulouse. In 1249 and 1259, as will be seen again, the Jew Astrug from Toulouse was lending money in nearby Llobregat.[9] A final example is Bernard Raymond Baranonus of the Bourg, sometimes called "de Burdegala" because he resided for a time at Bordeaux. He returned to Toulouse in the twelve-sixties and in 1274 testified to the Inquisition about his long contact with Waldensians in Toulouse and Bordeaux. In that year and the next, also, he was obliged to sell his tolls in the Bourg of Toulouse to the count's government in return for a substantial annual rent of sixty-five shillings on the Bastide of Castillon near Cépet north of town.[10]

What Baranonus was doing in Bordeaux is not known, but he could very easily have been in the wine trade. Twelfth century charters about farming around Toulouse mention new vineyards or "maloles" quite as frequently as vineyards or "vinee," so much so that modern historians believe that the production of wine for export was being introduced at just this time. They are probably right. Surveying the Toulousan and English documents used in the family histories in my *Repression of Catharism* one finds no less

[7]Published in my *Liberty and Political Power*, pp. 209-210, No. 16, original in E 569 (May 1216).

[8]Arbois de Joubainville, *Histoire des ducs et des comtes de Champagne* 5: Nos. 1521 (dated 1222 ?) for the wife, and 1911 (June 1229) for Signarius; ibid., No. 1803 (December 1227) for the papal letter; and ibid. 4: 841-842 (dated 1228 and 1229) listing creditors, mostly Sienese, an abbot, two Jews and some laymen from Besançon, Cahors, Lyon and Toulouse, the latter being the smallest, having invested 249 pounds of Tours.

[9]Lladonasa Pujol, "Marchands Toulousains à Lérida au XIIe et XIIIe siècles," *Annales du Midi* 70 (1958) 227-229 about the "alfonduk" and the "capitulum civitatis Tolose et suburbii."

[10]Baranonus' history is described in my *Repression of Catharism*, pp. 134-135 and touched on again on p. 206 below.

than seven Toulousans, some of them notables like Bertrand de Palatio and Hugh de Roaxio, of the patrician family of that name, who, testifying in 1279 to 1283, had been in the business for thirty-five years.[11] Lastly, a Toulousan named William Molini petitioned Count Alphonse of Poitiers in 1270 for help because the Lord Edward (King Edward I in 1272) had confiscated sixty "tonelli" of wine to pay some merchants at Waterford in Ireland, an unhappy event, according to an excessively succinct text, precipitated by a theft of forty marks sterling by a knight from Saintonge from some Dublin merchants.[12]

Wine was the main export commodity, but woad or the dyestuff pastel was being introduced and had begun to follow the same profitable route northward to the Atlantic. A protest made to Alphonse of Poitiers by the parishioners of Toulouse against unjust clerical taxation between 1251 and 1255 concerned the "primiceria de pastelleria," as well as the same levied on wine and linen.[13] The issue was not solved by the count's finding in favor of the laity, which he did, because in 1308, tithes on woad were still being fought over by the consuls of Toulouse and the canons of Saint-Sernin.[14] In short, during the period treated in this book, commerce flourished and two major export crops, one well established and the other being implanted, are attested in the sources.

B. Expansion and Contraction

Significant exceptions apart, Toulouse expanded into the mid-fourteenth century and fits the pattern of expansion and contraction familiar to today's historians of western Europe in the middle ages. Evidence of this can be seen in the history of the town's bridges. Marked on the map of Toulouse in the Introduction as number 21, the so-called Old Bridge was built at an

---

[11]In my *Repression of Catharism*, see Jordan de Castronovo or Caramanno, p. 201; Bertrand Bequini, p. 250; Raymond Arnold de Ponte, p. 250; Hugh de Roaxio, p. 261, Bernard de Roaxio, p. 265; Arnold Unde and Bertrand de Palatio, pp. 265 and 291.

[12]*Enquêtes administratives d'Alfonse de Poitiers*, ed. Fournier and Guébin, No. 128, roll of parliament held at Toulouse in April-May 1270: no. 386: "apud civitatem Waterfort in Ybernia 60 tonnellos vini, quos ibi conduxerat dictus Guillelmus causa mercature, et tradidit pro emenda dictos tonellos quibusdam mercatoribus dicte civitatis, pro eo quod Gaufridus de Talneio, miles Xanctonie, abstulit quibusdam mercatoribus Ybernie, civitatis Develina, 40 marchas sterlingorum et amplius, unde petit apponi consilium." Alphonse told him to take it up with Louis IX at Aiguesmortes.

[13]PAN, J 318 78, published in *Layettes du Trésor* 2: 306ff., No. 2428, 308b.

[14]Saint-Sernin 689 (21, 73, 6) (October 1308), where a syndic "dominorum de capitulo regie urbis et suburbii Tholose" appeared in the vicar's court.

undetermined date across the Garonne river somewhere on or very near the northern end of the Ile-de-Tounis.[15] The New Bridge was that of the Daurade, further downstream; it was erected after the town and the prior of the Daurade were granted the right to build a tollfree bridge by Count Alphonse-Jordan sometime between 1119 or 1123 and 1130.[16] The Daurade Bridge had not been opened to traffic in 1152 when an official document refers to a fruit market "ad pontem," thus implying that the town still had only one bridge.[17] Later documents show that this new bridge had opened by 1180.[18] Within a few years, texts attesting the bridge multiply.[19]

A third bridge, this one named after the Bazacle, was constructed sometime after 1212.[20] Although projected or in the process of being built, the Bazacle Bridge had probably not been completed in September 1217 when Count Raymond VI entered Toulouse from the south by fording the river at the Bazacle.[21] By 1218 this bridge, that "of Saint-Pierre de Bazacle," benefited from a bequest.[22] According to the verse history of the Albigensian Crusade here identified as the Canso, the new facility was integrated into the defenses of the town in 1219.[23] The bridge probably left the right

---

[15]Wolff, *Commerces et marchands de Toulouse (vers 1350–vers 1450)*, p. 92, conjectures it was on the location of the present Pont Neuf, whereas, following a document of 1271 seen below on p. 15, I put it slightly to the south, but archeology will someday settle the question.

[16]An undated original privilege is in Daurade 145 and was published by Catel, *Histoire des comtes, avec quelques traitez et chroniques anciennes, concernans la mesme histoire*, p. 194. Mentioned in the document, Alphonse-Jordan was in Toulouse in 1119 and 1120 but was not fully in power there until 1122 or 1123, and Raymond, prior of the Daurade, died in 1130 accoding to *Gallia Christiana* 13: col. 101.

[17]TAM, AA 1 4 (1152 no month mentioned).

[18]Ibid. 19 and PAN, JJ 21, fol. 39v (both dated November 1180) referring to a street "versus pontem veterem," thus implying that there was a new one.

[19]Ibid., fol. 41v (March 1182 or 1183) refers to a stretch of the Garonne bank between the New Bridge and Saint-Michel "de Castello" south of the City. TAM, AA 1 22 (April 1199) speaks of mills located "inter pontem novam et pontem veterem."

[20]Testamentary bequests show that it was not there in 1208 and 1212: see Appendix 8, Nos. 27 (January 1208) and 34 (June 1212) where testators mention only the Old and New Bridges.

[21]William of Puylaurens, *Chronique*, ed. Duvernoy, p. 101: the count and his party entered "non ponte, sed vado sub Vadaculo." The picture is rounded out by the poet's remark in the *Canso*, ed. Martin-Chabot, 2: 276, line 62, that the party "came out from the water": "E can eison de l'aiga son e·l prat restortiz ... ."

[22]Appendix 8, No. 41 (August 1218) granted sixpence each to the Old, New and Bazacle Bridges.

[23]*Canso*, ed. Martin-Chabot, 3:316, line 100: "pont del Bazagle qu'es faitz novelamens."

bank from somewhere in the Bazacle toward the church of Saint-Pierre-des-Cuisines.[24] It reached across the Garonne river to a place somewhat above the hospital called La Grave in Saint-Cyprien on the left bank. In 1228 the Daurade granted the Hospital of Novellus a stretch of the left bank between the "barbacana pontis novi" and that of the Bazacle Bridge, describing the latter as running from the Grave Hospital to the head of the Bazacle Bridge.[25] Because, as seen above, Raymond VI's party had waded the Garonne river in this region, the bridge very likely followed the diagonal path across the river traced in part by the later Bazacle barrage.[26] Whatever its precise location, the early Bazacle Bridge was a temporary construction. A testament in 1253 recorded the bequest by a wealthy smith of a mass of bricks to be used in building the "first pillar" of the bridge.[27]

A fourth bridge, called Comminges, was built in the late thirteenth century. Jules Chalande, the historian of the streets of the City, conjectured that it was one of two spans that merely crossed the branch of the Garonne that separated Tounis from the bulk of the City.[28] Wolff rightly dismissed Chalande's opinion by noting that an arbitral decision of 1284 describes the span as crossing the Garonne.[29] In 1322 a gild statute stated that fines levied on butchers were assigned, half to the denouncer, and half to the four bridges over the Garonne: the Old, New, Bazacle and Comminges.[30]

[24]Documents relating to this end of the bridge clarify little. Arnold Guilabertus sold the town the "castrum" of the Bazacle in TAM, AA 1 37 (March 1205) and surrendered his rights to the emplacement of the Bazacle Bridge in ibid. 74 (December 1222), calling it all that he had "in illo loco in quo pons Basaclei est constructus."

[25]Daurade 68 (September 1228): "de superiori capite cornu muris eiusdem barbacane quod est usque Hospitale de Grava usque ad aliud capite cornu muris eiusdem barbacane quod est usque pontem Badaculi ... ."

[26]The barrage at the time of the Saguet map lay below the Grave, but earlier maps show it above and I follow them.

[27]Appendix 8, No. 84 (August 1253).

[28]Histoire des rues de Toulouse, p. 149. Chalande was reacting against the contrary opinion of Alexandre Du Mège, a wildly inaccurate historian who published in the period 1846 to 1848.

[29]Commerces et marchands de Toulouse, p. 92. The document of 1284 is in the archives of the mills of the Château Narbonnais presently housed in the Town Archives at Toulouse, and the pertinent passage reads: "per quem tenditur de carreria Convenarum versus Sanctum Cyprianum." Wolff also added another document of a much later time, namely 1414, stating that the bridge was useful for defending the town.

[30]Mulholland, Early Gild Records of Toulouse, pp. 66 (dated March and April 1322): half of the fines to the "denunciatori et medietas operibus pontium novi, veteris et de Badacleo et Convenarum supra flumen Garonne constitutorum aplicetur."

Although wrong about location, Chalande may well have been right when he conjectured that the Comminges Bridge was begun sometime after 1275. A charter of 1271 records a grant at fief by the vicar of Toulouse and members of the Tolosa family to a Bernard Raymond Fusterius. The property was about six meters or just under eighteen feet in breadth and extended from the Garonne branch on the Toulouse side to the Garonne on the side of Saint-Cyprien next to the weir. It was therefore on the Ile-de-Tounis, or, as the document states, on the island or sandbank in front of the Dalbade Gate.[31] The lords also promised not to construct any bridge or obstruction that might harm the said tenant's interest.[32] They further allowed him to build a bridge or up to three bridges over the Garonne, and to erect a suitable bridgehead or bridgeheads as long as these did not interfere with boat traffic on the river. The permission to make two or three bridges presumably refers either to arches or to bridges over both the main Garonne and the Petit Garonne flowing between the town and Tounis.[33]

---

[31]Malta 7 117 (March 1271): "locum seu locale in illa insula sive albardillo, que insula sive albardillus est ante villam Tolose videlicet, et ante portam de Albate, qui locus seu locale habet et habere debet .iii. brachiatas in latitudine sive in amplo et est inter locum seu locale quod Raimudus de Insula de Servuneriis eodem die a dictis dominis adquisierat et locum seu locale quod Perrinus Botelherii subvicarius Tolose ab eisdem dominis similiter adquisierat et tenet seu ducit de illa partita fluminis Garonne que est versus villam Tolose usque ad illam partitam eiusdem fluminis Garonne que est versus Sanctum Siprianum circa paxeriam que est prope dictam insulam ... cum exessibus, ingressibus et accessibus suis per dictum flumen Garonne cum nave vel per pontem seu pontes, si quem vel quos ipsum feodotarium et alios qui in dicta insula locum seu localia habent vel habuerint facere contingit, supra dictum flumen Garonne adeundum et redeundum versus insulam predictam videlicet et tenendum et possidendum et quicquid eidem feodotario eiusque ordinio deinceps placuerit perpetuo faciendum ... et specialiter ad construendum et hedifficandum ibi domum vel domos seu alia hedifficia faciendum pro voluntate dicti feodotarii et eius ordinii."

[32]Ibid.: "Dederunt siquidem et concesserunt in feodum dicti domini ... dicto feodotario eiusque ordinio dictum locum seu locale, ita videlicet quod nemo quoad jus dicti domini comitis et aliorum dominorum predictorum possit antedictam insulam ex parte dicte ville Tolose nec ex parte Sancti Sipriani citra paxeriam predictam in dicto flumine Garonne vel supra eundem flumen facere aliquid opus novum vel hedifficium aliquid construere quod posset facere aliquid preiudicium vel impedimentum dicto feodotario eiusque ordinio ... ."

[33]Ibid.: the lords "dederunt ... plenam licentiam et liberam facultatem faciendi et construendi ibi ... pontem vel pontes, unum vel plures usque ad tres in dicto flumine Garonne et supra ipsum flumen et refficiendi si necesse fuerit et tenendi in perpetuum si voluerint et eis expediens videatur. Et quod possit ydem feodotarius ... capud pontis vel capita pontium si unum vel plures usque ad tres ibi fecerint vel facere voluerint ut est dictum firmare in ripis et cum ripis et super ripis dicti fluminis Garonne versus dic-

Bernard Raymond and his associates were also allowed to construct weirs and other defenses for the island, which is described as being about 359.25 meters or 1178 feet.[34] Finally, the landlords gave Bernard Raymond and settlers on Tounis a space of nearly eighteen meters or a little over fifty-two feet for a square at the head of the bridge.[35] As is obvious, this contract also shows that housing was envisaged for Tounis and that the island was itself being defined.

These bridges also illustrate Toulouse's late medieval decline. Over-crowded during a religious ceremony, the Old Bridge collapsed in 1281.[36] A flood in 1298 is said to have reached the top of the Daurade Bridge and temporarily destroyed all the others.[37] The vicissitudes of these bridges in the fourteenth and fifteenth centuries are sketched elsewhere, but it seems that the Comminges Bridge had been washed out or damaged by 1364, that it was thought of as being there or about to be there again in 1374 and that town government envisaged restoring it in 1414.[38] In short, the fourteenth

---

tam villam Tolose et versus Sanctum Subranum et in illis videlicet locis que ipse feodo-tarius et alii ... duxerint eligenda et specialiter cum ponte et in ponte et super pontem veterem, ita videlicet quod naves et alia quarigia decendentia et acendentia per dictum flumen Garonne vel per flumen Arigie possint per eundem flumen Garonne expedire transire et acendere sine eminenti periculo."

[34]Ibid.: "dictus feodotarius et omnes alii ut est dictum possint ... facere paxerias et alias deffensiones et opera versus utramque portam dicte insule usque ad ripas et in ripis eiusdem insule, et versus utramque partem ipsius ut est dictum tantum quantum prefata insula durabit et apparuerit infra tantas metas et bozelas ipsius insule, ad deffendendum ipsam insulam et domos et hediffacia, et res que ibi fuerint, que quidem insula habet ut ibi dictum fuit ducentas brachiatas in longitudine sive in longo." On the Tolosa family and their holdings along the Garonne river, see my *Repression of Catharism*, pp. 268ff.

[35]Ibid.: "dederunt et concesserunt necnon dicti domini nomine quo supradicto feodo-tario et omnibus illis qui in dicta insula locum vel localia habent vel habituri sunt in futurum decem brachiatas de amplo predicte insule versus pontem veterem uti tenent seu durant de una ripa ipsius insule usque ad aliam ad firmandum et hedificandum ibi capud pontis et ad habendum et tenendum ibi similiter plateam, ad opus sive ad usus dicti feo-dotarii et omnium aliorum qui in dicta insula locum vel localia habent vel habituri sunt."

[36]Dominicans 111, fol. 1 of two paper leaves inserted in the beginning of a leather-bound register, reading: "Pons fractus: anno domini 1281 in vigilia Ascensionis fractus est pons antiquus Tolosae pro multitudine gentium ibi existentium et expectantium descensum crucis per aquam ubi submersi et mortui sunt 400 personnae utriusque sexus et status."

[37]Ibid.: "Diluvium: 1298 Garonna tam crevit in ingressu mensis Junii ut ascenderit super pontem Deauratae ita quod homines super dictum pontem existentes aquas de dicto flumine cum manibus propriis sine alio vase recipiebant, et omnes pontes qui erant in dicta civitate excepto novo ponte Deauratae ceciderint et fracti sunt infra unam diem."

[38]See Wolff, *Commerces et marchands*, pp. 92-93. On the above, see TAM, II 61 (April 1364) where fines on the butchers are to be put toward the Old, New and Bazacle

century witnessed the collapse of all of Toulouse's bridges save for that of the Daurade. By 1444, moreover, it too was in a pitiable condition, much of its masonry having been replaced with wood beams.[39]

By 1500 the population of Toulouse is said to have dropped by as much as a third.[40] This was the town's nadir. By the mid-sixteenth century things were picking up, and a good bridge was being built: the present Pont Neuf being under construction from 1543 to 1614. Like much else in early modern times, this bridge was far larger, more stable and better engineered than its medieval predecessors, being designed for two-way carriage and wagon traffic. Still used and until recently supporting two tram or trolley lines, it was as broad, or almost, as all its medieval predecessors put together, and hence rather more efficient. Fine though this was, however, the town had lacked facilities it had enjoyed around 1300 for a century and a half.

C. THE TOWN'S REGIONS

To turn now to examine patterns of settlement: Toulouse, like other towns in the Midi, was initially a congeries of settlements implanted around its most ancient part, the City or "civitas" initially fortified in Roman times. Around this original nucleus, an unusually large one for France, the City was bounded by and in part composed of the cathedral and Close of Saint-Étienne to the east, the count's Château Narbonnais (overlapping the Roman wall) to the south, the church and monastery of the Daurade to the north on the Garonne bank and finally the site of the present Place du Capitole. The last was then built up with the Roman gate called the Portaria on its northern edge. The early thirteenth century witnessed the building of a town hall on land to the east of the Portaria that reached across the frontier into the Bourg.

Three words were employed to describe the new quarters or growths: "salvetat," "barrium" (vernacular "barri") and "suburbium." The first term appeared during the eleventh century and meant an area of special or exempt jurisdiction frequently demarcated by crosses placed around its frontiers. "Barrium" described a faubourg outside a community's walls and was

---

Bridges, with no mention of that of Comminges. A document in the Hospital Archives 1 B/2 (July 1374) records the election of the "baiuli" of the Hospital of Saint-Jacques at the head of the New Bridge, and, when listing the parts of the town, included the "partida del pont de cumenge vas sent subra." Lastly, TAM, II 46 60 (April 1414) where the order to restore the Comminges Bridge was published.

[39]*Commerces et marchands*, p. 95.

[40]Ibid., p. 71.

commonly used at this time for village and town extensions everywhere. The Roman term "suburbium" had undergone a change from meaning the whole territory around a "civitas" to designate a town faubourg in the early middle ages, and, at Toulouse, it was more or less restricted to the Bourg, an area to be discussed shortly.[41] The meaning similar to "barrium" and the present English word "suburb" was just beginning to re-emerge in the latter period treated in this book.[42]

Of the specific settlements, a "salvetat" designed to attract settlers was founded just south of the Château Narbonnais in 1115. This area centered on the chapel of Saint-Antoine of Lézat, but seems to have had only a brief independent life.[43] Although the abbot of Lézat appears to have retained a jurisdiction similar to those of the other ecclesiastical closes in the town, his "salvetat" was soon absorbed into the growing suburb or "barrium" south of town.[44] In the twelve-hundreds, the region was called that of the Château Narbonnais, as in a document of 1285 which mentions a property "in barrio castri Narbonensis."[45] It was later named Sainte-Catherine's after the hospital and church of the Fontevrault sisters of Longages founded in or after 1180.[46] According to Catel, Sainte-Catherine's served parish functions under the cathedral parish of Saint-Étienne, but, in 1331, the cure went to the newly built church of Saint-Michel.[47] Saint-

---

[41]Ordinary usage is seen in my *Liberty and Political Power*, pp. 209-210 (May 1216) where a man received all properties "in civitate Tolose et in surbubio aut de foris Tolosam in aliquo loco."

[42]Carmelites 30 (October 1264): the charter recording the initial installation of the Carmelites stated that it was "extra moenia et suburbium civitatis Tholose" at Férétra just outside the southwestern corner of the "barrium" of Saint-Michel (near today's Saint-Roch). The word "suburbium" therefore refers to Saint-Michel. See also the charter of 1358 in the next note.

[43]Ourliac and Magnou, *Cartulaire de l'abbaye de Lézat*, No. 1343 (August 1115). It was founded by the monks of Lézat with the aid of William, count of Toulouse, in "illam plateam et loco ante portam Castri Narbonensis." Catel, *Mémoires de l'histoire du Languedoc*, p. 131, noted that the original chapel was destroyed in 1358 because of the threat of foreign invasion, and that its altar was relocated on the Place du Salin. The act of 1358 which he cited describes the old chapel as "sita est in suburbiis Tholose extra villam prope Castrum Narbonense, infra parochiam ecclesiae Tholosanae, fundata et constructa anni sunt ducenti et quadraginta elapsi opere non modicum sumptuoso."

[44]See my *Men and Women*, p. 55, for an abbot's arrest there of a woman named Ricsenda.

[45]Malta 20 56 ii (March 1285, copied in 1289).

[46]See my "Charity and Social Work," pp. 217-218.

[47]Saint-Michel was the patron of the count's chapel "in castro Narbonensi" according to Malta 7 96 (May 1232). Catel, *Mémoires de l'histoire du Languedoc*, pp. 235-

Michel's name was only gradually given to the region because as late as 1387 a charter refers to the "recluses of [the church of] Saint-Michel of Sainte-Catherine's faubourg."[48]

Sometime between 1123 and 1141, Count Alphonse-Jordan created a "salvetat" within and on the edge of the City.[49] The only document describing the territory of this "salvetat" is a confirmatory act by Raymond VI of 1195 in which the count quotes part of the initial grant. From this passage, it may be presumed, first, that the "salvetat" lay both within and without the later walls of the City; second, that within the City its eastern frontier ran roughly from the Dalbade church to the Château Narbonnais; and third, that it included all the land from that line over to the Garonne river.[50] The "salvetat" also grew over the small branch of the Garonne (the Petit Garonne) to the sandbank that became the island of Tounis.[51] Even though the area initially had a jurisdictional identity of its own rather like that of the various "claustra" or closes of the major churches in the

---

237, tells about Sainte-Catherine, and an entry in the Hospital Archives 1 B/2 (July 1374) says: "partida del barri de santa catharina." I grasped this history on rereading Catel and transcribing the Hospital document, for which see my "Parishes of Toulouse," p. 194, where I had not yet understood the role of Sainte-Catherine's in the parish of Saint-Étienne.

[48]Catel, *Mémoires de l'histoire du Languedoc*, p. 196: "reclusae Sancti Michaelis barrii Sanctae Catherinae."

[49]Roschach, "Sur la commune de Toulouse" in *HGL* 7: col. 216, dated it before 1141 because the count suppressed an impost on the sale of wine abolished for the whole town in TAM, AA 1 1 (November 1141). For Alphonse-Jordan's presence in town see note 16 above.

[50]TAM, AA 1 11 (dated 1195) reads "sicut signata est et bodulata per crucem et de cruce in cruce infra muros civitatis Tolose et de foris, et a flumine Garonne usque ad ipsum murum civitatis, et de intus ad supra castellum Narbonensem." My observation about the Dalbade derives partly from the act of 1195, where it states: "Set retinuit ibi dominus Raimundus prefatus comes illa feoda et dona, que in eadem salvetate dominus Raimundus comes, pater ejus, dederat et concesserat Bernardo Arnaldo et aliis probis hominibus, quod ibi habeat unusquique illorum suum ius, sicut ibi debet habere," and from PAN, J 413 (February 1194) wherein the count granted at fief to an individual named Bernard Arnaldus "totum illud planum et locale, sicut sese extendunt a furno quod tenebatur fevaliter de domina Sarracena, usque ad capellam ecclesiae beatae Mariae de Albate" for the purpose of setting up a meat market. Raymond or his agent was obliged to note this exception in 1195 because the original grant of the "salvetat" permitted any individual to exercise any trade, including that of butcher, within the frontiers.

[51]A location on the "Insula Thonisii sive Salvitatis" in 1289 is seen in Julien, *Histoire de la paroisse Nôtre-Dame la Dalbade*, p. 11, and Catel, *Histoire des comtes*, p. 21. See also the document dealing with the Comminges Bridge in 1271 cited above on p. 15.

town, the Daurade and the cathedral, for example, it was fully absorbed in the City by the late twelfth century, as indeed were all the other jurisdictional areas in or around the City.[52]

Lastly, on the left bank of the Garonne river another settlement, Saint-Cyprien, began to take shape around the heads of the bridges from the City. Soon well endowed with hospitals, Saint-Cyprien was described as a "villa" as late as 1177 in documents by local scribes, and was probably initially under the jurisdiction of the priory of the Daurade.[53] Its parish of Saint-Nicholas boasted a parish priest from 1188 or 1189, and it had become a "barrium" under town government by that time or shortly thereafter.[54] Perhaps unaware of the change or unwilling to recognize it, a papal confirmation of the Daurade's rights dated 1240 still called it a "villa."[55]

By the late twelfth century, the only remaining part of the town that retained a significant distinction and a clear identity was the Bourg ("burgus" in Latin). Since it had grown up adjacent to the Roman "civitas" from late antiquity onward, the Bourg was also called "suburbium" throughout its history. This section of the town had its original nucleus in the Close and monastery of Saint-Sernin that was fortified in Carolingian times and later expanded southward down the Bourg's "carraria maior de Freneriis" (the present Rue du Taur) as far as the area to the south of the church of Saint-Sernin-du-Taur (the present Nôtre-Dame-du-Taur). This extension brought it to the very edge of the City at the later town hall and the present Place du Capitol.

The region toward the river and to the east of Saint-Sernin-du-Taur, later enclosed in the Bourg and called the quarter of Saint-Pierre-des-Cuisines, was not part of the Bourg in the mid-eleventh century. In 1067 Count William IV and his mother confirmed a grant by his predecessor Count Pons (d. 1061) of the allod (freehold) and church of Saint-Pierre-des-Cuisines to the monks of the famed monastery of Moissac, member house of Cluny. The gift liberated Moissac's "famulantes persone" in the "villa" of Cuisines from rent charges, taxes on hides and military service and granted them two servile families.[56] After this date, however, nothing more is heard of the "villa," and the village grew to link together the Bourg

---

[52]My *Liberty and Political Power*, p. 138.

[53]"Villa Sancti Cypriani" in Catel, *Mémoires de l'histoire du Languedoc*, p. 146, and similarly in an undated early twelfth century act in E 579 by the scribe Vitalis.

[54]My "Parishes of Toulouse," p. 198.

[55]In *Gallia Christiana* 13: col. 29 (June 1240) Gregory IX confirmed the "temporalem jurisdicionem villae Sancti Cypriani et loci qui dicitur claustrum Sancti Mariae."

[56]*HGL* 5: No. 277.

and City in the region along the bank of the Garonne. The area between Saint-Pierre in the Bourg and the Daurade in the City was apparently only being built up just before or around 1200, a fact recorded in its name Bourguet-Nau or Borguet-Nau. Saint-Pierre's individuality was slow to be obliterated because it retained its Carolingian designation into the twelfth century.[57] This absorption of the "villa" of Saint-Pierre shows that, like the City, the Bourg was able to swallow neighboring communities.

Information becomes available about the northern and eastern frontiers of the expanding Bourg – Lascrosses, Arnaud-Bernard, Pousonville (Posamila), Matabiau and Villeneuve – during the eleventh century. One of them, Lascrosses, appears sometime shortly after midcentury.[58] The same is true of the gate of Arnaud-Bernard to which an undated but undoubtedly late eleventh century act refers when describing a property "at the head of the Bourg before the Arnaud-Bernard Gate."[59] All the gates defining the Bourg were seen by the mid-twelfth century.[60] Where there were gates, a wall must have been being built. A document of around 1106 from the monastery of Saint-Sernin adverts to a lay notable who was forced to surrender the archdeaconry he held while "captive in the Bourg of Saint-Sernin within the fortifications."[61] An agreement between the "parishes" of

[57]See Douais, *Cartulaire de l'abbaye de Saint-Sernin de Toulouse*, No. 564 (October 1131): "in burgo Sancti Saturnini, in termino de Quoquinis."

[58]*HGL* 5: No. 277 (dated 1067) mentions a "casal" there at the end of the allod of Saint-Pierre-des-Cuisines bounded in part "sicut via tendit usque ad Crosam et usque in Garonna." Catel in his *Histoire des comtes*, p. 122, remarks that this lot was outside of Toulouse.

[59]Douais, *Cartulaire de Saint-Sernin*, No. 188: "in capite burgi ante portam Arnaldi Bernardi." One of the witnesses to the charter was William Bernard de Claustro and a person with that name is seen in ibid., No. 133 (dated ca. 1080) and also in No. 548 (solidly dated between 1080 and 1098).

[60]Ibid., No. 567 (February 1136) records a property "extra portam Arnaldi Bernardi." References to those of Villanova and Pousonville in August 1145 are in ibid., No. 498: "in decimario Sancti Stephani ad portam Ville Nove, extra vallum suburbii et extra murum civitatis"; to that of Crosis or Crosarum in December 1152 in Grandselve 52, Roll Ir, xv; and that of Matabove in April 1161 in Saint-Bernard 138, fols. 1r-2r. Houses were outside the Posamila gate by May 1159 in Douais, *Cartulaire de Saint-Sernin*, No. 87. Even the Bazacle, the terminal point of the perimeter on the Garonne, was noted as early as around 1080, the presumed date of the foundation of the Hospital of Saint-Raymond signaled in ibid., No. 547. A reference to the "porta canonicorum" in March 1182 or 1183 in Grandselve 1, 2 of 3, probably refers to a gate in the Close of Saint-Sernin.

[61]Ibid., No. 131: "staret captus in burgo Sancti Saturnine infra vallos." This could refer to the Close of Saint-Sernin itself, and not the general enclosure of the Bourg, but one doubts it.

Saint-Étienne and Saint-Sernin dated 1145 leaves no doubt about the Bourg's wall. It describes the eastern juncture between the fortifications of City and Bourg as "the walls of the City and palisades of the Bourg."[62] The Bourg's walls were surely less substantial than the Roman brick and fill ones of the City.[63]

To sum up, Toulouse grew in size and population starting somewhere in the tenth or eleventh century and continued into the fourteenth. Even around the Bourg, Toulouse's least populous region, housing in new "barria" or faubourgs sprang up outside its gates during the late twelve-hundreds and early thirteen-hundreds.[64] Although sometimes nearly as productive of hardship as contraction, expansion probably imposes the following conclusion: the evolution of the town's institutions and of its religious beliefs in this age did not take place in a context of economic despair and psychic defeat, but instead in one of economic progress tinctured by a relatively sanguine view of human prospects.

D. City and Bourg

Toulouse proves the commonplace that geographical distinctions root themselves in society. The two units, City and Bourg, were wholly unequal in population and wealth. The evidence dealing with the fourteenth and fifteenth centuries has been reviewed by Wolff, who estimated that in 1332 the

---

[62]Ibid., No. 498 (August 1145): the parties agreed not to build a church "a Sancti Salvatoris ecclesia et a vertice montis versus muros urbis et vallum suburbii, usque ad portam Podamilan, sicut ascendit via Sancti Salvatoris versus podium Sancti Germani, et a porta Podamilam versus ulmum oratorii." The church of Saint-Sauveur or Salvador lay due east of the cathedral, so the area marked went all the way from roughly the Saint-Étienne Gate in the City to the Pouzonville Gate in the Bourg. Saint-Bernard 138, fols. 101-103 (August 1191), referred to the perimeter as the "clausura suburbia."

[63]TAM, AA 1 4 (dated 1152 without month) interdicted sales "extra muros civitatis et portas suburbii." William of Puylaurens observed in his *Chronique*, ed. Duvernoy, p. 99, that Simon de Montfort dismantled the "muros civitatis et parietes burgi" in 1216.

[64]Note the "barrium" of the Matabiau Gate mentioned in Appendix 8, No. 100 (July 1282). The Cistercians of Grandselve also developed properties outside the Bourg owned by the College of Saint-Bernard. In charters dated from 1303, the monks contracted with private persons to create two zones of new housing by renting lands in return for rapid construction, one outside of the Pouzonville Gate called the "bastita" of Saint-Bernard and another near the church of Saint-Sauveur, a "bastita" on the "carraria Grandissilve" otherwise called "Stella," today's "Rue de l'Étoile." See Saint-Blanquat, "Sur L'établissement de deux Bastides aux portes de Tolouse, en 1303," *Recueil de L'Académie de Législation de Toulouse*, n.s. 1 (1951) 164-165.

population of the Bourg was about a quarter of the whole town's, holding a fifth of its taxable wealth.[65] This configuration is confirmed by figures from a document of 1285 wherein the royal treasurer in the Toulousain receipted the town's contribution to the crown of 10,000 pounds of Tours. To round out the sums involved, the consuls themselves provided 37 pounds, and the twelve quarters (usually "partite," earlier called "divisiones," later "capitularie" and "partidas" in the vernacular) into which the town was then divided gave 9,963, of which 73.2% came from the City, and 26.8% from the Bourg. In fact the "partite" of the City along the river, ie. Daurade, Old Bridge, and Dalbade, together with Saint-Rome and Saint-Pierre-Saint-Géraud, the "partite" on or near the "carraria major" running from the Portaria to the level of the market called La Pierre (today from the Place du Capitole to the Place Esquirol), gave no less than 65.5% of the whole assessment.[66] That the quarter of Saint-Étienne gave the least of all the parts of the City (only 10%) and was by far the largest (running down the whole eastern side of the City), moreover, proves that the town's real center of population and wealth reached from the river to the blocks on and just east of "Main Street" (now called Saint-Rome, Change and Filatiers).

Given the disparity in wealth and population, one is surprised that, when the areas represented by the chaptermen (later consuls) were mentioned just after the mid-twelfth century, the two parts of the town were treated as equal.[67] And this curiously inaccurate representation of their true inequality persisted through the fiscal "reform" of 1269 and 1270. Later on, in 1336, royal arbitration reorganized the town's representation and taxation. Instead of being divided into two parts with an equal number of divisions or "partitas," the City was divided into eight quarters, and the Bourg into four, thus reckoning that the Bourg was approximately a third of the community. Numerical rationality did not wholly triumph even then: one consul from the Bourg was to accompany all deputations to king or pope, for example and, for votes about weighty matters, one consul from the Bourg always had to join the majority. The Bourg, in short, had a veto.[68]

---

[65] *"Estimes" toulousaines*, p. 54, and *Commerces et marchands*, p. 71.

[66] TAM, II 62 (December 1285).

[67] See the lists of 1163 or 1164 and of 1175 or 1176 in Appendix 4.

[68] Royal patent letters issued at Béziers in AA 3 228 (February 1336). The eight "partitas" of the City and four of the Bourg were to have each one consul; two civil assessors were assigned the City and one to the Bourg, with a similar distribution of notaries and police, etc. Notaries for criminal cases, however, and nightwatchmen remained equal in numbers between the town's parts.

This curiously persistent division split the two areas. As early as about 1082, the City's ecclesiastical authorities headed by the bishop had invaded the Bourg and especially its cult center of Saint-Sernin to replace the canons with the Benedictines of Cluniac Moissac.[69] Although this initiative was defeated and Saint-Sernin soon recovered its independence, similar conflicts continued to be seen. A formal capitular law (one issued by the chapter, the later consulate) of 1184 insisted that inhabitants of either half were not obliged to carry their rents to lords in the other part. This contradicted a common practice of delivering rents to a lord's domicile.[70] In short, a change in the way rent was paid at this time was rather absurdly attached to the geographical or jurisdictional division. Again, at the beginning of the Albigensian Crusade, a confraternity called Black in the Bourg sided with Count Raymond VI and helped defeat the initial crusader attack on the town. In the City, Bishop Fulk had evoked, and profited from, the support of a White Confraternity to aid the Crusade and attack the prince as well as both divergent religious thought and usury.[71]

In my first study of Toulouse published in 1954, I attributed this division to social motives, describing them as expressions of class or economic divisions. To repeat myself rather more schematically than my earlier study warrants, the City was the center of the greater or aristocratic families and also of the artisan working population whereas the Bourg was "dominated by the new rich of business [and] commerce."[72] In an article first published in 1977, Wolff advanced somewhat similar conjectures. Treating Toulouse as an example of divided towns in the middle ages, he argued that the two areas differed in their balance of social classes, that the City was richer and had more trades- and craftsfolk than the Bourg, and that the latter was, in comparison with the City, "gangréné par l'hérésie."[73]

We were both right about the greater wealth and population density of the City. My case was overstated in regard to the "new rich of business and commerce." If the new rich in the Bourg are well represented by Pons de Capitedenario, it is sure that the distinguished Roaxio family of the City came from modest origins in the early twelfth century to become truly patri-

[69]The most recent study of these events is Magnou, *Reforme Grégorienne à Toulouse, fin XIe–début XII siècle* published in 1958.

[70]AA 1 15 (May 1184). For these practices, see the Raissaco family history, Appendix 1, No. 13.

[71]See the discussion in my *Liberty and Political Power*, pp. 82-85, and in Chapters Ten and Eleven.

[72]My *Liberty and Political Power*, p. 84.

[73]Wolff, "Civitas et Burgus, l'exemple de Toulouse," *Regards sur le Midi médiéval*, p. 206.

cian and even knightly by about 1200.[74] To speak of business, commerce
and the usury so savagely attacked by Bishop Fulk, if Pons profited from
it, so also did members of the Roaxio family, especially Grivus de Roaxio.
Again, if Pons was notable for his extraordinary charities, offering as he did
10,000 shillings of Toulouse, Bernard de Miramonte who lived in the
Portaria in the City disposed of no less than 25,000 thousand (1250 pounds
of Toulouse, 2500 of Tours).[75] Even if most patrician families boasting
knights (or which were to do so by the end of the thirteenth century)
inhabited the City, similar families lived in the Bourg. The Turribus lived
in the City and the well-nigh equally notable or noble Vital Galterius
inhabited the region of Cuisines in the Bourg.[76]

Artisans as well as patricians also lived in the Bourg. True enough,
more lived in the City and therefore large-scale export industries such as
that of hides and leather were concentrated there.[77] Starting in the early
thirteenth century, moreover, the relatively cheap land of the barely settled
Bourg invited the implantation of the mendicants, especially the Dominicans
(on the frontier of the City and Bourg) and the Franciscans. In the fourteenth century, also, most of the colleges of the University of Toulouse
were built there. This huge attribution of real estate to institutional purposes further distanced the Bourg from the City and reduced its comparative
weight. On the whole, however, the difference in this earlier period was
probably caused by the fact that the Bourg's population was smaller than the
City's and, like Denmark today in comparison with Germany, some rich
were richer and some poor, poorer in the latter than in the former.

Although one wonders if those given to divergent thought ought be described as "gangréné" by anything, there is no reason to think that, because
the Black Confraternity of the Bourg aided the count against the Crusade,
the Bourg favored Catharism or Waldensianism more than did the City.
Reality is subtle. Capitedenario's charity went largely to the church and he
was even politely churlish about his widow's portion. Miramonte was a
family man who gave only five percent of his huge bequest to charity and
assigned the rest to relatives and other layfolk. Besides, he arranged the

[74]See the Capitedenario and Roaxio family histories in my *Repression of Catharism*,
pp. 155-167 and 251-287.
[75]See Appendix 8, Nos. 51 (March 1229) of Capitedenario and 68 (August 1237) of
Miramonte.
[76]The Turribus history is in Appendix 1, No. 15, and Vital Galterius in the Carbonellus history, ibid. No. 3, as well as Appendix 8, No. 72 (March 1243).
[77]See Wolff's "Fortunes et professions vers 1400," *Regards sur le Midi médiéval*,
pp. 269-278.

marriage of his only daughter with a nearly baronial dowry to a member of a family he could not help but know leaned toward Catharism.[78] Again, the motives of those who supported, indeed, of those who led, Bishop Fulk's White Confraternity were more complex than they appear at first glance. Its main leader, one of two celebrated knights, an uncle and a nephew, both named Aimeric de Castronovo, is known to have dabbled in Catharism and one of them eventually led the town's resistance to the Crusade.[79]

Statistics may show whether the Bourg was more given to divergent religious thought than the City. Readers are reminded that extant archival documents overestimate the weight of the Bourg. Whereas that region contained only about a third of town population, if that, twenty of the family histories I wrote up concern the Bourg and only twenty-five the City. Statistical weakness aside, twenty-three town families had members who were Cathars or were investigated as such.[80] This high rate of over fifty percent does not represent the true degree of divergence, but instead the fact that, to the eye of a researcher, the divergent stick out like sore thumbs. On the other hand, I was not looking for the ratio in each region of the town, mainly because I did not know that it was an issue when I did the research. Of the twenty-five families fingered by the ecclesiastical police, eight (about thirty-five percent) lived in the Bourg and, of the twenty-two not subject to that treatment, twelve (about fifty-five percent) in the same area. In short, it cannot be proved and is inherently doubtful that the Bourg was more inclined to heresy than the City. In spite of that, these two parts of the town fell out over the issue at a decisive moment in its history.

To conclude, the measure of unity achieved by the City and Bourg undoubtedly helped the town to win self-government or freedom from the count in the past. And it is therefore not surprising that, when the French crown had drastically curtailed town liberty, the Bourg's equality with the City all but vanished. On the other hand, internal social reasons for the durable singularity and occasional hostility of the City and Bourg cannot be found. Perhaps, like many unrepresentative bodies in today's oligarchic republics, this seemingly irrational division was a way of blocking an egalitarian distribution of political authority. Perhaps also, as again today, natives often believe that places, even those wholly ordinary to a foreign eye, are the deity's or nature's cradles for the brave or intelligent.

---

[78]See the history in the Curtasolea family history in my *Repression of Catharism*, pp. 199-200.

[79]See ibid., especially pp. 188-189.

[80]In Appendix 5, Part 1, the figures are rough because some families have lengthy and broad trees and others either very slender ones or do not go over two generations.

Part One

SOCIETY

2

Regional History

A. Contexts

Views about the nature of western European society on the north shore of
the Mediterranean Sea have recently changed. A significant voice is that of
Pierre Bonnassie, who has popularized a new view of the origins of the
rural lordship and servility.[1] Bonnassie naturally depends on earlier scholars and especially specifies Marc Bloch, cofounder of the well-known
journal *Annales* and martyred hero of France during the Second World War,
as well as the more immediately antecedent George Duby.

Sometime ago, Duby called the medieval rural community a "seigneurie
banale," meaning a community not simply composed of landlords and their
dependents but instead one whose inhabitants are best defined as dependent
subjects of a petty state.[2] Prompted by ideas expressed by a Marxist economic historian or sociologist named Pierre Dockès, Bonnassie has used
this conception to prorogue antiquity and begin the feudal age somewhere
around 1000.[3] By the latter tenth century, in this view, the rural population
had won freedom and destroyed the slave "mode of production" characteristic of ancient times. And, indeed, recent research has shown that farmers
of that period were rarely described as servile in large parts of France,
Catalonia and central Italy.[4]

---

[1]*La Catalogne du milieu du Xe à la fin du XIe siècle. Croissance et mutations d'une
société*, 2 vols. (1975-1976). His popular *From Slavery to Feudalism in Southwestern
Europe* is a translation in 1991 of an earlier French work introduced by T.N. Bisson,
who subsequently, as Paterson, *The World of the Troubadours*, p. 15, remarks, discovered that Catalan feudalism was not as systematic as Bonnassie believed.

[2]*La société aux XIe et XIIe siècles dans la région mâconnaise* of 1953.

[3]Dockès' most pertinent work is *La libération médiévale* published in 1979.

[4]For Italy, for example, especially the work of Pierre Toubert, *Les structures du Latium:
Le Latium meridional et la Sabine du IXe siècle à la fin du XIIe siècle*, 2 vols., and various
essays in the colloquium published as *Structures féodales et féodalism dans l'occident méditerranéen (Xe-XIIIe siècles)* held at the École française de Rome in 1978 and published in 1980.

Centuries-long though its gestation had been, the new rural freedom is claimed to have collapsed within a century. During and after the last great invasions, those of the Muslims, Hungarians and Scandinavians, farmers were subjected to a renewed dependency, the servitude of the "feudal mode of production." Rural workers were forcibly brigaded into lordships centered on newly built fortifications and witnessed the replacement of the people's old foot militia with a privileged martial elite, the mounted knights. Usually called "rustici," ordinary farmers were deprived of access to the old courts of weakening central governments and were prohibited from moving freely, both socially (by marriage) and geographically (away from their villages). Lastly, the fruits of their labor were largely attributed to the lords who, retaining much for themselves, monopolized the distribution of the surplus to society at large.

Older theory had envisaged that fortification was a response to the barbarian raids, but the new analysis argues that written proof of the existence of castles largely postdates the invasions.[5] Lacking function, this militarism is now viewed as a tyrannical imposition on the mass of the population by magnates and their "familiae." Again, liberals usually imagined that economic growth and the expansion of the area under cultivation ineluctably advanced liberty. The new view, however, denies this easy parallel, arguing that renewed servitude was not precipitated by economic hardship. Quite the contrary, as the economy picked up after the year 1000, the wealthy and powerful reduced the working population to dependency because "enrichment [leads] to covetousness."[6]

Because humans, especially the rich, are always covetous, one wonders if that quality suffices to explain this great change. But ideology rarely invalidates realities evident in the documents, as may be the case here. The curse may anyway be expunged from this vision, one mildly reminiscent of *Tintin en Amérique*, by adducing a broader context earlier provided by N.-D. Fustel de Coulanges (d. 1889). Because he detested Jean-Jacques Rousseau (d. 1778) and the romance of brotherly equality among Europe's original peoples, this great liberal's views always excite opposition. The

[5]For example, Bonnassie's work cited above, Jean-Pierre Poly and Éric Bournazel, *La mutation féodale: Xe et XIe siècle* in 1980, Robert Fossier, *L'enfance de l'Europe (XIe-XIIe siècles): Aspects économique et sociaux* in 1982, Guy Bois, *La mutation de l'an mil* in 1989, and articles by Monique Gramain, "'Castrum,' Structures féodales et peuplement en Bitterois au XIe siècle," *Structures féodales*, ed. Toubert, pp. 119-134, Christian Lauranson-Rosaz and André Debord in *The Peace of God: Social Violence and Religious Response in France around the Year 1000*, ed. Thomas Head and Richard Landes in 1992, to name a few.

[6]Bonnassie, *From Slavery to Feudalism in Southwestern Europe*, p. 118.

invading Germans, fancied by some to be the fount of liberty, were to him mere "primitives" incapable of continuing Rome's government, economy and law. Coulanges nevertheless knew that the rural lordship of medieval Europe was the successor of the weakening, but still unitary government of the Carolingians and, earlier on, of that of the Roman Empire. He therefore truthfully observed that the devolution of antiquity's centralized governments and economies had gradually transformed Rome's large landed proprietor into a medieval lord who "within the limits of his domain [became] a kind of head of state."[7]

To this liberal vision enlarged by a partially Marxist lens may be added the views of Susan Reynolds. Reynolds asserts that, contrary to the canonized opinion of French historians, the construction of the feudal hierarchy, the close relationship of land to public office, not to speak of the oaths associated with "vassalage" and "fidelity" were not systematized before the centralizing efforts of the French (and other) monarchs took hold during the twelfth century.[8] Applied to Languedoc, this scholar's perception is reinforced by Elisabeth Magnou-Noirtier's accent on the long persistence of Roman and Carolingian institutions and her choice of a similar late date for the introduction of feudalism.[9] Regardless of these rightist caveats limiting the significance of Bonnassie's radical change sketched above, the date of the mutation proposed by him and his followers coincides with that of the Gregorian attempt to overturn the clergy's past subordination to secular authority and the rise of the ecclesiastical order to lead Latin Europe for two or three centuries. If these events are joined, it may be that Latin Europe experienced what Eugen Rosenstock-Huessy long ago called a "revolution," Europe's first revolution, in fact.[10]

The revolution sparked violence, to use today's catchword.[11] Bonnassie and others have accented the mistreatment of the farming population and the duration and intensity of the wars between the greater regional princes

[7]*L'alleu et la domaine rural* of 1889, p. 458: "dans les limits de son domaine, une sorte de chef d'état."

[8]*Fiefs and Vassals: The Medieval Evidence Reinterpreted*, published in 1994, an interesting book marked or marred by a curious hostility to lawyers.

[9]Her basic work is *La société laïque et l'église dans la province ecclésiastique de Narbonne [zone cyspyrénéenne] de la fin du Xe à la fin du XIe siècle* of 1974.

[10]For the full title, English translations with enlargements of his strange *Die Europäischen Revolutionen* of 1931, see the Bibliography below.

[11]In the debate on "The 'Feudal Revolution,'" *Past and Present* 142 (1994), Bisson americanized Bonnassie's tenth century revolution, stripping ideology from early feudalism to underline instead the wickedness of its protagonists. Dominique Barthélemy and Stephen D. White in ibid., 152 (1996) seem about to cause violence itself to fade away like the Cheshire cat as a causative factor.

and lesser notables in the age of political devolution when, in effect, private individuals seized public power to hold it hereditarily. These feuds or social wars prompted the movement of the Peace of God, an attempt by the church and its allies to act in lieu of the dissolving general government or governments of the time. Against this, it has been asserted that just as, so to speak, the new rural lordships were settling in for a long stay, substantial regional authorities such as the counts of Barcelona (and later kings of Aragon), the counts of Toulouse-Saint-Gilles on a lesser level and still lower down the counts of Foix, the viscounts of Béziers and Carcassonne and the lords of Montpellier rose to head reasonably stable governments.[12] Subdivided into baronies and smaller rural lordships, these eleventh century principalities used service contracts, such as the fief, to build clienteles, but also relied on the service demanded of all freemen characteristic of Carolingian days.[13]

These events have been briefly rehearsed here because they are the "mise en scène" for the twelfth century with which this study begins. That the eleventh century suffered social dislocation is undoubted, but, unlike Catalonia or Provence, Toulouse itself was not deeply scarred. Its only serious disorders were the Cluniac and Gregorian struggle in the local church and the intermittent Poitevin interventions of William IX of Aquitaine from 1090 to 1123. Thereafter, the relatively durable local government of the house of Toulouse-Saint-Gilles stilled warfare for a time.[14]

B. Classes and Orders

Although documents deriving from Toulouse are relatively few, codes and charters from other communities and regions define the different social groups around 1100. To go far afield, to Milan in Lombardy, the social orders there under the prince-archbishop were the "ordo capitaneorum" or barons, the "ordo militum" or "valvassorum" of the rural and urban knighthood, the "ordo populi" of the town dwellers and the "ordo rusticorum" of the farmers.[15] At Carcassonne something similar is seen around 1107,

---

[12]Magnou-Nortier's "The Enemies of the Peace: Reflections on a Vocabulary, 500-1100," *The Peace of God*, ed. Head and Landes, p. 58.

[13]A point well and often made by both Magnou-Nortier and Reynolds.

[14]Like Magnou-Noirtier and Reynolds, Bisson, "Feudalism in Twelfth Century Catalonia," *Medieval France and her Pyrenean Neighbors*, pp. 170-171, remarks how nonfeudal these local states were.

[15]Keller, *Adelsherrschaft und städtische Gesellschaft in Oberitalien: 9. bis 12. Jahrhundert*, especially pp. 379-381.

where the viscount headed the "noti homines" or barons, "milites," "burgenses," the "universus alius populus" and the "suburbani," an antique term here still meaning as the Romans would have the countryfolk outside of the city walls.[16] Unusually systematic was the Catalan *Usatges de Barcelona*. There, viscounts followed after the count, each being worth two "comitors," each "comitor" being worth two "vasvassores" and each "vasvassor" having five "milites" being worth four knights. In the same text, also, viscounts, "comitores" and "vasvassores" are all termed "magnates" and are distinguished from the "milites."[17] The slots reserved for urban and rural folk in this code will be seen later.

Around Toulouse, beneath the count of Toulouse, the highest echelon of lay society was composed of princes such as the counts of Foix or Comminges and, below them, notables, some of whom were titled viscounts and some simply "domini," "magnates" or "seniores." The barons of Isle-Jourdain west of Toulouse, for example, were always simply "domini" in the long period treated in this volume. All of these notables were "nobiles" or sometimes "principes et nobiles" as the counts of Foix and Comminges and the lords of Marquefave and Montaut southwest of Toulouse were described in 1139. [18] Earlier the lords of Marquefave were termed "quidam homines nobilissimi et secundum seculum famosi et robustissimi," but this pomposity boils down to the same thing.[19]

Under magnates or barons were "milites" or, to use the Latin word reflecting the vernacular, "cabalarii" (later, "cabalerii"). Obviously meaning a mounted soldier or horseman, the word "cabalarius" described a knight or "miles" in Languedoc just as it did in Catalonia and Provence.[20] "Cabalarii" often held "cavalaria," a word employed throughout the Midi to mean their holdings or allotments.[21] Far more numerous than magnates, "cabalarii" were of different grades. Barcelona's *Usatges* speaks of "inferiores milites" and, in 1056, a council held at Saint-Gilles on the Rhone

[16]*HGL* 5: No. 429 (ca. 1107).

[17]Bastardas, *Usatges*, Articles Nos. 4, 5, 60 and especially 73.

[18]PBN, Collection Doat 99: fol. 382 (April 1139).

[19]Cau-Durban, *L'abbaye de Mas d'Azil*, No. 1 (dated to the late eleventh century).

[20]Kiener, *Verfassungsgeschichte der Provence seit der Ostgothenherrschaft bis zur Errichtung der Konsulate – 510-1200*, p. 107, Duby, "La diffusion de la titre chevaleresque sur le versant méditerranéen de la Chrétienté latine," in *La noblesse au moyen-âge: XI-XV siècles. Essais à la mémoire de Robert Boutruche*, ed. Philippe Contamine, pp. 45-69, and Bonnassie, *La Catalogne du milieu du Xe à la fin du XI siècle*, pp. 805-806.

[21]Bonnassie, *From Slavery to Feudalism in Southwestern Europe*, p. 109: "caballarias" in Catalan.

refers to "milites maiores et minores."[22] The humbler "cabalarii" were
surely close to the classes below them, sharing a dependent station little
above that of the farmers from whose group many must have derived.[23]
Eleventh century information from the frontiers of the Empire and in south-
eastern France and Provence likens "cabalarius" to "ministerialis" and
"serviens" and the same was doubtless true in western Languedoc.[24] In
Catalonia, where institutional evolution was precocious, a line based on
wealth separated noble from non-noble: "milites" already constituted an
order there, that is, a group of peers.[25]

The honorific "nobilis" was gradually being generalized in Languedoc
and around 1100 only greater magnates were called so. Although the sources available are few, to be noble, it appears, was to be free to dispose of
one's property and person as one saw fit. An eleventh century charter repeated an old formulary stating that, as Roman, Frankish and other law
declared, "every nobleman has the capacity of giving his own property to
whomsoever he pleases."[26] At that time also knights around Toulouse
were already consequential enough to have their names enriched by other
adjectives expressing worth. Where the monastery of Lézat held property
to the south of Toulouse, barons were called "noble" and "powerful," but
knights only "very prudent" or "very strong."[27] By the mid-twelfth century or somewhat earlier, however, knightly militiamen were viewed as
"nobiles," as in a charter dated 1140 where the baron of Marquefave acted

[22]Bastardas, *Usatges*, Article No. 27. Philippe Wolff, "La noblesse Toulousaine:
Essai sur son histoire médiévale," *Essais ... Robert Boutruche*, p. 156, cited the council
of 1056.

[23]Bonnassie, *La Catalogne du milieu du Xe à la fin du XI siècle*, pp. 800-801,
conjectures they derived from the freeholders, those with allods. In his *From Slavery to
Feudalism*, pp. 156-157, he opines that this group, like recent Russia's perfidious kulaks
(!), "changed sides ... to join ... the nobility."

[24]Kiener, *Verfassungsgeschichte der Provence*, p. 107, and Poly and Bournazel, *La
mutation féodale: Xe et XIe siècle*, pp. 216-217.

[25]Bastardas, *Usatges*, Article No. 52: for the word "par," see note 41 below.

[26]Douais, *Cartulaire de Saint-Sernin*, No. 47 (dated to the tenth or eleventh century)
reading: "Multum declarat auctoritas romana vel salica, seu qualicumque lege vivet homo, ut unusquisque vir nobilis de rebus suis propriis potestatem habeat donandi, cedendi
cui illi placuerit."

[27]Ourliac and Magnou, *Cartulaire de Lézat*, No. 545 (1072/1081) "quidam homo
nobilis"; No. 288 (March 1084–March 1085) "nobiles viri"; and No. 1055 (June
1075/1081) an "homo quidam nobilis atque potentissimus," a "miles prudentissimus,"
and several "milites fortissimi."

"with the consent of my noble men."[28] As an honorable title, "miles" was not applied to, or carried by, individuals at this period.

The elevation of this soldiery was expressed not only by the well-worn commonplace of the brotherhood of arms, but also by the equally familiar notion that their duty was to protect the poor and weak and maintain the peace at home and abroad. Associated with the Peace of God, these ideas were everywhere expressed in this period, by Bonizo of Sutri (d. 1089), for example, and John of Salisbury (d. 1189) later on. The mounted militia, however, did more than defend rural and urban communities from inimical outsiders: it also served as internal police. This point is often made nowadays, but near contemporaries of the history being described here believed the same.[29]

Lastly, although most properties or salaries attributed to "cabalarii" by princes were located in, or derived from, the countryside, knights and magnates, just as princes, were often town denizens. At Toulouse, a convention about burial rights dated 1093 specified that the bishop, count and knights inhabiting the City were to be buried in the cemetery of Saint-Sernin, unlike the rest of the parishioners of Saint-Étienne.[30] The condition of these urban knights was surely like that of the soldiers assigned property by a viscount of Béziers and Carcassonne in 1225 and 1226 in return for an eight months' "statio" or garrison service in a tower annually.[31] And residence in town also meant being attracted to business there. In or after 1102, to cite a well-known case, the lord bishop of Puy-en-Velay (well to the north of Languedoc) and the citizens joined to tear down the towers and great houses of the "proud knights, called minters," but also cautiously bought them off with 10,000 shillings of Puy.[32]

[28]Douais, *Cartulaire de Saint-Sernin*, No. 212 (dated 1140), has the lord of Marquefave give property to Saint-Sernin "cum consilio ... nobilium virorum meorum," some of whom are named.

[29]See the Catalan Ramon Llull's opinion in the Conclusion, pp. 289-290.

[30]Douais, *Cartulaire de Saint-Sernin*, No. 2 (December 1093): "in cimiterio Sancti Saturnine ... sepeliantur. Ceteri autem omnes qui in parrochia Sancti Stephani infra muros supradictos habitant, unus autem etiam miles Ugo Guillelmi [with wife, issue and successors] illius qui in eodem casali quo nunc ipse habitat manserint, sine contradictione hominum quorumlibet infra muros vel extra in cimiterio Sancti Stephani sepulturae tradantur."

[31]*HGL* 5: No. 489 i (January 1125) for which see note 63 below. Montpellier also had urban knights, for whom see *Liber instrumentorum memorialium. Cartulaire des Guillems de Montpellier*, ed. A. Germain, No. 104 (April 1139) where William V excluded the "districta ct firmancias militum Montispessulani et uxorum illorum" from his grant to the vicar.

[32]The text is in Chapter Six, note 68 below.

Beneath nobles and "milites" were the other classes, headed by the "ci-ves" or "burgenses."[33] Because most towns of this area were "civitates" of ancient foundation, the word "cives" usually designated all denizens, even "milites." The term "burgenses" was also employed, but normally designated persons who were not nobles or "milites." This is not as simple as it sounds because "burgenses" also meant those who lived in burgs, that is, in communities or in newly fortified centers that had grown up adjacent to older "civitates." An example is the Bourg of Saint-Sernin located hard on the northern frontier of the "civitas" or City of Toulouse. A result was that the "cives" resident in the Bourg of Toulouse were for long also called "burgenses."[34] This specific meaning apart, however, the word "burgen-ses" was often employed to mean all town inhabitants except knights.[35] Lastly, although sometimes rich, burgesses were not considered noble.[36]

Burghers owed economic services to prince and fatherland and hence, in early eleventh century charters, the word "burgenses" was almost inter-changeable with "mercatores," and so economic was their service that they were likened to Jews.[37] Along with that function, they owed military ser-vice. Exemption from tax, toll, military service and also fees in justice were granted at Toulouse by the count to persons who founded hospitals and hospices from around 1080 to 1157.[38] Unlike the mounted "cabalarii" of

[33] *HGL* 5: Nos. 339 and 351 (dated around 1000) show that society in the Narbonnais was normally divided into "milites," "cives" and "rustici."

[34] For a similar usage, see *HGL* 5: No. 515 (dated 1131) where the count of Tou-louse adjudged a dispute between the bishop and the viscount of Béziers about the bi-shop's "burgenses qui stabant in suis burgis." Van Werveke, *"Burgus": Versteking of Nederzetting?* argued that "burgum" never meant a fortified center, but he was probably wrong.

[35] Hence, when the mid-twelfth century chronicle of Nîmes described the peace of 1166, the text in *HGL* 5: col. 30, refers to a "concordia militum et burgensium Nemau-sensium."

[36] Kiener, *Verfassungsgeschichte der Provence*, pp. 170-171, where at Arles in 1067 the population was called the "gens civitatis, nobiles sive ignobiles." Sometimes called "maiores," the knights of the famous Arènes were noble, the rest being non-noble.

[37] Long ago well explored by Mayer, *Deutsche und französische Verfassungs-geschichte von 9. bis zum 14. Jahrhundert* 2: 227-228, 257, 280-281, and 286-287.

[38] The founder of the Hospital of Saint-Raymond in the Bourg was granted "quod tu nec tuus filius non ambuletis in ost ne en cavalgada nec donetis questa ne tolta" in Douais, *Cartulaire de Saint-Sernin*, No. 546 (ca. 1080). The endower of the hospice of the monastery of Grandselve, published in my *Liberty and Political Power*, p. 194, No. 1 (May 1157), was promised "ut numquam Bernardus predictus neque post eum habitantes in predicto casale pergant in comitali cavalcata vel exercitu nec pro clamore donent iusticiam aliquam michi vel meo successori neque alicui meo vicario."

town and country, most burghers served on foot and, at Barcelona, "pedones" had half the value of "caballarii."[39]

The *Usatges de Barcelona* compared the values of burghers and knights.
An article there shows that burghers like knights were considered worthy
of serving in court.[40] An earlier article shows that the average knight was
better off than a burgher. He also had more honor because knights are to
defend their word, sword in hand against their peers.[41] Those too old or
poor, however, were to take oath, their oaths being valued at the same rate
as that of a burgher, namely five ounces of gold.[42] The code also notes
that wives of burghers charged with infidelity could summon a footman to
defend their honor, whereas a knight's consort called on a knight, and a
footman was worth only about half as much as a knight![43]

Lastly, although rarely signaled as such in the charters of this time,
crafts- and tradesmen in the towns were probably dependents because the
prince's rights over them were extensive and durable. Materials elsewhere
explored not only show that the count of Toulouse taxed and controlled
what a modern would consider public functions, like the mint, but also
certain trades, especially those of the bakers, butchers and millers.[44] The
best evidence comes from the building and siege service owed the count of
Toulouse in 1188 by the stonemasons of Nîmes in lower Languedoc. As late
as the twelve-twenties and thirties various trades in Toulouse, the butchers
on the rue Saint-Rome in the City and the boatmen on the Garonne river,
owed him special service in time of war and peace.[45]

[39]Bastardas, *Usatges*, Article No. 23.

[40]In the D'Abadal y Vinyals and Valls Taberner edition of the *Usatges*, Article No.
144 records twelfth century legislation about the prince's courts. Decisions were published "de consilio et approbatione nobilium, magnatum, etiam civitatensium nostrorum
.... " Article No. 80 describes the members as "principes, episcopi, abbates, comites et
vicecomites, comitores et vavassores, philosophi et sapientes atque judices."

[41]Bastardas, *Usatges*, Article No. 52: "manibus propriis defendant ad illorum parem."

[42]Ibid., Article No. 51: "senex miles qui non potuerit se defendere per semedipsum,
seu pauper qui se non potest preparare de bello." Ibid., Article No. 53: "Sacramenta
burgensium credantur ut militum usque ad .v. uncias. Deinde quicquid jurent, per bellum
defendant, scilicet per pedonem."

[43]Ibid., Article No. 89 for the wives, and Article No. 23 puts the pledge for a
judicial battle at 200 ounces of gold for "milites" and at 100 for "pedones."

[44]In my *Liberty and Political Power*, Chapter 3, especially pp. 243-245, notes 7-16.

[45]Ibid., p. 244, note 14.

C. SERVICE AND DEPENDENCY

As "villani," farmers were members of the "villa;" as "rustici," they were countryfolk. Some were called "servi" and, in Catalonia, these could not plead in the courts outside those of their "ville." Theirs was not a unique deprivation, however, because ministerial cadres and knights also depended on local lords. The advantage of many knights and town dwellers (but, as shall be seen, not all) was that they served regional princes and not local lords. An example is the Jews, who fell under the "potestates," the counts of Catalonia and Toulouse, the viscounts of Béziers and Carcassonne, etc.[46]

Save for a few princes and magnates, in fact, everybody was dependent, a result of two long-term institutional evolutions. The first was the late Roman and early medieval attempt to extend obligatory service for prince and republic to the whole population. The second was the devolution or decentralization of political power started in those early days, that had finally come to rest in local circumscriptions, in rural lordships and small towns. Although only the lowest groups were called "servi," the language describing the various classes and their activities was strikingly similar.[47] A few examples will suffice to show what is meant.

Unlike Catalans, rustics around Toulouse were not termed "servi" in the early twelfth century. Some, although how many cannot be ascertained, were like serfs. Treated as income-bearing possessions, individuals, together with their families and tenancies, were pledged, sold or given as gifts by those who "owned" them. Typical was a sale in 1135 of a half share of two dependent brothers, inhabitants of Braqueville across the Garonne from Toulouse, for five shillings of Toulouse.[48] Of the twenty-seven "servicia" or rents owned by the Tolosa sisters of Toulouse in 1187 or 1188, some deriving from their grandfather, a minimum of eight were paid by farmers, ranging in number from one to eight household heads with wives, children

[46]Bastardas's *Usatges*, Article No. 9, where fines for wounding or killing them accrued to the prince. For the condition of the Jews in Toulouse, see Chapter Four, pp. 58-60, and, for their similarity to burghers and rustics, later in this chapter.

[47]Magnou-Noirtier, *La société laïque et l'église dans la province ecclésiastique de Narbonne*, pp. 225-226, notes the similarities between rural and urban inhabitants.

[48]Saint-Étienne 227 (26 31 2) 59 (November 1135): "vendimus tibi Raterio et tuo ordinio totum hoc quod habemus in Petro de Bracavilla et in Ramundo fratre suo, hec est medietas predictorum hominum quam ibi habemus, quam tibi et tuo ordinio vendimus per .v. solidos decenos Tol. quos de te precio accepimus, et nos faciemus inde guarentiam de totis amparatoribus sine vestro enganno." For Raterius, see Appendix 8, No. 1 (August 1150).

and tenements.[49] Town service charges initially bore the same names as those paid by farmers. When in 1115 the count gave the Benedictines of Lézat an emplacement outside the southern wall of Toulouse, he specified that those "ex civibus atque urbanis" who settled there were to pay "servitium" and "census."[50]

Properties held by "rustici" were usually called tenements, "tenenzones" or "tenencie." Nor were tenements uniquely rural: burghers and Jews held the same. They and their holdings, moreover, were disposed of in the same way. In 1078 the count of Toulouse gave a king of Aragon "four Jews and four burghers" with all their property and the charges they paid.[51] In 1121 a viscount of Nîmes endowed his daughter and her husband from Béziers with "a Jew and a burgher and their tenements, and their successors with the same tenements" to which was later added some "'villani' with their tenements."[52] A little over thirty years later, a viscount of Béziers dowered his daughter with "a Jew and a man with his tenement in Béziers."[53]

Yet another example of the similarities between classes concerns the fief, a term already current elsewhere but rare around 1100 in western Languedoc.[54] The cartulary of the Benedictines of Lézat records acts about Comminges and adjacent regions south of Toulouse and first mentions the word in 1079. At about the same time "feudum" appears in the cartulary of Saint-Sernin designating properties near Toulouse.[55] Following the standard article on this subject by Hubert Richardot, to "dare ad feodum" meant

[49]See Appendix 6, No. 2, Nos. 4, 6, 8, 10, 11, 13, 22 and 24.

[50]Magnou and Ourliac, *Cartulaire de Lézat*, No. 1343 (August 1115), the priory of Saint-Antoine.

[51]Rosell, *Liber feudorum maior*, No. 2 (May 1078) where Bertrand pledged the king "ad suam propriam dominicaturam quatuor iudeos et quatuor burgeses cum omni earum hereditates et cum totos illos foros et illos usaticos quos facere debeant ad illo comite de Tolosa."

[52]*HGL* 5: No. 475 (without month 1121): ".i. judeum et .i. burgensem ... ambos cum tenezonibus eorum et successores eorum in eisdem et cum eisdem tenezonibus ... [and] villanos de Margarida cum tenezonibus eorum."

[53]Ibid., No. 599 (April 1154): the dowry was cash, a toll at Montpellier "et ad Beders unum Judaeum et unum hominem cum sua tenentia ubi hospitetur."

[54]Early seen in Rouquette, *Cartulaire de Béziers*, No. 43 (dated ca. 978): "Hic est breve de ipso fevo, que tenet Poncius de Bernardo episcopo in villa Paleriis vel in suo terminio."

[55]Magnou and Ourliac, *Cartulaire de Lézat*, No. 1096. Douais, *Cartulaire de Saint-Sernin*, No. 99 (eleventh century), about Combe Salomon just outside the Bourg "quas tenebam de preposito ... ad feudum" and No. 270 (dated 1060-1108) wherein family members "donaverunt a fevo duos aripentos" at Saint-Caprais just north of the same.

that the grantee received a piece of property in return for a rent in service, kind or money called a "servicium" ("servitium") or "oblia" (the usual term for a rent appraised in money), a mutation charge on the death of both the fiefholder and the "dominus," a percentage of the sale price or that of pledging and a fine for infraction of justice."[56]

The normal words for what was transmitted were a "feodum" or an "honor" and remained so throughout the period treated in this book.[57] A gift at fief was one of several contracts seen in this area wherein property or any productive good, including persons, were assigned for a term, for life or in perpetuity in return for a money rent or service.[58] As is obvious, also, the idea of service applied not only to farmers but also to lords. In 1139 a castle at Brusque far away from Toulouse in the Rouergue was given at fief and the contracting parties reminded each other that it was a "service fief."[59]

Such grants were frequently used by princes and magnates to build military clienteles, and hence both to reinforce and replace the ancient "defensio patriae," the general service obligation incumbent on every freeman. Especially rich information is available regarding the fiefs of the Trencavel viscounts of Béziers and Carcassonne, dependents of the counts of Toulouse, as well as the lords, all named William, of Montpellier. An example is the contract of a substantial fief renegotiated around 1107 by the viscount of Béziers and the archbishop of Narbonne.[60] "As a man should be who

---

[56]"Le fief roturier à Toulouse," *Revue historique de droit français et étranger*, 4th series, 14 (1935) 307-358 and 495-569. Around Lézat an earlier and overlapping terminology was that of the "acaptatio," "acapte," etc., a term meaning acquiring or a thing acquired. "Dare ad acapte" or "acaptare ad feodum," in short, was similar to the Toulousan "dare ad feodum." The use of the term that persisted in Toulouse was "retroacaptatio" (many spellings), the word for the mutation charge (or relief) described above.

[57]Douais, *Cartulaire de Saint-Sernin*, No. 132 (dated ca. 1106): "Nam honorem eorum [of the monks] unde solummodo serviens esse debebat, pro feudo diu per vim retinuerat [a usurper], nec feudum suum esse ullomodo iuste poterat probare."

[58]Magnou and Ourliac, *Cartulaire de Lézat*, No. 48 (dated 1102-1113) records that [several persons] "acquirimus" several other persons "de ... abbate ad fevum ut teneamus in vita nostra et post mortem nostram teneat ... filius noster; post mortem vero ejus remaneat Deo." I have found no example of a money fief around Toulouse, but they were common elsewhere, as in Catalonia from the early eleventh century in Bonnassie, *La Catalogne du milieu du Xe à la fin du XI siècle*, p. 757.

[59]*HGL* 5: No. 543 iii (without month 1139): "istum fevum est sirventale."

[60]Ibid., No. 427 (ca. 1107): "fevum sicut ab antecessoribus ejus adquisierat ... et vicecomes accepit fevum, et cum venit vicecomes archiepiscopo, ut ... fecit ei hominium et iuravit fidelitatem et sacramentum."

commends himself to his 'senior' with his own hands," the viscount promised aid to the archbishop "for forty days, there where you or your 'missi'
summon me," against any save his principal lord, the count of Toulouse.[61]
This service is for war, as is seen when a notable in the Narbonnais pledged
service to Béziers a little later on.[62]

A striking example shows how a local prince used such contracts to
protect his capital. Having repressed a revolt of his service cadre, a viscount of Béziers and Carcassonne replaced the traitors in 1125 and 1126,
granting the new soldiers in perpetuity towers, houses and "honores" with
dependents in return for eight months "statio" in Carcassonne annually.[63]
Similar contracts are also seen near Toulouse, but examples are few because
of the nearly complete loss of the archives of the counts. A partial substi-
tute exists, however. For reasons that escape this observer, the great cartulary of Montpellier's lords recorded the marriage of Mary, daughter of
William VII, to Bernard IV, count of Comminges, in 1199 or 1200. Her
"dotalicium" of 500 silver marks was guaranteed on the town and castle of
Muret, some eighteen kilometers southwest of Toulouse, and on other nearby places like Rieumes and Samatan.[64] Individual notables and the leading

[61]Ibid.: pledging himself "adjutor esse tibi [archbishop] per fidem sine enganno infra
xl dies la ou tu m'en comonrias per te aut per tuum missum vel missos, et de commoni-
mento non devedarei et fidelis adjutor ero tibi per fidem sine enganno de omnibus, exceptis comite Tolosano ... . Et de ista hora in antea tunc fidelis ero sine enganno, me
sciente, sicut homo debet esse ad suum seniorem cui se propriis manibus commendavit."

[62]Ibid., No. 483 ii (ca. 1124): two brothers "juramus vobis [the viscount and family]
quod ab hac hora in antea recti adjutores erimus vobis, omnibus diebus vitae nostrae cum
nostris castellis et cum nostro honore et cum hominibus nostris qui nos adjuvare voluerint ... excepto archiepiscopo ... de ista guerra quam hodie habetis cum eis vel in antea
habueritis et de totis aliis guerris quas cum ipsis habueritis in vita nostra."

[63]Ibid., No. 489 i (January 1125): "donamus tibi [name] ad fevum et propter castel-
laniam ipsam estagam et ipsum mansum qui fuit [of the 'traditor'] in civitate Carcasson-
na, cum ipsa turre et cum exitibus et redditibus suis ... et totum illum honorem ... ubicumque sit; hoc sunt homines et feminas cum suis tenentiis et cum suis usaticis et servi-
ciis ... ut per quemque annum cum tuis hominibus et tua familia facias stationem in Carcassona per viii menses et praedictam turrem custodire et gaitare facias omni tempore
et ipsam urbem custodias ... et suprascriptum honorem ... non possis dare vel vendere
aut impignorare, nisi cum nostro consilio." Ibid. iv (March 1126): a similar oath by the
new soldier reads "juro vobis vitam et membra ac fidelitatem, et juro vobis Carcassonam
et forcias ipsius atque suburbios ... et ut ipse meus haeres qui post me ipsum praedictum
honorem tenuerit et habuerit similiter juret vobis et eamdem fidelitatem faciat vobis et
posteritati vestrae per eamdem suprascriptam convenientiam in perpetuum."

[64]*Liber instrumentorum memorialium*, Nos. 206 (March 1199 or 1200), 207, 208,
209 and 210 (all four dated December 1201). In the mid-twelve hundreds notaries at

men in these towns swore fidelity, service and protection to Mary and her daughters in feudal contracts, reserving the right of male issue, if she had such.[65] The same source contains a charter of 1139 showing that tower or garrison grants similar to those in Carcassonne were customary near Toulouse, at Muret just to the south.[66]

Ecclesiastical institutions in this region enjoyed few baronial jurisdictions and hence the two cartularies illuminating this area have only sparse information on this subject. In an undated twelfth century act, however, that of Saint-Sernin refers to the "feudum de cabalariis" at Castillon just north of town.[67] Again, in 1140 a lord of Marquefave southwest of Toulouse donated property to Saint-Sernin but expressly exempted the "knights' fees and the lordship of the castle."[68] In the late eleventh century, a notable gave the abbot of Lézat a horse and promised service, fidelity and homage for his "honor" of Montaut.[69] Early in the twelfth century, the abbot of Saint-Sernin gave at fief to several persons half of an "honor" composed of properties stretching along a wide arc from Le Buguet near Montaudron just east of town to a property at Saint-Quentin hard on the Bourg of Toulouse's northeastern edge, an arc of fragments of rights stretching almost five kilometers. This composite "honor" brought with it the obligation of feeding and quartering ("albergum" or "gîte") ten knights annually, of whom the abbot could choose one to be his "man."[70]

Muret used Toulouse's first of April dating style for the start of the year and acts Nos. 207 and 209 were written by a public notary of Toulouse. If the style was April first, the document is to be dated March 1199 just as did A. Germain, the editor of the *Liber*.

[65]Ibid., No. 207, where they swore "quatinus ... vobis fideles permaneamus, et vitam et membram vestram custodiebimus et salvabimus ... [in Muret and nearby] ita scilicet ut fideles et coadjutores ... ." In ibid., No. 210, an Arnold Mascaron promised: "afizels om lur sia, et lur vida et lur membra lur gar et lur salve, a mon poder, siens gien e sens engan; et Murel ... e tota la sennoria de Murel ... . E d'aizo serai fizels e ajudaire ad ellas ... ."

[66]*HGL* 5: No. 541 (April 1139) two "castella" are given as part of the dowry of a daughter of a count of Comminges. One was held by a man who remarks that "pater meus ... et ego tenuimus et habuimus turrem et castellum de Murello de genitore tuo ... vicecomite et fuimus inde sui homines."

[67]Douais, *Cartulaire de Saint-Sernin*, No. 335.

[68]Ibid., No. 212 (dated 1140): "preter feuda militum et castri dominium."

[69]Magnou and Ourliac, *Cartulaire de Lézat*, No. 1714 (dated 1061-1108): this was a "carta acaptionis de illo honore de Montaut ... quem acaptavit a feus Ramundus Rogerius de abbato ... et dedit ei acaptationem .i. equm adpreciatum propter .xx. sol. et fuit homo de duabus manibus suis, et in tali convenientia ut fiat fidelis Deo et Sancto Petro et abbati ... et det ei receptum per legatum mandatum unumquemque annum honorifice et faciat fidancias et prestet equas et pergat cum eo et serviat ei sicut lex est."

[70]Douais, *Cartulaire de Saint-Sernin*, No. 85 (January 1129 or 1130): "honor cum

Nor were fiefs primarily military. In the Lézat cartulary, most fiefs concern churches, tithes, mills, forges as well as ordinary rental property.[71] The picture is similar in the cartulary of Saint-Sernin, in which, among other non-military properties and rights, a priest's endowment was described as a "presbyteral fief."[72] It is obvious that to give at fief was simply to contract for service in return for a grant of land or income.[73] This helps explain how it was that, in western Languedoc, "feodum" together with "honor" became terms associated with any and all rental property, noble and non-noble.

Further evidence of similarities among the classes is that, like "milites" and "burgenses," rustics served in arms. A passage in the Barcelona *Usatges* enforces agreements made between "milites" and "pedites" "who wished to go on campaign or to hunt," and, although burgesses occasionally hunted, this provision must mainly refer to rural folk.[74] In 1067 the inhabitants of the "villa" of Saint-Pierre-des-Cuisines, a village under the lordship of the Benedictines of Moissac soon to be absorbed into the Bourg of Toulouse, were exempted from military service as footmen.[75] Again, limitation of marital freedom was a mark of rural servitude, but was also known in town, even among the nobility. For both knights and "burgenses," marriage across social frontiers required a prince's grace. A charter of 1115

---

uno albergo quod omni anno faciant ad .x. milites; et unus eorum sit homo abbatis, ille scilicet quem abbas voluerit." Le Buguet and the Close of Saint-Denis are near Montaudran, but "Belangard" and "Campdolent" have not been identified. See Caster's invaluable "Le vignoble suburbaine de Toulouse au xiième siècle," *Annales du Midi* 78 (1966) 215-217.

[71]A chronologically arranged list from Magnou and Ourliac, *Cartulaire de Lézat*, reads: No. 1096 (dated 1079) a church; No. 1650 (dated ca. 1090) the forge of Saint-Germier near Muret; No. 408 (dated to the beginning of the twelfth century) a mill; No. 367 (dated 1102-1105) vineyards; No. 1095 (dated 1102-1105) a lot to clear and cultivate; No. 1209 (dated 1130-1140) a part of a church; and No. 712 (August 1171) a quarter of a tithing.

[72]Douais, *Cartulaire de Saint-Sernin*, for a similar catalogue: No. 65 (dated 1117-1140) three parts of a tithing; No. 530 (dated 1120-1125) an allotment in return for rent, mutation charges, etc.; and No. 77 (May 1121), where a tithe and other properties at La Bastide-Saint-Sernin north of town and nearby Grisolles and Bessens "et feodum presbyteralem totum" were given.

[73]As in Reynolds, *Fiefs and Vassals: The Medieval Evidence Reinterpreted*, pp. 156, 165, 205 and *passim*, and Bonnassie, *La Catalogne du milieu du Xe à la fin du XI siècle*, p. 747, who finds commoners' fiefs in Catalonia in the mid-eleventh century.

[74]Article No. 66 in Bastardas' *Usatges*: "in cavalcatas vel in venationes ire volentes."

[75]*HGL* 5: No. 277 (ca. 1067): "neque in hostem vel expeditionem pedistrem homines ibi manentes pergere cogerent."

witnesses the marriage of a burgher's daughter to the son of a vicar of Montpellier, who was a knight, and the act required the approval of the town's lord.[76] Dated to the same year, Montpellier's customs show that impediments to marital freedom were designed to keep the classes separate. Burghers were prohibited from transferring property to clergy and knights and forbidden to allow daughters dowered with property to marry knights.[77]

Overlapping functions and classes are everywhere illustrated. In the small community of Montauriol, for example, not far from Montauban north of Toulouse, about thirty-two knights and sixteen commoners owned and enfeoffed property, including allods or freeholds, from 1125 to 1140. In 1120, moreover, about twenty-two rustics held land there in fief from the nearby monastery of Saint-Théodard.[78] Most of the military fiefs seen above were also hereditary. To have an income or productive good as an hereditary right was to enjoy private property, but the bliss was mitigated by an equally hereditary service requirement. Although this detrimental aspect surely affected knights who were summoned to war, today's writers often call such obligations servile only when field or domestic labor is demanded. Hereditary right is great, but there are those who want to abrogate contracts or quit communities. The terms of later law will be seen in forthcoming chapters, but a contract of 1140 between the bishop of Maguelonne and the lord of Montpellier concerning the "homines" of Les Palus, near modern Lattes, owned by the canons of Maguelonne, shows the normal way of handling the problem: permit what cannot be prevented, but make them pay. Dependents wishing to settle in growing Montpellier could do so, the two lords said, if substitutes were provided or tenancies relinquished.[79]

[76]Ibid. 5: No. 448 ii (March 1115) where Faiditus "burgensis" married his daughter Ajalumis to William Aimonus, the vicar's son.

[77]Ibid. 5: col. 839, commands "quod alicui burgensi non liceat honorem suum aliqua occasione dare vel vendere nec impignorare militi vel sancto vel clerico, nec filiam suam liceat in uxorem dare militi cum honore Montispessulani ... ." On alienating property to clerks and knights, see Chapter Three, pp. 50-51.

[78]Galabert, "Le nombre des hommes libres dans le pays de Tarn et Garonne aux XIe et XIIe siècles," *Bulletin archéologique et historique de la société Tarn et Garonne* 29 (1901) 30-31.

[79]*HGL* 5: No. 545 (September 1140): "substituant unum de liberis vel consanguineis, cui donent honorem quem habent de Sancto Petro, isque fungatur ruralibus obsequiis et hic homo beati Petri et in honore vel in manso commoretur; vel si neutrum facere voluerint, liceat eis praedictos mansos vel honores cum consilio canonicorum alienare vel honorem omnino relinquere."

D. Social Differentiation

One suspects that nearly all, from "milites" through "burgenses" to "rustici," not to speak of the special group of the Jews, were in someway dependent from about 1050 to 1100. One can, in fact, assert that the same was true of the clergy (an order not treated in this study), a condition that helps explain the vehemence of Gregorian revolutionary or reformist ideology. The fact that the word "servus" only rarely appeared in documents may indicate that the term was still associated in literate minds with older, perhaps Roman or German, traditions of slavery and remained so until the neologism "sclavus" was generalized as a result of the slaving on Europe's eastern frontiers. Save for a few princes and magnates, then, all social groups were dominated by a tradition of service that came to them from late Rome. The program enunciated or the hope expressed by late Carolingian monarchs that all society should be organized on the basis of dependency and service to lords had almost been realized.

Because almost everybody owed it, what distinguished rustics from the others, then, was not that they owed service. It was instead the circumstance in which they performed it. Although their sweat made the world go 'round, thus eliciting acclaim from society's moralists, everyone leaned on them. Rustics, the Catalans of the *Usatges* said, "had no dignity," no honorable function, that is.[80] Their dependency was heavier than that of knights, burgers or Jews. Charged with adultery, Catalan farmers' wives could not claim trial by battle, as could those of knights or burghers, but were reduced to the cauldron.[81] Rustics also had a different age of majority, being, as it were, put to work earlier than their betters, as they were later called.[82] Dependency removed rustics from the larger community and only emancipation returned them to it. In 1149 three notables in the Toulousain freed a man together with his issue and property and, as the scribe put it in the conventional formula, gave him to the community, that is, to God, the Virgin, Saint Stephen, Saint Sernin, Count Raymond of Toulouse, Bishop Raymond of Toulouse "and to all the other people of Toulouse."[83]

---

[80]Bastardas, *Usatges*, Article No. 11, the farmer "qui nullam habeat dignitatem."

[81]Ibid., Article No. 89: wives of knights "per militem; uxores civium et burgensium et nobilium bajulorum, per pedonem; uxores rusticorum, manibus propriis per caldariam."

[82]Ibid., Article No. 92, the knights' age was twenty and rustics' fifteen.

[83]Grandselve 58, verso roll 3 v (June 1149) where Augier de Calvomonte, Pons de Villanova, "nepos" of Augier, and his wife Mabriana "solverunt et libertati vere dederunt quendam hominem nomine Arnaldum Ainerii de Columbario et omne genus suum quod iam ab eo exierat vel in antea ab eo exiet, et quicquid suum est vel suum erit, domino omnipotenti deo ... et omni cetero populo Tolose ibi presenti atque futuro."

Although sharing service with the richer classes, "rustici" and even
some ministerial persons were usually poor or modest. In Catalonia, to use
the celebrated example, an offense against a bailiff who is "noble, and who
eats white bread and rides" is to be compensated at twice the rate that of a
"non-noble bailiff."[84] But how much poorer were simple farmers or even
townsfolk? As noted earlier, the estimates of wealth in the *Usatges* state
that, below the count, each viscount was worth two "comitors," each "comitor" two "vasvassores," and each "vasvassor" having five "milites," four
knights. Another rough passage sketched the distribution of rural property.
Viscounts and "comitores," barons or lesser princes, that is, were responsible to the count of Barcelona for up to a hundred ounces of gold for each
of their "castra" with associated property or "honores." Knights were estimated at ten ounces for each knight's holding or "cavallaria terre" and
another ten for each "castrum" attributed to them, and rustics were pegged
at five shillings.[85] Viewing this material, Bonnassie has systematized Catalan monetary compensations for death or injury as:[86]

GRADE	DEATH	INJURY
Viscounts	160	120
"comitores"	80	60
"vasvassores"	40	30
"milites"	12	6
"rustici"	6	2

On Calvomonte, his family and relationship to the Tolosa and Villanova families of
Toulouse, see my *Repression of Catharism*, pp. 271 and 292.

[84]Bastardas, *Usatges*, Article No. 10: "Bajulus ... si nobilis est et panem frumenti
comedit cotidie et equitat, emendetur sicut miles. Ignobilis vero bajulus huius composi-
tionem medietatem habeat."

[85]Ibid., Article No. 20: "Omnes homines debet firmare directum senioribus suis
ubicumque seniores eorum illis mandaverint in suo. Ad potestatem quoque vicecomites
et comitores sui, per unumquodque castrum cum honore suo, per centum uncias auri
Valencie. Miles vero per decem per unamquam cavalleriam terre, et per castrum eum
adempramento eius per alias decem; per fevos minores secundum eorum valorem; per
hominiaticum namque per mediam cavalleriam terre, de hoc quod ad fidem pertinebit.
Rusticus namque per quinque solidos." See also Bonnassie, *La Catalogne du milieu du
Xe à la fin du XI siècle*, pp. 799-802.

[86]*La Catalogne du milieu du xe à la fin du xie siècle*, p. 908.

Looking beyond these categories, the value of "burgenses" must have varied. In the passages of the *Usatges* cited earlier in this chapter, the oath of a burgher was said to be equivalent to that of a knight who could no longer serve in arms and "pedones" (foot militiamen such as burghers largely were) were only half as valuable as mounted knights. In short, urban folk had about half the value of knights, but the difference between merchants and crafts- or tradesmen is nowhere spelled out. It is even more difficult to estimate rustic wealth. According to Bonnassie, the only "rustici" whose oaths are listed in the *Usatges* are those with a manse and a pair of oxen valued at seven shillings, and those called "bachalarii" valued at up to four "mancusi" of Valencian gold and thereafter trial by the cauldron.[87] How many farmers owned two oxen?

In short, although its authors knew what they were talking about, the indeterminate figures there cited, the span of time over which the articles were written or assembled and their marked succinctness limit the *Usatges de Barcelona* to providing only impressionistic figures. One nevertheless divines that, in terms of wealth, the various classes clearly overlapped and, moreover, when the relatively few nobles above the knightly grade are removed, social differentiation seems not to have been stark. What probably made the universalized service ethos of this age difficult to bear was that a larger percentage of the poor hovered on cliff's edge than in modern western European society.

[87]Bastardas, *Usatges*, Articles Nos. 49-50.

3

Townsfolk

A. EVOLUTIONS

To repeat what was said in the previous chapter, twelfth century society in and around Toulouse was divided into "milites," "burgenses" and "rustici." The first and last of these social categories were largely rural, but not a few "milites" lived in town or had habitations there. Although largely urban, burghers likewise owned property outside of town, invested heavily in rural business and also often lived in communities so small as almost to be villages. Legal differentiation aside, town and country overlapped at this time. Even later around 1200 legal documents usually called towns with episcopal sees "civitates" and those without bishops "ville"; and in the countryside fortified centers were designated "castra" and unfortified ones "ville." In brief, the word "villa" referred to any built-up area with a uniform jurisdiction and was therefore applied to both town and village. Thus the town of Toulouse was a "villa" in 1158 and so was the hamlet of Braqueville across the Garonne south of town somewhat earlier.[1]

Within urban centers, the twelfth century witnessed an equalization in law of the body of the citizenry, which partly reflected the political evolution of Languedocian society. It may be recalled that, in the decades before 1100, substantial towns and rural lordships began to undermine princely authority. Seen elsewhere in the partial dismantling of some monarchies and principalities, this devolution of political authority was especially marked in the extensive dominions of the counts of Toulouse, extending from Provence in the east to inland Languedoc in the west. The striving of Gregorian churchmen to unchain themselves from lay domination deprived old governmental structures of public justification and was accompanied or followed

---

[1]*HGL* 5: No. 511 (dated 1158): "in villa Tolosa, tam in urbe quam suburbio," and Bracavilla in Saint-Étienne 227 (26 DA 2 79) (dated to the early twelfth century). On this point in the Midi generally, see Dupont, *Les cités de la Narbonnaise Première depuis l'invasions germaniques jusqu'à l'apparition du consulat*, pp. 633ff.

by a general, if usually quiet, push toward local independence by secular society. This liberation was expressed by magnates reducing the service and taxes owed their princes. To use Coulange's idea, they also obtained independence by subjecting the inhabitants of their little states. More modestly, the ministerial militia with whose aid they built their power also profited from this role to enhance its status, becoming by about 1200 a knightly aristocracy, to use a meliorative term. This was accomplished both by making salaries or fiefs hereditary and by building family property.

In this devolution or decentralization of power, a leading role was played by what can best be described by Arthur Giry's felicitous phrase as the "collective lordships" of the towns and especially, for the present purposes, by the city that was the capital of the western and inland reaches of Languedoc, Toulouse itself. From its initial steps just after 1100, the stages of the political emancipation of this community have already been explored, and it suffices to say here that the high point of Toulousan political liberty was attained in the decades around 1200. From 1189 until 1229, the leading families of the town, although somewhat impeded by the authority, at once durable and recalcitrant, of the count of Toulouse, created institutions describable as quasi-republican and self-governing. In the period from 1202 to 1205, indeed, the consuls or board of governors of this community even launched the town militia against twenty-three towns and lordships of the Toulousain, clearly designing in the Italian style to conquer a "contado," the "patria Tolosana," as the town fathers called it.[2] Although slowed both by the aggression of Toulouse, their powerful capital, and by their own simple social structure and modest wealth, small towns and even villages in the countryside eventually evolved in much the same direction.[3]

Centralization and the growth of local autonomy would have been difficult without the achievement of a measure of unity. There were differences, for example, within the "universitas populi" of Toulouse. Foremost of these, as seen in Chapter One above, was the distinction between the old Roman "civitas" and the Bourg or settlement around the monastery of Saint-Sernin. The words "civitas" and "urbs" were usually reserved for the old City; "burgus" or "suburbium," on the other hand, meant the Bourg.[4] And

[2]For this history, see my *Liberty and Political Power*, pp. 733-738, and for the general political history of Toulouse in its region, the early chapters of the same book. For analogies see Dilcher, *Entstehung des lombardischen Stadtkommune*, especially pp. 134-141, where he speaks about the unification of the "milites" and "cives" of the different Lombard towns in the late eleventh century and the development of a community.

[3]See the observations on the country town of Isle-Jourdain in my "Village, Town, and City," pp. 142-190.

[4]Terminology was more complex than this. "Civitas," for example, early meant the

the emotional division separating the "burgenses" of the Bourg and the "cives" of the City remained significant, even central, in the life and constitution of the community. Other special regional identities were less durable, but clearly had a role to play during the twelfth century.

The town's persistent class divisions were just as weighty. Just as elsewhere, a difference between the militias of the "milites" and "pedites" divided the population in terms of service for defense. Some of the citizens of the community were knightly and even baronial, owning property and lordships outside of town.[5] Within any community, such notables retained qualities setting them apart from the mass. This was noticeable in the countryside as shown by the terms used in the treaties between the town of Toulouse and the small rural towns or lordships from 1202 to 1205. These documents usually described the parties as the "milites et probihomines," the "milites, probihomines et barriani" or simply the "milites et homines" of such and such a locality. The "barriani" were those who lived in "barria," places either outside the community's fortifications or in unfortified villages.[6] The same terminology was also used to describe the inhabitants of Toulouse.

That this social division was real, quite as real as in the earlier days discussed in the previous chapter, is also proved by documents transferring real property. These often specified that real property was not to be alienated to knights or, for that matter, to the members of the greater social order, the clergy.[7] Although a reason for this prohibition may have been that

---

whole town and continued to do so, but this usage rarely invaded documents written for the urban administration. From antiquity, also, "civitas" and even "urbs" meant the region around town and had the significance of "county" in the early twelfth century. For this, see Dupont, *Les cités de la Narbonnaise Première*, especially pp. 501ff. and 633ff.

[5]See family histories of the Tolosa and Villanova in my *Repression of Catharism*, pp. 268-283 and 292-304, and also those of the Falgario, Noerio and Turribus in Appendix 1, Nos. 7, 10 and 15.

[6]For example, TAM, AA 1, the treaties dated from June to December 1222 including No. 30 Villemur, No. 38 Aubiet, No. 41 Blanquefort, No. 60 Corbarieu, where the variant "domini, milites, et homines," is seen, and No. 81 Saverdun "milites et barriani," headed by their consuls. In a small community, the latter formulation seemed suitable. In PAN, J 314 22 (November 1241) where three knights and four consuls of Saverdun appear together with "quidam alii milites et barriani ejusdem castri," and TBM, MS 609, fols. 99 and 100v, where a knight reports in May and July 1246 that, forty years ago, many "tam milites quam barriani" were buried in the cemetery of Montesquieu in the Lauragais.

[7]A typical example at Toulouse is in E 896 (November 1183) where the fiefholder "non debet hunc honorem vendere aut inpignorare nec ullomodo a se alienare ullo homini vel femine de religione nec alicui persone litterate neque militibus."

alienation or gifts to the clergy fell under the dead hand, it is hard to see how knightly property differed from that of other laymen at this time. The blanket prohibition was clearly more honored in the breach than in the observance and was sometimes expressly revoked, but it surely asserts that property possessed by knights was different from that owned by commoners.[8]

Excluding the above, twelfth century charters, public or private, were remarkably free of references to social orders or social distinctions. They nevertheless existed in Toulouse, and surfaced as politically significant when a popular party gained control of the consulate, hitherto in the hands of the limited group of families comprising an informal patriciate that had emerged during the century. The consular term of 1202-1203 saw the appearance of a more popular consulate, one in which merchants and money-changers were not bashful about listing their specialties in public documents. During this period, the town not only identified itself in a new and vigorous way by attempting, as noted earlier, to conquer the "patria Tolosana," but also insisted on the superiority of the court of the consuls over all jurisdictions both in town and nearby, starting with that of the count's vicar but also including the courts of the ecclesiastical closes.[9] In addition, the once free courts of arbitration wherein the leading families and institutions of the town had settled much of their litigation about property came under consular scrutiny and regulation. More significantly in the present context, a hitherto never and, indeed, never to be, defined group of Toulousan "cabalerii" is seen to exercise or to have exercised jurisdiction. Issued about 1204, an informal memorandum (emanating from the consuls of the town but not inserted in the official cartularies of the City and Bourg) distinguished between the "cabalerii" and their elected judges called the "consules cabaleriorum" and the "alii probihomines" of the town and their consuls, that is, the town consulate. In this document the town consuls asserted their superiority over the "consules cabaleriorum" before whose courts suits of "cabalerii" were brought and regulated them just as they had the other non-political and private arbitral courts.[10]

---

[8]E 506 i (February 1181, copied in 1260), also in Saige, *Juifs du Languedoc*, No. 6 from Malta 2 155, states that the "feodotarius habeat licenciam vendendi vel impignorandi cuicumque voluerit, scilicet domui milicie vel ospitalis vel infirmis vel quibuscumque aliis hominibus voluerit." Such freedoms had also been previsioned in local law elsewhere, as in *Usatges de Barcelona*, Article 145, which permits knights and rustics to give allods to churches.

[9]This history is discussed in my *Liberty and Political Power*, pp. 66-68.

[10]The pertinent document is in *HGL* 8: No. 125, and is also published in full in my *Liberty and Political Power*, pp. 355-356, note 50.

Exemplified especially clearly in Italy's city states, the desire of the richer knightly citizenry who served as mounted militiamen to have their own courts handle their own cases (limited only by the Roman legal principle "actor sequitur forum rei") had surfaced in Toulouse.[11] Because of the continuing though declining imperial power, such class or order jurisdictions were far more long-lived in Italy than in Toulouse where no efficacious princely authority was able to support the "cabalerii" against the mass of the community. At Toulouse, in fact, consular legislation rendered so nugatory the power of the "consules cabaleriorum" that neither the "cabalerii" or their judges are ever heard of again.[12] After 1204, it seems, all free citizens shared a common law and a measure of real equality, until the radical changes in the thirteenth century explored below.

In spite of lingering differences between knights and commoners, twelfth century Toulouse witnessed the growth of a community within the City and Bourg, one seen in many towns of the time.[13] All citizens had similar rights and duties and all were simply described as "cives" or sometimes, referring to the two divisions of the town, as "cives et burgenses." In 1203 two persons testified in court what it meant to be a citizen, namely that they paid the common taxes and served in the militia.[14] Presumably one of the lords of Verfeil, their opponent in the same case, described how he had become a citizen: he had acquired property in town and then petitioned the consuls to receive him, which they did. He also took care to have a public notary record that fact.[15]

[11]For analogies, see my *Liberty and Political Power*, pp. 357-358, note 56, and especially for Italy, Dahm, *Untersuchungen zur Verfassung und Strafrechtsgeschichte der italienischen Stadt im Mittelalter*, pp. 59-60.

[12]My *Liberty and Political Power*, pp. 144-146, and, regarding Italy, especially note 56.

[13]Described, for example, by Dilcher, *Lombardischen Stadtkommune*, pp. 158-160, where he says that the unification of the "milites" and "cives" made the average north Italian town into an "örtlich bestimmter Rechtsbereich" in which the community was a "Körperschaft." This was not invariable, however. Some communities leaned toward the "milites," others to the "pedites," and some, such as Mantua (p. 140), failed to unify at all.

[14]TAM, AA 2 84 (April 1203): charged with being serfs at Verfeil, they stated that they had long done their duty as citizens because "in hac villa Tolose stabant et steterant xx annos et amplius et, quando habuerunt potestatem, fecerant exercitus huius ville et consuetudines et husus sicut alii habitantes in Tolosa, secundum suum locum et posse bona fide."

[15]Ibid., where Arnold Ysarnus stated that "postmodum adquisierat domos et alios honores in Tolosa et preparaverat se ante consules Tolosanos, ut eum pro de Tolosa cog-

Further information on what defined a citizen awaits the later thirteenth century. In 1282 an oath taken by a new public notary was inserted in the matricule of the notaries of Toulouse. By then the king of France was Toulouse's lord and hence the notary swore service and obedience to him as well as to the town's consuls. As to the latter, a "civis Tholose," he avowed, owed military service, advice or counsel, which meant taxes and service as a militiaman, town officer, judge delegate, etc.[16]

B. MINISTERIAL DEPENDENTS

Dependency in the Toulousain will be investigated anew in the next chapter, but what may be examined here is whether dependents played a role in town society. I note in Chapter Twelve below that in 1229 the owners of raw material put out to be manufactured in the cloth industries were called "domini" and "domine," and that the artisans who worked their cloth were obliged, just as was often the case of dependent farmers, to deliver the finished goods to the master's or mistress' house, there to be weighed on their scales.[17] One is initially tempted to wonder if these workers were legally dependent, but it is obvious that they were not. Here, however, social conceptions are being talked about, not economic reality: although rarely recognized in law, a measure of economic dependency or servitude is shared by everybody but the richest and most powerful in most medieval and modern societies.

Later on in 1286 when the *Custom* of Toulouse was published, two articles dealt with the agents or "recipientes" of the presumably senior merchants called "domini mercandarie." These passages proposed that such agents are entitled to a fourth of the profit of a venture and adequate maintenance.[18] Their word, furthermore, is to be trusted in rendering accounts as long as the books are examined by two or more reputable merchants.[19]

---

noscerent quod fecerant, de qua cognitione ipse Arnaldus Ysarnus quoddam autenticum instrumentum manu publici tabellionis factum consulibus produxit ... ."

[16]TAM, BB 204, No. 210 16 (June 1282), owing "consulibus Tholose fortiam, adiutorium, consilium, et celare," he stated that "ego sum civis Tholose et de foro civium Tholose et ... dem et contribuam in omnibus collectis, expensis, et missionibus communitatis Tholose ad voluntatem consulum ... iuxta facultates et divitias meas sicut unus ex aliis civibus Tholosanis."

[17]Chapter Twelve, p. 221 below.

[18]Gilles, *Coutume de Tolouse*, Article No. 72: "ad quartum denarium quem de lucro recipere et habere," and sufficient food and wine.

[19]Ibid., Article No. 73: to render account "super administratione et lucro et damno dicte mercandarie, reddito primitus computo et ratione domino dicte mercandarie ex

Significant for the present purpose is that such conventions were made between a merchant and his "mancipium" or "socius," these being defined as
persons owning none of the merchandise.[20] The fact that "mancipius," a
word sometimes meaning slave, was linked with "socius" implies that it was
used to describe somebody whose services were bought. The term nevertheless had another meaning, namely that of a junior member of a family or
"junior." Nor was it pejorative: one of the most distinguished patrician
families of Toulouse, the Maurandi, favored "Bonmacip" as a first name
generation after generation.[21] Lastly, "mancipius" was paralleled in the
Bordelais and England by "valettus," a term once applied to a wealthy wine
merchant named Arnold de Unde when he was an associate of the initially
greater merchant Bertrand de Palacio in the twelve-fifties and sixties.[22] In
short, the "mancipii" of Toulousan merchants have nothing to do with servitude, save perhaps economic, but about that the documents are silent.

If dependent townsfolk were few at Toulouse and elsewhere, urban
servitude was clearly a political problem and not just an interesting social
oddity. In 1254 an arbitration of disputes between the baronial lords of
nearby Isle-Jourdain and the town's elected consuls illustrates the issue.
Future questions were to be settled by arbitrative panel, of which half was
chosen by the consuls and half by the lord, but expressly not by his vicar,
not from his family and not from among his dependents.[23] The latter
might well be unreliable citizens. Such serfs, furthermore, sometimes
enjoyed privileges because the baron's vicar in Isle-Jourdain had prohibited
them from paying the community's common tax assessments.[24]

---

predictis laudabili videlicet et rationabili, ad notitiam duorum proborum aut plurium mercatorum."

   [20]Ibid., Article No. 73: "videlicet si dictus recipiens mancipius aut socius talis
extiterit qui nullam partem habeat in dicta mercandaria ex conventione sed ad voluntatem
domini mercandarie."

   [21]Recorded in the family history in my *Repression of Catharism*, pp. 229-241.

   [22]Ibid., p. 291.

   [23]MADTG, A 297, fols. 7 and 151, partly published in Cabié, *Chartes de coutumes
inédites de la Gascogne Toulousaine*, p. 24 (September 1254).

   [24]Ibid.: the vicar "inhibet hominibus propriis dicti domini ne respondeant vel dent
aliquid missionibus in dicta villa ab universitate comuniter facta." The settlement provided that, save for the expenses incurred in providing the present arbitration, "homines
proprii Jordani, qui eidem tenentur et subjiciuntur ratione homagii, obligentur et etiam
teneantur respondere, exsolvere seu satisffacere omnibus expensis, missionibus, collectis
seu talliis quas faciet seu fecit comunitas seu universitas dicte ville Insule, sicut alii
homines de dicta universitate."

The previous chapter noted that well into the thirteenth century the count enjoyed close relations with some Toulousan trades- and craftsmen, such as the boatmen on the Garonne river. The link, furthermore, between the prince and the town's workers and their crafts and trades had both economic and political significance.[25] In addition to this, individual inhabitants of the town were in ministerial bondage to the prince until into the thirteenth century. In 1236 Arnold Natalis, son of a Natalis "mercator de Salvitate" (the "salvetat" in the City), confessed himself to be, "that is, his own body, a man" of the count of Toulouse, and that, furthermore, his father and his predecessors had been the count's dependents.[26] Perhaps, however, Arnold's act and his assertion about his forebears was prompted by a wish to avoid the confiscation of family property for reason of heresy. Still alive in 1230 but dead by the time of his son's act of voluntary servitude in 1236, Natalis was to be condemned posthumously for his beliefs in 1237.[27] The inheritance of "Natalis de Salvitate" was listed among those of the Toulousan citizens amnestied in the royal diploma of 1279 and, for what it's worth, the rubric in the count's cartulary, not the act itself, describes his son Arnold as a "citizen."[28] Arnold probably hoped that the count would extend himself to protect his dependents.

Records concerning the count's Christian bailiffs and vicars remind historians that princes usually entrusted government to three kinds of officers: hereditary, ministerial and appointed ones, of which the last often farmed or bought an office for a term. The history of the vicars of Toulouse, the count's premier officer there during the twelfth century, records the use of all three methods.[29] When first seen, the vicarage appears to have been

[25]See Chapters Four, Five and Ten of this study and my *Liberty and Political Power*, pp. 109-111.

[26]PAN, JJ 19 173v-174r (December 1236): a typical act of voluntary subjection (for these, see the next Chapter) wherein Arnold "concessit ... se, scilicet suum proprium corpus, esse hominem" of the count, and also claimed "quod pater suus et alii antecessores sui ab antiquo erant homines a patre et aliis antecessoribus ipsius domini comitis."

[27]Saint-Étienne 227 (26 DA 2 47) (November 1230, copied in 1249 and 1256): "Natalis mercator de Salvitate."

[28]This case is described in my *Repression of Catharism*, p. 104, No. 188.

[29]Readers are reminded that the hereditary viscounts of Toulouse had been pushed out of the town early in the twelfth century by the counts as described in my *Liberty and Political Power*, pp. 23 and 193; for the history of the vicarage, see ibid., pp. 33-35, 52-53, 171 and 193. This treatment contains an error because I read back late twelfth century circumstances when defining the earlier vicarage, mistakenly saying that the office "was not given in hereditary fief." The desire of lords to replace or destroy hereditary vicars was also experienced elsewhere. In Montpellier in the *Liber instrumen-*

held by the Tolosa family of the City. Their hold must have been well established, because by the time evidence is available the family no longer acquired it directly from the count. In 1132 or 1133 the barons of Calmont well south of Toulouse granted the husbands of two sisters of the Tolosa family the "vicaria Tolose et Burgi," one of whose scions, Gerald Engilbertus, appears in a charter as the "vicarius civitatis Tolose" in 1125 and 1127.[30] In short, during the early twelfth century, a baronial line exercised a major comital office and entrusted it to a related knightly family inhabiting Toulouse. Seen holding office in 1138, the next named vicar, Pons de Villanova, was also related to the Calmonts and in 1164 was both vicar and chapterman, a member of the board that in 1189 was to become the consulate of Toulouse.[31]

During Villanova's vicarage, however, the count appears to have begun to free the office from this family linkage. An initial indication of the change occurred in 1164, when the vicar was assisted by a subvicar named Espanolus. Espanolus was a minter, conceivably of foreign origin and assuredly not of an old family like Villanova.[32] He became full vicar in 1167 and was the first known non-hereditary vicar of Toulouse. One therefore guesses that this minter and vicar was ministerial, that is, a dependent of the count. Evidence also exists that succeeding vicars were in the same position. The English chronicler Roger of Hoveden (Howden) described Peter Seilani, one of the bailiffs of the count of Toulouse captured by Richard the Lion Hearted in 1188, as a "serviens."[33] Peter was from a family living in the "salvetat" in the City (where, incidently, Natalis had come from), two of whose members, William and Bernard, were bailiffs and vicars of Toulouse from 1176 to 1186.[34] Later on, in 1251, the inher-

---

torum memorialium, No. 123 (October 1197), William VIII bought the vicarage from a hereditary vicar.

   [30]For the early history of the vicarage see my *Repression of Catharism*, pp. 270-271, in the Tolosa family history, where mention is made both of the above Gerald, the Calmont grant and Peter Regimundus (or Raymond), a vicar in the late years of the eleventh century and presumably a member of the same family. For its business interests, see also Appendix 6, No. 1.

   [31]*Repression of Catharism*, pp. 292-293.

   [32]Although his name and that of other minters, notably Amoravis and Florranus, are foreign to Toulouse, the conjecture that he was in origin Jewish is based on a mistaken interpretation of a charter mentioning another minter, Pons David, in my *Liberty and Political Power*, p. 53, which is corrected in my *Repression of Catharism*, p. 203.

   [33]Roger of Hoveden, *Chronica*, Rolls Series 51, part 2: 339.

   [34]See the vicarial lists in my *Liberty and Political Power*, pp. 171-172, and the Seilani in Appendix 1, No. 14.

itance of a vicar named Peter Rogerius, who served from 1194 to 1208 and
was long since dead, was claimed by the count because, he asserted, Peter
was subject to him "by the yoke of servitude."[35]

Memories of earlier actualities aside, it is certain that the ministerial
status of the vicars did not last long after 1200. When the consuls were as-
cendant and relatively independent of the count, they imposed an oath on
the newly chosen vicars and probably participated in their election. Since
they themselves were certainly not ministerial (not, at least, after their
victory over the count in 1189), it is hardly likely that their and the count's
vicars were.[36] In the period after 1189, furthermore, the ministerial quality characteristic of comital officers was clearly collapsing. Although, for
example, the money of Toulouse was formally the count's, he had lost control of it by 1205 and 1208 when it fell under the oversight of the consuls.[37]
What is more, the old minters were themselves evolving. The David family
were minters and documents show that its members treated or had come to
treat their portion of the mint as heritable property. In 1180 Bernard David
emancipated his son Pons, giving him a share in the family property which
included a portion of the mint of Toulouse. In 1199 Pons bought a quarter
of this once-public facility from the sons of the onetime vicar and minter
Espanolus (one of whom had married his sister) as well as from seven other
heads of family and their male issue.[38]

Nor were the minters the only ones to lose their service vocation. Durand de Sancto Barcio, who held office as vicar in 1214 and then again after the ejection of the crusaders from Toulouse from 1228 to 1235, seems
to have stepped over the frontier between ministerial and appointive office.
He may even have bought or farmed his vicarage. In 1227 the count released him from the "villicatio" of his office, and recognized that he owed
the ex-vicar no less than 4000 shillings of Toulouse.[39] A further indication is that a member of a onetime ministerial family turned against the

---

[35]Malta 118 8 (May 1251): "cui Ramundus tunc comes in solidum heredis jure
successit," the count had held all his property "suo juri et ratione dominii, cum dictus
Petrus Rogerius esset ei servitudinis iugo subjectus."

[36]My *Liberty and Political Power*, pp. 111-114.

[37]Ibid., pp. 108-109.

[38]Ibid., pp. 53 and Published Document No. 9 on p. 203, and also by Boyer in his
Mélanges I: Mélanges d'histoire du droit occidental, p. 152. Espanolus had retired into
the Hospital of Saint John in Malta 116 9 (dated September 1186), and had divided his
goods among his sons in ibid. 11 (December 1187). A history of the David family is in
my *Repression of Catharism*, pp. 203-208.

[39]PAN, J 317 16 (November 1227). His dates of office are given in Chapter 13,
pp. 241-242 below.

count during the Albigensian Crusade. Peter Seillanus, scion of a family
that, as noted several paragraphs above, served as comital vicars and bailiffs, was among the first companions of Dominic, the sainted founder of
the Dominican order. So devoted to his new religion was Peter that he remained in Toulouse to preach even during the Albigensian war when the
founder was usually sheltering in the crusaders' camp. His animus against
Count Raymond VII was notorious. When the count objected to his serving
as an inquisitor in Toulouse, he did so, according to the Dominican Pelisson's chronicle, because Peter had become his enemy, he who had been
both "a member of his predecessors' court and a Toulousan citizen."[40]

Natalis and presumably others in his station recall to mind the Jews
who, as seen above, were likened to Christian burghers and merchants dependent on local princes including the count of Toulouse around 1100.[41]
Although available documentation is thin and is not to be compared to the
rich notarial registers for Perpignan used by Richard Emery, the Jews of
Toulouse are known to have busied themselves as long-range merchants and
also as moneylenders. An action dated 1200 dealing with property at Fontanas just north of town owned by the brothers Isaac and Moses was witnessed by co-religionists from Verdun-sur-Garonne and Carcassonne, the
former place located about thirty kilometers north of town and the latter
about ninety to the south.[42] These witnesses were surely merchants. Forty
and more years later near Lérida far to the south in Catalonia, an Astruc
"judaeus de Tolosa" is seen busy as a merchant and moneylender.[43] As
to moneylending, two examples will suffice. Ispaniolus, Jew of Verdun-sur-
Garonne, and his son Solomon acquired prime properties on the present rue
du Taur fronting on the Portaria from 1178 onward and their transactions
provide clear evidence of moneylending. Desiring to return to Verdun presumably to avoid the Albigensian war, then centering on Toulouse, Solomon sold this property in 1212 and 1213.[44] In a charter dated 1207, a
Toulousan resident named Alacer acquired a "curia" (a large farm) near the
"caminum Francigenum" leading south of town because of a debt owed by

---

[40]*Chronique*, ed. Duvernoy, pp. 68-70: "qui fuerat de curia patrum suorum et civis
Tolosanus." Peter's history is in my *Repression of Catharism*, pp. 23, 31-33, 50-51, 54
and 60, and below in Appendix 1, No. 14.

[41]See Chapter Two, p. 36.

[42]Appendix 2, No. 4, p. 366.

[43]Ibid., No. 2, p. 364, the acts being dated 1249 and 1251.

[44]Ibid., No. 3, p. 365.

the monks of Roncesvalles. Later, in 1227, the count gave his vicar in Toulouse all debts owed to Abraham and Belitus, Alacer's sons.[45]

These Jews were dependents of the count, a local ownership of this people seen elsewhere in the French kingdom. Although charter evidence awaits the thirteenth century, they could not alienate (and probably could not acquire) real property without the count's consent. When Solomon, son of Ispanolus, sold his substantial house and its attachments in 1212, the document records the count's express consent, and the same was true when Alacer's son Belitus alienated a farm near Montaudran in 1231.[46] Again, in 1249 when the Jewish community was forced to sell an emplacement to the citizens financing the installation of the Carmelites in the City, its agents were licensed to do so by the count.[47] A license of this kind was a tax on Jewish transactions, one systematized by the count in 1242. At that date Raymond VII granted all Jews, male and female, the right to alienate property, requiring in return five percent of the sale price and two and a half percent of a mortgage.[48] This tax was not as exploitative as it sounds because it was domanial: landlords normally took a percentage of the sale and pledge prices from their tenants, free or servile.

Dependents though they were, Jews enjoyed a certain amount of self-government, as is shown in actions representing the religious community. When Alacer acted in 1217 for the Jews of Toulouse, he was described as their "bailiff" or agent, or when, at a time of greater legal sophistication in 1281, three Jews sold a rent for the group, they were called "proctors, syndics or legal representatives of the university or community of the 'scola Iudeorum'."[49] In the latter case, the agents are described in terms similar to those employed for solicitors among Christians, thus showing that Christian notaries knew that the Jews had their own law.

Although no evidence exists other than that they frequently appear as witnesses to comital acts, Jews surely provided the count with administrative and fiscal services. The excellent archivist and historian Gustave Saige

---

[45]Ibid., No. 1, pp. 361-362.

[46]For Solomon, see ibid., No. 3, p. 366, and for Belitus, No. 1, p. 362.

[47]Catel, *Mémoires de l'histoire du Languedoc*, p. 237 (June 1249).

[48]Saige, *Juifs du Languedoc*, No. 35 from PBN, *Collection Doat* 37: fol. 120 (June 1242, copied in 1260 and 1279, all attested by the apposition of the consuls' seal): twelve pence per pound "de qualibet libra denariorum Tholose" for a sale and sixpence for a pledge or mortgage.

[49]For Alacer in 1217 see Appendix 2, No. 1, p. 360. E 506 (January 1281) in Saige, op. cit., No. 42.: three "procuratores et syndici universitatis seu communitatis scole iudeorum Tolose seu actores eorumdem et actores ... constituti ... ."

remarked that they did not hold office in the domains of Raymond VII.[50]
He was right as far as the documents show because they never carried titles
of office in Christian government, but this was probably obeisance to the
well-known papal anti-Jewish legislation. Issued during the pontificates of
Alexander III (d. 1181) and Innocent III, especially in the Fourth Lateran
Council of 1215, this extensive body of law prohibited, among much else,
the employment of Jews in princely administration.[51] Judging from documents concerning Provincialis and his son Bonuspuer, however, these Jews
are known to have served Raymond VI and VII's government for over fifty
years, from 1191 to 1247. That this relationship was known to their contemporaries is probably why a street in the City was named after Provincialis. Their function may also have been reflected in a title because a
Bonuspuer, perhaps Provincialis' son of that name, was once called "jugerius" in a charter.[52]

In brief, although old functional distinctions between the social orders
had assuredly not been obliterated, a measure of equality, especially among
citizens, seems to have triumphed in the law administered within the city of
Toulouse before the Albigensian Crusade.

C. Vocabularies and equalities

Even when the difference between town and countryside is admitted, it is
remarkable how simple the social vocabulary of the charters had become before 1200. What had emerged as the principal method of characterizing or
identifying individuals was that some of the lower and many of the middle
and upper ranks of the population both in town and countryside were identified only by surnames, surnames that often became family ones. Other than
names, a subject to be discussed in Chapter Nine below, the charters drawn
by public scribes are remarkable for the absence of social identification.

Some titles were naturally retained. The count of Toulouse was always
identified by his title and so were visiting notables such as the counts of
Foix or Comminges, although one rarely sees viscounts gratified by a mention of their dignities. As had been true in the past, these worthies were also
often described as "viri nobiles."[53] The various grades of the clergy were

---

[50]Saige, *Juifs du Languedoc*, p. 20.

[51]Discussed in Gilles, "Commentaires méridionales des prescriptions canoniques sur
les Juifs," *Cahiers de Fanjeaux* 12 (1977) 24-50.

[52]The family history is recorded in Appendix 2, No. 2, pp. 362-365.

[53]For example, TAM, AA 1 80 (September 1222) where one reads "nobilis dominus
Centullus, dei gratia comes de Astariaco," and *HGL* 3: No. 174, col. 651, where the
count of Foix and his son are described as noblemen.

also mentioned, as was the office of the vicar and that of the "capitularii" or "consules" (as they began to style themselves from 1175 or 1176) of the town, but the mention of such functional titles is hardly of more significance than the identification of a craftsman by the name of his business. A baker usually baked for his working life; a consul was elected to serve for a year or two and, by about 1200, a vicar was appointed for a term. The only group designation common to lay individuals in the decades around 1200 was that of "judeus" to describe a member of the Jewish community, a subject sketched above.

Although themselves rare, the most common titles attributed to individuals around 1200 are those of "dominus" and "bonushomo" or "probushomo." The first was usually applied to counts and princes and, as "dompnus," to prelates and choirmonks.[54] "Dominus" was also occasionally applied to senior scions of knightly families and, on one occasion, was even attributed to a very rich Toulousan, Pons de Capitedenario.[55] This restricted use of the word "dominus" or "Monsieur" remained normal until the latter decades of the thirteenth century. An exception to this rule is the common use of the singular "domina" in notarial charters. Every senior and married woman, however humble her social status, was normally so titled in the charters, unless described as a wife or daughter, for example, in a testament.[56]

In the plural, however, "domini" was much more democratic than in the singular. Similarly, the vernacular words "baros" or "senhors" were thought by the author of the *Canso* of the Albigensian war to be the normal way of addressing the citizenry.[57] The count of Toulouse so addressed a general assembly at Montaudran and a similar word was put in the mouth of Simon de Montfort when he spoke to a group of Toulousan hostages.[58] The local magnate Pelfort de Rabastens began his oration to the citizenry assembled in "parlamens" with "Baros, vos de Toloza ... ." – "You men

[54]See Grandselve 4 (April 1203) where a sale to the Cistercians of Grandselve was witnessed by three "monachi," each one called "domnus," and by three "fratres," not so titled. This distinction was infrequent in the charters where both the monks and "conversi" were usually simply called "fratres." The vernacular equivalent is seen in PBN, MS lat. 11010, fol. 52 (February 1262) where mention was made of "lo senhor N canonges" of Agen.

[55]TAM, AA 1 81 (December 1222).

[56]In my *Men and Women*, p. 37.

[57]*Canso,* ed. Martin-Chabot, 3: 190, lines 49-50: "Dels baros de la vila e de los poestatz / Cavaliers e borzes entendutz e celatz ... ."

[58]Ibid. 2: 4, line 26; the count of Toulouse: "'Senhors,' so ditz lo coms ... ," and ibid. 2: 218, line 53: Simon: "'Baro,' so ditz lo coms ... ."

of Toulouse ... ."⁵⁹ The Latin equivalent of these vernacular words was
"Domini." The Dominican William Pelisson has John Textor beginning
his complaint to the crowd about his arrest for heresy with "Domini! Lis-
ten!"⁶⁰ Later on in 1269, defending himself against a charge of incitement
to sedition, a citizen named Guarnerius described his attempt to save a
town policeman from an enraged mob. He rushed, he says, to stop the
mob that was dragging the "nuncius" down the street, crying out to them
"Domini! Don't do it! For the love of God don't do it!"⁶¹

"Bonushomo" or "probushomo" are more complicated. Historians have
often asserted that these terms have a class connotation, meaning the rich
and prepotent. And it is certainly true that, as in a series of treaties between Toulouse and other communities of the Toulousain from 1202 to
1205, the "probihomines" mentioned by name, who together with the "milites" stood for these places, were surely the more consequential inhabitants.
The same was true in legal matters as well, as in a charter of the late
twelve-twenties in which one actor was a "knight and the other a worthy of
the town."⁶² It is also obvious that, in a list of "probihomines" witnessing
an important public document, a rising businessman or usurer will have his
name spelled out whereas the not inconceivably honest humble craftsman
waving his blue nails in the air will only be a shadow among the "alii
quamplures qui ibi erant."

In spite of these inadvertences, the term "probushomo" itself had no
class connotation whatsoever, being applicable to any kind of group considered collectively. When in 1223 a privilege granted the town by the
prince provided that the count could not choose consuls "except with the
consent of the 'probihomines' and the university," this does not mean that
there is a class of "probihomines" within the "universitas."⁶³ The consuls

⁵⁹Ibid. 3: 213, lines 33-38.
⁶⁰*Chronique*, ed. Duvernoy, p. 52: "Domini! Audite me!," sometime early in the
great repression in 1232. For this event see my *Repression of Catharism*, p. 60.
⁶¹PAN, J 192b 21 (March 1269), a role recording a trial: "Item quod idem Garnerius, cito currens, obviavit eis qui nuncium trahebant. Item quod dixit trahentibus:
'Domini! non faciatis, non faciatis, amore Dei!'" One witness said that "Garnerius
predictus surrexit coram predicto populo, dicens eidem 'Domini! domini! ...'" and
another that Guarnerius "locutus fuit populo sic: 'Domini mei! dico vobis ego ... .'"
Later in the same role of testimony, the subvicar reported that Guarnerius began
"Domini!," but then went on "Senhors! ... ."
⁶²Brunel, *Les plus ancienne chartes en langue provençale*, No. 343, an action dated
by two actors, one of whom was last mentioned in 1225 and the other in 1227, states:
"E aisso sabo cavaer et altri home ondrad d'esta vila e de fora."
⁶³TAM, AA 1 87 (April 1223): "nisi ex voluntate proborum hominum et universitatis urbis Tolose et suburbii illud evenerit."

of Toulouse were often called "probihomines." But so were the four "comunarii" (also "comunalerii") elected for tax and financial purposes in each division or "partita" of the town and, indeed, so was the whole body of the citizenry.[64] The term was used similarly elsewhere, at nearby Montauban, for example.[65] At far away Tarascon in the Rhone valley, the admirable Fritz Kiener long ago noted that the two parties to a treaty in 1199 were the "domini et milites" and the "consules et probihomines de plebe."[66]

In regard to the term's employment in private matters, "probushomo" was normally applied to a father with a son or an uncle with a nephew who bore the same Christian and surname.[67] All sorts of groups were called "probihomines": the executors of a will, groups of artisans, tradesmen, and shareholders in the mills of the Garonne river.[68] The word was used in the same way in the countryside and this is true from at least the early eleventh century.[69] Sometimes mixed with their betters, as Jane Austen's age called them, villagers were invariably called "probihomines" when functioning as members of their communities.[70] Indeed, the term was applied

[64]Ibid., 75 (March 1222).

[65]Galabert, "Le rôle des bons hommes dans le pays du Tarn et Garonne," *Bulletin archéologique et historique de la société archéologique de Tarn et Garonne* 29 (1901) 247-248, where the Abbé discusses the utilization of the term in the customs of Montauban of 1195. To replace the "capitol" or board of consuls, the old board is instructed to "enlegir autres proshomes" believed useful to the lord and the community, "e devo los retraire devant lo comunal poble de la vila."

[66]Kiener, *Verfassungsgeschichte der Provence*, p. 288 (October 1199).

[67]Examples are too numerous to quote and are to be found in the family histories published in my two recent studies, namely the *Repression of Catharism* and *Men and Women*. Two persons in a prosperous leatherworking family will illustrate the matter: Serninus Aissada seen in TAM, II 44 (February 1239) listed among those of his craft dealing with the count; in PAN, J 305 29 (February 1243) he swore to maintain the Peace of Paris; in Grandselve 9 (May 1252) he was described as a "probushomo"; in ibid. 9 (August 1256) a Serninus not so described; a person of that name was consul in 1255-1256; and, lastly, in PAN, J 328 47 (April 1280) a Cernin Ayssada is seen among the leatherworkers, surely a successor of the Aissada bearing the same name.

[68]In Appendix 8, No. 78, the modest group of executors ("sponderii") of a woman's will in 1247 were all called "probihomines" and included a "pelherius." For millers and mill shareholders, see PAN, J 330 5 i (December 1192, copied in 1277). Lastly, TAM, II 44 (February 1239) was addressed to forty-six "probihomines cervunerii, peleganterii, affaitatores, et paratores coriorum."

[69]*HGL* 8: Note 46, col. 208, where the "boni homines, tam nobiles quam rustici" of the Carcassès appear in 1037.

[70]To report some references in chronological order: PBN, MS lat. 9994, fols. 164r-v (March 1183 or 1184), a settlement between the monastery of Grandselve and the

to simple farmers in almost any context.[71] Lastly, as is the case in town, the members of an individual rural family were designated by this word.[72]

In fine, it is well-nigh certain that in the plural "bonushomo" or "probushomo" has no class connotation whatsoever. But what about the singular? It is tempting to believe that, in the singular, "probushomo" implied distinction, the term conferring an honor which it was not suitable to grant to just anybody. Such was the case with the word "dominus," why not with "probushomo" also? The histories of the families of Toulouse I have collected will convince any reader, however, that the attachment of "probushomo" to an individual merely replaced the words "maior" or "senior" for an older person who had to be distinguished from a younger relative, "junior" or "juvenis," who bore the same Christian name and surname. As an example, an Arnold Guido first appears in the twelve-twenties as a "junior," because an older Arnold Guido was then alive; by 1259 he is called "probushomo."[73] In the singular, one concludes, the word simply and only means "senior," and was therefore applied to members of demonstrably modest families.[74]

Even when titles of nobility were being introduced, this word retained its traditional sense. In 1262 near the monastery of Grandselve, the monks

"homines" of Saint-Jory just north of Toulouse involved, on the side of the village, eight named inhabitants designated "supradicti probihomines Sancti Jorii"; PBN, MS lat. 11008, fol. 213r (June 1187) where the contract handling disputes between Grandselve's herders and the grain farmers closes with the clause "quod si animalia vestra in segetibus vel in vineis nostris fecerint damnum, cognitione et arbitrio vicinorum proborum hominum nobis emendetur"; and PBN, MS lat. 6009, fol. 340 (July 1204) reports that five of the rustic worthies of the village of Aussonne near Toulouse were summoned before the lord along with "alii probi homines ejusdem ville."

[71]PBN, MS lat. 6009, fols. 369rff. (July 1204) has the bailiff of Cornebarrieu for Raymond VI congregating the men of Aussonne in order to get information about the "tenencie" held of the count. Of these, five were named and the rest were called "alii probihomines." In Saint-Étienne 227 (26 DA 2 53) (October 1205) fourteen men and one woman are described as the holders of vineyards in Saulonare near Toulouse. Two of these "probihomines" had plots of one arpent and the rest of a half arpent.

[72]E 65 (May 1239) notes the thirteen pence rent and six "gallinas censuales" owed the landlord by the "probihomines de Cairadz qui vocantur Fabri."

[73]In my *Repression of Catharism*, pp. 226-227, especially note 6.

[74]Malta 2 147 i (June 1251, copied in 1253) where a Bernard de Trageto "probushomo" is called "senior" in the next instrument on the same parchment. For the modesty of this family, see the family history in my *Repression of Catharism*, p. 284. Examples are legion, see, for example, the William Vasco "olerius probushomo" in Grandselve 7 (March 1235).

reached agreement in the vernacular with "los nobles baros En Gautier del Fossat lo prohome, en Gautier del Fossat lo masip," "en" meaning "dominus," and "masip" junior.[75] To return to town, the highest honor ever rendered a citizen in a public document occurred when a famed leader during the Albigensian wars was listed as "dominus" Aimeric de Castronovo "probushomo." It will be noted that Aimeric was not there called knight, although he was one, and that the adjective "probushomo" was added to distinguish him from an equally knightly nephew with the same Christian and surname.[76]

Apart, then, from the modest elevation implied by the word "dominus," the social topography of Toulouse and the Toulousain was almost wholly devoid of landmarks around 1200 and retained this quality for some time thereafter. Officially speaking, the word "burgensis" was only very rarely affixed to individuals because, in relation to outsiders, every "burgensis" of Toulouse was a citizen or "civis." An unusual exception is seen in the eleven-eighties when two of four arbiters chosen by the bishop are called "burgenses." This use was clearly designed to show that both the City and Bourg had contributed members to this important panel.[77] In private documents drawn by the scribes of Toulouse and the nearby rural districts also, occupation or status titles were very rare indeed. Naturally, this does not apply to those artisans and tradesmen who bore no surnames and therefore had to be identified by their occupations, but these, together with an occasional merchant, moneychanger, lawyer and notary, were really the only exceptions.[78]

Titles of honor and status attached to individuals were also exceedingly rare in the charters. After its disappearance early in the twelfth century, "miles" or knight was not to be seen before 1200 and rarely thereafter and that of "domicellus" or squire waited even longer. The exceptions are worth noting. The distinguished Aimeric de Castronovo mentioned above as being

[75]PBN, MS lat. 11010, fol. 48v (February 1262).

[76]The history of these persons and their family is in my *Repression of Catharism*, pp. 182-189, citing TAM, AA 1 72 and 77 (both dated April 1222), in the former of which his nephew was mentioned.

[77]Malta 25 19 (undated) where the bishop of Toulouse chose four notables to settle a dispute between the Hospitalers and the Dalbade church. These were Bernard Peter de Cossa "burgensis Tolose," Pons de Villanova, Toset de Tolosa, and William Rotberti "burgensis." Villanova and Tolosa were knights who inhabited the City; both of the others lived in the Bourg. The Cossano family history is in my *Repression of Catharism*, pp. 193-196, and the Roberti are in the index of the same work.

[78]Notaries were always so designated at the base of the acts they wrote, but this observation concerns the use of the title "notarius" in the body of an act.

called "dominus" was also called a knight in 1200.[79] Wholly exceptional
was the designation "armiger," meaning squire, applied to an individual at
Castillon just north of Toulouse in 1182.[80] More understandable was a
phrase in Count Raymond VI's testament of 1209 referring to his brother
Baldwin (who had been raised in France) as the "knight and man ... of my
son [Count Raymond VII]."[81] None of this means that knighthood was un-
important, but it was typical of this politically decentralized society that it
was relatively informal and not directly tied to greater princes. Almost any
magnate could educate boys derived from what are still today called "good
families" and train them to be knights. In 1222 William Unaldus, the lord
of Lanta southeast of Toulouse, stated in his testament that his godson,
Alaman de Roaxio of the noted Toulousan City family, was, together with
another youth, to be placed in the charge of his executor, Sicard de Montealto, lord of Montaut, and instructed Sicard to "make them knights." It is
therefore not surprising that this weighty baron and knight is described in
his charters, including his testament, simply as William Unaldus.[82]

It was a telltale mark of the modestly republican and patrician society
of the town as well as of the authority of the gentry and magnates of the
countryside that private and public documents in both Latin and the vernacular only rarely described individuals as knights and squires in this period.
As in the cases of the patrician Aimeric de Castronovo and William Unaldus, lord of Lanta, seen above, it was enough to be a senior member of a
notable and distinguished clan. For such personages, titles were not needed.

[79]Saint-Sernin 599 (10 35 16) 5th of 8 acts tied together iii (January 1200, copied
in 1219 and 1220). On Aimeric's history, see my *Repression of Catharism*, pp. 188-189.

[80]Malta 3 76 (January 1182).

[81]In a note to p. 230, Guilhermoz, *Essai sur l'origine de la noblesse en France au
moyen-âge*, had picked this up from *HGL* 8: No. 146, col. 574: "miles et homo ...
Raymundi filii mei." Quite inexplicably, I described the unhappy Baldwin as a natural
child in my *Men and Women at Toulouse*, p. 79.

[82]Appendix 8, No. 47 (November 1222), and the Roaxio family history in my *Repression of Catharism*, p. 256.

4

Dependents

A. RUSTICS

If the danger of ministerial or political servitude to the count or prince was obviated shortly before or just after 1200, the town still faced a less dangerous but troublesome problem, namely the ownership of dependents by private persons living in town, some of whom were rural lords. In describing this category of the population, the author is obliged to rely on others, especially Paul Ourliac.[1] Noting that the word "servus" does not make its appearance in this region until Simon de Montfort's so-called reforms of the *Statutes of Pamiers* in 1212, Ourliac has proposed that a new law of servitude spread largely after 1150.[2] Servitude was introduced, he believes, by the enrichment of the region, its growing village population scarred by the new money economy with its loan sharks or usurers from towns like Toulouse. To this is added an additional motive: a need for security during the upheaval of the Albigensian Crusade.[3] As partial proof of this contention, the number of charters dealing with servitude preserved in ecclesiastical archives multiplied in the hundred years before and after 1200.

[1] His "L'hommage servile dans la région toulousaine," originally published in the *Mélanges Halphen* of 1951, and his "Le servage à Toulouse aux xiie et xiiie siècle," first in *Mélanges Perroy* of 1973, both republished in his *Études d'histoire du droit médiéval*, pp. 125-130 and 131-144. To some extent, Ourliac starts from the base provided by Hubert Richardot's, "Le fief roturier à Toulouse," *Revue historique de droit français et étranger*, 4th series, 14 (1935).

[2] For Pamiers, see *HGL* 8: No. 165, Article 27, col. 631, where it refers to those "qui dicuntur proprii homines sive servi."

[3] *Études d'histoire du droit médiéval*, pp. 136-139. One notes how similar this process, as one loves to say nowadays, is to Pierre Bonnassie's origins of Catalonian serfdom. That two scholars, one from the right and the other from the left, should blame the rich for imposing servitude might seem strange, but Ourliac's villains are urban usurers whereas Bonnassie's are rural lords, devils harmonizing with the authors' respective ideologies.

Ourliac has also claimed that rural servitude weakened or all but vanished by the late thirteenth century, citing as proof the efforts of the crown to raise money from the "homines de corpore" in the Toulousain in 1297 and 1298. Although the texts concerning this incident and its context have been only sketchily investigated, persons clearly demarcated as serfs did not constitute (no longer or had never constituted?) a majority of the population. In an age when rural consulates were everywhere being established and village and small town liberties generally grew, it looks as if it may have been profitable to liberate dependents.[4] Although the research has yet to be done and quantification is probably impossible, a few charters of group emancipation are extant.[5] At Laurac near Castelnaudary in 1297, where an assembly of heads of household mustered from 150 to 300 persons (depending on the witness), the village consuls and others asserted that no more than four or five men were of this condition, although an interested royal notary maintained that there were sixty or more.[6] In the late twelve-hundreds, servitude certainly had little significance for Toulouse's lawyers. The rubric "De homagiis" (which dealt with personal servitude) in the *Commentary* of 1296 on the *Custom* of Toulouse had really very little to say. Its author limited himself to emphasizing the need for written proof and listed Roman law's many terms for rural and servile persons.[7] He closed his dismissive treatment by saying that "it would be more laborious than useful" to go into detail, and referred readers to an Italian treatise by Roffredo of Benevento (d. ca. 1243).[8]

[4]See my "Village, Town, and City," pp. 164-166, with pertinent literature.

[5]Malta 138 24 (May 1265) where the preceptor of the Hospital emancipated eleven men of three families at Cugnaux and two others at Pouvourville, the former in the vicarage and the latter in the "gardiage."

[6]Langlois, "Les doléances des communautés du Toulousain contra Pierre de Latilli et Raoul de Breuilly (1297-1298)," *Revue historique* 95 (1907) 30-32.

[7]Gilles, *Coutumes de Toulouse*, p. 272, from the *Commentary* of 1296: "Verumptamen ad declarationem predictarum consuetudinum sciendum est quod agricole quidam sunt ascripticii seu ascripticie condicionis" etc., closing with "Omnia alia nomina species sunt et sic intitulatur primo genus et postea species."

[8]Ibid., pp. 272-273: "Item queritur an tales homines possunt dare vel alienare vel vendere et testamenta facere et ista et alia que circa materiam istam sunt dicenda, pocius si vobis recitarem, esset laboriosum quam utile, et ideo causa brevitatis vos remitto ad titulum *de officio judicis que datur vassallis et colonis* in libello Refredi ubi copiosius invenitur. Hiis breviter jam dictis pro summa, videatis consuetudines vestras." The learned editor notes that this refers to Roffredo's *Tractatus libellorum*, Fifth Part, *De officio judicis quo subvenitur censito et vassallo si dominus exigit ultra quam debet exigere* (Avignon 1500), fols. 114-116.

As described by Ourliac and is everywhere seen in the charters, the characteristic rural servitude of the latter twelfth and early thirteenth centuries was an inherited status by which an individual or family was placed under the protection and government of an owner. Save for its inherited condition, the serf's was a position similar to that of oblates in the church and therefore employed the same terms for subjection, notably "captennium," "manutenere et amparare et defendere per hominium," "sub potestate," etc.[9] Dependents of private persons were of two kinds: "homines de corpore *sine* casalagio" and "homines de corpore *et* casalagio," the latter word referring to their allotments, "tenencie" or, to use the customary Toulousan terms, "feoda" or "honores." Of the two, according to the *Custom* of Toulouse of 1286, the category "de corpore" gave a claim to service superior to "de casalagio" because a man's body was held in a stronger grip than his land.[10] Although most were "de corpore *et* casalagio," dependents "de corpore *sine* casalagio" were common. A woman at Cayras in 1257 owed three shillings annually "because she was for her body only ... and not for her holding."[11]

Often called a "homo proprius [et] ligius" or "femina propria ligia," a dependent performed an act of homage, joined hands and exchanged kisses with the master, swearing fidelity.[12] Omitting only the kiss, an especially full list of the formalities appears in an act of voluntary servitude dated 1268. This act was made by an individual from Pechaudier near Castres to the Templars who, in an unusually explicit way, asserted that before his pledge of service he was not bonded to anybody in the world from pope to burgher.[13] He then performed "omagium" and, kneeling, placed his joined hands in those of the Templar. Reciting a renunciation of exceptions, he then swore that, "whether in church, City, Bourg, market,

---

[9]*Études d'histoire du droit médiéval*, pp. 121, 127, 128 and 130.

[10]Gilles, *Coutumes de Toulouse*, Article No. 148: "De immobilibus, scilicet casalagio vel feudis que tenent a domino suo et aliis," where the text argues that the lord of a "homo de corpore" "jure potior [est] secundum consuetudinem Tholose quam" another who is merely lord of a "homo de casalagio."

[11]E 65 (April 1257) has two Toulousan knightly notables claim that persons at Cayras and Marville south of town owe five shillings "nomine queste," and that of these the woman owed three "quia erat femina de corpore ... solum et non ratione casalagii."

[12]Ourliac, *Études d'histoire du droit médiéval*, p. 126, with the kiss being first seen in the late twelve-thirties.

[13]E 508 (May 1268): he, "interrogatus a fratre Willelmo de Sancte Iohanne si sub dominio Romane ecclesie nomine servitutis omagii esset submissus vel obligatus nec archiepiscopi vel eciam regis, comitis, vicecomitis, militis, burgensis nec sui filii nec alicuius alius viventis, et ipse asseruit iuratus super sancta dei evangelia dominum non habere."

cloister, or public road and highway," he and his issue were liege men of the Templars.[14] Similarly, just as had been seen in earlier years, charters of emancipation stress the return or translation of the individual from private ownership to the community of Toulouse, a body viewed, consequently, as being composed of the free.[15] By the late thirteenth century, the language of emancipation shared the qualities common throughout western Europe. In Toulouse on his way to crusade against Tunis in 1270, Alphonse of Poitier manumitted a serf in Castelsarrasin in terms borrowed from Roman law: "By nature all men are free, but the 'ius gentium' made some into slaves."[16]

Like lords and rural folk, town citizens owned dependents. An example is William de Turribus, a notable whose family history is recorded in this volume and whose property at Pouvourville just south of town was operated by servile tenants. Running from 1194 to 1207 four men underwent the formalities mentioned above in return for tenures.[17] Together with the

[14]Ibid.: "Flexis genibus suisque iunctis manibus et eciam manibus eiusdem fratris Willelmi positis et misis, predictus Petrus devocione habita erga ordinem Milicie Templi non choactus nec deceptus et nec metu nec verbis alicuius seductus, set mera et simplici ac gratuita voluntate, dedit, concessit atque fecit se cum omni sua progenie genita vel genitura in perpetuum hominem ligem corporis fratrum et domus supradicte ... . sine omni exceptione iuris et facti canonis et civilis scripti et non scripti in ecclesia et extra, in civitate et extra, in suburbio et extra, in foro et extra, in claustra et extra, in carrariis publicis et extra, in caminis et extra ..." recognizing himself to be the "homo liges [normally ligius] corporis" of the Temple by this "omagium."

[15]Saint-Sernin 502 (1 1 57) (April 1212): "Hec libertas fuit ita data" on the above date. "Ad honorem dei omnipotentis patris et filii et spiritus sancti et beate gloriose virginis Marie genitricis dei et Sancti Stephani et Sancti Saturnini et omnium fidelium dei, et Ramundi Tolosani comitis et Fulconis episcopi et tocius populi Tolose urbis et suburbii presentis et futuri, ego N [a notable] ... dono veram et irrevocabilem libertatem sine omni fraude et dolo tibi ... et omni progeniei que de te exivit et exierit ... ."

[16]Catel, *Histoire des comtes de Tolose*, pp. 394-395 (April 1270): "Natura omnes homines sunt liberi, sed ius gentium aliquos s[er]vos fecit, et quia de facili res ad suam naturam revertitur, notum facimus quod nos intuitu pietatis ... N hominem nostrum de corpore et casalagio liberaliter manumittimus et ab omni iugo servitutis absolvimus et quittamus ipsum et heredes suos." The passages in the *Corpus iuris civilis* are I. 1, 2, 2 and D. 7, 1, 4.

[17]Malta 12 23 vii (December 1194): two men "iunctis manibus miserunt eas iunctas in manibus Willelmi de Turribus et sic <ac> flexis genibus concesserunt ei et suo ordinio hominium ..." Ibid., iii (April 1197): "Johannes de Manevilla se fecit homo Willelmo de Turribus et suo ordinio et dedit se et illud genus quod de eo est egressum vel egressurum Willelmo ... et convenit ei ... servire pro hominio in ecclesia vel extra ecclesiam et in claustro et extra claustrum et in salvitate et extra salvitatem et in villa ista et foras istam villam et in omnibus locis de inter et de foris ad totam voluntatem et ad cog-

Raissaco family whose history is also recorded in this study, these charters show that servile labor was well-known around Pouvourville and Castanet, villages just south of town in the "gardiage," the part of its "dex" under consular administration, not that of the vicar.[18] This servitude was also durable. The William de Turribus seen above acquired three servile families in the same region in late 1196 and, in the spring of 1227, their heads confessed themselves to have been his serfs for over thirty years.[19]

Most owners of servile labor seen in the charters had extensive rural holdings or themselves derived from the countryside.[20] Not all were primarily landlords, however. In 1205 an inhabitant of Capdenier, a small center north of town, performed an act of voluntary servitude in favor of the very rich Pons de Capitedenario. A moneylender and entrepreneur who invested in animal husbandry, Pons is not known to have had more than a substantial suburban farm.[21] Far more modest town and countryfolk also possessed dependents. In 1191 five men and three women, only one a wife, freed Peter de Yspania, of whom more anon.[22]

Previously mentioned, the chapter "De homagiis" in the *Custom* of 1286 defined dependency at Toulouse, but did not touch on the widely variable "servicia" or rents in kind and/or money, mutation charges and inheritance taxes owed by serfs. "De homagiis" prohibited servitude within the walls and in the suburbs or "barria" of Toulouse, the area, that is, later

---

nitionem Willelmi de Turribus et eius ordinii et mandavit et iuravit Johannes de Manevilla stadium et fidelitatem et quod non defugiat super Sancta Evvangelia et quod ei sit verus et fidelis." Ibid., vi (January 1207) with similar clauses.

[18]See the families in Appendix 1, Nos. 13 and 15.

[19]Malta 12 23 – one of several acts sewn together in a package (December 1196): Bestiacius, son of the deceased Arnold de Sancto Dyonisio, "vendidit Willemo de Turre omnes homines et feminas quos habebat apud Populivillam et totum ius et dominium et rationem quam super illos habebat, videlicet omnes Barradas et eorum tenenciam et omnes Molnarios et eorum tenenciam et Tabastam et eius tenenciam et ipsos et eorum infantes et omnia eorum bona mobilia et immobilia que habebant vel habituri erant." Ibid. (May 1227): Peter Barrada, Arnold Molnarius, his brother Raymond Molnarius and their sister Sibilia, and William Tabasta say that "semper extiterant homines Bestiacii et sui generis et de dominio eius fuerant semper ipsi et eorum antecessores," having been sold thirty or more years ago.

[20]Saint-Sernin 502 (1 1 57) (April 1212) where the notable Bertrand de Montibus emancipated a man. For Bertrand, see my *Repression of Catharism*, pp. 144-145. In E 266 (August 1190), a Bernard and his brother Peter de Rocovilla emancipated a woman. These were among the brothers "dels Rochovilas," rural knights from the Lauragais south of Toulouse.

[21]See the history of Pons' economic activity in my *Repression of Catharism*, p. 157.

[22]Appendix 1, No. 16.

embraced by the "partite" into which the City and Bourg were divided and
which extended beyond the walls to include the several "barria" outside the
gates. Servitude's hold began in the "dex" of the town and spread throughout the Toulousain.[23] Toulousan servitude was hereditary, transmitted by
either parent, the status following the one who was servile, male or female.[24] Dependents were not permitted to own a freehold (an allod or
"honor liber") although they could hold fiefs or rent them from landlords
other than their personal one.[25] This custom was long established because,
a century before its publication, the servile Raissaco family from Pouvourville both held tenures from lords other than their principal one and also
had others holding from them.[26]

Most private transactions by dependents were overseen by their lords.
Serfs could make wills and dispose of moveable property without interfer-
ence as long as the goods had been transmitted before death; if not, the
lord's claim took precedence.[27] Testamentary disposition or gifts "inter
vivos" of real property required a lord's express consent and assuredly cost
fees not mentioned in the *Custom*.[28] The reference to "formariage" in the
Custom is both subtle and effective: no dependent may assign his wife a
return of dowry or marriage gift without the express consent of the lord,
because, without prior arrangement, her right cannot be legally established.[29] A charter of a dying woman in 1168 shows how and when a lord
gave assent. Herself a widow, she transmitted to her second husband a half
arpent of vineyard given him as dowry "in the presence" of the lord and "in
his hand."[30]

---

[23]Gilles, *Coutumes de Toulouse*, Article 154: "in villis, barriis seu castris que sunt
infra dex Tholose, scilicet extra Tholosam et barria Tholose ... ."
[24]Ibid.: if "aliquis homo ligius de corpore et casalagio vel de corpore sine casalagio"
should marry an "uxor libera" and beget children, they are "homines ligii" of the lord,
and the same is true of a "femina ligia de corpore." A similar provision is found in
Article 150.
[25]Ibid., Article No. 155 provides that, if a serf had such a holding, "ille fundus seu
honor liber tenetur a domino suo ... sicut alii honores de casalagio ... ." Article No. 148
allows the serf to hold of others than the lord of his body.
[26]Appendix 1, No. 13.
[27]Gilles, *Coutumes de Toulouse*, Article 147: without a "traditio," "prevalet occu-
patio domini et precluditur via petendi donatario vel legatario."
[28]Ibid., Article 148: "De immobilibus, scilicet casalagio vel feudis que tenent a
domino suo et aliis ... ."
[29]Ibid., Article 153: "nomine dotis vel dotalitii aliquam summam peccunie sine
assensu et consilio expresso domini aut cujus est homo." The word is "assignamentum."
[30]Saint-Étienne 227 (26 DA 2 116) (October 1168): Dying, Arsenda, widow of John

Toulouse's serf owners wanted to have their cake and eat it too. If a lord occupied a deceased serf's property, he was not liable for the latter's debts, a provision protecting the lord, but also impeding the latter's capacity to grow economically.[31] On the other hand, in this region where animal husbandry was extensive, the *Custom* expressly allowed dependents to busy themselves in this kind of enterprise, indeed in any business that did not involve real property, even without their lords' agreement.[32] Lastly, although the lot of dependents may have been hard, citizens could not arrest, tax, fine or in any way force dependents within the walls, gates or "barria" of Toulouse.[33] And these terms clearly go beyond economic matters: "to force," for example, also meant "to ravish."

Lastly, like others, this urban community found it profitable to welcome servile emigrants from the countryside and protect them against their lords, as long as the latter were not citizens of Toulouse. In 1203 the consuls heard a suit brought by a notable from Verfeil to the east of Toulouse who had become a citizen. This worthy claimed he had bought a man and his sons who regularly spent their summers in Verfeil and wanted them to recognize their dependency. The presumed serfs countered by arguing that, although they may have been sold, the lord was not yet a citizen at that time and they themselves were then living in Toulouse and indeed had done their duty by the community for twenty or more years. The consuls rejected the plaintiff's suit simply by saying that he had not proved his case by Toulousan witnesses![34]

This town right was recognized by the count in 1226 when he allowed the expansion of the "salvetat" of Toulouse. In that law, the consuls stated that rural folk often wanted to come to town, asserting that persons "having lords" but living in Toulouse were to be protected against their masters.[35] Later on, when the town customal was accepted by the crown and

---

Taliato, gave a half arpent of vineyard to her husband Arsivus, a gift she had given him when he married her, and she gave it "Arsivo viro suo in presentia Bertrandi Ferriolli qui est inde dominus et in sua manu."

[31]Ibid., Article 151.

[32]Ibid., Article 149. The text is reproduced below in Appendix 7, note 7.

[33]Ibid., Article 152: No citizen "potest auctoritate sua hominem suum proprium de corpore infra villa Tholose vel in aliquo loco dicte ville intus muros seu portas Tholose vel barria capere, questare, pignorare aut in aliquo modo forciare."

[34]TAM, AA 2 84 (April 1203): "quia [the plaintiff] nil probaverat per testes illius ville."

[35]See my *Liberty and Political Power*, pp. 132-133, and especially TAM, AA 1 102 (June 1226), in which, having noted "quod multi homines et femine habentes dominos ... ex multis terris et diversis locis et partibus ... venerunt quondam in hac villa Tolose

published in 1286, a provision confirmed this right.[36] More forthright is
a paragraph under the rubric in the *Custom* reading "The Privileges of Toulousan Citizens." There a person residing outside of town who declares "I
want to enter Toulouse and become a citizen of Toulouse" is to be taken
under consular protection "as if he were a citizen," saving only the right
of the lord of his body ("dominus corporis") if he has one.[37]

If Toulouse encouraged serfs to come to town and there find freedom,
it nevertheless conducted no crusade to impart liberty to rural folk. Its de-
sign was instead to increase town population and also, covertly because
never stated, to weaken rural jurisdictions and lordships. Nothing in town
policy equals the generosity advocated by Simon de Montfort in his *Statutes
of Pamiers* of 1212. There, in his basic constitution for the recently conquered dominions (at that time not including Toulouse), the northern invader proposed that free farmers could leave their communities, even against
their lords' wishes, on surrendering their real property; serfs could do the
same, on leaving behind all property.[38] Though surely no "Great Emancipator," Montfort was trying to rally townsfolk and villagers against his
most stubborn enemies, the local barons and knights of his new domains.

---

causa ibi omnino permanendi," the consuls ordered "infra quos terminos homines et
femine manentes in [Toulouse] habentes dominos euntes et redeuntes extra predictam
civitatem et suburbium et operantes extra et manentes in eorum operibus vel in alienis
operibus et facientes alia sua negocia, ita erant securi a suis dominis vel dominabus quod
... nullatenus debebant nec poterant esse capti ... ." The count specifically added to this
right animals and property.

[36]Gilles, *Coutumes de Toulouse*, Article 155b, providing "quod homines venientes
in Tholosa causa habitandi et ibi habitantes undecunque venerint, quamvis habeant dominos, possunt et debent ihi stare liberi a dominis suis et facere negotia sua sine petitione
et impedimento et contradictione dominorum suorum, et quod dicti domini non possunt
nec debent ipsos homines sic in Tholosa habitantes vel in barriis in aliquo fortiare ratione seu occasione dominii."

[37]Gilles, *Coutumes de Toulouse*, Article 156: "dicens: 'Ego volo intrare Tholosam
et facere me civem Tholose' et aliquis vivens in itinere illo – excepto domino corporis
si forte habet – illum hominem ceperit ... consules et communitas Tholose debent illum
hominem talem petere, manutenere et, si captus est, recuperare et universa bona sua,
tanquam si esset civis Tholose."

[38]*HGL* 8: No. 165. col. 631 (December 1212), Article 27: "Item licitum erit omnibus hominibus qui possunt talliari transire a dominio unius domini in dominium alterius
pro voluntate sua, ita tamen quod illi qui dicuntur liberi cum mobilibus suis poterunt
transire sine aliqua contradictione ad dominium alterius, relicta hereditate et hostisia
priori domino suo cum omnibus his que tenent ab aliis. Alii vero qui dicuntur proprii
homines sive servi, poterunt similiter transire ad dominium alterius, non solum hereditate relicta et hostisia, set mobilibus priori domino suo."

Although an undoubted problem, then, it is curious that no Toulousan law concerning servitude talks about the conditions under which a dependent can leave a lordship. The town law of 1226 taking rural folk coming to Toulouse under protection merely remarks that such immigrants sometimes brought property with them, and sometimes not.[39] Perhaps town legislators wanted to leave well enough alone, preferring to decide cases that came up on their merits or, rather, on how they suited their interest.

However ungenerous Toulousan attitudes were, it is obvious that the town was something of an island of freedom in a world of rural communities and small towns most of whose inhabitants were subject to the petty monarchies of their lords. Putting aside the ministerial servitude of a political kind discussed above in the previous chapter, one wonders, in fact, if private serfs were found in town. The *Custom* of 1286 contains a provision wherein a person and his or her issue who voluntary entered into personal dependency must serve a citizen "in church, cloister, 'salvetat' inside and outside and in all places" as befits "a liege man and proper."[40] Curiously, but probably intentionally, this article omitted a phrase customarily found in such acts of enserfment, one stating that service was also owed in town.[41]

It is also puzzling that town institutions and persons received voluntary pledges of servitude without describing what the functions of the newly enserfed persons were. The Templars' "liege man of his body" whose elaborate "omagium" of 1268 is delineated above pledged only a modest annual "servicium" of sixpence to the house.[42] Service equaling that was obtained by emancipating serfs! In 1190 members of the knightly Rocovilla family seen above emancipated a woman and her two sons, retaining sixpence every All Saints day.[43] One guesses that the acquisition of a dependent or two assured a towndweller a "servicium" rather like rental income on real property. Thus the well-known Mascaronus, cathedral provost

---

[39]TAM, AA 1 102 (June 1226): "quidam cum rebus suis et quidem etiam sine rebus."

[40]Gilles, *Coutumes de Toulouse*, Article 155a: to serve his citizen lord "in ecclesia, claustro, salvitate et extra vel in cunctis locis et hoc cum carta publica que inde fiat [so he and his will be] homo ligius et proprius [of the citizen]."

[41]An example of March 1214 is cited in note 45 below. Another is in an act of 1268 cited in note 14 above.

[42]E 508 (May 1268): a promise "annuatim dare uti homo liges corporis et servire dicte domui Templi et festo Sanctorum Omnium .vi. den. tol."

[43]E 266 (August 1190) where the brothers Bernard and Peter de Rocovilla "solvimus et derelinquimus et vere libertati damus unam feminam Venguda" and her sons "et omnem eorum progeniem que de illis exivit vel adhuc exierit" retaining "nisi tamen .vi. den. tol" to God, etc. and all the people "in vera et in firma et irrevocabili libertate."

during the Albigensian Crusade, was given a holding by a country gentle-man together with its tenants and possibly a young woman, if she refused to marry the husband designated by the donor.[44]

A year later a town notable gave Mascaronus a serf from Blagnac just outside of town. This gift makes one suspect that the good provost was recruiting domestic servants.[45] Entry into such service may have been the reason Peter de Castilhono gave himself and his children save two daughters to Raymond de Recalto for the count of Toulouse in 1190.[46] Whatever the case, domestics are decidedly worth investigation: they may have been the only kind of serfs permitted within the town's walls.

B. DOMESTICS

Speaking loosely, domestics were between free and servile. As in modern times, they ranged from persons of authority and even privilege to slaves. In the *Usatges de Barcelona* "familiares vel servi" are likened to each other.[47]

Evidence about servants is not ample and is especially meager for the town. That "ancille" and (wet)nurses were common is obvious and, perhaps because close to masters and mistresses, are gratified in testaments, sometimes even being called "mother."[48] A gentleman's gentleman is also seen when the rich Pons de Capitedenario in 1229 endowed a "scutifer" for his chic son-in-law Roger Barravus, a nearly knightly patrician.[49] In fact, Pons' testament not only provided a valet for his son-in-law but also three personal maids, one for his wife and two for his daughter. About the rest of the working staff, one knows nothing, but Pons was rich enough to live almost like a baron. A William Sancius "de Capitedenario" voluntarily

---

[44]Appendix 8, No. 34 (September 1214) records the gift to Mascaronus.

[45]Saint-Étienne 230 (27 4 1 12) (March 1215, copied January 1238) where, "manda-to et prece" of his lord Bernard Raymond Pilistortus, Raymond Guilabertus of Blagnac "flexis genibus dedit et dando concessit domino proposito Mascarono ecclesie Sancti Stephani ... se ipsum et omnem suam tenentiam ... ad totam suam voluntatem ... in Tolosa vel extra, in ecclesia et extra, in claustra et extra, in salvitate et in omnibus locis ... ."

[46]E 508 (August 1190, copied in May 1267): "se ipsum scilicet suum corpus et omnes suos infantos exceptis .ii. filiabus ... ."

[47]D'Abadal i Vinyals and Valls Taberner edition of the *Usatges de Barcelona*, Article No. 164.

[48]Appendix 8, Nos. 15, 51, 69 and 98 for "ancille"; No. 27 for a "pedisecca"; and Nos. 63, 98, 99 and 103 for "nutrices," one of whom is called "nutrix et mater."

[49]Appendix 8, No. 51, and see the Barravus and Capitedenario family histories in my *Repression of Catharism*, pp. 136ff. and 155ff.

entered himself and his family into the servitude of this urban "nouveau riche" in 1205.[50] Possibly a domestic, William could also have been one of Pons' rural staff.

Some servants can be shown to have been dependents. Another charter of voluntary servitude is seen in 1262 when the town notable, citizen and lord in Gascony, the knight Guy de Turribus, entered the Hospital of Saint John of Toulouse together with his wife Mabriana as oblates. Mabriana and Guy lived in considerable state in their retirement home and, doubtless to enhance its comforts, two of their dependent families voluntarily became serfs of the order.[51] On the other hand, in town or the countryside, servants were often both free and salaried. In 1246 a rural knight had a "hired domestic," a person of some worth, and even an urban "ancilla" seems to have been paid, although not on time, another durable characteristic of the domestic family.[52]

Because of better sources, the status of domestics becomes clearer by the mid-thirteenth century. Out in the Lauragais, the countryside south of Toulouse, other than the old term "famulus," the usual designation for a servant was "serviens," a word that has been seen to have had ministerial or servile connotations in the twelfth century.[53] In the thirteenth century, however, "serviens" had no such connotation, at least not necessarily. In 1271 the testament of a burgher, really a rural patrician, named Raymond Arguanhati of Isle-Jourdain placed a nephew in charge of his minor children at a specified salary, calling him "serviens."[54] Another common term was "nuncius," a word applied across a wide spectrum, ranging from hired teamsters, for example, to household domestics.[55] The wealthy built hierarchies of domestics. A lord at Montréal had a "key keeper and dispenser of his house," analogous to a modern butler perhaps, and a similar officer served as the chief domestic of the baronial magnate Jordan of Lanta.[56]

---

[50]My *Repression of Catharism*, p. 157.

[51]The family history is in Appendix 1, No. 15.

[52]TBM, MS 609, fol. 103v (July 1246) where William de Casals reports that he was a "famulus conductorius" in the house of Arnold de Vilela, knight. The "ancilla" in Appendix 8, No. 15 was owed money by the testator, almost surely her salary.

[53]TBM, MS 609, fols. 163v and 216, for example, in the mid-twelve-forties.

[54]In my "Village, Town, and City," p. 187, note 87 (May 1271).

[55]See MADTG, A 297, fol. 808r (January 1224) for the teamsters who worked for the nuns at Lespinasse at Mondonville and were paid "merces nunciorum." For a "nuncius domus" as a member of a "familia domus," in company with an "ancilla domus," in Toulouse about 1225, see TBM, MS 609, fol. 202v.

[56]In TBM, MS 609, fol. 252v: "claviger et dispensator ipsius domus," and fol. 110 refers to the "claviger tunc temporis domini Jordani de Lanta."

The servants at the Unaud castle in Lanta also included a maid, a nurse and a "nuncius," all described as being of "the household."[57]

As has been true in recent times, some types of public officers were also thought of as domestics. The "nuncii" of the town of Toulouse, for example, functioned as a composite of modern police and court bailiffs. They accompanied town criers and are once seen in 1213 when recalcitrant tenants were ordered to pay their rent and one was evicted.[58] In about 1226 at Fanjeaux well south of Toulouse, an Isarn de na Estela, associated with a local knight, was called both "nuncius" and "scutifer" or squire.[59]

Warm though the terms domestic, household and "familia" are, relationships between servant and master are obviously not always happy. Life sometimes conspires to weaken the mutual loyalty of any two parties and external pressure can break almost any link between persons. In testimony given in late February 1245, an Arnold de Bonahac with his wife Ramunda reported to the Inquisition about a knight from near Lanta named Peter de Resengas and his wife Austorga, a Toulousan. Peter stated that the lord, now deceased, had a son named Peter de Resengas "junior" and a daughter named Orbria who had married another local lord named William Sais.[60] Several others appeared in the house, including one of Austorga's bailiffs, for example, and two maids, Finas "ancilla dicte Austorge" and Jordana "ancilla domus." The impression is given that Arnold and Ramunda were outside domestics unlike the inside maids who presumably belonged to a group that surely included other persons not mentioned because the inquisitors were not told of, or did not ask about, those who prepared the meals, etc. of what was obviously a substantial household. Whatever the case, Arnold and Ramunda saw four men enter and, having heard that Austorga was a believing Cathar, concluded that they were "heretici" or perfects of the cult. After all, the "ancilla domus" had told Ramunda that Orbria so loved the Cathars that she had left her husband and wanted to become a "perfecta."[61] Arnold then went to the bailiff of Caraman, Peter Dellac, and reported the presence of the presumed heretics. Peter told him that, after he'd talked it over with his brother, he'd come by to arrest them.

---

[57]Ibid., fol. 202r: "ancilla domus … nutrix domus … et … nuncius domus."

[58]In my *Liberty and Political Power*, pp. 208-209, Published Document No. 12.

[59]TBM, MS 609, fol. 163v: testimony of March 1246.

[60]For Austorga, see my *Repression of Catharism*, pp. 63, 86, 92, 105, 107-108 and 111.

[61]TBM, MS 609, fol. 200r: Austorga a "credens," and Orbria "diligebat tantum hereticos quod propter monitionem hereticorum dimiserat maritum suum, et voluit fieri heretica."

When he did, he said, he'd compensate Arnold with a silver mark and the salary he was owed by Resengas.[62] As it turned out, he came late, arriving on Easter Saturday, the four "perfecti" having left on Good Friday (April 1, 1244).

C. JEWS

It was shown in Chapter Three above that the status of Christian towndwellers was improving before 1200 and that the same probably obtained among the Jews. One wonders, however, especially because, with the gradual liberation of the Christian urban population from the prince's domanial hold, this long-disfavored minority may well have been left behind in a condition resembling that of only one other class, rural serfs. Besides, since antiquity, the Jews were a separate order of society, as stated earlier, almost constituting a religious caste, and it was surely difficult for society to set aside this long tradition. Even in the best of times, Jews and Christians were kept apart: they did not eat together and, unless conversion took place, did not intermarry.

Such being the case, one may perhaps go further to assert that the relationship between the Jews and their local prince, one never explicitly defined in any local law text or charter, was one of mutual use verging on abuse. Probably so, but, if so, Jews nevertheless constituted a very privileged group of serfs. Extant documents show that their community was mainly composed of the well-to-do, of persons equal in wealth to Christian urban patricians. In 1243 the dowry of Gauzios, the widow of Abraham, amounted to 1550 shillings of Toulouse, a sum in the middle range of Christian patrician marital portions.[63] To turn to male Jews, the owners of the tolls collected in the burghal markets were forcibly bought out by the crown in 1274. The shareholders involved in that transaction were the canons of Saint-Sernin and thirteen layfolk among whom was the Jew Durand, son of the deceased Moses "de Curia." Estimated at 200 pounds of Toulouse or 4000 shillings, Durand's share was just a tad below the average holding (4200 shillings) of the sometimes noble and always rich partners.[64]

---

[62]Ibid.: "daret sibi unam marcham argenti et persolveret totum mercedem quam debebat habere ipse testis a dicto Petro de Resengas."

[63]Published in Saige, *Juifs du Languedoc*, No. 36, and recorded in my *Men and Women*, No. 147 (July 1244), and also pp. 165 and 169 for comparative figures. For her family, see the family history of Alacer and his sons Appendix 2, No. 1, pp. 360-362.

[64]PAN, J 324 26 ix (July 1274), and his history in Appendix 2, No. 4, p. 367.

The values of houses owned by Jews seen during the twelve-hundreds were also priced above average, good solid values, although not great.[65]

The charters even seem to show that the traditional line separating this caste or religious group from Christians had become rather relaxed by 1200. An owner's freedom to alienate a "feodum," that is, an ordinary piece of property, was sometimes limited by contract, it being provided, as noted above, that a burgher or farmer could not transfer real property to knights or monks. An occasional charter went further to exclude Jews as well, thus implying what is known to be true, namely that public persons, such as notaries (medieval solicitors), recognized that Jews could acquire and own real property.[66] Another jot of evidence is that, in spite of the almost universal identification of members of this community as "judei," an exception occurs in just this period, a charter of 1202 mentioning Ispaniolus and his son Soloman without identifying either as Jews.[67]

Fragmentary though they are, these exceptions to the rules (which were, one notes parenthetically, soon to be reinstituted again with additions) invite conjectures. If Jews were usurers in Toulouse, so also were not a few prestigious Christians. Competitors are not usually mutually tolerant, but they may well have been so at this time when the ecclesiastical attack on usury was gearing up, so to speak, but had not yet been visited on the town. Besides, those given to divergent religious thought are known to have been more tolerant in their views about Jews and Saracens than were the orthodox.[68] At this time, also, although Jews and Christians never socialized (as today's high-school principals say about their charges), the housing of the former was not yet separate from that of the latter. No ghetto existed at Toulouse. Although most Jews apparently lived in the seven-odd blocks adjacent to their synagogue, the documents prove that their housing was commingled with that of Christians. At least one Jewish family, furthermore, acquired a house and property in a different area just north of the Portaria on the Bourg's Main Street from 1178 to 1213.[69] Nor did it seem shameful to Toulousans to call the most southern street of

---

[65]See Chapter Eight, p. 150.

[66]Malta 9 94 i (February 1206, copied in 1238) permitted alienation to all "excepto milite et excepto domo religionis et iudeo"; ibid., 17 55 iii (December 1242) is another example. For the exclusion of knights and monks, see Chapter Three, pp. 50-51 above.

[67]For these persons see Appendix 2, No. 3; the charter is Grandselve 4 (December 1202).

[68]My *Europe in the High Middle Ages 1150-1309*, p. 373, has several examples.

[69]Dossat, "Juifs à Toulouse," *Cahiers de Fanjeaux*, pp. 126-127, with a good map on p. 139. For the Portaria see Appendix 2, No. 3, pp. 365-366.

the main Jewish quarter the "carraria Provincialis [Provensal] judei," after the notable who was a servant or officer of the count of Toulouse.[70]

These and other signs encouraged Gustave Saige to look for evidence of toleration and even of open and equal relationships between the members of the two religions. He seized on the fact that male Jews were sometimes called "domini" and females "domine" in the charters.[71] Partly right, he was also partly wrong. What he overlooked was that "dominus" was not an individual's title in the cited cases, but simply recorded that renters owed money or kind to Jewish landlords, who like all of this category, no matter how humble, were normally called "domini." "Domina," however, was an undoubted personal title. Usually affixed in notarial charters about property to the names of married women of a certain age, it is pleasant to see that it was applied to Jewish ones as well.[72] But this is about as far as the breaching of the caste frontier went.

This tolerant or rather somewhat relaxed relationship between the two communions was limited by the attitudes of the traditionally somewhat anti-Jewish majority. If the Jews were richer and lived in ampler housing than ordinary Christians, their synagogue was modest in comparison not only with the magnificent basilica of Saint-Sernin and the cathedral, but also with the many smaller but often elegant churches of the Christians. When sold in 1310 together with five stores in very good locations, the synagogue brought 700 pounds of Tours, hence about 7000 shillings of Toulouse.[73] This reminds readers that, unlike Christians who could vaunt theirs, Jews were well advised to keep their religion more or less to themselves, and hence the external decoration of their temples was similar to that seen in private houses.

On balance, then, the period being discussed was the best in the history of medieval Toulouse's Jewry. And, as is often the case, if it is good for minorities, especially those usually suffering discrimination, it is good for everybody.

[70]See Appendix 2, No. 2, p. 364, and Chapter Three, p. 60.

[71]Saige, *Juifs du Languedoc*, p. 58.

[72]See the family sketches in Appendices 1 and 2 *passim* and the word "domina" in my *Men and Women*, p. 37.

[73]In PAN, JJ 46, fols. 105v-105 (December 1310) published by Dossat, "Quelques documents inédites sur les Juifs à Toulouse," *Eglise et hérésie en France au XIIIe siècle*, No. 19, Document No. 2, pp. 791-792.

D. CONDITION OF LIFE

Judging somewhat superficially from the materials in the last two chapters, the measure of equality attained in town contrasts with that in the countryside where a similar unification was not as complete. Residents foreign to the community weighed more heavily on village populations than on urban ones. Among these were the clergy, the lord and his agents, an occasional privileged family, such as rural knights and even some relatively well-to-do commoners. Some of this was true in town, but the proportions were vastly different. Since town governmental form had become a quasi-republican collective lordship in this age, also, many urban folk participated in governing their community, but villagers clearly felt less loyalty to the petty lordly monarchies in which they lived. Although most urban legislation about the relationship of town to countryside concerned farmers wishing to enter town and live there, the village law administered by the lords tried to prevent inhabitants from leaving either the community or their social class.

As noted above in Chapter Two, the word "servus" was not used in this region during the twelfth century. Still, economically speaking, farming families were treated as possessions: taxes and charges owed by individuals, families and their tenements were pledged, sold and given as gifts by the wealthy.[74] Typical was the action of a testator in 1214 who, as seen above, granted Mascaronus, the cathedral provost, a family with its "casalis" and tenement.[75] As in earlier times, the phrase "homines proprii" or even the simple word "homines" meant serfs: in 1245 a notary of the Inquisition described the dependents of the lord of Cambiac in the Lauragais as "his men."[76] Similarly, an individual dependent could be owned by more than one person, up to eight, as was seen above in a document of 1191.[77] Although families seem to have been kept together in the extant transfers of service or land, servitude was profitable for lords and investors. The heir of a family sold in 1207 was still paying a modest but reliable annual "servitium" of five shillings over twenty years later.[78] Lastly, reflecting the mixed feelings one has toward those one uses, the term "villani," meaning persons inhabiting a "villa," was pejorative. A

---

[74]How a dependent, family and tenement were transmitted among owners in August 1185 is seen in Appendix 1, No. 15, note 17 below.

[75]Appendix 8, No. 34 (September 1214).

[76]TBM, MS 609, fol. 238r (December 1245): "homines ipsius testis [ie. the lord]."

[77]Appendix 1, No. 16, and also, for an early example, the charter of 1135 cited in Chapter Two, p. 38 above.

[78]Malta Garidech 1 ii (November 1207) first records the sale of a man, wife and child, and then in v (December 1230) the annual payment by the heir.

young gentleman once went to a chamber in which the lord of Mireval-Lauragais well south of Toulouse lay dying and, seeing two "heretici" there, asked "what kind of villains are those?"[79] For that crack, he was asked to leave.

Not that dependents were abjectly miserable or powerless. One sometimes forget that, oppression aside, dependents in this region usually enjoyed hereditary right to their land when relief (death duties) had been paid, a right to work often hungrily sought by modern workers. Besides, people serve others for many motives, not always because they must. In the face of what one may assume to have been the hostility of rustic males, the lords of Cambiac, father and son, had mistresses recruited from among the wives of their villagers. Were, one asks, these excellent women beaten into it? Or what? But Cambiac also shows how nuanced servitude really was. There, in this almost wholly Cathar community, the farming folk, especially the "homines proprii," were subject to the petty monarchy and occasional tyranny of the gentlefolk.[80] When the inquisitors began to grill them, the "rustici" testified that they had been afraid of their lords, Jordan Sais (Saissius) and his son William, and blamed their Catharism on them.[81] Very possibly so, but two of the serfs were "perfecti," Cathar clergy, that is, and had, in fact, been "adored" by one of their lords ten to a dozen years before.[82] Nor is this a unique case. In the same body of testimony, Raymond de Rocavilla, a knight and lord of Cassers in the Lauragais well south of town, testified that about sixteen years before his testimony of July 1245 he both saw and "adored" among the Cathar "perfecti" an individual named "Ramundus Sirvens rusticus ipsius testis."[83] True, the ceremony of "adoration," a term applied by Catholics, did not mean that the men were themselves being worshipped, but rather that the Holy Spirit in them was being saluted. All the same ...

Censoriousness blinded the orthodox. Writing about the years before the Crusade, the clerical historian William of Puylaurens did his best to blame

[79]See, for example, TBM, MS 609, fol. 198v, testimony of July 1246: "cujusmodi villani essent illi?"

[80]See my *Men and Women*, pp. 42-43 and 71.

[81]TBM, MS 609, fols. 237v-240, the testimony being given in two sessions in December 1245 and July 1246 in part by the men of the village and then by Aimersenda, the woman who turned them all in to the Inquisition.

[82]Ibid., fol. 238v, where Jordan Sais "dixit etiam quod vidit Petrum Gausbert et Arnaldum Faure, hereticos, homines suos, in domibus ipsorum hereticorum apud Cambiacum, et ipse testis ... adoravit ipsos hereticos."

[83]Ibid., fol. 216.

the spread of heresy on the local clergy, a sentiment then favored by
prelates not in the actual arena and also by the Cistercians and mendicants
who were cranking up the repression, as well as common among today's
historians. Rather ludicrously, Puylaurens says that rural priests let
Waldensians help them preach against the Cathars, and blames them for
doing so, calling them ignorant.[84] He also complained that gentlefolk
rarely put their children in the clergy, but instead presented the sons of their
dependents to complaisant bishops to serve the churches in their lordships,
whose tithes those same lords were anyway stealing![85] Lords indeed loved
tithes and servile youths wanted careers in the church. The lords of Noé in
1197 possessed the right to present candidates for their parish church to the
bishop. It must have been rare for that local family to find one who had
been to the schools of Montpellier or Paris.[86] Besides, fair minded people
knew then (and surely know now) that local recruiting has both advantages
and disadvantages. Thirteenth century documents show that rural parish and
monastic schools prepared students for the clergy or the public notariate
throughout the region south of Toulouse.[87] More pertinent here is what
the practice shows about society: if the rich and powerful usually exploit the
humble, ambitious and obliging youths also often make use of their betters
as stepping stones.

Although evidence is sparse, furthermore, the poor certainly did not
wish to remain poor, and some escaped their lot. An example is to be seen
in the history of four generations of a servile family living just to the south
of Toulouse at Pechabou. The father, Arnold de Revigono, died in 1192,
leaving three sons, Peter, Arnold and Bernard Arnold, who identified
themselves as "de Raissaco." Peter and Arnold were dead by 1200, but
their brother was still alive at that date and, as had his brothers, had left
issue. Arnold's son named Stephen is seen in the charters from 1171 or
1172 on. As "homines proprii" of the abbot of Lézat, a status they initially
denied, this family fought a long and eventually losing battle about what
they owed to Saint-Antoine of Toulouse, Lézat's priory on the edge of

---

[84]*Chronique*, ed. Duvernoy, p. 24: "Et illi quidem Valdenses contra alios [Cathars]
acutissime disputabant, unde et in eorum odium aliquando admittebantur a sacerdotibus
ydiotis."

[85]Ibid.: "Milites enim raro liberos suos clericatui offerebant, sed ad ecclesias, qua-
rum tunc ipsi decimas percipiebant, hominum suorum filios presentabant, et episcopi
quales pro tempore poterant clericabant."

[86]Appendix 1, No. 10, p. 330.

[87]The history is sketched in my "Village, Town, and City," pp. 156-157 and 159-
160.

town. All the same, Peter de Raissaco in 1179 was said to be a "clericus," and other members both rented property to other farmers and rented from other lords than the monks of Lézat.[88]

Others were liberated, as in the case of Peter de Yspania. Peter began as a serf, but was enfranchised in 1191, and then or thereafter came to town. By 1202 he had acquired property in and around the Bourg of Toulouse. In 1215 he and his wife Garsenda, no doubt worried by the tumult occasioned by the Albigensian Crusade, entered the monastery of Saint-Sernin as "brethren and oblates." In return, they gave the abbot their property, reserving 200 shillings for deathbed gifts. The charter listed their wealth, which consisted of several small houses and shops fronting on Main Street in the Bourg (the present rue du Taur), a vineyard near the Villanova leprosery just outside the town walls, and a nearby plot of land. That their accumulation was typical of modest businessfolk or substantial artisans is shown by their property outside the Bourg's walls. It was next to subdivided properties each paying an average annual rent of just under fivepence. While an oblate, Peter had also given the canons much cloth including linen, some hens and at least 300 shillings in cash to help the canons receive new brethren and the abbot visit Rome. He further recorded that, owing to the crusader occupation of his home, he lost much moveable property, including a bow and arrows, personal armor and documents recording the debts that others owed him. One concludes that, had not Peter and Garsenda's retirement coincided with a major war, this onetime serf and his spouse would have done nicely indeed.[89]

Whatever their condition, serfs and farmers were surely poorer than those higher in the social scale and, even when relatively well-to-do, visibly disadvantaged. Even for the unfree, however, just as for the free, bread was more significant than status. In 1212 the *Statutes of Pamiers* issued by the conqueror Simon de Montfort, set the fines for the main categories of the subject population guilty of illegal seizure of property and of forbidden assembly or "conjuratio." The crusader legislator divided the population into four very rough categories, "barones," "milites (simplices)," "burgenses" and "rurales" and imposed the following ratio of fines:[90]

[88] Appendix 1, No. 13.
[89] Appendix 1, No. 16.
[90] *HGL* 8: No. 165, col. 632 (December 1212), Articles 34 and 35.

FINE FOR	PROPERTY IN £	"CONJURATIO" IN £
"Barones"	20	10
"Milites simplices"	10	5
"Burgenses"	5	2
"Rurales"	1	1

Even if anywhere from five to ten times poorer than knights, dependent farmers were not hopelessly separated from the other classes. Their tenurial contracts were similar to those of knights and burgesses not only in the vicarage right around the walls of Toulouse but also in purely rural areas. An illustration is a sale in 1209 of "fiefs and allods of knights and rustics" by Isarn Jordan of Verfeil to William de Turre Bestiacius in which the locations involved extended from the outlying community of Isle-Jourdain to Portet close to Toulouse.[91] An apparently feudal vocabulary was widespread in the Toulousain around and after 1200 but had little to do with the nobility. At that time, it was especially used to define the relations of servile people to their lords.[92] In the *Custom* of Toulouse the title "De homagiis" treats only of servitude. Until the full development of class or order distinctions in the later middle ages, all under service contract owed "hominium," just as they all also held fiefs.

[91]MADTG, A 297, fols. 866-867 (June 1209): "feuda et alodia militum et rusti-corum." See also the Turribus in Appendix 1, No. 15.
[92]For servile homage, see the Raissaco family in Appendix 1, No. 13.

5

Nobles

A. WEAPONS AND STATUS

As seen above, the distance between social orders was not great during much of the twelfth century. Armies composed of militiamen divided by wealth into horse and foot were described as "milites et pedites," at least, until the Albigensian Crusade which began in 1209.[1] The citizen soldiers of Toulouse and its region became experienced in war during the early thirteenth century. In 1202 through 1204 the town attacked some twenty-three rural lords and communities, a moment describable as Toulouse's attempt to conquer a "contado." Thereafter its militia was involved in even bigger events. Much divided at the start of the Crusade, Toulouse went to war in 1211 and two years later its militia was crushed or massacred in the battle at Muret. Less dramatic but grindingly difficult were the later campaigns in and around the town. Briefly occupied by the crusaders, the town rose against them abortively in 1216 and successfully in 1217 and then withstood the great siege of 1218 during which Simon de Montfort was slain. Thereafter, through 1224, a southern counterattack led by the young Raymond VII was momentarily victorious and Amaury de Montfort, Simon's son, resigned his domain into the hands of the French crown. Worn down by the subsequent campaigns of Louis VIII, king of France, and successive armies led by royal officers, the southerners weakened and finally capitulated in 1229.

In spite of all these campaigns, the sources are relatively uninformative about military equipment and organization. This is especially true of those who fought on foot in spite of the fact that the "pedites" of the militia were heard of as early as 1067.[2] A few testaments by Toulousan citizens refer

---

[1] See PAN, J 428 12 (dated 1211 without month) published in *Layettes du Trésor* 1: 370a, where the consuls of Toulouse described both the crusader army and the town militia in this way.

[2] *HGL* 5: No. 277 (dated 1067): service once owed by the inhabitants of Saint-Pierre-des-Cuisines "in hostem vel expeditionem pedistrem."

to mail coats, but only one has more detail, listing a coat of mail, leather coats and swords.[3] A petition by a modest pensioner who had retired into the monastery of Saint-Sernin tells more. The crusaders, he asserted, had plundered his house, causing him to lose his "good leather coat, [leather?] helmet and iron hat" together with his "bow and arrows."[4] In short, the "pedites" were bowmen and swordsmen and perhaps spearmen, although spears are never described in the sources.

More information is available about mounted soldiers. At Toulouse, as elsewhere, twelfth century knights or "cabalarii" were a mixed lot, some being truly knightly and heavily equipped and others a kind of light horse. No sharp line divided the various types of "cabalarii" and probably not much of one divided the poorer horsemen from the foot militia. Presumably published between 1128 and 1135, a list of donors to the newly founded Temple in Toulouse promising annual contributions and eventual deathbed gifts will illustrate what is meant.[5] Seven donors promised obits of less than a shilling, averaging nine pence, and eight of more than a shilling, averaging considerably more, namely 45 s 2 d (542 pence). One individual promised a dependent and his tenement. Eight others pledged no money but instead warhorses and "arma" with an average value of 78 s 1 d (937 pence). Five gave the same but only described the value of their mounts. Most generous of all was Curvus de Turribus who promised at death "his best horse and arms or one hundred shillings [1200 pence] of Toulouse if I do not leave a horse."[6] The animals averaged forty-four shillings (528 pence) each, but went down from a hundred to twenty shillings. In brief, as stated above, the old mounted militia ranged all the way from what moderns would later call heavy cavalry to light horse.

[3]See Appendix 8, Nos. 9, 15 and 27. Dated 1208, the last testament is that of a wealthy burgher and minter named Pons David who may have served mounted, but mentions no horse. For his history, see the family history in my *Repression of Catharism*, pp. 202-208.

[4]See Yspania in Appendix 1, No. 16.

[5]Malta 1 45 published in Albon, *Cartulaire général de l'Ordre du Temple 1119-1150*, No. 20. The document mentions Master Hugh of the Temple and Aicard, provost of Saint-Étienne. The former being master from 1128 to 1135 and Aicard being provost from 1118 to 1135, the document may be dated between 1128 and 1135. The annual gifts are too stereotyped to be of use in this context, but the obits have greater variation.

[6]Ibid.: "in fine equm suum meliorem et arma vel .c. sol. Tol. si non habuerit equm, et laudat hoc super bovariam suam de Pabulvilla [Pouvourville]; et si derelinquerit seculum, laudat se pro fratre domus Templi, et ad alterum non veniat habitum." The Turribus history is in Appendix 1, No. 15.

The Albigensian Crusade seems to have fallen on a society in which there had been no serious wars for much of the previous century. An intermittent struggle against the Plantagenet princes of Aquitaine and England, those of Aragon-Catalonia and occasionally of Navarre had stretched from 1156 to 1196. With peaks in the eleven-sixties and eighties, these long if intermittent hostilities had decidedly weakened the extensive state of the Raymonds of Toulouse-Saint-Gilles. They owed homage for Agen and other lands to the north to the Plantagenets, their hopes in Provence were blocked by Catalonia-Aragon and the Pyrenean principalities and the Trencavel lords of Béziers and Carcassonne gravitated toward that Iberian power.[7] Except briefly in the early eleven-sixties when the Toulousans thought themselves really threatened by England, causing their leaders to appeal to the king of France, this protracted series of heavy skirmishes hardly involved the town and region. The worst took place in 1191 when a Navarrese raiding party captured the fortified farm of Braqueville, just across the Garonne immediately to the south of the City. This event was noticed by the English chronicler Roger of Hoveden and was also reflected in a suit for breach of contract in 1193 between the canons of Saint-Étienne, the owners of the grange, and the "custos" hired to protect it.[8] The relative insignificance of this engagement is shown by the fact that, although it had been planned to defend Braqueville with a garrison of up to twenty-five "homines armati," only eight were on hand to defend it. They nevertheless held it for a whole day, but finally surrendered because the buildings caught fire.[9]

A second threat was the intervention of the church against religious divergence, especially Catharism. Undoubtedly threatening, this took time to develop, although in hindsight one may say that the evolution of the Cistercian missions showed where things were going. The change from Bernard of Clairvaux's preaching mission in 1141 to the police intervention in Toulouse with the count's aid in 1178 and especially the armed expedition against nearby Lavaur east of Toulouse in 1191 clearly showed the militarization of the church's effort. But Toulousans were too busy within to look

---

[7]See Benjamin, "A Forty Years War: Toulouse and the Plantagenets, 1156-96," *Historical Research: The Bulletin of the Institute of Historical Research* 61 (1988) 270-285, who gives the dates given above. The earlier treatment in my *Liberty and Political Power*, pp. 51-52 and 59-60, ran the dates from 1158 to 1194 and played down the military importance of these wars.

[8]*Chronica magistri Rogeri de Houedene*, Rolls Series 51 iii: 194.

[9]The pertinent document is published by Saige, "Une alliance défensive entre propriétaires allodiaux au xiie siècle," *Bibliothèque de l'Ecole des Chartes* 2 (1861) 374-440, and the original is in Saint-Étienne 227 (26 DA 1 19) (March 1193).

around outside and therefore the Crusade starting in 1209 fell on them like a thunderbolt.

This long war was a watershed in the military history of the region. Quite good scholars have maintained and others denied that the equipment of the militia armies of the Midi was inferior to that of the crusaders.[10] With the pitiable documentation available, however, one is reduced to wringing one's hands and affirming that foreign attacks on divided peoples are likely to be successful, at least initially. But it is sure that what was happening – or perhaps what had happened – in areas other than the Midi happened there during the war. The heavier armament and larger horses required by the appearance of "balistarii" or crossbowmen, mounted or on foot, separated the old militia of the "cabalerii" into heavy cavalry and light horse, into knights as against mounted sergeants.[11]

Signs of this change are that the Latin word "cabalerius" disappeared and the term "miles" became firmly linked to nobility, a change implying that to be a knight was more consequential or expensive than it had been before. An example of the new reality and terminology is seen in the grant of Verfeil by Simon de Montfort to the bishop of Toulouse in 1214. Especially interested in reinforcing the episcopal office, Montfort demanded from this village only "one well-equipped noble knight."[12] The single knight Simon required contrasts strongly with the traditional dimensions of the mounted militias of "cabalerii" in Languedoc. In 1199, in a little town like Muret, a bailiff, two clerks and 113 other men swore fidelity to the wife of the count of Comminges. One of these persons, Arnold Mascaronus, was surely a noble because he later gave an individual oath of fidelity, but what of the rest?[13] And who were the 101 cojurors from the small Gascon town of Samatan well to the west of Toulouse who pledged loyalty to the same princess in 1201?[14] Surely not knights, one would say, but instead a listing of the community's male inhabitants. One wonders,

---

[10]Delpech's *La bataille de Muret et la tactique au xiiieme siècle*, p. 100, denied such was the case, but see *HGL* 7: Note 48, "La bataille de Muret d'après les chroniques contemporaines," p. 259, where Auguste Molinier states that "l'armement militaire était beaucoup plus soigné dans le Nord que dans le Midi."

[11]This explanation is advanced tentatively because both old and new treatments of the history of medieval warfare make little of the spread of this new technology.

[12]*HGL* 8: No. 176 (June 1214): "nobilis miles unus bene munitus."

[13]*Liber instrumentorum memorialium*, Nos. 206-207 (respectively dated March 1198 or 1199 and December 1201). On Mascaronus' oath, see ibid., No. 210 (no date given, but roughly the same time).

[14]Ibid., No. 209 (December 1201).

however. At Gaillac on the way to Albi, thirty-two or three persons, an astonishing number, called themselves "the knights of Montagut" when they took the oath of fidelity and service to the count of Toulouse in 1229.[15] These were surely "cabalerii," and it is little wonder that the Latin word began to disappear in this period.

In the age of the crossbow, knights with horse armor and the larger mounts to carry it were more valuable than those without such equipment. Although narrative sources about western Languedoc provide little information, a contract of 1214 providing for soldiers in a war against the town of Arles in the valley of the Rhone explains the matter clearly. One party, Nuñez Sanchez, son of the count of Provence, pledged to provide for the duration thirty soldiers, "knights and crossbowmen." The other, Hugh de Baux, proposed that "a knight whose person and horse are fully armored is worth two knights with unarmored horses or eight sergeants, and an [ordinary] knight or an archer with an armed squire, four sergeants."[16] That the southern armies caught up quickly with the evolution of war's style is shown by an up-to-date garrison promised by the count of Toulouse to the town of Agen in 1221. This prince engaged to send a force of twenty knights fully equipped, thirty armed mounted sergeants and ten mounted crossbowmen.[17] The testimony of thirty-two elderly citizens in about 1274 concerning the war also shows the significance of crossbows. Ten had fought, one, in fact, on the side of the Crusade. Five of the ten had been wounded, two recording that they had been struck by quarrels, one also observing that that cost him his horse.[18]

Surely as a result of the greater wealth required, the number of those who could legitimately be called knights diminished sharply. As the old term of "cabalarii" disappeared, the mounted arm became double. Writing the famous *Canso* of the Albigensian Crusade, the poet now spoke of knights and sergeants and, with poetic license, distinguished between them and burgesses and footmen.[19] Words like "scutifer" (a squire or assis-

[15]PAN, JJ 19, fols. 178r-v (June 1229): "nos milites de Monteacuto."

[16]Bênoit, *Recueil des actes des comtes de Provence appartenant à la maison de Barcelone* 2: No. 18 (August 1214): "quod miles, qui ipse et suus equus sint muniti ex toto, debet accipere per duos milites cum caballis desgarnitis vel per octo servientes, et alius miles vel arquerius et scutarius cum armis debet accipere per quatuor servientes."

[17]*HGL* 8: No. 213 iii (August 1221): "garnizo de xx cavaers garnids del tot e de xxx sirvents armada a caval e de x balesters a caval."

[18]PAN, J 305 32, fols. 3r, 6v, and 8r (dated ca. 1274): "equum suum amisit in dicta guerra."

[19]*Canso*, ed. Martin-Chabot, 2: 96, line 79: "cavalers e sirvens e borzes e peos."

tant), "serviens" and "cliens" no longer reflected the old distinction between freemen and dependents, but instead the development of the military household or "familia," the "curia" or "societas" of the greater knights and lords.[20] In the early twelve-thirties a "societas" or company is seen going from Fanjeaux to Limoux. The unit consisted of four knights, four "balistarii" and some "scutiferi pedites," thus showing that the crossbowmen were mounted.[21] The vernacular equivalent of the Latin "societas" was "companhia" or company.[22]

The word "serviens" was loosing its old servile or ministerial overtone and becoming a way of designating a subordinate soldier, a sergeant or a relatively lightly equipped soldier but one of worth. Some of these, being professionals, were especially prized by princes. In 1249 the oath of allegiance to the new count Alphonse of Poitiers was taken by eleven "balistarii et servientes" of the deceased Raymond VII, one of whom was a "francigena" (Frenchman).[23] To these may be added "venatores" (huntsmen), "nuncii" and other specialists. The count's "venatores" obviously doubled as rural police because they hunted men as well as beasts.[24] In 1243 at Montgaillard near Villefranche-de-Lauragais, a William Cassaire, "huntsman of the lord count of Toulouse," is said to have captured a heretic.[25] Already discussed above, "nuncii" meant many things, including the police of the consuls and vicars of Toulouse.

In town, patricians and knights were mounted and went to war as heavy cavalry. And so, naturally, did the local rural lords. What strikes readers is that the documents show more of their equipment than they did in the past. One knightly patrician left a nephew his "charger and palfrey."[26] In 1254 the testament of Ferran Dalfaro, a knight and one of the lords of Saint-Jory just north of Toulouse, records that the decedent left his "best beast" and other equipment to one heir and his arms, including a "crossbow

[20]In TBM, MS 609, fols. 232v and 245r a Pons "scutifer," also called "scuderius," appears during the Albigensian Crusade.
[21]In ibid., fol. 164r (March 1246) about an event fifteen years previously. Both "curia" and "societas" also meant the court of a magnate or prince. For "curia" see Pelisson's *Chronique*, ed. Duvernoy, p. 68. See TBM, MS 609, fol. 53v, where, about 1231, a man reported seeing some knights and others "de societate domini comitis."
[22]*Canso*, ed. Martin-Chabot, 3: 298, line 84: "las companhias dels sirvens logadiers," as the consuls described hired sergeants.
[23]PAN, J 308 71 published in *HGL* 8: No. 415, col. 1264 (December 1249).
[24]TBM, MS 609, fol. 44v and *passim*, frequent references to "venatores domini comitis."
[25]Ibid., fol. 44v (testimony of June 1245).
[26]Appendix 8, No. 72 (dated 1243).

made of horn" perhaps acquired in the Holy Land, to another.[27] Pledging himself to duel in 1260, a Gascon knight listed his offensive weapons as a lance, sword, mace and knife.[28]

B. KNIGHTS AND NOBLES

No matter how many "balistarii" appeared on the field of battle, this transformation of the upper classes was surely not wholly due to technology or to changes in the way of making war. Thirteenth century society, led by its jurists, seems to have wanted to delineate social station more accurately in terms of wealth, occupations, interests and privileges than ever before. It also seems that, within the ranks of the well-to-do, wealth was becoming more concentrated. Readers are reminded that, by modern times, the numbers of western Europe's nobility had been reduced to a small part of the population, rarely more than from one to two percent. Only occasionally did nobles still constitute larger percentages, as in Castile or Navarre, for example, or Hungary and Poland.

In 1202-1205, as has been seen, the "milites et probihomines" of each community made peace with the "milites et probihomines" of Toulouse; the communities, in short, made peace. In 1249 the oath to the new count Alphonse of Poitiers was taken "before many barons and nobles and others, both clerical and lay." More significantly, the local princes, barons and knights swore loyalty individually apart from their communities, whose magistrates or consuls took their oaths separately.[29] By the time the Toulousain was joined to royal France in 1271, the oaths of alliegance were taken by bailiwick, the vicarage of Toulouse and the town and "gardiage" of Toulouse before the assembled "barones, milites, nobiles et populi."[30] The "barones et milites et nobiles" of the county swore individually by bailiwick (or vicarage and town in the case of Toulouse), and the consuls

---

[27]Grandselve 41 (dated without month in 1254): "meliorem bestiam quam habeo et omnia munimenta mea exceptis illis que sunt de ferro," and "lausberc e las calsas e las cubertas ... et balestam del corn." For Alfaro see Chapter Six, p. 119 below.

[28]PBN, MS lat. nouv. acq. 2406, p. 3 (January 1260): Gerald de Maloleone with a "lancea et spata et clava et cutellum" and "alia munimenta militis ad opus sui corporis et equi ... sufficiencia."

[29]PAN, J 308 71 also in *HGL* 8: No. 415 (December 1249): "coram multis baronibus et aliis nobilibus et aliis tam clericis quam laicis."

[30]Dossat, *Saisimentum comitatus Tholosani*, No. 6, p. 88 (October 1271). The count of Comminges was called "dei gratia comes Convenarum," and the lords of Astarac, Isle-Jourdain, Marquefave and Puylaurens were simply titled "domini."

of the "populi" of the individual communities swore for them. The so-called reform ordinance of 1270 refers to barons as being nobles of a higher order than others, barons "having jurisdiction" or lordship.[31] To be investigated in the final chapters of this book, this gradual change weakened the onetime independence of the communities in decentralized regions and, within them, encouraged the division of society into orders and classes.

This change was accompanied by another. In 1255, for example, a power once claimed and even exercised by the consuls of Toulouse to judge all cases between citizens and those of other communities in the county of Toulouse was curbed by an assertion of the right of the count and his officers to adjudicate such cases. Those especially protected against the consuls' authority were described as the "nobiles" and "milites de terra domini comitis." The distinction between the "nobiles" and the "milites" in this legislation was reflected in the fact that the consuls applied marque and reprisal to the inhabitants of the territories of the "nobiles" when their lords were in debt to a Toulousan creditor, whereas they ordered ordinary knights to appear directly before a town court. The count's spokesmen observed that such knights were willing to appear before the seneschal "in the court of the lord count," and, considering that that sufficed for justice, he thereby vetoed the consuls' claim. In effect, he had inserted his court between rural knights and the consuls.[32]

The climax of this transformation of gentlefolk and lords into a nobility is to be seen, to cite one of several examples, in legislation of 1279 that refers to the counts, viscounts, barons, knights and "alii nobiles" of the seneschalsy. Earlier, in 1263, a knightly citizen of Toulouse, Curvus de Turribus, lord of Endoufielle, together with other notables including the lords of Isle-Jourdain and Noé stood as surety for the count of Armagnac before the court of the seneschal of Toulouse. Readers of the record were there informed that Curvus and the others were all "nobiles et potentes de terra vestra." As his successors into the eighteenth century were to be, Curvus was called a "noble et puissant sire."[33] To exemplify the moderni-

---

[31]In Bressolles and Jouglar, "Étude sur une charte inédite de 1270 contenant les statuts de la réformation du comté de Toulouse," *Recueil de l'Académie de Législation de Toulouse* 9 (1860) 317-328 (November 1270): "barones vel alii jurisdictionem habentes."

[32]*HGL* 8: No. 452 (dated before December 12 1252): "licet illi milites in curia domini comitis coram senescallo parati sint stare juri." See also ibid., No. 456 (December 1255) and TAM, II 61 (March 1259).

[33]Fournier and Guébin, *Enquêtes administratives*, pp. 135-136a, No. 39 4 and 6 (January 1263).

ty of these titles, a vernacular address of 1251 in the neighborhood of Agen adverts to the "tres noble baro [such and such], senhor de Clarmont."[34]

Although, as seen in Chapter Two above, the term "noble" had once had the acceptation of "peculiarly free," by the early thirteenth century it had come to mean "especially noteworthy." Public acts habitually called the consuls of Toulouse "noblemen" and sometimes described all the town's notables as "a very noble" group.[35] In a privilege of 1222, written by a consular notary, the count of Toulouse confirmed the liberties of the town, especially in regard to military service. This celebrated act was attested by the consuls, the count of Comminges and by several rural and urban notables, including commoners, whose names were recorded. The formula of attestation ended with "and many other noble men, knights and burghers, who were there present."[36]

What texts like the above did not reflect was the opinion of the gentlefolk that they were above, and apart from, the other classes. There is no doubt, however, that they thought they were and, what is more, that their opinion was applauded or at least admitted by society generally. The detailed inquisitorial register of the midcentury recording events dating back to the years of the Crusade in testimony collected in the Lauragais to the south and east of Toulouse shows what is meant. Reversing their usual practice in Latin documents where women of all classes were called "domine," public notaries, hastily translating testimony given in the vernacular, there called only gentlewomen by this title. Even in wartime, ladies portrayed themselves as apart from other women. At the siege of Montréal in 1240, "domina" Ermengarda, soon to be the widow of a knight from Puylaurens, reported that she and "alie domine" had carried stones for the defensive artillery. What the notary meant by calling her "domina" is sure, but what did Ermengarda mean by "alie domine?" One might today hope "other women," but she surely meant "other ladies," ladies like herself.[37] To derive from a noble family, moreover, seems to have been

---

[34]PBN, MS lat. 11010, fol. 23v (October 1251).

[35]An example is in PAN, J 428 12 published in *Layettes du Trésor* 1: 369b in 1211 where the consuls of Toulouse wrote the king of Aragon to report how they had attacked heresy. They remarked, in passing, that, "ad mandatum episcopi [Fulk] magna pars de nobilioribus hominibus Tolose" had aided the crusaders in the siege of Lavaur in 1211. For the ordinary use, see Saint-Étienne 227 (26 DA 1 1) (December 1198) where litigants came "ante presenciam nobilium virorum capituli."

[36]TAM, AA 1 81 (December 1222): "et plures alii nobiles viri, milites et burgenses, qui ibi erant presentes."

[37]TBM, MS 609, fols. 183r-v (testimony of May 1246).

thought to excuse or mitigate one's presence at anything, even Cathar conventicles. A knight of Fanjeaux told the inquisitors that he and other young blades had attended a Cathar service solely out of "familiaritas" or family duty, but reported that they got the giggles and had to leave the house when an overly devout lady toppled over when genuflecting.[38] Another knight reported that his Cathar mother had been captured in a woods by a gentleman, who let her go "because she was a lady," that is, of noble birth.[39] This strong, if largely private, tradition penetrated public law by the twelve-sixties and seventies and, by the latter decade, individual knights and squires had normally come to be identified by their rank in private charters drawn by public notaries.

Either more responsive to social reality or more given to using titles, however, literary sources, such as the *Canso* of the Albigensian war, used "cavaer" and "donzel" to describe both individuals and groups. Reflecting what was remembered of the first thirty years of the thirteenth century, the later historians William Pelisson of the Dominican Order (writing in the twelve-forties) and William of Puylaurens, chaplain of Raymond VII (writing between 1249 and 1272), hardly ever fail to identify individuals of that period with their appropriate knightly titles. The latter clerk carefully distinguished between knights and commoners even when listing the leaders of Bishop Fulk's confraternity in 1211, thus providing information about social status that no contemporary document bothered to.[40]

Perhaps because they were aiming high, the testimony amassed by the inquisitors against heretical pravity in the midcentury always meticulously recorded the social status of those under investigation.[41] That the Cathar Sicard de Tolosa was a "miles" – although never so titled in a notarial document – was not only known to Pelisson, but also surfaced in an inquisitors' text of 1237.[42] Four years later another Toulousan magnate,

---

[38]Ibid., fols. 164r-v.

[39]Ibid., fols. 67r-v (April 1245) about events some twelve years previously: "quia erat de nobili genere."

[40]Puylaurens' *Chronica*, ed. Duvernoy, p. 64: "Propositisque baiulis confratrie Aymerico de Castronovo, qui dicebatur Copha, et Arnaldo fratre eius, militibus, et Petro de Sancto Romano et Arnaldo Bernardi dicto Endura, viris quidem strenuis et discretis atque potentibus." On how infrequently Castronovo was called a knight, see my *Repression of Catharism*, pp. 182-187.

[41]For conjectures on the class policies, possibly inadvertent ones, of the inquisitors, see ibid., pp. 54-61.

[42]Pelisson, *Chronique*, ed. Duvernoy, pp. 72 and 100. For the text, see Percin, *Monumenta conventus Tolosani ordinis fratrum praedicatorum*, p. 201.

Raymond Arnold de Villanova, is so described by the inquisitors.[43] The inquisitors' notaries also regularly employed the second noble title, that of "domicellus," squire or esquire, and its female equivalent of "domicella."[44] That the sons and daughters of knights had always been important is not what is new here. From late antiquity, indeed, the children of those under contract, such as, for example, Visigothic "bucellarii" and Frankish "antrustiones" normally acceded to their parents' functions, if only because family means and education advantaged or trained them. In the mid-twelfth century, when the bishop of Béziers, a lord who exercised secular jurisdiction, "held court, [his seneschal or steward] was to serve at the banquet together with a knight or a knight's son."[45] What is new or different in this later time is that the generalization of the title "domicellus" and "domicella" confirmed that a hereditary right to parental status, office and remuneration had been recognized. Once recognized, furthermore, the titles of knight and "domicellus" also begin to be used by notables in the town of Toulouse, starting just about midcentury. Early examples are the Brugariis, Castronovo, Turre, Turribus and Villanova families and they were soon followed by other patrician clans.[46]

An especially good illustration of the use of titles is found in the official lists of the consuls of Toulouse. Of interest here is the fact that, long before the lists begin to attribute the titles "miles" or "domicellus" to individual consuls, other persons were described as merchants and moneychangers, crafts- or tradesmen of various kinds, and members of professions such as notaries and jurists. Whereas non-noble folk were early tempted to accentuate the functions they performed in and for society, gentlemen were not. Perhaps the procrastination of the latter class was linked to a conviction that their place in society was transmitted by prestigious families or lineages. Perhaps also the separation of the old "cabalerii" into those who

[43]PBN, Collection Doat 21, fol. 172v (dated 1241).

[44]TBM, MS 609, fols. 189v and 202r, both in the early twelve-forties, for example, mention a "domicellus" at Bram and a "domicella" at Lanta.

[45]Rouquette, *Cartulaire de Béziers*, No. 178 (July 1153): "curiam tenuerit, serviat Poncius ad epulas cum uno milite vel filio militis, et post primorum prandium commedant; sed de his que ad mensam apponuntur, nichil extrahat."

[46]Lespinasse 3 (June 1244): Raymond Berengar de Brugariis "miles" and Jordan de Villanova "domicellus," both Toulousan citizens. TAM, AA 1 103 (dated 1248 without month): a member of the count's court named Bernard de Turre "miles." MADTG, A 297, fol. 221r (April 1265): the Toulousan William de Castronovo "domicellus." The Toulousans are from notable families, for whom see my *Repression of Catharism*, pp. 178-190 for the Castronovo, pp. 285-289 for the Turre and pp. 292-303 for the Villanova.

were truly knightly and those who were not took time. It is certain,
however, that, once they bit the bullet, they came to love what they had
neglected and honorifics multiplied apace. The term "miles" was first used
for a councilor of the consuls when Peter de Castronovo served in the term
of 1255-1256 and for a consul when Raymond de Castronovo served in the
term of 1268-1269.[47] Even more indicative of the transmission of nobility
from father to son is the honorific "domicellus"; the first such person in
extant consular lists is Raymond Ato de Tholosa in 1271-1272.[48] The
prefixed title "dominus" was likewise being adopted at the same time. In
the term of 1282-1283, the consulate was graced by the "dominus" William
Garcias de Aurievalle, knight, and by Bertrand de Turribus, squire.[49] The
form favored throughout later centuries was soon stabilized. In 1290-1291,
for example, the twelve consuls included no less than four "messieurs" or
"domini," the knights Arnold de Castronovo and Arnold de Falgario and
the squires Hugh de Palacio and Peter de Tholosa.[50]

With these changes, it is not surprising to see that the charters multiplied titles to exalt the members of the nobility. Whereas, in the early thirteenth century, the adjective "nobilis" when applied to individuals fitted
only persons of comital grade (and even there largely reflected speech and
not notarial practice), in the twelve-seventies, a baron and even a simple
knight or squire was addressed or described as "vir nobilis" even in common business documents.[51] There was also increasing accent on the style
of life of the nobility. In 1268 a family battle within the lordly line of Le
Fauga, who will soon be seen as troublesome citizens of the capital, led
Arnold de Falgario to cut off his son Thomas. Overriding Arnold's decision, the count's court ordered him to honor Thomas' marriage contract
with the daughter of the lord of Montaut and to provide him and his bride
means and sustenance "according to their noble condition."[52]

---

[47]See the consular lists in Appendix 4. Called both "dominus" and "miles," Peter
was also a consul in 1275.

[48]Appendix 4, specifically Saint-Étienne 239 (30 1 nn) (June 1271) and TAM, II 61
(October 1271).

[49]TAM, BB 189, fol. 16v (June 1282).

[50]Archdiocese 347, fol. 42v (October 1290).

[51]For a "dominus" and "miles" whose daughter had married a burgher, see Aranhano in Chapter Six, note 3 below. See also an act drawn by a public notary of Toulouse
in PBN, MS lat. 11010, fol. 37, recording an action of the "nobilis vir Sicardus Alamanni domicellus, filius quondam bone memorie domini Cicardi Alamanni, et dominus
Bertrandus vicecomes Lautricensis avunculus et curator ... ."

[52]In 1268: "secundum condicionem nobilitatis [eorum]," for which see the Falgario
history in Appendix 1, No. 7, p. 323.

Style of life embraces many things, but must always include economic means. Although Giovanni Boccaccio (d. 1375) and others lauded the generosity of poor but noble knights, the manualist of knighthood, Ramon Llull (d. ca. 1315), was sure he knew better. Wealth is needed because "without harness and money, a wicked knight will become a robber and traitor."[53] Although Llull conveniently forgot how many poor men-at-arms became famous knights, nobles were on average wealthier than others. They not only gained more, they also paid more. Along with town patricians, for example, they were charged more for church services, according to a convention of 1296 between the clergy of the Dalbade parish and its parishioners.[54] And things they touched or handled became expensive. Toulousan tenants paid rent for their "feuda," a fee for succession, a percentage of the sale or pledge value and a fine if condemned in justice. As specified in the *Custom* of 1286, all were limited by tradition and all were uniform for noble or commoner. The fine in justice, however, was different. Set at fourpence for commoners' fiefs, "if the said fief had been given initially by a knight or a son of a knight, the justice of the said property is to be five Toulousan shillings" – fifteen times greater![55]

C. ORDER DEFINITIONS

Nor were these titles semi-private or customary as they had been in the past. When Berengar de Promilhaco, appointed in 1243 as vicar of Toulouse, was called a "miles," he was the first such officer to be so addressed. The title clearly shows that he was not ministerial as past vicars had been, but rather that he was an officer whose status was recognized by the prince and who either received a salary or farmed the office.[56] In line with this, dubbing or making knights not only became more formal, but also gradually ascended from local lords to greater princes. A testament of 1222

---

[53]*Livre de l'ordre de chevalerie*, ed. Minervini, Chapter Four, p. 133: a squire without means should surrender his desire for knighthood "car par deffaulte de richesse deffalt hernois, et par deffaillement de harnois et de despens mauvais chevalier devient robeur, traiteur ... ."

[54]See Daurade 91 Register, 9v (December 1296) in Julien, *Histoire de la Dalbade*, pp. 143-145.

[55]Gilles, *Coutumes de Toulouse*, Article 144d: the tenant or fiefholder was held to "dare dicto domino pro clamore feudi fidem et justitiam iiii[or] d. tol. si feudatarius inculpabitur. Tamen, si dictum feudum ab initio per militem vel filium militis datum fuerit, justitia dicti feudi debet esse de v s. tol."

[56]*HGL* 8: No. 364 (April 1243).

noted that Alaman de Roaxio and another youth was to be knighted by the
lord of Lanta or that of Montaut. In short, around 1200, baronial families
were quite capable of training young knights and performing the ceremony,
just as artisans did with their apprentices.[57] It seems likely, of course, that
the counts of Toulouse had always knighted many of the barons and knights
of the Toulousain, although one may well doubt whether many "cabalerii"
had really been dubbed at all. It is nevertheless improbable that the great
court held by Raymond VII at Toulouse on Christmas 1248 wherein he
knighted perhaps as many as two hundred "nobiles et alii plures" had been
customary in the past.[58]

Gentlemen also wanted it known that they were the prince's men, thus
emphasizing or adding a statist authentication to their nobility. In 1259
Jordan de Rabastencs stated that "I am the 'domicellus' of the said lord
count" of Toulouse.[59] This desire represents a need on the part of local
magnates and notables to associate themselves with ever greater princes,
thereby recognizing that it was no longer sufficient to be a member of the
local upper class. What this meant for the gradual centralization of the
kingdom was already shown when a lord of Isle-Jourdain, whose predecessor had been dubbed by Raymond VII in 1248, styled himself in the twelve-
eighties "miles illustris regis Francorum."[60]

Linked more closely than heretofore to the crown of France, knights
and magnates were called the king's "feodotarii," thus adopting the style of
their class in northern France.[61] This title means that the fief, homage and
other elements that, in the past, typified the service contracts of every class
were now being captured or adapted to define the nobility. As seen above
in Chapters Two and Four, contracts based on these rituals or using these
ritual phrases had been long known throughout the Midi and around
Toulouse to describe the relations of the unfree with their lords as well as
that of notables with their knights. During and especially after the
Albigensian Crusade, well before the Capetian take-over of the county, it

[57]Noted in Chapter Three, p. 66 above.

[58]Puylaurens, *Chronica*, ed. Duvernoy, p. 176. The passage cited above derives
from the title of Puylaurens' Chapter 45. The text tells the date and remarks that the
knights, including the count of Comminges, a viscount of Lautrec, Sicard Alaman,
Jordan de Insula, etc., were "accincti cingulo militie nove."

[59]Guilhermoz, *Origine de la noblesse*, p. 230: "sum domicellus predicti domini
comitis."

[60]For the title, see MADTG, A 297, fol. 36r (November 1272) among other
references.

[61]TAM, II 61 (dated 1273 without month).

seems, noble fiefs and rituals were being separated from ordinary ones. In 1213, for example, the notable Aimeric de Castronovo received Castelnau-d'Estretefons "pro beneficio, honore et servicio," and the count retained "de predicto castro in causa et guerre auxilium et valenciam."[62] Closely related to a town family, a lord of Noé gave homage for his castle and community to the counts of Toulouse in 1245 and again in 1249.[63] Later in 1288 another Toulousan, Pons de Villanova, received Mérenvielle in the Save valley on similar terms from the lord of Isle-Jourdain, showing, as one would expect, that the contracts the greater princes employed had attracted the attention of local barons.[64] Naturally, the term "fief" could not be restricted to the nobility, but there are fiefs and fiefs. Perhaps reflecting northern French usage, Count Alphonse of Poitiers granted a commoner fief in 1270, felicitously calling it "a rent-paying fief."[65]

As consequential was an aspect of the continuing attempt to distinguish noble from common land. It was noted above that this difference was traditional, but that it did not seem to be a matter of great moment. Even in this later age, as will be explained, the new rich always managed to "buy in." An additional terminological reinforcement, however, was introduced to strengthen the contracts, and perhaps raise the price of the property being acquired. Into the teens of the thirteenth century, it was thought sufficient to mention that land ought not be alienated to knights (and clergy, of course). Thereafter and especially in the twelve-forties, it became customary to refer not only to knights, but to their issue as well: "to a knight or his son."[66] As is obvious, the express and repeated mention of knights' children in these common contracts is clear evidence of society's desire to accentuate the existence of an hereditary order.

[62]PAN, J 330 13 (May 1238) containing a "vidimus" of the act of February 1213. See Aimeric in my *Repression of Catharism*, p. 185.

[63]See Appendix 1, No. 10.

[64]MADTG, A 297, fol. 153v (March 1288).

[65]Catel, *Histoire des comtes de Tolose*, p. 394 (April 1270): a rent of two pennies of Toulouse "pro qualibet sextariata terrae ... casalagii sui ... nunc a nobis eidem [the tenant] concessi in feudum censuale."

[66]Examples in Malta 17 28 (January 1222) and ibid. 2 162 (February 1267) where exclusion is directed to "militi nec suo filio nec domui religionis nec clerico nec leprosis." Compare the above with Malta 9 81 (December 1224, copied in 1225) reading "militi nec suo filio nec clerico nec leprosis neque domui religionis." On the exclusion of Jews, see Chapter Four, p. 80 above. It may be remembered, as shown in my *Men and Women*, pp. 28-29, that groups of children of both sexes were normally described as "filii."

During this period, also, the prince's government began to regulate, or profit from, the ability of the wealthy to buy land and nobility. The acquisition of knightly property continued throughout the thirteenth century, but was now increasingly regulated and taxed by a growingly efficacious government. The issues involved are shown by petitions to the crown dispatched by the consuls in 1273.[67] One requested confirmation of the right of citizens to buy possessions owned by knights and another asked the crown to confirm the lordly powers of "high and low" justice acquired by citizens.[68] The consuls requested a prescription period of twenty years for fiefs already acquired, a provision admitting that more recent and future acquisitions required the express assent of the crown.[69]

Debates about these questions continued into the fourteenth century, but it seems that wealthy burghers could and still did acquire noble or military fiefs.[70] Less pleasurably, such owners could also be summoned to serve in knights' arms for their property. In 1303 royal legislation stated that "feudal men, noble or non-noble," having an annual income of one hundred pounds of Tours (fifty of Toulouse) must appear with horse and arms.[71] Other "nobiles" having smaller incomes were to appear in arms as best they could, thus showing what is almost self-evident that some urban patricians were better off than some rural nobles.

The consular petitions of 1273 mentioned above also touched on another mark of the age, namely knightly or noble exemption from taxes. The issue was partly new because the general tax or tallage was itself new, having first appeared during the Albigensian Crusade. Thereafter, it was not seen again until generalized throughout the area at the time of Count Alphonse

[67]The petition preceded the document of June 1273 cited two notes below. TAM, II 61 which contains a copy of these petitions is dated by the inclusion of the consuls Arnold and Raymond de Castronovo among the petitioners, both being in office in the term of 1274-1275.

[68]Ibid., Article 6: "Item supplicant quod cives Tholose possint emere a militibus possessiones." Ibid., Article 26: "Item cum aliqui cives Tholose in castris, villis et locis suis habuerint et exercuerint iurisdictionem altam et bassam."

[69]Ibid., Article 18: "Item supplicant quod de possessionibus militum emptis a civibus Tholose a viginti annis citra quod dominus rex litteram suam concedat quod rata maneant huiusmodi empciones, et si placet usque ad diem presentem." Among others, this request was granted by the crown in *HGL* 10: No. 12 (June 1273).

[70]See Wolff, "Noblesse Toulousaine," pp. 169-170, where, basing himself on TAM, AA 7 16, the author notes that in 1298 and again in 1324 the crown admitted that commoners were able to acquire noble fiefs including jurisdictions in the seneschalsy of Toulouse.

[71]TAM, II 41 (January 1303): "homines feodales, nobiles sive ignobiles."

of Poitiers (1249-1271). The consuls of Toulouse, for example, insisted that all were obligated to pay taxes on all property, including those citizens, knightly or other, who held property outside the town and its "gardiage" and those who held fiefs of the count or later of the crown. In 1273 the consuls asked the king to confirm this principle in spite of the fact that some "claim to be fiefholders of the king and rendered homage in order to avoid sharing the [town's] common charges."[72] Although the principal families of the older Toulousan gentry and rich burgesses and some of the knightly and even baronial lines that had long lived in Toulouse seem to have paid taxes on all properties in or out of town, the issue came to a head at the time of the royal assumption of the county in 1271.

The protagonists of freedom from taxes for extramural properties were William and Arnold de Falgario. Brothers of Raymond of Falgar, the first Dominican bishop of Toulouse (1232-1270), these contentious men were to be seen in town from the late twelve-thirties, and surely became citizens shortly thereafter.[73] Although citizens, they served in the knightly militia called to campaign in Gascony and retained their rural lordships.[74] The tolls collected at their lordship of Venerque on the Ariège river from citizens of Toulouse led to a major lawsuit begun in 1268 or 1269 against the consuls of the town in which they had settled. The disposition of this case is not known, but is mentioned in a document of 1274 that adverts to a decision of the seneschal's court of that year. Another dispute is evidenced by a long roll of testimony dated 1271 and 1272 given by witnesses speaking for the consuls against the brothers' claim not to be citizens (although both residence and service in the consulate spoke against them) and not to be obligated to pay taxes on their rural property. Presumably pleaded before the seneschal's court, the outcome of this case is not known, but the brothers and their heirs later served as consuls and continued to reside in town. They also sometimes won judgments against the consuls, being awarded in 1273 a fine of 4130 shillings for a reason not explained in the charter. In 1279 a later scion of this recalcitrant line was ordered to serve a term as consul of Toulouse by the "parlement" of Paris and did so.

What this lawsuit and the other battles between the town and the Falgario (Le Fauga) family show is that the battle was not only between

---

[72]In ibid. 61 (dated 1273 without month), Article 6: some citizens "nunc se asserent feodotarios de novo domino regi et recognitiones fecerunt ut possint evitare predictas communes expensas."

[73]On the material in this paragraph, see this family's history in Appendix 1, No. 7.

[74]TAM, II 10 (datable from March 1271 to July 1272) where Arnold "fuit in exercitu cum omnibus militibus in Vasconiam."

town and countryside, but also between noble and commoner. In this
struggle, the lawyers at first sight seem to have sided with the knights or
nobles. An undated "responsum" of the law professors of Toulouse opined
that a knight did not have to pay taxes if he had enjoyed exemption for forty
years, as long as he and his heirs had been expressly exempted by a
privilege from the prince. The prince named in this "responsum" was
Raymond VII who had died in 1249.[75] In fact, however, the lawyers had
so hedged their opinion that one understands why noble citizens still paid
taxes on rural properties in the fourteenth century. Furthermore, apart from
any special royal privilege given specific persons and their families, the
crown generally supported the consuls' right to tax feudal properties owned
by their citizens.[76] Practical limits on freedom from taxation aside,
however, it is nevertheless clear that nobles had come to differ sharply from
commoners in late thirteenth century law, and that local princes and the
crown of France had played a decisive role in building this distinction.

[75]Meijers, *Responsa doctorum Tholosanorum*, quaestio 39, p. 85ff.

[76]Archdiocese 347, fol. 42v, contains a "vidimus" dated October 1290 of a royal
letter issued at Paris on the Tuesday before the decollation of John the Baptist without
the year being given. The letter asserted that the consuls were "in possessione vel quasi
imponendi et exigendi collectas a civibus Tholosanis pro modo facultatum suarum ubicumque eas possident etiam si possessiones dictorum civium essent feudales episcopi
predicti."

6

Commoners and Urban Style

A. BOURGEOIS AND WORKERS

Paralleling the emergence of a nobility and of a language to describe it was a change in the meaning of the word burgher or "burgensis." The town of Toulouse gives better and earlier evidence of this change than the villages and small towns of the Toulousain. This is partly because insufficient work has been done on the latter and partly because the category of the village "bourgeois" was only being introduced in just this period, the social division normally being simply that between the gentry or "milites" and the "rustici." Signs of the future were to be seen, however, as in the case of a Garsia Faber of the very small town of Lézat who will appear below.

The relative rarity of the term "burgensis" to define social status may inspire one to think that it was introduced or re-introduced to this region by the French during the invasion called the Albigensian Crusade. In 1212 just under four years before the brief crusader occupation of Toulouse, Simon de Montfort issued the *Statutes of Pamiers* to apply to the conquered territory and there described the orders of society as "barones, milites, burgenses, [et] rurales."[1] There is also some evidence that northern social terminology was having a modest effect in this region: the widespread use of "scutifer" or "écuyer" that competed with the more typically southern "domicellus" or "donzel" to describe the son of a knight illustrates this.[2]

In regard to "burgenses," moreover, it seems true that the Capetian administration did not at first understand the somewhat Italianate urban scene of Languedoc. It must have given the sometimes knightly citizens of

---

[1] *HGL* 8: No. 165, cols. 628 and 632-633, "tam inter barones et milites quam inter burgenses et rurales succedant heredes," etc.

[2] In Dossat, *Saisimentum comitatus Tholosani*, the word "scutifer" alternates with "domicellus." An example is No. 7, 25, p. 95, where in October 1271 Jordan de Villanova "scutifer" and William de Falgario "domicellus," both, incidently, citizens of the town of Toulouse, are seen in the bailiwick of Caraman.

Toulouse a decided shock when, in 1262, Alphonse of Poitiers addressed them all simply as "les borgeois de Tholose," or, in 1269, when he directed his attention to a group of twelve patricians, including one Jew and two of knightly family, blandly stigmatizing them all as "quidam burgenses."[3] And this northern French usage was always favored by his chancery.[4]

In spite of this, the French had introduced nothing new here. The vernacular "borzes" or "borguezes" and the Latin "burgenses" had long had the meaning of townsfolk in the charters of the region.[5] These words were, one must confess, relatively rarely employed, but that was simply because most of the cities were "civitates" of ancient origin and consequently "cives" was the normal term, as stated above, to describe their inhabitants. At Toulouse, furthermore, the social employment of the term "burgenses" had next to no currency because it was the well-nigh invariable practice in documents issued by the consuls to use "burgenses" to refer to those who lived in the Bourg and "cives" to those in the City.

Although the sources were almost wholly silent until the twelve-hundreds, everybody knew that patricians, substantial burghers and workers, especially if the latter were valets, apprentices or journeymen, differed profoundly. A rough awareness of class difference had long been expressed in literature. This is exemplified in a commonplace found in "ars dictaminis" treatises and those on the notary's art by which society was divided into high and low, or into high, middle and low. Both very ancient documents and fairly recent ones, moreover, habitually partitioned society in this conventional way. Philippe Wolff cited a document from Aspiran near Lodève of the year 897 describing the population as "omnes homines eiusdem territorii commanentes, tam maiores et nobiliores quam mediocres et minores" and Fritz Kiener long ago found an act of 1194 describing the

[3]Molinier, *Correspondance administrative*, No. 1314 (July 1269). In PAN, J 324 6, some of the individuals or families described in the act of 1269 as "borgeois" are listed as a notary (act numbered i dated November 1273); a son of a quondam "civis" (iv March 1274); a son of a quondam "burgensis" (vi November 1273); a "domicellus," son of a quondam "dominus" who was also a knight and a "domina," the daughter of another knight (vii November 1273); a "burgensis" (viii November 1273); a son of a notary (ix March 1274); a "civis" (x February 1274); a "domicellus" son of another of the same grade (xi November 1273); and, lastly, a William Vitalis "parator burgensis" and "domina" Condors, his wife, daughter of the deceased "nobilis viri domini Bertrandi de Aranhano militis et domine Gaude" his wife (xii April 1274).

[4]Fournier and Guébin, *Enquêtes administratives*, No. 35, 126b (dated 1262).

[5]Note, for example, PBN, MS lat. 11010, fols. 12v and 22v (respectively dated November 1250 and March 1263) in which a "borgues" of Auvillars and another of Moissac appear.

population of Arles as "omnes homines tam maiores quam minores."[6] So common indeed were such formulations that they penetrated private legal documents. In 1199, for example, a hospital at Toulouse was placed under the protection of a patron lest "anyone, whether high, middling or low, by force of arms or in any other way should be tempted to harm it."[7]

Even though formulaic, these modes of speaking were also used to, or had come to, articulate divergent interests within society and were so employed in midcentury Toulouse. When Count Raymond VII capitulated to the town in 1247 and 1248, for example, he was compelled to restore the free election of the consulate, but in turn obliged the victorious magistrates to state that half of their college was to be chosen from the "maiores" and half from the "mediores."[8] By 1265 this language had become customary.[9] Later when, in 1270, Alphonse of Poitiers' administration had forced a general reform, to use the word favored by medieval lawyers, of taxation and fiscal administration on Toulouse, the consuls confessed that they had acted in a general assembly on the prompting of the "universitas," the whole body of the citizenry composed of the "maiores, mediocres et minores."[10] Similar distinctions spread elsewhere, for example, to the nearby country town of Isle-Jourdain. There, in 1275, after a long and gradual loss of consular independence to the lords of that community, a new form of election was adopted. The seven consuls were to be selected by lot from a group of forty notables (the ancient word "proceres" was thought adequate to describe them) chosen by the lord or his vicar and the outgoing consuls. The forty were not only to be chosen from among the "milites, burgenses et barriani," but also from among both the "maiores" and the "mediores."[11]

Things ripen rapidly when society is under strain. During the Albigensian war social reality tended to penetrate into the charters at the expense of constitutional principle. The great privilege of 1222 granted by the count to the town and drawn up by a town notary was, as seen above, witnessed

---

[6]Wolff, "Noblesse Toulousaine," p. 156 and Kiener, *Verfassungsgeschichte der Provence*, p. 190.

[7]E 973 (February 1199, copied in May 1200): "si aliquis sublimis vel mediocris vel infimus illam domum ... armata vi vel ullo alio modo molestare temptaverit."

[8]TAM, AA 1 101 (July 1247). See also ibid., 102 (January 1248) where the consuls elected in each of the twelve "partita" of the town were to be "medietas ... maiorum et alia medietas mediorum."

[9]*HGL* 8: No. 515, col. 1554 (dated 1265): "medietas esset majorum et alia medietas esset mediorum."

[10]TAM, AA 3 128 196-197 (June 1270).

[11]MADTG, A 297 1r-6v (May 1275) summarized in Cabié, *Chartes de coutumes inédites de la Gascogne Toulousaine*, pp. 25-26.

by specified princes and rural and urban worthies and by "many other
noble men, knights and burghers" there present.[12] Further legislation of
1226 issued by both the count and the consuls was addressed to the "universitas" or all the inhabitants, which was now divided into the "knights,
burghers and other good men."[13] The "alii bonihomines" is what interests
historians here. These were not the "burgenses" but instead the people or
plebs, a fact more clearly defined in the *Canso* of the Crusade. There the
town militia is described as the "knights, burghers and the people of the
town" and the "pobles de Tholose" as the "knights, burghers and commonalty."[14]

There were, in short, three classes in Toulouse: knights, burghers and
the commons. Who the commons were is made clear in another passage of
the *Canso* where the poet defines the townsmen as the "knights, burghers
and the artisans and tradesfolk."[15] The clear implication of this passage
is that, ideally speaking, burgesses were those who may well have been in
business but did not directly "work at" a craft or trade. Although there is
no legal text or charter from the Toulousain asserting this to be the case,
what was earlier alluded to by the author of the *Canso* was spelled out in
1247 by a Vidal Mayor of Canyellas in the customs of Huesca in Aragon.[16]
There, this Catalan jurist and later bishop defined citizens as

> those who live in cities or in towns equal to cities; of which group those are
> called burghers who, although they have masters and workers through whom
> they exercise their professions, do not work with their own hands. There
> are, however, some who, although they do use their hands, are not excluded
> from the order of the burgesses, such as cloth merchants and moneychang-
> ers, and especially lawyers, medical doctors, or surgeons, and others equal
> or superior to these.

[12]TAM, AA 1 81 (December 1222): "plures alii nobiles viri, milites et burgenses."
[13]Ibid. 102 (June 1226): "milites, burgenses, et alii bonihomines."
[14]*Canso*, ed. Martin-Chabot, 2: 6, line 6: "cavaer e borzes e'l pobles de la vila,"
and ibid. 14, lines 19-20: "li cavaer e'l borzes e la cuminaltatz."
[15]Ibid. 3: 8, line 14: "cavalers, borzes e menestrals."
[16]Tilander, *Los fueros de Aragon*, p. 380: "Cipdadanos son todos aqueillos qui
moran en las cipdades o en las villas que son como cipdades, de los quoales logares
aqueillos son ditos burgeses los quoales, maguer ayan cabdaleros et servientes por los
quales trayen los sus offitios, empero no usan eillos por sus manos aqueillos offitios.
Empero son unos offitios que, maguer por sus manos usen, non son itados de la orden
de los burgeses, assi como son aqueillos qui venden los paynnos de pretio et camiadores
et sobre toto esto vozeria o fisica o cirùrgia et otras cosas iguales d'estas ho mayores."

Somewhat later in 1294, the constitution of Alès in maritime Languedoc has much the same distinction. Burghers or – to use the anglicized French term that seems increasingly suitable here – bourgeois were described in this code as "those living off their own incomes who exercise no profession" and were placed in the first "échelle," sharing this grade with money-changers, innkeepers, etc. The second "échelle" contained the drapers, merchants, etc. and the third included the medical, legal, and several other professions. These were the bourgeois notables of the town of Alès."[17] Being simpler, rural society differed somewhat. In the country town of Lézat, a smith named Garsia was vainly asked sometime before 1254 by the only too lively abbot of the monastery in that place to give over his daughter to him. One witness of the event called this staunch worthy "Garsia burgensis Lesatensis" and another "Garsia Faber."[18] In large villages or small towns, in short, the term "burgensis" was beginning to be applied to commoners of more than usual wealth.

The clearcut class distinction between bourgeois and ordinary townsman gradually replaced the older term "probihomines" with its accent on a unified social community. The consular petitions of 1273 mentioned earlier in this essay are instructive in this regard. It will be recalled that it was there requested that citizens or "cives" could acquire knights' properties. Another passage petitioned that "bourgeois gentle on their mother's side" could be knighted.[19] The later the time, the more obtrusive the new social vocabulary became. Seemingly indifferent to the old distinction between the City and the Bourg, the consuls of 1273 viewed every inhabitant, knight or commoner, as a "civis," but spoke in class terms when they asserted that some "burgenses" were more gently born than others. Indeed, the term "burgensis" already meant individuals of substantial wealth and old family. Although most of the Toulousans who sold their tolls to the crown in 1273 are described, according to immemorial custom, as "cives" if they lived in the City and "burgenses" if in the Bourg, one of them, a member of the distinguished Roaxio family was called a "burgensis Tholose qui moratur

---

[17]"Burgenses seu et illi qui propriis suis vivunt redditibus, nullum infrascriptorum officiorum in aliquo exercentes" in Dupont, "L'Evolution social du Consulat nîmois du milieu du XIIIe au milieu du XIV siècle," *Annales du Midi* 72 (1960) 306.

[18]MADTG, G 712 bis (testimony dated 1253 and 1254), witnesses Nos. 10, 13 and 22, the latter being his son named William Garsie.

[19]TAM, II 61 (dated to 1273 – for which see Chapter Five, p. 102 above), Article 19: "Item supplicant quod generosi burgenses Tholose ex parte matris possint esse milites." Guilhermoz, *Origine de la noblesse*, p. 353, note 14, offers a northern French charter of 1280 mentioning an individual "nobilis ex utroque parente."

in Tholosa prope Roycium," now the Place Rouaix, a square located in the City.[20] A further illustration is a passage in Toulouse's *Custom* published in 1286 that defined a category of the town's inhabitants as "a knight or bourgeois, a citizen of Toulouse or another citizen," the latter obviously not being, or not being equal to, a "burgensis" in the new sense of the term.[21] Of such patrician origins were the Paul de Castronovo, "bourgeois of Toulouse and lord of Beaulieu" in 1307, and the Raymond de Roaxio, son of the "deceased lord Raymond de Rouaix, bourgeois of Toulouse," in 1319.[22]

Bourgeois, both Paul and Raymond were "domini" or "messieurs," and one may be sure that, as such, they were able to "vivre noblement." To live in the style of nobles was to be rich, to be privileged and to pay as much for services as did gentlefolk. As it was put in a compromise between the five proctors of the parishioners and the clergy of the Daurade parish in 1296, fourpence was to be paid for a marriage by all persons "of any condition whatsoever except nobles or citizens of gentle birth, which nobles and others who are counted among the nobles" are to pay more.[23] Such bourgeois also had the dubious pleasure of owing the same kind of military service gentlemen did. In that regard Toulouse's patricians must have shared the rights and duties sketched in the statutes of Avignon issued in 1251 by Alphonse of Poitiers and Charles of Provence. There, "knights or military persons or even lawyers" were not obligated to parade in the town militia and the same goes for "honorable bourgeois who are accustomed to live like knights."[24] Such persons were clearly thought of as similar to the "feodotarii" and "homines feodales, nobiles sive ignobiles" referred to in the royal documents applying to Toulouse dated 1273 and 1303 described above.[25] Other citizens were to serve in the militia, unless it was not suitable for them to go as footmen, in which case they could send substitutes.[26]

[20]Ibid. 12 (November 1273). For the Roaix family history, see my *Repression of Catharism*, pp. 251-267.

[21]Gilles, *Coutumes de Toulouse*, Article No. 152: "Item est usus et consuetudo Tholose quod aliquis miles vel burgensis, civis Tholose aut alter civis ... ."

[22]Two acts dated in 1319 without month in E 1307: "burgensis Tholose et dominus de Belloloco," and E 439: "quondam dominus Raimundus de Roaxio burgensis Tholose."

[23]See Daurade 91 Register, 9v (December 1296), discussed in Julien, *Histoire de la Dalbade*, pp. 143-145, and my "Parishes of Toulouse," pp. 189-190. All were to pay "per matrimonium ... cuiuscumque conditionis nisi nobiles et generosi civium, qui nobiles et alii qui nobilium numero habentur ... ."

[24]Maulde, *Coutumes et règlements de la république d'Avignon*, p. 269 (May 1251): "milites vel militares persone vel etiam advocati," and "burgenses vero honorabiles qui ut milites vivere consueverunt."

[25]Chapter Five, p. 102 above.

[26]Maulde, *Coutumes et règlements de la république d'Avignon au treizième siècle*,

These worthies, in short, are the bourgeois notables of late medieval and early modern society. "Les bourgeois des cités" were described by Christine de Pisan in 1404-1407 as persons with established lineages, family names and coats of arms, some of whom were called nobles "if they were well-to-do and of good renown for a long time."[27] Nor were these distinctions wholly new around 1300. In the schools both of canon and Roman law, "senatores" or "viri consulares" were clearly separated from the "plebs." Unlike the distinction between the nobles and the commons, however, these categories were joined together under the rubric of the "populus" or the people.[28]

As a result, the bourgeois did not constitute a social order as did the nobles; their separation from the mass of the people was a class distinction. Although used in private charters, for example, "burgensis" was not appended to describe individuals in public ones, as, for example, in consular or other similar lists. Typical is the consular list of 1274 and 1275 where, among the twelve, a knight, three merchants, three craftsmen and two persons described by the quarters where they lived are all identified not only by their names (both Christian and family, if they had the latter), but also by their grades or professions. The three remaining were listed by name only and are all of good patrician lines.[29] In Toulousan lists, furthermore, the merchants, money-changers, lawyers, etc. included among the "burgeses" by the custom of Huesca adverted to above were, together with the

---

p. 269 (May 1251): "ceteri vero in cavalcatas ire debebunt, nisi tales sint, quod non deceat ire pedites; qui siquidem, si ydoneas pro se miserint."

[27]*Les livre du corps de policie*, ed. Lucas, 3, 6 (p. 183) where she discusses "le .ii. estat du peuple [qui] sont les bourgeois et les marchans des cités" saying: "Bourgois sont ceulx qui sont de nacion ancienne en lignages es cités et nom propre, surnom et armes antiques, et sont les principaulx demourans et habitans es villes rentés et herités des maisons et des manoirs, de quoy ilz se vivent purement; et les appellent les livres qui parlent d'eulx citoiens ... . Et en aucuns lieux s'appellent els anciens d'aucuns d'eulx nobles quant ilz ont esté de long temps gens de bel estate et de renommee."

[28]A familiar canonist source is the distinction between the "populus" and the "plebs" advanced in the *Summa 'antiquitate et tempore'*, cited in Post, *Studies in Medieval Legal Thought: Public Law and the State, 1100-1322*, pp. 374-375. The unknown jurist was commenting on a phrase of Isidore of Seville carried in Gratian's *Decretum* (D. 2 1-3 in Friedberg 1: 3) of which the ultimate source was Institutes 1 2 4.

[29]See Appendix 4, especially TAM, II 9 and 15 (respectively dated January and September 1274). The names were Arnold Barravus, Raymond de Castronovo (Curtasolea) and Berengar de Portali. See, in my *Repression of Catharism*, pp. 136-154 and 197-202, the history of the Barravi and Curtasolea families. The Portali family did not offer coherent materials for examination, but the name (spelled Portallo, Portale, etc.) is everywhere seen in the lists of consuls, the oathtakers of 1243 and the index of this study.

notaries, the most frequently identified businesses and professions. In short, in Toulousan usage, "burgensis" in the singular was relatively rarely employed in public documents, being largely restricted to times when the authorities wished to state that a particular person was a man of worth but not noble. In the plural, "burgenses" was not or, rather, was no longer a suitable word for describing all non-noble citizens. In smaller communities, such as nearby Isle-Jourdain, however, this term could still serve for a time to describe that category.[30] In general, however, at Toulouse and else-where in southern France, town population was described as commoners, burghers and nobles, the last sometimes being called "the military."[31]

In the meantime, around 1300, it had become common to refer to the "menestrals" of the *Canso* in both public and private charters by both their names and the terms designating their crafts or trades. This was a change from around 1200 when, although sometimes seen, such professional desig-nations were not frequent.[32] Along with this went an increased tendency to record the street addresses and the specialties of the persons mentioned in the charters.[33] Yet another is a change in the first names used in Tou-lousan families, a subject treated in Chapter Nine below. If, then, a man's name and especially his family name was the prime method of identification around 1200, by 1300 it was instead his title, functional or honorific. This desire or need to make explicit what had once been merely implicit shows again that a family-centered society was changing into an order-centered or corporate one.

---

[30]See the texts discussed in my "Village, Town, and City," pp. 165-166.

[31]According to Dupont's "L'Evolution des institutions municipales de Beaucaire du début du XIIIe à fin du XVe siècle," *Annales du Midi* 77 (1965) 265, the population of Beaucaire in 1307 was described as a "universitas militarium personarum, burgensium, et popularium." The "militares persone" were the knights and squires.

[32]A few acts will illustrate what the new styling required. Grandselve 14 (January 1289) was witnessed by six persons including Peter Vasco "sabatarius," Peter Ramundus "frenerius," William John Fusterius "notarius" and Peter de Terrasona "saumaterius," Ibid., 15 (June 1297) included "Magister Servinus massonerius," Raymond Adalbertus "magister fuste" and Peter de Ayres "publicus Tholose notarius."

[33]Street addresses and/or specialities are exemplified in Grandselve 9 (December 1256) with Peter Textor de Posamilano and William Bernardus "mercator pannorum lini," in ibid., 15 (September 1290) Pons de Rivis "qui manet in carraria qui dicitur Montis Galhardi," and ibid. (July 1292) William Poma "textor de carraria furni Bastar-di." Although previously rarer, the practice of giving rough addresses had long been known. Note, for example, Grandselve 5 (July 1214) where a William "de furno de Pe-leganteriis" appears and E 65 (May 1239) a Pons Furnerius "sutor de cruce Baranone."

As a final example of what has been said above, one notes that, although notarial registers are succinct and abbreviated, not a few fully engrossed documents, especially those recording significant events, are weighed down with status information. In 1297 the "nobilis vir dominus" Bertrand Mascaronis "miles" bought a town house, tower, hall and attached stores from a solid burgher of good family for 10,000 shillings of Toulouse. In addition to the notary who naturally subscribed the act himself, this important sale was witnessed by the "discreti viri Magistri" Bernard Armanni and Bernard de Garda "jurisperiti," "dominus" Arnold de Alid "miles," and Stephen de Maura "campsor."[34]

B. STYLE OF LIFE

This enrichment of the vocabulary of social identification seem to have been paralleled by an evolution of social ethos. Naturally, uniformities were to be seen throughout this long period. The songs of war, romance and social commentary that flourished among the troubadours and "ioculatores" around 1200 continued to attract both the gentlefolk and the commons throughout the period. It is nevertheless sure that the production of great vernacular literature in Languedoc was languishing by 1300. Neither prince nor pauper was seen any longer among the authors: poets like the tailor Guillem Figuera and, greatest of all, Peire Vidal, the son of a Toulousan furrier, were no longer duplicated.[35] Work had become more didactic, less combative and critical. Among mendicant preachers, a measure of hostility to the old literature surfaced. A manual of business casuistry composed for Toulouse by a Dominican named Guy around 1311 recommended that his strictures against usury were better reading than the romances the workers obviously liked: "I wish you to read or at least hear [my *Regula mercatorum*] instead of the useless stories and romances usually read in workshops and stores and listened to by those working there."[36] The friar's cause was probably hopeless, but his work repesents a trend.

[34]E 502 (March 1297).

[35]The Toulousan authors of troubadour literature are treated in my "Urban Society and Culture," pp. 235-238.

[36]Oxford, Lincoln College, MS Latin 81 fol. 34 and Cambridge, Gonville and Caius College, MS Add. B. 65 fol. 1: "quam compilationem ... legere vel saltem audire cuicumque vestrum consulo loco fabularum et romantiorum inutilium que consueverunt legi in operatoriis et ab asistentibus ascultari." For literature on this text see Chapter Ten, note 53 below.

Similarly, it is obvious that, around 1200, wealthy townsmen emulated the ethos and style of life of the martial elite, the gentry on the land. Perhaps rural life was attractive, but more significant was surely the fact that ownership of land and the concomitant possession of lordship was one of the most stable and richest investments not only in this period but also well into modern times. It is probable, however, that even the wealthiest and most ambitious member of the greater urban families would not have applauded the ritual wastefulness of the magnates at a great assembly held by Count Raymond VI at Beaucaire in the Rhone valley in 1174. There, according to the historian Geoffroy de Vigeois, one lord burned wax candles for his household's cooking, another employed twelve teams of oxen to sew the fields with 30,000 shillings and yet another, "causa jactantiae," burned thirty horses, etc.[37] To borrow a term from the Aleutian Indians, potlatching always inspires envy, even if Vigeois' account was obviously hot air.

At any rate, it is certain that the good bourgeois wanted to be gentlemen, if that's the word for it. In December 1259, the paramount lord of the barony of Isle-Jourdain, Jordan IV, reported to the court of Peter Bernardi, vicar of Toulouse, that his cousin Isarn Jordan had challenged him to a duel. Jordan baldly stated that Isarn, the son of the deceased Bertrand de Insula, had no claim to a share of the family's goods because he was illegitimate. In actual fact, the noble lord asserted, he was the son of a subdeacon and deacon who was also a canon in the cathedral of Toulouse and had there advanced to the grades of prior and archdeacon.[38] Later in the next month, Isarn responded by charging that Jordan was four times a traitor: against the Blessed Virgin because he had killed pilgrims, against the count and his wife because he had impugned her honor, against the plaintiff himself because he had slain one of his squires and against his own family because he had dispossessed a cousin and allowed him to die in misery. Reserving a right to appeal to the count, Isarn threw his gloves toward the vicar, who promptly called for the guarantors of the parties.[39] Having gasconaded each other, so to speak, the parties declared themselves ready to settle the quarrel "per duellum vel pugnam" in harness. Champions were then summoned and twenty of those on Jordan's side were heard in late January 1260.[40] In April, Isarn Jordan appeared before the vicar and contested the jurisdiction of his court, pending his appeal to the count of

---

[37]*Chronicon*, Ch. 69, in *Recueil des historiens des Gaules et de la France* 12: 444.

[38]PBN, MS. lat. nouv. acq. 2406, p. 1, the first sitting of the court being dated December 24, 1259.

[39]Ibid., pp. 1-2 (January 12, 1260).

[40]Ibid. (January 27-28, 1260).

Toulouse, and demanding that the lord of Isle-Jourdain pay a hundred marks in legal costs.[41]

There are two points of interest here. The first is that the parties to this trial acted in the traditional manner of the Gascon nobility anent judicial duels.[42] The champions of the side of the lord of Isle-Jourdain not only contradicted the assertions of the opposing party but also expressed their willingness to do battle "cors a cors" against any worthy knight or "scutifer" chosen by the enemy. Pelfort de Rabastens claimed, moreover, that the lord of Isle-Jourdain had slain the pilgrims to avenge the death of his brother Bernard Jordan, and that Isarn should have done the same "were he as strong in his body as he is in tongue and mouth." A near relative, Bertrand de Rabastenquis, repeated the same defense, concluding that, when the two were slain, they were no longer on pilgrimage but were instead going home![43] Several of the knights and squires prepared for the "bellum" with Isarn by comparing their physical capacities to his. Peter de Rama wanted to fight "body to body although he was smaller."[44] Either because of size or experience, the knight Gerald de Maloleone was supremely confident. He pledged to duel without offensive weapons, save those he would take from Isarn there in the lists. If Isarn appointed a champion to fight in his stead, he'd fight him, but with full equipment for self and mount.[45]

Among the witnesses and participants in this lively affair were not a few Toulousan citizens. Isarn's "fideiussores" were Stephen Barravus, a grand bourgeois of Toulouse, Pons de Gamevilla of a knightly town family and Fulk, son of the deceased Curvus de Turribus, a citizen knight of

---

[41]Ibid., p. 5 (April 12, 1260).

[42]This kind of duel persisted in a wide reach of Languedoc south and west of Toulouse, for which see Ourliac, "Le duel judiciaire dans le sud-ouest," *Études d'histoire du droit médiéval*, pp. 253-258.

[43]PBN, MS. lat. nouv. acq. 2406, p. 3: "pro vindicta vel venganza," and the conclusion reading "si ita probus esset corpore sicut lingua et ore." Bertrand's testimony stated that they were slain "quia dicti occisi tempore mortis sue erant capitales inimici ipsius domini Jordani, et fratrem suum quondam scilicet dominum Bernardum Jordanum interfecerant."

[44]Ibid.: "pugna cors a cors licet sit corpore minor [than Isarn]."

[45]Ibid. He would fight "tali etiam modo quod absque lancea et spata et clava et cutelo que ipse Geraldus non habeat nisi in campo posset ipsa adquirere ab eodem Ysarno vel auferre, dummodo ipse Geraldus alia munimenta militis ad opus sui corporis et equi habeat sufficiencia vel decencia paratus est cum dicto Ysarno facere dictam pugnam, vel quod recipiet inde militem se maiorem si dictus Ysarnus dictam pugnam modo predicto facere noluerit, set hoc casu nullis armis dimissis ... ."

Toulouse. Jordan's guarantors were the rural lord Sicard de Montealto, and two town knights and "domini," William de Falgario and Jordan de Villanova. In the beginning of the case, three champions stood beside each principal prepared to duel. All but one of the six were rural, but that one was the younger Curvus de Turribus, citizen of Toulouse, lord of Endoufielle and knight.[46] Alarms and excursions aside, a compromise imposed by the crown finally settled the matter, but the case shows that patrician townsfolk were closely tied to the life and mores of the rural aristocracy, if that's the word for it. They were, in fact, members of it.

And there was more to it than that. In 1265 or thereabouts, a skirmish took place between two mounted parties, one led by two bourgeois notables, members of the Maurandus family, Bonmacip and Bertrand, and a group of about fourteen Hospitalers, including a "capellanus," three brothers and at least three "donati" of the order, one of whom was a "domicellus." The preceptor of the Hospital reported that Bonmacip had come at him with his "lancea" leveled and that he actually struck one of his party with it ("cum hasta lancee seu teli"). The "capellanus" was hit by a quarrel ("cayrellus") from a crossbow ("balista") fired by one of the Maurand party. Bertrand Maurandus struck another "in capite" several times "with an unsheathed sword" ("cum ense quem deferebat evaginatam") and, had the Hospitaler not been wearing a "pilleus de ferrero," he would have been killed. Another wound was inflicted "cum clavis seu macis" or "cum bastone seu massa," but nobody was slain.[47] Earlier on, other grand bourgeois, the Barravenses, protected their family interest in the Benedictine monastery of the Daurade, by swarming in the streets around that institution wearing swords and accompanied by armed footmen.[48] Such families, moreover, were among those who ascended into the nobility in the latter decades of the thirteenth century.[49]

---

[46]Ibid., pp. 1-3. See the family histories of the Barravi, Gamevilla and Villanova in my *Repression of Catharism*, pp. 136-154, 221-225 and 292-304, and those of the Falgario and Turribus in Appendix 1, Nos. 7 and 15.

[47]Malta Garidech 8 1 (August 1265). The Maurandi family history is in my *Repression of Catharism*, pp. 229-241.

[48]Raynald Barravus reported in MADTG, G 713, fol. 312v (dated late in 1247) that he went to the monastery "accinctus ense suo cum quodam pedite qui defferebat telum in manu."

[49]See the discussion of the acquisition of noble land by patrician families above, and also note that members of both the Barravi and the Maurandi families were knightly in the later thirteenth century. The family histories are in my *Repression of Catharism*, pp. 131-135 and 229-241.

The more or less aristocratic way of life characteristic of the well-to-do, moreover, influenced architecture as well. Endowed with lordly symbols such as dovecotes or "columbaria," the towered fortified farms or "forcie" of the countryside were properties that rich families domiciled in town ardently desired to have. Some, indeed, had surely possessed them from the days when, as members of the ministerial group, they owed service to the prince.[50] As elsewhere in the Midi and in Italy, these rural fortified structures found their parallel in town probably because the towers of town walls had originally been entrusted to the guard of knightly families of mixed rural and urban origins. It is evident, furthermore, that not a few of the knightly and patrician families of the town aristocracy had their origins in the prince's service cadre, the Castronovo (Castelnau-d'Estretefons), Tolosa, Turribus, Villanova and others, and were deeply imbued with its quasi-military ethos and aesthetics, or were derived from families that had important and wealthy rural origins.[51]

The town towers mentioned in the sources and owned by particular families were found in locations that once served defensive functions: around the old Bourg of Saint-Sernin, the Saracen Wall between the City and Bourg, around the Close of Saint-Étienne, and on the southern edge of the City where new fortifications were built in the twelfth century. No towers from this early time are extant, but their dimensions may be seen in an "ex voto" model of the choir of the church and the Close of Saint-Sernin dated 1541 now hanging in the basilica by the lady chapel. The Maurand family tower on the edge of the Close of Saint-Sernin on the corner of the present rue du Périgord must have been similar. By this time, moreover, the towers on the Saracen Wall between the City and the Bourg were near the center of the town and so was, for example, the Roman Gate in the Portaria, razed to make place for the modern Place du Capitole. Typical of old Toulouse, the twin-towered Portaria was sometimes called the "castellum Portarie."[52]

Because Toulouse was the major city or the capital of the province, many of the rural upper classes spent much time there. It was probably there that they met their brides and the families into which they were to

---

[50]An example is the farm at Valségur owned by the Maurandi family of the Bourg in the Maurandi family history in my *Repression of Catharism*, pp. 229ff.

[51]Shown in the Turribus in Appendix 1, No. 15, and in the Castronovo and Villa-nova histories published in my *Repression of Catharism*, pp. 178-191 and 292-304. One town family, the Noerio (Noé) in Appendix 1, No. 10, derived from the lords of that community to the south of Toulouse.

[52]Grandselve 2 (September 1179).

marry, held their political or other assemblies and lived part of the time, especially, one guesses, during the winters. Jousts or tournaments brought to town rural knights and their families and were also participated in by the young patricians of the city. Not only the need to train the urban militia, but also their love of martial sport and its attraction to rural folk, one imagines, led the town fathers to improve facilities. In 1240, they acquired from the heirs of Pons de Capitedenario the right to demolish stores attached to his ample house to enlarge for such exercises the square in the Bourg just in front of the cloister of Saint-Sernin.[53]

Intermarriage of the rural and urban wealthy resulted in wives retaining town citizenship and houses there or in its immediate vicinity. One was Austorga de Vadegia (Baziège), wife of the lord of that place, who had houses at Baziège, Gardouch and also on Montaygon square (the present Place Saint-Georges) in town.[54] Another was Austorga de Resenquis (Resengas) who, while still a citizen, was the wife of a rural lord and had a house in Lacroix-Falgarde in the vicariate.[55] An orthodox example is the long-lived Sarracena, a child of the notable Tolosa clan, who married a lord of Noé well south of town, lived in Toulouse and engendered two branches of the Noé clan, one of towndwellers and the other of rural lords.[56]

Even a casual glance at the documents shows that rural worthies acquired and maintained houses in town and thus helped set its social tone. Some had determined to become citizens. Arnold Ysarnus from nearby Verfeil to the east reported in 1203 that he had bought a house in town as part of his program to become a citizen, and the history of the Noé and Le Fauga families, some of whose members did just that, have been seen throughout this essay.[57] Others were not necessarily citizens, just people who found it profitable to have a house in the provincial capital. A modest pastor from Aureville near town to the south maintained a house in Toulouse for twenty-five years and the knightly Rocavilla of the southern Lauragais, so open to crusader attack, rented houses there during the

---

[53]TAM, AA 1 100 (August 1240): three stores and tables acquired "ad evitanda infinita pericula equitantium currentium in astiludiis vel aliter per plateam maiorem suburbii, cum armis vel aliter, invenientium in introitu claustri" of Saint-Sernin.

[54]Austorga was condemned for Catharism as a citizen of Toulouse in March 1246. For her activities and homes, see my *Repression of Catharism*, p. 108, No. 219.

[55]For her, see ibid., pp. 63, 86, 92, 105, 107-108, 111 and No. 216, and, for a correction, my *Men and Women*, pp. 115-116 note.

[56]Appendix 1, No. 10.

[57]TAM, AA 2 84 (April 1203) and the pertinent text is cited in Chapter Three, note 15 above.

Albigensian Crusade.[58] Although altogether probable, it cannot be shown that the counts of Comminges or Foix had homes there until later, but the baron of Isle-Jourdain maintained a substantial establishment near the Portaria.[59] Some notables with town residences came from quite a distance. The testament of Saix de Montesquivo, a lady from Puylaurens over forty kilometers to the east of Toulouse, mentioned her town house.[60] Others had domiciles all over the region. Scion of a lineage descended from the Navarrese captain Hugh d'Alfaro of Albigensian Crusade fame, Ferrand Dalfaro, a lord of Saint-Jory just north of Toulouse, left houses in Condom, far to the northwest, and in Toulouse itself.[61] In town, in fact, the name of the "rue Pharaon" in the City derived from a corruption of Ferrand's family name.[62]

With all these gentlefolk, rural and urban, living in town, urban architecture naturally reflected their taste, the larger houses being modeled both on town towers and on rural castles or fortified farms. In 1297 a wealthy rural gentleman like the knight Bertrand Mascaronis acquired a town house with hall and tower in the City.[63] Although there were surely important town houses not graced by towers, rich and notable town families shared the joys of having towered houses and stone halls just as much as their peers of the countryside. Two rich heiresses of the Tolosa clan in 1187 or 1188 had two town houses, both with towers.[64] Charters mentioned towers almost as addresses even on the Main Street of the City, the "carraria maior".[65] Although the practice weakened in the later twelfth century, a notable in 1146 found it appropriate (as Americans love to say nowadays) to instruct farmers to bring the annual rent to his tower.[66] New wealth

---

[58]Both are in my "Village, Town, and City," p. 153.

[59]Chapter Eight, p. 152 below.

[60]PBN, Collection Doat 24, fol. 126v (December 1243).

[61]See his testament drawn by a priest at Condom in Grandselve 41 (dated without month in 1254). Ferrand had been in the count's court at Toulouse in PAN, J 304 75 (March 1249) and ibid., 459 6 (April 1253) and also in the Holy Land in ibid., 318 47 (December 1252). On the lordship of Saint-Jory, see Contrasty, *Histoire de Saint-Jory, ancienne seigneurie féodale erigée en baronnie par Henri IV*, Part Two *passim*.

[62]Chalande, *Histoire des rues de Toulouse*, Section 101, pp. 194-195: "carraria Ramundi de Alfaro" in 1276, etc.

[63]The *Liber instrumentorum memorialium*, No. 210 (dated from 1198 to 1201) has a notable named Arnold Mascaronis at Muret and, given that the name is rare, this may well be where Bertrand came from.

[64]Recorded in Appendix 6, No. 28, p. 427.

[65]For an early twelfth century example of a private tower on the "carraria maior" of the City, see Appendix 6, No. 2, p. 428 below.

[66]E 573 (April 1146) where William de Brugariis gave at fief "ad plantandum" a

also sought this authentication. Seen several times in these pages, Pons de Capitedenario did not find his ascension complete until he had acquired an old towered house with a stone hall and chapel (great hall?) adjacent to Saint-Sernin.[67]

Things were to change, however, and Toulouse never developed into what Michelangelo called San Gimignano so many years later, a "città turrita." This is probably because, unlike Bologna, Siena, and other Italian towns, Toulouse only enjoyed a relatively brief period of true self-government during which the vanity of its leading families could be expressed at will and in which the rural knights and barons of the town's "contado" were partly obliged and partly enticed to serve as citizens or clients of the republic. The weakening of the tower cult began during the Albigensian Crusade when free rein was given to the well-nigh universal hostility to private towers on the part of princes, a resentment shared, to a degree, by a town's ordinary inhabitants. This aversion was early evinced when, after his installation in 1102, Pons of Tournon, prince bishop of Puy-en-Velay, had allied with the people of that center to level the towers and houses of the town's "proud" knights.[68] When a prominent burgher named Peter Maurandus was condemned as a Cathar in the basilica of Saint-Sernin in 1178, the prelates and magnates there assembled not only made him retract his purported heresy and undertake a stiff penance, but also ordered his towers torn down.[69]

Sharing the usual ambition to divide in order to rule, northern French princes especially disliked the Italianate urban landscape of the Midi in which the towers of families equally at home in town and countryside signified the function of a city as the capital of a united province. According to the nearly contemporary William of Puylaurens, when Simon de Montfort

---

half "arpent" at Lespinet south of town with the proviso that, at the end of four years, the rent should be delivered "ad suam turrem."

[67]Saint-Bernard 138, fols. 91r, 93v and 94v, a series of acquisitions partly from the monastery of Saint-Sernin and partly from the Astro family dated October 1225 through May 1226. For his history, see my *Repression of Catharism*, pp. 144-161.

[68]Chapter 427 of the Chronicle of Saint-Pierre du Puy in Chevalier, *Cartulaire de Saint-Chaffre du Monastier*, p. 165: no sooner unctioned than he "milites superbos, monetarios vocatos, magnis injuriis affligentes cives urbis, in tantum humiliavit ut turres eorum et maximas sedes quas in urbe fecerant, facta caede pugnantium civium, terrae coaequaret et eos subditos ecclesiae faceret; datis eis pro pace decem millibus solidis Podiensis monetae."

[69]See my "Noblesse et hérésie – Une famille cathare: les Maurand," *Annales E.S.C.* 29 (1974), 1212-1214, and *Repression of Catharism*, pp. 230-231, and, anent the tower, 239, note 49.

took over the government of Toulouse in 1216, he dismantled the walls, filled the fosses, and leveled the "towers of the fortified houses in the town."[70] Later on in 1226 when King Louis VIII replaced the unhappy crusader in the conduct of the Albigensian Crusade, the Capetian invader razed the private towers in Avignon and Nîmes.[71] The postwar collapse of Toulouse's ambition to create and preside over the "patria Tolosana" appears to have meant that, although towers decorating private town houses were built there into the eighteenth century, the tall skyscrapers raised in Italy by the great "popolani" and "magnati" families were not to define the urban profile or "aspectus ville" of this southern French community. Even at best, however, to judge by the "ex voto" of 1541 hanging in the basilica of Saint-Sernin mentioned a few paragraphs above, Toulouse's towers were modest in size compared to those found in northern Italian towns. They seem like those still extant in Danubian Regensburg or Lorraine's Metz.

* * *

Society's boundaries having been sketched, three major institutional ingredients or manifestations will now be placed within them. The first of these is the family, an entity whose evolution in this period was defined in terms of its structure, modest size and changing modes of identification. The second is economics, a sphere in which individualism weakened or was subordinated by the prohibition of usury and the rise of corporate social organization. The third is government where urban self-rule failed, princely authority revived and the church suppressed divergent belief while partly instrumenting and reflecting society's needs. Finally, a brief conclusion summarizes the subjects treated in this book and closes with general conjectures about this history.

---

[70]Puylaurens, *Chronica*, ed. Duvernoy, p. 92: "turres domorum fortium infra villam." Another example is found in Bernard Gui's De fundatione et prioribus conventuum provinciarum Tolosanae et Provinciae ordinis praedicatorum, ed. Amargier, p. 32: "Ortus predictus claudebatur ex parte suburbii magno muri sarracenico aliquando; et erat turris rotunda ibi que fuit Arnaldi Guilaberti et uxoris eius Gentilis, set comes Montisfortis destruxit turrem et murum ... ."

[71]Michel, *L'administration royale dans la Sénéchaussée de Beaucaire au temps de Saint Louis*, pp. 132-133.

Part Two

FAMILY

7

Structure

A. SOLIDARITIES AND HEIRS

The jurist and philosopher Leibnitz once remarked that last wills and testaments were a proof of man's individual immortality. One does not know what Toulousans thought about that dubious proposition, but it is certain that they used these instruments to build their families or to determine, sometimes willfully, their shape after their deaths. They even went beyond their own families to create or strengthen fictional ones, those of their godchildren.[1] As they did with their own children, testators sometimes tried to direct the lives of these beneficiaries. They encouraged them to marry, sometimes offered them the choice of entering marriage or a religious order and at least one testator, a baron, the Unaud of Lanta, instructed an executor to knight two young gentlemen squires, one from the rural gentry and the other from the urban patriciate.[2]

Decedents usually invested much effort to build or consolidate their own blood groups, wishing them to follow their footsteps or those they fondly imagined they had followed. Family resources were not to be risked, and hence clauses stipulating the transmission from an heir who died without succession to other family members abound in the testaments. In all classes conventions asserted lineage rights. In 1216 a widow of decidedly modest social class assigned her property to her sons. The three brothers agreed that, if one died without legitimate children, his share of the estate was to go to the sibling or siblings who had such.[3] In 1206 two sets of cousins from a well-to-do family resident both in town and at Cornebarrieu

---

[1]Appendix 8, Nos. 41, 66, 68, 71, 84, 85, 93 and 101. See also the testaments mentioned in the next note.

[2]Especially in regard to goddaughters for which see Appendix 8, Nos. 22, 31, 34, 48 and 88. On the knighting, see p. 66 above.

[3]Appendix 9, No. 30.

across the Garonne from town agreed to offer each other first option to
buy family property if it was to be sold.[4]

The blood group interesting the testators was larger than the unit created
by a husband and wife. Individual examples and family histories show that,
in well-to-do families, great efforts were made for nieces and nephews, and
cousinage involved serious duties. Just under a third of the 103 testaments
calendared in this book contain bequests to nephews, nieces and cousins.[5]
In 1218, for example, the distinguished knight Aimeric de Castronovo
"maior" dowered a niece to help her marry.[6] All people, humble or rich,
moreover, were faced by death among their parents and the irregularities
of normal life. The will of a childless artisan in 1195 remembered his
"matrina" (step-mother or godmother) and her husband, persons who had
probably raised or endowed him.[7]

This seems impressive testimony to the importance of the larger family
in Toulousan minds. It is apparent, however, that the decedents who favored collateral relatives were largely those who had no heirs of their own
bodies or whose only heir was female.[8] In 1227 an unmarried testator requested his mother and brother to raise his nephew for five years, at which
time the two could divide his estate.[9] Marcibilia Rossella (to use her family
name) left her property in 1282 to two grandnephews named Rossellus, a
niece and three other grandnephews named Ruffus.[10] In 1243 the very
rich Vital Galterius passed over his illegitimate son or sons to institute as
heirs his nephews and a cousin.[11] In his testament of 1237, Bernard de
Miramonte de Portaria, surely one of the richest men of his generation in
Toulouse, listed huge bequests from which he endowed for marriage his
only child Francisqua and then, being without a male heir, proceeded to
gratify relatives. These were three cousins and six nephews, all males and
all of whom, since they have surnames differing from his, were his sisters'

---

[4]MADTG, A 297, fol. 722v (January 1206) involving Raymond de Lambes and
Aton de Lambes and his brothers.

[5]Nephews in Appendix 8, Nos. 9, 17-18, 25, 29, 34, 48, 53, 57, 63, 66, 68-69, 72,
77, 86-87, 89-90, 96 and 100-102; nieces in Nos. 11, 34, 41, 47-48, 57, 59, 61, 83 and
100; and cousins in Nos. 34, 63, 68-69, 71-72 and 87.

[6]In my *Men and Women*, No. 79, p. 144.

[7]Appendix 8, No. 15.

[8]Two-thirds of the testaments gratifying nephews, nieces and cousins were those of
childless persons.

[9]Appendix 8, No. 48.

[10]In the Sobaccus family history in my *Men and Women*, pp. 189-190. The word for
both nephew and grandnephew was "nepos."

[11]Appendix 8, No. 72.

children and those of other closely related women.[12] In fine, the larger family beyond that created by man and wife was well represented in the testaments only when a married pair lacked male heirs and/or when a testator was rich.

Another mechanism reinforcing family solidarity is the "fratrisca" ("frairesca," "-escha," etc.), a term referring to common possession of an inheritance by siblings, including sisters. One is tempted to believe that the fraternal sharing exemplified by this institution reflected conceptions derived from the primordial enlarged family or clan. Perhaps it also could perpetuate or create large families in which siblings and collateral relatives lived or owned property together. Truth to tell, there is something appealing about this conjecture. "Fratrisce" were specifically instituted only in the earliest testaments of my collection (the last one is dated 1166) and never thereafter.[13] Although several times mentioned in later documents, it was not included or mentioned by name in the *Custom* of Toulouse published in 1286.[14] One guesses that the term had come to mean something implicit, a right shared by all siblings, valid until expressly invalidated, something no longer deliberately created by decedents.[15] As late as 1284 documents concerning jointly held estates refer to the rights or claims of groups of heirs as being "pro fratrisca successionis."[16]

The rights and properties kept in community, whether in "fratrisca" or not, are varied. They include the secular patronage of a church, a share in the mint of the town of Toulouse, the pasture and water of a large farm or "curia" and rights over rural serfs and property in what seem to be lordships.[17] Only the first uses the word "fratrisca." Two and part of a third of the four cases listed above involved fiscal or administrative rights associated with local government, ecclesiastic or lay. The others were principally shared economic rights, such as the continued common holding of the pasture and water of the "curia" mentioned above. Although some seem to

---

[12]Appendix 8, No. 68.

[13]Appendix 8, Nos. 1 and 3.

[14]The only passages touching problems similar to those served by "fratrisce" in the *Custom* do not employ the word itself. See Gilles, *Coutumes de Toulouse*, Articles Nos. 90 and 125. There is also no mention in the documents or the *Custom* of "parage," a similar institution described in Ourliac and Malafosse, *Histoire du droit privé* 3: 404-405.

[15]See Appendix 9, Nos. 1, 4, 18-19, 22, 28, 32, 36, 43, 54 and 56.

[16]Appendix 9, Nos. 32, 54 and 56.

[17]Appendix 9, Nos. 1, 9-10 and 51.

have been durable, most of these possessions seem to have been eventually split up by the succeeding generations.

Why communitarian family arrangements were created or persisted is not altogether clear. Lordly rights, such as the secular patronage of a church, and some economic facilities like water and pasture are naturally best held in common if there are several heirs. More consequential is that a family faced a crisis if minor children were left when its head died. Eight testaments specify that adults, including siblings, are given charge of minors who, if more than one in number, were to be kept together until ten, seven, six, five or three years have passed.[18] When a metal worker died in 1219 leaving a widow and five children, the widow and oldest son were instructed to raise the other heirs for five years after the decedent's death. For this service, the son was awarded fifty shillings and, together with his mother, "maioria" over the other children. Although some were apparently over fifteen years of age, the father stated that any child so "stupid" as to leave was to be disinherited (the word naturally not being employed) with the customary sum of five shillings.[19] Most such arrangements merely specify that the children and their property were to be kept together and in tutelage until they reached majority, surely meaning that individuals could spin off when they attained that state.[20]

Whatever its ancient origins or meaning, by the time being treated here, then, the "fratrisca" like any other brotherly and sisterly communitarian estate was, or had become, a mechanism for looking after minors or adolescents. Two early "fratrisce" illustrate this perfectly. A testament of 1166, for example, provides that a son who had attained majority was obligated to hold the paternal inheritance in "fratrisca" for his brother and to "keep company" with him for ten years.[21] The widow Prima Rateria's will of 1150 invoked a similar arrangement.[22] There, although she gave individual donations, especially to her oldest son, the bulk of the property was shared by her five children in "fratrisca," the youngest son being placed under the control of his elder brother for ten years. This brotherly community, moreover, lasted for the specified time, ending in 1160.[23]

[18]Appendix 8, Nos. 1 ("fratrisca"), 3 ("fratrisca"), 13, 26, 28, 31, 36 (one only), 48 (a nephew to be raised) and 62.
[19]Appendix 8, No. 43. For the five shilling rule, see p. 131 below.
[20]Appendix 8, Nos. 13, 17, 19, 32, 68, 70-71, 76, 90, etc.
[21]Appendix 8, No. 3.
[22]Appendix 8, No. 1.
[23]Appendix 9, No. 4.

Given the rarity of the documents, it is difficult to say how long such communitarian arrangements normally lasted. Ten years appears to have been the maximum proposed by decedents; there were shorter terms than that, however, ranging down to two years.[24] Of greater interest is the fact that property was held undivided far longer, the documents exhibiting durations of thirteen years and over thirty, the former figure being that of a family of decidedly middle class quality, and the latter that of a knightly and lordly one, the brothers Turribus (Lastours).[25] Furthermore, one of the cases, that lasting about thirteen years, involved an uncle and nephew, thus reminding one of the possibility that the fraternal community could create enlarged families.[26]

All the same, neither case proves that the institution really pointed in that direction. The "fratrisca" between the uncle and nephew only involved some vineyards and did not include their houses. To what fraternal warmth or dependency the thirty year term of the three brothers of the great Turribus family may be attributed is not known, but the members of equally prestigious families, such as the Castronovo, Tolosa and Villanova, normally divided estates after each death.[27] A glance at the testaments clearly shows that most testators with issue divided their estates in their wills or prepared for the eventuality of such division. Not, however, that inheritances were always quickly divided. In the mid-twelve-thirties, it took a year and a half for the heirs of a leather worker to effect the division of a small uncluttered estate.[28] Still, division was encouraged by town custom. There, the unemancipated heirs of a decedent were held jointly responsible for the action of the group or of any one sibling unless they or their father had already divided the property. They were also to share in the possible profits of such action.[29] Indeed any acquisition made by one of the children was presumed to derive from the paternal inheritance.[30]

---

[24]Appendix 9, Nos. 19 (nine at least), 36 (approximately nine) and 47 (two years).

[25]Appendix 9, Nos. 28 and 51, and also the family history in Appendix 1, No. 15.

[26]For the history of the middle-class Tolosa family (which is not to be confused with the patrician Tolosa), see my "Urban Society and Culture," p. 244.

[27]The brothers Fulk, Curvus and Guy de Turribus divided their inheritance in 1255 and their father William Bestiacius de Turre or de Turribus is last seen in October 1222 and had vanished by July 1224, for which see Appendix 1, No. 15. The histories of the other significant families named above are in my *Repression of Catharism*, pp. 178-190, 268-283 and 292-303.

[28]Appendix 8, No. 60 and Appendix 9, No. 40.

[29]Gilles, *Coutumes de Toulouse*, Article No. 90: "quod dampnum et emolumentum ad omnes fratres pertinet ... ."

[30]Ibid., Article No. 91.

In short, twelfth and thirteenth century documents argue that the "fra-trisca" did not promote the creation of family groups larger than that of husband and wife, their issue and one or two other adult relatives, the typical small western European family. Nor did the other later and unnamed arrangements for common management or ownership of real property and productive means by siblings or by parents and children. Even when such relationships lasted more than ten years, they were not of as much significance as "societates" or business partnerships such as the one built around investment in land and rents that Bernard and Pons de Capitedenario and their "socii" of the Aiscii family kept going for over forty years.[31] Whatever their significance in earlier times, the "fratrisca" and other means of joining together in a family unit more persons than those created by the bond of man and wife were not used to create large clans at this time. In spite of a real measure of lineage solidarity, the evidence presented above shows that the Toulousan family was based on a man and wife and their children and was usually small.

B. LIMITING HEIRS

The *Custom* of Toulouse stated that the male issue of a married pair were the heirs and that all were normally equal.[32] There were several limitations, however, to this equality. Sometimes one son was favored, one child, for example, of a well-to-do family being given the family town house, a matter investigated in Chapter Nine below. In fact, the system tended to favor the eldest sibling or siblings, a practice sometimes functional because an older heir was often charged with helping to raise the junior ones.

The nature of the goods to be transmitted also played a role here. It may be that military fiefs often went to single persons, but one cannot say because they did not show up in the testaments of this period. Still, a movement toward single succession or primogeniture, a practice more common in north France, seems to have been underway, probably because properties owing service or possessing jurisdiction were best not divided up. In 1200, for example, Jordan III, lord of Isle-Jourdain, acting with the express consent of the count of Toulouse, stated in his will that the first born legitimate male child was always to have the major holding or property of the family, namely the town of Isle-Jourdain and its region.[33]

---

[31]Described in the family history of the Capitedenario in my *Repression of Catharism*, p. 155.

[32]About the exclusion of females, see my *Men and Women*, pp. 28-33 and 105-112.

[33]Appendix 8, No. 21.

The transmission of an inheritance could also be interrupted by disinheritance. Although extant cases do not record the motives of the testators, some "filiifamilias" were barred. What the law was on this point is not known, at least until the promulgation of the *Custom* of Toulouse in 1286, but what amounted to disinheritance was practiced before that time. In 1218 a testator gave a son, apparently his only child, five shillings "pro hereditate" and no more, his mother (his father's widow) receiving the house and other property.[34] This conformed to the *Custom*, wherein disinheritance was obviated, but its actuality permitted by the payment of this modest sum or the gift of an object of that value.[35]

It also seems likely that younger children were relatively underendowed by their parents. Faced by a gaggle of three boys and four daughters, the leather merchant Raymond de Podiobuscano in 1297 gave his real property to his two older sons and assigned the third only 500 shillings and the right to remain at home until paid off.[36] One cannot tell whether this was a partial disinheritance or merely an assignment of cash not far short of the value of the real property his elder siblings had received. Whichever the case, there is another example in which an older sibling was clearly being advantaged. In 1206 William Raymond de Insula gave his son Bernard 1000 shillings to be invested in a partnership for seven years until his majority. Not one to forgo a chance to manipulate others, he bound his son to the contract with the "societas" managing the investment by threatening him with the loss of all but 100 shillings were he to break it within the stated term.[37] An as yet unnamed child with whom his wife was pregnant was allotted 600 shillings and nothing more; 500 of that sum was to come from Bernard Raymond Garnerius, a friend and debtor of the decedent, who was also to raise the child. The latter provision of this curious will makes one wonder who the testator thought the father of his second child was. In all likelihood, however, the parent was merely putting the larger resources behind his already living child, a procedure not wholly irrational given the high death rate for babies in this age.

This kind of disinheritance was only one way of pruning the group of heirs to what a father or family council thought was a reasonable size. Possible heirs and sharers of an inheritance could be excluded "bona mente," as the lawyers said, by putting them into religion. Although one may pre-

---

[34]See Appendix 8, No. 41.

[35]Gilles, *Coutumes de Toulouse*, Article No. 123c-d, passages rejected by the crown when the *Custom* was submitted for confirmation.

[36]Appendix 8, No. 103.

[37]Appendix 8, No. 26.

sume that siblings were expected to continue to offer help to those of this
group long after they had entered the convent, this was a relatively inexpensive method of exclusion. Many examples concern daughters, but sons are
seen too.[38] In 1220 the patrician Stephen Astro dowered one daughter
with 1000 shillings and sent the other to the sisters of Lespinasse with
about 400.[39] Nor was this practice limited to the rich. In 1212 a baker,
blessed with three sons, chose two as his heirs and gave the third 100
shillings to enter religion.[40]

How a wealthy individual could take care of his children's needs and
not dissipate their inheritance may be seen in Hugh Johannes' testament of
1235.[41] This weighty citizen and onetime vicar of Toulouse had three
daughters and three sons and, being a widower at time of death, was
obliged to plan more than most fathers did. There was no need to bother
about one child; his daughter Ramunda had been married in 1221 to one of
the wealthiest men in town.[42] The others had to be provided for. Two
sons were to be his heirs and the third was to be made a canon of Saint-
Sernin at the modest cost of 300 shillings. One of the remaining daughters,
either already married or in religion, was given a decent gift of 200
shillings. The last female was directed toward religion with the usual
endowment of 200 shillings, or, if the executors so wished, was to be
dowered with 1000 shillings and married, about 2000 shillings less than her
more fortunate sister Ramunda had received in 1221 – 300 for a monk, 200
for a nun and from one to two thousand for a married woman!

Some young men were disinherited in another and possibly quite pleasurable way by being emancipated, ie. given their share of the parental
estate before their fathers composed their testaments. The charters show
that all classes, rich and poor, practiced this kind of emancipation. The
examples include the rich minter and usurer Pons David, a middle class son
from the Grillus family and a humbler person who was the son of an "ortolanus" or gardener, although that professional designation may merely have
been his surname.[43] This habit permits one to comprehend why, in 1201,

---

[38]Appendix 8, No. 3 where, in 1166, Bruno Trenca put one of his daughters in
religion with 150 shillings endowment or, if his executors so wished, allowed her to
marry with 200.

[39]Appendix 8, No. 45. The daughter was given five arpents of arable, a value
estimated at about what is stated above.

[40]Appendix 8, No. 31.

[41]Appendix 8, No. 62.

[42]See my *Men and Women*, p. 146-147, No. 93.

[43]See Appendix 9, Nos. 8, 9 and 13.

another humble testator gave one son twenty shillings and no more while his brother and mother were accorded the family property. Whatever the real reason for his action, the father's proposal was soon changed because, in 1206, the two brothers switched places with the consent of their mother.[44]

C. MINORITY

It has been seen in an earlier study on the sexes at Toulouse that widows were frequently entrusted with raising minors left behind on the death of a father.[45] Another practice that contributed to the continuity of the family is nearly as common. Testators sometimes gave an older sibling, already a major, responsibility for the juniors together with "ancabada" or "antecaba-da," that is, the right to a prior or preferential share of the property given the coheirs.[46] For a parent to call on an older child, male or female, for this kind of service was clearly considered altogether normal.[47]

If there was no willing mother on whom the testator could rely or older siblings available, moreover, orphans were often left in charge of other relatives, who were presumably compensated for their labor in ways not described in extant documents. When the widower Peter Arnaldus was dying in 1194, he entrusted his two sons, one eight years old and the other three, to his brother-in-law and sister until majority, specifying that thirty shillings Toulouse was to be spent on each child annually.[48] A rare use of a relation, presumably a relatively poor one, is seen in the testament of Raymond Arguanhati from Isle-Jourdain west of Toulouse dated 1271. Raymond was a small town bourgeois, members of whose family were notaries, village pastors and merchants. He made his wife "domina et potens" of his estate and assigned one of his nephews to be the "servant of his children," the latter being promised keep and clothing as long as he performed his duties.[49]

---

[44]Appendix 8, No. 23.

[45]In my *Men and Women*, pp. 37-38.

[46]Appendix 8, Nos. 1, 28, 38, 62, 70 and 87, for example. Also Gilles, *Coutumes de Toulouse*, Article No. 125.

[47]As an example, see the case of Bordolesia, daughter of Raymond de Podiobuscano, whose history is in my *Men and Women*, pp. 38 and 40, and in Appendix 1, No. 12 below.

[48]Appendix 8, No. 13.

[49]In my "Village, Town and City," p. 168, based on the will in MADTG, A 297, fols. 439v-450 (May 1271). As the "serviens suis infantibus," this nephew was granted maintenance "quamdiu ad eorum servicium exercendum se habebit."

Were family members unable to raise orphaned minors by themselves, the system of business partnership current in the town could be called on for supplementary help. In 1216 Bernard Balderia placed his two boys and widow in an association with his erstwhile business partner ("socius") to manage or dispose of his shares in the mills of the Château Narbonnais and other property.[50] This curious alliance of partner, widow and children seems to have worked out well, at least financially. In 1225 the "fratrisca" between the two brothers ended, and they are seen to have done well economically.[51] If no family of any kind was available, a testator could call on executors. A curious example of this was William Raymond de Insula, a man who clearly did not trust his widow. In his will of 1206, this testator invested 1000 shillings in a "societas" whose active partners were to work for seven years partly for the benefit of one of his children. He also stipulated that his executors were to conduct an annual audit of the management of this partnership.[52]

Town law ordered that minors left unattended were to be assigned guardians.[53] If, as was not infrequently the case, a decedent had left minors, female or male, as heirs and had not empowered his "sponderii" to sell property, the consuls were to assign "tutores," chosen from among the executors or others, to perform this function in case of need.[54] Evidence of consular action in this matter is found in the documents. In 1259, for example, the consuls assigned two "curatores" to Bernard de Murello, the son of a carpenter who had died intestate, until he reached majority. In 1261 the two "tutores," one a weaver, reached agreement with William Pelisson, the famous Dominican historian and inquisitor, then "locumtenens" for the prior of his order, about a house Bernard shared with the Dominicans "in barrio castri Narbonensis."[55] The law also protected tutors and the transactions undertaken by them involving the alienation of their charge's property when done with consular authorization.[56]

[50]Appendix 8, No. 37.

[51]Appendix 9, No. 36.

[52]Appendix 8, No. 26.

[53]Gilles, *Coutumes de Toulouse*, Articles Nos. 5 and 6 and the *Commentary* on pp. 184-186, where the author cites the case of a consul named Pons de Villafranca who was charged with neglect in administering a tutorial charge before the consuls. This section of the *Commentary* also treats other aspects of tutorial responsibility.

[54]Ibid., Article No. 100, and the conditions of such sales are also described in Article No. 101.

[55]TAM, DD 1 1 3 i and ii (respectively dated August 1259 and January 1261, copied in 1268 and 1270) the Dominican's name being spelled "Pellissonus."

[56]Gilles, *Coutumes de Toulouse*, Article No. 101.

The *Custom* carefully spelled out the powers of tutors and executors. Their testimony was valid only if their own interest was not involved.[57] Sales of real property belonging to heirs under tutelage were to be publicly proclaimed three times and performed under consular supervision.[58] Another article obligated a "sponderius" to follow the customary order when paying creditors of an estate. Were he to fail, he was liable to the sum of the debt.[59]

With all its care, the *Custom* was curiously incomplete and indeed almost seems to have opened the door to family or tutorial corruption. Although usually obliged to prepare an inventory of the goods entrusted him in order to render accounts to the consuls, an executor who failed to do so was neither necessarily punished nor deprived of his administration.[60] The Commentator on the *Custom* reports that this oversight resulted from a lawsuit around mid-century in which a Pons de Villafranca was charged with failing to render a complete inventory. His lawyer was a legal luminary named William de Raina, and the consuls gave in on the issue partly because of who he was. They probably also themselves served in the same capacity without too much care.[61] The same source notes, however, that this mistaken judgment was subsequently reversed in order to increase the protection of those under tutelage.[62] Still other weaknesses in the system were done away with in the fourteenth century by royal legislation incorporating the protections of canon law.[63] One has the impression that, no matter how good intentions were, ways around them could always be found. The law on executors required them to swear that they had executed a

---

[57]Ibid., Articles Nos. 40 and 42: "dum tamen ipsorum testimonium predictum non spectet ad commodum eorumdem spondariorum."

[58]Ibid., Article No. 5.

[59]Ibid., Article No. 83, noting also that the preceding article dealt with the payment of debts by "spondarii."

[60]Ibid., Article No. 6 states that a "tutor testamentarius qui vulgariter appellatur spondarius" can conduct the "administratione negociorum pupillorum," acting, for example, against their debtors, especially "si pupillus sit de parentela tutoris seu spondarii."

[61]Ibid., p. 185: William "de Narraina ... erat unus de quatuor candelabris Tholose tempore suo," and the consuls "forte erant percussi de eadem infirmitate male administrationis pupillorum et adultorum ... ." On William, see the family history in my *Men and Women*, pp. 184.

[62]Ibid., saying that the consuls, the vicar and his ordinary judge made "tutores et curatores jurare quod de bonis dictorum pupillorum et adultorum inventarium facient et rationem reddent," etc.

[63]See Boyer, "La nature juridique de l'exécution testamentaire" in his *Mélanges*, pp. 186-187.

decedent's wishes, but testaments almost always expressly exempted them from that obligation.[64] The real situation, one guesses, was that the laws were satisfactory, but that the persons applying them could circumvent them. Such is the case today and people of this earlier age were probably no better.

What these arrangements together with the need for consular regulation conclusively prove is that, in matters concerning the raising of minor heirs, the small Toulousan family tried to rely on itself or one or two close relations. There is no evidence of a large or broader group of relatives being summoned to aid in such circumstances. Aside from the key role of widows in educating children, a topic treated in my *Men and Women*, the executorial and tutorial systems were the most commonly employed ways of effecting the desired end.

D. MAJORITY

Young men usually became heads of family at the time they married and young women also acquired their share of their family's estate at that time. A daughter's inheritance was the dowry her parents gave her to help create her family and, on marriage, she was thereby emancipated.[65] Young men were also given something with which to enter the marital state and, like young women, were considered emancipated when they married because they or their parents provided a gift to the bride which, once given, could not be taken back.[66] Sons given "donationes super matrimonio" by their fathers "habentur pro emancipatis" and can testate, buy, sell, act, borrow, etc. in court and out "ac si essent per patres eorum cum omni sollempnitate juris emancipati." This emancipation differed from that of a wife because the principal endowment of a male heir usually waited until his father's death. The dowry given a bride by her family at her wedding was normally her inheritance unless no other heirs existed when her parents died.

The basic requirement for civil acts such as setting up a family was majority. When the *Custom* was published in 1286, it stated that the age of majority was fourteen for males and twelve for females and set the age

[64]See Gilles, *Coutumes de Toulouse*, Article No. 49, and the editor's comment in footnote 1.

[65]My *Men and Women*, pp. 30-31 and 100, and Gilles, *Coutumes de Toulouse*, Article No. 122: "Filia dotata a patre habetur pro emancipata et, mortuo marito suo, de dote sua potest facere omnes suas voluntates, scilicet dare alii marito vel testari et facere testamentum vivente patre vel non."

[66]Ibid., Articles Nos. 86 and 121.

of emancipation at twenty-five for both sexes.[67] As in canon law, the numbers twelve, fourteen and twenty-five referred to the completion of these years.[68]

To talk first about the idea: a major was one who had become legally capable and was responsible in law for his or her actions. Society's supposition was that minors lacked sufficient judgment to decide important matters. Evidence from the Lauragais, the region southeast of Toulouse, taken by the Inquisition in the twelve-forties proves this point repeatedly. A witness from Fanjeaux told the inquisitors that he had often "adored" Cathar "perfecti," but had never before avowed it "because he was [then] a boy and knew nothing about heresy."[69] At Pexiora a woman noted that she had believed in Catharism for a few months when about age seven, but gave that belief up when no longer young.[70] Later evidence from Foix remarks that girls below nine years of age were too young to be taken seriously in matters of religion.[71] Testimony indicates that Cathars also thought children to be either too unreliable or too young to participate in their religion's mysteries. A witness reported that, when receiving heretics, her father ordered her to leave the house because she was a mere girl.[72] Youth was also grounds for refusing a young person entry into the coveted grade of a "perfectus" or "perfecta." In the early twelve-hundreds, Dulcia fled her husband, Peter Faber, to take refuge in the homes or houses of female "perfecte," first at Villeneuve-la-Comtale, then at Castelnaudary, and finally at Laurac where she spent two years "in probatione." In the end, the "perfecte" refused her, she reported, "propter iuventutem."[73]

---

[67]Gilles, *Coutumes de Toulouse*, Articles Nos. 7-8, 31 and 100 and p. 217 for the *Commentary* of 1296.

[68]Ibid., Article No. 7: "maior xiiii annis." Mansi, *Sacrorum conciliorum ... collectio* 23: Article 28, col. 201, Toulouse council of 1229: "Ut omnes ab anno XIV jurent servare pacem."

[69]TBM, MS 609, fol. 165r (April 1246) Bernard Recort "junior": "quia puer erat et nihil noverat de heresi." Ibid., fol. 168 (April 1246) tells a similar story. An Isarn de Villanova "junior" records that he was converted by his mother, but that he subsequently rejected the belief having then been "ab annis discretionis citra."

[70]Ibid., fol. 190 (July 1246): "cum esset septennis" or "juvenis."

[71]Pales-Gobilliard, *L'inquisiteur Geoffroy d'Ablis et les Cathares du Comté de Foix (1308-1309)*, p. 354, where two sisters saw some heretics, "tamen erant puelle et nulla ipsarum erat etatis ix annorum."

[72]Ibid., fol. 237 (December 1245): "expellebat ipsam testem de domo quia puella erat et iuvenis."

[73]Ibid., fol. 184v.

Significant in matters of the mind and belief, majority was important in all criminal cases. Without the consent of a parent, a minor could not be tried for a criminal offence. This was illustrated in the *Commentary* on the *Custom* by the case of a baker's apprentice from Foix condemned to death by the consuls for adultery with the wife of the baker in whose house he lived. Although these magistrates were eventually able to put him in the stocks and run him out of town, their harsher earlier judgment was quashed by the vicar on the grounds that the apprentice's father had not consented to the trial.[74] The same was true in the case of a Raymond de Marcurin-hano who was justly accused of murder, summoned and tried legally in his absence and condemned to death by the consuls. The "reus" subsequently appeared, claiming that he was a "filiusfamilias" at the time of the trial and hence unjustly sentenced. Three well-known and learned jurists consulted by the consuls agreed with the plaintiff and their finding was upheld on appeal to the court of the vicar of Toulouse.[75]

Majority also played a principal role in civil relationships. In 1190 a Peter Sancius, son of the deceased William Johannes, affirming that he was fifteen and more years old, confirmed a sale earlier made by his guardians.[76] In 1243 a Peter Martinus, also the son of a dead father, was declared of "legitimate and perfect age" at fourteen and more years, thus empowering him to do business as an adult.[77] In 1194 a dying father provided for the maintenance of his minor children up to the age of fourteen, a testamentary disposition that clearly implied the parent thought they would be capable of looking after themselves at that age.[78]

The attestation of parents and relatives authenticated by the magistrates or consuls of Toulouse could establish the attainment of majority by citizens.[79] This type of action is frequently seen in the charters. In 1196 Terrenus Martinus appointed three persons "sponderii" of his will, naming

[74]This decision had to do with Articles Nos. 7 and 8 and the passage from the *Commentary* in Gilles, *Coutumes de Toulouse*, pp. 187-188.

[75]The passage in the *Commentary* is in Gilles, *Coutumes de Toulouse*, pp. 178-179 concerning Article No. 2.

[76]Malta 3 44 (March 1190) where Peter stated that he "se cognitus perfecte etatis .xv. annorum et de plure."

[77]Malta 15 133 (January 1243) Peter "erat perfecte legitime hetatis .xiiii. annorum et amplius et quod de tempore nativitatis ipsius Petri Martini hucusque habebat .xiiii. annos et amplius ... ."

[78]See Appendix 8, No. 13.

[79]In conformity with the passage in Gilles, *Coutumes de Toulouse*, Article No. 31.

them tutors of his three male children until they reached majority.[80] At the beginning of the next year, the executors enfeoffed a piece of Terrenus' property, an action confirmed in 1203 when a decision of the consuls recognized one of his sons as a major.[81]

The documents concerning majority cited in the paragraph above all dealt with the children of deceased fathers, that is, young persons who were no longer under the "patria potestas." Those, however, whose parents or fathers were still alive, "filiifamilias," as the lawyers said, were under parental authority until emancipation, a happy condition attained at age twenty-five in the case of both sexes. A recent historian of law, Mireille Castaing-Sicard, has succinctly stated that, in the latter half of the thirteenth century, emancipation was becoming legally more significant than majority, indeed, was even partly replacing it.[82] An example of how true this is was to be seen in 1273. In that year, being less than twenty-five and more than twelve, Salamandra de Villanova, wife of Bertrand Maurandus, acted with her mother's consent, her father being deceased. Furthermore, her husband's consent was rendered with the agreement of his father, because he, although over fourteen, was younger than twenty-five.[83] In 1327 Pons de Garrigiis with the consent of his father alienated a property bequeathed him by his uncle. Older than fourteen, Pons promised to confirm the action when he reached twenty-five years, the age of emancipation.[84] Minors below twenty-five were even described as "inpuberes filii" in a consular enactment of 1274.[85] Strangely, given that conception, a minor below twenty-five was obliged to renounce the Roman "exception" of minority rights, but anyway promised to confirm his action later when emancipated.[86]

Further evidence of the soundness of Castaing-Sicard's opinion about the matter is the fact that public acts of emancipation replaced similar acts concerning majority in the charters. In 1287 a litigant named Bernard de Marcello "textor" presented the court with a consular decision dated 1283. The magistrates had there applauded and registered the statement of the litigant's father emancipating his son, surrendering all rights of tutelage

---

[80]Appendix 8, No. 17.

[81]Ibid. at the bottom of the entry.

[82]Castaing-Sicard, *Contrats dans le très ancien droit Toulousain*, pp. 409-411.

[83]PAN, J 324 6 vii (November 1273): "quia minor erat .xxv. annis, maior tamen .xii."

[84]Daurade 117 (March 1327).

[85]Saint-Sernin Canonesses 9 (January 1274 copied in 1286).

[86]Malta 4 226 (June 1266): "Et cum dictus venditor sit major .xiiii. annis et minor .xxv. annis renunciavit expresse beneficium restitutionis in integrum et minoris etatis ... ."

and giving him a piece of property as his full anticipation.[87] Three years
later, Galhard de Noquerio from Villeneuve-la-Comptal (well south of Toulouse near Castelnaudary) appeared before the judge of the vicar's court in
Toulouse. He there related that his son John, a barber who lived in the
"barrium" of the Château Narbonnais, there present with him, wished to
be emancipated, a wish he was happy to grant. The judge so decided and
gave the young man a document to this effect signed by the notary and
sealed by the court.[88] Similarly, in 1289, Vital Senherellus, son of the
deceased Raymond Senherellus, appeared before the consuls. Proving by
witnesses that he was twenty-five or more years, he petitioned for the right
to administer his property. The consuls therefore elevated him to the status
of a "pater familias tanquam maior."[89]

These materials show that the change from majority to emancipation,
from fourteen to twenty-five, involved more than the free disposition of
property; it also concerned a citizen's civil status. The *Commentary* on the
Custom refused a minor of less than fourteen years the right to testify in a
civil suit and extended the prohibition of testifying in criminal cases to age
twenty.[90] As seen above in the case of John de Noquerio, formal emancipation by a parent may well have been able to change this, giving him the
right to stand in court and give testimony as a major.[91] It is nevertheless
hard to determine the practical law about witnesses because the consuls
themselves sought to reject the testimony of someone testifying for Hugh
Dalfaro on the tolls of Saint-Jory in 1273 on the grounds that he was not
yet twenty-five years of age.[92] Another example is the case of criminal
libel levied in 1287 against the weaver Bernard de Marcello by his neigh-
bor on the "carraria Putei Carbonelli" in the Bourg, Guillelma, wife of
Raymond Guillelmus "mercator."[93] Both the "actor" and the "reus" were

---

[87]TAM, II 92 (November 1287).

[88]Malta 20 56 ii (March 1286, copied in 1289): the parent "a se emacipavit et a sua
manu et potestate sua eum dimisit et penitus liberavit et a sacris paternis potestatibus et
nexibus relaxavit dando licentiam et plenam potestatem testandi, testificandi, et standi
in judicio," etc.

[89]E 502 (January 1289), the petitioner having "ad etatis viginti quinque annorum et
pluris devenerat complementum."

[90]See Gilles, *Coutumes de Toulouse*, p. 217, where the right of a minor to levy a
suit against someone for a crime is based on his right to tutorial protection.

[91]See the document in note 88 above.

[92]TAM, II 46 (April 1273).

[93]TAM, II 92 (November 1287) partly published in Gilles, "Une cause d'injure à
la fin du XIIIe siècle," *Annales de la faculté de droit à Toulouse* 17 (1969) 121-144. See
also my *Men and Women*, p. 27, for the context of the trial.

at pains to prove that they were of sufficient age and, as noted above, the defendant had presented the court with a consular attestation of his emancipation.[94] The defendant protested that, being less than twenty-five years old and therefore a minor, the plaintiff had no right to initiate a suit, but the latter insisted that she had because she was a major over twelve years of age. Although, as was the custom dealing with women in Toulousan courts, she anyway appointed proctors with consular approval, she was surely right according to the town *Custom*. That law states that a woman not under parental tutelage or that of "curatores" can act freely in regard to property.[95]

Although emancipation had become more consequential, simple majority still had a role to play. In 1277 a testator bequeathed his grandchildren a sum of money to spend as they wished "after they were fourteen years of age."[96] Furthermore, the age midway between fourteen or fifteen and twenty-five was important in law. The *Custom* records that a young man could serve as an arbiter in a judicial matter when twenty years of age.[97] It has been noted above that the *Commentary* on the *Custom* dated 1296 states that, among males, minors less than fourteen years old cannot testify in civil matters and minors less than twenty, in criminal ones.[98] In short, it seems probable that the age of twenty years played a role in Toulouse in this period. Perhaps it was considered to be the natural or average age for young men to marry.

Further evidence reinforces this supposition. Lacking documents, one divines by guesswork or analogy that age fourteen was considered sufficient for such duties as service in the militia, but that the administration of property was sometimes remanded to twenty and that this was so even before the rise of the emancipatory age of twenty-five. An example may be seen in charters concerning Raymond de Capitedenario, the son of Fort. Burdened by debts and wracked by protracted illness, Fort died in 1195,

---

[94]The act of 1286 in the paragraph above.

[95]Gilles, *Coutumes de Toulouse*, Article No. 69 which, however, deals only with property. But see the *Commentary*, p. 217, where the author explains why minors can accuse someone, but are forbidden to offer testimony in a criminal trial, by saying that "in accusatione quod deest minori etati suppletur per auctoritatem tutoris," citing D 41 2 32 and C 5 59 4.

[96]In Appendix 8, No. 98.

[97]Discussing Article No. 10 on arbitration, the Commentator in Gilles, *Coutumes de Toulouse*, p. 192, notes that a person less than twenty years old may not arbitrate and then adds: "Minor autem xx et v annorum, dum tamen sit major xx, potest esse arbiter ... ."

[98]Ibid., p. 217.

leaving his son Raymond at the age of about two.[99] In 1201, when the boy was about eight, his guardian sold some of his charge's property, arranging for young Raymond to receive the income from the alienated property until the age of twenty, and then, on confirming the sale, to get the full price of the property from the purchaser.[100] Accordingly, in 1213 several witnesses including his uncle, the respected Pons de Capitedenario, testified that Raymond had twenty or more years, upon which Raymond confirmed the sale mentioned above.[101]

Whatever their ages, it is certain that when young persons, both male and female, married and set up households, they were partially emancipated in the opinion of the *Custom* of Toulouse. A final consideration is relevant here. According to the *Commentary* of 1296 on the *Custom*, "inpuberes" and "filiifamilias," minors, that is, below twenty-five years, were among the categories of persons ruled incapable of drawing a testament. The exceptions to this rule are important. They include married couples as described above and also those who benefited from the right to have special properties, such as the knight's or soldier's "peculium castrense" or the "peculium quasicastrense" gained in return for exercising other professions, ecclesiastical, legal, clerical, etc.[102]

In conclusion, although the formal age of majority was fourteen, twenty was the age at which most men began to act somewhat independently of the families by which they had been nurtured. Around 1200, furthermore, the law on emancipation was obviously not yet introduced into practice, coming into its own only later, during the thirteenth century. Although mitigated by

---

[99]The context of this history is the Capdenier family history in my *Repression of Catharism*, pp. 163-164. The specific document is E 538 ii (May 1196 copied in 1197).

[100]E 538 (August 1201, copied in 1202). The document does not mention the legal capacity of the seller, whether he was tutor or simply "spondarius" of the father's will.

[101]E 579 (June 1213) together with other copies in the same "liasse" and also one in E 896. The witnesses "dixerunt pro testimonio quod Raimundus ... habebat .xx. annos et amplius et quod erat etatis .xx. annorum et amplius." The actual history is more complex because Bernard, the father of Pons de Capitedenario, had picked up one of the debts of Fort and his relative William Faber in E 538 ii (May 1195) and acquired some property from them and from other of Fort's creditors in Grandselve 2 (January 119? – the date is erased) and in Saint-Bernard 138, fols. 78r-80r (November-December 1197). These acquisitions were guaranteed in the act of 1201 noted above and the sale was confirmed in ibid., fols. 80-81 (January 1213).

[102]See the *Commentary* in Gilles, *Coutumes de Toulouse*, p. 259. On the subject of these kinds of "peculia," consult Fitting, *Das castrense peculium in seiner geschichtlichen Entwicklung und heutige gemeinrechtlichen Geltung*, pp. 527ff., and Ourliac and Malafosse, *Histoire du droit privé* 3: 76.

the importance of age twenty, the change from the earlier date of majority to the later one of emancipation was significant. It illustrated the increasing desire of society to define status and was therefore in harmony with the growing rigidities of social structure at this time. This change paralleled the replacement of the amateur or lay judges or assessors by professional lawyers and judges in the courts of law around and after 1200. The new courts not only sought to prosecute crime more actively than in the past, but also to protect those in their charge more vigorously.[103] And protected people are also very easily reduced to being under tutelage.

In a sense, although the family was the foundation of it all, the impediments inspired by the need to define status had become a weightier burden on that institution than ever before. A time when a young man between fifteen and twenty-five years of age could be described by the lawyers as an "immature child" is one where the protection of status and property was considered more significant than the reality of bodies and minds. When men of that period went to war they did not refuse to recruit or call up these youths, but they did not permit them to dispose of property as easily as their elders. The Roman law of emancipation at age twenty-five was only one example of this. Another, seen in my earlier study on the position of women in Toulousan law, is that the law taught in the schools and used in the courts put the good of the family and of its issue well ahead of that of wives. Quite apart from the weakening of a woman's own status, what cut especially deep was that, to the lawyers of the time, maternal love of a child was inferior to a father's. A mother's wishes could therefore be set aside because "no love conquers paternal love."[104]

[103]The growth of the university in this period and that of the legal professions, notaries, lawyers, and judges is sketched in my *Liberty and Political Power*, pp. 116-119 and 147-148, "Village, Town, and City," p. 157, and "Urban Society and Culture," pp. 233-234.

[104]In my *Men and Women*, pp. 38-39, 95, 99, 109-110 and 114-115.

8

Size

A. HOUSING

The measure of cohesion possessed by the Toulousan family in this period has been investigated above, as has the way its individual cells were constituted. An examination of the size and character of Toulousan housing may now distinguish further between the rich and the poor and obtain a general idea of family size. What the reader will learn is that the typical family was small and that even the patrician and noble clans in and around Toulouse, although in some respects similar, did not equal the "consorterie" of the Italian city republics in size. A reason for this difference may have been that, because Toulouse never became as free of princely power as did the Italian republics, her greater families never built such extensive structures to mobilize the power of blood, clientage and the economy.

Individuals live in rooms but families, save those of the very poor, inhabit apartments or houses. Unlike the later middle ages, the poor do not seem to have crowded the social scene at this time. Still, little is known about them because the available documentation deals largely with real property and therefore veils them.[1] The material on the Toulousan apartment and house therefore tells something, but not really enough, about the size of the family in this area. By nature's invariably harsh definition, however, it is sure that the families of the very poor were small.

Little evidence about Toulousan housing exists for this period and what there is requires an examination of terms, terms whose meanings are indistinct. A common vernacular word was "casal." Perhaps originally meaning "house," it referred to the whole complex of a house, attachments and lot or emplacement. In 1187 or 1188, two Tolosa heiresses divided two houses, one a "tower, 'camera' and 'casal'" and the other a "tower, 'domus' and 'casal.'"[2] A charter of 1217 mentions the "casalis scole Judeorum," not

---

[1] A few humble persons will be seen below and note also the mute pair mentioned at the beginning of Chapter Nine below.

[2] Appendix 6, No. 28, p. 427 below.

only the synagogue, then, but also all attachments.[3] A rural "casal" was a farm or allotment, as in 1193 when a farm was called the "honor casalis de Raissaco," of the Raissaco brothers.[4]

The primary word for house in this period was "domus." This term was indiscriminately used for houses both small and large. The ample house sold by the heirs of Berengar Astro in 1226 was a "domus."[5] A solid burgher family named Embrini bought a new residence, as today's real estate agents like to say, with a tower and stone hall in 1255. Next door to the towered home of the distinguished clan of the Maurandi, this domicile was also a "domus."[6] In 1271 a patrician sold a "domus" on the "rue des Couteliers" to the knight Arnold de Falgario, a scion of a family far more elegant than the Embrini. The emplacement was approximately 141 by 88 by 23 feet.[7]

The "domus" mentioned above were those of the well-to-do; smaller ones were legion. In 1225 a wealthy pair sold a "domus et casalis" with attached buildings to William Raymond Calavus who is otherwise unknown. Two streets partly bounded the edifice, their fronts being approximately 29

---

[3]Barrière-Flavy, *L'Abbaye de Calers*, pp. 151-153 (July 1217): sale by the cellarer of Calers to a non-Jew of a "casalis et honor ... cum omnibus clausuris que sunt ex parte casalis iudeorum."

[4]Ourliac and Magnou, *Cartulaire de Lézat*, No. 1499 (January 1193).

[5]Saint-Bernard 138, fol. 93 (May 1226).

[6]Saint-Sernin 600 (10 36 12) i (January-March 1255).

[7]Grandselve 11 (March 1271). The seller was John de Castronovo (Curtasolea) for whose family see my *Repression of Catharism*, pp. 197-202. The actual measurements are 24 "brachiate" x 15 x 4, being 43.1 x 26.9 x 7.18 meters, if one follows the calculations of the conversion of the "brassa" of Toulouse into meters stated in Vitry. This author's "Recherches sur l'ancienne mesure Toulousaine appellée 'brassa,'" *Mémoires-ASIBLT* 3 (1847) 336-345, estimated the "brachiata" or "brassa" of the fifteenth century (itself composed of eight "palmi") to equal 1.7961 meters or .7363 feet. This proposal seems reasonable from the evidence he has cited and also is in accord with the figures given in Zupko, *French Weights and Measures before the Revolution*, s.v. "brasse" and "palme" (pp. 30 and 126) where he employed the "palme" of Nîmes as a guide. These calculations seem further confirmed by a compromise between two parties found in Saint-Sernin Canonesses 45 (August 1295) concerning a wall between the properties of two artisans. The arbiters proposed "quod in dicto meiano non fiant nec fieri possint viste seu fenestre per quas capud hominis possit transciri et si fenestras vel vistas in dicto meiano facere voluerint quod faciant a novem palmis tamen vel amplius de terra vel de solerio in alto ... ." Following Vitry nine palms equals 6.62 feet or 2.02 meters, just about right for privacy. Gilles, *Coutumes de Toulouse*, Articles Nos. 158 and 159, in the version approved in 1286 stated that such walls should be ten palms in height, say about 7.3 feet or 2.24 meters.

and 45 feet.[8] Passable figures are found in the meticulous history of the
Dominican convent of Toulouse written by the noted inquisitor and historian
Bernard Gui. Of the nearly forty houses acquired by the order from 1229
to 1263 in the then socially modest quarter where the magnificent church
of the Jacobins still stands, nine entries dated from 1248 to 1263 record
both the size of the property and the price of the purchase. The area in
which these gifts and purchases occurred was obviously one that had been
surveyed and divided in a somewhat uniform manner: all the lots were
twelve "brachiate" deep, say seventy feet. Of these lots, one was about 35
by 70 feet, four were 23 by 70, one 17 by 70 and three 12 by 70.[9] These
were ordinary or modest houses. One of the 12 by 70 footers, for example,
once housed a cobbler's shop and now had a tailor's.[10]

Shops or "operatoria" marked the urban scene, indeed, the charters
assert that a typical street toward the center of the town was lined by
shops of every description for professionals as well as artisans.[11] Just
before a major riot in February 1268, the citizens, including burghers,
artisans and tradesfolk, were summoned from their shops by the consuls or
their "nuncii" to attend a general assembly.[12] As to the height of these
unpretentious domiciles, the documents occasionally mention cellars and
top story rooms or "solaria."[13] There is, however, no way of knowing
how many houses had two or three levels or stories.[14] Some also had

[8]Grandselve 6 (May 1225). Five "brachiate" less a "palmus" "ad virgam
mercatoris," and seven "brachiate" plus five "palmi." The sellers were Bertrand de
Cossano and "domina" Bernarda, daughter of Stephen Astro, both possessors of patrician
names (for the Cossano history, see my *Repression of Catharism*, pp. 193-196, and for
that of the Astro my *Men and Women*, pp. 173-183). In meters, this is 8.75 x 12.69.

[9]The information is in *Bernardus Guidonis de fundatione et prioribus conventuum
provinciarum Tolosanae et Provinciae ordinis praedicatorum*, ed. Amargier, pp. 32-41,
and is partly summarized in Vicaire, *Dominique et ses prêcheurs*, pp. 338-339. In
meters, the figures are 10.77, 7.18, 5.38 and 3.59 all by 21.55.

[10]*De fundatione*, ed. Amargier, No. 28, p. 36: "In ista est sartoria et fuit sutoria
parvula et ortulus parvulus."

[11]MADTG, G 713 Unnumbered Register, fol. 37v (July 1247) where the notary
public John Gaitapodium stated that "quadam die esset in operatorio suo ... ."

[12]PAN, J 192b 21 contains the record of the trial in the vicar's court about this riot
of February 28, 1268.

[13]See Gilles, *Coutumes de Toulouse*, Article No. 157, where a "solarium" is so defined,
the law providing that it may not overhang the front of the house more than a palm.

[14]E 501 (November 1232) records the sale of a property as being composed of (to use
the accusative of the charter) "totas illas domos et solerium et cellarium cum puteo qui ibi
est, cum loco in quo sunt, cum omnibus hedificiis et bastimentis petrinis et ligneis que ibi
sunt." Daurade 174 (July 1236) mentions an "operatorium et solarium quod est desuper."

small courtyards and many must have had facilities such as latrines, rarely though the latter are mentioned.[15]

Prices permit a comparison between these ordinary houses and the many very small ones. Gui's history of his order's acquisitions has given the prices of the "domus" described immediately above. The one 35 x 70 feet cost 475 shillings of Toulouse, those 23 x 70 averaged 327, one 17 x 70 cost 280, and three 12 x 70 averaged 200. In the same list, there were eleven small houses, lots obviously smaller than 12 x 70. The prices of these "domunculae" or "domus parve" ranged all the way from 200 to 46 shillings, with an average price of 96 shillings sixpence. An additional example shows a person of obviously modest means in 1227 bequeathing 150 shillings or a "domus" to a niece.[16] People of the time and just afterward observed that the town's streets were lined by many little houses. A wealthy testator proposed to found a college for the university in 1243, an institution that was never created. He set aside the emplacements of eighteen houses for this installation. All of them were located on one block in the region of the Bazacle and Saint-Pierre-des-Cuisines, thus showing that some houses were very small indeed.[17]

A late copy of some entries about noteworthy events in Toulouse records a fire in the street of the Borguet-Nau in 1242 and another in 1297 that burned the whole waterfront from the Bazacle to the New Bridge, the mills of the Daurade and the Capella Rotunda. This source asserts that 500 houses were destroyed in the first conflagration and almost 1147 in the second.[18] These exaggerated figures are surely not to be believed, but the testimony indicates that contemporaries knew that there were many houses in relatively small spaces. This evidence prompts one to conclude that, apart from occasional overcrowding such as that seen today in the slums

[15]Daurade 189 ii (March 1236, copied in 1240) mentions a "domus, solarium et curtile." Saint-Sernin Canonesses 45 (August 1295) records that one of the two artisans whose differences were being arbitrated was instructed to promise that, in his half of the courtyard, "mutet et mutare teneatur latrinam que erat circa dictum meianum vel si ibi ultra teneret latrinam quod faciat a duobus palmis extra meianum et quod faciat versus meianum murum de duobus palmis de spisso cum morterii franco scilicet de fundo usque super terram ... ." See a further passage from this charter in note 7 above.

[16]See Appendix 8, No. 48.

[17]Appendix 8, No. 72.

[18]Dominicans 111, a Register with loose notes bound into it. Written in an eighteenth century hand, the notes copied information from other presently undiscovered sources listing floods, plagues, fires, etc. in Toulouse and the region. The houses were called "hospitia," for which term see below.

of Mexico City or New York, the family living together in one domicile
was not large.

This conclusion is reinforced by the fact that people also often lived
in apartments or flats or in houses shared by several families. "Domus"
were divided. In 1237 two brothers who had married related women split
what the charter called the "domus et casales" they held jointly. One pair
received the shop ("operatorium"), a portico (or passageway – "porgeus")
next to it and a great room or hall ("aula"). Their share also contained
half of a room ("camera") with an adjacent "second story [?]" ("escagium
casalis"), both together just under 18 feet in size, along with all of another
"casal" behind the "camera" (about 20 feet in size) with the right to draw
water from the well there. The other pair were given "all the rest" of the
property.[19] Divided houses were common.[20] Such divisions also help
explain the frequency of two or more "houses" owned by a single family,
sometimes a modest one, on the same street.[21]

Flats or apartments of this kind were apparently investments for a
family that took its name from a butcher named Petricola.[22] In 1262 the
butcher's sons sold property presumably in the City. One of the two charters concerning this transaction recorded the alienation of fixed rents
("oblie") on ten "half" houses averaging just under two pennies (1.72)
annually.[23] The second charter sold three "quarter" houses with an annual
rental average of just over three pennies (3.3).[24] These rents were proba-

---

[19]Malta 4 203 iii (June 1237): Bernard and Raymond de Podio and their wives
"venerunt ad divisionem et ad portionem ... de illis domibus et casalibus" they held
jointly. Bernard received "totum operatorium et porgeus qui est iuxta operatorium, et
aula que est iuxta honorem Arnaldi de Bosqueto, et medietas camere cum escagio casalis
qui est iuxta, et totus ille casalis qui est retro cameram sicut est inter aliam partitam et
honorem Vitalis de Serris et Willelmi sui fratris et tenet usque ad casalem Ramundi de
Monte Galharda; et predicta camera cum escagio casalis habet de amplo .iii. brachiatas
ad communem virgam Tolose, et predictus casalis habet de amplo iuxta honorem
Ramundi de Monte Galharda .iii. brachiatas et .iii. palmas, et habent [Bernard and
Bernarda] suum pozaticum in puteo que ibi est, totum hoc ... cum omnibus hedificiis et
bastimentis." The other brother and his wife received "totum superplus de predictis
domibus et de casale." 5.38 meters for the "camera" and "casal" and 6.06 for the
"casal" with the well.

[20]See Appendix 8, Nos. 20, 23, 37, 61, etc.

[21]See Appendix 8, No. 60, for example, and Appendix 9, No. 40. In Grandselve 2
(March 1189) a wife gave her husband a house adjacent to his brother's and his own
house which had been acquired from a third party.

[22]See Appendix 1, No. 11.

[23]E 510 (March 1262): the form reading "pro medietate tocius illius domus et honoris."

[24]E 504 (February 1262): "quarta pars domus et honoris" or "quarta pars feudi."

bly not the real fees, rents or "premia" that those occupying houses or apartments paid. "Premia" were always far higher than fixed rents, but are also only rarely seen in the charters because they had nothing to do with the basic rent of the "feodum" or "honor" that had been fixed long before. The two houses of an individual named Deusaiuda in 1251 and 1253 will illustrate this. One or the other of his houses bore a fixed rent of nine pennies yearly, and the other was leased by him for two years by the contract called a "conductio" for an annual "premium" of twenty shillings![25] Most of these small City houses or apartments may well have been leased to modest persons, but one at least went to a well-to-do professional, the jurist "Magister" Benedict de Insula "legista."[26] Master Benedict either leased his quarter house as a pied-à-terre for himself or in order to sublease it. All these "quarter" houses seem to have been rented to single persons, but the "oblie" of two of the "half" houses were paid by a man and his sister or sisters.

In 1227 the monks of the Daurade compiled a list of the rent charges due on December twenty-first from their town fiefs. A total of 135 quantifiable entries about layfolk were made, and the rents averaged about seven pence, but ranged all the way from a quarter of a penny to two shillings tenpence, which was the largest layman's rent, that of a medical doctor.[27] As expected, also, the rents paid by the thirteen women with sole ownership of a house averaged below that for the men, at just under five pennies. As stated above, this evidence has the weakness of not showing the real or practical day-to-day rent of a house or facility, but what it does tell is the number of tenants and the relative size of the plot on which a house or facility rested. It therefore argues strongly that the housing mentioned in these rent rolls was mainly suitable for small family groups, ideally for a husband, wife and children, although an occasional sibling or two or aging relative could also be housed.

[25]See Appendix 1, No. 1. Another verb for this kind of lease is "collocare" as one sees in Appendix 8, No. 80 (dated 1251).

[26]In E 504 (February 1262) as above.

[27]Daurade 189: "Anno .m°.cc°.xxvij°. ab incarnatione domini fuit facta hec commemoratio obliarum Sancti Thome." There were actually 139 entries but four concerned were for institutions, the Hospital of the Grave (4 s 8 d), the Hospital of Saint-Jacques (2 s 7 d 1 "pogesatz"), the hospital "ad caput pontis [veteris]" (14 d) and the lepers at the Arnaud-Bernard Gate (11 d) whose rents were above average. This is merely a rough count because several of the entries in my photographic copy, one made in 1946 and now deteriorating, are too unclear to read with confidence. The doctor was Raymond "de Moisag medges."

The homes of the rich were different. One mark of their domiciles was that, for a time, the word "domus" seemed too common or undistinguished. For these elegant homes terms like "albergum" and "hospitium" became current in the course of the thirteenth century.[28] As is usually the case, however, the word "hospitium" was soon debased, being applied to all town houses.[29]

A second quality of the houses of the well-to-do was more significant: they were expensive. Located in the town's center near the modern Bourse, a house and tower was bought by a "nobilis vir dominus Bertrandus Mascaronis miles" in 1297 from a notable named William Durandus for 10,000 shillings of Toulouse. This complex "honor" consisted of a hall, tower, mansion and stores contiguous to the tower.[30] Earlier, in 1255, a large house near Saint-Sernin went for 6600 shillings of Toulouse and another paying a fixed rent on the "carraria Gaitapodiorum" in the City sold for 900 shillings.[31]

Illustrating the values characteristic of a rather cohesive minority in the middle range of the patricians of Toulouse is the evidence dealing with the Jews, a generally well-to-do group. A Jewish widow named Aster and her sister Galda bought a house in 1200 for 1200 shillings.[32] Other figures derive from 1277 and afterward when the Jewish situation was difficult, their properties either being confiscated or sold off, and when the values expressed in the charters may not really be comparable with those of a half a century earlier. Two otherwise unknown brothers, Assanellus and Samuel, sold a house with a hall and some stores located right near the Carmelite church in the City (the center of the Jewish community) for 100 pounds of Toulouse (2000 shillings).[33] The final sales by the crown in 1306 and 1307 provide figures for the sales of three onetime Jewish homes that went for 720, 1500 and 3300 shillings respectively.[34]

[28]Pons de Capitedenario's large home was called both "domus et albergum" in 1229 in Appendix 8, No. 51. "Albergum" appears again in Appendix 8, No. 82 (dated 1252) and "hospitium" is seen in No. 101 (dated 1283), MADTG, A 297, fol. 89 (June 1287) and E 502 (September 1296).

[29]Note as typical Saint-Bernard 13 (May 1362) where an "hospitium" on the modern rue Romiguières was located next to other "hospitia," one owned by a tailor.

[30]E 502 (March 1297): "ad capellam Ugoleni," with the property described as "aula et turris et hospitium et operatoria dicto turri contigua."

[31]Saint-Sernin 600 (10 35 12) (January & March 1255) and Malta 15 78 (January 1274).

[32]Appendix 2, No. 4, p. 366.

[33]PAN, J 328 44 (June 1277) published in Dossat, "Quelques documents inédites sur les Juifs," pp. 789-790, Document No. 1.

[34]Appendix 2, No. 2, pp. 364-365: possibly in the hands of the brothers Bonmacip and Solomon.

The residences of the wealthy were also large. Many were made of stone, a fact often signaled in the instruments. The possession of a tower, a "sala petrina" or "aula lapidea" or a "capella" (a chapel or large chamber?), in fact, was a token of an individual's success or high status.[35] The "nouveau riche" Pons de Capitedenario in 1225 completed his social ascension by buying from the abbot of Saint-Sernin a house near that monastery described as a stone hall, tower and chapel, together with attached properties.[36] Capdenier's installation was, one recalls, extensive enough to become the College of Saint-Bernard for Cistercians studying at the university in the late thirteenth century.

As in most medieval towns, Toulouse's richest and most heavily populated quarters ("partite") lay toward the center of town and the town's outskirts or suburbs ("barria") were poorer. This distribution nevertheless meant that relatively large town houses were placed cheek by jowl with the very modest housing of crafts- and tradesfolk in the town center, and that the social classes were not separated as in many modern cities after the introduction of mass transportation. A fine example of this mixture of facilities and classes is seen in 1271 and 1272 when all sorts of persons from almost every walk of life testified about the Falgario town houses and life in the quarters of the Old Bridge and the Daurade, along the riverine center of the City.[37] A certain percentage of the wealthy nevertheless lived in relatively uncluttered parts of the town, although never in the suburbs. Their ample homes were in choice places removed, as it were, from the centers of industry and trade. One of these was in the Bourg, around the basilica and cloister of Saint-Sernin where families such as the Astro, Capitedenario and Maurandi clustered.[38] Two others lay toward the northeast corner of the City, the squares named Montardy ("planum Montarsini," later Pré Montardy) and Montaygon (the modern Place Saint-Georges). Around the former were some of the homes of the Escalquencs, Gamevilla and Turribus clans and around the latter those of the Castronovo de Strictis Fontibus, Montibus and Villanova lines.[39]

[35]See Daurade 166 i (October 1180 copied in 1322) and ibid. 171 (February 1187 copied in 1210, 1235 and 1303) in which the words "sala" and "aula" are employed to describe the same hall. See also Appendix 8, Nos. 62 (dated 1235) and 80 (dated 1251).

[36]Saint-Bernard 138, fol. 91r (October 1225): "tota illa aula lapidea et turris et capella."

[37]See Appendix 1, No. 7.

[38]See the family histories in my *Men and Women*, pp. 173-182, and *Repression of Catharism*, pp. 155-167 and 229-241.

[39]A rich will concerning Montaygon is in Appendix 8, No. 64 (dated 1235). For the Turribus, see Appendix 1, No. 15, and for all the rest, my *Repression of Catharism*, pp. 178-190, 209-216, 221-225, 242-247 and 292-304.

Whatever their location, the large installations of the well-to-do were not only expensive but also profitable. Figures for real rents or "premia" are lacking for this period and what little evidence there is late and partial. In 1278 a noble squire rented from the Hospital a house once owned by Guy de Turribus at the Montardy Square at an annual charge of ten pounds of Tours, that is, 200 shillings of Tours or 100 of Toulouse.[40] Besides, large parts of such substantial housing were not lived in by the occupying family, but instead subleased. The great house sold in 1297 for 10,000 shillings mentioned above not only had an "aula et turris et hospitium" but also ten "operatoria," shops or workshops, all of which were surely usually rented.[41] Pons de Capitedenario's capacious new mansion adjacent to Saint-Sernin also had attached houses and shops, some of wood and others of stucco or stone. In 1240 Pons' heir tore down three of them to oblige the town's magistrates who wanted to widen the "platea maior" of the Bourg to facilitate jousts.[42] In 1287 the lords of Isle-Jourdain acquired a house right near the Portaria (now erased by the Place du Capitole) near the church of Saint-Quentin and not far from the town hall, on the frontier between the City and Bourg. This stone "hospitium" also had attached stores.[43]

Divisions between heirs or other circumstances sometimes broke up the old great houses. The basilica and monastery of Saint-Sernin was initially surrounded by towered stone buildings derived from, or built on, early medieval fortifications. One has the impression that some, probably most, of these structures housed the rich – the Astro, Capitedenario, Claustro, Maurandi - but some were split up and some may have even fallen on hard times. With the consent of two brothers, for example, two other brothers sold their portion of an ample property adjacent to the "planum claustri Sancti Saturnini," fronting on their brothers' home and on those of patrician families named Astro and Claustro. What was sold was a half of a third part of a tower and half of a stone house once owned by a Claustro.[44] Some-

[40]Appendix 1, No. 15.

[41]See above, note 30.

[42]Saint-Bernard 18, fol. 91 (October 1225): "tabule cum locis in quibus sunt et domus et operatoria et casales ... tam de petra quam de terra quam de lignis ... ." For the future of these shops, see TAM, AA 1 100 (August 1240).

[43]MADTG, A 297, fol. 89 (June 1287) records the sale of the fixed rents paid "ratione illius hospitii lapidi et operatoriorum ... ."

[44]Douais, *Cartulaire de Saint-Sernin*, Appendix No. 55 (May 1171). For the sellers of the Castronovo family, see my *Repression of Catharism*, p. 182, for the Claustro my "The Farm of Fontanas at Toulouse: Two Families, a Monastery and a Pope," *BMCL* n.s. 11 (1981) 29-40, and the Astro family history in my *Men and Women*, pp. 173-183.

times, a group of relatives who lived together in large houses determined late in life that they had better divide their homes, presumably in view of their own demise and the needs of their heirs. In 1255, after over thirty years of living together, the three sons of the very rich William de Turribus divided up their large house in town on the Pré Montardy and also their rural "castrum" of Cugnaux.[45] Such decay or subdivision of old great houses sometimes enabled relatively modest individuals to acquire parts of such facilities.[46]

If the modest size of the houses of the middle and humble classes seem to imply that society was divided into small family groups, one can expect that, since the rich enjoyed the possession of larger properties and houses, relatives would tend to cluster there. In the history of the Falgario family, a young wife of a son died in one of her parents-in-law's homes sometime before 1271 or 1272.[47] The three Turribus brothers shared urban and rural houses for thirty or more years. In 1237 the testament of the rich Bernard de Miramonte de Portaria expressly provided for a cousin and a nephew to reside in his great house. These relations were there to look after the estate of his only daughter whose future husband the testator also chose or approved. Over and above this, his house was to accommodate his aged mother, possibly his widow and, of course, his daughter and her husband. Without adding possible spouses and children, this makes a minimum of five or six related persons.[48] This is as close as readers of Toulousan charters get to the entended family.

Bernard's will assuredly reflected current attitudes and, as significantly, the value of centrally located housing. All the same, his disposition was clearly inspired by the fact that a daughter was his only heir and he clearly wanted to make sure that his home would go to a male. Other patricians, perhaps most, favored keeping the large family home in the hands of one male heir. However much they divided the rest of the inheritance among all the male issue, the big town house was left to only one child. In one exaggerated example of 1252, indeed, the testator left the family "albergum" first to his oldest son and then, if he died without male issue, seriatim to one after the other of his other three sons and their male children.[49]

[45]The family history is in Appendix 1, No. 15.

[46]Malta 1 34 i (July 1253) records the "aula lapidea" and "stabulum" of Deusadiuva, for whom see Appendix 1, No, 1, and Appendix 8, Nos. 13 and 80, dated respectively 1194 and 1251.

[47]See Appendix 1, p. 323 below.

[48]See Appendix 8, No. 68.

[49]See Appendix 8, Nos. 62-63 and 82, a sampling of new and old rich: Hugh

On the other hand, when heirs divided their properties, they sometimes partitioned the onetime family house as well.[50] In fine, even the ample homes
of the rich were usually inhabited by a husband and wife and their issue,
together with a few siblings or older relatives.

B. FAMILY DIMENSIONS

The average size of the Toulousan family household, of the group that
shared housing and bore the same name, is difficult to determine. One
observation almost goes without saying: the families of the rich were larger
than those of the poor. Rich or poor, however, the typical Toulousan family
of the early thirteenth century was small, often unicellular. Although biased
in favor of modest social levels, statistics offer additional proof for this
contention, one still occasionally questioned by today's scholarship about
the medieval family. Of the 135 rental properties listed by the Daurade
priory in 1227, the vast majority were held by single individuals, many
perhaps heads of family. Only four were owned by two brothers, two by a
male and his mother, one by a man and wife and a final one was held by
a woman and a man whose relationship is not spelled out.[51] A rent roll
with a relatively large percentage of women (nine cases) acquired by Pons
de Capitedenario in the war year of 1218, when death must have been common, listed sixty-five houses or pieces of real estate owned by individuals
or men and wives. Of these, three were being held for minor infants, four
by groups of brothers and one by an uncle and his nephews.[52] In short,
to repeat what was said above, the typical household consisted of either an
individual or a married pair with children and perhaps one or more older
parents or an occasional collateral relative.

How large, then, was the typical group of heirs, the children or young
adults who were to create the families of the future? Although limited, the
charters give some information. The appendix of estates published in this
book contains fifty-six entries mostly recording divisions of estates by heirs
or their actions. Of these, two cannot be used for quantification because
they lack reasonably full counts of such heirs.[53] The remaining fifty-four

---

Johannes and Vital Rotbertus in 1235 and Bertrand Descalquencs in 1252. This kind of
"préciput," as the French say, was common in the customary law, for which see Ourliac
and Malafosse, *Histoire du droit privé* 3: 402.

[50]Appendix 9, No. 51 (dated 1255) involving the Turribus.

[51]Daurade 189 (dated 1227).

[52]Saint-Bernard 138, fols. 181v-188.

[53]Appendix 9, Nos. 27-28.

give an average family heir group of about 3.25. The charters used are also biased against women because females were usually heirs only when males were lacking.[54] The result is that males constitute a trifle over eighty-two percent of the heirs mentioned.[55] If one corrects for the shortfall of women, the average family of heirs amounts to 5.33 persons.[56] This estimate is high and one suspects that the deformation is probably due to the fact that instruments recording divisions of inheritances largely concerned the upper classes.

The calendar of testaments balances this picture of society.[57] Although the wills of some very wealthy persons are included among the documents and the collection is biased toward the well-to-do, many people of relatively modest means are also seen. Of the 102 testators, thirty-eight (of whom about a half were alone when they rendered their wills) were childless, and two additional ones had only illegitimate issue.[58] The remaining sixty listed about 130 legitimate children, thus giving an average of 2.16 children per testator or, if the numbers are again corrected, so to speak, to repair the loss of female issue in the records, 2.5.[59] In short, the documents testify that the poor had fewer surviving children than the rich. But how many more did the rich have? One cannot say.

Documents permitting an estimation of how many persons bore the same identifiable family name at one time are also very few. In 1243, 1028 Toulousans assembled to take oath to maintain the Peace of Paris. The oath took place in late February, a date when even most merchants and landlords were likely to be in town and not abroad or in the countryside.[60] Although the oathtakers were numerous, the poorer elements of the citizenry were probably very inadequately represented. Insufficiencies aside,

[54]See my *Men and Women*, pp, 32-33 and 111.

[55]144 males and 31 females.

[56]An unsubtle, even perhaps mistaken, equality in the numbers of women and men has been assumed.

[57]Appendix 8 presents 103 documents produced by 112 persons, Nos. 86 and 87 having been created by the same testator.

[58]The childless testaments are Nos. 2, 4-5, 10-12, 14-16, 22, 24-25, 27, 29-30, 33, 34-35, 39, 44, 48, 50, 53, 56-58, 61, 64-65, 69, 73-74, 80-81, 84, 89, 92, 95-97, 100 and 102. The four testators with natural children were Nos. 66, 72, 85 and 101, and the second and the fourth of these testators had no legitimate offspring.

[59]Of the 130 only 55 were female. Useless for these statistics were the legitimate pregnancies and the natural children.

[60]Appendix 3. Note that the 1028 names are there listed according to the lines in the manuscript where they were placed by the recording notary, thus showing those who stood together. See below on p. 368.

the list shows that, the older and wealthier the family, the larger the number of adult males bearing the same surname alive and active at the same
time. The families whose names are seen in consular lists before 1202
average just short of four adult scions; those achieving office after 1202,
something under two. These figures are, however, very crude. Not all the
Barravenses listed there were members of the City family bearing that
name. Twelve persons with this surname took oath, only eight or nine of
whom can be shown to be of the City patrician family.[61] Similar caveats
apply to a number of other Toulousan noble or patrician families, as, for
example, the Villanova.[62] Of the nine listed in 1243, only one cannot be
shown to have been of the true-blue Roays.[63]

One therefore feels entitled to assert that, however rich an occasional
individual of a family of humbler origin (Pons de Capitedenario, for example) may have been, the middle range family was modest in size and
was therefore markedly exposed to life's accidents and to political and economic disturbance. Since they were both more numerous and collectively
wealthier, the greater families were able to exhibit more resilience in the
face of difficult or changing circumstances.[64]

It is also true that, quite apart from their capacity to call on domestics
and members of the "familia," old and wealthy families could mobilize substantial numbers of adult males to act in the family interest. The Barravenses had extensive interests in the New Bridge and generally on the waterfront of the Garonne just north of the Ile-de-Tounis. In 1239 eight males of
the clan and three brothers-in-law appeared to applaud a settlement between
the town and the monastery of the Daurade concerning the bridge.[65] The

[61]This estimate is based on the family history in my *Repression of Catharism*, pp.
136ff. and especially p. 137 note 9. At this oath, Peter, Aimeric, Roger, Bernard,
William, Stephen, Bertrand and Arnold, brother of Peter Arnold, are seen together on
line 19; Durand and William, line 25; Vital line 27; Elias line 31.

[62]See ibid., pp. 292ff. and especially p. 297 note 12. Only a house with as distinctive
a name as Roaxio was unlikely to have had strangers using their surname in the oath.

[63]The contiguous Roaxio on lines 30-31 are Hugh, William, Grivus, Hugh, Roger,
Bertrand, Stephen and Peter. On line 50, there was a Peter de Roais. For the family
history see my *Repression of Catharism*, pp. 251-267.

[64]See the history of the Capitedenario in my *Repression of Catharism*, pp. 155-167,
where the rich Pons whose testament is dated 1229 was only one of several brothers, all
of whom predeceased him. Pons had only one child, a daughter, who survived him, but
who died shortly after his death.

[65]Daurade 117 (May 1239). Peter and his brother Arnold, Arnold, son of Arnold,
Roger, Bernard, Peter, son of the deceased Durand, Raymond de Montetotino, Arnold

family was also much interested in the Daurade monastery and actively intervened to protect one of its scions named Bernard Barravus who won the priory of that religious house for a time, but then lost it to another contestant in June 1248 by a decision of a cardinal judge-delegate appointed by the pope.[66] In testimony about this case rendered in 1246 and 1247, the Baravenses are not only seen swarming about during the crisis wearing swords and accompanied by armed retainers, but also ten of them appeared as witnesses, one being Bernard's brother.[67] Not that all families of this social level were able to gather such large contingents. When, in 1271, arrangements were made to build a new bridge across the Garonne from the Ile-de-Tounis, the interests of the knightly Tolosa family were represented by five male heads of household and the husbands of two female Tolosa.[68]

To conclude, in terms of the group of married couples and parents that visited, acted, or lived together, the families of the different classes followed the rule that, the higher the social scale, the greater the family size. The humbler levels of society doubtless loved their relatives as much as did the rich, but it is obvious that, just as flies cluster around a honey pot and not around the salt, the members of successful and rich clans could view their collaterals with eyes whose benignity was much reinforced by the hope of gain. Size apart, however, the families of middling and lower class townsfolk were institutionally very similar to those of the rich.[69]

Guido, and Bertrand Balsanus. Known to be a relative (see the family history in my *Repression of Catharism*, pp. 135ff.), Vital Barravus attested the settlement.

[66]See my "Village, Town, and City," pp. 152-153, and also *Men and Women*, pp. 199-201 and 202.

[67]MADTG, G 713, a roll of testimony dated 1246 and 1247, and, for the document's context, my *Men and Women*, p. 199. The witnesses were Raymond, brother of the prior Bernard, Bertrand their cousin, Arnold "maior," Dominic, Roger, William, Arnold, brother of Peter, Aimeric, William, son of Raymond, and Bernard.

[68]Malta 7 117 (March 1271). They were Macip senior and his "nepos" Peter, the knight Bernard Raymond, the squire Bertrand, son of the knight Bertrand, Macip junior, Bernard de Turre, husband of a Tolosa, and Stephana, wife of a Maurand. See the Tolosa family history in my *Repression of Catharism*, pp. 268-283.

[69]In Appendix 1, Nos. 1, 2, 3, 4, 8, 9 and 12, families named Arnaldus, Barbaordeus, Cerdanus, Davinus, Marcillus, Najaco and Podiobuscano (the latter above the average level by the late 1200s) could assemble up to six siblings for important occasions, but were mostly smaller than that, and only four of them are represented among the oathtakers of 1243. Similar information is conveyed by the modest Tonenquis family in my *Men and Women*, pp. 190-194, as well as those named or designated Corregerius, Guido and Trageto in my *Repression of Catharism*, pp. 191-192, 226-228 and 265.

9

Names

A. NOMENCLATURE

Everybody, one thinks, has a name and such seems to have been the case in Toulouse at this time. A curious exception is a document of 1217 which refers to a certain "mute man and woman," neither being named, who owed rent to the notable William Pons Astro and his widow for an apartment or house on the street now called Coq-d'Inde in the City.[1] This is clearly Arnold J. Toynbee's celebrated exception, the one that proves the rule: persons are always named.

As was noted in the introduction to my *Men and Women at Toulouse*, the archives tell little about the Toulousan family until the genesis of the public notariate in the early years of the twelfth century.[2] As a result, the original character or structure of the family in this region is veiled in silence. One may guess that a change occurred around 1100 in which a small family, centered about a man and wife, replaced larger or more extensive clans. Maybe so, but the existence of a putative earlier larger family structures cannot be proved from available fragmentary sources.

More to the point than hazardous conjectures about a purported modernization process that created the small or unicellular family around 1100 is an attempt to tie the well-documented relaxation of institutional and external controls over families and their properties during and after the Gregorian age to the character of the family. The triumph or very considerable expansion of hereditary right in the eleventh and early twelfth centuries meant that the regime under which Toulousans lived was increasingly that of private property. This conventional phrase means the family exploitation of land and other sources of income and means of production, including monopolies, tolls, servile labor, and, typically medieval, lordly or governmental

---

[1] Ourliac and Magnou, *Cartulaire de Lézat*, No. 1451 (March 1217): "quidam mutus et muta qui manent in carraria de Sescariis."

[2] On p. 8ff.

rights. It therefore seems probable that the decline of the service owed the prince by the higher social orders and the weakening of past servitudes characteristic of the lower orders combined to individualize social life and exalt the family. This increase in freedom perhaps allowed what may have always been families based on unicellular nuclei to become prominent and identifiable for a time. Coinciding with this was the introduction of new methods of family identification, especially or initially among the leading families of town and countryside. Although it is known that the modes of expression differed in the varied parts of southern France, at Toulouse this identification took two forms, the introduction of the surname or family name and the development of special name patterns for individual families.

In 1900 a study rightly reported that, in documents from the Toulousain, the first surnames made their appearance in the tenth century and that the employment of these as family names waited until the twelfth century.[3] In the archives of Toulouse, the extant cartulary of the monastery of Saint-Sernin contains the first substantial number of surnames that were family names. There, documents dated from the latter decades of the eleventh century contain many of the appellations that became familiar during the next two centuries, Astro, Barravus (Barrau), Caraborda, and, preceded by the particule "de," Claustro, Noerio (Noer), Tolosa, and Turribus (Lastours), to cite some examples.[4]

Historians and philologists have long argued that the early employment of surnames at this time merely reflected a need to have additional identification in a growingly crowded society and asserted that truly hereditary family names awaited the fifteenth century and even later.[5] Their opinion seems partly valid for Toulouse. There, as elsewhere, family identification was not mandatory until the establishment in modern times of the police characteristic of the nation-state and its attendant state church.[6]

[3]Duffaut, "Recherches historiques sur les prénoms en Languedoc," *Annales du Midi* 12 (1900) 182-183.

[4]See Douais, *Cartulaire de Saint-Sernin*, Nos. 270 (dated 1060-1108), 131, 546 (both 1080), 548 (1080-1098), and 290 (July 1083).

[5]Expressed in 1934 by Weber, *Personennamen in Rodez um die Mitte des 14. Jahrhunderts*, p. 26, and derived from a tradition that included the diplomatist Arthur Giry. The old arguments were also resumed in Michaelsson, *Études sur les noms de personne français d'après les rôles de taille parisiens* of 1927, p. 127. The same author also cites Gaudenzi, *Sulla storia del cognome a Bologna nel secolo XIII* in *Bollettino dell'Istituto storico Italiano* 19 (1898) 2, where this distinguished historian advanced the same proposition.

[6]This teaching seems generally accepted. See Reichert, *Die deutschen Familiennamen nach Breslauer Quellen des 13. und 14. Jahrhunderts* (1908) and Ekwall, *Early London Personal Names* (1947). The patterns by or in which I have organized Toulousan names derive from these various sources, especially Ekwall on p. 118.

At Toulouse around 1200, nomenclature was similar to that in other west European communities. Expressing what was in effect a religious caste, the names carried by Jews differed somewhat from those of Christians. Although they first appear in charters from the early twelfth century, Jews were identified by a first name followed by the word "judeus" or "judea" and rarely or never carried surnames and family names. "Alacer judeus" is a typical identification among this group, although there is also, from time to time, mention of the given name of a parent or other relation.[7] Less frequent, a similar simple practice was true among Christians also. Individuals of all social levels appeared in the charters identified only by a single name, sometimes unusual, as Deusaiuda, for example, or Ugolenus, and sometimes common, as Arnaldus and Guido.[8] Still, identification by first name only was or had become rare. Just over two percent of the names of the 1028 citizens of the town taking oath to maintain the Peace of Paris in 1243 bore single names.[9]

These rather simple ways of identifying persons may have continued the earlier custom of the late eleventh and early twelfth centuries, whereby many, if not most, townsmen were identified in extant charters by two given names, the first being that identifying the individual, and the second the name of his father in the genitive case.[10] It may also be noted here that, although the employment of the genitive case clearly weakened for a time, indeed, almost vanished, not a few persons seemed to be sufficiently identified by two or more given or Christian names. About thirteen and a half percent of the oathtakers of 1243 were so named. Some of the second

[7]The first example to my knowledge is Douais, *Cartulaire de Saint-Sernin*, No. 335 (dated early in the twelfth century) where a vineyard near Castelginest just north of Toulouse paid a quarter of the fruits to an Abraham "judeus." In Magnou and Ourliac, *Cartulaire de Lézat*, Nos. 1364 and 1365 (dated respectively December 1160 and February 1172) at Lespinet near Pouvourville a vineyard of Glaniolus (Clarionus?). Thereafter references become common.

[8]For Arnaldus, see Appendix 1, No. 1. For Guido, see the family history in my *Repression of Catharism*, pp. 226-228.

[9]See the list in Appendix 3 and the names in the general index marked with a *: twenty-two persons.

[10]Douais, *Cartulaire de Saint-Sernin*, Nos. 550 and 551 (June 1122) where Arnold Bernardi "elemosinarius" of Saint-Sernin is seen. Ibid., Nos. 161 and 155 (respectively dated 1126 and March 1128/9), the first referring to Bernard Arnaldus de Capite Pontis, and the second to Bernard Arnaldi. Here and in subsequent notes, note the case endings of the second names. Given here in English, the Latin cases of the first names are all nominative.

names used in this way were common first names, like Arnold or Raymond, but among the most popular was Vasco, a name derived from place or group of origin and also used as a forename.[11] In fact, some families defined both their families and their members merely by reversing two given names generation after generation, an Arnaldus Bernardus, for example, being the son of a Bernardus Arnaldus.[12] Seen frequently early in the twelfth century, this practice persisted throughout the period treated in this essay.[13] One suspects that, although such families are difficult to trace in the documents, they were of some pre-eminence.

Similar to this was yet another method whereby a person was named after his father, a system also persisting throughout the period with which this history deals. Although infrequent, this method of identification sometimes created new surnames or family names. The Christian name of a person could be joined to that of his father recorded in the genitive case (as described above) or by the use of the possessive particule "de." Until the revival of the genitive for the father's name in the second half of the thirteenth century, the particule was more common. Typical is the family name Marcillo employed with the particule, the origin of which was an individual named Marcillus, and the identifying name of an individual alternately called Bernard Garcionus and Bernard den Garsio (d'enGarsio).[14] Although such persons are hard to spot, slightly more than one percent of the persons in the list of 1243 were so identified.[15] These methods of identification persisted and were naturally interchangeable with other ways of effecting the same end.[16]

[11]By a rough count, 140 persons, including six Arnaldi, five Raimundi, twelve Vascones, etc.

[12]Douais, *Cartulaire de Saint-Sernin*, No. 548 (dated between 1098/1100) mentions Arnold Bernardus, Gerald and Arnold Bernardus de Capite Burgi, sons of Bernard Arnaldus.

[13]See Benedict Arnaldus, son of Arnold Benedictus, in 1269 in Molinier, *Correspondance administrative d'Alphonse de Poitiers*, No. 19, and, as deceased, in August 1279 in my *Repression of Catharism*, p. 114.

[14]See Appendix 1, No. 8 and for Garsionus TAM, II 9 (November 1270 and January 1271).

[15]Fifteen with "de," "den" and the genitive. See also Malta 133 42 (September 1230) where Bertrand de Eleazaro and his brother Peter Durandus, sons of the deceased Heleazarius acted together. A final example is seen in the will of a butcher in Appendix 8, No. 85 (February 1256) where the butcher's brother was named Peter Johannes, and his nephew Arnold de Petro Johanne.

[16]See also the Najaco and Petricola family histories in Appendix 1, Nos. 9 and 11.

A variant of this somewhat rare method was the identification of a person by the name of a woman, usually (invariably?) a mother. In 1234 and 1237 the two brothers Bernard and Raymond de Podio appear. They were both once called "de Podio de Boysazo" and one of the brothers was also named Raymond de Boissazone.[17] As in the case of a male parent's name, a female's name could evolve into a family name. Thus in 1196 a "Ramundus Willelmus de Laura" who was earlier described in 1178 as a son of Laura appears, and there is one modestly prominent family graced by a jurist and several public notaries named "de Rayna," "Raina" or "naRayna."[18]

Two cases derived from the countryside south of Toulouse illustrate other dimensions. Mas-Saintes-Puelles (near Castelnaudary) boasted the house of Willelma "filia quondam d'en Companh," concubine of Arnold Maiestre. Another reference calls this woman Willelma Companha and her mother Aymengarda Companha.[19] An unmarried or husbandless woman, in short, could carry her mother's married name, the name, that is, of her father. Again, although none of the individuals mentioned above was of that humble grade, it seems probable that not a few servile persons were designated by their mothers' names, an echo perhaps of onetime uterine succession or origin. In 1230 a group at Colomiers just west of town has no less than three of seven serfs so identified.[20] A parent's nickname could also be utilized for identification. A family bearing the name of Amigo produced a member and perhaps a branch preferring to be called "de Abbate." This name derived from a "Bernardus Amigo de Rivis qui vocabatur Abbas," whose son styled himself "Poncius de Abbate de Rivis."[21]

Exceptions apart, surnames were often family names and, by 1200, family names had become the ordinary and most frequent method of identification at Toulouse. This is shown not only by the statistics rehearsed

[17]See Marriage No. 119 in my *Men and Women*, p. 151.

[18]Grandselve 3 i (August 1196) Raymond William de Laura as a witness, also in ibid. ii (February 1178) as the son of Laura. See also Grandselve 9 (September 1255) for Sanche de naProvincia. For the Rayna or Raina, see TAM, II 9 (November 1270 and January 1271) where the syndic of the consuls is William de Naraina who is also described as William de Raina. For the history of this clan of notaries and jurists, see my *Men and Women*, pp. 183-185. Another possible instance is the Arnold de naRica seen in the Guido family history published in my *Repression of Catharism*, p. 226, whose other name may have been Arnold Guido.

[19]TBM, MS 609, fols. 2v and 5 (May and June 1245).

[20]TAM, II 97 (January 1230), all using the apheresis "na" for "domina," as in Vital de naDepertz.

[21]Daurade 189 ii, iii and iv (dated respectively March 1236 and 1237, copied in 1240).

above, but also by individual cases giving evidence of conscious choice by
quite ordinary citizens. In 1216 an individual normally called Bernard
Stephanus was once referred to as Bernard Balderia. In 1225 his sons
were respectively named Peter Bernard Balderia and William Balderia.[22]
Another example, one that also illustrates the ways of identification available, is the "Adam de Petro Boneto filius Petri Boneti" (or, in the vernacular, "Azam den Peire Bonet") seen in 1227 and 1240.[23] At that latter
date, moreover, Adam's son was named Peter Bonetus, showing that the
family was reverting to the more normal method. It is not improbable that
the peculiar usage adopted by Adam was inspired by the fact that there had
once been two Peter Boneti, one an "olierius" and the other the "mercator"
from whom Adam sprang.[24] One of these earlier Peters was called Peter
son of Bernard Bonetus in 1225.[25]

B. SURNAMES

Very common Christian names, such as "Arnaldus" and "Gasco," could
and did became family surnames.[26] And even some patrician families
carried quite ordinary names, the Rogerii, for example, and Rotberti.[27]
As has been seen above, the system of naming a person after a parent
could likewise be employed to generate a family name.

The most frequent family names were probably those derived from localities. These were sometimes places in town. Examples are the family
called Claustro, after the Close of Saint-Sernin, for example, or Ponte,
Porta, or Sancto Romano, all either preceded by the particule or written
in the genitive.[28] Other placenames, the vast majority, in fact, simply re-

---

[22]See Appendix 8, No. 37 and Appendix 9, No. 36.

[23]Daurade 189 (1227 dated without month) for the vernacular reference, and ibid.
91 (March 1240) for the Latin.

[24]Ibid. 191 ii (dated 1191 without month, copied in 1242, 1260 and 1322).

[25]PAN, J 329 39 (December 1225).

[26]Grandselve 5 (January 1219) lists Bermunda, daughter of William Gasco, whose
uncle is Bernard Gasco. See the case of the Bonetus family in the paragraph above and,
for the Arnaldi, see Appendix 1, No. 1.

[27]For the Rogerii, see what little information exists in my *Repression of Catharism*,
pp. 83 and 91-92, and also p. 172 below. For the Roberti, see the consular lists in
Appendix 5.

[28]For the Claustro, see my "Farm of Fontanas at Toulouse," pp. 29-40. The normal
presentation was "de Sancto Romano," for example, but see Malta 58 1 (March 1179)
for the "Sancti Romani" variant. This name referred to the church of Saint-Rome; the
church of Saint-Martin similarly named a family, etc.

ferred to places whence immigrants had come to town and hence names with the particule were not necessarily gentlemanly in this period. The higher the social level, however, the more the localities were those where families possessed substantial properties or lordships. The result was that several of the greatest families carried the particule, the Castronovo de Strictis Fontibus (Castelnau-d'Estretefons), for example, and the Noerio (Noé).[29] Perhaps the most curious example of a family name derived from a locality is that of the patrician clan called Tolosa. The name was presumably adopted because the family was the urban branch of a notable rural family from which it initially wished to be distinguished.[30] Whatever the origin, family names derived from placenames were probably the most frequent single group seen in documents from Toulouse. They constitute over thirty-six percent of the names listed in the role of 1243 cited above.[31]

Next in frequency was what may be described as second or third names serving as surnames, about twenty-eight percent of the list of 1243.[32] Because names were of all sorts, problems abound. Geographical names, for example, were also used as first names: Catalanus, Tolosanus, etc. Placenames often marked rural nobles, but such was the power attached to a family name in this period that some clans of this class favored them and were not named after their rural lordships or castles. The lords of Isle-Jourdain to the west of Toulouse invariably followed their Christian names, usually Jordan, with "de Insula" or the phrase "dominus de Insula," but the equally baronial line of the Unaud of Lanta always used their family name and not that of their village and castle. To return to town, many second names or surnames derived from a placename. An example is that of the substantial burgher, and eventually knightly, family called Maurandus, a name derived from a village to the south of Toulouse. The same was probably the case of the equally distinguished family initially called Roais (Roays, Roaxio or Rouaix), to which name, however, the particule was soon prefixed.[33]

Persons bearing surnames as family names were of every class from the lowest to the highest. Note, for example, the patrician lines of the Astro

[29]See the family history of the Castronovo in my *Repression of Catharism*, pp. 178-190, and that of the Noerio in Appendix 1, No. 10.

[30]See the family history in my *Repression of Catharism*, pp. 268-283.

[31]378 persons, but there are problems distinguishing place from personal names.

[32]Some 288 names.

[33]For these clans, see the family histories in my *Repression of Catharism*, pp. 229-241 and 251-267.

and Caraborda.[34] It has been seen above that very common given names sometimes served as family names. At other times, the names chosen were altogether special. Note, for example, in 1244, a person named Arnold Deus Nos Signet who acted with the consent of his nephew, another Arnold Deus Nos Signet.[35] Other and somewhat comic examples are a Peter Centumoves, Terrenus Pulcher Cifus also called Belenap, and an Arnold Lavavaisel.[36] But things considered odd today were not so considered then. As can be seen in the history of the patrician Descalquencs family, the name Bastard was rather chic, but it was also used by quite ordinary people.[37]

Craft, trade and professional designations were also commonly used for purposes of identification. Just over sixteen percent of the persons on the list of 1243 were so identified, bearing, that is, a Christian name and a craft or trade designation.[38] Naturally enough, such titles could also be appended to two Christian names or to first names used as surnames.[39] Not a few persons bearing craft or trade titles also carried other surnames they used when convenient. To judge from the list of 1243, however, the employment of vocational titles often impeded or replaced the employment of other surnames.[40] This does not imply, however, that individual crafts- or tradesmen did not have them; there is, indeed, ample proof they did.[41]

---

[34]The Astro family history is published in my *Men and Women*, pp. 173-183, and the Caraborda in my *Repression of Catharism*, pp. 167-177.

[35]Malta 278 (February 1244) at Grisolles. The name sounds oddly Latin African.

[36]Ourliac and Magnou, *Cartulaire de Lézat*, No. 1457 (May 1176) at Lespinet (l'Espinet). Grandselve 7 vi (August 1198 copied in 1198 and 1236, as above) and vii (January 1192 or 1193): Terrenus Belenap (Hanap). Malta 9 81 i (January 1204 copied in 1224) as Arnold Lavavaxellos; ii (September 1218). Note also Peter Fugiens, son of Bertrand Fugiens, in E 538 (May 1230).

[37]See my *Repression of Catharism*, pp. 209ff. For the non-patrician use, see Peter Bastardus, son of Raymond Bastardus, whose uncle was Peter Bastardus de Portaria in Grandselve 9 (March 1254).

[38]167 persons.

[39]As examples, see MADTG, G 717 ii and iii (respectively dated December 1226 and February 1256, copied in 1269). The first has Peter Johannes "macellarius" (butcher) and his brother Arnold William buying property once owned by William Johannes "affachator" (tanner) and the second records the testament of Arnold Willelmus "macellarius." Note also Malta 3 176 (June 1238) containing a sale by Raymond Rainaldus "sartor" witnessed by Bernard Rainaldus "mercator," and the William de Claromonte "corderius" in the oath of February 1243.

[40]Only four persons there had both placename-surnames and craft or professional titles.

[41]An example is E 461 vi and viii (respectively dated September 1208 and February 1222) where Bernard de Luganno "textor" is once simply called Bernard Textor and his son-in-law is named both William Martinus and William Raditor. Note also in Malta 4

Occasional documents show that, if a person had a surname, craft or professional titles were often used simply to distinguish between two persons bearing the same first name and surname. One hears in 1254, for example, of a William de Castello who was once called William de Castello "mercerius" to distinguish him from his son Peter de Castello "campsor."[42] Because bakeries were fixed local establishments, bakers' craft titles were almost always mentioned in the parchments.[43] Exceptions are to be found even there, however. An example is the Raymond Bascol "furnerius" who bought a bakery in 1202 from the heir of another baker.[44] Craft, trade and professional names also functioned as family names, thus hiding the true profession of the bearer. A Pons Molinerius (miller) "pelliparius" (pelterer), Pons Furnarius (baker) "sutor (tailor) de Cruce Baranone," Vital Pelliparius "mercator," Arnold Mercerius "argentarius" (silversmith), Raymond Ganterius (glover) "tegularius" (tile maker) and others are seen, all of whom presumably appeared in quite a number of charters sufficiently identified without the use of their professional title.[45] It goes without saying that the Peter Ovelherius who lived on the Main Street of the Bourg in 1245 was not a shepherd.[46]

The most frequent craft name employed in this way is clearly that of Faber or Smith. The names of Fabri who are in other lines of metal work, cutlers, armorers, etc. give evidence of the growth of related crafts. Such persons are seen in both town and countryside. A Toulousan act of 1188

---

205 i, ii and iii (March 1237 to September 1240) also in Saige, *Juifs du Languedoc*, Nos. 22-24, where a Bernard de Roquis first appears as that and then later as a "textor." See also the Peter de Iustarete "sartor" in Malta 3 176 (June 1238).

[42]Ibid. 4 220 iii, iv, v and vi (respectively dated April 1239, July 1239, March 1245 and April 1254). No. iv has the mercer together with his son.

[43]See the note below and also E 501 i (1224 dated without month) and ii (August 1239 copied in 1239 and 1255), respectively recording a William Furnarius "de furno Roaxensium" and a witness named Peter Arnold "qui manet ad furnum Bastardi."

[44]Malta 14 104 i, ii, and iii (respectively dated January 1200, March 1201, and May 1202). The earliest transaction records the sale of the bakery by Peter Furnarius to Raymond Furnarius. In March 1201 Raymond wrote his testament and, in 1202, his brother Peter sold the bakery to Raymond Bascol with the consent of a Bernard Furnarius and another Bernard "Furnarius de furno Sancti Petri Sancti Geraldi."

[45]Daurade 189 ii (March 1236, copied in 1240), E 65 (May 1239), PAN, JJ 21 No. 25 (November 1246), Grandselve 11 (July 1263), TAM, AA 6 94 (March 1247), and for a few additional references not mentioned above, see E 509 (July 1264) Vital Furnerius "mercator," Malta 9 137 1st of a group of membranes tied together (February 1255) William Ortolanus (gardener) "sabaterius" (shoemaker), and Grandselve 14 (January 1289) William John Fusterius (carpenter) "notarius."

[46]Appendix 8, No. 75.

was attested by a Raymond Faber "crosolerius" (refiner?) dealing with a purchase by a Raymond Faber "coltellarius" (cutler), an individual who subsequently drew a testament in which he was simply called Raymond Coltellarius.[47] Deep in the country at Laurac, far south of Toulouse, a Peter Faber "coteler vel garrus" is heard of, a cutler and "faber ... qui aliter nominatus [est] Petrus Gairus."[48] Others bearing this common name had nothing to do with the metal industries, but were instead gardeners, weavers and notaries.[49]

To ordinary craft and professional titles one may add that of "magister." A vexation here is the difficulty of distinguishing between the "magistri" trained in letters or the liberal arts and those deriving their appellation from their mastership in a craft, art or trade. Generally speaking, the title "magister" carried by someone trained in the liberal arts preceded the name, and followed it in the case of crafts and tradesmen.[50] Only one person titled "magister" appears in the list of 1243, "Magister" Raymond Capellerius. This person was not a hatter or a helmet maker as one might judge from his last name, but instead a jurist. Master Raymond Capellerius served as the judge of the seneschal of Toulouse in 1264 and a sentence of his was cited three years later.[51] In addition, "magister" was easily converted into a second or even a family name. Nine of the craft and professional persons in the list of 1243 carried it as a second name.[52]

---

[47]Malta 3 147 i, ii and iii (respectively dated February 1188 and May 1188 copied in 1224), and see Appendix 8, No. 10. Other examples are Malta 9 137 1st act of several membranes tied together (February 1255) with Arnold Faber "capellerius" (hatter or helmet maker) and ibid. 1 335 (February 1258) where a Peter Faber de Carcassona "cultellarius" appears.

[48]TBM, MS 609, fols. 76v-77v (November 1245).

[49]Malta 1 17 (March 1208) and ibid. 9 150 i (January 1230, copied in 1250 and 1257) William Faber "notarius," E 501 (November 1232) Peter Faber "textor qui manet ad portam canonicorum" and Malta 9 137 1st of group of membranes tied together (February 1245) Pons Faber "ortolanus."

[50]Note Grandselve 9 (September 1255) where a Raymond de Balsca "magister texenderie" is contrasted with the renter of one of his houses, a "Magister" Durand Ispanus, clearly a jurist. Note also Grandselve 15 (June 1297) Raymond Adalbertus "magister fuste," a carpenter or builder.

[51]TAM, II 79 (April 1264) and the sentence in Molinier, *Correspondance administrative* 1: 178, No. 286 (July 1267).

[52]For another example, see AADML, Lespinasse No. 10 (February 1236) and Grandselve 9 (October 1253) where is seen a William Magister, son of Pons Magister, the latter sometimes being also described as a "pelherius" (old clothes merchant). See also E 509 i (July 1263) with William Magister, now called the son of the deceased Pons Magister.

In spite of this effort to identify persons, so repetitive were the names applied to Toulousans of this period that even the members of the greatest houses had need of additional identification to mark them off from their siblings or older relatives who carried the same first names and surnames.[53] Persons were therefore often identified in terms of their relationship to others of the same family, as nephew, etc. to effect the necessary distinctions. Note as an example the Bernard Sancti Romani called "nepos Palatini" to distinguish him from his cousin german, another Bernard Sancti Romani.[54] And, as the family histories amply demonstrate, words like "maior," "probushomo," "senior" as against "junior" and "juvenis" were beaten to death in attempts to distinguish between relatives bearing the same names. This need was naturally felt by all social orders and the family histories published in my volumes show that both humble and distinguished persons were so identified. Hence, to take an instance from a famous knightly clan, Aimeric de Castronovo, the nephew of Aimeric de Castronovo, was called "junior" or "juvenis" in the documents to distinguish him from his uncle, the latter being termed the "probushomo."[55] Other families bore distinctive Christian names perhaps derived from origins outside of Languedoc. Scions of the Turribus carried the strange name of Curvus (Couve ?) and the Tolosas often named a child Toset.[56]

The nickname was another way of distinguishing between persons. An example is the nickname "Copha" (meaning, a knight's cap) given to the Aimeric de Castronovo "junior" described above by the historian Puy-laurens in his chronicle. This name never appears in legal documents and it may therefore be that a nickname was considered too familiar for formal use, at least among persons on Aimeric's level. Elsewhere nicknames found a regular place in the documents. In 1221 a William Gitbertus "qui vocatur Piper" is seen who is surely the William Gitbertus "macellarius" mentioned in 1226.[57] Sometimes, indeed, persons had such hopelessly

[53]See the discussion of male and female first names in my *Men and Women*, pp. 39-40, wherein the numbers of male first names are shown to be very limited in comparison with female ones. A peculiar example I did not explore at the time was the fact that the name William appears in two forms in the documents, as Guillelmus and as Willelmus. In the often-cited list of 1243, the latter spelling occurs 171 times, and the former only fifteen.

[54]Malta 58 1 (March 1179).

[55]See the family history in my *Repression of Catharism*, pp. 178-190.

[56]For the Lastours, see Appendix 1, No. 15, and the Tolosa history is in my *Repression of Catharism*, pp. 268-283.

[57]MADTG, G 712 iii (February 1256) and ii (December 1266). See also the Raymond de Insula "qui vocatur Migos" in Daurade 145 (January 1221).

common names that nicknames were almost mandatory. Note the Stephen Bernardus "qui vocatur Stephanus Rubeus" of 1209.[58]

C. FAMILY PRIDE

It was remarked above that public authority did not insist on surnames and family names at this time. The sources available, moreover, privilege the family names of the upper classes. There are obvious reasons for this. Possessing relatively little real property, individual members of modest or poor families were conveniently identified by their occupations, their crafts and trades. Poor families were also normally smaller and less durable than rich ones, and hence did not leave such clear traces in the archives. Where there is wealth there are documents. All that being said, however, it is obvious that one of the marks of Toulousan society around 1200 was the desire to use such family demarcations and they were therefore both common and prized.

The veracity of this assertion may be illustrated on the popular level. It has been remarked that crafts- and tradesmen often had surnames other than those of their professions. This practice seems to have increased. A list of the earliest mentions of persons carrying vocational designations in the late twelfth and early thirteenth centuries shows that only about a quarter of such persons carried additional surnames.[59] Later, in 1239, two-thirds of the forty-six leaders of the leather industries bore family names.[60] Approximately thirty years after that, in 1271, the charitable confraternity of Saint-Sernin lists 117 officers and members. To add to the very occasional patrician in this popular organization, all the notaries, merchants, silversmiths, mercers and five out of the six smiths carried surnames. Of the humbler crafts- and tradesmen, over half boasted the same.[61] The histories of the Arnaldi, Cerdani, Marcillo, Najaco and Petricola families published in this volume also attest to the penetration of the employment of a surname into the lower social orders.[62]

---

[58]Malta 1 123 vi (June 1209, copied in 1232).

[59]See my *Liberty and Political Power*, pp. 273-275, note 22. Although obviously incomplete, this catalogue has the advantage of having been collected simply to list by date the first mention of each craft title appended to an individual's name and sometimes surname in the documents I had read up to that time.

[60]TAM, II 44 (February 1239).

[61]See the two documents Saint-Sernin 625 (14 43 14 and 15) (respectively dated March 1270 and May 1271).

[62]The respective family histories are published in Appendix 1, the oath of 1243 to uphold the Peace of Paris in Appendix 3 and the general index of this book.

Craft and trade designations pose obvious problems for social historians. They soon became family names and were therefore carried by wealthy persons who had little or nothing to do with the original vocation. One among many examples is the Peter Feltrerius who lived on the street called Peyras in the City. When he sold his share of the town's tolls to the crown in 1271, one learns that he was not a felter but instead a public notary (analogous to a solicitor) and a rich one at that.[63] The instrument containing a sale by William Vital Parator "burgensis" and his wife Condors gives an even better example. Daughter of Bertrand de Arzinhano knight and "domina" Gauda, she acted with the consent of her brothers, one a knight and the other a squire. It may be imagined that, in William's eyes, to be named "Finisher" was not shameful, but instead testified to his respect for ancestral manual or mercantile labor.[64] And the same is to be seen in the well-to-do gens of the Prinhaco (Preignac) and related lines who did not despise the name Carbonellus, a progenitor's name that smacked of the smithy.[65] On the other hand, such names were sometimes replaced or disguised. Seen before in these pages, a family of modest millers was named Balderia. It is likely that the original name was "bladerius," meaning a grain dealer or miller, but "balderia" may have reminded those who heard it of the baldric or soldier's sword belt.[66]

Family piety or pride played a role here. An example was the adoption by the Descalquencs family of the name Sancto Barcio on the extinction of the male line of that clan, presumably from a mother of the Sancto Barcio line.[67] As is the case today, such piety was surely largely upper class.[68] The well-to-do also changed their names to fit both an improvement of social status and the places where they acquired or held property or lordship. Examples abound. Note the transformation of the Carbonelli into the "de Prignaco" or the Curtasolea into "de Castronovo."[69] As noted above also, the males of the greater rural clans were customarily named after their larger properties or lordships. This is exemplified by an action taken

[63]PAN, J 324 6 (November 1271).

[64]PAN, J 324 6 xii (April 1274).

[65]Appendix 1, No. 3.

[66]PAN, J 330 12 i-iii (respectively dated October 1216, April 1225 and July 1228, copied in 1250 and 1277).

[67]See the history of the Descalquencs in my *Repression of Catharism*, pp. 211, 213 and 215.

[68]One thinks of the recent German fieldmarshal "von Lewinski genannt von Manstein," born Lewinski but given by his parents to their friends the Mansteins because the latter clan lacked a male heir.

[69]Carbonellus in Appendix 1, No. 3 and the Curtasolea in my *Repression of Catharism*, pp. 197-202.

in 1257 by the baron Sicard de Montealto for himself and his knightly
cousin Raymond Aton de Altarippa, the son of the knight Gilbert de Montealto. Auterive was Raymond Aton's principal seat whereas Montaut was
Sicard's.[70] It is reasonable to assume that the change of names by the
Curtasolea, being based on wealth, was primarily social, whereas that of
the Montaut may have been initially or primarily functional because it
designated the fiefs for which the lords were responsible. Since fief service
of a feudal kind is rarely seen in the documents before the latter thirteenth
century, there is little chance of proving this proposition.

Indeed, persons could use different names at different times and
changed them for reasons that often elude the observer. Above, for example, a man variously called Bernard Textor or Bernard de Luganno
"textor" was seen. In 1213, also, a "Poncius Seger de Caniaco" drew his
testament, the same person being referred to in his daughter's will of 1215
as "Poncius de Venerca qui vocabatur Poncius Seguer de Caniaco."[71]
Another example is that of Petrona de Tonenquis, the daughter of William
de Tonenquis and sister of Raymond de Tonenquis. The widow of a baker,
this woman obviously wished to retain her parental name and not that of her
short-lived husband. Petrona also had several other brothers who, although
seen in other charters, are not known to have been called Tonenquis.[72]

Family histories also make it clear that family names early developed
a substantial measure of stability. Because Toulouse was a small world
where well-to-do families were more or less able to protect their chosen
names, there was more than a hint of monopoly here. Even a name as common as Barravus (Barrau) seems largely to have been restricted to one or
two clans. With rather late exceptions, all those who bore the name Maurandus in extant charters can be shown to fit into the direct line of the true-
blue Maurandi. It is certain, however, that even great families such as the
Castronovo and Villanova were unable to prevent others from bearing their
names simply because there were so many places called Castelnau and
Villanova in the countryside around Toulouse.[73] Lastly, since the town

---

[70]Saint-Etienne 242 (32 B 2) (February 1257). See also PAN, J 324 6 xii (April
1274) where are seen the two sons of the knight Bertrand de Arzinhano, one being
Sycred de Lerano and the other Arnold William de Arzinhano.

[71]Appendix 8, No. 35 (February 1215). See also Ourliac and Magnou, *Cartulaire
de Lézat*, No. 1417 (May 1232) where Saptalina, daughter of the dead Raymond de Ven-
tenaco "qui vocabatur Ramundus de Murello," appeared.

[72]The family history is in my *Men and Women*, pp. 190-194.

[73]See the histories of these families published in my *Repression of Catharism*,
pp. 136-154, 178-190, 229-241 and 292-303.

was divided into the City and the Bourg, it seems to have been customary to allow two branches of one family or two independent families to carry the same surname, one being domiciled in the City and the other in the Bourg. This was exemplified in the patrician names and clans of the Caraborda, Barravus and Turre (Latour).[74]

So common had family names become that it was customary to describe families by a version or adaptation of their surnames. Called the "Roaxenses," the Roaxio family had a square named after them called the "planum" or "platea Roaicencium" as early as 1181, on or near which was a bakery called the "furnum Roaxensium."[75] Testifying to the violent events around the Daurade monastery in May 1247, three witnesses in a judicial investigation described the Barravi who swarmed about to protect the interest of a relative as the "Barravenses" or "multi Baravenses consanguinei."[76] Other well-known clans of the town were similarly treated. Among these was the family whose scions were all called Rogerius (preceded by a first name) the "Rogerii," and there are not a few others.[77] The possessions of Arnold Signarius, son of the deceased John Signarius, another patrician, were described as properties "den Sigarania" and "den Segarania."[78] On occasion, a family's property was identified by the particule together with the family name as, for example, an "ortus de Turribus," a small fragment of the holdings of the knightly Lastours.[79]

---

[74]These family histories are in my *Repression of Catharism*, pp. 136-154 and 285-289.

[75]See Chalande and Cau, *Rues de Toulouse*, pp. 268-271, citing TAM, AA 1 19 (November 1180) and note a house "prope Roycium" owned by a Roaxio in TAM, II (November 1273). The bakery is mentioned in E 501 i (1224 dated without month) and other property of the "Roaxensium" in E 538 (July 1192).

[76]MADTG, G 713, fols. 10v, 15, and 16v.

[77]See Douais, *Trauvaux pratique d'une conférence de paléographie*, No. 7 (July 1181) where Peter Rogerius, son of Bernard Rogerius, has possessions at Montaudron called "de Rogeriis," Malta 116 11 and 16 (respectively dated December 1187 and August 1192) where an "honor Capiscolorum" is also called "honor de Capiscolis" (for this family see my history of the Villanova family in my *Repression of Catharism*, pp. 290, 299-300). See also Malta 3 167 i (April 1190 copied in 1218 and 1233) referring to the "pratum Albertensium," Saint-Etienne 227 (26 DA 1 10) (December 1198) the "condamina Rateriorum" in Braqueville (see Appendix 8, No. 1), and Saint-Sernin 600 (10 36 5) iii and vii (respectively dated February and July 1200) mentioning tithings at Castillon owed by the "Rocenses."

[78]Puybusque, *Contribution à l'histoire du vieux Toulouse. Généalogie de la famille de Puybusque*, pp. 10, 15-16, and 19-20 (respectively dated December 1196, February 1205, and August 1206).

[79]Malta 1 92 (June 1195), and see below Appendix 1, No. 15.

Rural families were also normally so identified. Charters of 1205 record the sale of a third of the ninth part of the fief of Cépet by Bernard de Mallaco. This property had been held by the "Mallaguensi" (variant: "Malhaguenses") for thirty or more years.[80] During the late twenties in the Albigensian war, the house (or houses) at Toulouse near the Croix Baragnon and the Gate of Saint-Etienne rented by the knightly brothers of the Rocovilla family, lords of Cassers and Montgiscard in the Lauragais south of town, was (or were) several times called "dels Rocovillas (Rochovillas)," and a housemaid of the lords was identified as an "ancilla dels Roqovillas." What is more, the rented house (or one of them) was named after its owners, the Boneti, being called the "domus dels Bonets."[81] As modest were the Bertrand Guilabertus, his brothers and "alii Guilabertenqui," who had property at Cornebarrieu just northwest of Toulouse.[82]

Given today's' exaggeration about the medieval sense of privilege, it is pleasant to record that this method was also employed to describe persons of modest social class. Of such were the Boneti mentioned in the previous paragraph. In fact, the practice reached well into the lower ranks of the population, including ordinary farming and even servile families. In 1239, the "probihomines de Cairadz qui vocantur Fabri" were not the smiths of Cayras just south of town, but instead a family named Smith.[83] In 1196 William de Turribus bought from a relative "all the men and women he had at Pouvourville ... , namely all Barradas [to use the case in the document] and their tenement and all Molnarios ... and Tabastam ... ." In 1227 Peter Barrada, Arnold and Raymond Molnarius, their sister Sibilia and William Tabasta testified that the above sale had transferred them thirty or so years earlier.[84] These surnames had persisted at least two generations in these dependent families.

So significant was the family name that it was customary to call individual children by it. Examples of this practice abound, especially in the

[80]PAN, J 328 23 ii and iii (respectively dated April and June 1205).

[81]TBM, MS 609, fols. 66, 201v, 216, 201v and 223v.

[82]MADTG, A 297, fol. 620 (July 1231), a witness added that the land had been rented "de ipsis Guilabertenquis" for upwards of thirty years.

[83]E 65 (May 1239).

[84]Malta 12 23 (December 1196): "omnes homines et feminas ... et totum ius et dominium et rationem quam super illos habebat, videlicet omnes Barradas et eorum tenenciam et omnes Molnarios et eorum tenenciam et Tabastam et eius tenenciam et ipsos et eorum infantes et omnia eorum bona mobilia et immobilia que habebant vel habituri erat." Ibid. (May 1227) where, individually named as above, the dependents recorded that "semper extiterant homines Bestiacii et sui generis et de dominio eius fuerant semper ipsi et eorum antecessores ... ."

patrician families of the town. They employed it not only to designate male scions, but female ones as well, such as the "Caraborda mater Grivi," the mother of a Peter Grivus de Roaxio, a Caraborda woman who was listed among those whose inheritances had been confiscated for heresy.[85] The complications invited by utilizing a family name as the sole identification led to the introduction of additional appellations referring to property. In the Maurandi family history, for example, several generations of individuals named "Maurandus de Vallesecura" (after the family property at Valségur) and "Maurandus de Bellopodio" (after the property at Belpuy) appear. This practice was not frequent among families who drew their surnames from placenames, but was exemplified by at least one example. This is the Christian name or sole identification adopted by the family of Castronovo (Castelnau-d'Estretefons). A child of almost every generation was called Castellusnovus or Castrumnovum (Castelnau or -nou in the vernacular) and, as is obvious, this person had no need of a placename with a particule.[86] Another interesting variation is the employment of a placename in lieu of both a Christian and a surname. In 1254 Rabastencs de Villanova, a son of the patrician and knightly family of that name, was also called Raymond de Rabastenquis.[87] In fine, the practice of identifying both property and groups by family name was common in the twelfth and thirteenth centuries.

D. FAMILY CORPORATISM

During the thirteenth century, the names describing individuals began to change. One change was the generalization of the use of the genitive case for the second given name. A passage above explained that this method was one of the ways of naming a person after his father, an ancient practice that continued a half-life throughout the period treated in this essay.[88] This custom had weakened in the Latin charters of the latter twelfth century, but then mysteriously recurred to become frequent again around the mid-thirteenth century. This change had not been imposed by law, at least not as far as available legal texts say. Although, for example, the gradual or general triumph of this method of identification may be seen in the more

[85]See for example, the histories of the Caraborda, Embrini and Maurandi in my *Repression of Catharism*, pp. 168-177, 217-220 and 229-241.

[86]For the Castronovo, see my *Repression of Catharism*, pp. 178-190.

[87]The Villanova family history is in my *Repression of Catharism*, pp. 301-303.

[88]See Malta 10 26 ii (May 1259, copied in 1259) where John de Companha's minor sons are named Bernard, Raymond and William, all having the second name "Johannis," thus "Bernardus Johannis," etc.

or less annual lists of the consuls, at least two lists in the twelve-seventies still retained the older practice of using the nominative for all names.[89]

Reasons for this change are difficult to discern. Perhaps the older tradition, still alive in the vernacular, surfaced again in mid-thirteenth century notarial Latin. An instance showing the persistence of this usage in common speech occurred when a rural knight testified to the Inquisition about the wife of Bernard Raymond de Tolosa, a notable who appears as such in many charters. The witness referred to him as "Bernardus Ramundus Tozez de Tholosa," a name obviously recording the name of his father Toset de Tolosa.[90]

What brought the vernacular practice to the surface again or gave it renewed vigor was probably that it imitated foreign fashions. It will be recalled that the Italian and Provençal way of describing a person was similar, an individual being called, for example, "Petrus Johannis Olivi," Peter of John Olivi, that is, Peter, the son of John Olivi. Curiously, at Toulouse, this style, even after its adoption, appears to have been largely without function because the genitive second name often had no relation to the father's actual name. So bemused or indifferent were Toulousan scribes that they were capable of describing a notable person in a public document as "Bernardus Raimundi Baranhoni filius Bernardi Raimundi Baranhoni" or inserting a more humble "Bernardus Fabri carrugerius" (carter) into a consular list.[91] What probably inspired the notaries was that, performing functions similar to those of modern solicitors, they were influenced by the law taught in the Italian schools and at the new university of Toulouse which brought with it Italian or Provençal styles in nomenclature.

A second and perhaps more consequential change was that patrician and knightly families began to exchange first names. It was remarked in my *Men and Women at Toulouse* that male first names lacked much of the color possessed by female ones. Three practices, however, partly saved the day for the men. As has been remarked above, unlike the women seen in property documents, men used special names and, just as did women, employed family names as single or first names, which sometimes became Christian names characteristic of families. Generation after generation, the knightly house called Tolosa boasted a scion named Tosetus (vernacular Tozes). Obvious indications of the strength of family solidarity, family

---

[89]Appendix 4, dated November 1270 and September 1271.

[90]See the Tolosa family history published in my *Repression of Catharism*, pp. 275 and 283. Bernard Raymond was active from 1192 to 1217, but had died by 1230.

[91]Bernard Raymond was among the petitioners and proctors to the crown published in PAN, J 313 95 (March 1279) (this document is summarized in my *Repression of Catharism*, p. 122), and the carter was among the consuls in 1261 in Appendix 4.

names were even more common. The names Castellusnovus and Maurandus, for example, tell that those carrying them derived from the knightly Castelnau-d'Estretefons and the patrician Maurandi. Curvus, a rare name, was a mark of the Turribus house, and there are others. In the course of the twelve hundreds, however, some of these rare names were adopted by other knightly or patrician clans.

To look at the patricians named Roaxio whose line had risen from modest early twelfth century origins, one scion was seen bearing the name Toset as a Christian name as early as 1230.[92] His mother may have been a Tolosa, because there are not a few cases of daughters carrying the names of their mother's families. In 1284 a Ramunda, widow of Bernard de Turre, for example, had among her children an unmarried "Mauranda de Turre." It seems all but sure that Mauranda had been given her name to honor her mother, presumably a Maurandi woman who had married a Turre (Latour).[93] If daughters, why not sons also? To this may be added that the Roaxio family was pushing at the gates of the knightly nobility as early as 1222, notably in the case of the famous Cathar named Alaman, who had been given to the Unald family to be trained as a knight.[94] Later on, other alliances are seen reflected in the nomenclature of this lineage. An especially striking instance is seen in 1271 and 1273 when Castrumnovum de Roaxio's brother was named Aimeric de Roaxio, both siblings therefore bearing names traditional in, and indeed hitherto characteristic of, the Castelnau-d'Estretefons family.[95]

Because these families had always intermarried, these changes in nomenclature obviously reflected a different view of society from that obtaining in the past. Once, it had been enough to be a Roaxio and to carry the first names traditionally used in that clan, names like Alaman. Important though the lineage or family still was, it had now become meaningful to adopt first names borrowed from other equal or even more distinguished lineages to express membership in a class or social order. A private and family-structured society was evolving toward one based on order and class, both, it should be added, defined and regulated by the crown or by state authority. Just as did the introduction of titles of nobility and of a bourgeoisie of urban notables, subjects investigated earlier in this study, these gradual changes represented or reflected the increased formalism of late medieval corporate society.

---

[92]See my *Repression of Catharism*, p. 263.
[93]Malta 123 19 one of several membranes tied together (November 1284).
[94]Mentioned in Appendix 8, No. 47 (November 1222).
[95]In my *Repression of Catharism*, pp. 265-267.

Part 3

ECONOMY

10

Usury

A. History

The aspect of economic life that best illuminates the capacity of individuals and families to do what they like with their property is their right to gain wealth for themselves by lending money or goods to those needing it. In social terms, the exercise of this right measures the strength or ability of such persons to withstand the hostility of their debtors or of those who profit from this enmity to mobilize society against them, in order to shake them down. In economic terms, usury is what is being talked about, namely the capacity of persons to demand a return in kind or in money above and beyond the value invested to compensate them for taking a risk and for their putative loss from other or foregone investments. In this sense, the prevalence of usury in twelfth century Toulouse shows the vitality of both economic individualism and family economic authority at that time. The position adopted here reflects Henri Pirenne's celebrated argument about the "epoch of free capitalist expansion" as characteristic of the middle ages up to about 1300, one so much deplored by Max Weber, not to speak of the Marxists. Of the two views, I think Pirenne's better reflects reality because his is the simplest and clearest definition of what is found in the documents. I eschew the use of the word "capitalism," however, partly because it has again become today's deceptive Golden Calf and partly because it tradition-ally involves things, such as the technological revolutions of modern times, that have no real parallel in the middle ages.

A first step toward examining the situation in Toulouse in this regard is to rehearse the medieval law on usury. The background context and treatment of the general conception and law on usury derives from two books. The first is Benjamin Nelson's inspired but very general *Idea of Usury* and the second, John Noonan's fine *Scholastic Analysis of Usury*, a work at once close to the Scylla of Catholic apologetic and the Charybdis of capitalist self-congratulation. Usury at Toulouse preoccupied my own research in 1946 and 1947 and was soon illuminated by Mireille Castaing-Sicard's study of Toulousan contracts. Castaing-Sicard's book, like my own research, was in debt to Georges Boyer, a onetime dean of law at Toulouse who had seen all the documents, but for whom publishing was decidedly secondary to teaching or even perhaps to knowing.

In Roman and early medieval times, usury was forbidden to the clergy and this prohibition, together with the notion of restoring ill-gotten gains to the victims, had been extended to the laity in the Carolingian age.[1] After these initial steps, important for the growth of theory, the real attack on usury began after the triumph of the church during the Gregorian age. Starting at that time, popes and church councils began to legislate systematically, thus beginning the gradual elevation of the prohibition of usury into a major characteristic of the medieval economy. The first general council to treat the subject was the Second Lateran Council in 1139 whose canons initiated a spate of papal conciliar legislation and judicial decisions on usury that culminated at the Council of Vienne in 1312-1313.

The clergy especially attacked the "mutuum" and the "pignus." Roughly similar to a mortgage, the latter was initiated either by the debtor or creditor, and enabled a creditor to collect the income deriving from a pledged property as his interest (in today's sense of that word) on the capital loaned to the debtor. This division into capital and interest is reflected in the charters. In 1185 a notable in Toulouse was said to have received the "cabalis et servicium," the former term meaning "capitalis" or capital and the latter the annual rent or interest owed, in this case, by an individual.[2] Although widely used by both clergy and laity, this contract had been declared usurious by councils and pontiffs, especially by Alexander III in the mid-twelfth century.[3]

---

[1]For the history of early laws on usury such as the canon *Ne hoc quoque* of Leo I in 444, Charlemagne's "Admonitio generalis" of 789 and the conciliar legislation at Pavia in 850, see Schaub, *Der Kampf gegen den Zinswucher, ungerechten Preis und unlautern Handel im Mittelalter von Karl des Grossen bis papst Alexander III* and Lestocquoy, "Les usuriers du début du moyen-âge," *Studi in onore di Gino Luzzato* 1: 69ff.

[2]See late twelfth century usage in Appendix 1, No. 15, note 17 below and the entries in Appendix 6 concerning the "servicia" owed the Tolosa sisters. "Cabalis" or "capitalis" derives from the classical "caput" and means the capital invested as against the accruing interest.

[3]In 1142 Eugene III forbade mortgages in a letter contained in PL 180: 1567. Alexander III's enactments were in X. 5 19 6, a canon issued at the Council of Tours in 1163 and extended to the laity in a letter to the archbishop of Canterbury carried in X. 5 19 2. See Noonan's *Scholastic Analysis of Usury*, pp. 17-19, and Castaing-Sicard's *Contrats dans le très ancien droit Toulousain*, pp. 318-319. Unlike a mortgage, the contract called "vifgage" was permitted precisely because the income from the pledged property or labor counted toward paying off the debt.

Condemned even before the "pignus," the "mutuum" with openly stated "lucrum" (profit or interest, to use the modern term again) was paradigmatically the usurious contract and hence was everywhere decried. Because it proposed that a creditor could openly receive profit or lucre, the old Toulousan "mutuum" was often frankly usurious. What creditors got for their investment was, as some of the charters put it and has been mentioned above, "cabalis et lucrum," in today's language "capital and interest."[4] Having been especially sharply censured both in antiquity and the middle ages, anatocism or compound interest rarely appears in the documents, but there are cases.[5] Because usurers were obliged to make restitution, churchmen and others were ordered to refuse gifts from such illegal sources even for charitable purposes. In fact, money derived from such contracts was not even supposed to be used to ransom prisoners from the Saracens.[6] Even if

---

[4]The subject is well treated in Castaing-Sicard, *Contrats dans le très ancien droit Toulousain*, pp. 248-255. For examples of these documents see E 508 (November 1197), published in ibid., p. 592. See further examples in Saint-Étienne 227 (26 DA 2 21) ii (September 1184, copied in 1197): "Poncius Raimundus de Rocas debet dare et reddere Raimundo Durando et eius ordinio .l. sol. tol. bonos pro quibus debet dare ei et suo ordinio .viii. d. tol. de lucro in unoquoque mense dum illos tenuerit; et est terminus in quo predictus debitor habuit predictos denarios .xii. dies ad exitum mensis Septembris; et quando Raimundus Durandus ... voluerit suos denarios recuperare, predictus debitor debet ei reddere illos cum omni lucro quod ibi factum fuerit." The interest rate is 1.3 percent monthly or 15.9 annually not compounded. No. iii records the closing of this debt by one of the guarantors ("pro ... fidantia") of the whole original debt "inter cabalem et lucre pro barata predicta" in May 1191, a quittance that implies that the September deadline may have been fictional. A typical short-term loan is E 538 (May 1201) where a debtor admits he owes Pons de Capitedenario sixty shillings to be paid on the Virgin's feast in August "et si illos deinde tenuerit, convenit ei dare .xii. d. tol. de lucro pro unoquoque mense dum illos deinde tenuerit." Payment "de cabale et de lucro" was guaranteed by pledging the debtor's body and black mare. The rate here is 1.6 percent monthly or 19.2 annually.

[5]The matter is discussed with examples in Castaing-Sicard, *Contrats dans le très ancien droit Toulousain*, pp. 251-252, but it is possible to add an example of delayed compound interest. PAN, J 1024 1 (May 1200) has two debtors confessing that John Barravus had lent them twenty shillings and that they had agreed to pay him four pence monthly "de lucro." They had received the money on the last day of April and, "si ultra .i. annum supradictam pecuniam tenuerint, convenerunt ei dare de cabale et de lucro lucrum panalium dum deinde tenuerint." Without the penalty payment, the monthly interest was 1.6 percent and the yearly 19.9 percent.

[6]The basic legislation was that of Alexander III (d. 1181) and was carried in the *Decretals of Gregory IX*, notably in X. 5 19 6, X. 5 19 4 (on Saracens) and the round-up law on usury in Canon 25 *Quia in omnibus* issued in the Third Lateran Council of 1179 in X. 5 19 3. This was all confirmed by Urban III (d. 1187) who in X. 5 19 10 abbreviated the famous passage of Luke 6 35 into "Date mutuum, nihil inde sperantes."

debtors agreed to forgo restitution, furthermore, the concession was considered illegal and was to be overridden by judges, according to Innocent III (d. 1216).[7]

As is obvious, condemnation is blanket, but practical needs mitigate its incidence. Although banned, contracts like the "pignus" enjoyed a kind of half-life for quite a time, especially out in the countryside away from the schools of the larger towns. An example of rural persistence is seen in 1241 when a magnate, Bernard de Saisses, mortgaged his possessions in the castles of Le Foussaret and "Savars" (Savères?) far southwest of Toulouse to the baron Roger de Noerio.[8] Again, and more significantly, a special provision of canon law allowed the use of the "pignus" for recuperating ecclesiastical property, especially tithes.[9]

None of this papal law on usury is directly signaled at Toulouse, but the new compilations of canon law and other recent laws were cited there during the eleven-eighties in legal suits concerning matters other than usury.[10] The Toulousan clergy, furthermore, knew and used the option of employing the "pignus" to recuperate ecclesiastical goods. Among other cases, the cellarer of the cathedral chapter, Mascaronus, acquired a tithe by means of this contract in 1200.[11] A mortgage loan was also made by the abbot of the monastery of Nizors far southwest of Toulouse near Saint-Gaudens in 1235 and the Hospitalers of Poucharramet near Rieumes to the southwest held one in 1239.[12] Lastly, in 1181 Pope Celestine III cast a glance at Toulouse and commented adversely on the town's usurers. Sent

[7]X. 2 24 20 and 5 19 13.

[8]Pledged in PAN, J 330 20 (July 1241), "pro tenere et explectare." If the pledge was not redeemed within a year, the debtor was to pay for "missiones ... in operibus de terra et de fuste in hoc predicto pignore in bonis denariis infra Tolosam vel ad Noerium vel in predicto castro de Fossareto si forte aliqua missio ibi facta fuerit ab ipso Rogerio de Noerio ... ."

[9]Alexander III's X. 5 19 1 of 1163 prohibited this kind of usury to churchmen "nisi forte ecclesiae beneficium fuerit, quod redimendum ei hoc modo de manu laici videatur." There was much debate about this and also other legislation in X. 5 19 8 and 3 20 1, which is discussed in Noonan, *Scholastic Analysis of Usury*, pp. 102-103, who also remarks that, by the time of Hostiensis (d. 1271), some layfolk were allowed to use this contract.

[10]See my "Parishes of Toulouse," pp. 178-179 and 202-204.

[11]Cresty, *Répertoire des titres et documents concernants les biens et droits du chapitre de Saint-Étienne*, fol. 164v (December 1200) at Lisiac, wherever that may be.

[12]Nizors, a single "liasse" (February 1235), and Castaing-Sicard, *Contrats dans le très ancien droit Toulousain*, p. 598, No. 32 (dated 1239).

to Bishop Folcrand of Toulouse, the letter urged that prelate to reform the administration of his cathedral church whose wealth, the pope asserted, was being dissipated because of the negligence of the canons, the aggression of usurers and the malice of parishioners.[13]

In a primitive form, deathbed restitution of wrongfully acquired wealth also made an appearance, an early example being dated 1123. The testator was a rural lord who had lent money to the countess of Toulouse in return for the pledge of the market in Baziège southwest of Toulouse. His victims, it appears, were not only the countess and the canons of Saint-Sernin of Toulouse, but also those using the market.[14] Not until over forty years later, however, is a real, if still somewhat undeveloped, example of testamentary restitution found at Toulouse. In 1166 Bruno Trenca ordered his heir to pay off his "conquerentes," those harmed by his usury who requested restitution.[15] In this context a "conquerens" always meant a person with a claim on an individual or estate for reason of usury or other violence.

These early attempts to repair social damage already depict what clerks and utopians in this period thought to be society's two main enemies: usurers and soldiers. The former are the subjects of this chapter, but it is

[13]Douais, *Cartulaire de Saint-Sernin*, pp. lx-lxi, with a copy in 4G Saint-Étienne 407 (April 30, 1191 – Jaffé No. 1668a): "precipimus quatinus ... que in Tolosana ecclesia tum ex negligentia canonicorum, tum feneratorum ambitione, tum etiam parrochianorum malicia faciente, tam circa spiritualia et temporalia dissipata sunt et consumpta ... corrigas et emendes."

[14]Ibid., No. 5 (dated 1123): "Ego Guilabertus de Lauraco, positus in extremis, reminiscor omnia scelera mea que gessi; inter que et tot reminiscor quoddam scelus quod ego miser et infelix feci, scilicet de pignora que feci cum Tolosana comitissa. Inpignoravi etenim ab ea per tria milia solidos medallas quas illa habebat et tenebat in mercato atque in villa de Vadega. Ego vero, suadente diabolo, supra pignus quod ab ea accepi, plurimos malos usagios misi et auxi; et propterea omnia mala usagia que miseram in mercato, in stratis, vel in salinis, ex toto dimitto et reddo propter medallas quas illa habebat et tenebat in mercato atque in villa de Vadega. De .iii^a.m^a.ii^o. solidis quos ipsa accepit a me pro pignore, medietatem michi reddidit. De alia vero medietate que remansit, dono Domino Deo et Beato Saturnino et clericis qui modo ibi sunt et in antea erunt, quingentos solidos, propter remedium anime mee, et propter violentiam quam feceram Deo et Beato Saturnino et clericis eius. In tali vero convenientia ut, quando comes Tolosanus vel clerici Sancti Saturnini hoc pignus tradere voluerint, quingenti solidi sunt ad ipsos; c. vero dentur monachis Beate Marie Deaurate; alii autem c. dentur canonicis Sancti Stephani, sedis Tolose; octingenti vero qui remanent, sint infantibus meis. Ego igitur Guilabertus supradictus sic dimitto atque laxo omnia mala usagia suprascripta propter remedium anime mee ... in manu Amelii episcopi Tolosani."

[15]Appendix 8, No. 3.

worth recording here parenthetically that, like economic aggressors, lordly magnates were also commanded to bandage the wounds they had inflicted on the body social. And, like usurers in and around Toulouse, they are known to have offered testamentary restitution for the damage wreaked on their subjects and others. In 1228 and 1237, for example, two successive lords of Isle-Jourdain, Bernard Jordan II and III, made testamentary restitution, the first restoring to the community rights he had usurped and the second compensating persons harmed by him.[16]

In this period of change, moneylenders were well aware of the threat posed by the canons against usury. This may be shown by the fact that the word "usura" was sedulously avoided in Toulousan contracts.[17] As a result, not a few contracts introduced in lieu of "lucrum" or "usura" a "pena" or penalty payment ("lucrum penalium") for nonfulfillment of contract.[18] As will be seen below, the replacement of the term "pena" by that of interest ("interesse") awaited the end of the century.

B. PROHIBITION

In spite of the gradual penetration by the canons against usury sketched above, the decisive moment in this history at Toulouse awaited the episcopate of Fulk of Marseille. It was during the early days of his reign that the town really received, as legal historians say, the canons against usury and put them into practice. Fulk's attack echoed that of the popes. In 1209 Innocent III wrote the archbishop of Narbonne and his suffragans urging them to combat heresy and also usury, the latter prohibition being viewed by the pontiff as a defense of economic brotherhood. He especially militated against defending loan contracts simply because the debtors had sworn to

[16]See Appendix 8, Nos. 49 (March 1228) and 67 (February 1237).

[17]This practice differs from that obtaining elsewhere, for which see pp. 203-204 below.

[18]A local term for "lucrum" was "gazain" and the word "gravium" was used in lieu of "pena," for which terms see Castaing-Sicard, *Contrats dans le très ancien droit Toulousain*, pp. 104-109. See an example in Saige's *Juifs du Languedoc*, No. 36 4 (April 1244) where the Jew Belitus promised to pay the notable Guy de Turribus ninety shillings on the feast of the Virgin in August and "si deinde illos tenebit, convenit inde ei dare pro unoquoque die duos denarios Tolosanorum de pena." The rate is about 67.5 percent annually, but, having been contracted for the limited span of time from April 22 to August 15 was really a rate of about 21.5 percent. The debt was guaranteed by a pledge of vineyards "ad recuperandam inde omnem suam pecuniam et predictam penam." See also the Turribus history in Appendix 1, No. 15, and that of Belitus in Appendix 2, No. 1.

pay and also urged restitution for usury.[19] This program was already being introduced at Toulouse by the time the pontiff wrote.

Fulk of Marseille had become bishop of Toulouse in 1206. A Cistercian, his appointment to this see reflected the already long association of his order both with crusading and with the repression of divergent religious thought or heresy in the Midi, an example of which was seen as early as Bernard of Clairvaux' preaching mission in 1145.[20] While at Toulouse, Fulk looked about for stronger medicine than that provided by his Cistercian brethren. He fostered Dominic's mission at Toulouse and thus prepared the ground for the largely Dominican-led inquisition of the twelve-thirties. It was fitting that, on Fulk's death in 1231, he was replaced in the see of Toulouse by the Dominican, Raymond of Falgar, one of the founder's early companions and an equally ardent foe of the heretics.

As suited one during whose episcopate Toulouse was invaded by crusaders originating principally in northern France, Fulk was also in close touch with the northern French church. He was a friend of James of Vitry and, like that prelate, an admirer of the early Beguines in the Low Countries.[21] He was influenced by the movement for the renewal of the crusades and the polemic against the violence of the knighthood and against the usury of businessmen promulgated by the circle of Robert of Curzon, the Parisian master and papal legate. Contemporary propaganda against usury may be instanced by the exaggerated report about Stephen Langton, before he gained fame as archbishop of Canterbury, whose preaching is

---

[19]PL 216: 158 (November 1209): "Cum autem pro fraterna defensione pugnantes a fraternis deceat injuriis expediri, volumus et mandamus ut si qui nobilium clericorum seu eciam laicorum contra pestilantes hujusmodi procedentium ad prestandas usuras juramento tenentur astricti, creditores eorum in vestris diocesibus constitutos, cum ab ipsis fueritis requisiti, per censuram ecclesiasticam, appellatione postposita, compellatis, ut, eos a juramento penitus absolventes, ab usurarum prorsus exactione desistant. Quod si quisquam creditorum ipsos ad solutionem coegerit usurarum, eum ad restituendas ipsas, postquam fuerint persolute, simili censura, sublato appellationis obstaculo, coartetis, creditores talium quam diligentius poteritis inducentes, ut terminos ad solutionem debitorum prefixos, donec illi labori vacaverint huiusmodi pietatis, elongent; quo sic demum retributionis eorum gaudeant participio quorum certamen tali promoverint adjumento."

[20]On this history, see my *Liberty and Political Power*, pp. 59-92, and, for Fulk's background, see Stronski, *Le troubadour Folquet de Marseille*; for a brief review of these events together with new material, my *Repression of Catharism*, pp. 11-18.

[21]On the Beguines, see McDonnell's *The Beguines and Beghards in Medieval Culture*. The information about Fulk derives from the "Vita Mariae Oigniacensis" in the *Acta sanctorum* 24 (June 23, v) 542-572, and also Lejeune, "L'évêque de Toulouse Foulquet de Marseille et la principauté de Liège," *Mélanges Félix Rousseau*, pp. 433-448.

said to have "largely cleaned usury from Italy and France."[22] The attack
on usury was also a theme used in the propaganda for the Albigensian
Crusade, a war that, launched in 1209, only affected the Toulousain directly two years later.[23]

The only known decision of the bishop's court against a usurer was
dated 1215 and was directed against the deceased Pons David, or rather
against his heirs, the Hospitalers of Saint John.[24] There is also evidence
that a similar decision was rendered by Mascaronus, provost of the cathedral chapter and vicar of the bishop, concerning an illegal "pignus" sometime between 1211 and 1221.[25] Charters containing promises by debtors
not to sue their creditors before ecclesiastical courts also instruct their
readers that usurers had been threatened with prosecution from at least
1211.[26] Although forbidden by canon law, such promises were even witnessed by the local clergy who for reasons at present unknown clearly
doubted the validity of the new law.[27] One debtor even went so far as to
forgive the soul of his creditor, and another absolved the creditors "here

[22]This circle derived from Peter Cantor, on whom see Baldwin, *Masters, Princes
and Merchants: The Social Views of Peter the Chanter and His Circle*. The story was
told by Master Gervais of Melkeley in Matthew Paris' *Vita sancti Stephani archiepiscopi
Cantuariensis*, ed. Liebermann in his *Ungedrückte Anglo-Normannische Geschichtsquellen*, pp. 327-328: "mundavit in magna parte ab usuris Ytaliam et Franciam," being
aided in Flanders and northern France by Robert of Curzon, both being helped by
James of Vitry.

[23]Latin texts about the Albigensian war are full of this propaganda. See also a vernacular passage in William of Tudela's *Canso*, ed. Martin-Chabot 1: 150, lines 25-26,
reading: "et tuit li renoier lo renou laicharan / E si gazanh an pres tot primer lo ren-
dran." For the meaning of the word "gazan," see Appendix 7 on "The Early 'Gasalha'
Contract."

[24]See the David history in my *Repression of Catharism*, pp. 207-208, and also, for
the charter recording the decision of the court, my *Liberty and Political Power*, pp. 208-
209, No. 15 (November 1215).

[25]See my "Un usurier malheureux" in *Hommage à M. François Galabert*, pp. 123-125.

[26]The earliest example is Bernard Barravus' charter of forgiveness housed in E 508
and published in Castaing-Sicard, *Contrats dans le très ancien droit Toulousain*, No. 25,
p. 592 (February 1211). On Bernard, see my *Repression of Catharism*, p. 146.

[27]Witnesses to the charter dealing with Bernard Barravus mentioned in the previous
note were Dalbis "capellanus" of the Daurade and Raymond de Lubers "presbiter."
The career of Dalbs or Dalbis ran from 1209 to 1235 as may be seen in my "Parishes
of Toulouse," pp. 194-195, and *Men and Women*, pp. 196-197. The rejection of such
contracts by canon law is described in McLaughlin, "The Teaching of the Canonists on
Usury," *Mediaeval Studies* 2 (1940) 17.

and before God!"[28] These layfolk must have received somewhat aberrant counsel from their ghostly advisors.

During this period, however, the testamentary restitution of usury became both relatively frequent and explicit, thus showing that the church was moving to enforce its laws.[29] Of the 103 testamentary dispositions calendared in this study, sixteen contained explicit restitutions, to which may be added one doubtful case.[30] Although less frequently busy in credit operations than men, women were also called on to make restitution.[31]

Having become legally enforceable, claims against usurers were willed by testators and sometimes precipitated equivocation. One decedent, a rural gentleman named Raymond de Montelauro, not only bequeathed money to satisfy those who protested his usury, but also willed his right to recuperate the usuries he had paid on a debt owed to Peter Grivus de Roaxio, a notable Toulousan businessman. The debt entailed an annual charge of fifteen percent and had run for twelve years.[32] That restitution was actually made is shown by extant quittances given for payment by the heirs of dead usurers.[33]

---

[28]E 508 (March 1211): "Notum sit quod Raimundus de Castaned sua bona voluntate solvit Raimundum Andream et eius ordinium et suam animam de omnibus illis usuris et lucris que ei dederat pro aliquibus debitis absque omni retencione quam ibi non fecit, et non debet inde de eo facere querelam domino episcopo nec alicui literate persone nec alicui viventi ullo modo." In Grandselve 5 (February 1212) Pons de Murello, then deceased, and Peter Sobaccus (see the latter's history in my *Men and Women*, pp. 185-187) acquired a letter from a widow which forgave them "hic et ante domino ... totum illud lucrum et usuram quam de eis unquam habuerant" from her husband and self.

[29]Appendix 8, No. 45 (March 1220) has Stephen Astro assigning a sum to his wife to distribute to his "conquerentibus." See also my *Men and Women*, pp. 173-182.

[30]Appendix 8, Nos. 3 (dated 1166), 27 (dated 1208), 34 (dated 1214), 36 (dated 1216), 45 (dated 1220), 51 (dated 1229), 56 (dated 1232, a woman's testament), 62 (dated 1233), 64 (dated 1235, the doubtful case), 68 (dated 1237), 72 (dated 1243), 80 (dated 1251), 95 (dated 1265), 98 (dated 1277), 99 (dated 1278), 100 (dated 1282, a woman's testament) and 101 (dated 1283).

[31]An example is one of the two cases listed above, Appendix 8, No. 56 (March 1232). On the role of women in business, see my *Men and Women*, pp. 24-27, and another case is that of Bona, seen on p. 199 below.

[32]See Appendix 8, No. 34 (September 1214), and the Roaxio history in my *Repression of Catharism*, pp. 259-260.

[33]E 538 ii (June 1230), published in Castaing-Sicard, *Contrats dans le très ancien droit Toulousain*, p. 593, No. 25, where Elias Barravus "dedit et solvit ... Poncio de Capitedenario qui fuit et domine Aurimunde sue uxori et domine Stephane eorum filie totum hoc quod eis ... petere poterat vel putabat pro lucris nec pro usuris nec pro explectis pignorum nec pro redditibus quicquid esset ullo modo" for himself and his deceased brother Arnold Barravus. These persons are in my *Repression of Catharism*, pp. 137 and 159.

In this atmosphere, creditors not only abandoned the traditional "pignus," but also changed the terms used in their charters containing loans,
the old "mutuum" being considered far too naked for practical purposes.
Although not really usurious, words derived from the vernacular like the
verb "gadanare," and the nouns "gazanha" or "gazaille" (meaning to acquire, profit or contract for profit), slowly all but lost their old generic
sense, to become terms designating investment in animal husbandry.[34]
The much more ancient word "lucrum," which simply meant "gain" or
"profit" and was not of itself usurious, came to appear far too frank an
expression of the creditor's real intentions or hopes and therefore disappeared.[35] So associated with illegal usury had the term "lucrum" become
that a consular law of 1197, while prosecuting debtors, allowed creditors to
imprison them "in irons" only for the capital of their debts.[36] Later legislation of 1214 expressly excluded the "lucrum" or interest a debtor owed.[37]
In fact, charters issued by the consuls of Toulouse in the later twelve-
twenties simply describe lucre as usury.[38]

What replaced lucre in the documents were terms specifying the loss to
the creditor caused by the debtor's inability to meet the deadline specified
in the contracts, and notaries who drew them up were careful to specify that
usury was not involved.[39] Similar clauses were used in all kinds of con-

---

[34]See Appendix 7 on "Gasanha."

[35]As meaning profit or gain, the term "lucrum" is seen in Appendix 8, Nos. 1
(August 1150), 2 (January 1164), 11 (May 1199), 34 (September 1214) and 45 (March
1220), after which it is not seen in my collection. Lucre was therefore the ordinary word
for interest on a mortgage or loan.

[36]TAM, AA 1 18 (November 1197), in which the recalcitrant debtor was given to
the creditor to be put in latter's house "in ferris ... scilicet pro cabale ... ."

[37]TAM, II 45 (March 1214), where the consuls determined "quod omnia illa debita
que debentur pro venditionibus et emptionibus domorum vel vinearum vel terrarum vel
aliorum honorum vel equorum vel aliorum animalium vel pannorum vel blati vel vini
vel pro aliquibus aliis rebus et negociationibus de quibus debitis lucrum non datur nec
capitur nec ibi numeratur vel includitur vel remuneratur, omnis illa talia debita persolvantur ... ."

[38]As in the decisions of 1225 and 1228 cited in notes 54 and 55 below.

[39]E 508 ii ("actio" in February 1212, "conscriptio" in August 1212) where Pons de
Capitedenario and his partner Arnold Aiscius rented a vineyard to Bernard Massus, and
then lent him sixty shillings. Payment was to be made within three years in three annual
payments of twenty shillings. If he failed to meet the deadline, Bernard was to "eis
reddere et reficere omnem miscionem et gravium quod deinde predicti creditores ... inde
fecerint excepto fenore et usura." On Pons de Capitedenario's business activities, see my
Repression of Catharism, pp. 158-162.

tracts, notably leases.[40] As was the case elsewhere in Europe, the term "interesse" to describe such a penalty ("pena" or "lucrum penalium" or its variant "panalium") became current and was accepted in law during the thirteenth century.[41] The corresponding penitential change was signaled in Raymond of Peñafort's renowned manual where he describes interest as "not lucre, but instead the avoidance of loss."[42]

Probably reflecting nothing more than the weakness of documentation typical of thirteenth century Toulouse, the term "interesse" is not seen there until 1281.[43] It is nevertheless easy to show that the law about it was known there. Deriving, as it did, from Roman law, the canon law on "interesse" permitted a creditor to recuperate not only lost capital but also lost probable profits.[44] And indeed, even before the term "interesse" itself appeared in Toulousan charters, the law allowing it had been received there and even exceeded. In a document of 1208 the well-known Jew Provincialis recognized that he owed the Christian patrician Peter de Roaxio thirty-five shillings to be paid within a year's term, and spelled out the terms of a penalty payment and accompanying pledge. Although this transaction may have reflected the normal relationships in business of Jews and Christians in which economic individualism held unusual sway, it looks strikingly like the "lucrum" clause in contemporary charters.[45] In fine, although evi-

---

[40]In Saint-Sernin 599 (10 35 5) (January 1234) the archdeacon Master Pons bought the "collocatio" of the "bovaria" of Valségur, recently acquired from Maurand "vetus," for ten years, and was obligated to pay 2700 shillings in a series of stipulated payments. If he defaulted on the payments and "si ultra constitutos terminos illos tenuerit, [Pons] debet et convenit eis [the canons of the basilica] reddere et reficere omne gravamen et missionem que ipsi inde fecerint excepto lucro et usura." Other good examples are found in Castaing-Sicard, *Contrats dans le très ancien droit Toulousain*, pp. 263-269.

[41]Note the discussion in Noonan, *Scholastic Analysis of Usury*, pp. 104-109. Roman law had the notion of "quod interest," that is, the difference between what would have been the case if the debtor had not defaulted on the contract by delay or other nonfulfillment in D. 46 8 13 and especially C. 7 47 2, in which law it states: "Et hoc non solum in damno sed etiam in lucro nostra amplectitur constitutio ... ." The term "interesse" was standardized by the famous jurist Azo around 1220.

[42]*Summa de poenitentia et matrimonio* (Rome 1603) 2 7 3, p. 228b: "id est non lucrum, sed vitatio damni."

[43]E 508 (December 1281) where a debtor promised to "restituere omne gravamen et missionem atque interesse ... preter usuram" to his creditor, William Gafa "cultellerius," if he defaulted. Some aspects of the poverty of documentation at Toulouse in this period are discussed in my *Men and Women*, pp. 10-14.

[44]As in X. 3 22 2 of Lucius III of 1181, although the pontiff there spoke only about what a debtor owed his "fideiussor" or guarantor, if that person had had to pay the creditor.

[45]In Malta 18 23 (December 1208) giving the term of payment as a year beginning

dence is sparse, a new language describing old economic actualities was making its appearance.

C. Enforcement

Ample evidence shows that the law on usury was generally enforced and that businessfolk never openly challenged it. The episcopal court continued its work, actively prosecuting a usurer in 1269. Replete with the copious tears of the debtor's son and protestations by the creditor that nothing untoward would happen (reminiscent of today's comforting TV ads for personal loans), the evidence was presented before the bishop's judge or "officialis" of Toulouse and concerned a fictional sale of property in Lavaur well to the east of Toulouse consummated sometime from 1245 to 1247.[46] Witnesses testified to the usurious nature of both the sale and the creditor and, in fact, the moneylender Pons Isarni was a Toulousan citizen. A witness to the original contract was Pons Palmata, another well-known citizen usurer.[47]

The tribunal of the "officialis" of Toulouse was supplemented and possibly kept to the mark by the archiepiscopal court at Narbonne. In 1255 the

---

on December 24th, "et si deinde illos tenuerit, convenit inde ei dare lucrum panalis [read 'panale'] deinde ... ." And for this sum "pro cabali et pro lucro," the debtor is to pledge a piece of land. At the end of the act there is an additional note: "Item Petrus de Roaxio recognovit et concessit quod isti .xxx.v. sol. tol. debent persolvi in lucro illorum .c. sol. tol. quos ipse Provincialis ei debet pro quibus habet de eo in pignore maloles et, si aliquid inde superabit, paccato lucro illorum .c. sol. tol., Petrus de Roaxio debet ei reddere residuum." Quite apart from what Peter may have gained from the newly pledged piece of land to guarantee the payment of his thirty-five shillings, the interest on this loan amounted to thirty-five percent over a period whose length cannot be ascertained. On Provincialis, see Appendix 2, No. 2.

[46]An indistinct roll of testimony "coram Magistro Bertrando de Ferreriis officiali Tholosano noviter creato" in TAM, II 92 (late March and April 1269) concerned a sale "in ripparia de Vileta" by a Peter de Vileta to Pons Isarni. Peter's sister reported that her brother "sub ficta venditionis specie obligabat eidem reo" his property for 300 shillings of Toulouse. She had not seen the sale consummated "in operatorio Massoti de Vauro," but immediately afterward saw the "venditorem et vidit quod dum Guillelmus de Vileta [his – Peter's – son] ploraret, idem Poncius [the creditor] dixit eidem Guillelmo quod non fleret quia ipse redderet eidem Petro dictos honores cum dictos .ccc. sol. tol."

[47]Ibid.: witnesses remarked that the creditor promised to return the property once the capital was repaid, but that, in the meantime, he kept its fruits. One, "inquisitus si sciret quod idem reus sit usurarius vel consueverit exercere usuras, dixit quod nescit sed audivit dici." On Pons Palmata, see my *Repression of Catharism*, pp. 22 and 82-83.

parish priest of Saint-Étienne's of Toulouse recorded and transmitted to the archbishop's court for trial there testimony against three Toulousan money-lenders.[48] As will be seen below in a case involving the farm of Fontanas in 1256 and again in a letter of Nicholas III in 1278, the popes also inter-vened directly in the region of Toulouse to strengthen the attack on usury.[49] It was, in fact, the opinion of the popes that no authority could dispense from this fault save themselves and even privileged orders bowed to them in this regard. A letter of Gregory IX's received at Toulouse dated 1237 confirmed the privileges of the military orders, recalling that they could bury members and remit part of their penitence even when the town or region where they lived was under interdict. The members referred to were not so much the clerical brethren as the lay "collegae" who, as deathbed oblates, sought to be buried in the order's robes. Among such were surely

---

[48]Alphonse Blanc, *Livre de comptes de Jacme Olivier* 2: 333-344, published testi-mony collected at Toulouse for debtors and guarantors harmed by usury. Dated May 1255, the evidence was sent with this address: "Reverendo in Christo patri ac domino G [William I de la Broue], Dei gratia sancte Narbonensis ecclesie archiepiscopo, A[melius] ecclesie Sancti Stephani Tholose capellanus, salutem et reverentiam cum debita hobediencia et honore. Noverit vestra reverenda paternitas nos auctoritate vestra et mandato super quibusdam positionibus a Petro Sayseti factis testes recipisse, quorum depositiones sunt hec prout inferius continentur." The moneylenders are known. One was Arnold Raymond Boumer, the vernacular form of the name Bosmundus. See Saint-Bernard 138, fols. 167v-168 (May 1219) where "Bosmundus et Arnaldus Ramundus eius frater, filii Petri Ramundi Bovismundi," sold property to Pons de Capitedenario. His associate was Ptolemy of Portalli. In Saint-Sernin 599 (10 35 10) (November 1233), Maurand "vetus" owed 800 shillings to a Vital Geraldus, then defunct, a debt which Vital's son Raymond Geraldus, acting for himself and his brothers Berengar de Portali, Ptolemy ("Tolomeus") and Gerald, sold to Saint-Sernin. A Berengar de Portali was a petitioner for heretical inheritances in 1279 for which see my *Repression of Catharism*, p. 124. For the "capellanus" Amelius (de Favariis), see my "Parishes of Toulouse," pp. 191-192.

[49]Daurade 7, an original (dated March 1, 1278) with seal still appended: "Nicolaus episcopus servus servorum dei dilecto filio . . priori de Burgo Caturcensis diocesis salu-tem et apostolicam benedictionem. Conquestus est nobis . . prior prioratus Beate Marie de Aurate quod Attonus Riquier laicus Tholosane diocesis super terris, debitis, posses-sionibus et rebus aliis iniuriatur eidem; ideoque discretioni tue per apostolica scripta mandamus quatinus, partibus convocatis, audias causam et, appellatione remota, usuris cessantibus, debito fine decidas, faciens quod decreveris per censuram ecclesiasticam firmiter observari. Testes autem qui fuerint nominati si se gratie, odio vel timore sub-traxerint censura simili, appellatione cessante, compellas veritati testimonium perhibere. Datum Rome apud Sanctum Petrum, kalendis Martii, pontificatus nostri anno primo." The letter is signed on the "plica" "Sy. Ven.," identified by Gerd Nüske as Simon Vena-frenus (of Venafro), a papal scribe.

gift-bearing usurers hoping to give a relatively inexpensive protection to
the heirs of their accumulations as they were about to depart this life.
The exception to the pontiff's generous terms was that such penitents could
not have been personally excommunicated, named as interdicted or "manifest usurers."[50]

Preventive inspection strengthened enforcement. As ordered by canon
sixteen of the Council of Toulouse published in 1229, wills were to be
rendered in the presence of an appropriate clerk, especially a parish priest.
This grant to ecclesiastical police of a favored place at a decisive moment
in the lives of penitents was made obligatory by a constitution issued at the
same time by Count Raymond VII of Toulouse and Cardinal Roman ordering that notaries were not permitted to render testaments unless clergy
participated.[51] Although regular clergy also served as testamentary executors and counselors, "capellani" or parish priests frequently held these
positions in the early thirteenth century.[52] The high point of this penitential discipline was attained when the first specifically Toulousan manual of
business casuistry appeared around 1300. This was a compilation by an
otherwise unknown Dominican named Guy called the *Rule of Merchants*
dealing with usury and related topics. Guy's tract had been culled from the
large *Summa of Confessors* written by the better known Dominican John of
Fribourg around 1290 and the compiler's intention was to instruct Toulousan businessmen and workers by means of examples to understand and obey
the law on usury.[53]

---

[50]Gregory IX's letter (March 21, 1237) is copied in Malta 6 51. Individuals who "in
eorum sancta fraternitate statuerit se collegam" can be buried "si tamen nec excommuni-
catus nec nominatim fuerit interdictus aut etiam usurarius manifestus."

[51]Mansi, *Sacrorum conciliorum nova et amplissima collectio* 23: 198, and Catel,
Histoire des comtes de Tolose, pp. 352-353. The pertinent passages from these texts are
discussed and presented in my "Parishes of Toulouse," pp. 184-185.

[52]In the testaments calendared in Appendix 8, the executors or counselors who were
not "capellani" were a monk of Grandselve in No. 3 (dated 1166), Hospitalers in No.
279 (dated 1208), the abbot of Saint-Sernin in No. 36 (dated 1216), the abbots of Saint-
Sernin and Grandselve in No. 51 (dated 1229), a "capellanus" assisted by two Dominicans and two Franciscans in No. 60 (dated 1234), the abbot of the Cistercian house of
Feuillans in No. 64 (dated 1235) and the abbot of Grandselve and a Dominican in No.
86 (dated 1256). "Capellani" initially served merely as witnesses in Nos. 2 (dated 1164),
4 (dated 1168), 11 (dated 1191) and 24 (dated 1202), and as executors in Nos. 29 (dated
1209), 35 (dated 1215), 40 (dated 1217), 49 (dated 1228), 50 (dated 1228), 53 (dated
1230), 58 (dated 1233), 60 (dated 1234) (along with four friars as seen above), 70 (dated
1240), 75 (dated 1245), 78 (dated 1247) and 91 (dated 1259).

[53]For this source, see Michaud-Quantin, "Textes penitentiels Languedociens au XIIIe
siècle," *Cahiers de Fanjeaux* 6 (1971) 160-161.

Church law was generally accepted in local secular courts. Suits before the consuls of Toulouse and their appointed "curia jurata" frequently adverted to the prohibition of usury. In 1225 a consular "curia jurata" found for two creditors against a widow for a debt owed by her deceased husband, but obliged them to swear that they had gained "neither lucre or usury from the debt."[54] Three years later a similar court awarded a creditor what he asked for, but added that, if he had given the debtors less than was stated and had collected "lucre or usuries," the court would see that the debtors were compensated.[55] One wonders how effective such reservations were, but some evidence exists that the avoidance of usury and restitution for it were realities that the business community had to take seriously. In 1241 the consuls had awarded a plaintiff a stiff fine because of a criminal assault. The defendant having failed to appear, they appointed a "curia jurata" to enforce their judgment and find the money for the award.[56] Knowing that the defendant's maternal grandfather had made testamentary restitution for usury, the court determined to draw on that to pay the fine, but also insisted that the claims of those who had suffered usury, if such there were, were also to be paid.[57] In 1228 a civil court condemning a debtor expressly exempted his right to sue his creditor for usury.[58]

The reader may have noted that the cases mentioned in the preceding paragraph all record victories of creditors over debtors and might therefore think that there is more to the matter than meets the eye. In support of this feeling is the fact that the consuls, or individuals on that board, sometimes

---

[54]TAM, II 45 (March 1225): the creditors of Bonafos Bertrand de Pozano and his brother were each obliged to swear that "inde aliquid non habuerit pro persolutione nec lucrum nec usuram non habebat ... ."

[55]TAM, AA 6 131 (March 1228): "si ... minusfalliebant pro persolutionibus vel solutionibus vel etiam pro lucris vel usuris que inde essent date vel facte ... Poncius Vasco teneatur eis [debtors] illud minusfalliamentum reddere et refficere ratione fori ... ."

[56]Malta 21 15 (March 1241) where John Vasco claimed before a consular "curia jurata" 100 shillings and damages from Raymond Capella "pro quodam vulnere et dampno et contumeliis" visited on him.

[57]Raymond Capella's grandfather's testament was cited as follows: "Bernardus Brunetus disposuerat .d.v. sol. tol. ut redderentur suis conquerentibus pro usura quos .d.v. sol. Bernardus Brunetus habebat tempore mortis sue, et residuum bonorum suorum exceptis .c. sol. tol., videlicet omnia sua bona, relinquerat dicto Ramundo Capelle et matri sue nomine Englesie, filie ipsius Bernardi Bruneti; sub tali vero conditione eis ipse Bernardus Brunetus relinquerat sua bona ut si dicti .d.v. non sufficierint in reddendis usuris suis conquerentibus quod alia eius bona distribuerentur conquerentibus donec esset inde omnibus satisfactum."

[58]See above note 55.

dragged their feet when questions of usury arose. Examples are the consuls Raymond Caraborda and William Durandi, who gave testimony to be sent to the archiepiscopal court at Narbonne in 1255, and who had not only decided an earlier case in favor of the creditors involved but also fined the guarantor of the debt. Astonishingly, these worthies stated that they knew little about the case.[59] Again, one of the public notaries in the service of the consuls at the time they decided in favor of the creditors was asked whether or not the original transaction was usurious. Curiously succinct, he said he did not know, "but nevertheless believed that there was a little bit of usury."[60] And the suit before the consuls concerned a "mutuum" involving compound interest, a loan made about five years before the witnesses were being interviewed! All of the witnesses, furthermore, agreed that the two creditors were well-known usurers, one saying that this had been their reputation for fifteen years or more.[61]

What, as much as possible, exerted pressure on the consuls was that, as seen above, the ecclesiastical courts breathed down their necks. The case involving the coy municipal officers seen in the paragraph above was clearly an appeal to the archbishop of Narbonne or his courts against a consular decision. There is no doubt, also, that the consuls were obliged to act in concert with the judge or "officialis" of the episcopal court in regard to usury. What seem to be draft notes for consular legislation in the mid-century contain a provision prohibiting citizens who had an apostolic rescript or other ecclesiastical censure in hand from citing other citizens to attend a court outside of Toulouse.[62] Were they to do so, plaintiffs were to refund the defendants' losses and expenses "unless [the latter were] usurers." If in that unhappy category, they should act "on the advice of the consuls and of the "officialis" of Toulouse."[63]

[59]Blanc, *Livre de comptes de Jacme Olivier* 2: 333-344, witnesses nos. 4 and 19. Raymond Caraborda may have been the one of that name mentioned in my *Repression of Catharism*, pp. 171-172.

[60]Ibid.: William Durandi was witness No. 5: "tamen bene credit quod ibi esset aliquantulum de usura."

[61]Ibid: one of the two guarantors or "fideiussores" of Peter Sayseti's debt was Hugh d'Endura, who was also a witness (No. 12) and the other was a priest. Hugh remarked that the consuls had forced the debtor to pay the creditors, and his testimony was confirmed by Vital Durandus, witness No. 19, a consul at the time of the trial, and by Vital Catalanus (No. 20), a "nuncius" of the consuls who enforced their judgment on d'Endura.

[62]TAM, II 70, undated notes. By the look of the hand and the spelling of "Tolosa" (without the "h"), these notes probably derive from around or before the midcentury mark.

[63]Passages from ibid. state that plaintiffs "teneantur resarcire dampna, missiones et expensas que citatus passus fuerit cognitione consulum nisi fuerint usurarii manifesti;" if so, they are to act "de consilio consulum et officialis Tolose."

In fine, reservations aside, the business ethos at Toulouse had not only changed, but had changed irreversibly. Once creditors had more or less had a free hand, largely answerable only to courts staffed by themselves or their friends. Now, ecclesiastics had invaded their economic freedom and policed their activities.

11

Reception of the Law on Usury

A. Casuistry

The age of business casuistry, if one may call it so, had dawned at Toulouse, and had dawned suddenly. A contract written before the time of Bishop Fulk pretty much told a reader what it was about; after Fulk, a long second look was required to find out not what it said, but instead what it meant. The effects of this program on the provision of credit are hard to discern.

As often happens with what passes for moral legislation, it certainly encouraged Toulousan businessfolk to be secretive or canny. Since much of their wealth had been derived from mortgage service payments and loaned money, they protected themselves against possible loss because of past usury.[1] Even very careful or devout creditors played games with the new rules. Pons de Capitedenario gave a loan of 200 shillings without stated term of payment to one of his partners in the Ascii family, stipulating that the debtor was to donate two pennies daily to a woman until the debt was repaid.[2] Although clearly usurious, this playful (?) loan was not to be condemned according to some who, like the Parisian teacher Peter Cantor (d. 1197), emphasized intention or motive and hence distinguished between moneylending "pro humanitate" as against "pro solo lucro."[3] Besides, just

---

[1]In Malta 5 252 ii (February 1209 copied in 1230), substantial properties involving "pignora" to the east and south of the town were alienated to the brothers Bernard Raymond and Peter de Tolosa in a charter that added to the usual guarantees against lawsuits, etc. whatever the sellers had there "ratione vel occasione usure sive ullo alio modo."

[2]E 508 (September 1213): "une domine cotidie pro suis necessariis dum predictos denarios tenuerit," amounting to about 30.4 percent annually.

[3]In his *Summa de sacramentis et animae consiliis* 3 2 a *Liber casuum conscientiae* 3 ("de usura") (ed. Dugauquier 3: 182, paragraph 213), Peter asks the question: "Si mutuum tibi decem ut des inde pauperibus aliquibus elemosinam, et postea reddas michi summam, ecce hic aliquid accrevit sorti non michi, sed alii. Estne usura?" The answer is "No!"

as was the case with the abolition of the "pignus," people used "pro anima" giving to the church to avoid the usury sanction. In return for clearing a mortgage from the brethrens' land, a Bernard de Gavalduno and his mother and two sisters received two and a half arpents of vineyard in "commendatio" for life from the Hospitalers. For this investment "pro anima," Bernard received twelve percent annually.[4]

Liberal or laxist opinion such as that of the Chanter and likewise practices such as the above were rejected by the majority of the doctors and many local clergy. That the clerical attack made Toulousan businessfolk highly sensitive is easy to show. Trips to Rome involved expensive travel and equally costly judicial decisions by the court, most of them financed by Italian merchant bankers there assembled.[5] It is both entertaining and significant that one of the few times Toulousans could bring themselves to talk frankly of usury in the age of enforced casuistry was when they described the debts incurred by visits to the Roman "curia."

It is also sure that the new clerical law was resisted. Periods of relative quiet in the pursuit of usury, for example, invite a careful second look. Oddly, one such time accompanied the crusader Simon de Montfort's occupation of the town from March 1216 to September 1217 when his courts of collaborators, as such people are called since the days of German National Socialism, not only continued the practice of confiscating and selling debtors' property in order to pay off creditors, but also included several important moneylenders, namely Pons de Capitedenario and Peter Grivus de Roaxio.[6] To conquer is one thing perhaps; to govern another. But financing his campaigns during the early days of the crusade had involved Simon de Montfort with a financier from Montpellier named Raymond de

---

[4]Malta 58 2 (February 1195): clearing the title: "Item Bernardus ... pro ista predicta venditione fecit de caritate de .d. sol. tol. qui fuerunt paccati Arnaldo Barravi." The return: "Item de unoquoque anno faciebant [the vineyards] de lucro .lx. sol. tol."

[5]See Saint-Bernard 4 (November 1320) where the cellarer of Grandselve alienated property for sixty-five shillings which he "asseruit se fore conversos in utilitatem dicti monasterii et pro relevatione eiusdem et in debitorum usurariorum solutionem faciendam videlicet quibusdam creditoribus usurariis quibus dictum monasterium camere domini nostri pape fuerat obligatum et quibusdam aliis creditoribus in curia romana ... ." It is not known to whom the Cistercians were in debt, but a charter of the Hospitalers records a famous name. Malta 118 343 (March 1327) has the prior raising money to go "ad socios societatis Bardorum de Florencia et quosdam alios creditores dicti prioratus ... in curia romana ... ." These are special cases having to do with the "curia." Note an earlier case of the same involving the abbot of the monastery of Lézat going to Rome in the twelve-fifties in my *Men and Women*, pp. 200-201.

[6]See my *Repression of Catharism*, pp. 158-159 and 159-160.

Salvanhac.[7] Raymond's loans were repaid by the plunder of Lavaur when it was taken in 1211 and in the next year of Pézenas and Torves.[8] Later on, Genoese bankers as well as the Templars and other papal financial agents helped out and none of these gave service for nothing. The "potestas" of Genoa intervened in 1237 with the preceptor of the Temple in Montpellier, for example, to settle the unpaid debts Guy de Montfort, Simon de Montfort's brother and companion in the crusade, owed to a consortium of Genoese bankers.[9]

Besides, usury continued, being practiced not only by laymen but also by clerical institutions. An example of this is seen in a charter dated 1256 dealing with the farm or "bovaria" of Fontanas. This document reports that the abbot of Saint-Sernin and a layman named Bernard de Barreggiis had agreed to share all expenses caused by an appeal against them to Pope Innocent IV for reason of usury by their debtor, Walter Raimundus. The pope had assigned the case for settlement to the prior of the Daurade monastery in Toulouse. Although the result of this case is not known, it is evident from other evidence that the plaintiff was not able to prevent Saint-Sernin and the Barreggiis from garnering the lion's share of the farm of Fontanas.[10] One may perhaps conclude that, as constituted at that time, society required lending for profit, which, when forbidden, continued in disguised forms.

Lastly, the enforcement of law, especially law that is well-nigh impossible to obey, leads to all sorts of problems. Toulouse's parishioners, it has been seen, were obliged by the legislation of 1229 to make testamentary restitution and, furthermore, their wills were to be witnessed by the parish clergy. These laws led to new conflicts between the clergy and the people.

---

[7]On Raymond, a Cahorcin by origin, see chapter 72 of the *Canso*, ed. Martin-Chabot, 1: 174-175: "Ramon de Salvanhac, .i. riche merchaant / Que fo natz de Caorts, ric borzes e manant; / Lo coms de Montfort l'i deu l'aver fer e gran. / Cel mantè la crozada, que li prestá l'argiant, / e pois pres ni en paga draps et vi e fromant: / tot l'aver de Lava[u]r li mes om dedenant."

[8]Denholm-Young, "The Merchants of Cahors," *Medievalia et Humanistica* 4 (1946) 38, where he notes this information. To this add *HGL* 8: No. 157 (dated 1212) and Albe, *Inventaire raisonné des archives municipales de Cahors*, p. 9.

[9]The late Robert Reynolds of the University of Wisconsin in Madison sent me the transcription of this Genoese act in the Archivio di stato, Archivio notarile, Register of Januinus de Predono, volume 1, fol. 168r. Entered by the hand of Palodinus de Sesto, the act is dated March 18, 1237. The consortium consisted of the well-known Genoese businessmen William Niger Embriacus, his brother Hugh and two Scoti brothers, William and Lanfranc.

[10]In my "Farm of Fontanas," pp. 29-40.

Restive under the rule of their rectors, the parishioners listed their protests in "gravamina" presented to their recently installed count, Alphonse of Poitiers, in the early twelve-fifties.[11] Among their protests was a complaint against Raymond de Ferrariis, rector of the Daurade church, concerning usury. According to the charge, the rector had pocketed a restitution of twenty or more shillings made by a woman named Bona instead of distributing it.[12]

A final difficulty is that businessfolk clearly favored restoring what the clergy and public opinion called "ill-gotten gains" by means of setting aside a lump sum for "conquerentes" and by giving bequests to specific persons without mentioning usury or other violence wreaked on them.[13] The weakness of restitution to specific people was that, if conscientiously done, it was time consuming, possibly ruinous and certainly embarrassing to the usurer's family. Of the sixteen sure testamentary restitutions in the calendar of wills published below, only one named specific beneficiaries.[14] The advantage of lump sums to a usurer's heirs was that onetime debtors were obliged to prove their right to the decedent's executors and to the clergy participating or remembered in the will. Executors, especially relatives or beneficiaries, were naturally slow to surrender the property of the deceased, and clerical ones were surely sorely tempted to favor the charity given their institutions.[15] Testators were aware of this problem, and one of them tried to get around it by providing that claimants who took oath

[11]PAN, J 318 78 (after June 1251 and before June 1255) published in *Layettes du Trésor* 2: 306-309, No. 2428. For the dating of this act, see my *Men and Women*, p. 19, n. 39.

[12]In PAN, J 307a the testator had ordered restitution to three persons. When her executor "Bernardus Vitalis pro ipsa domina Bona promisisset et fidejussisset dictam usuram persolvere et illud gratis postmodum vellet facere, dictus capellanus dictos denarios accepit et postea illos nec aliquid ex eis reddidit nec reddere voluit."

[13]The appropriate passages are in Appendix 8, Nos. 72 (dated 1243) and 98 (dated 1277). Some testators hid it almost altogether, for example, No. 64 (June 1235), for a possible case.

[14]Appendix 8, Nos. 3, 27, 34, 36, 45, 51, 56, 62, 68, 72, 80, 95 and 98-101. The exceptional example is No. 98 (May 1277) where Peter Raymond Descalquenquis gave restitution to four named debtors or their heirs and then provided for additional claimants who might turn up.

[15]The persons in charge of restitution in the sixteen testaments were usually heirs, family members and/or clergy. Note, for example, that in Appendix 8, No. 45 (dated 1220) Stephen Astro assigned that duty to his widow, and in ibid., No. 62 (dated 1235) Hugh Johannes entrusted it to his sons and heirs.

were to be believed without further proof.[16] Another decedent insisted "that restitution should be made to complainants from whom I appear to have extorted something not due me as long as they appear within three years after my death and do this easily and without any judicial contest."[17] Still, these fine sentiments are not all that impressive. The first testator limited all charity including restitution to the modest sum of 200 shillings and the second had no children anyway.

In spite of the problems posed by covert usury, even today some believe that the poor are helped by its excision. Contemporary Muslim and Orthodox Jewish laws still condemn usury, as a breach of brotherhood. Although one cannot surely know about economic effects, it is doubtful that prohibitions of this kind achieve their objectives. Areas where usury has been forbidden in modern times, Muslim lands like Bengal, for example, have suffered widespread near servitude for debt. Furthermore, medieval businessmen may have had to employ costly subterfuges such as the letter of exchange to get around the law on usury, thus increasing the cost of capital.[18] Lastly, it seems that, although the prohibition was still very much alive, western Europeans were clearly worried about its effect. In the fifteenth century the "mons pietatis," not wholly successfully, was created to help modest people get credit on easy terms.

Oddly, in spite of the prohibition of usury, neither at Toulouse nor elsewhere did the church's attack visibly impede economic growth. Few can doubt that, around 1300, after a century of ecclesiastical pressure, business in the Midi was more mature and developed than it had been in 1200. The emergence of investment or deposit contracts and of many forms of the partnership or "societas" is the primary indication of this expansion. In addition, the gradual replacement of the "pignus" by the "census," and that of the forthright "mutuum" by contracts involving penal interest are other evidence of the same. The evidence for Toulouse is slight because of the poor preservation of private documents in the thirteenth century, and the position taken here largely depends on analogies drawn from the well-known economic history of Italy and the study of Perpignan by Richard Emery cited earlier in these pages. Trace evidence of improvement is nevertheless seen even at Toulouse, as, for example, the matter of "interesse" touched on in the previous chapter and the emergence of specialized deposit

---

[16]Appendix 8, No. 98 (dated 1277).

[17]Appendix 8, No. 99 (dated 1278) by a wealthy notary named Paul.

[18]This position reflects Raymond de Roover's well-known conjecture that the letter of exchange evolved partly to sidestep the prohibition of usury.

and "gazalha" contracts.[19] To these local advances may be added the influence of foreign, especially Italian, business techniques, deposit and merchant-bankers associated with urban republics, the papacy and crowned heads. These new means of mobilizing capital exemplify new ways of providing credit. Might the argument therefore be turned upside-down to assert instead that the churchmen's attack on usury had actively aided the growth of trade and business? "Objectively," as Marxists once loved to say, had the clergy subvented entrepreneurs?

Although what would have happened had the attack not taken place cannot be known, it must be confessed that, insofar as they were conscious of the possible effects of the law they were adumbrating, the clergy and their allies among the people evinced no love of individual enterprise, of the accumulation of capital or of investment mechanisms. In spite of the fact that churchmen were often acute observers of the economic scene, investment partnerships, for example, were treated in canon law in ways that demonstrate a monumental indifference to the needs of businessmen. A well-known example is the loose or mistaken phrasing of Gregory IX's *Naviganti* of 1236 wherein a partner's assumption of risk was said not to justify a share of the profits.[20] Although this kind of insurance and credit contract is not to be seen in the charters from Toulouse, it is self-evident that an economy based on the private ownership of land and of other means of production could not exist without loans and that loans require compensation for their providers.

To turn to the "pignus," it may have been that it was detrimental in yet another way, one that far transcended the fact that moralizers found it usurious. With it, it has been said, debtors risked losing pledged real property precisely at a time when population was growing and land was becoming ever more rare and expensive. This point will be argued at length below but, for the moment, it is worth noting that the "pignus" differed only formally from the "census" or "rente" that replaced it, because a "census" was a sale and not a loan like the other contract. From a purely legal and rational viewpoint, then, the condemnation of such widespread contractual forms as the "mutuum" and the "pignus" is difficult to explain.

Lastly, to call medieval lenders and entrepreneurs "usurers" beclouds the issue because it borrows far too heavily from the language of the rigorist clergy and of their allies among the people. Although serving to remind

[19]On the latter, see Appendix 7.
[20]X. 19 19: "Naviganti vel eunti ad nundinas certam mutuans pecuniae quantitatem, pro eo, quod suscipit in se periculum, recepturus aliquid ultra sortem, usurarius est censendus."

today's rich and powerful (not to speak of their humbler imitators fighting for what they believe is *their* place in the sun) that their actions often wound human brotherhood severely and that they owe more in restitution than occasional philanthropy, it caricatures reality because it leaves the impression that usurers were wholly exceptional people. From what can be seen at Toulouse and elsewhere, almost everyone in business, high or low, practiced usury before the application of the canons in the period discussed above. Although the proposition cannot be proved from the exiguous materials available in thirteenth century Toulouse, it is known that, after the application of the law against usury, moneylending, although veiled by the casuistry of the teaching on intention, was a daily business in the rural Toulousain and its towns. In the town of Foix and the nearby villages around 1325 not only did Toulousan credit providers work the region, but also, just as they did for education, people from these foothills of the Pyrenees mountains went to Toulouse to bank and do business.[21]

B. The Crusade and Heresy

Other questions are raised by the prohibition of usury and among these is why clerical law was received at Toulouse with such harsh rapidity. Part of the answer has to do with the institution and idea of a holy war. To review the issuance of church law on usury once again, the really practical legislation on this purported crime was elaborated in a specific period, namely, from the Gregorian age to the council of Vienne in 1311-1312. Much of this law expressed the desire to protect the crusade and was therefore designed to strengthen peace at home in order to make war abroad. The attack on Jewish moneylending, Christian usury and on the violence of the rural magnates was all part of this mobilization of the Christian republic to recuperate, to use the word contemporaries favored, once-Christian and once-Roman lands, or, to speak with candor, to subject neighboring Islamic and even Greek peoples.

In the late twelfth century, however, the crusades were faltering and the authorities were peering about within Latin Europe trying to point a finger at those obstructing them. Often doubting the validity of holy war, those criticizing the church or even favoring beliefs divergent from its newly promulgated orthodoxies were soon characterized as secessionists, heretics to be eradicated. Another enemy was the usurer whose business, it was thought, multiplied inordinately the cost of mounting crusading expeditions.

---

[21]See Pales-Gobilliard, *L'inquisiteur Geoffroy d'Ablis*, p. 380.

When Philip Augustus expressed annoyance at the vehement crusade preaching of the legate Robert of Curzon and especially his attack on usury, Pope Innocent III explained to the king in a letter of May 1214 that he had appointed this especially radical preacher because, "unless an efficacious medicine can be applied to the grave sickness of usury, the property of the church will not suffice to aid the Holy Land."[22] Bowing to all the complaints, the pope shortly dismissed Curzon and stilled a radical preaching that not only appealed to the poor, the sick and even to children but also infuriated the rich and noble in France. Once preached, however, the linkage of crusade, heresy and usury set the stage and, from 1214 on, Curzon's themes appear in the propaganda directed against the southern French.

Although the propaganda joining divergent religious thought and usury in a common condemnation was uniform, the experience of different areas threatened by the attack varied. To judge from rather sparse evidence, it seems that, where there was a relatively vigorous central state or monarchy, the canons on usury were quickly received or imitated, just as was the law on heresy. Because it was advantageous for them to have a stick to hold over their subject moneylenders, princes sold exemptions, just as the clergy sold dispensations. Or, sometimes, it was because it was financially and institutionally possible for a prince to entrust much of the lending function to a dependent minority, to Jews, for example, or foreigners like the Lombards. In substantial regions of northern Italy and southern France, where princely states were relatively ineffective and where urban republics had won great independence, however, the law was received more reluctantly. In both of these regions twelfth and early thirteenth century legal codes, notarial manuals and business practice show that church legislation on usury was being resisted, circumvented or was running into ingrained habits of economic individualism that braked its reception. Although Toulouse shared many of the qualities described above as typical of northern Italy and the Midi, it nevertheless suffered an attack whose speed and impetuosity had no parallel in other communities.

At other places, the reception was much slower. In nearby Perpignan in Catalan Roussillon, for example, Richard Emery's classic treatment has shown that the frank use of the word "usura" continued throughout this period.[23] At Marseille in Provence, according to Joseph Shatzmiller's

---

[22]Dickson, "Le cardinal Robert de Courson," *Archives d'histoire doctrinale et litteraire du moyen-âge* 9 (1934) 99: "... nisi tanto languori [of usury] adhiberetur efficax medicina, [facultates ecclesiarum] intendere non sufficerent ad subsidium terre sancte." The article treats the history of Robert's legation.

[23]*The Jews of Perpignan*, pp. 54 and 84ff.

detailed study, the clerical program on usury was only adopted in 1318, when threatened by the severe canon *Ex gravi* issued at the Council of Vienne.[24] A further contrast is that between the region of Languedoc, hit by the crusade, and northern Italy. Although even more lively in northern Italy, heresy was repressed there more gradually than in Languedoc because the greater Italian cities were needed by the popes as allies in their long combat with the Empire. As at Toulouse, Italian town authorities initially resisted the ecclesiastical inquisition. Again, as at Toulouse, this opposition began to collapse during the course of the twelve-thirties, but it is note-worthy that the Italians fought longer, especially the great maritime centers. Genoa delayed the introduction of inquisitors until 1256 and Venice until 1289.[25] Languedoc's towns, their capital Toulouse among them, were not so advantaged. Rome's initiative resulted in the Albigensian Crusade, the summons to which inadvertently touched off a northern French conquest of the Midi. And, once the northern French had begun to intervene, the political history of the Midi began to differ radically from that of Italy. The cities and little regional states of that peninsula gained freedom largely because of the struggle between the Empire and the papacy. In the Midi, the combination of the two powers of Rome and Paris destroyed both the independence of Languedoc and Toulouse's liberty.

The mechanism of this assault was the Albigensian Crusade, the first holy war of great magnitude since Gregorian days directed against an area where the majority of the population was Latin Christian. Being potentially both crusaders and those crusaded against, then, the inhabitants of Toulouse and its region were treated to a double dose of this medicine. The crusade propaganda and actions against usury and heresy fell on them at the same time as did the crusaders. In brief, then, when generously defined, the crusade may be called one reason why the church's law on usury was so rapidly received at Toulouse.

As seen above, the church thought to protect the crusade by abolishing usury and many churchmen in this period believed that usury flourished because divergent or secessionist belief did. They especially charged the Cathars with usury as well as religious deviation from orthodoxy. Otherwise very different, persons such as Joachim of Fiore (d. 1202) and the orthodox Waldensian Durand of Huesca (fl. 1180-1210) were sure Cathars

---

[24]*Shylock Reconsidered: Jews, Moneylending, and Medieval Society*, pp. 120-121: issued in 1311-1312, the canon was published as authoritative in 1317 and cited in a statute at Marseille in 1318.

[25]Borst, *Die Katharer*, pp. 130-131.

were usurers.[26] These polemical attitudes are typified by James of Vitry (d. 1240), the friend or associate of Bishop Fulk of Toulouse mentioned in the previous chapter. In fiery sermons, James excoriated town citizens for their sins, noting their lust for usury and their leaning toward heresy, implying that this was partly because heretical sectaries did not oblige them to make restitution.[27] In spite of the obvious polemic of this famed preacher, moreover, he had something there. Persons who question one set of beliefs or restraints are likely to question others and the same is true of dissident cults or religions.

The Cistercian historian and propagandist of the crusade, Peter de Vaux-de-Cernay, is another example. He remarked that "credentes" or ordinary believers did not have to follow the rigors of the "perfecti/-e" and, confident of salvation without penance and restitution, even on the deathbed, gave themselves up to usury and other crimes.[28] In spite of the obvious interest that Peter and clergy like him had in asserting this opinion, he may have been right. Unlike Catholics on whom the developing penitential system imposed heavy burdens, Cathar believers did not have to live the ascetic self-sacrifice practiced by their clergy. In the "consolamentum," the rite of conversion or sometimes of final reception on the deathbed, moreover, believers were not asked to confess their sins but rather to repeat the Lord's Prayer and expressly forgive those who had harmed them.[29] Difficulties could obviously multiply for a consoled penitent who recovered

[26]Thouzellier, "Polémiques autour de la notion de pauvreté spirituelle," *Etudes sur l'histoire de la pauvreté*, ed. Mollat, 1: 383-384.

[27]*Sermo ad cives et burgenses* in Giry, *Documents sur les relations de la royauté avec les villes de France* citing from BN MS lat. 17509, fol. 112v and ibid., 3284, fol. 146v: "Quod vix invenitur aliqua communitas in qua non sunt fautores, receptatores, defensores vel credentes hereticorum ... . Alii libenter eis credunt, quod rapinas, furta et usuras non jubent resitutere, sed per manus impositionem, absque aliqua satisfactione, salutem eis promittunt in morte .... ."

[28]*Historia Albigensis*, ed. Guébin and Lyon, 1: 15 "... credentes hereticorum dediti erant usuris, rapinis ... ; isti quidem ideo securius et effrenatius peccabant, quia credebant sine restitutione ablatorum sine confessione et penitentia, se esse salvandos, dummodo in supremo mortis articulo 'Pater noster' dicere et manuum impositionem a magistris suis recipere potuissent."

[29]Pales-Gobilliard, *L'inquisiteur Geoffroy d'Ablis*, pp. 126 and 276. The first incident records a deathbed reception where the "credens" and the "perfectus" join hands, pray, and the latter says: "Tu debes parcere omni homini et ego parco tibi et remitto omnia peccata tua, ex parte Dei, a quo habeo plenariam potestatem." A second case records the heretication of a dying man: "Tunc dictus hereticus dixit dicto infirmo quod parceret omni homini et omni persone que sibi dixerat vel fecerat malum et dictus infirmus totum concessit dicto heretico."

from what had seemed to be a mortal illness, but Cathar penitence generally
rested more lightly on its believers than did Catholic. Because of their lack
of economic censoriousness, René Nelli, apparently wishing to congratulate
them, has even asserted that, had they triumphed, the Cathars might well
have begun to introduce "bourgeois capitalism"![30]
     Although Cathars may have had advantages over Waldensians and simi-
lar cultists, Waldensian usurers or moneylenders surely existed. To use an
analogy, both the French Huguenots and English Quakers were later famed
for banking, that is, for usury. Waldensians in this very period were
charged with that offense by the Cistercian Caesarius of Heisterbach who
reported that rich usurers at Metz adhered to this faith.[31] Occasional
usurers aside, the desire of the members of this religion to imitate here on
earth the life of the apostles and to experience apostolic poverty following
the prescriptions of the *Acts of the Apostles* clearly inhibited members who
hungered for wealth and power. Doubtless a similar impediment was placed
in the way of Cathar "perfecti" if they went beyond building the church and
sought personal advancement in the marketplace, but the difference between
the ordinary adherents to the two faiths is that the Waldensians, animated
by something close to the idea of a priesthood of all true believers, were
expected to live as virtuously (as they would have put it had they read
philosophy) as their leaders. As Peter of Vaux-de-Cernay both knew and
asserted, the same was not true of the Cathars.
     These conjectures sound reasonable, but do Toulouse's documents show
that usurers were Waldensians or Cathars? As to the former, a Toulousan
merchant named Bernard Raymond Baranonus resided at Bordeaux for a
time before returning home in the twelve-sixties and was there called on by
the inquisitors in 1274 to tell about his long-standing Waldensian connec-
tions. These dated back to 1224 and Bernard also owned a copy of the
famous anti-papal poem "D'un sirventès far" of Guillem Figuera. Like any
merchant, this member of a good family may have doubled as a usurer, but
the remaining evidence does not show it.[32] Some Toulousan moneylenders
were also Cathar believers.[33] I once conjectured that such usurers had
been converted before the attempt to repress both usury and heresy had

---

[30]*L'erotique des troubadours*, p. 236: "Si le Catharisme avait triumphé, il aurait sans
doute favorisé l'essor d'un premier capitalisme bourgeois."
     [31]*Dialogus miraculorum* 5 20, ed. Strange, 1: 301.
     [32]In my *Repression of Catharism*, pp. 134-135, and Dossat, "Les vaudois méridio-
naux d'après les documents de l'Inquisition," *Cahiers de Fanjeaux* 2 (1967) 207-226.
     [33]See Peter Sobaccus in my *Men and Women* pp. 185-187, Pons Palmata and Peter
de Roaxio in my *Repression of Catharism*, pp. 82-83 and 259-260.

developed. Intelligent and ambitious individuals, I thought, seem unlikely to have risked a double condemnation. But that is just what a religious mind might well do. They were not many, however. Even before Fulk's attack was launched, the two most successful businessmen recorded in Toulousan documents were unusually generous donors to the church. Pons David made the Hospitalers his principal heir and Pons de Capitedenario provided a positive bonanza for the Dominican mother house and other orders, only partly because his daughter and heiress had no issue. The significance of Pons' role in the church is evidenced by his contemporary William Pelisson, the Dominican inquisitor, who called him "dominus" when recording his gift to the early Dominicans, and also by the later Dominican inquisitor and historian Bernard Gui, who designated him "patron of the house" and "of the brethren," that is, of the Dominican order.[34] In short, to speak the language of the orthodox, profoundly Christian layfolk were usurers.

Even if inexact, however, the Catholic confusion of heresy with usury was efficacious because it enlisted popular support against heresy. Persons in rapidly expanding economies, like that of Toulouse in the late twelfth century, often suffer from indebtedness, a subject that attracted the attention of both the consuls and the count in this period. The link between usury and Catharism seemed real to the people of the time, but it is hard to know how that conviction was spawned or what it meant. Perhaps usury helped promote Catharism because debts probably caused some, well-to-do or plebeian, to question society's values and structures and therefore to lean for a time toward religious dissent. On the other hand, the vigorous attack on usury during this very period by Catholic authorities, an attack that had no counterpart among the Cathars, may have won back some, perhaps many, for orthodoxy.

Whatever the case, the introduction of the clerical law on usury twice coincided with social troubles at Toulouse. During the eleven-seventies and eighties both usury and heresy were condemned. At that time a partly foreign invasion and a reassertion of princely power were preceded and accompanied by evidences of turmoil or discontent among artisans and tradesmen and a struggle between the City and the Bourg. A patrician named Peter Maurand was condemned at Toulouse in 1178 and it is note-

---

[34]Pelisson, *Chronique*, ed. Duvernoy, p. 40, and Gui, *De fundatione et prioribus conventuum provinciarum Tolosanae et Provinciae*, ed. Amargier, p. 32 (in the *Tractatus fratris Guillelmi Pelisso*) where "dominus" Pons de Capitedenario, together with his wife and daughter, are credited with the founding gift "sicut patronus loci" and then later on p. 48 in his *Fundatio conventus Tholosani* where the donor is twice called the same.

worthy that the clergy and their lay allies believed his crimes to be those of both Catharism and usury.[35]

A similar period marked by social troubles, division between the City and Bourg and foreign intervention occurred at the start of the Crusade in 1209, repeating the turmoil of the eleven-seventies and eighties. Bishop Fulk took part in these troubles by creating an association called the White Confraternity to combat both heresy and usury and accorded its members the advantages granted crusaders.[36] Headed by scions of the town's older aristocracy and eliciting popular support, this confraternity set the City against the Bourg. The latter region responded by creating a Black Confraternity supporting the count. Until the crusaders assaulted Toulouse directly in 1211, the City's White Confraternity also actively aided the crusade, even with arms. Although Fulk and his supporters did not get far with heresy (that waited until after the defeat of the southerners and the Peace of Paris in 1229 when Cardinal Roman and the Dominicans jumped into the work), it won much popular support by harassing usurers, going so far as to provoke a rent strike against one of them, Pons David.[37]

To conclude, that there was a necessary relationship between heresy and usury as propagandized by the orthodox may not have been wholly true to real life, but it was undoubtedly efficacious in evoking popular support for the clerical cause at the time of the crusade.

C. MORAL RIGOR

The social troubles seen at Toulouse were also aspects of the rise of the trades and crafts affecting the whole of western Europe at this time. This movement stimulated moral rigorism, itself an aspect of a longing for social justice or equity and therefore for community and fraternity, a wish often

[35]See my "Noblesse et hérésie. Une famille cathare: Les Maurand," *Annales ESC* 29 (1974) 1211-1223, especially 1211 where the contemporary *Gesta regis Henrici secundi Benedicti abbatis*, Rolls Series 40 (1867): 219, notes that Peter was condemned to "usuras omnes quas acceperat reddere; damna pauperum quos afflixerat resarcire." For the Maurandi family history, see my *Repression of Catharism*, pp. 229-241.

[36]According to William of Puylaurens' *Chronica*, ed. Duvernoy, pp. 64-66, Bishop Fulk acted so "quod omnes ejus cives Tholosani ista que extraneis [crucesignatis] concedebatur indulgentia non carerent, utque per hanc devotionem eos ecclesie aggregaret, atque facilius per eos expugnaret hereticam pravitatem et fervorem extingueret usurarum ... optinuit Tholose magnam fieri confratriam, confratres omnes consignans Domino signo crucis .... ." For the general history, see my *Liberty and Political Power*, pp. 82-85.

[37]See the context in ibid., p. 83, with Published Document No. 14 (June 1213) on pp. 208-209.

evoked by, or that often provoked, utopian dreams. These ideas or ideals had always moved religious folk, but became positively effervescent among Latin Christians during the twelfth and thirteenth centuries when the church was raised to lead Europe. Linked to the many attempts of monks, friars and associated lay groups to restore the "vita apostolica" or to build an earthly paradise "ad instar Jerusalem," the idea of brotherhood was part of the "mise en scène" of the medieval assault on usury. Robert of Curzon, a prelate whose relationship to Fulk of Toulouse has been mentioned above, was an enthusiastic utopian and tried to express his belief in his legatine mission in France from 1213 to 1216. Lamenting the failure of the crusades, the threatened secession of dissenters from the church and the dearth of true charity, Robert cast about for a way to recall man to his duty and rebuild the world. It seemed to him that a start on this program could be made in a general council of all bishops and princes under the leadership of the pope. There, sanctions were to be levied on resisters, all were to eat only the bread earned by their own mental and bodily labor and all were prohibited from profiting from another's work.[38]

Were that teaching promulgated and enforced, Curzon thought, usurers, heretics and robbers would vanish, charity and the church would flourish and all things would again be brought back to their pristine state.[39] The pristine state is that of the *Acts of the Apostles* 4 32-35, the widely commented on passage to the effect that no member of the original community had his own property, "but all was in common among them" and that each contributed to the community according to his means, placing his gains before the feet of the apostles whence "it was divided to each according to need."[40] In brief, although Curzon's utopian hopes failed to find expression in France during his legation and found no place among the canons issued by the Fourth Lateran Council of 1215, it is sure that a longing for equality, fraternity and the "vita apostolica" constituted a foundation for the moral rigorism of the time. Still, one wonders if even this required the outright abolition of the "mutuum" and "pignus." Surely, since even Cur-

---

[38]The section "de usura" of Robert's penitential "summa" was published in "Le traité 'de usura' de Robert de Courçon," ed. Lefèvre, *Travaux et mémoires de l'Université de Lille* 10 (1902) 35: "ut unusquisque panem suum, id est sui laboris, manducaret, sicut praecepit apostolus [2 Thessalonians 3 10-12], et ne aliqui essent curiosi aut otiosi inter nos."

[39]Ibid.: "Et sic tollerentur omnes foeneratores et seditiosi et raptores, et sic possent fieri eleemosyniae et fabrica ecclesiarum, et omnia sic reducerentur ad pristinum statum."

[40]Acts: "sed erant illis omnia communia," and "dividebatur autem singulis, prout cuique opus erat."

zon did not advocate distributing property to level private wealth or abolish it, intelligent regulation would have been more useful than the impossibility of outright abolition.

Along with an express ideal of brotherhood, however, a touch of fratricide was probably also found in the minds of the rigorists. One believes, rightly I think, that although basic solidarity is always required for social life, each social order exercising a particular duty looks on the performance of others with the eye of denigration. Certainly, tension and conflict marked the relationship of social groups in the middle ages just as today. To speak only of one party to these conflicts, censoriousness toward other social orders by the clergy was exacerbated when, in and after the Gregorian age, the church was raised up to rule Europe, trying not only to channel her wars into the crusade, Hostiensis' "bellum Romanum," but also to police her marketplaces. Other than princes, those most severely criticized were the two most active elements of lay society, the gentleman and the trader, ie. the soldier and the businessman.

To deal here with the latter only, the merchant's function and due remuneration were naturally never condemned; indeed, they were often lauded. To do otherwise would have destroyed society and, besides, a laborer is worthy of his hire. On the other hand, this recognition was vitiated by a rigorism that found the practitioners of the trader's profession almost beyond hope of salvation. Transmitted to posterity by such widely read compilations as Gratian's *Decretum* and Peter Lombard's *Sentences*, a passage from a canon of the Roman synod of 1078 conveys the censorious tone of this message. It states that a soldier, businessman or one given over to any function that cannot "be exercised without sin" may not perform a penance sufficient to enable him to enter heaven unless he gives up his profession and restores what he has unjustly taken.[41] Derived from an ancient theme, this law or recommendation censured businessmen in the market place and the military, in short, those who dominated the productive

---

[41]Gratian's D. 5 de poen. 6 (Friedberg 1: 1241), Gregory's *Registri VI* 5b in Jaffé, ed., *Bibliotheca rerum Germanicarum: Monumenta Gregoriana* 2: 333-334, and the Lombard's *Sententiae in IV libris distinctae* 4 16 88 (3) in 1: 339-340. Friedberg's version reads: "Falsas penitentias dicimus, que non secundum auctoritatem sanctorum patrum pro qualitate criminum imponuntur. Ideoque miles, vel negotiator, vel alicui offitio deditus, quod sine peccato exerceri non possit, si culpis gravioribus irretitus ad penitenciam venerit, vel qui bona alterius iniuste detinet, vel qui odium in corde gerit, recognoscat, se veram penitenciam non posse peragere, per quam ad eternam vitam valeat pervenire, nisi negotium relinquat, vel offitium deserat, et odium ex corde dimittat, bona quidem que iniuste abstulit, restituat, arma deponat, ulteriusque non ferat, nisi consilio religiosorum episcoporum pro defendenda iusticia."

workers or led the active life of secular society.[42] This sentiment was, in fact, an egregious expression of the moral usury that the socially supervisory or religious person or order customarily exacts from the rest of the world's inhabitants. The saving grace of the papal text was that it closed with a significant caveat on which a whole system of casuistry and dispensations could be, and was, built.[43]

Although the impulse toward moralizing rigorism is present in every society, its incidence or intensity is related to immediate circumstance. One suspects that the clergy could not do without it in this period. One reason for this has been mentioned above: rigorists were the natural allies of utopians. Another was that this expression of rigorism was partly functional. The financial basis of the cult was changing because of the moralizing impulses revived during the Gregorian age. Before that time, princes had both exploited and looked after their profitable state churches. They had also, as evidenced in 1143 by a royal French privilege to the burghers of Tours, protected usurers in return for cash.[44] At that time also, it had never seemed harmful that monasteries were rich or that entry to the secular and regular clergy was partly acquired by gifts or purchase. Churchfolk, especially monks, had also been busy in credit operations, sharing with well-to-do layfolk the profits derived from mortgage and other loans. As has been seen in the previous chapter about twelfth century papal law and as can be seen in regard to monastic finance, the dialectic of Gregorian reformism destroyed these easy admissibilities.[45] To rule the world, the church had to be nearly perfect: the utopian urges of what was thought to be the Christian spirit consequently gradually affected its financial structure.

---

[42]An earlier version of Gregory's statement is found in *Sancti Gregorii magni XL homiliarum in evangelia* 2 24 1 in PL 76: 1184: "Sunt enim pleraque negotia, quae sine peccatis exhiberi aut vix aut nullatenus possunt." The earlier pontiff, however, did not speak about soldiers and merely contrasted the virtue of those who produce things for human consumption with the vice of tax collectors and dealers in money or business.

[43]Friedberg as above: "Ne tamen desperet, interim quicquid boni facere poterit hortamur ut faciat, ut omnipotens Deus cor illius illustret ad penitenciam."

[44]In Giry, *Les Etablissements de Rouen* 1: 190: "... burgensibus nostris beati Martini de castro novo ... concessimus, quod neque nos nec aliquis successorum nostrorum ... ab eis pecuniam queramus nec causabimus eos de usura neque de turpi lucro neque de aliqua multiplicatione pecunie sue .... Facta vero hac conventione predicti burgenses bona nobis voluntate dederunt xxx milia solidorum."

[45]Curzon and others including popes were much agitated by this behaviour of the regular clergy, for which see Lynch, *Simoniacal Entry into Religious Life from 1000 to 1260: A Social, Economic and Legal Study*, especially pp. 200-201.

The period of transition began in the later eleventh century and continued during much of the twelfth. Happily for the church, it was a time when the clergy, and especially the newly endowed monastic orders, were in the position of promoting and profiting from the founding of new villages and towns and the settlement of virgin lands. Traditional purchase of office and entry to ecclesiastical institutions was gradually veiled, becoming a customary, even laudable, gift: testaments of both the rich and modest show that entry into an order required an endowment of property or cash, a wardrobe and payment for a celebratory dinner.[46] However gradually, moreover, mortgage loans were given up, although as noted above they were accorded a half-life for a time in order to recuperate tithes presumably lost to the church in this and earlier ages of turmoil and war. Limited though these improvements were, ecclesiastical moral rigor was driving churchmen out of the land market and commerce.

Again, the recuperation of tithes that had suited the alliance of the wealthy and the church in the age of the Gregorians eventually ran into increasing opposition. This has been the subject of some polemic, some having argued that the rural nobility were hostile to these taxes and fortified their resistance by means of divergent belief.[47] In Toulouse's urban and mercantile patriciate, some of the well-to-do from families that undoubtedly leaned toward Catharism fought the church over this issue.[48] Even those wholly orthodox like the Astro family and Pons de Capitedenario seem to have profited and perhaps even profiteered from clerical tithes.[49] The opposition to this kind of taxation, moreover, was more general than that of a few wealthy folk because, even when orthodoxy triumphed after the Albigensian war and the ecclesiastical inquisition was

[46]See Appendix 8, Nos. 27 (January 1208, a wealthy testator), 31 (July 1216, a baker placing a son in the Daurade), 45 (March 1220, a rich person placing a daughter in Lespinasse), 61 (April 1235, a modest endowment for a niece to enter either a monastery or marriage) and 62 (May 1235, a rich man placing a daughter in a nunnery for 200 shillings – or allowing her to be married with 1000 shillings – and a son as a canon of Saint-Étienne for 300 shillings "sine plure"). Note that entry banquets required more financing than the contributions of those entering the house, for which see Peter de Yspania in Appendix 1, No. 16.

[47]An argument stated by both medieval and modern persons from Bernard of Clairvaux's secretary Geoffrey of Auxerre through Elie Griffe, *Les débuts de l'aventure cathare en Languedoc 1140-1190*, p. 172.

[48]A member of the Castronovo family, the knight Raymond Garsias, was in conflict with Saint-Étienne over the tithes of Braqueville and Balma, for which see my *Repression of Catharism*, pp. 179-180, and John Curtasolea in ibid., p. 196.

[49]Ibid., p. 162 on Pons, and, for the Astro, my *Men and Women*, pp. 173-183.

enjoying its greatest successes, Toulouse's townsfolk fought their parish clergy to a standstill over the attempt to extend the tithe to things other than crops produced on the land.[50] And much the same hostility toward tithes was later seen among the farming population in the Pyrenean piedmont near Montaillou.[51] In these circumstances, the economic position of the church was that of a rentier, a weak position in a growing economy. The church, in short, needed other sources of revenue.

Radical minds might well imagine that churchfolk should have answered their need by laboring in the world. Easier said than done, however. Save in exceptional cases, legal and scribal services had fallen from clerical hands during and after the Gregorian age, largely to protect the ecclesiastical order from secular justice which naturally insisted on the responsibility of notaries, lawyers and judges for their actions in civil or criminal matters. Even the physical labor formally permitted to clerks by the canons and practiced by the quasi-lay Beguines in the Low Countries, the Italian Humiliati and Francis of Assisi's early brethren was closed to the majority of the clergy. This was partly because of their specialization in other functions, but, more decisively, because layfolk wished to reserve the profits of labor, industry and commerce for themselves. This was well exemplified, for example, by the hostility of gildsmen, once their corporations were well established, to economic competition by those under the protection of canon law.[52]

One area, however, could grow with the economy as long as churchmen were able to lead Latin Europe. This was the penitential system, the court of conscience, that is, and a variety of related mechanisms, deathbed restitution, penitential obits, for example, and indulgences. Intellectually speaking this system was expressed or enforced in terms of casuistry, an alternating application of rigor and laxity in judgment, both extremes eliciting from society benefactions for the cult, charity and education, causes that were relatively or immediately unprofitable to entrepreneurs. In this context, the impossibilism of the outright prohibition of usury favored by rigorist clergy had a function. The advantage those who play the ideologue's role of moral supervisor acquire from proposing unattainable ideals is that men and women working in the world are unable to establish a schedule of fixed fees whereby they can buy more than momentary solace. Needing

[50]In my "Parishes of Toulouse," p. 187, and note also my "Urban Society and Culture," pp. 240-242. The matter is reviewed again in my Conclusion below.

[51]*Le registre d'inquisition de Jacques Fournier, évêque de Pamiers (1318-1325)*, ed. Duvernoy, see index under "dîmes."

[52]For some brief remarks on the failure of this kind of labor utopianism, see my *Europe in the High Middle Ages 1150-1309*, p. 137.

constant renewal, the cost of such solace may therefore increase in a manner commensurate with the rising prices of a growing economy. It can even, and for a time did, outpace them.

In the long run, the lawyers found in their ancient texts ways of circumventing, or limiting the damage done by, the rigor of this law. Echoing the great lawyer Azo, Cino of Pistoia (d. 1336) believed that, although usury was prohibited by divine law, Roman law or the emperor thought it equitable in order to avoid yet greater evils.[53] After all, God, everybody said, does not demand the impossible.

[53]In his *Super codicis* cited in McLaughlin, "The Teaching of the Canonists on Usury," *Mediaeval Studies* 1 (1939) 92-93.

12

Corporatism

A. Gains and Losses

A commonplace familiar to many economic historians of the recent past argues that the clerical program prohibiting usury had a practical function. Twelfth century "mutua" and "pignora" did not provide capital for economic growth but only for consumption, loans, it is said, being made principally to the poor, to improvident gentlefolk or declining monasteries and churches, and not to economically productive industry or agriculture.[1] Although there is something to this argument because society obviously cannot exist without what today calls "consumer credit," one wonders how much. To refer to an analogous case, Richard Emery's study of Jewish loans in late thirteenth century Perpignan clearly shows that borrowing at usury was engaged in by all classes and that the most successful Christian businessmen of the community were among the borrowers.[2] Evidence from Toulouse before Fulk's episcopate argues the same case. There, for example, members of every class were both creditors and debtors. The documents concerning the lords of Isle-Jourdain and the Tolosa family cited below in this chapter will clearly show readers that members of this region's rural and urban upper social classes both lent and borrowed money. Quite humble persons were also in the business.[3]

At Toulouse, the realities of the credit market and the possible exploitation of debtors are veiled, largely because the documents are both few and terse. Profits on "mutua" are also notoriously difficult to ascertain because, since the starting date of the interest is frequently not recorded, one can

---

[1]A strong statement of this view is found in the otherwise fine pioneering study of Généstal, *Le rôle des monastères comme établissements de crédit étudié en Normandie* of 1901.

[2]*The Jews of Perpignan in the Thirteenth Century*, pp. 39ff.

[3]See Appendix 8, Nos. 56 (dated 1232) involving a wife named Willelma, and 95 (dated 1265) concerning the modest Arnold de Podio.

only conjecture the length and rate of gain of each investment. An example occurred in 1209 when Bernard Raymond de Tolosa surrendered to the Hospitalers his rights to seven stores and a farm that he had acquired by fulfilling his duty as a "fideiussor" for a debt of Bernard Barravus de Hospitale to Peter Maurandus. Peter had given the debt to the guarantor because the Hospital of Saint John paid 851 shillings to replace Bernard Raymond "in that gift ... of 720 shillings and the lucre ... which the said Bernard Barravus owed Peter Maurandus." The minimum profit on this loan was just over eighteen percent, but one has no idea how long the debt had been running.[4] "Mutua," in short, are nearly useless for economic analysis.

More information is available about the "pignus," however. Although the documentation is also light, it seems to show that few contracts were as useful and as flexible. It was, for example, a method of borrowing money in exchange for granting an income from property, real or moveable, or from the labor of economic or social dependents. In terms of these functions, indeed, it is almost impossible to distinguish between the "pignus" and the "census" or other contracts that replaced it, since the distinction, as noted earlier, was essentially legal; the "pignus" was cast in the form of a loan, the "census" in that of a sale. Numerous charters attest the popularity of the "pignus" in the twelfth century. One also notes that the creditors were not only those a modern person would call urban credit providers but also wealthy landed families. An example is an undated list of pledges and incomes from property compiled for the lord of Isle-Jourdain, a small town and great lordship, later termed a viscounty. The magnate involved was Bernard Jordan I who was replaced by his son Jordan by 1191. The list was copied into the celebrated *Saume de l'Isle* and contained twenty-eight "pignora" or "acapta" valued at a total of 2500 shillings of Toulouse and Morlas. Only two small loans of twenty shillings each record the amount of the annual interest – "servicium" or "acaptum" – which in both cases is twenty percent of the invested value.[5] Among the rich, whether urban or rural, furthermore, service charges or rents from "pignora" were often a

---

[4]Malta 1 108 (May 1209): "in toto illo dono quod Petrus Maurandus ei fecerat de .dcc.xx. sol. tol. et de lucro quod fecerant quos predictus Bernardus Barravus eidem Petro Maurando debebat sicut melius in cartis illorum debitorum et pignorum continetur." On these patrician families see my *Repression of Catharism*, pp. 140-141, 232 and 275.

[5]MADTG, A 297, fol. 290v, headed: "In nomine patris et filii et spiritus sancti. Carta commemorationis pignorum et acaptuum que fecit Bernardus Jordanus." There were also several other individual "pignora" funded by Bernard Jordan recorded in the same source, fols. 376v-377.

substantial part of a family's inheritance. Nothing proves this point more conclusively than the division in 1187 or 1188 of their inheritance by the daughters of the rich magnate Peter de Tolosa who lived in the town of Toulouse. Other than much real property and houses, the two sisters were assigned a total of twenty-six contracts, all "pignora" save for two "mutua," comprising rents in money and commodities and the labor of over twenty-six dependents, totaling in value 1359 shillings of Toulouse. These investments involved communities and families from the whole region of Toulouse in a wide circumference reaching from Isle-Jourdain, around thirty kilometers west of Tolouse, to Verfeil, about eighteen kilometers to the east, with most of the properties and dependents being located eastward and southward of town.[6] Such "pignora" were also customarily willed in testaments.[7]

Following the late nineteenth century commonplace, one is inclined to believe that the rate of profit on invested capital typical of such "pignora" shows that these medieval moneylenders were skinning those desperately in need of capital. But this is unlikely. Of the twenty-six contracts inherited by the Tolosa sisters described above, sixteen can be evaluated. Averaging 126 shillings 15 pence, these loans purchased annual "servicia" ranging in value from three to twenty-three percent of the capital invested, with an average of around fifteen percent, the interest being higher the smaller the capital invested. Given that rates of interest or profit could range widely at this time, as indeed they can today, these profits seem reasonable. They were neither as high as those allowed in Roman law and sometimes permitted elsewhere, nor as low as those seen in other communities.[8] The same document makes it also seem unlikely that only those whose prospects were poor were borrowers. Of the approximately twenty-five "pignora" and "mutua" listed in the Tolosa document, only six borrowers cannot be recognized. Of the nineteen remaining, one contract went to a Tolosa of the creditor's family, two to the barons of Lanta, one to those of Isle-Jourdain and two to Toulousan Turribus (and the related Sancto-Dionisio line), all of which families were rich and flourished into the thirteenth century.[9] Other contracts were with persons less well known but surely not less well-to-do.

---

[6]See Appendix 6, No. 2, with a map.

[7]See, for example, that of 1150 by "domina" Prima, Appendix 8, No. 1.

[8]For high rates of interest or profit, see Shatzmiller, *Shylock Reconsidered*, pp. 53-54, and for low ones, Emery, *Jews of Perpignan, passim*, where he estimates that deposit contracts in late thirteenth century Perpignan in Roussillon offered investors around ten percent annually.

[9]See the Turribus in Appendix 1, No. 15.

One was with a Toulousan patrician clan called Montibus, four with the lords of Saissac and no less than eight with those of Verfeil. The last were esteemed by contemporaries to be rich, although they were to lose out when Verfeil was taken from them by Simon de Montfort during the Albigensian Crusade and given to the bishop of Toulouse.[10]

Nor were "pignora" necessarily ruinous for debtors. Although assuredly durable, they were often redeemed and did not result in an inevitable loss of the real property or income pledged. A checklist called "Breve de pignori[bu]s" contains abstracts of twenty-six "pignora" and related contracts datable to the latter eleventh century or the early twelfth. The actors in the actions summarily described in this list were members of the Tolosa family, probably related to the notable sisters seen above.[11] The majority of the twenty-six abstracted acts contained in the "Breve," twenty in number, dealt with debt, and three named individuals as personal guarantors of debts or loans. A total of seventeen dealt with "pignora" and, of these, eight contained pledges, but, what is important here, no less than nine recorded the cancellation of "pignora" by means of payment.[12]

This list of pledges did not contain true investment contracts like those of the Tolosa sisters studied above but instead ones designed for internal family finance, something that perhaps helps explains the rather low annual rate of return (8.3 percent) on the only "pignus" actually recorded.[13] One debt contract helped a family member acquire a horse, presumably a warhorse.[14] Another relative needed money to go to Spain, either to the very

[10]Concerning Montibus, see the family history in my *Repression of Catharism*, pp. 242-247. A note on Verfeil is to be seen in the Turribus history in Appendix 1, No. 15. The properties of the Saissaco mentioned here were just east of Toulouse.

[11]Saint-Étienne 227 (xxvi DA 2 79), (dated in Appendix 6, No. 1. For the history of the Tolosa family, see my *Repression of Catharism*, pp. 269-270.

[12]Ibid.: the first two contracts read: "Odegarius et frater eius Petrus miserunt in pignus ad Petrum Benedictum Astarium .iiii. aripentos vinearum qui sunt ubi vocant Flaugas per .lx. et .v. sol. denariorum Tolosanos atque decenos. Post multum vero temporis ego Regimundus frater Odegarii et Petri abstraxi supradictas vineas a pignore et solvi munus Petro Benedicto Astario, vidente Guillelmo Leodegario et Petro Benedicto camarario."

[13]Ibid.: "Iterum Raimundus inpignoravit de Guillelmo fratre suo unum casalem in Braca villa quem tenet Poncius Arnaldus per .ii. sol. de denariis decenis et dat census .ii. denarios."

[14]Ibid.: "Iterum Gaucelinus fecit mercatum unius caballi de Regimundo Stephano et de fratribus suis per .c.xx. sol. de denariis ramondenchis qui debuerunt esse soluti per terminos et si non erant soluti, totum illius honorum habuisset Raimundus in pignus donec universum fuisset redditum, videntes Odegarius et Hugo Arman." The coinage mentioned is that of Albi that was, at this time, about half the value of that of Toulouse, hence sixty shillings.

profitable wars against the Muslims or to settle there.[15] In short, among other things, a means of financing family adventures or investments, the "pignus" was not intrinsically exploitative.

If the arguments advanced above are valid, one wonders why church-men promulgated and society embraced a law that weakened, destroyed or drove underground such excellent devices as the old "mutua" and "pigno-ra." Viewed practically, it would surely have sufficed to police these contracts by extending the traditional conception of the just price from commodities to credit transactions. Indeed, although the names or the terms of the contracts had changed, this is roughly what happened as the secular state rescinded or attenuated church regulation of the economy during the centuries of the late middle ages and early modern times. The question is, therefore, why it was that the moral theory of twelfth and thirteenth century church law and society was so extraordinarily rigorist. To answer this, one must go beyond the rather slender material available in Toulouse's archives and examine broader perspectives. They show that others than ecclesiastics were involved in this history.

B. CORPORATE STRUCTURES

It cannot have escaped the reader that the arguments advanced above have been one-sided, proposing a world in which the clergy acted without regard to the laity. It is nevertheless surely true that churchmen could not have acted alone in matters of such moment, nor that they alone could have forced layfolk to jump through the inconvenient hoop of the absolute prohi-bition of usury. As has been implied above, it seems probable that the growth of a corporatist ethos in the economy and society during the late twelfth and thirteenth centuries provided or elicited a necessary and funda-mental popular support or even impulsion for the clerical program. Popular adhesion, it seems, was animated by two closely related motives. The first was that rigorist doctrines and programs of Christian utopianism were clearly needed as polemical weapons by the middle and lower ranges of the population in their battle against entrepreneurial elements and against the rich, old and new, in the age of the first creation of gilds, the very time being examined here. The second is that the emphasis on the virtues of eco-nomic brotherhood and the consequent attack on usury expressed a desire of substantial elements of society to limit economic individualism, a phrase

[15]Ibid.: "Iterum inpignoravi de fratre meo Petro quartum de duobus aripentis vinearum, unus fuit T[er]reni et alter Poncii Aleta in Chanal de Boc per .xiii. sol. de denariis tolosanis decenis, quando perexit in Ispaniam, vidente Stephani Benedicti."

taken here to mean the right of men and women to do what they wish with what they are convinced are their own means.

To discuss the second matter first, it was remarked above that, before the introduction of the canons on usury, every businessman at Toulouse was a usurer and, it may be added, there is reason to believe that, although now disguised, the same was true even after those canons were introduced. Not every businessman, however, was usurious in the same way. Devout though he was, Pons de Capitedenario was obliged to restore his usuries, but the sons of the William de Turribus, the knightly Curvus, Guy and Fulk de Turribus, whose elevated social station was clearly based on their father's past usuries, were not so embarrassed.[16] In part, this merely proves what has been advanced before in this book, namely that the families rising to prominence in the twelfth century normally used "mutua" and "pignora," contracts forbidden in the thirteenth century, just as their successors were to use more covert devices and that Capitedenario was caught out when the mechanism changed.

But there was surely more to it than this. The cases of Capitedenario and the Turribus as well as those of many of their peers show that new men were peculiarly exposed to social censure. The records of court cases in thirteenth century Toulouse reveal some who had clearly been singled out as notorious usurers, men, that is, popularly considered to be given over to that vice.[17] A survey of known creditors and especially of those either charged in court or known to have made restitution in their testaments or otherwise makes it clear that, although everyone sought a profit on invested capital, there were relatively few manifest usurers among the humble and not many among the town's knightly families. Those singled out for hostile attention were the new rich, sometimes scions of good burgher families, sometimes not, sometimes those ascending from the middle ranges of the population. The humble, it may be guessed, were preserved for virtue because of their incapacity to be vicious, and well-to-do patricians and knights by the transfer of their ambitions to government or war. It therefore seems that the harassment of the manifest usurer both slowed the accumulation of wealth by new men and taxed their gains for the benefit of charity, education and the cult by means of the penitential system. In fine,

---

[16]See the history of Pons de Capitedenario in my *Repression of Catharism*, pp. 155-163, and the Lastours in Appendix 1, No. 15.

[17]The papal law on manifest usurers derived from the canon of the Third Lateran Council embodied in X. 5 19 3, for which see Chapter Ten, note 6 above. For the meaning of the category "manifest," see Christiani, "Note sulla legislazione antiusuraria Pisana (secolo XII-XV)," *Bollettino storico pisano* 22 (1953) *passim* especially p. 13.

although utopian hope never triumphed and the economic individual was not extirpated, the relatively free economy of around 1200 in which a Pons de Capitedenario or a William de Turribus operated had been replaced by a more corporate and regulatory one by the decades before 1300.

To return to the gilds, it is certain that, at Toulouse as elsewhere in western Europe, the corporate structure was growing at this time. The first evidences of a rapid development of the crafts and trades are to be seen in the late eleven-seventies through the nineties.[18] The first extant Toulousan statute on an industry, that of cloth, dates from 1227 when its provisions were received and issued by the consuls.[19] Typical of the time, it favored those who provided the raw material to be processed, calling them "domini" or "domine" and required the manufacturer to collect the raw material at the home of the "dominus" or "domina" and return the finished commodity there, just like a rural rent or share-cropping contract. In short, the statute favored entrepreneurs. Somewhat earlier, in 1221, the consuls legislated against the economic freedom of craftsmen, perhaps sometimes for their own good, by preventing them from pledging or otherwise alienating the materials entrusted to them for manufacture.[20] Thereafter, although the picture is muddied by lack of documents and research, the craft structure grew.

Part of the reason for this growth was that artisans needed protection against entrepreneurs. The old regulatory system based on dependency to the count had unraveled as private and entrepreneurial interests arose and weakened the prince during the twelfth century. Shaky though it was, however, the count still exercised vestigial authority over the crafts and over business and trades in the town. This nearly moribund remnant of an erstwhile general power was reanimated by the rise of the crafts and trades and the formation of an alliance between these workers and the prince against the business community. An example may be seen in the case of waterfront rights.

The count of Toulouse had retained significant interests in the Garonne river and its confluents, including inter-regional business such as that of the boatmen.[21] These interests enabled him to take a stand against the pri-

---

[18]See my *Liberty and Political Power*, pp. 64ff., 82ff., and 111.

[19]Mulholland, "Statutes on Clothmaking: Toulouse 1227," *Essays in Medieval Life and Thought*, ed. Emery, Mundy and Nelson, pp. 168-181, with the text published pp. 172ff.

[20]TAM, AA 1 90 (August 1221).

[21]See my *Liberty and Political Power*, pp. 30-31 and especially 244, note 14, where evidence that butchers, leather workers and boatmen owed the count special service especially in time of war may be seen. The last enactment concerns the boatmen and is dated 1231.

vate property of the rich. In 1239 Raymond VII asserted the right of the
leather workers of the town to use the banks of the Garonne to wash and
prepare their hides, granting them a house or shed at the place called
Viviers (near the New Bridge in the center of town), guaranteeing them
against all comers, among whom the consuls were uppermost in his mind.[22]
Behind the consuls, it may be added, stood rich families like the Barravi
and Tolosa that owned large stretches of the waterfront which they thought
they were free to do with as they liked.[23] A curious example was Raymond Galterius who, early in 1193, claimed the right of wreck and wrack
on his riverine shores.[24] The conflict between private property and public
use stirred much excitement among the crafts and trades. In 1268, for example, one of the petitions presented to the count by the popular party
against the consuls concerned the right of all citizens, especially, it may
be guessed, butchers and hide and leather workers, to pasture the animals
being imported for slaughter freely near town on the lands and in the
woods owned by local landlords.[25]

Probably owing to resistance by private right orchestrated before the
midcentury by the consuls, Toulousan trade and craft corporatism was
slow to attain maturity.[26] It was attained only when some nineteen gilds
recorded their statutes in the period from 1270 to 1322.[27] These statutes
no longer refer to "domini" and their relationship to artisans, and it is noteworthy that princely or royal encroachment on consular authority in this
sphere was on the increase.[28] As in nineteenth century Europe, the mere
building of economic organizations often excited intense resistance, but

[22]TAM, II 44 (February 1239, copied in 1239 and 1267) where the count granted
the leather crafts "ut domum predictam ... et aquam de Vivariis et aquam Garonne et
rippas citra Garonnam et ultra semper habeant, possideant, et explectant" so that they
could "taneant, lavent et parent eorum coria" there. See Roschach's observations about
the consuls in Note 47 in *HGL* 7: 240-241.

[23]The Tolosa and Barravi histories are in my *Repression of Catharism*, pp. 136-154
and 268-283.

[24]TAM, AA 1 20 and 21 (February and March 1193), and the Carbonellus-Prignaco
family App 1, No. 3.

[25]*HGL* 8: No. 521 ii (July 1263), col. 1653, where petition No 14 is directed against
the rights of the "domini terrarum et nemorum."

[26]Toulouse's gilds grew much more slowly than those in Montpellier and Paris
where the princes had weakened the power of the local patricians with the aid of the
crafts and trades.

[27]These are published and annotated by Mulholland in her *Early Gild Records of
Toulouse*.

[28]Ibid., pp. xli-xlii.

the growth of charitable ones, burial societies and the like, did not provoke the same opposition in spite of the fact that the latter were often essential prerequisites for gilds or unions. It is in this context that, allowing for the difference of an economy based on the household workshop and not on the factory system, one also notes the astonishing development of charitable agencies in thirteenth century Toulouse.[29]

To review this history, the growth of the court of conscience and the system of casuistry developed in the church during the thirteenth century drew money from the wealthy, especially the new rich, those most exposed to the threat of social retribution and consequently to the pricks of conscience. What was gained went to the cult itself and to charity and education which were relatively or immediately unprofitable. Here were causes dear to some of the older rich and especially to the humble many who sought in the securities of social and economic corporatism an answer to the insecurities of rapid economic growth, the exploitation of entrepreneurs and the aggression of the powerful. As will be argued later when dealing with the relationship of the prince to the people, also, political action was as important in instituting these changes as was ideological pressure and the cult.

C. REGULATED ENTERPRISE

Willfully unpaid debt had been considered close to criminal injury by the synods and councils of the Peace of God and this idea was still very much alive in Toulouse around 1200.[30] In 1197 the consuls legislated that a recalcitrant debtor was to be put in the vicar's prison for eight days. If proved to be without means, he was then to be given to the creditor to be kept in irons in his house, there to receive only bread and water until two-thirds of the consuls ordered his release.[31] Nor could a debtor flee into the sanctu-

---

[29]See my "Charity and Social Work," *passim*.

[30]Huberti, *Studien zur Rechtsgeschichte der Gottesfrieden und Landfrieden* 1: 319-320.

[31]TAM, AA 1 18 (November 1197): This "constitutio" reads "Quod si aliquis debitor responderit suo creditori se non habere aliquid quod ei possit persolvere, quod vicarius, si clamorem inde habuerit, eum in castello viii diebus teneat et si ad viiii diem creditor potest probare quod debitor aliquid ei possit persolvere, quod debitor illud ei persolvat." The debtor in the creditor's house was placed "in ferris ... [and the creditor] non teneatur ei dare ad comedendum aliud nisi panem et aquam, nisi voluerit." For the general history of this subject, see Molinier, "Condition des debiteurs à Toulouse selon deux chartes du XIIe siècle," *Recueil de l'Académie de Législation de Toulouse* 6 (1857) 156-193. This scholar notes that such constraints were not permitted in the custom of Montpellier dated from 1172 to 1196 where it is stated in article no. 13: "Item si aliqui fuerit captus pro causa pecuniaria, non debet in compedibus ligneis vel ferreis ponere."

ary of an ecclesiastical close (the cathedral, the Daurade, Saint-Sernin and Saint-Pierre-des-Cuisines each had such an area) and, if he did, the creditor could arrest him there. Being, as is obvious, more than a civil disagreement between two individuals, debtors and their guarantors were likened to criminals and could not be chosen by citizens to serve as guarantors for their loans, etc.[32]

These laws were issued at the very moment the consuls had begun to take control of indebtedness from the failing hands of the counts of Toulouse and their officers. Before 1189 the count's vicar had judicial as well as police power over it and, in fact, the first known reference to debt shows this officer in command. In 1174 the vicar Espanolus gave Bernard de Capitedenario possession of a debtor's land and awarded him first claim over other creditors.[33]

The chaptermen or consuls subsequently began to interfere, at first without harming the rights of the count or his vicar. The first consular judicial decision dealing with debt was dated 1195, and permitted the alienation of property for cause of debt.[34] The consuls' first recorded legislation about debt was a "constitutio" of 1197 which, however, adverted to previous edicts of that body.[35] The novelty of consular intervention in this field was shown by the fact that the vicar Peter Rogerius gave express consent to this law, presumably as a function of his traditional police power

[32]TAM, AA 1 13 (March 1198): a citizen who chose as an "obses" one who is a "malefactor, debitor, nec fideiussor" must pay the requisite fine, namely the property if a "pignus," an "emendatio" if a "malefactor" and the "debitum" if a debtor.

[33]E 538 (September 1174) wherein Bernard assumed a debtor's liabilities, paid off the creditors, and then received in pledge the properties the creditors had seized: "quia in predictis vineis ceperant posse cum vicario pro istis debitis." "Hoc fuit factum consilio vicarii, scilicet Ispanoli qui tunc erat vicarius pro ipso domino Raimundo Tolosano comite constitutus in urbe Tolosa et in suburbio, qui Ispanolus pro domino comiti et pro seipso laudavit istos .cccc. sol. Bernardo de Capitedenario et suo ordinio in predictis vineis et dedit inde ei potestatem ante omnes creditores."

[34]E 501 (January 1195) in which Bernard Espertus told the consuls that he and his deceased brother Peter Stephanus owed money which he could not repay save by the sale of property in the close of Saint-Sauveur: "dicens quod non habebat aliquid de Petro Stephano unde debita posset persolvere nisi venderet predictum malolem, unde volebat ut cognoscerent [the consuls] quod illa vendicio quam faceret de predicto malole haberet firmitatem."

[35]TAM, AA 1 18 (November 1197): "Et alia instrumenta que alii consules posuerant super facta debitorum, posuerunt consules quod huic nec aliis huiusmodi factas [read factis] non nocerent."

in cases of unpaid debt.[36] The consular "stabilimentum" of a year later about debt and related matters was enacted in the presence of the count thereby proving that the count and his vicar exercised police power over debtors as late as 1198.[37]

Thereafter, the count and vicar vanish for upwards of thirty years from recorded Toulousan legislation or judicial action regarding debt, and all one hears about is the consuls. The first extant consular settlement of a dispute among creditors over the property of a debtor by judicial act was written in 1206.[38] From then on judgments about debt and assignments of property for cause of debt became perhaps the most frequent of all extant lawsuits in Toulouse, and were soon deputized by the consuls to courts of sworn lay judges.[39] Such assignments of property in payment of debt by "curia jurata" appointed by the consuls were definitive sentences, expressly forbidding appeals to any other tribunal.[40]

---

[36]Ibid.: "Hoc totum fuit factum consilio et voluntate Petri Rogerii, tunc vicarii, qui totum hoc laudavit et concessit pro domino Raimundo, Tolosano comite, et in loco eius, et pro se ipso, et voluit quod esset factum."

[37]TAM, AA 1 13 (March 1198).

[38]Malta 15 107 (March 1206): the debtor had absconded.

[39]An example of such suits is in TAM, II 45 (March 1225) where the case was "in presentia virorum de curia jurata constituti, que curia erat a consulibus urbis Tholose et suburbii constituta, super causis ac controversiis debitorum ac baratorum determinandis, inter creditores videlicet et debitores ... ."

[40]An assignment of property for debt began in E 573 (March 6, 1225, copied in September 1233) with the following harangue: "quod [two named persons] venientes ante presentiam virorum de curia quos consules urbis Tolose et suburbii constituerant judices ad iudicandos et assignandos honores debentium creditoribus pro debitis iudicatis que eisdem creditoribus debentur, que debita viri de curiis quondam iudicaverant persolvi creditoribus quibus debentur, et pro illis iudiciis que consules Tolosani iudicaverant vel domini claustrorum pro sponsaliciis dominarum, quibus viris de curia ipsi consules urbis Tolose et suburbii, habito prudentum virorum consilio, iudicio dixerant et cognoverant atque diffinierant quod quicquid viri de curia predicta scilicet [twelve] NN iudicaverant vel assignaverant ex quo fuerant de hac curia vel deinceps dum de hac curia fuerint iudicaverint vel assignaverint creditoribus de honoribus debentium pro debitis que debent iudicatis a consulibus vel a curiis eorum vel ab aliis curiis vel a dominis claustrorum vel pro aliis quibuslibet iudiciis a consulibus promulgatis vel pro sponsaliciis dominarum maritos habentium vel non habentium, et etiam de honoribus illorum qui unanimes et concordes venirent ante eorum conspectum licet non adierint primam curiam super iudicandis debitis constitutam, et de honoribus similiter illorum debentium vel illarum qui commoniti et citati bis vel ter vel pluries ab ipsis viris de curia vel eorum nunciis rebellione vel contumacia coram ipsis contempserint comparere, auditis rationibus tantummodo alterius partis quod illud totum ut premissum est quod idem viri de curia iudicaverant vel assignaverant vel transegerant vel composuerant vel iudicaverint vel

Consular legislation on this subject no longer mentioned the count or his officers. In 1201 a law prohibited persons under the jurisdiction of parents and tutors from borrowing and pledging.[41] In 1208 the consuls protected citizen investors by proposing that those living outside of town could not refuse to be pledged by a Toulousan.[42] Far more significantly, the consuls responded in 1214 to a petition from Toulousan creditors and businessfolk, and rescinded antecedent legislation by the count (of which not a trace remains) granting debtors longer delays for payment.[43] Lastly, in August 1221, the consuls acted alone to prohibit artisans from selling or pledging materials given them to manufacture.[44] Debt had become a consular case; the count had been replaced and his vicar reduced to being an agent of the consuls.

During the Albigensian Crusade, things began to change and resurgent comital power began to invade what had become the consuls' sphere. An initial sign of this basic recasting of social balances may be seen during the administration of the crusader Simon de Montfort. In 1217 a court of four Toulousan citizens empowered by Gervais de Chamigny, seneschal of the Toulousain, and the eight "viri de curia" of Simon's town government assigned a vineyard at Bonne Gazagne at Montaudran in the "gardiage" in part payment of a debt to Peter Grivus de Roaxio of 700 shillings.[45]

---

assignaverint vel transegerint vel composuerint de honoribus prelibatorum ut superius est expressum efficaci robore et firmitate inviolabiliter perhennetur, ita quod illa iudicia et assignamenta et compositiones et transactiones ullo tempore valeant nec ab aliquo apellari nec contradici nec contraveniri sicut melius in carta illius iudicii et cognitionis quam Raimundus de Sancto Cezerto scripsit continetur; et ibi prius ab ipsis prestito sacramento ostenderit et dixerit eisdem viris de curia ipse [the plaintiff] ... ."

[41]TAM, AA 1 23 (March 1201).

[42]TAM, AA 1 88 (March 1208): if a citizen "pignoraverit vel pignorare voluerit aliquem manentem extra villa Tolose" the pledged person may not reject his condition.

[43]TAM, II 45 (dated March 1214), the consuls, "viso et intellecto instrumento forme et compositionis quam dominus comes Tolose fecerat et posuerat inter acomodatores et manulevatores, ... cognoverunt et iudicio dixerunt quod ... " that payment "pro venditionibus et emptionibus domorum vel vinearum vel terrarum vel aliorum honorum vel equorum vel aliorum animalium vel pannorum vel blati vel vini vel pro aliquibus aliis rebus et negociationibus" must be made "sine omni dilatione, quam aliquis debitor ibi non mittat pro forma nec pro temporibus a domino Raimundo Tolosano comite constitutis ... ."

[44]TAM, AA 1 90 (August 1221).

[45]E 501 (September 1217, copied in December 1243): " ... Grivus venit ante presenciam Bernardi Petri filii Bernardi Ortolani et Poncii Astronis et Willelmi Aimerici de Pegulano et Ramundi de Fumello qui a domino Gervasio de Chameniaco senescalco in Tolosano et a viris de curia vicilicet a Bernardo Ramundo de Tolosa et Poncio Berengario et Bernardo Caraborda et Bernardo Arnaldo de Portaria et Raimundo Rotberto et Peregrino Signuario et Poncio de Capitedenario et Poncio Guitardo qui a domino Sy-

Although nothing more was heard of such intervention by the count until the war was over, a document of 1230 mentions a tribunal designed to assign land and property in payment of debt "in the whole of the diocese of Toulouse," constituted by the "venerable lord Raymond by the grace of God count of Toulouse," whose members acted to enforce a decision by a consular "curia jurata."[46] In a way, this court was advantageous to Toulousan creditors and may be regarded as a way for them to ensure the collection of debts owed them outside of the "gardiage." The judges were all Toulousans and two were frequent consuls.[47] It is noteworthy, however, that Toulousans felt it necessary to use a comital agency to effect their ends. What began in 1230 was continued afterward, moreover, the same judges being active in another case a year later.[48]

This forum, furthermore, is the first known example of a comital court dealing with debt in Toulouse since Raymond V's capitulation in 1189. And, although the intervening history is not represented in the charters, the powers of the vicar, as will be seen in Chapter Thirteen, had been wholly revived by mid-century. In the past, furthermore, the consuls had held that their judgments and those of the courts appointed by them were beyond appeal.[49] This doctrine was still alive around 1254 or 1255. Notes for a consular "supplicatio" of about that time presumably to the count clearly stated that "appeal from their sentences had never been known."[50] The consuls' claim was also being overridden at about this time. In 1254 or just

---

mone comite Tolosano ad audiendas et terminandas causas et controversias erant judices constituti et commissionem et plenam receperant potestatem super assignandis honoribus pro debitis ... ." For Peter see my *Repression of Catharism*, pp. 259-260.

[46]Saint-Étienne 227 (xxvi DA 2 47) (November 1230) wherein the case was pleaded "ante presentiam virorum de curia super honoribus assignandis statuta scilicet Bernardi Caraborda de Portaria et Ramundi de Sauzeto et Vitalis Rotberti et Vitalis Willelmi, qui a viris de alia curia a venerabili domino .R. dei gratia comite Tolosano statuta, erant super honoribus et debitis et baratis et obliis assignandis in toto episcopatu Tolosano judices constituti." The debtor was the distinguished Jordan de Villanova, for whom see my *Repression of Catharism*, pp. 296-297.

[47]Ibid.: Bernard Caraborda de Portaria, Raymond de Sauzeto, Vital Rotbertus, Vital Willelmus. Bernard Caraborda and Vital Rotbertus were often consuls around this time, for which see Appendix 4.

[48]E 501, ii (October 1231, copied in November 1233).

[49]See, for example, TAM, AA 1 20 and 21 (February and March 1193) ("quod a nemine possint removeri") and also the decision in the case cited above in note 40 (dated March 1225) written by Raymond de Sancto Cezerto.

[50]PAN, J 896 31 (undated but the consuls named are those of 1255 and 1256): "Item, quod consuetus honor Tholose consulibus observetur quod ab eorum sententiis nequeat appellari sicut fuit obtentum a tempore quo non extat memoria."

after, Count Alphonse of Poitiers' administration flatly asserted that cases could be appealed to the vicar's court from that of the consuls, and from that court to that of the seneschal and even to the count.[51]

At this very moment, a case was appealed from the consuls to the vicar's court. A notable, Bernard Aimeric Astre, sued Ricarda, the widow of Bernard Gastoni, for thirty-five shillings of Toulouse in 1258.[52] Ricarda admitted the debt but claimed it was usurious, which Bernard Aimeric denied.[53] In 1261, Bernard having taken oath that the debt did not involve usury, the suit was brought before another consular court (the document says "afterward in another consulate") and apparently decided in Bernard's favor.[54] Finally, in February 1261, Ricarda's proctor and Bernard appeared to hear the sentence read, upon which her proctor straightway appealed to the vicar's court.[55] In short, comital power had been renewed, thereby giving debtors an alternative to the courts of the consuls, a body usually allied to creditors.

Not that the law on debt softened materially but, as in northern France, the reinvigoration of the monarchical principle mitigated the private imprisonment of debtors by their creditors. In 1268 three of the petitions brought to the count's administration by the people and responded favorably to in 1269 requested protection for debtors and another sought to lessen the incidence and ameliorate the conditions of precautionary imprisonment, a matter of much moment for debtors.[56] Although nothing as elaborate is

[51]*HGL* 8: No. 447, col. 1353. See the discussion in Chapter Fourteen, p. 260 below.

[52]TAM, II 45. The date elements are indistinct and the document has been dated November 1259, but I prefer 1258 because one session of this complicated lawsuit was held "in die martis post festum Sancti Martini," a date which works for 1258 but not for 1259.

[53]Ibid.: Ricarda "concessit instrumentum debiti esse verum et publicum; dixit tamen debitum esse de usura et ultra hoc quod [the creditor] habuit de ea .ii. sol. tol. de usura." On Bernard Aimeric and his family, see my *Men and Women*, pp. 182-183.

[54]Ibid.: "cum juramento quod [Bernard] faciat super altare ... quod isti non sunt de usura predicti .xxxv. sol. tolosanorum et post in alio consulatu, anno domini .m.cc.lx.i."

[55]Ibid: "et post die sabbati in crastinum Beati Mathei comparuit Estultus [Gastoni] predictus nomine procuratorio dicte domine et dictus Bernardus pro se ex altera, et de eorum voluntate fuit lecta dicta sententia, a qua quidem sententia dictus procurator illico appellavit ad dominum vicarium Tholose nomine et loco domine supradicte."

[56]*HGL* 8: No. 526, ii, col. 1652 (July 1268): petition No. 11, col. 1652, was really directed against unjust imprisonment and was not limited to imprisonment for debt, but the count's response in effect abolished precautionary imprisonment for debt as well as other offenses. For ibid., No. 526, v, col. 1655 (March 1269), see Chapter Fourteen, p. 259 below. On cautionary imprisonment for debt in the vicar's court, see my *Liberty and Political Power*, p. 100.

seen in Toulouse, the customs of the Beauvaisis composed by Philip de Rémi, lord of Beaumanoir, around 1283 illustrates the northern French law on this subject that was in the minds of Alphonse's administrators. This learned provincial governor proposed that imprisonment for debt was a monopoly of government not to be granted to private persons, that it was not to be punitive as if exacted from criminal perpetrators, and that detention was to be limited to forty days.[57]

The preaching against and prosecution of usurers was welcomed by the Capetians who, under Louis IX, seemed to wish to be more Christian than the clergy. In his reform edict of sometime around 1254, Alphonse of Poitiers repeated the strictures his brother Louis had borrowed from the church: "Usury is not to be paid by Christians, and usury is whatever is received beyond the capital."[58] In spite of the probably sincere veneration of the idea of economic brotherhood expressed by these princes, no secular government could long be expected to go right down the line. What is found in the archives on this subject instead shows that the crown followed the traditional and useful course of regulating interest rates (to use the modern phrase). In 1312 a royal ordinance against usury was published and a copy found its way into the town's archives. Although illegal in the view of canon law, the crown followed Roman law's tradition and established maximum rates of interest. Given what humble borrowers of today sometimes experience, these rates, while not generous, were not bad, ranging from fifteen percent annually to over twenty-one percent depending on the duration of the loan.[59]

These rates may remind readers that, although medieval princes often protected the plebs, their motives were not love of the poor half so much as a desire to control the rich and powerful. In exchange for a modest measure of support, the obvious requirement was that the humble should not threaten to disrupt social order. In short, governments defended social

---

[57]*Coutumes de Beauvaisis*, ed. Salmon, 2: Paragraphs 1538-1539: the government may not imprison a debtor of a private person unless the matter has been so decided by a court. The prisoner for debt is not to be reduced to bread and water as is a common criminal, but is instead to receive from the creditor "pain et vin et potage tant comme il en puet user au meins une fois le jour." Whether or not a debtor can pay, he may not be held more than forty days "car ce seroit contraire chose a humanité que l'en lessast tous jours cors d'homme en prison pour dete ... ."

[58]*HGL* 8: No. 447, col. 1355: "Item quod Christianis non solvantur usure, usura autem intelligitur quodquid recipitur ultra sortem."

[59]TAM, AA 3 161 (January 1312), the rates being one penny a week per pound, fourpence a month, and three shillings a year.

peace, a peace confirming private property, of which a substantial, if not the larger, part was in the hands of those they tried to restrain, namely the well-to-do. The gains for debtors were therefore modest: to be protected in their poverty was the advantage princes and governments offered the poor. When government offered anything, however, it thereby invaded the private right of economic individuals to do what they wanted with their property and means and hence expressed economic corporatism.

That the renewed monarchy of the thirteenth century controlled the economic actions of the well-to-do to the satisfaction of the poor may well be doubted, but readers are nevertheless invited to remember that there is a world of difference between an economy in which individuals can do what they wish with what they think is theirs and be praised for it, and one in which they find it advisable to limit and sometimes even to camouflage what they do. In this circumstance, as can be seen in Chapters Five above and Fourteen below, the well-to-do for the first time began grudgingly to admit the right of the government to collect taxes from them for its support and probably thereby avoided hostile regulation. Politically speaking, the first situation, that of doing what one wishes, is oligarchy; the second, monarchy.

Part 4

GOVERNMENT

13

Constitutional Defeat

A. The old constitution

Whether one looks at Provence or maritime Languedoc, at, for example, the cities of Avignon or Marseille or those of Beaucaire, Alais, and Nîmes, the thirteenth century generally witnessed a decline in self-government or urban liberty and a rise in the authority of princes. This southern region was also penetrated by the Capetian dynasty whose heads in the mid-thirteenth century wore not only the crown of France but also the princely tiaras of Provence and Toulouse. When, furthermore, it is recalled that royal seneschalsies had been installed in Beaucaire and Carcassonne at the end of the Albigensian Crusade, it is obvious that, by midcentury, the whole of this region save Montpellier and one or two other enclaves was in the hands of the northern French monarchy. The same or a similar pattern of institutional evolution was to be seen in western Languedoc, especially in regard to Toulouse but was also evidenced there in smaller communities such as Isle-Jourdain in Toulousan Gascony. An investigation of the history of Toulouse, however, will show that the decline in urban self-government and the rise of monarchical centralization was part of a much larger and more complex process than one suspects at first glance.

In this chapter, the words "republic" or "republican" will be employed to define the institutions and age of a town or region when it attained a substantial measure of self-government at the expense of its hereditary prince. Although situated in a vastly different setting, the institutional structures designated by these terms were not unlike those of a modern constitutional monarchy. The model is that of the Italian city republics whose history, however, departs from that of Toulouse and almost all communities in southern France because the peninsula's greater cities, as the jurists said with some exaggeration, "recognized no superiors on earth" and thus were real republics. That the more modest measure of freedom

from princely power attained by Toulouse was for a moment similar to that
of an Italian town republic was signaled by Petit-Dutaillis in 1941.[1]
    During the period from 1189 until 1229, Toulouse experienced its re-
publican age, when this town almost became free of its princes, the counts
of the house of Saint-Gilles. Many things are unclear about the constitution
of the town in this period. The remnant powers and political role of the
count are not fully known. The penetration of the consulate by a group of
new men and new families in 1202 and the weakening of the hold of older
families illustrates this. This change may well have been orchestrated by the
count, motivated by a desire to offset the power of the quasi-oligarchy that
had defeated him in 1189. If so, the prince must soon have been much
disappointed. In the period from 1202 to 1205, the new consulate exhibited
the fervor and aggressiveness one associates with republics, trying to
conquer the small towns and villages of the "contado," to use the familiar
Italian term for county, or, as its leaders called it, the "patria Tolosana,"
almost until the very eve of the Albigensian Crusade in 1209.
    Although the "patria Tolosana" is not defined in extant charters, it is
easy to guess what it was. It did not englobe the traditional territories of
the count who was, one remembers, duke of Narbonne and marquess of
Provence as well as count of Toulouse. It was instead the large bishopric
of Toulouse. In 1230, when Count Raymond VII appointed a court of Toulousans to settle disputes about debts owed to townsmen by persons in the
county, that entity was described as the episcopate of Toulouse. The same
was true as late as 1285 when the *Custom* of Toulouse defined the area
wherein Toulousan public notaries claimed superior competence.[2] Because
the diocese of Toulouse was then vast and remained so until divided into
eight dioceses and erected into an archdiocese by papal actions running
from 1295 to 1318, it is not surprising that western and southern counties
like Astarac, Comminges and Foix and baronies like Montréal and Laurac
to the southeast, Rabastens to the northeast and Isle-Jourdain to the west
bowed to Toulouse's commercial pretensions in the last desperate years of
the Albigensian war.[3]
    Another significant limitation of princely power was the loss of control
over Toulouse's consulate, the board of magistrates which governed the

---

[1] "La prétendue commune de Toulouse," *Comptes rendus des séances de l'Académie
des Inscriptions et Belles-Lettres de Paris* (1941) 57.
    [2] Saint-Étienne 227 (26 DA 2 47) (November 1230): "in toto episcopatu Tolosano
judices constituti," and Gilles, *Coutumes de Toulouse*, p. 90, tit. 14a and 14b, articles
refused by the crown in 1285: "ubique in diocesi Tholosana."
    [3] In my *Liberty and Political Power*, p. 89.

town, in both the executive and judicial spheres, beginning with the defeat of Count Raymond VI in 1189.[4] Whatever the count's continuing role in choosing the "capitularii," as they were initially called, or the "consules" as they styled themselves after 1175 or 1176, the enlargement of their college to twenty-four members sometime around 1180 clearly weakened his control, especially because the change was accompanied by the practice of annually replacing the whole group. For a prince to find twelve loyal servitors every so often is one thing; it is altogether another to choose twenty-four every year.[5]

The culmination of town freedom, however, awaited the formal surrender of the count's right to choose the consuls in 1223 and lasted only until just after the Peace of Paris ending the Albigensian Crusade in 1229.[6] During this period, town statutes speak only vaguely and generally about the election of the consuls, that of 1223 merely observing that the electors, meeting in a body not otherwise defined, were henceforth never to choose members of their own families or households as consuls.[7] This provision strongly implies that the outgoing consuls chose their successors, because the provision about relatives would have been absurd had the people chosen them in an election. A later attempt by townsmen to define the election of the consuls occurred when the old free consulate was re-established in 1248 at the time of a later defeat of the count. The consuls then stated that the "communitas et universitas" of Toulouse was to elect twelve consuls from each of the two halves of the town, or two from each of the six "partite" or divisions into which the two parts of the town were divided.[8] They rehearsed this law again around 1265 during a battle with the new count, Alphonse of Poitiers, stating that Raymond VII himself had admitted that the community itself alone had the right to nominate and institute new consuls.[9] Alphonse or his officers replied that this was only partly true, assert-

---

[4]See Chapter Five of my *Liberty and Political Power*.

[5]See Appendix 4.

[6]TAM, AA 1 83 (April 1223): where he promised not to intervene "nisi ex voluntate proborum hominum et universitatis."

[7]Ibid. 75 (March 1223).

[8]Ibid. 103 (January 1248): "Immo ipsa sola communitas et universitas Tolose urbis et suburbii, presens et futura, nunc et in perpetuum, sua propria auctoritate et libera voluntate eligat, nominet, instituat, creet, mutet, reducat, faciat, et teneat, et possit eligere, nominare, instituere, creare, mutare, reducere, facere, et tenere consulatum et consules in Tolosa, in urbe et suburbio, scilicet de ipsa urbe et suburbio et de communitate et universitate ipsorum annuatim xxiiijor viros ... ."

[9]*HGL* 8: No. 515, col. 1554 (dated ca. 1265) where Raymond was quoted as asserting "quod totus consulatus Tholose ... erat et esse debebat in perpetuum in proprietatem

ing instead that the consuls had usually elected four new consuls, who had themselves then chosen the remaining twenty.[10] Although both methods of election are seen in other towns in south France and elsewhere, the count's view has a ring of truth, but so also does that of the consuls.

In addition to the consuls, the town's general assembly, variously called a "public parliament" or "common colloquy" played a major role here. Evidence for this assertion is twofold. The actual naming or institution of the new magistrates took place before such an assembly and its role may well have been more than merely acclamatory. Around 1241 a tumultuous assembly took place at a time when Count Raymond VII had seized control of the consulate. Testifying in about 1274 Bernard Aimericus, the count's onetime personal notary and thereafter a constant member of the comital administration and a consul in 1258-1259 and 1266-1267, gave an eyewitness account. According to his surely reliable statement, persons in the parliament were of the decided opinion that they should be consulted about the choice of these officers and did not hesitate to contradict the count on this point.[11] Extrapolating from this, it may well be that, having been chosen by the outgoing consuls or by some of their number, the successors were then presented to be received or acclaimed by a general assembly. Although hardly a wholly free election, this procedure implies prior consultation with interested parties to assure a harmonious result. An outright refusal of the nominees by a "public parliament" must have been rare, although the radical change in the consular board of 1202 makes it more than likely that something like it sometimes happened.

---

et possessionem communitatis et universitatis urbis Tholose et suburbii ... et ... communitas et universitas poterat et debebat eligere, nominare, instituere ... et tenere consules ... scilicet annuatim xxiiii viros, medietatem de urbe et aliam medietatem de suburbio, de qualibet partita duos viros ... quorum medietas esse majorum et alia medietas esset mediorum ... ."

[10]Ibid., col. 1556: "Verum est quod ab antiquis temporibus cum predecessoribus domini comitis tam tempore pacis quam tempore guerre facta est electio consulum per ipsos cives, non sub forma ab eis proposita sed aliter, videlicet quod consules exituri de regimine, qui tunc erant viginti quatuor, eligebant quatuor consules pro anno futuro et illi eligebant viginti."

[11]PAN, J 305 32, lr (part published in *HGL* 10: Note 35, pr. no. 1, 163ff.): Bernard reported "quod vidit quod dum quadam die dominus Ramundus comes esset in domo communi Tholose, vocato publico parlamento ibidem, fuit discencio inter aliquos cives quia quilibet ipsorum procuraba[n]t quod idem dominus ... poneret consules in villa Tholose de consensu ipsorum vel aliquem seu aliquos de amicis ipsorum. Tandem dominus comes Raimundus motus aliquantulum dixit quod aliquos consules non poneret ad ipsorum civium instanciam et sic recessit, aliquibus consulibus in consulatu minime positis."

Whatever the mode of election, the names in the consular lists instruct one that there were alternations between the scions of old and new families. This reflection of the existence of different groups with differing policies was exemplified, as noted above, in 1202 and also in subsequent consulates during the Albigensian Crusade when quite modest people were in office.[12] Unlike the situation in Italy where the division between the Guelph and Ghibelline parties marked all thirteenth century politics, however, there was relatively little difference in political ideology. The men of 1202 and the war years were in office during the greatest age of Toulousan republicanism, but the earlier victory over the count had been won by the old families in 1189. Besides, if the new group had led in the attempt to conquer the "patria Tolosana" from 1202 to 1204, they shared with the older families the burden during the wars against the crusaders and the crown of France. Just before the collapse of southern resistance in 1229, however, those from the families of 1202 led Toulouse in a last hurrah.[13]

By that desperate time in the war, Toulouse had itself become the only real center of resistance to Capetian or northern French power, other than notables already expropriated by the crusaders or those who, like the count of Foix, were greatly threatened. The consuls profited from their role to demand every conceivable privilege as the price for continued support. They asserted their right to elect their successors freely and multiplied their controls over the count's principal executive officer, the vicar of Toulouse, thereby almost erasing their prince's powers. They repeated their earlier action of reaching out into the countryside, wringing from the count freedom from tolls in his domains for all the citizens of their town. They asserted the superior jurisdiction of their courts over all civil and criminal litigation between their citizens and any other subject of the prince. They also assumed the right to protect churches and monasteries in the vicarage around the town and the addition of this spiritual role implies that this elected board of magistrates threatened to replace the count's authority in much

---

[12]See the discussion of these changes in my *Liberty and Political Power*, especially pp. 66-68 and 88-90.

[13]To put the matter rehearsed in more detail in my *Liberty and Political Power*, Chapters Five and Six, somewhat too schematically: up to the term of 1213-1214, during which the southern side was defeated at Muret, the consulates of the war years were largely dominated by the old families who had been in office before 1202. Thereafter, excluding the years of Simon de Montfort's occupation, the old and new families alternated until 1218-1219 when the new men took over, sharing the consulate with the old families only twice during the great sieges until 1229, once in the term of 1222-1223 and again in 1225-1226.

of western Languedoc.[14] In brief, to continue to fight the war would have cost the count too much: the consuls were driving their prince into his enemy's arms.

B. RAYMOND VII

Reaction was not slow in coming. From the very moment Toulouse admitted its defeat in 1229, there are unmistakable signs of a revival of princely power. In spite of a temptation to believe that Alphonse of Poitiers and his successors, the kings of France, were those who deprived Toulouse of its freedoms, it is certain that the first weakening of Toulousan republicanism occurred during the aftermath of the Albigensian war in the reign of Raymond VII, the last member of the house of Saint-Gilles. Raymond's policy necessarily asserted local independence, that is, a measure of autonomy for his house within the Capetian realm, and tried to break free of the bondage to Paris he had accepted on the defeat of the southern cause. To destroy the terms of the Peace of Paris imposed on him in 1229, he tried to arrest or reverse the decentralization of his realm and to weaken the traditional liberties possessed by the urban and landed families of his remaining towns and provinces. In brief, for his family's traditional freedom from the Capetian French and perhaps also for what he conceived to be the liberty of the Midi, the count undertook, or was obliged, to limit the liberty of its leading subjects.

Nothing could have been more hopeless than Raymond's ambition. The attractions and needs of France's new centralization and the inadvertent alliance of the Roman church and the Parisian monarchy defeated and even turned to ridicule the actions of an individual who had shown decision and capacity in the days of the Albigensian Crusade. Faced by his great opponents and their allies, Raymond was unable to maintain a consistent or coherent policy. His means were inadequate, his allies unreliable and his subjects used to a measure of freedom so great that they could not unify in the face of the northern French monarchy. How and in what ways the count was distressed by his failures may only be divined, but, in their censorious way, the clergy, notably, in this case, the historian Puylaurens, blamed him for blowing hot and cold in prosecuting heresy and obeying the terms of the Peace of Paris.[15]

---

[14]For a treatment of these themes, see my *Liberty and Political Power*, especially Chapters Five, Six and Eight.

[15]Puylaurens' *Chronica*, ed. Duvernoy, p. 146, remarked about his policies in the early twelve-thirties: "Sed habens comes quandoque latera Aquilonis circa se, idem ex

Puylaurens was right and Raymond's inconsistency towards Catharism and the clerical repression of this divergence made him oscillate from side to side with marked intemperance. Although from the war years he had friends and courtiers who were Cathars, he could not afford to protect them. Catharism and divergent thought generally, it had been proved, invited foreign intervention. And those one cannot help and who inadvertently hurt one easily become the objects of one's rage. Right after the war, Raymond was obliged to support and even amplify Cardinal Roman's actions and legislation of 1229 and appears to have abetted the lynch-like actions of his first postwar vicar, Durand de Sancto Barcio. The growing rage the consuls directed against the inquisitors in the mid-twelve-thirties and the fact that one Dominican, Peter Seillanus, seemed about to zero in on Raymond himself or his immediate entourage, caused the count to change his tune. Always hostile to foreign intervention in his realm, Raymond and his new vicar, Peter de Tolosa, tried to restrain these friars. The latter even aided the consuls when they expelled the Dominicans from the town in 1235 and was excommunicated along with them for this act.

Although this policy with its appeals to Rome won some victories by precipitating conflicts between the pope and the inquisitors and within the Dominican order itself, Raymond enjoyed only a momentary success, one dependent on the shifts of papal policy. The count was momentarily lucky there because, although Gregory IX (1227-1241) could concentrate on Toulouse to defeat the heretics, Innocent IV (1243-1254) was unable to do so because Hohenstaufen threats made him turn back to Italy.[16] Raymond was nevertheless in no position to move with consistency. He was embroiled unsuccessfully in Provence and with the Capetians in the early twelve-forties, and Toulouse rose against him in 1245. In 1249, the last year of his life, he had clearly become frantic. He had momentarily crushed Toulouse, but it was bubbling with opposition. He had been discomfited in Provence. His new marriage had failed to produce a male heir, his attempt to reverse the terms of the Peace of Paris had miscarried and he was entering his fifties. It is not surprising that, in these difficult circumstances, Raymond allowed or perpetrated the burning of eighty purported Cathars (the numbers are surely exaggerated) in a village near Agen in the spring of 1249. There is also evidence that his officers in Toulouse, probably the vicar and his staff, were exceeding the punishments meted out by the inquisitors. As a

---

calido aliquando redebatur tepidus et remissus, ut minus fervens inveniretur in negocio pacis et fidei prosequendo."

[16]See Dossat's detailed articles published from 1955 to 1960 and reissued in his *Eglise et hérésie en France au XIIIe siècle*, Nos. 20-22.

result of such indiscriminate killing of Cathars and those suspected of that belief, the inquisitors themselves, moved by the distaste within their order for this unpleasant work and by pontifical censures of inquisitorial excesses, reacted by favoring moderation and the rule of law.[17]

Raymond then may be thought to have been the villain. But this is surely to overstate the case. Both in town and countryside, the well-to-do who led society in the years around 1200 were as incapable of handling their problem as the count was of handling his. In Toulouse, on the defeat of the southern cause in 1229, the relatively popular elements that, mixed with scions of older families, had led the town during the war were quickly replaced in the consulate by members of old and traditionally more pacific families. But the problem of these families was, as shall be seen in Chapter Fifteen below, that they were among those most heavily committed to divergent religious thought. When the repression of Catharism began in earnest under Cardinal Roman in 1229 and was vigorously continued by the newly founded Inquisition in the twelve-thirties, the consuls joined with the count against their common foes at the cost of throwing their onetime political liberty to the winds. Raymond VII's domination of the consulate began in 1229, the very year of the Peace of Paris and that of Cardinal Roman's mission to root out aberrant belief. Available consular lists state that the consulate was reduced from twenty-four to twelve members and this reduction of its membership, one so useful to the prince, was retained through 1245.[18] The traditional practice of rotating the board of consuls each year was at first retained, but the count soon began to appoint his consuls for terms up to four years.[19]

As consequential was the count's attempt to prise the office of the vicar of Toulouse from consular control. By the time of the wartime vicarages of William de Roaxio and Hugh Johannes (1218-1226), the vicar had almost become a creature of the consulate.[20] Although information is spotty until around 1265 when the consuls explained what they thought had been the position of the vicar, it seems sure that he was usually a citizen who took

---

[17]On the change in the inquisitors' attitudes from the early angry days of Peter Seillanus, see the letter written to Alphonse of Poitiers by the inquisitors Reginald of Chartres and John of Saint-Pierre in *HGL* 8: No. 465 (January 1255). Dossat, *Les crises de l'inquisition toulousaine*, p. 191, has emended this date to January 1257.

[18]The last consulate with twenty-four members is 1227. From 1230 to 1245 twelve is the number, with twenty-four reappearing in 1246. For this, see Appendix 4.

[19]Appendix 4's lists for the long term from 1235 to 1238 or 1239 and from 1243 to 1245.

[20]My *Liberty and Political Power*, pp. 111-114, treats this history.

oath to the consuls and was to be judged by them if he harmed citizens.[21] Some of this, especially about the oath, was admitted by Alphonse's administration, as being true not only during the war years but even afterward.[22]

After the crusade, things had begun to change, to the consuls' detriment. The agent of this change was Durand de Sancto Barcio who first appeared as vicar briefly in 1214 just before the crusader occupation of Toulouse, but began another term in 1227 to hold office until 1235.[23] He aided the bishop and Dominicans in their first massive attack on the Cathars. According to the Dominican William Pelisson's frank account, he busied himself burning persons condemned by the friars for Catharism immediately after what seem like hasty trials. These events naturally evoked widespread popular indignation. In one well-known case, that of John Textor, who won the crowd over by his pleas, the vicar was forced to back off. In another he got his way and a smith or artisan of the Croix-Baragnon who had elicited much popular support was burnt.[24] An event in 1234 will illustrate the tenor of the times. After a mass honoring the founder's canonization, the Dominican bishop of Toulouse, Bernard de Falgario or Miramonte, and his brother friars were called away from their repast to convert a dying Cathar woman. They condemned the recalcitrant woman and the vicar, summoned by the friars, promptly carted her on her sickbed from her son-in-law's house and burned her just outside of town. The bishop and the brethren then repaired again to the refectory and dined happily there, "giving thanks to God and the Blessed Dominic."[25]

---

[21]*HGL* 8: No. 515 (ca. 1265): "Item quod vicarius ... tempore sue novitatis seu ingressus sui officii, jurabat et jurare tenebatur ... ibidem dictis consulibus forciam et consilium ... et quod vicarius se tornabat specialiter et tornare debebat seu desistebat et desistere debebat cognicioni consulum ab omni forcia et violencia et injuria, si quam faciebat vel fecerat civibus Tholose et alicui eorumdem, et emendam inde faciebat cognicioni consulum eorumdem."

[22]Ibid.: "Verum est quod de patiencia domini comitis bone memorie juraverunt vicarii consulibus sub certa forma, que scripta poterit inveniri, et etiam tempore domini comitis qui nunc est aliquis vicarius dicitur jurasse."

[23]Although not titled vicar in a charter until MADTG, A 297, fol. 730 (December 1227), he occupied the post during the month before in PAN, J 317 16 (November 1227). His retirement is seen in J 320 48 (April 1235).

[24]Pelisson, *Chronique*, ed. Duvernoy, pp. 50-62 (John Textor) and 58-60, where in 1234 the condemned "faber" kept shouting his innocence: "Unde commoti sunt multi de populo contra fratres et vicarium, et nichilominus vicarius combussit eum."

[25]Ibid., p. 64: "Vicarius autem eam [the sick woman in Pictavinus Borsier's house on the modern rue Romiguières], cum lecto in quo erat, sic ad ignem ad pratum Comitis portari et statim eam comburi fecit ... . Episcopus vero et fratres et socii, hoc completo, venerunt ad refectorium, et que parata erant cum letitia comederunt, gratias agentes Deo et beato Dominico."

Given the circumstances, the violence of Dominic's friars is understand-able, but why the vicar shared it is not. He may have been prompted by the count's initial policy after the Peace of Paris and the Council of Toulouse of 1229 and failed to catch up with its later change. He may also have bought the vicarial office. He is known to have been a creditor of both Raymond VI and his son and perhaps tried to recoup the investment from properties confiscated from condemned Cathars. Whatever the case, Du-rand's vehement attacks on the Cathars undoubtedly frightened the consuls. As will be discussed below, many consuls in office from 1235 to 1238 were from families already, or about to be, lashed by the inquisitors' whip. Besides, it was more than self-defense. It was remarked earlier in this study that the great maritime republics of northern Italy, Genoa and Venice were slow to admit the inquisitors and, by the time they did, had all but drawn their fangs. Republics are usually more solicitous of their subjects' rights vis-à-vis third parties than other kinds of government. Even when the con-suls were unable to protect individual Cathars from the church, they jealous-ly tried to protect their citizens and their rights. Initially designed to re-strain the count's confiscation of property, this resistance was applied to heresy trials as well.[26] In 1203, even before the Albigensian Crusade and the subsequent systematic repression, these magistrates had persuaded a papal legate to promise to uphold the custom of Toulouse and in 1205 had sought to prevent the condemnation of dead heretics.[27] Lastly, the vicar's impetuous actions surely represented a reversal of the long evolution of the consuls' relations with this comital officer. Before these events, vicars, according to the views expressed by the consuls in 1265 or thereabouts, depended on them, protected Toulousan citizens and admitted the consular monopoly of criminal cases involving them.[28]

After Durand's term ended in 1235, a Guilalmonus Dalart was appoint-ed to that office. Unlike most of his immediate predecessors, Guilalmonus was not a Toulousan, being from the region of Cahors, and it is remotely possible that he, like his twelfth century predecessors, was one of the count's "servientes." The count's initiative may have faced consular resis-

[26]See the discussion of Toulouse's criminal law in my *Liberty and Political Power*, pp. 106-108.

[27]PAN, JJ 21, fol. 77 (the legate took oath in December 1203, and the act was written in March 1204), and TAM, AA 1 52 (March 1205), both being treated in my *Repression of Catharism*, pp. 17-18.

[28]See the passage in *HGL* 8: col. 1553, cited above. Note also ibid., col. 1554: "Item quod consules Tholose ... audiebant et diffiniebant omnes causas criminum et injuriarum civium Tholose."

tance, because Guilalmonus is seen as vicar in only one charter of 1235.[29]
In September of that year, Peter de Tolosa, a citizen and member of that
distinguished town family, is seen in office. This appointment shows that
the count had changed from the policy typified by Durand de Sancto Barcio
to join with the consuls against the Inquisition. Battling the Dominicans,
Peter was excommunicated together with the consuls but appears to have
anyway remained in office for a reasonable length of time.[30] He was replaced in 1243 by Berengar de Promilhaco, the first vicar regularly
described as a knight. Although he perhaps burned a few Cathars illegally,
he held his office until the assumption of the county by Raymond VII's
successor, Alphonse of Poitiers in 1249. Berengar's vicarage was an undoubted victory for the prince because he, deriving presumably from Pro-
millac in the Rouergue, was another noncitizen.[31]

Although things were clearly getting out of hand, Toulousans had not
forgotten their erstwhile freedom. Profiting from Raymond's defeated
attempt to ally with the Angevins against the Capetians, his failure in
Provence and his humiliation by the crown of France in 1243, Toulouse
asserted its independence. Between September 1245 and January 1246, the
count's consuls were summarily ejected and the number of these magistrates
rose again to twenty-four. In the term of 1247-1248, the count capitulated
to one of the few boards dominated by the old families.[32] He was also
forced to exculpate the rebels of 1246, to aver that his control of the
consulate had been temporary, undertaken only at the invitation of Toulouse
itself, and to restore the old free election and yearly term of office.[33]

Protestations of good will notwithstanding, Raymond was unreconciled.
In 1249, the last year of his unhappy life, he took over the town govern-

[29]PAN, J 322 56 (July 1235). The name Dalart derives from J 314 75 (August 1238)
where he, no longer vicar, served as a witness. The rarity of his name makes it probable
that he was the Wilalmonus among the "balistarii et servientes dicti domini Raimundi
quondam comitis Tholosani" who swore loyalty to Alphonse of Poitiers in December
1249 in HGL 8: No. 415, col. 1263.

[30]For Peter's life and term of office, see my Repression of Catharism, pp. 280-282.

[31]The act appointing Berengar is in HGL 8: No. 364, cols. 1123-1124 (April 1243),
and he was last mentioned taking oath in ibid., No. 415, col. 4261 (December 1269).

[32]Although the rise of yet further new families complicates the picture, the older and
newer groups alternated in this manner in Appendix 4: 1230 mixed old and new, 1230 or
1231 old, 1231-1232 old, 1235-1238 or 1239 old, 1239-1240 new, 1243-1245 mixed but
new, 1246 new but nearly balanced, 1247-1248 old, 1248-1249 new, and 1249-1250 new.

[33]TAM, AA 1 101 (July 1247), and AA 1 103 (January 1248), the first being the
count's forgiveness before a general assembly "in domo comuni," and the second the
basic statement promulgated in a "comune Tolose colloquium."

ment again and appointed a consulate of twelve members. On the news of his premature death in September of that year, his appointees were expelled from office by a popular revolt and the old free consulate of twenty-four members reappeared – a sad memorial to "lo jove," the town's young hero of wartime fame and popularity.

C. ALPHONSE OF POITIERS' VICTORY

Toulouse's attempt to restore its political liberty soon failed. After Raymond's death, Paris took over in the person of the Capetian, Alphonse of Poitiers, an absentee prince who, in the twenty-odd years of his reign (1249-1271), spent only about a month in the Midi, most of that short time at the very end of his reign just before going to Tunis on crusade.[34] A vigorous exponent of princely government and of northern French centralization, this brother of Louis IX was as hostile to urban quasi-republican self-government as his predecessor of the house of Saint-Gilles had been and was in a far better position to do what he wanted.

The constitutional issues dividing Alphonse's administration and the town of Toulouse were addressed during the twelve-fifties. Alphonse first requested that the troublesome points between the consuls and himself be submitted to arbitration. The arbiters he nominated show that the count's offer was anything but ingenuous: one arbiter was the bishop of Toulouse, a harsh persecutor of religious divergence, and the others were Sicard Alaman and Pons Astoaudus, members of Raymond VII's old government, all three notorious enemies of the gains the Toulousans had made (on paper) in the late days of the Albigensian Crusade.[35] This suggestion having gone nowhere, the count tried again ca. 1265 when he denied the validity of the charter restoring the liberty of the consulate in 1248, because it was not authenticated by his predecessor's seal.[36] Given the way Toulousan

---

[34]The assumption of power was taken by Queen Blanche of France in her son's name in *HGL* 8: No. 415, col. 1260 (December 1249). Alphonse went to Toulouse on his way back from the Holy Land and held a public assembly there late in May 1251, being in town from May 23 to 29. He then reached Verdun-sur-Garonne on his way north on May 30. He returned south only in 1270, being at Toulouse sometime between April 21 and 31, remaining there until between May 13 and 16, to be at Aimargues on his way to Tunis on May 17. These dates are taken from Fournier and Guébin, *Enquêtes administratives*, pp. xix-xxi.

[35]*HGL* 8: No. 450, col. 1371 (June 1255).

[36]Ibid., No. 515, col. 1558: "Non creditur quod dictum instrumentum de consciencia domini comitis bone memorie fuerit factum sicut in petitione consulum continetur, nec in dicto instrumento sigillum prefati domini est appensum."

public notaries drew valid acts for both the count and civil society from the early years of the twelfth century, the requirement of a seal almost seems like a polemical attempt to impose the northern French "regime of seals" on this citadel of the public notariate.

It really had nothing to do with diplomatic, however, because the count's seal was a banner around which rallied the natives of Provence and Languedoc who had earlier served Raymond VII. Of these, other than the seneschal Pons of Villanova studied below, the major figures were Pons Astoaudus, Raymond's onetime chancellor and a jurist from Marseille and Avignon, and the baron Sicard Alaman, who had been close to Raymond from 1231 and was to hold both the office of vicar of Toulouse and seneschal of the Toulousain.[37] In addition, Alphonse also called on Guy Folcoldius, the later Pope Clement IV, a jurist who had also served Raymond VII and, like the others, went into Capetian service. The battle for Languedoc's independence having failed, these officers were probably hostile to Catharism that, they may have felt, had brought such misery on their homeland. They assuredly favored the renewal of princely government, whether Raymondine or Capetian, and probably also wished to reinforce rural freedom and reduce Toulouse's economic dominance of the Toulousain. Sometime just after the events of 1255 recited above, Folcoldius rendered a legal decision at Lavaur against the town and favoring the count. No copy of this decision has been found, but what it contained is known because a note on the dorse of the count's complaints against the consuls dated sometime before December 1255 contains the phrase: "approved by 'dominus' Guy Folcoldius."[38]

Building on Raymond's foundation, then, Alphonse's administration restored princely authority. The first requirement was to establish a hierarchy of officers free from the grasp of the town magistrates. As readers already know, a key officer was the vicar of Toulouse. Around 1265 Alphonse of Poitiers admitted that his first vicar had taken oath to the consuls, but canceled that avowal by declaring that he had acted of his grace.[39] Shortly before that observation was made, in fact, the count had taken over the appointment of this office. Pons Astoaudus reported that the vicarial oath to the consuls was abrogated when Odart de Ponpagne became vicar

---

[37]Thumbnail sketches of these two persons with bibliography are to be found in Fournier and Guébin, *Enquêtes administratives*, pp. xliii and lxxxii-lxxxiii. Astoaudus, whose family were rural gentry in the Venaissin, was knighted for his service.

[38]Ibid., No. 452 (before December 12, 1255): "Hec sunt capitula in quibus consules Tholosani injuriantur domino comiti." And on the dorse: "Laudat dominus Guido Fulcoldius."

[39]See note 22 above.

in 1253 and he almost certainly told the truth.[40] Furthermore, with the exception of the Toulousan William de Escalquencs who served as a "locumtenens" briefly in 1264 and Sicard Alaman who was general trouble-shooter in 1268 and 1269, all of Alphonse's vicars were outsiders and most of them came from northern France.[41] When one realizes that most of Alphonse's administration's other officers, the all-important investigating "clerici" and judges, also came from northern France, the degree to which the Toulousain was invaded by the French, as a modern would put it, is obvious.[42]

Crowning this effort was the rebuilding of the seneschalsy or provincial governorship. This office had been instituted by Raymond VI before the Albigensian war, as part of his attempt to reassert control in the period when the vicarage of Toulouse was falling into the hands of the consuls of Tolouse. Although noble stewards were known in southern France, the count had probably imitated the continental administration of the English Angevins.[43] The seneschalsy of the Toulousain evolved from the vicarial office in the period from 1202 to 1210 and its first holder was the well-

[40]See Fournier and Guébin, *Enquêtes administratives*, No. 35, 127a, 130b-131a (dated June to September 1262) and also in *HGL* 8: No. 506, col. 1516 (dated ca. 1264) where copies of the old oath may be read and where Astoaudus "dist que il n'i ot point de serment puis que Odart de Ponpogne fust vigier."

[41]The vicars were Odart de Ponpagne (perhaps Pomponio or Ponpona), a knight from the Vaucluse, from 1253 to June 1256 in Fournier and Guébin, *Enquêtes administratives*, pp. 127a-b; Peter Bernard, burgher of Chartres, from 1256 to 1261 in ibid., p. xlii; William de Nantolleto, knight (Nantholet near Meaux), from January 1263 in ibid., p. 135b, to May 1269 in Molinier, *Correspondance administrative* 2: 11-15 (November 1223 and April 1231 and May 1269); interim officers, ie. William de Escalquencs in *HGL* 8: No. 509 v, cols. 1530-1541 (April 1264), and Sicard Alaman as seneschal, vicar and general "locumtenens" in 1268 and 1269 in Fournier and Guébin, *Enquêtes administratives*, p. lxxxii; and, lastly, the knight Peter de Roceio from May 1269 in Molinier, *Correspondance administrative* 2: 16, No. 1231, to April 1271 in TAM, II 77 (April 1271, copied in February 1299).

[42]Fournier and Guébin, *Enquêtes administratives*, pp. xxxiv-xlv, summarize the histories of the investigators or "missi" employed by Alphonse. Thirty-nine were there listed: six laymen (including five knights and one burgher), seventeen secular clerks and sixteen regular clerks (seven Dominicans and eight Franciscans). Although some of the secular clerks like the future pope, Guy Folcoldius, may have been laymen when in service or, at any rate, not yet in higher orders, clerks constituted 84.5 percent of the sample. Over half (at least twenty-one of these officers) were from regions north of the Loire, especially the Ile-de-France.

[43]Rouquette, *Cartulaire de Béziers*, No. 178 (July 1153): the bishop of Bézier's "feodum quod vocatur senescalera," was an example of the older stewardship. On the origins of the Toulousan seneschalsy, see my *Liberty and Political Power*, pp. 111-112 and 125.

known knight Raymond de Recalto, a rural notable foreign to Toulouse who first served as "vicarius Tolosanus" and then as seneschal. His fortunes were reversed by the defeat of the southern side: he fled the field of Castelnaudary in 1211 and retired after the southern side was crushed at Muret two years later. That he was a person of consequence was shown when the abbot of Moissac arranged to have him retire into the Mainaderie Hospital in Toulouse in 1214 and Bishop Fulk angrily vetoed the idea.[44]

Raymond's first postwar seneschal was Pons de Villanova (Villeneuve-la-Comptale) of Montréal in the Lauragais, not a member of the town's Villanova clan. The historian Puylaurens described him and the more famous Oliver de Termes as "energetic men" when they helped animate the unsuccessful defense of Labécède-Lauragais near Castelnaudary against the French in 1227.[45] Pons served as "senescallus Tolosanus" from the spring of 1235 to that of 1241 and after that time appears in the court of Raymond VII.[46] Unfortunately for his career, he was an active Cathar believer. Various witnesses in the twelve-forties testified that they had seen him salute heretics and organize a transport of grain to the famous Cathar fortress of Montségur which fell to a force under the French seneschal of Carcassonnne in 1244.[47]

In short, the seneschalsy never really flourished under the house of Toulouse-Saint-Gilles, but, under Alphonse of Poitiers, it really took off. Of this Capetian's seven seneschals, all save Sicard Alaman were northern Frenchmen.[48] Although Sicard, a baron from the region of Albi, held the

[44]For these events and Fulk's acid wit, see my *Repression of Catharism*, pp. 21, 25 and especially 279, and Appendix 6 below which deals with Raymond's Toulousan wife's property and the *Canso*, ed. Martin-Chabot, 1: 234-237, about his flight from Castelnaudery to Montferrand.

[45]See Duvernoy's edition of Puylaurens' *Chronica*, p. 124: "viri strenui." Duvernoy's note 4 on p. 125 has led to the following footnotes.

[46]See PAN, J 320 48 (April 1235), *HGL* 8: No. 317 ii (August 1236) serving at Narbonne as "senescallus et procurator domini comitis Tolosani," *HGL* 8: No. 322 v (February 1239) at Saint-Gilles on the Rhone in PAN, J 314 76 (February 1241) as "senescallus Tolosanus" and again in *HGL* 8: No. 339 i (April 1241) not described as seneschal. According to Duvernoy, Pons is seen until 1248.

[47]PBN, Collection Doat 24: fol. 86, where a lord of Niort testified that Pons had adored in about 1232 at Villeneuve-la-Comptale and thereafter, on fols. 88v-89, arranging for transportation near Laurac in 1233 or 1234. TBM, MS 609, fol. 124v, testimony of the lord of Gaja-la-Selve near Fanjeaux in 1246, stating that "circa pacem" he himself had adored together with Pons "senescallus olim."

[48]The careers of Alphonse's seneschals running from 1251 on are sketched in Fournier and Guébin, *Enquêtes administratives*, pp. lxxvii-lxxxvi. One other seneschal,

seneschalsy only from 1268 to 1270 and even then partly as "locumtenens" for Thibaut de Nangeville, his several special missions for the count make it sure that he was devoted to the policies associated with Alphonse's name and may perhaps have been their main initiator.

The reduction of the consulate took longer, but was no less sure. Sometime around 1265, matters came to a head when the so-called "Articles of the Citizens of Toulouse" were presented to the count by two consuls and two members of their council, who there rehearsed the arguments of the consulate.[49] Traditionally, they said, and following Raymond VII's grant of 1248, the outgoing consuls "toward the end of their administration annually elected the succeeding chaptermen or consuls."[50] The count's position was that, although that was sometimes true, Raymond VII had himself sometimes chosen these magistrates. And, furthermore, that he had done so just before his death and that, on news of this sad event, his consuls were "violently" removed before the expiration of their term of office.[51] True enough, but the count's was a truncated version of the past: he or his informants failed to note that Raymond VII had violently installed the consuls who had been later tossed out.

The victory of the count's party was remanded until after a later grinding and exhausting constitutional crisis extending from 1261 to 1270, with its peak in 1268 and 1269. The consuls were again defeated. Alphonse's government restored the situation which obtained during Raymond VII's personal government, reduced the number of consuls to twelve and directly appointed these magistrates. Sometime after the royal assumption of power

---

Hugh d'Arcis, in office from 1254 to 1256, presumably came from northern France but possibly from the Rouergue. The seneschalsy of Toulouse was often combined with that of Albi, sometimes with Agen and Cahors.

[49]*HGL* 8: No. 515 (ca. 1265): "Articuli civium Tholosanorum."

[50]Ibid., col. 1553: "capitularii vel consules, qui ex parte dicte communitatis urbis et suburbii in dicta urbe et suburbio pro tempore fuerant, circa finem sue administrationis annuatim alios capitularios vel consules de eadem urbe et suburbio eligebant et creabant et nominabant et instituebant ... ."

[51]Ibid., col. 1556: "pluries autem facta est electio consulum per dominum comitem. Et eo tempore quo dominus Ramundus comes ... migravit a seculo, ipse creaverat consules qui iuxta morem Tholose debebant regere villam per unum annum. Et post obitum dicti domini comitis cives Tholosani consules creatos per dictum comitem expulerunt violenter de consulatu et de domo communi bene per dimidium annum ante finem sui regiminis, et privaverunt indebite dominum comitem, qui nunc eat, sua possessione ... propter quod dictus comes fuit restitutus ad illam possessionem."

following Alphonse's death in August 1271, Master Aimeric de Robiano, a lawyer in the count's service, rightly testified that, under Alphonse, the consuls were chosen by the count's vicar and officers and served merely as his "officiales."[52] After these severe defeats, Toulouse tried to restore its freedoms several times again, especially at the time of the royal assumption of power by Philip III in 1271. The settlement of the intermittent negotiations in 1283 between the prince and the town was, in fact, somewhat more favorable to the consuls than the Alphonsine regime had been. The parties agreed that the outgoing consuls would elect three from each of the twelve "partidas" of the town from whom the vicar would choose one for the final body of twelve.[53]

To conclude, constitutionally speaking, by 1285 Toulousan republicanism was nevertheless all but dead and, decorated by the egregious title of "royal city," the town was on its way to becoming just another modestly privileged urban community in the new France of the later middle ages.[54]

[52]TAM, II 9 contains an undated roll of testimony about the consulate and the rights of the count. This note may be dated to the early twelve-seventies, no later than 1274, because seven of the sixteen Toulousan citizens who gave testimony were the same as those testifying at about 1274 in PAN, J 305 32. In the TAM, II 9 roll, Robiano testified that "consules Tholose pro suis temporibus fuerunt electi per vicarium Tholose et curiam domini Alfonsi comitis Tholose et sunt in consulatu Tholose officiales domini comitis."

[53]TAM, AA 3 4, ibid. II 35, a "vidimus" of August 1335, and Archevêché (G 1), Register, f. 45r, both dated October 1283.

[54]Typical formulas in Saint-Sernin 689 (21, 73, 6) (October 1308) where a syndic "dominorum de capitulo regie urbis et suburbii Tholose" appeared in court concerning a tithe of pastels or woad and Saint-Bernard 36 (February 1312) where the "domini consules regie civitatis et suburbii Tholose" authenticate an act of February 1307.

14

Social Defeat

A. TOWN AND COUNTRY

The mention of the southerners who favored the diminution of Toulouse's liberties brings to mind another element in the failure of Toulousan republicanism, namely the countryfolk, especially the gentlefolk or nobility. Disciples of the playwright Gênet are accustomed to view the world in terms of a plot by malevolent judges (princes or magistrates), generals (soldiers, nobles or knights) and priests against the liberties or the naturally free spirit of the people. The princes have been active in the previous chapter and the priests will wait until the next one; the nobles are dealt with here. One is tempted to believe that the failure of Toulouse's republicanism was caused by a reaction of a feudal landed aristocracy against the rising bourgeoisie of the town, to employ a time-honored terminology.

As is obvious, conflicts of interest between town and countryside abounded and the counts of Toulouse had long tried to exploit them. These had erupted into open warfare when Toulouse had attempted to conquer a "contado" in and after 1202 and it is noteworthy that the popular elements that entered the consulate in that year were both republican and expansionist. From 1202 to 1204, they attacked and in the main defeated twenty-three rural lordships and small towns of the region. There is also evidence to show that, had they not been arrested by the Albigensian Crusade, they planned an even greater expansion. This trend culminated in the later stages of the Albigensian Crusade, the great war against the northern French. At that time the count had become almost wholly dependent on Toulouse for support. As noted above, he therefore granted the town jurisdiction of all cases involving her citizens and foreigners. Other local princes and rural lords also joined him by promising Toulouse's merchants and citizens complete freedom from tolls and tariffs in their domains.[1]

---

[1] See my *Liberty and Political Power*, pp. 66-72, and especially Chapter Ten. The old counties and baronies affected by the treaties of the early twelve-twenties are listed in Chapter Thirteen, p. 234.

Once the war was over Raymond VII determined to rescind these con-
cessions. From 1245 through 1248, the period of a brief restoration of
consular freedom, the consuls tried to reverse the erosion these privileges
had begun to suffer after 1229. They despatched the town militia to destroy
facilities and communities from Verdun well to the north on the Garonne
river to Auterive and Venerque on the Ariège in the south, and more than
half way toward Lombez at Saboneres in the county of Comminges. This
effort to revive the glory of an earlier age failed at the time of Alphonse of
Poitiers. His spokesmen, clearly reflecting the attitudes of Raymond VII's
administrative officers, charged that Toulouse's actions in the places mentioned above had stabbed Raymond in the back when he was busy in Provence trying to re-establish his realm.[2]

Alphonse therefore resumed Raymond's policies. He mobilized the villages and small towns of the countryside against the more concentrated
economic power of the town by stripping the townsmen of their wholesale
exemption from tolls and tariffs. During his reign, Toulouse's commercial
advantages narrowed and tolls became a constant preoccupation of the consuls. After the royal government took the town over, following Alphonse's
death in 1271, their unhappiness erupted in public protests. The first took
place in the Château Narbonnais and the second in the full publicity of a
public assembly in the Town Hall.[3] The consuls there pledged loyalty to
the king if he did not diminish the town's rights over its consulate, criminal
justice and tolls and other praiseworthy customs.[4] In the negotiations leading up to the final settlement in 1278, the proctor for the town rightly re-

[2]*HGL* 8: No. 452, col. 1376 (dated before December 1255) refers to the castle of
Saboneres; ibid., No. 455, cols. 1382-1383, in 1255, Saboneres again and Raymond's
properties at Venerque and Verdun No. 515, col. 1558 (dated 1265): "Et cum dictus
dominus comes Raimundus esset in partibus Provincie magnis et caris et periculosis
negociis occupatus, cives Tholosani immunitatem dictorum pedagiorum violenter
usurpaverunt et paxeriam ... quam habebat apud Verdunum ... destruxerunt ... ."; and
ibid., No. 522, x and xiii, cols. 1615-1616 (June 1268): the baron Sicard de Montealto
claimed that the consuls had destroyed property in his lordship of Auterive "quondam
tempore bone memorie Raimundi, quondam comitis Tholosani" and the consuls
responded by charging that he had imposed new tolls at Auterive.

[3]In TAM, AA 66, inserted parchment fol. 3, the "prima protestatio consulum fuit
facta in Castro Narbonesio" to this effect on September 16, 1271, and the "secunda
vero protestatio fuit in palatio comuni Tholose universitate ibi congregata" on September 20, 1271.

[4]Ibid.: "quod ius suum sit eis salvum in facto consulatus et cognitione criminum et
pedagiis et leudis et libertatibus et bonis et aprobatis consuetudinibus et usibus non de-
crescat."

ported to the crown that, when Alphonse had become count, the citizens had imported and exported their goods without toll or tariff, but had been despoiled of this right by the deceased royal uncle whose "officers [had] maliciously and cleverly" interpreted his regulations so as to tax everything not brought into town for immediate consumption.[5] The royal officers tactfully bowed and agreed to abolish tolls on goods bought and sold at Toulouse, but retained them on goods transhipped there.[6] When one remembers that Toulousan merchants and producers were trying to dominate the wine, leather and other trade down the Garonne to Bordeaux and all trade in the Toulousain, it is obvious that this purported rectification merely systematized the controls and left townsmen mildly privileged but prevented from easily dominating the countryside.

In line with this, many of the legal advantages over the countryside built up or acquired by the town were undermined or removed. From the late twelfth century, for example, the consuls insisted that citizens were bound in law only by instruments drawn by Toulousan public notaries.[7] Stigmatizing this as absurd and unjust, Alphonse of Poitiers' administration abrogated it as early as 1255.[8] Because the law greatly advantaged Toulousan citizens doing business with outsiders, however, a passage in the *Custom* of Toulouse continued to enshrine it and the crown had to reject it again with some asperity in 1285.[9] What in the long run finally served to strip Toulousan moneylenders and others operating in the countryside of

---

[5]*HGL* 10: No. 22, cols. 147-148 (April 1278): the proctor said "adportabant et adducebant res suas ad civitatem Tholose et etiam extrahebant inde mercimonia et omnes mercaturas suas libere et sine omni prestatione pedagii seu leude" and that Alphonse's "curiales [acted] malitiose et astute."

[6]Ibid.: "per minutas partes vel pecias" as against goods "que transeunt in grosso per Tholosam."

[7]Exemplified by a case of 1196 discussed in *Liberty and Political Power*, pp. 131-132.

[8]Molinier, *Correspondance administrative* 2: 607, No. 2100 (December 1255) where the count wrote: "Quia vero multam absurditatem continet et multis iniuriis viam parat quod apud vos dicitur usitatum, ut videlicet instrumenta extra Tolosam facta, quamvis sint publica, super solucionibus debitorum que Tolosanis civibus debebantur, fidem non faciant nisi de dictis debitis instrumenta monstrentur confecta per notarios Tholose, volumus et mandamus id apud vos omnino non servari. Cum enim par sit aliorum notariorum auctoritas et major forsitan aliquorum, fidem parem habere volumus omnium instrumentis."

[9]Gilles, *Coutumes de Toulouse*, p. 90, tit. 14a and 14b: "... quod ratione obligationis contracte sub publico instrumento per manus publici notarii Tholose confecto vel recepto et facto civi Tholosano, potest contrahens vel promittens vel qui se obligavit ubique in diocesi Tholosana et sub dominio domini comitis Tholosani, vel alterius qui sit de dominio ejusdem domini comitis cum predicto instrumento conveniri et ratione dicti contractus in civitate Tholosana coram consulibus Tholose, et coram eis tenetur etiam respondere."

privileged documentation was the creation in this period of rural judicial circumscriptions and notariates.

Toulousan commercial liberty, as modern liberals would call it, or domination of the countryside depended on the town's control of the courts whose writ obtained in the whole county. As early as 1230 Raymond VII instituted a court to adjudicate disputes over debts between citizens and foreigners. Proceeding cautiously, his court was composed of town citizens. His successor launched a far more vigorous program: a marked renewal of the vicar's judicial functions and, especially, a new expansion of the seneschalsy. New and reformed courts reflected the growth of the business brought before them. From 1255 or 1257, the ordinary judge of the vicar ("judex ordinarius," or, earlier, "judex Tholose" or "judex vicarii") makes his appearance in the documents.[10] From 1264, the seneschal's judge ("judex senescalli"), the higher judge of appeals for the whole province ("judex appellationum," the later "judex maior" or "juge mage"), is seen.[11]

These innovations changed things radically. Now, cases involving citizens and foreigners within the vicarage went to the "judex ordinarius," those within the seneschalsy to the "judex appellationum" and, indeed, as the titles of these officers indicate, the system allowed appeals from the con-

---

[10]The first reference to this judge in Toulouse is in the letter of the inquisitors of 1255 or 1257 mentioned above in Chapter Thirteen, note 17. Thereafter this officer is seen in Grandselve 9 (December 1257) recording an action of a Master Peter de Regio "iudex Tholose" wherein reference is made to an earlier action by Master Gaufridus "tunc iudex Tholose domini comitis Tholosani." Peter is heard of once again as a quondam judge in Molinier, *Correspondance administrative* 2: 112, No. 1379 (December 1269). Gaufridus is unquestionably the Geoffrey Maleti, nephew of Peter Bernard of Chartres, vicar of Toulouse from 1256 to 1261, who, according to Fournier and Guébin, *Enquêtes administratives*, p. xlii, aided his uncle during his administration, as is seen in *Layettes du Trésor* 3: 404a (April 1258). In 1264 a Master Rigaud Bellus served as "judex Tholose" in Fournier and Guébin, op. cit., pp. 170b and 180b. In 1265 or 1266 a Berengar Peutrici served in this post in ibid., pp. 188a and 234b. The latter is undoubtedly the Berengar styled "legum professor, judex curie domini vicarii Tholose," who acted in Grandselve 10 (June 1265). This is the office of the later "judex ordinarius," as in PAM, II 42 (October 1304).

[11]The first "judex senescalli" or "appellationum" was a Toulousan jurist named Master Raymond Capellerius who served as judge in PAM, II 79 (April 1264) and is cited as having rendered a sentence in Molinier, *Correspondance administrative* 1: 178, No. 286 (July 1267). The next one was Master William de Furno who was in office in September 1264 and still there in 1270 according to Fournier and Guébin, *Enquêtes administratives*, pp. 170b and 291b, and see the index of the eighth volume of the *HGL*. The later title of "judex maior" or "juge mage" is seen in PAM, II 61 (documents of September 1279, copied in March 1280 and January 1285).

suls to the vicar and then up one further step to the seneschal. Furthermore, on a local level in the countryside, the prince's government promoted the establishment of a whole system of rural jurisdictions and courts, together with the attendant services of local public notaries and legal counsel.[12] "Promoted" is the word that characterizes the role of the prince's government in this matter because the maturing small towns and villages of the province favored and aided this expansion of legal institutions to answer their own needs as well as to help control the economic aggression of their capital.

To add to this, an aspect of the evolution of social orders at this time helped the prince set town against countryside. The rural nobility and those of this order who lived in town as citizens began to claim that, unlike the rest of the community's inhabitants, they owed no taxes to the town on their rural properties. At first sight, some notables seem unmoved by this opportunity. The noble Curvus de Turribus, sometimes called "de Andosvilla" from his lordship of Endoufielle, apparently remained a contented tax-paying citizen.[13] He was nevertheless of so high a social level that he served in 1263 in the seneschal's court as a guarantor of the count of Armagnac along with other worthies including the lords of Isle-Jourdain and Noé, who, as the record said, "omnes sunt nobiles et potentes de terra vestra."[14] Turribus' placidity, however, may have merely reflected the fact that his principal lordship of Endoufielle lay near Isle-Jourdain in a jurisdiction beyond Toulouse's reach. Surely more representative of their class, the Le Fauga were more contentious. Battles between the two Falgario brothers and the consuls over the latters' right to tax their rural properties and lordships extended from the twelve-fifties into the seventies and exemplify what was really a growing division of social orders.[15] Lastly, in spite of the durable tradition of knightly and lordly families enjoying town citizenship, it seems likely that the princes, from Raymond VII through the kings of France, fostered the separation of the noble order from the other classes. This helped to produce something analogous to what

[12]Boutaric, "Organisation judiciaire du Languedoc au moyen-âge," *Bibliothèque de l'Ecole des Chartes* 16 (1855) 200-230 and 532-560, and 17 (1856) 97-122. On the as yet to be studied rural notariate, see my *Liberty and Political Power*, p. 344, notes 38-39, and my "Village, Town, and City," pp. 142-190.

[13]The family history is in Appendix 1, No. 15.

[14]Fournier and Guébin, *Enquêtes administratives*, pp. 135-136a, No. 39, 4 and 6 (January 1263).

[15]The family history is in Appendix 1, No.7, and see references in Chapter Five, pp. 103-104 above.

had long obtained in northern France, namely the artificially sharp separation of town and countryside.

One must confess then that, after about 1250, the social corporatism that split what modern historians call the bourgeoisie from the nobility had something to do with the loss of Toulousan political liberty. Interestingly, this division was almost invisible in the early part of the century. Then, when townsmen were really rising and, just as in Italy, were thirsting to become rural lords and landowners, rural notables were hastening to become Toulousan citizens, inhabitants of a capital from which they could rule the province. By this later date, circumstances, aided by the prince, had divided the well-to-do into rival groups. A relatively oligarchic structure that held power both in Toulouse and in the countryside (the Toulousain's villages and small towns) was beginning to split apart and monarchy took root in the division.

Doubtless monarchy flourishes when princes can divide in order to rule, but that does not explain why the people of this area, both gentle and commoner, submitted to a power they had done so much to diminish in past times. Actuality was probably more subtle than that stated above and the combat between town and country, between burgher and gentleman, reflected the fact that both groups fell out because they were under pressure from those both above and beneath them. Certain it is that well-to-do landed lords derived relatively little advantage from what happened in the thirteenth century. Their class's members were as, or more, inclined toward heresy as town leaders and suffered quite as much from confiscation and other punishment. Although the matter has yet to be seriously investigated, lordly rural franchises were as much the object of attack by the prince as was the consulate of Toulouse. If some notable families like that of Sicard Alaman profited very considerably from their alliance with the counts, one merely needs to look at the cartulary of Raymond VII and the various inquisitorial materials used by Yves Dossat and earlier by Célestin Douais to know that many barons and landed gentlefolk had a terrible time during and after the Albigensian Crusade. As noted above, this began well before the Capetian assumption of power. The sources record forced sales or alienations of rural farms and lordships and substantial rural properties to Raymond VII, some of which were actually returned to their old owners by Alphonse's government. These involve urban families (many of them landed) such as the Baranoni, Barravi, Castronovo, Curtasolea, Gamevilla and Maurand and the rural gentlefolk like the Miramonte and Noerio.[16]

---

[16]Raymond's cartulary is PAN, JJ 19. With the notable exception of Dossat, *Les crises de l'Inquisition*, Chapter 13, little has been done on this question. See also PAN, JJ 21, pp. 7-8, 13-14, 20, 25, 31, 39 and 43. A systematic survey would disclose much more.

The subjects of these rural lords had also found an ally in the prince. To profit from the growing economy, the local magnates were themselves involved in refounding or building new settlements called "bastides," usually in conjunction with the count. Alphonse of Poitiers was especially active in this regard and was also devoted to multiplying rural consulates with rights of low and sometimes even of high justice often exercised by officers either elected by the farming population or in whose election that group participated. In the Lauragais southeast of Toulouse before the Crusade, there were few or no rural consulates, but nine were to be seen at the death of Raymond VII in 1249. By that of Alphonse of Poitiers in 1271, no less than ninety-six existed.[17] It looks as if the prince helped weaken the independence of the rural well-to-do by applying the same social and democratic solvent he will be seen to have used so successfully in town.

B. POPULAR PARTICIPATION

It seems likely that, had the people, the middle and lower ranges of the population, pushed for the continuation of the evolution toward political freedom and the provision of alternatives to the established religion, the story of Toulouse would have been very different. Ever hungry for careers, the upper ranges of society would have furnished the requisite leaders had the plebs provided the indispensable mass support. They did not, and the puzzle is then to discover why the many were relatively indifferent to political freedom and religious diversity.

The counts had long sought to direct the discontents of the middle elements of the population against the upper classes and those of the plebs against the political and social leadership of the town. In the period from 1178 to 1181, Raymond V, just as Bishop Fulk was to do later on, attacked both heresy and usury, and profited from the division between the City and Bourg. But this attempt to restore comital authority collapsed with the victory of the consuls in 1189.[18] Raymond VII and especially Alphonse of Poitiers were more fortunate than their predecessors. Raymond pointed the way by favoring the crafts and trades and Alphonse was to profit from this in the two constitutional crises in the mid-twelve-fifties and the twelve-sixties. Then, although private property was naturally not itself attacked, the private ownership of public services and rights characteristic of the twelfth century was deprecated and propaganda was launched against pur-

---

[17]Ramière de Fortanier, *Chartes de franchises de Lauragais*, p. 44. See also Saint-Blanquat, "Comment se sont crées les bastides du sud-ouest de la France," *Annales: ESC* 3 (1949) 278ff.

[18]My *Liberty and Political Power*, pp. 59-66.

ported economic Bourbons, to borrow a phrase from American socio-economic polemic.

One battleground was the mint of Toulouse. Although nominally the count's, the money of Toulouse was in the hands of hereditary mint masters before 1200 and had come under the legislative authority of the consuls just after that date.[19] Raymond VII invaded the mint masters' rights in 1240 by nominating a supervisor, in all likelihood a Toulousan.[20] Alphonse went further: he rejected the recommendation of the mint master Peter Feuterii on the profits the masters were to make and ordered the mint to harmonize its practices with those of the royal mint of Nîmes.[21] He also twice appointed new mint masters, some of them foreigners, from 1251 onward.[22] In 1255 the count's government abruptly repudiated an attempt to restore consular controls by arguing polemically that French princes did not share *their* mints with "*their* subjects."[23] Toulouse had lost its mint to the prince and its private minters their golden goose.

By 1269 the comital government directed its aim at the collection of tolls in the town's markets and of the harbor or mooring dues along the Garonne river front. On the grounds that they were gouging the public, the vicar investigated a group of toll collectors that included the canons of Saint-Sernin, one wealthy Jew and twelve Toulousan citizens of good family or substantial means. Although the negotiations took time and these rights were not finally lost until the owners sold out to the crown in 1273 and 1274, the propaganda value of such an attack is evident.[24] Finally, Ray-

---

[19]See ibid., pp. 108-109. The names of the old hereditary mint masters are listed in a document of March 1199 published on pp. 203-204, No. 9.

[20]*HGL* 8: No. 330, v (December 1240): Arnold Trunnus "cambiator" received the "sagium" or right to inspect the money of Toulouse.

[21]In Molinier, *Correspondance administrative* 2: 599, No. 2090 (dated 1251).

[22]In August of 1251 in *Layettes du Trésor* 3: 138-139, No. 3955, the seneschal gave the "fabrica monete" to foreigners, but surely unsuccessfully because, in ibid., pp. 178-180, Nos. 4048-4049 and 4051, a different group of mint masters was in litigation with the seneschal. At least one of these masters was a citizen of Albi, as is stated in ibid., pp. 188-189, No. 4064 (July 1253), and the names of the rest seem foreign to Toulouse as well.

[23]*HGL* 8: No. 515, cols. 1558-1559: "Mirandum est quia de moneta domini comitis, que pleno jure ad ipsum pertinet et ad predecessores suos et semper pertinuit sine cujusdam consorcio, volunt consules ordinare, maxime cum nunquam in regno Francie ab aliquibus dominis qui monetam habent istum fuerit per eorum subditos postulatum."

[24]Molinier, *Correspondance administrative* 2: 68, No. 1314 (July 1269) where it was reported to the count that "portagium seu leudas ... percipiant, et exigant nonnulli ipsorum plus debito, et aliqui ut dicitur, minus juste ... ." For the names of the holders, see above Chapter Six note 3.

mond's earlier favoring of the leather craftsmen's desire to use the Garonne waterfront reappeared in the form of one of the so-called reforms proposed by the popular party in 1268. There the "populares," clearly reflecting the interests of butchers and of artisans in the leather and cloth industries, petitioned the count for the free use of forest and pasture in the immediate vicinity of the town at the expense of landowners.[25]

The revival of the vicar's office and the creation of his court explored above seems to have had support among the people. Not that that had anything to do with the prince's initiative. What inspired him and his government was probably annoyance that the consuls regularly insisted that either party convoked before the vicar's court could instead claim arbitral judgment before a consular "curia jurata." The count's successful attempt to subject the consular court to that of the vicar during the constitutional crisis of 1255 was a direct affront to Toulousan self-government, but was veiled by a program typical of thirteenth century legal reform. Legal professionalism was underscored, sometimes in language offensive to the citizenry. "Curie jurate" appointed by the consuls, for example, were disparaged because the sworn judges were sometimes "cobblers or furriers" or other "common or uneducated persons."[26] Although echoing the attitudes of professional jurists, this invidious language was not drummed home by repetition and, indeed, never recurred again. The offense could also be overlooked, especially by a largely illiterate citizenry, because, although crafts- and tradesfolk sat on these courts, most judges were chosen by the consuls from the middle and upper classes.

Although professionalism is often malignantly elitist (being partly motivated by a desire for fees), such reform was generally advantageous for the middle and lower ranges of the population.[27] Alphonse's legislation not only published the first public tariff of court costs in Toulousan history, but also discreetly failed to mention what was indeed a fact, namely that professional jurists were to monopolize the advocatorial and judicial functions, thus weakening the oligarchic amateurism of the old consular system. It also ordered, moreover, that the new vicar's court was henceforth to

[25]*HGL* 8: No. 526, ii, col. 1653, Petition No. 14 directed against the "domini terrarum et nemorum."

[26]Ibid., No. 452, col. 1376 (before December 1255): "... scilicet quemdam pelliparium, sutorem aut quamlibet vilem personam et imperitam de villa Tolose ... ." A similar passage is found in the actual legislation in ibid., No. 456, col. 1386 (December 1255).

[27]On the early origins of legal and scribal professionalism, see my *Liberty and Political Power*, pp. 100-103 and especially Chapter Nine.

provide paperwork gratis for the poor. It even repeated the ever popular but rarely enforced rule first trumpeted by Rome's lawyers whereby courts were ordered to furnish "advocates to those lacking them."[28]

Later, during the constitutional crisis of 1268, the "populares" of Toulouse petitioned the count about matters involving the overlapping jurisdictions of the consuls and the vicar, the officer who, as is known, served as the enforcer of the consuls' judgments.[29] Three of the popular petitions requested protection for debtors and another sought to lessen the incidence and ameliorate the conditions of precautionary imprisonment, a matter of moment for both debtors and perpetrators of offenses. A year later, the count responded to another petition and ordered his vicar to prevent the imprisonment of persons not charged with notorious crime as defined in custom or [Roman] law, who could put up bond for his appearance at the trial, thus reinforcing or instituting a practice reminiscent of modern bail.[30] The Alphonsine monarchy was not being inventive here. Hardly beloved by Toulousans, Simon de Montfort had included this idea in the *Statutes of Pamiers* of 1212: "no man may be imprisoned or kept as a prisoner as long as he provides sufficient pledges that he will stand trial."[31] A further popular demand was to have the law of Toulouse redacted into a publicly available document, a request that did not bear fruit until the royal review and publication of the *Custom* in 1286.[32] It is worth repeating that all of these requests for facilities protecting defendants were not legal arcana

[28]*HGL* 8: No. 457, col. 1390 (dated 1255): "Citationes et pignorationes gratis facient pro pauperibus hominibus intra Tolosam, non habentibus unde solvant eis, ad cognitionem curie, etc. ... Item quod curia det advocatum non habenti, etc."

[29]Ibid., No. 526, ii, col. 1652 (July 1268): petitions Nos. 8-10 involved a wide variety of questions; No. 10, for example, concerned protection of the dower rights of wives.

[30]Ibid.: petition No. 11, col. 1652, was directed against unjust imprisonment. See ibid., No. 526, v, col. 1655 (March 1269): the count orders his vicar "ne aliquis in civitate Tholose captus detineretur, nisi in notoriis criminibus vel in casibus a jure vel consuetudine concessis, dum tamen parati essent prestare ydoneam caupcionem de stando juri de se conquerentibus coram vobis [vicario]." This position had been voiced in the reform edict of ca. 1254 in ibid., No. 447, col. 1355. Imprisonment for debt has also been treated in Chapter Eleven above.

[31]Ibid., No. 165, Article No. 128: "Item nullus homo mittatur in carcerem aut retineatur captus, quamdiu poterit sufficienter plaegios dare quod stabit juri."

[32]The petition in PAN, JJ 24, f. 134a, is reconstructed by the editors of *HGL* 8: No. 526, ii, col. 1651, as follows: "Item supplicant, quod adinveniuntur et fruguntur aliquid (corr. fruuntur aliquibus) minus bene quam [si] per aliquem vel aliquos bonos viros ... compilarentur omnes in uno registro seu libro, ideo ut sciretur in quibus et que habent (corr. debent) consuetudines Tholose observari." See Gilles, *Coutumes de Toulouse*, pp. 15ff., on the long negotiations.

known only to the few. They were everywhere characteristic of medieval reform legislation, especially in Italy's towns and legal schools.

Constitutionally speaking, the main result of these battles was that the old order of the courts had been overthrown. Until 1230 the nearly sovereign consulate's only rival had been the count himself. After the so-called reform edict of Alphonse of Poitiers of around 1254, citizen litigants were to advance from the court of the consuls to that of the vicar and, if need be, could appeal from there to the court of the count's seneschal.[33] Somewhere between 1271 to 1274 the jurist Master Aimeric de Robiano claimed that the count was the "iudex ordinarius" of the town and county of Toulouse and that the consuls had themselves often been summoned to appear before the vicarial court in Alphonse of Poitiers' time.[34]

That this sequence of appeals was real and not just theoretical is undoubted. Toulousan citizens fell into the habit of appealing from the consuls' to the count's courts, especially to that of the vicar. In 1258 or 1259, for example, a modest widow appealed from the consuls to the vicar on the grounds that the city fathers were permitting usury.[35] Sometime in the twelve-seventies, a well-to-do widow threatened the consuls that, if right were not done to her and her sister, they would appeal to the vicar or even the king.[36] The count's government also controlled access to the consuls' court. In 1269 the count informed the consuls that, after a citizen named Bernard Gaitapodium had won a case before their tribunal, he had appealed to the vicar seeking a better decision. Bernard had subsequently changed

---

[33]*HGL* 8: No. 447, cols. 1353-1354 (tentatively dated by Molinier as about 1254, but obviously possibly 1255 or even later): "Item quod a consulibus Tolose appelletur ad vicarium domini comitis, et quod judex curie vicarii cognoscat de omnibus illis appellationibus autoritate vicarii. Item quod sententiis domini vicarii appelletur ad senescallum et quod judex qui continue est cum senescallo Tolose, cognoscat de illis appellationibus, autoritate senescalii." Provisions follow about appeals from the seneschal's judge to "bonis personis non suspectis" appointed by the seneschal himself and to the count, as the final judge.

[34]TAM, II 9 (from 1271 to 1274 – on which dating, see Chapter Thirteen, note 52 above). Robiano said the consuls were convoked "super multis actionibus coram domino vicario Tholose vel eius iudice tamquam coram ordinario."

[35]On Ricarda, widow of Bernard Gastonus, against Bernard Aimeric Astro, see Chapter Twelve, p. 228.

[36]On Mateva and her sister, see the Sobaccus family history in my *Men and Women*, pp. 185-189. Their case in E 569 is undated, and the petitioners informed the consuls that, if they were not gratified, "ex tunc ad dictum dominum vicarium vel ad dictum regem dominum Francie appellamus in scriptis," putting their property "sub protectione domini vicarii Tholose et domini regis."

his mind and now wanted the consuls to enforce their judgment, which the count instructed them to do.[37]

Lastly, in 1276, a substantial wine merchant named Arnold Unde complained that Stephen Galterius, consul for the "partita" of Saint-Pierre-Saint-Géraud, together with the two "comunalerii" and the notary of the quarter, had come to his house to inform him that he owed forty shillings for the tax being raised to support the king's campaign in Navarre. He protested that the consuls had not assessed his taxes fairly and, far more significantly, that, when they changed his tax estimate, they had not consulted the "universitas," probably meaning thereby that tax estimates had to be confirmed by the town's general assembly.[38] Unlike the petitions of the widows mentioned above who claimed that a prince should defend the poor or those suffering from usury, Unde's appeal proved that some citizens attributed to the count's government the right not only to relieve the oppressed but also to judge the constitutionality (if that unsuitably modern word fits the case) of consular actions. Although nothing is known about the outcome of this case, the principle is pretty clearly stated.

The merchant's argument was really based on a long conflict between the consuls and the count over taxes in the political crisis of the twelve-sixties. Unde's complaint aside, the battle was not really over the weight of the taxes imposed; they seem to have been moderate. Sometime before 1271 William de Falgario had been called on to pay a halfpenny per every thousand shillings, hence about one percent of a fortune estimated at 60,000 shillings.[39] The debate between town and prince over taxes was about

[37]Molinier, *Correspondance administrative* 2: 7, No. 1219 (April 1269).

[38]TAM, II 63 (dated August 1-15, 1276). His house was located on the "carraria de Forguas," a street I have been unable to find. The tax was "pro talia comuni seu traita que fiebat in Tholosa pro illis qui erant ituri in Navarram in exercitum domini regis." At the time of his protest, the consuls were not "in eorum consistorio," so he "viva voce appellavit ad dominum vicarium Tholose" with the following written schedule: "Quoniam appelationis remedium idcirco est institutum ut sit relavamen oppressorum," he appealed against the dimension of his "coma" or tax because it was not "per solidum et libram." It was, he said, unjust "respectu ad patrimoniam aliorum concivium ut moris est" and "ultra iustam extimationem patrimonii mei, maxime cum non fuerit vocata universitas Tholose nec statuerit ut a me dicta quantitas peccunie exigeretur, sed dicti consules inter se predictam ordinaverunt, non vocata dicta universitate nec ejus consilio super hoc adhibito," and he therefore proposed to appeal to the vicar's court within ten days.

[39]In the Falgario family history in Appendix 1, No. 7, and TAM, II 10 (datable from March 1271 to July 1272): testimony in which the notary of the quarter of the Pont-Vieux recited from the "librum comunaleriorum" of that quarter the fact that William de Falgario "dederat quondam in aliquo como pro omnibus bonis suis et ibi dicebatur ad extimacionem .lx. milia sol. tol., .xxx. sol. tol. pro miliario .vi. den. tol."

principle because there had been no general taxes of this kind since the defense of Toulouse during the Albigensian Crusade. This conflict began in 1261 when the count requested a crusade subsidy and was not finally settled until the new law on taxes of 1270 and until the Toulousan hearth tax ("focagium, subsidium, vel donum gratuitum") was receipted by the count at Aiguesmortes in that year.[40]

"Donum gratuitum" simply meant a voluntary contribution, a conception implying somewhat inaccurately in terms of institutional growth that the hearth tax was not to create a precedent, as was stated by the count as early as 1267.[41] Shrewdly, the count's government began by ordering the seneschals to raise the tax through agencies directly appointed by the people and not by traditional authorities. It was furthermore specified that the citizenry was to be taxed according to wealth.[42] Graduated taxation was not only favored by princes like the Capetians and the celebrated northern French jurist and monarchist Beaumanoir, but was also a normal demand of the popular parties in Italian town republics.[43]

Because the distribution of the tax burden had been hidden in the hearts of the consuls in the past, this appeal to the people provoked both opposition and fear. Sometime in 1266, the consuls won back their right to collect the tax by promising the count the rather modest subsidy of 6000

[40]Alphonse receipted the "don gratuit" in TAM, AA 5: 289 (June 1270). Explored by Auguste Molinier in vols. 6 and 7 of the HGL, Alphonse's taxes were studied by Wolff, "Estimes" Toulousaines, pp. 23 ff. and Bisson, "Negociations for taxes," Medieval France and Her Pyrenean Neighbours, pp. 52ff.

[41]HGL 8: No. 517, i, cols. 1261-1262 (October 1267), the count observing that the transmitted sum "de quibus tenemus nos plenarie pro pagatis, nos subventionem hujusmodi profitemur ab eisdem gratis et liberaliter nobis factam nec volumus seu intendimus nomine focagii vel promissionis ab eis nobis facte super eodem vel cujuscumque alterius servitutis nunc vel in posterum occasione dicte subventionis, spontanee ab eisdem facte, ipsis prejudicium generari."

[42]See especially Wolff, "Estimes" Toulousaines, pp. 23 ff. and the Alfonsine program in HGL 8: No. 495 (dated ca. 1261) where the seneschals are to appoint "qui miaux sachent et conoissent la povrete et la richesce de chascun des homes de la vile en moebles et en non moebles et leur feront jurer seur sainz, que il asserrons bien et loiaument a leur escient seur chaucune person, selonc ce que elle sera, une some certaine de deniers et feront metre en escrit ... ."

[43]As in Enrico Fiumi, "L'imposta diretta nel comuni medioevali della Toscana," Studi in onore di Armando Sapori 1: 332, who cites a Volterran statute of 1239 instructing collectors of a "datium" or tallage to record for, or get estimates of taxable wealth from, "divitibus secundum divitias, pauperibus secundum paupertates, aspiciendo equitatem et commoditatem et incommoditatem cuiusque."

pounds of Tours by November of that year.[44] The delivery of the tax was then held up until February 1268 because the town's magistrates tried to profit from the occasion to prove their right to tax every resident of the "dex" or immediate vicinity of the town, as well as all property held by town citizens beyond that limit.[45] The payment of the subsidy was apparently delayed even further because, according to a letter sent to Sicard Alaman by the count, the consuls hoped to use it to force him to restore consular liberty.[46] It looked as if things had reached an impasse, and that the prince's need for money had impeded his ability to get his way.

The consuls' hopes, if they really had any, were soon dashed, however. A group of proctors representing the "populares" or the "communitas popullarium," a party claiming to be popular, that is, appeared before Alphonse in July 1268. These spokesmen were clearly hostile to the consuls, actually delated to the count and proposed a series of general popular reforms.[47] Among these was the adoption or emplacement of taxes graduated according to the taxpayers' means, "by shilling and pound" as the documents say.[48] In March 1269 Alphonse wrote his local orchestrator Sicard Alaman to order the consuls to convoke four "probihomines" from each quarter elected by the whole "communitas" and to render to the "whole body of citizens (tota universitas)" an accounting of the money raised and the names of those entrusted with holding it.[49] Although modi-

[44]*HGL* 8: No. 517, i, cols. 1561-1562 (sometime in 1266).

[45]Ibid., iv and v, cols. 1564-1565 (November and December 1267) in which the count at first argued that the consuls should not raise a fourth part of the "focagium ... ab hominibus villarum et boeriarum infra le dex Tholose et extra existencium ad cives Tholose pertinencium," but then allowed it in December, giving the consuls an extension until February 2, 1268.

[46]Ibid., No. 522, xix, col. 1620 (March 1269) telling him that the consuls had not turned the money over to him "cum sperarent super consuetudinibus suis sibi a nobis aliquam gratiam concedendam, sicut missi nobis procuratores communitatis Tholose asserebant." Addressed to his seneschal, letter xviii is of the same date and concerns the same matter.

[47]Ibid., No. 526, ii, col. 1651 (July 1268) and see the "procuratores communitatis" in the previous note.

[48]Ibid.: where the petition reads "quod quandocumque aliqua summa pecunie extrahetur ... ab hominibus civitatis et suburbii, exigatur per solidum et libram secundum eorum facultates." A similar phrase is found in ibid., iv, col. 1654 (March 1269), and in the two originals in TAM, II 23 and 62.

[49]*HGL* 8: No. 522, xix, col. 1620 (March 1269), sent to Sicard Alaman, queried what had happened to the money raised under the consuls of 1266 and 1267 (there is no list for 1267 and 1268, so these worthies may have been in office for two years) and ordered the consuls of 1268 and 1269 that, "convocatis ab eisdem consulibus quatuor

fied in another draft, the count's proposal effectively circumvented the consuls by calling directly on the citizenry.[50]

This thunderbolt destroyed the already wavering resistance of the consuls.[51] The fiscal unification of the City and Bourg necessary for such tax reform was achieved before a huge public assembly in December 1269.[52]

---

probis hominibus de qualibet partita civitatis, a communitate ejusdem civitatis ad hoc electis, de dictis collectis compotum audiant, ita quod dicti homines ac tota universitas predicta sciant quod residui fuerit et eorum nomina, qui illud residuum penes se detinent, necnon in quos usus collecta exinde pecunia posita fuerit et conversa."

[50]Letter xviii, cols. 1619-1620 (March 1269) is a less extreme draft of the same, proposing that four "probihomines [be chosen] a communitate" and four by the consuls.

[51]Wolff, *"Estimes" Toulousaines*, pp. 25-26, feels that some part of this reform may have been started as early as 1264. He may be right, but the evidence is ambiguous. Some light is shed on this by TAM, II 10, an undated document containing testimony against the Falgario brothers but datable to between March 1271 and July 1272. There the notary Pons de Albeges testified that the consuls had increased the valuation of an individual's property ten years before the Falgario suit, that is, sometime between 1266 and 1271, probably the earlier date, and then added that "nunquam ipse vidit fieri extimationem a civibus ... in talhiis ... usque fuit levatum fogagium," that is, not until the count raised the hearth tax in 1266 or 1267. That the tax was actually collected during the consular term of 1266 and 1267 is learned from the same document where the notary Bernard Aimericus remarked that he was among the consuls – "de quibus consulibus idem testis erat tunc quando subvencio domini comitis exigebatur in Tolose." The consular list of 1266 and 1267 in Appendix 4 contains this notary's name. Wolff may nevertheless still be right because the same witness appealed to an earlier general tax to prove the consuls' case, remarking that, when the brothers contested the tax for the count, the notary of the quarter of the Pont-Vieux stated that William de Falgario paid a modest tax as on p. 261 above. As to the "terminus ante quem" for the "extimatio," William Amelius "servunerius" observed that, at the time of the consuls Arnold de Escalquencis and William Rotbertus "legista," "tunc non fiebat extimacio inter cives." According to the consular lists in Appendix 4, William was surely a consul in 1255 and in the terms of 1258 and 1259 and 1269 and 1270, and Arnold in 1259 and 1260 and 1265. Going through the lists from 1255 to 1270, only four are complete with twelve consuls, four name ten or eleven, three range from eight to nine and four terms present no lists at all. In principle, consuls could not serve two successive terms, so the two could have sat together a total of five times between 1254 and 1270.

[52]TAM, AA 3 129, cols. 197-200 (December 1269) where, a general assembly having been convoked ("convocato publice cum tubis et precone ... et congregato ut moris est in comuni palatio dicte ville generali et publico parlamento"), the two "universitates" of the City and Bourg met together in a mob so large that "ipsis duabis universitatibus totum predictum comune palacium tam in gradibus quam in solo seu planicie plenum erat" to entrust the unification of the town to the judgment of the consuls. The consular decision or legislation was thrice announced to the throng "alta voce" by the consuls' notary who also stated that "si aliquis vel aliqui de predictis

Shortly thereafter, in June 1270, the consuls formally admitted the principle of proportional or graduated taxation.[53] They also systematized the assembling and bookkeeping of the "extimationes" or records of each citizen's worth, providing elaborate safeguards for the citizens and for lowering or raising taxes in individual cases.[54] Lastly, they arranged for a public accounting of town income and expenditures. Their legislation described the "universitas" of the town as the "maiores, mediocres et minores" and the consuls confessed they had acted on the prompting of that "universitas."[55]

There is nevertheless an air of compromise about the new legislation. It failed to embody the democratic spirit of the count's proposal of March 1269. In the final law of 1270, the four "probihomines" of each quarter were not to be popularly elected as had been proposed the year before, but instead chosen by the consuls.[56] In spite of this mitigation, one typical of princely action once victory had been won and the money granted, it will be remembered that the litigious wine merchant named Arnold Unde of

---

universitatibus ibi congregatis ... dicte unitati faciende ... vellet contradicere vel se opponere, surgeret et diceret quicquid vellet et ab ipsis breviter audiretur," adding that, "si aliquis ibi non surgeret et expresse non contradiceret," the consuls could promulgate their decision. Finally, since "post quas requisitiones aliquis de predictis universitatibus non surrexit nec etiam in aliquo contradixit," the consuls signed the decision into law.

[53]Ibid. 128, cols. 196-197 (June 19, 1270). Meeting in the town hall, the consuls, "habito consilio generali ad instanciam et requisitionem universitatis prefate statuerunt" that all citizens and inhabitants "per solidum et libram solvant" for common expenses by whatever name the taxes are called.

[54]Ibid., the consuls ordered that "omnes et singule extimationes diviciarum et facultatum omnium et singulorum civium et habitancium ... sicut sunt scripte in libris seu papiris" of the town's twelve quarters or "partite" "correcte ita quod gravati et alleviati in extimationibus diviciarum et facultatum suarum diminuendo et augmentando ad extimationem facultatum suarum debitam reducantur" in twelve books, one to be locked in a chest in each "partita" for which there were five keys held by four "probihomines" elected by the consuls and the consul of the "partita." "Item si aliquis de civibus et habitantibus ... aliquo casu in facultatibus et rebus suis diminutionem seu detrimentum aliquod paterentur [read pateretur] vel alicuius facultates et divicie augerentur, quilibet talium in casu suo reducatur ad extimationem debitam ut est dictum secundum quod prefatis quatuor probis hominibus cuilibet partite et consulibus Tholose videbitur faciendum." That these estimations were revised may be seen in the testimony of the notary Pons de Albeges cited in note 51 above.

[55]Ibid., the annual accounting was to be effected by the consuls and also by the two "comunalarii" or "collectores" of taxes elected in each quarter "eo quod universitas supradicta, maiores scilicet mediocres et minores, non possit in extrahendis seu colligendis expensis communibus defraudari." See also the previous note.

[56]The document is cited in note 53 above.

1276 understood very well that the consuls could only change assessed taxes with the consent of the prince or with that of the "universitas" in a general assembly.

The notion that the "universitas" of Toulouse was not a uniform body did not await June 1270 with its "maiores, mediocres et minores." As recorded before in these pages, this division had already been seen back in the days when Raymond VII capitulated to the consuls of 1247 and 1248. It was then agreed or confessed by the victorious townsmen that half of the consulate was to be chosen from the "maiores" and half from the "mediores."[57] Although this arrangement of the consulate may have assured the count of occasional sympathy within that body or at least of some measure of class division within it, Alphonse of Poitiers' direct political appeal to the people was far more consequential. As early as the constitutional crisis of 1255, this prince had loudly objected to the tradition of sending his messages to *his* people of Toulouse through the consuls and had protested against the fact that he could not speak directly to the consular council or to a general assembly or public parliament when he wished to. By intercepting his messages and interpreting them, the consuls had not only, he claimed, suborned the assemblies, but also kept the people from their prince. Alphonse's argument was disingenuous because his counselors undoubtedly knew that all Italian and Provençal city republics limited the right of princes and even higher elected magistrates, such as "potestates," to address or summon general assemblies or "conciones" at will.[58]

In the later constitutional crisis of the twelve-sixties, the issue came to the fore a second time and again in circumstances wholly advantageous to the prince. As noted above, a group styling itself the "communitas popullarium Tholose" sent proctors to the count presenting petitions requesting not only a reform of the system of taxation in the town and the accounting of public moneys, but also other matters of interest to the people, most of them also examined earlier in this chapter. The count's favorable response was directed to his favorite lieutenant Sicard Alaman.[59] In July 1268 the

---

[57]Chapter Six, note 8, cites the pertinent text.

[58]*HGL* 8: No. 456, cols. 1387-1388 (December 1255): the count complained that "quando dominus comes mittit litteras de credentia vel alias per aliquos bonos viros universitati vel consilio generali Tholose, nunquam illi nuncii possunt suam credentiam dicere consilio vel universitati vel litteras suas ostendere, donec omnia solis consulibus revelaverint, et tunc postea consules loquuntur quibus volunt et subornant eos, taliter quod nichil respondetur nisi quod ipsi dictant."

[59]Ibid., No. 526, ii, cols. 1651-1653 (July 1268), lists the petitions sent to Alphonse from the "procuratores communitatis popullarium Tholose."

count instructed his vicar to present his response to this petition before a general assembly or public parliament.[60] In August of the same year, the vicar William de Nantolleto summoned the consuls to a meeting attended by Sicard Alaman and other notables and ordered them to convene the general assembly, where he presented the matter himself at a mass meeting held in September.[61]

The proposals must have engendered much opposition because in March 1269, the count ordered another assembly convoked in the town hall before which any "contradictores" of the five most important reforms were to appear and state their case. Such "contradictores" or their proctors were then to attend the count's court to be held in or near Paris in May where they were to present their case and stand ready to receive the prince's judgment concerning the articles containing the petitions.[62] Since all the petitions invaded financial and jurisdictional areas traditionally exercised by the consuls, it is evident that the count had seized the opportunity to arbitrate a conflict between the consulate and the "populares." *His* people had called on their "bon prince," so to speak, and he had answered with alacrity, inspired by a love much fortified by self-interest.

It is known, moreover, that there had been general assemblies or public parliaments in Toulouse before these dates. Not only were such bodies traditional in the Midi, but Toulouse's general assembly had in fact repeatedly met during the agonies of the Albigensian war when the citizens had been called on for military service and heavy taxes.[63] But what may be emphasized here is that there was a world of difference between the way of doing business under the old free consulate and that used at the time of princely intervention in the mid-thirteenth century. An act of March 1223 wherein the consuls regulated the election of the consulate and the management of the town treasury may be taken to illustrate the old republicanism. This important legislative act was performed by the consuls together with

---

[60]Ibid., iii, cols. 1653-1654.

[61]TAM, II 31, a series of "vidimus" dated December 1280, starting with the vicar's presentation to the consuls in August 1268. The second act copied on this document records the meeting of the general assembly on September 8.

[62]*HGL* 8: No. 526, iv, col. 1654, with originals in TAM, II 23 and 62 (dated March 1269): "plenum consilium communitatis Tholose in domo communi." The prince commanded "ut [contradictores] per se vel per procuratores legitime instructos compareant, si sua crediderint interesse, coram nobis, ubi tunc erimus, processuri super predictis quinque articulis prout justum fuerit, et recepturi quod super eisdem duxerimus ordinandum."

[63]See my *Liberty and Political Power*, pp. 150-153.

GOVERNMENT

their council, a total of just over 150 persons being named in the charter.[64] Twenty years later in 1243, a general parliament was summoned to take oath to maintain the Peace of Paris and 1028 adult males assembled there.[65] By the twelve-sixties even a lawsuit of no constitutional import required a "generale consilium" of fifty-three councilors as well as the consuls.[66] In September 1268 the count's generally favorable response to the petition presented by the "procuratores communitatis popullarium Tholose" was read in a public "parliament gathered in the town hall at the sound of the trumpet" of unstated but obviously large dimensions.[67] Given the passions of the time, such general assemblies could become mob scenes, almost out of control. A trial of March 1269 described a frantic public parliament angrily discussing the tolls to which Toulousan trade was being subjected. The meeting overflowed from the town hall to crowd into the nearby streets, things got out of hand and a consular "nuncius" was wounded in the riot.[68] Lastly, it will also be recalled that the so-called reform legislation on taxation of June 1270 had been issued by the consuls at the prompting of the "universitas" of the "maiores, mediocres et minores."

Given the circumstances, then, it is surely not too far from the mark to say that, at Toulouse at this time, the greater the participation of the many, the less the political freedom of the whole.

[64]TAM, AA 1 75 (March 1223).
[65]Appendix 3.
[66]Ernest Roschach in *HGL* 7: Note 47, cols. 242-243 (September 1264).
[67]TAM, II 31, No. 2 (August 1268) listed fifty-six names of those meeting "in parlamento in domo commune ad sonum tube seu tubarum congregato."
[68]PAN, J 192b 21 (March 1269).

15

Religion and Government

A. CATHARS

The jurist Guy Folcoldius, the future Pope Clement IV, was seen above as active in the service of both Raymond VII and his successor Alphonse of Poitiers. His advocacy of those prince's interests together with the role played by the early Dominican inquisitors in Toulouse and adjacent regions tells observers that not a few southern French clerks helped lead the party that militated against Toulouse's liberties, and that therefore clerical action did not await the northern French dominance seen after the accession of Alphonse of Poitiers. This seems to validate Gênet's catalog of the enemies of the people that began with the magistrates and nobles, and closed with the priests, unctuous deceivers who were perhaps the worst enemy of all. Anything but new, his view of history flourished in France in the late nineteenth century when secular anticlericalism joined with republicanism to defeat the collapsing alliance of crown and miter. Sure of a sympathetic audience among professors and indeed the public, Charles Molinier, scion of a distinguished family of scholars, wrote in his Paris thesis published in 1881 that the "ferocity" of the inquisitors "had smashed the cause of the unique genius of Occitania [the Midi], namely its liberty."[1]

It is surely impossible to imagine the rapid failure of Toulousan republicanism without the crushing defeat visited on this town and its region by the Albigensian Crusade, the intense pressures of the inquisitorial campaigns of the thirties and the continued threat of inquisitorial actions and confiscation, directed from 1255 from Paris and peopled by northern French inquisitors acting in harmony with the government of Alphonse of Poitiers.[2] This threat hung over Toulousan heads until 1279.

---

[1] *De Fratre Guillelmo Pelisso veterrimo inquisitionis historico Thesim*, p. xxix: "saevitia" wreaked by the Inquisition for over a century "ingenium proprium Occitaniae, videlicet ipsam libertatis ejus causam, fregerunt."

[2] Dossat, *Les crises de l'Inquisition*, p. 182ff. and my "Origins of the College of Saint-Raymond," p. 456.

Some have nevertheless questioned whether Catharism and the assault on that faith really had much to do with religion. It seems almost bizarre that, especially in a period of an expanding economy, a substantial part of Toulousan society seceded from the orthodox religious community, one six or more centuries old. Some probing this mystery are tempted to believe that the Cathars or other secessionist religious groups did not really espouse dissidence anyway. They even assert that the heresy was a fiction invented by ecclesiastical inquisitors to entrap the enemies of the ruling classes.

Views of this kind are surely largely mistaken because religious minds, which abounded among the Cathars and Waldensians just as among the orthodox, always talked (and still do talk) about salvation and sin, human free will and determination and other baffling questions that reflect irrepressible human curiosity and longing. That Cathar beliefs about such problems seemed (or seem to moderns) ludicrously wide of the mark cannot be used to show that the agents of orthodoxy stuffed the mouths of the sectarians with what they were forced to confess. It is assumed in this book that divergent belief was really preached, expounded and, as much as is possible among humankind, believed.

What one searches for, however, is objective evidence about the withdrawal of obedience from the ancient and orthodox cult. Perhaps such can be found in the ages of construction which show the inhabitants' devotion to the church and causes dear to it, notably charity to the poor, aged and sick. Sometime ago, Marcel Durliat outlined these ages. Outside of the late Roman and Visigothic Daurade church (named for its golden mosaics, unfortunately destroyed in the eighteenth century to make way for a fine new construction), most churches and cloisters were built or extensively rebuilt during the late eleventh century and the first half of the twelfth. Among these were the Daurade cloister, the churches of the Dalbade and Saint-Pierre-des-Cuisines, the huge and still extant nave of the cathedral and especially the great basilica of Saint-Sernin.[3] During the same years, the town witnessed the powerful intrusion of the Benedictines of Moissac in the late ten-hundreds and the implantation of the Hospitalers and Templars, the two major military orders, early in the eleven-hundreds.

This spurt was followed by an intermission, one often attributed to the rise of Catharism. Some evidence seems to contradict this view, however. The late eleven-hundreds and early twelve-hundreds, the cresting peak of Catharism, was a major age for the growth of charity, of hospitals (usually small and for the aged) and leperhouses. Seven hospitals appear in extant

---

[3]In Wolff, *Nouvelle histoire de Toulouse*, pp. 80-94.

charters up to and including 1153, two of which later changed their function. From that time into the Albigensian war, another seven were founded, the last one in 1213. Thereafter the number of new foundations diminished, there being only four additional ones by about 1250. Institutional numbers, however, do not tell the whole story. At least one of the mid-century foundations was to become the great general hospital and hospice called Saint-Jacques, thus showing that Toulousans were building fewer but larger institutions in that later time. Of leprosaries, four were seen after the mid-twelfth century and before the great war, and three appear afterward before 1250.[4] The years from about 1150 to 1215 were therefore those that witnessed the greatest building of institutions caring for the sick and aged.

That charitable institutions were built when new churches were not being designed may imply that charity and not the church attracted the support not only of the orthodox but of dissidents as well. Of the leperhouses, one notes, none were directly associated with churches or monasteries and three were named after their lay founders. Seven new hospitals were not affiliated to ecclesiastical institutions, and one carried its founder's name. The same period, however, witnessed the genesis of the town's several small "reclusanie" or sheds for recluses, celibate women sponsored by the church, located at gates or bridges and charged with collecting charity for good causes. The first of the town's six "reclusanie" appeared in 1193 and the last is first seen in 1246.[5] The appearance of the parishes of the town, five of which are seen before 1200 and the other two shortly thereafter, furthermore, may show that what was probably happening was that old foundations were continuing to fill out, but that no new large-scale initiatives had found support.[6] The late twelfth century rallentando in planning and building major ecclesiastical structures, in short, may have reflected the secession of the Cathars and other dissidents but was not as disruptive as might be supposed.

A renewed program of ecclesiastical building began right after the Albigensian war and, stretching into the mid-fourteenth century, lasted longer than that of any earlier period. It began with the introduction of the mendicant and other new orders. Founded at Toulouse by Dominic even before the great war, the Dominicans were the first, their initial installations being seen in 1212 and 1216, shortly followed by the Franciscans probably from 1222. By 1263, if one counts the Clares, Trinitarians and Mercedarians among them, ten mendicant orders had settled there of

[4]"Charity and Social Work," pp. 211-225 and 227-230.
[5]Ibid., p. 230.
[6]My "Parishes of Toulouse," pp. 172-174.

which three were to be abolished by papal legislation at the Second Council of Lyon in 1274. With the exception of the early and small house of the Clares, female monasticism was slower to start. Groups of female hospital workers and reformed public women and also the usual Beguines associated with the two large mendicant orders, the Dominicans and Franciscans, appear only after 1275.[7]

Mendicant building largely started after 1250 and continued well into the fourteenth century with churches, cloisters, chapterhouses and other buildings, including four huge complexes, those of the Dominicans, Franciscans, Carmelites and Austin Friars. The introduction of the new orders was accompanied by a revival of episcopal authority and the foundation of a new university, both of which soon busied themselves with construction: the new Gothic choir of the cathedral, for example, and, toward the end of this period, the university colleges and chapels mostly located in the Bourg.[8] To be added to again only in early modern times, this ancient Roman town had been converted during this age into a jewel box crowded with architectural monuments.

To turn from ecclesiastical and other monuments to the institutional history of the church, the start of this long period saw the orthodox clergy begin to divine that substantial elements of society were seceding from their church. Their first response inadvertently promoted divergent thought by failing to remember that, without police action, preaching, however persuasive it may seem to orthodox listeners, merely increases opposition. From Bernard of Clairvaux' preaching mission of 1145 through the growingly coercive and militarized Cistercian missions of 1178 and 1181, to the great crusade of 1209, followed closely by the developing inquisition after 1229, the ecclesiastics learned that, to be effective, repression must be severe and thoroughgoing. As the clerks' thinking and action evolved toward this unhappy objective, their eyes naturally focused on the political leadership of the society they were trying to bring to heel. Their charges against counts Raymond VI and VII have often been rehearsed, and it seems possible to show that they were rightly convinced that the government of the town of Toulouse was hostile to their cause.

The best evidence of the place of Catharism in town government is gained by comparing a list of deceased persons whose inheritances were confiscated for heresy found in a royal diploma issued in 1279 with the lists of the consuls starting in 1202 and continuing through 1249. This span

[7]Ibid., pp. 206 and 231.
[8]Again Durliat in Wolff, *Nouvelle histoire de Toulouse*, pp. 136-156.

of nearly half a century includes the attempt of the town to dominate the Toulousain, the war years of the Albigensian Crusade from 1209 to 1229, the first great repression of heresy around and after the latter date and the last and failing effort of Toulousan republican liberty in 1246 and 1248.[9] The condemnations recorded in the document of 1279 totaled about 278. Of these, the first 157 were condemned by February 1237 (with about a hundred, in fact, on or before 1229), the next thirty-eight from February to September 1237, the next fifty-seven from 1246 to 1248 and the remaining twenty-six by 1257.[10] The overlap is therefore nearly complete.

The fragility of this evidence is that, since individuals often carried similar first and family names, it is not sure that the condemned person was the same as the consul bearing his name. This weakness is partially offset because many or most such individuals can be shown to have been both a consul and a heretic, or, if not, that the two were closely related. A minor complication is that several persons bearing the same name were also listed among both the condemned and the consuls. Where the names are of persons whose family histories I have written, these individuals can usually be identified. More significant is that the individuals listed in 1279 who constitute the base of these statistics were condemned around or after 1229 in the years whose consulates are being studied. It is therefore obvious that the pool of names – not to speak of the persons! – was diminishing rapidly.

A final difficulty presented by these figures is that the time at which persons converted to Catharism cannot be known and hence a Toulousan condemned in the twelve-thirties or later may not have dissented when serving as a consul in 1214 or 1222. Besides, not all revolutionaries believe in the revolutions in which they take part, even as leaders, and many secede not because of belief but for other reasons, defense of family and loved ones, for example, or of property and social station. Toulousans changed according to war's fortunes. Some at times supported the Crusade and at other times resisted it and did so not necessarily as heretics but simply as Toulousans. An individual case will illustrate this. The Claustro family from the Bourg were "faiditi," persons who resisted the Crusade in arms after its victory and suffered dearly for it, but those who think they were active Cathars or Waldensians are almost surely wrong.[11]

These significant reservations aside, the statistics show that, until the start of the Crusade in 1209, the representation of those bearing the names of persons condemned for religious divergence among the twenty-four and

[9]Appendix 5, Part 2, especially the introduction.
[10]In my *Repression of Catharism*, pp. 49-50.
[11]See their history in my "Farm of Fontanas," pp. 29-40.

sometimes twelve annual consuls peaked at just over twenty percent, but, while slowly increasing, averaged only about twelve and a half percent. Only two consulates represent the war years before the occupation of the town by Simon de Montfort and they also stand at almost twelve and a half percent. Information is somewhat better for the rest of the war until the Peace of Paris and the defeat of the Midi in 1229. Although unorthodoxy reached a peak with a full third of the membership in the consular term of 1222-1223, the average for the period was about twenty-two percent and showed a substantial increase in the later years of the great war. In spite of the speed of the repression in the town, the peace precipitated no immediate collapse of religious divergence. Catharism, in fact, sustained a forlorn hope in the long term of 1235 to 1238. This coincided with the consulate's and Raymond VII's attack on the Inquisition when the names of condemned heretics amounted to two-thirds of the names of the consuls. The balloon then broke and the numbers quickly decline, averaging from 1243 on around seven and a quarter percent but falling to none by the end in 1249.

What must have worried and infuriated the pilots of the orthodox clergy was that government dragged its feet about helping the repression even after 1229. As seen above, Count Raymond VII had no consistent policy towards heresy. In the mid-twelve-thirties, he and his vicar Peter de Tolosa even joined the consuls in an attempt to restrain the Inquisition and appealed to Rome for help. How deeply Catharism penetrated the town's consulate of that time is shown by the twelve who held office from 1235 and possibly until 1238 or 1239, the term of Catharism's forlorn hope. I stated in the paragraph above that Cathar membership in this consulate amounted to two-thirds of the consuls. In fact, looked at more closely, only one member derived from a family not known to have a direct connection with Catharism, although the members of even that one married and did business with persons from families that had.[12] Three other individuals were probably themselves orthodox but two of them, Peter Grivus de Roaxio and Maurandus de Bellopodio, were from families shot through with Catharism, the latter even being the son of a Cathar believer.[13] The third person, Bernard de Miramonte, was one of the richest Toulousans of his generation and apparently orthodox, but nevertheless arranged to have his richly endowed only child, a daughter, married to Stephen de Castronovo, a Curtasolea, from a notoriously Cathar clan.[14] Lastly, people bearing the names of the

[12]The consul is Bertrand de Garrigiis, a member of a family whose history cannot yet be written, but see my *Repression of Catharism*, pp. 187 and 190.

[13]Ibid., p. 260 for Roaxio, and p. 233 for Maurandus.

[14]Ibid., p. 84.

eight other consuls of this list were condemned believers and most were surely the specific persons condemned by the inquisitors.[15] Although no other consulate can be shown to have been so heavily penetrated by members favoring this faith, it is self-evident that a clergy convinced of its right to monopolize religion would view its composition with horror and rage.

More significant for the present purpose is that the presence of so many consuls tainted by Catharism weakened the political will of that body. Even when Raymond VII supported their position against the Inquisition, the consuls were so dangerously exposed to ecclesiastical repression that they were unable to strike coherent bargains of a political kind. The price they paid the prince for his support was the surrender of Toulousan self-government. The period from 1229 through the late twelve-thirties, the time, that is, when Catharism was being extirpated in the town, was also the one when the consulate was altogether dominated by the count. In short, it seems that the political aim of Toulouse's leading families, those of the middle and upper ranges of the population, was hopelessly distracted by the assault on their Catharism by the Inquisition and that on their political liberty by the prince. They therefore capitulated gradually in the political sphere, happy to see that the protocol of surrender they signed at least protected their property and status.

Can one therefore say that the churchmen combined with the princes to ruin Toulousan republicanism? People of the time undoubtedly believed it. Raymond VII and especially his Capetian successors were said to have worked hand in glove with the church. Anger against popes and crusaders was exemplified by Guillem Figuera, author of the famous "D'un sirventès far," a major poet convinced that the church was destroying Languedoc.[16] A bizarre but perceptive hanger-on of the Franciscans named Peter Garcias of the Burgueto Novo in 1247 also raged against the church, rejecting miracles including those of Francis of Assisi, etc. and, more to the point here, condemning crusaders as murderers. Questioned about her Cathar background in 1274, even a very humble women named Fabrissa reported she

---

[15]Ibid., p. 99, No. 145, but many of this name are found in the Barravus family; pp. 98-99, No. 148, Pons de Suollio; p. 82, No. 6, Bernard Signarius; p. 81, No. 47 and also pp. 91-92, No. 81, both bearing the common name Raymond Rogerius; p. 88, No. 55, Raymond Borrellus; p. 97, No. 128, Oldric Maurandus; and p. 89, No. 59, Peter Embrinus.

[16]For his reception among Toulousans, see Dossat, "Les vaudois méridionaux," pp. 221-222.

276 GOVERNMENT

had been told by an artisan that the French or "Galli" had joined with the "clerici" to enslave Toulouse.[17]

That the repression churchmen set in motion was both fast and brutal does not show, however, that they directed their fire against anything other than religious liberty. The inquisitors of the earlier generations, those that dealt the really damaging blows to Catharism among the town population, had no demonstrable political or class objectives and would surely not have thought of themselves as being in the business of suppressing political liberty. The destruction of one freedom, however, often inadvertently eliminates another. In this case, the focus of the inquisitors' fire was fatally drawn toward the most conspicuous targets. Many of these were well-to-do persons from the families that had led the town as it achieved self-government and a measure of political liberty in the late twelfth century.

Other than coercion directed against divergence or heresy, the clergy also created, or rather helped to create, agencies that seemed to answer the needs of the middle and lower ranges of the population, thereby drawing the plebs away from those some might call its natural leaders. The prohibition of usury and the concomitant insistence on restitution launched by Bishop Fulk even before the Albigensian war undoubtedly attracted the mass of the people because, although the most scandalous usurers were arrivistes, those who lent money or provided credit were usually rich. This economic action, as seen above, coincided with the rise of a corporate economy and society, the appearance of the gilds and an increasing devotion of means to education and charity designed to help the middling and even the poor in society. To Toulouse's church, social reform and religious repression were wholly compatible: the Council of 1229 attacked religious divergence but also insisted that the courts provide lawyers for the poor.[18]

It is also true that all these initiatives were heartily applauded and forwarded by Alphonse of Poitiers and his successors the kings of France. Faced by urban and rural nobles and patricians wedded to their liberties, these princes gained support from the desires of lesser social elements. "Divide et impera" is as good a rule when applied to internal social structure as when used to exploit regional differences or the conflicting interests of town and village. Since, moreover, monarchical government always profits when oligarchic power is diminished, an alliance between church and state had much to do with weakening the republican aspirations of the town.

---

[17]For Garcias (or Garsias) and Fabrissa, see my *Repression of Catharism*, pp. 65ff.
[18]Mansi, *Sacrorum conciliorum ... collectio* 23: col. 202. The heading of Article No. 44 reads: "Ut curia det pauperibus advocatum."

It is nevertheless inherently unlikely and there is no evidence to prove that the churchmen and the princes consciously allied in order to rob the people of political freedom. Monarchs anyway rarely think in such terms, because to them, their own enhancement is really a way of enriching the whole society of which their subjects are part. Nor did churchmen necessarily favor monarchy. The relationship of Rome to the Italian city republics in the struggle with the Empire and the Aristotelian political teaching applauded by clerical intellectuals in the second half of the thirteenth century made many clergy favor, at least theoretically, republican political traditions. If church and state never saw eye to eye in theoretical matters, their practical relationships were also always full of friction, so much so that, if there was a plot in the style sketched in a Gênet play, it was a sadly mismanaged one. During the reign of Raymond VII the sheer incoherence of the relations between the count and the popes in regard to the inquisitors in Toulouse and especially Rome's renewed war against the Empire, its major enemy, show that the pontiffs, like the unhappy Toulousan prince, did not really know where they were going. With the Capetian takeover, relations became even more difficult. The church that Alphonse and the kings were visibly establishing in the Midi was far removed from the church of Innocent III's fond imagination, a church free from, above and even dominating secular powers. Theirs was instead the church of the future, the Gallican church ruled from the throne in Paris and peopled by its creatures. And the outline of this future evolution had been limned in the peace settlement of 1229.

In brief, circumstances allowed two rival groups, princes and churchmen, both wishing to rule society to their own advantage, to combine together to smash divergent religious thought and, at the same time, dissolve the political coherence of the middle and upper classes that had created Toulouse's oligarchic republic before 1229.

B. Jews

Although conjectural, the above may be a truthful picture, but one nevertheless wonders why there was no radical action, not to speak of a revolution, nothing except an occasional riot, to try to invigorate or even restore Toulousan republicanism. Or, for that matter, to go beyond it to create a really egalitarian republic. Given modern experience, it seems likely that something diverted or helped drain away the impulses of the people as a whole, that is, of both the rich and poor. One of these deflections, probably the major one, has already been examined, namely the church's attack on divergent religious thought, especially Catharism. Another, however, is more

familiar to contemporaries: an increase of anti-Jewish sentiment that prepared the way for the pogroms and expulsions witnessed at Toulouse in the
early fourteenth century. The effect of these two religious movements
seems to have differed. The anti-Cathar assault disarmed, or deflected the
aim of, the middle and upper classes; the anti-Jewish one may well have
appealed to, or affected, broader or more popular social levels.

Apart from its ups and downs, the Jewish community at Toulouse must
have always been small and was unusually so when the only extant figures
come to hand. They derive from the late twelve-eighties when the Jews
were being uprooted or eradicated, thus closing a period of mounting per-
secution from about the mid-century mark. At that unpropitious moment the
group's numbers are thought to have been from 425 to 500 persons, a count
that surely reflected a falling off of their original population.[19] Further
proof is that the real property confiscated from the Jews and sold by the
crown in 1306 and 1308 amounted to only seven houses and about eleven
stores, most of them in the region of the modern street called Joutzaigues
where the "carraria vocata scola Judeorum prope quadrivium de Fusteriis
[modern Paradoux]" was located. The "scola" (synagoge) was itself sold in
1310.[20] Illustrative of the light Jewish population in this whole region is
that of the nearby small town of Isle-Jourdain at the time of the expropria-
tion. There, in 1307 and 1308, three houses of two named persons and a
modest amount of real estate, vineyards, arable land, etc. were confiscated
and given to the local baron by the crown to pay off its debts.[21]

That the Jewish community was small may inspire critics to marvel
that an historian would spend any time on it at all today. Numbers are not
everything, however. To use a modern example, the Jewish population of
Weimar Germany including "Ostjuden" was less than one percent of the
whole and its numbers were declining rapidly before the National Socialists
gained power. Besides, like those of modern times, Toulouse's Jews were
relatively wealthy. One surmises not unreasonably that, like the assault on
the Cathars and on the rarer Waldensians, anti-Jewish action reflected in a
general way the frictions occasioned by the implanting of a corporative
social order in the years before and around 1300.

Sections of Chapters Three and Four showed that members of Toulouse's Jewish community played a role in the administrations of the last

[19]Dossat, "Juifs à Toulouse," p. 128.
[20]Saige's *Juifs du Languedoc*, No. 47; for the synagoge, see PAN, JJ 46, fols. 105v-
105 (December 1310) published by Dossat, "Quelques documents inédites sur les Juifs,"
Document No. 2, pp. 791-792.
[21]Saige, *Juifs du Languedoc*, No. 47, acts 9 (March 1307) and 13 (January 1308).

two princes of the house of Saint-Gilles-Toulouse, Raymond VI and VII. Under the Capetians, however, they had no place because Alphonse of Poitiers, in imitation of or spurred on by his brother Louis IX of France, was strongly anti-Jewish. Given the strength of the institution of the prince's Jews in late medieval Iberia and eastern Europe, not to speak of earlier practice in western Europe generally, this Capetian hostility is puzzling. One explanation is conjectural, but nevertheless likely. The papacy, it is known, had taken the lead in anti-Jewish legislation during the late twelfth and early thirteenth centuries. Affronting papal authority, secular princes like Frederick II Hohenstaufen and the later Philip the Fair of France vaunted themselves or their regimes by pretending to be more Christian than the popes themselves. And, to win their combat with the popes, princes were well advised to put aside their hitherto useful Jewish minority.

Coinciding with that ideological need, Jewish usefulness to secular princes was also declining because the latter's capacity to tax their citizens was growing. At Toulouse, for example, old direct taxes capable of growing with the economy had been surrendered as early as 1147 by Count Alphonse-Jordan. A result was that the count's right to license and profit from Jewish loans was, although indirect, one of the few ways open to him of taxing the rich by profiting from business activity. The first revival of direct taxation awaited the rule of the foreigner Simon de Montfort during the Albigensian Crusade, but, once started, his innovation was taken up by his enemies during the great sieges of Toulouse and resulted in basic consular tax legislation in 1222.[22] Once introduced during the war, moreover, tallage was not forgotten. Although Raymond VII's weak government was unable to use it after the Peace of Paris in 1229, Alphonse of Poitiers, as seen above, revived a general tax to finance the crusade against Islam. While surely not wholly obviated, the old economic function of the Jewish community for princes was being undermined.

Again, if the church's assault on usury was largely directed against Christian moneylenders, it also targeted Jewish ones, the popes having emphasized that secular government should force them to make restitution to Christian debtors especially for "severe and immoderate usury."[23] Al-

---

[22]This history is sketched in my *Liberty and Political Power*, pp. 31, 46, 85, 153, 298-299 note 52 and 367-368 note 28, with references to earlier works by Fons, Limouzin-Lamothe and Wolff as well as archival documents.

[23]X. 15 19 18, canon 67, of the Fourth Lateran Council: "graves immoderatasve usuras," and earlier in August 1198 a letter addressed to the archbishop of Narbonne in X. 5 19 12. A good guide to this subject is Grayzel, *The Church and the Jews in the Thirteenth Century*.

though secular princes sometimes continued to profit from Jewish loans to their subjects, those who both wanted to elicit the love of their subjects and also lead their churches, like Louis IX of France, became vehemently anti-Jewish and adopted the whole papal program. Besides, once the idea of general taxes had been accepted and the old function of the Jewish community had begun to decline, there was no reason why the Jews should not pay similar taxes themselves. Once he bit the bullet, since the Jews were his, Alphonse of Poitiers was not obliged to give ear to their reluctance to pay as much as he did to that of the magistrates of his great towns and the "gravamina" of his local nobility.

A result was that Jews of Toulouse came to be treated in intemperate ways wholly unlike Christians. Whereas, for example, the estimate of a Christian's tax was made under oath before elected public officers and notaries, the Jews suffered the obloquy of having to surrender their records or "libri" to the seneschal of Toulouse and Albi to be sent to Paris for examination, all simply at the count's command and all at their expense.[24] And this information was to be accumulated for the seneschal by "two Jews taken from among the richest Jews of the seneschalsy."[25] The actual collection of the estimated money was then entrusted to Jewish representatives chosen by crown officers. In 1270 Bonus, a Jew of Puylaurens well to the east of Toulouse, protested as iniquitous the assessment of 280 shillings of Tours assigned by the administration's three Jews, claiming that his wealth only justified a sum of 200. The seneschal was ordered to summon the three estimators and settle the question.[26] No parliaments or general assemblies of the Jews were called on these occasions.

Why these Capetian princes acted so harshly is hard to fathom. Their governments depended on loans and therefore on credit. Yet both were vehement opponents of usury, being especially hard on Jewish lenders. In Alphonse's reform edict of around 1255, the count ordered that Christian debtors could not be compelled to pay Jewish creditors and, even if the latter lived under the jurisdiction of a different lord or prince, could seize them as serfs if they tried to collect the debts owed them.[27] The degree

---

[24]*HGL* 8: No. 527, ii (October 1268): "in fardellis distincte vestro [the seneschal's] sigillo signatis."

[25]Ibid.: "duos Judeos captos de dicioribus Judeis ipsius senescallie."

[26]Fournier and Guébin, *Enquêtes administratives*, No. 128, roll of the "parlament" held at Toulouse in April-May 1270: p. 297, 70.

[27]*HGL* 8: No. 447, col. 1355 (dated ca. 1255): "Item quod nullus compellatur solvere debitum Judeis, et quicumque Judeum suum sub alterius dominio invenerit, eum capere possit tamquam proprium servum, nonobstante quod moram diuturnam sub alterius dominio traxerit."

to which this law was not a lane in a two-way street is seen when the count allowed Christian creditors to sop up the money owed them by Jews if any was left over from the tax then being collected, presumably maintaining that such Christian creditors were not usurers.[28] Punitive, even lunatic, recommendations of this kind nevertheless gave way in time to wiser, if not kinder, counsels. As both canonists and civilians said, laws impossible of fulfillment bind nobody. Administrative needs also played a role here. Capetian France was still politically decentralized and hence provision had to be made and was made in 1268 for Jews owned by local barons and princes.[29]

Given Capetian hostility, it is initially surprising that the Jews themselves preferred to be subject to the prince rather than to local authorities. Claiming that all inhabitants of their town were under their authority, the consuls of Toulouse tried to insist that Toulouse's Jews should plead in their courts, presumably, at least, for cases involving Christians or crime generally. And, just as they did regarding Christian citizens, they also wanted to enforce a Jewish creditor's right to collect debts owed him. This policy was expressly overridden by the count in 1268 when he ordered the vicar to prevent the consuls and their judges from forcing debtors to pay "new and old debts to Jews living in the town of Toulouse and even outside."[30] In spite of the obvious attraction of the consuls' policy to creditors, the Jews, according to the vicar in 1279, "now again say" that they want to be under the king and not under the consuls. Following a decision of the parliament of 1270, this put their cases in the seneschal's court instead of that of the consuls.[31] Why Jews wanted to be under regional princes and not local authorities, republican or lordly, was very probably inspired by what is seen in the following paragraphs.

In 1270 the count ordered the vicar of Toulouse to enforce the rule that Jews were to wear the sign showing the identity of their religion.[32] When one pauses to remember, however, that this legislation (if that's the word for it) merely repeats early thirteenth century papal law, one is reminded

---

[28]Ibid., No. 527, iv (March 1269).

[29]Ibid. i (October 1268): those "quos barones suos proprios esse probaverint."

[30]Ibid. No. 522, xi (June 1268): "debita nova vel vetera Judeis in villa Tholose habitantibus vel etiam extra villam."

[31]Molinier, *HGL* 10: Note 35, No. 26, xv, col. 156 (June-July 1279), and xvi, col. 163 (ca. 1279): "Nunc de novo Judei dicunt se ... ."

[32]Fournier and Guébin, *Enquêtes administratives*, No. 128 (April-May 1270) 162: "Vicarius Tholose faciat portare Judeis Tholose signa, prout datum fuit eidem in mandato per litteras domini comitis sibi super hoc directas."

that the worsening status of the Jews had much to do with the church. And, indeed, overt hostility to this minority was shown at Toulouse by the clergy's newest manifestation, the mendicant orders.

An example of how a popular mendicant order felt about Jews will illustrate what is meant. Having first settled just outside the "barrium" of Sainte-Catherine's or Saint-Michel, the Carmelites wished to move into town.[33] Floods disturbed them out there, they said, and they were too far away for their mission. The place they chose in 1247 for settlement was the Jewish quarter because, if the reader will forgive a porridge of their rhetoric, they planned to be right there "in the midst of the Jews ... praising the Virgin's most sweet name ... long blasphemed by Jewish perfidy, and exalting those of the Christian faith by confuting the Jewish rite."[34] And, in fact, these friars and their lay confraternity pushed hard against the Jews, requesting the vicar of Toulouse to threaten them with confiscating their homes unless they sold a rent of twopence on a house bought by the new religion.[35] Symbolic of their effort, the block taken over by the Carmelites lay squarely in the heart of the Jewish area of town, being bounded on the south by the street named "Provincialis judeus" and two blocks to the north by that called Joutzaigues on which the synagogue lay.

It is nevertheless mistaken to point the finger only at the monarchy and the church. At Toulouse, the Capetian count and his successors the kings were certainly of two minds about religious passion. In 1267 Alphonse urged his officers to look into and put a lid on the Carmelite confraternity, clearly worried by a report that it had swollen to about five thousand men and women.[36] Observantine religion without excess popular enthusiasm is what usually delights princes, and the Capetians, for all their ostensible

---

[33]Malta 1 103 (October 1255, copied in 1257) records a gift to the provincial prior for the houses being built "in Provincia" on either side of the Rhone river, and, at Toulouse, located "extra portam Narbonensem juxta caminum Gallicum," at Férétra, that is, not far from modern Saint-Roch.

[34]Carmelites 30 (October 1264): "propter inundationem aquarum que aliquando ibidem insurgebant et propter distanciam nimiam civitatis eiusdem necnon quia ibi non poterant fructuosius lucro querere animarum infra civitatem ipsam suum habitaculum et oratorium transtulissent ad domum videlicet sitam in medio judeorum ducti ad hec specialiter pro concepto firmoque proposito ut per eos beatissima virgo Maria mater salvatoris ... in eo loco ... laudaretur devote in quo fuerat per iudeos perfidos longo tempore blasphemata ... ." For the blessed virgin, the friars were to devote themselves "ad laudam sui dulcissimi nominis, et ad exaltandos Christiane fidei possessores Christianorum ... et ad ritum judaicum confutandum ... ."

[35]HGL 8: No. 522, xvii (March 1269).
[36]Ibid. i (June 1267).

Christian passion, shared that view. As for the church, apart from the mendicants, little is known about clerical attitudes. For all one knows, both the parish clergy and the older orders may not have been interested in inflaming anti-Jewish sentiments. The mendicants, however, were in their first age of growth and allurement. Although one is rightly skeptical of modern puffery about how popular religious orders were, it is nevertheless all but sure that the friars, if the elitist Dominicans are counted out, really attracted the plebs and not just selected elements or the well-to-do.[37]

Again, as to the people as a whole, one may surely guess that, although sometimes indifferent, they were anything but tolerant. What the historian William of Puylaurens said about lay attitudes before the Albigensian Crusade was still surely true. Layfolk so despised the clergy, he reports, that they swore "I'd rather be a 'capellanus'" [a parish priest] instead of the usual and wholly permissible "I'd rather be a Jew!"[38] Popular speech testifies to the same attitudes. According to testimony in 1269, the Guarnerius "campsor" who led a riot that nearly turned into a popular uprising cried out repeatedly that "we" Toulousans are taxed "like we're Jews," and that "we're more oppressed than any Jew in Joutzaigues."[39]

The ruin of Toulouse's Jews in the late twelve-hundreds evoked no opposition from either the secular government or the church. More profoundly, neither the rich or the poor acted to protect this group that had traditionally lived in their town. Because the rich were not powerless nor the plebeian many without the strength of their numbers, it is hard to know why. Perhaps it was easier to undergo a quasi-revolution or a partial one from which the rich could profit (which is what they do best) and in which the poor could mistreat or punish an exposed minority of the rich instead of

[37]Eleven testaments mention more than one of these new orders: Appendix 8, Nos. 51 (March 1229), 59 (January 1234), 60 (September 1234), 72 (March 1243), 84 (August 1253), 86 (August 1256), 90 (November 1258), 91 (May 1259), 93 (August 1261), 94 (November 1263) and 101 (January 1283). Of these, one was composed for a baron of Isle-Jourdain, three for patricians or nouveau-riche, two for wealthy persons in industry (including a Puybusque) and five for people in the crafts and trades or of modest social levels. When one recalls how underrepresented the last mentioned humble levels are in extant testaments, these few documents help prove the point made above.

[38]Puylaurens, *Chronica*, ed. Duvernoy, p. 24: "Capellani in tanto contemptu habebantur a laicis, quod eorum nomen, acsi Iudei essent, in iuramentum a pluribus sumebatur, ut, sicut dicitur: 'Mallem esse Iudeus,' sicut dicebatur: 'Mallem esse, quam hoc aut illud facerem, capellanus.'"

[39]PAN, J 192b (August to September 1269), part published in *Layettes du Trésor*, 5: 325, No. 5487: anent tolls on Toulousan trade: "quod sumus plus sosmes que nulh juzios de jusaigas," and "sicut si nos essemus Judei."

turning society wholly upside down (which is the worst they can do). In modern times, modest and poor folk have only rarely been able to confront the well-to-do who rule and often exploit them. On the other hand, they have been frequently free to assault the small minority of their richer neighbors who were Jewish. Perhaps something of that kind transpired in thirteenth century Toulouse.

Having experienced an increase of such hostile pressures for over a half century, by 1322 the Toulousan Jewish community had been so extinguished that, of a tax or fine collected from all the Jews in royal Languedoc, those of Toulouse contributed only a trifle over four percent.[40] The events in royal France take one's breath away: expelled in 1306, readmitted in 1315, massacred by the Pastoureaux in 1319-1321, expelled again in 1322 and readmitted in 1359, the Jews underwent in 1394 an expulsion that was to be final until modern times.[41] For the pogrom and massacre of 1320 in Toulouse, one has only to read the inquisitorial register dealing with the forced conversion and trial of the German Jew Baruch conducted by Jacques Fournier, then bishop of Pamiers and later Pope Benedict XII.[42] By the end of these persecutions, all that was left of France's onetime Jewish community were some groups along the German, Iberian and Italian frontiers.

To sum up, religion decisively helped destroy the town's traditional solidarity that had once contributed much to its political freedom. Although the classes were really quite intermixed, orthodoxy's erasure of Catharism had the effect of disrupting the political aim of the middle and upper classes. And the middle and lower ranges of the population were almost surely happy to be participants in the Christian anti-Judaism directed against Toulouse's small Jewish community.

---

[40]*HGL* 10: No. 223 (February 1322): the fine was estimated at 47,000 pounds of Paris, of which the seneschalsy of Carcassonne contributed 47.8%, that of Beaucaire 43.6%, Toulouse 4.3%, Rouergue 4.0% and Cahors .2%.

[41]Nahon, "Les juifs dans les domaines d'Alfonse de Poitiers, 1241-1271," *Revue des études juives* 124 (1966) 190.

[42]In *Registre d'inquisition de Jacques Fournier*, ed. Duvernoy, 1: No. 8, pp. 177-190.

Conclusion

A. Summary

To rehearse again the history sketched above in these pages, the church had arrested the threatened secession of substantial elements of the population in the town of Toulouse and the Toulousain into what the orthodox called heresy. This was accomplished by converting a program of preaching and voluntary conversion into a crusade in arms followed immediately by an inquisitorial police action directed against the dissenters. Under this pressure, a society in which diversity of belief about religion had been current gave way to one in which a revived and greatly developed orthodoxy both extirpated divergence and at the same time invented a religious ideology that for a time penetrated all levels of the population and won back many of its members. The church also appealed to the people by opening new educational and charitable doors to the enthusiasms and needs of those who for a time had been allowed to secede. Mendicant preaching, parish schools, university education and general hospitals like that of Saint-Jacques in Saint-Cyprien together raised the level of literacy and attempted to address the problems of health, old age care and burial.

At this time also, the old leadership and social tone of this society was radically altered. Once almost triumphant, the economic individual was first shackled by the attack on usury and then eventually forced to conform to, or hide his initiatives in, the corporatized economy of the thirteenth century. Along with this, a society centered on the family, especially the families of the middle and higher classes, was corporatized, replaced by one in which social order counted for more than it had in the past, perhaps even more than family identity. A parallel devolution of political power from the hands of the hereditary counts into those of landed and commercial gentlefolk and patricians reached its peak from 1189 to 1229 and then gave way to a renewed princely power whose ultimate manifestation was the monarchy of northern France.

At first sight, there is not much about Toulouse to distinguish its history from that of the average Italian city republic. The growth of a popular economic and social corporatism, the initial resistance to the Inquisition and the eventual popular approbation of the repression of divergent belief, all seem much the same. The only significant difference seems to have been the vehemence or rapidity of the attack on usury and the speed of the assault on heresy in Toulouse. Another and greater difference, however, was that the Italian town was spared the momentary combination of state and church that destroyed the quasi-republican government of Toulouse. The conflict of Empire and papacy did not exist in Languedoc where, to put it simply, the Capetians and the inquisitorial church worked for a time hand in glove. As a result, in Italy, the success of the popular parties in the war against the Empire created an unforgettable age during which a popular and almost democratic republicanism flourished, to be followed by hereditary principates or rigid oligarchies only later on in the fourteenth and fifteenth centuries. At Toulouse, although popular participation was everything in the thirteenth century, democratic or democratizing republicanism was stillborn. From the moment of the defeat by the northern French in 1229, the political indifference of the plebs and fear of the Inquisition on the part of the old and partly heretical patrician families weakened the spirit and muted the courage of Toulouse's leaders. Toulouse, in brief, skipped over the stage of popular republicanism and became monarchical in a long drawn out battle that began in 1229 and ended a half century later, an evolution that almost obliterated the memory of her brief republican moment, a matter of four to five decades, under patrician auspices.

B. RELIGION AND FREEDOM'S LOSS

To discover why Toulouse surrendered the joys of self-government and the relative freedom of intellectual or religious life that had marked the early years of that century is not easy. In answering this question, one is aided by the fact that, as noted above, although the Italian urban republics underwent the additional experience of a real measure of democratic republicanism, even the Italians in the long run shared Toulouse's experience. The problem is then of a general nature and is not limited to Toulouse.

That Toulousans refused to fight for the right to have several faiths within a quasi-republican constitution seems partly because of the Cathar religion. An alternative to the doctrine believed orthodox by the larger part of society, its dualist solution to the problems of free will and sin and its metempsychosis clearly appealed to many and also effectively obliterated the sacerdotal foundation on which the orthodox ecclesiastical order rested. One nevertheless understands why the people as a whole were not deeply moved by this faith. Unlike other medieval religions, it was devoid of utopia's traditional allurements. Cathars did not sing the praises of the *Acts of the Apostles*, to each according to his need, from each according to his means, did not attack usury, and, although demanding in regard to the "perfecti" or clergy, did not urge ordinary believers ("credentes") to imitate apostolic poverty or sharing. Unlike other faiths, also, such as the national cult of the medieval Jews or the regionalism of the later Protestantism of the Cevennes, Catharism appealed only to individual families or persons, those that wanted, dared or were impelled to set themselves against the orthodoxy of the time. Although itself a community of secession, it was nevertheless a non-communitarian faith.

The result was that, when attacked and left unsupported by external powers, Catharism vanished very rapidly indeed. Occasional persons and even one or two generations of a number of families died or suffered very considerably for their commitment. Since adhesion was divorced from real social support, however, it was only a person's pride, desire for consistency and self-respect that made her or him suffer martyrdom, while for families, even very heretical ones, it was all over in one or two generations.[1] Besides, some were surprised by the speed of the orthodox retribution and were unable to change gears in time. In these circumstances, not even the upper social elements that had initially welcomed this alternative to the ordinary church held on very long. Their members may have invented it, so to speak, but their need for careers and advancement made them drop it with alacrity. How much less, then, did the wide middle elements of society and the substantial workers or laborers wish to hold on to a faith that offered them little or nothing, one that was anyway tainted by being a gnosis somewhat more current among those they themselves probably thought of as their social betters. For such broad and modest social levels the church's founding of new religious orders and educational and charitable institutions was far more profitable.

That Toulouse returned to orthodoxy in the thirteenth century does not mean that its inhabitants were willing to let the clergy walk all over them, as it were. Because the Cathar religion could not withstand the assault of the Roman church, the citizens of Toulouse who faced problems with the church, and they were many, began to lean toward secular government, the traditional agency that had limited and sometimes defeated ecclesiastical demands in the past. At Toulouse, also, the Crusade had seen to it that the quasi-republican town government was in no position to withstand ecclesi-

---

[1]Proof for these propositions is repeatedly seen in the family histories contained in my *Repression of Catharism*.

astical initiatives. As a result, once the foreign Capetians – the adjective "foreign" verges on being too strong – had taken the county from the weakened hands of the local dynasty of Saint-Gilles, Toulousans began to look toward the French crown. Although Alphonse of Poitiers was assuredly conventionally devout and favored the work of the Inquisition, he was, like his brother Louis IX in royal France, no mere slave of the church. If he supported the inquisitors, he saw to it that they were now recruited in north France. He also actively employed them, sometimes to their regret, to control and inspect the lay officers of his government. Nor did he hesitate to support his subjects against the local church.

An especially significant issue was that of testaments. The church council meeting under the papal legate Cardinal Roman in 1229 at Toulouse had ordered that testaments were required of everyone, man and woman, and that they were to be rendered with the direct participation of their parish clergy. The cardinal's conciliar initiative was straightway confirmed by Count Raymond VII who was in no position to question it. Sometime between June 1251 and June 1255 parishioners of Toulouse, most of them quite humble, presented complaints about the parish clergy, "gravamina" stored up for nearly a quarter of a century, to their new count of the Capetian house and petitioned him to override this conciliar decision. By the latter date Alphonse did so, expressly stating that he had acted "notwithstanding the constitution of the onetime legate in the region of Toulouse, the lord cardinal Roman" and went on to assert formally that Toulousan practice anent testaments was consonant with Roman law.[2]

In the same list of complaints, the laity protested against the clerical attempt to increase tithes. Only tithes, the petitioners said, established by the time of the Peace of Paris, namely by 1229, were to be permitted, thus protecting town industry such as linen production and perhaps the blue dyestuff made from woad already being raised for exportation in the farms of the region. The count responded by deciding against the clergy, although petitioners noted that that body, headed by the bishop, persisted in trying to collect the new tithes, large and small. Writing to his favored agent Sicard Alaman in 1268, the count repeated his position on the matter, noting

---

[2]For this history, see my *Men and Women*, pp. 34-35, and "Parishes of Toulouse," pp. 185-188. Alphonse's reply is in Fournier and Guébin, *Enquêtes administratives*, p. 77, No. 12 (ca. June 1255), and reads in part: "nonobstante constitutione domini Romani cardinalis, legati quondam in partibus Tolosanis, que erat quod non valerent testamenta condita sine presentia capellani parochialis." The text began with: "Item super testamentis condendis serventur jura et consuetudo Tolosana, que a jure non discrepat hac parte."

that the bishop and clergy had been recalcitrant, and ordered him to persist in pushing the anticlerical initiative.[3]

In fine, their hyper-orthodoxy enabled Capetian princes to rally support among the mass of Toulousans against a church that the dynasty ostensibly and sometimes really did support. This relationship, one might conjecture, also helped shape or even deform the church. Because the clergy's demand in the matter of the tithe was surely designed to keep up with a growing economy and in no way breached any long-established principle, one sees an additional reason why clerics were obliged to develop the penitential system with its confession, indulgences, etc. to the degree they did.

C. THE PLEBS AND THE PRINCE

The actions of the "populares," the "universitas" or general assembly seen in the next to last chapter, make it seem as if, although probably without enthusiasm, the plebs sided with the prince against the middle and upper levels of the population, ie. against the Toulousan political class. To put the matter another way, historians who attribute the laying of the foundations of the corporate social and economic structures and monarchical government that grew everywhere during the later middle ages mainly or only to the initiative of princes and their allies among the noble or rich are probably very wide of the mark. Such an analysis underestimates the power and inventiveness of the people as a whole and even of their humbler members. How could Alphonse of Poitiers, an absentee prince who ruled an armed populace with hardly any police or permanent soldiery, have smashed consular liberty and Toulousan self-government so decisively in the twelve-fifties and sixties without popular support? To believe that the people were merely passive and that they were bemused by the institutions their leaders or betters thought good for them seems absurd.

Like some today, contemporaries of these events occasionally believed that society's lower orders were directly ruled by the higher ones. The late thirteenth century Catalan Raymond Llull observes in his *Order of Chivalry* that chivalry preserves the country because, fearing the knights, the people are afraid of destroying it, and that, for the same reason, kings and princes will not wage war. The fourteenth century French version of his tract was both more monarchical and more reactionary, affirming that the people both cultivate the land and fear kings and princes because they dread the

---

[3]*HGL* 8: No. 526, iii (July 1268) which repeats the rollback to the Peace of Paris and urges enforcement against a resisting clergy "licet vos pluries scripseritis domino episcopo Tholosano."

knights.[4] A measure of truth aside, the opinion of this famous apologist for the nobility is to be taken with a grain of salt, as is the harsher French version: both confounded what was with what they wanted to be. What had happened, it seems, was that a monarchy, ostensibly ruled by one and based on the quiet although surely not enthusiastic support of the many, overcame a relatively oligarchic government that had once exercised much of the power both in the town of Toulouse and in the small towns and villages of the Toulousain.

One also wonders what there was anyway in the older quasi-republican political liberty for the plebs, the lower reaches of the people. It seems likely that pressing economic needs and lack of leisure deprived the people of the only really enjoyable thing about that freedom, the ability and capacity to lead other men and to profit from that leadership. The matter should also be stated in other than negative terms. When one thinks of the social and political activities of the upper and middle ranges of the population in relation to those below, it sometimes seems that terms like freedom and liberty are beside the point. The fulfillment of those who led lay partly in personal freedom but mostly in their possession of the means and capacity to command, manipulate and use other men. A republic, one may say, was a collective or pluralistic principate, even a band of little tyrants. The more republican and the more free the middle and upper ranges of the population were to do what they wanted, the more despotic was their government of the humbler or poorer elements of the people, that is, of the plebs.

It follows from this that the indifference to political liberty of the lower and middle ranges of the population was little more than an expression of their desire to have the freedom to do or experience the intellectual, physical and technical things they wanted and for which they had the means, and to do them in their own good time, not under coercion. As or more compelling, given the modesty of the means at their disposal, was the consequence of their hands-on childhood education and adult labor in agriculture, crafts, trades, music and popular literature. Like that of modern scientists, medical

---

[4]*Obres essencials* 1: 531b reads: "Ofici de cavaller es mantenir terra, car per la paor que les gents han dels cavallers, dubten a destruir les terres, e per temor dels cavallers dubten los reis e ls princeps venir los uns contra los altres." Saying the same, a slightly variant text is in *Obras literarias*, ed. Balori and Caldentey, p. 115. The *Ordre de chevalerie*, ed. Minervini, p. 105, has: "Office de chevalier est de maintenir terre, car, par la paour que les gens de peuple ont des chevaliers, ilz labourent et cultivent les terres pour paour de estre destruictz et, par la cremeur ("tremeur" in Columbia University, Plimpton MS, fol. 86v) des chevaliers, ilz redoubtent les roys et les princes par qui ilz ont le povoir."

doctors, engineers, musicians, scholars and artists, their work was so time consuming and compelling that their practitioners had little need for anything else. Nor would it do to forget about modest folk what one knows about their betters, namely that they also wished to maximize the rewards due their service to society. It is therefore understandable that the plebs, a group whose principal property or force lay in the labor and artistry of its hands and in its children, was often inclined to entrust political direction to others with the education and experience to handle it, just so long as they did not invariably act in an arbitrary and heavy-handed manner. If these rulers were successful in external and other adventures and were not too obtrusive, the plebs could accurately affirm that, even if ruled from above, it was free, free, that is, to do what its members wanted.

From the point of view of what the people wanted out of government, it is also sometimes true that the most democratic regime was that of a prince. This is not because princes loved their peoples: they may have, but mainly to sate their appetites. Still, the thirteenth century reorganization of the courts propounded by the professional jurists and also by the prince who sponsored them undoubtedly appealed to the many. Alphonse's reform of around 1254 argued that the count's officers and judges should not bully citizens nor forcibly detain or imprison those willing to answer charges.[5] Against this interpretation is the fact that these steps of the government had overtones quite as elitist as those favoring professional lawyers against common persons serving as arbitral judges reported in an earlier chapter. Among Alphonse's citizens were "knights and other worthy folk," who, in his mind, obviously came before all the rest.[6] Again, the count's reform provides the first evidence of the use of the "quaestio," torture, that is, with which to acquire sufficient proof in serious criminal cases.[7] True, things were not quite that bald. The administration's statement on the "quaestio" was brief, recommended moderation and insisted that it be initiated by due legal procedure.

The introduction of legal torture may prompt an unwary modern reader to believe that princes imposed it on unwilling communities. Such was not case, however, because, after its long prehistory in antiquity, the medieval "quaestio" was first introduced in Italian city republics, an event occurring,

---

[5]*HGL* 8: No. 447, col. 1355 (dated ca. 1254): "Item ut homines non detineantur capti, qui parati fuerint satisdare, nisi qualitas criminis hoc requirat."

[6]Ibid.: judges were not to bully nor "dehonestent milites et alios bonos viros verbis contumeliosis."

[7]Ibid.: "Item ut non supponant facile homines questionibus et tormentis, nisi quod, si debeant, sententialiter fuerit pronunciatum."

for motives yet to be fully explored, at the beginning of the rise of their famous popular parties, either as an initial reaction against them or as their way of attacking their opponents. Certain it is that torture and other somewhat totalitarian jurisprudential manifestations had become completely at home in the most radically democratic Italian constitutions by around 1300.[8]

Harsh or rude though princes often were, also, the attractions of monarchy to the many are worth examining. Princely rule differed from that in republics governed by the middle and upper ranges of the population. In a social or functional sense, the loosely defined group directing republics had a near monopoly of higher mercantile, legal and military functions. Whether its members owned as property or instead directed as administrators the means of production and distribution or conducted other usually profitable social actions such as physical expansion or war, its members normally battled the rest of the people over the cost of capitalization, the partition of profits, plunder or wages and the duration and risk of service. In this the plebs shared a common interest with their princes who were likewise engaged in constant war with the well-to-do, those pretending to possess the blood or intellect of natural freedom. Princes always tried, often in vain, to lower the claims for excessively high profits or exemptions from service, taxes or controls over the means of production directed or owned by the rich or powerful.

The modes of living of the upper echelons of society also differed remarkably from those of the lower ones, a difference that served to set the teeth of the two groups on edge. As befits the pluralist political structure they favored, the higher classes were more conscious of individual family traditions. Because they nearly engrossed the organizational and intellectual functions of society and combined that near monopoly with a natural social and political pluralism, they constituted the main repository of society's intellectualism and freedom of thought, qualities for which neither princes nor workers were famed. The humbler classes instead often swung between the powerlessness of anarchic individualization, a condition in which no one had the means or the power to define him or herself and the collective mass passions of the corporations in which they were brigaded. The plebs shared this quality with their princes. Absolved from the prudent care and discretion imposed by family and class responsibility, a prince's heroic individualism best expressed itself in the uncontrolled infantilism of overriding self-gratification, characteristics also often seen in the intemperate movements

---

[8]For a sketch of the anti-magnate jurisprudence of the Italian popular republics, see my "Medieval Urban Liberty," in *The Origins of Modern Freedom in the West*, ed. R.W. Davis, p. 127.

of the humble in political and social life. This selfishness or, better, self-centeredness also empowered princes and tyrants to arbitrate the conflicts of the various classes over which they ruled.

If these conjectures are credible, one understands why the middle and lower ranges of the population at Toulouse and, at a later date, those of Italy's city republics, were indifferent to the rise of the monarchical form of government at the expense of the older tradition of republican independence. They were busy elsewhere: working at their compelling specialties, and helping to build the gilds that protected their economic interests and the charitable agencies answering their pressing needs. Nor may they have merely been indifferent: modest folk were often happy to witness the subjection of those who played the role of master, entrepreneur or employer.

Whatever motives inspired the people, the ideal hopes of a popular utopian of the early 1200s, if these were ever conscious, were surely not to be realized during the subsequent century. Gilds were certainly built in plenty, but, as has been seen above in the previous chapter, it has even been argued that the attack on usury may well have diminished the provision of cheap credit to the poor, those who needed it most. Gild brotherhood, also, was always limited by the desire of the masters to use to the point of abuse their laborers and those training to enter a craft or trade. Admittedly, these disadvantages were somewhat eased partly because rapid gild growth initially opened the way to workers and partly because of the benefits derived from the control of economic individualism such as the growth of education and charity based on charitable giving, restitution of usury and testamentary bequests to the church. It is nevertheless true that even a cursory examination of Toulouse around 1300 does not disclose a picture of a people's paradise.

There, although the rich had had to share a measure of their power with middling elements, wealthy families were still active and influential. As social corporatism grew, indeed, some patrician families were soon ranked among the newly privileged nobility. Lastly, when fourteenth century tax rolls are examined, one is struck by the fact that, in spite of the gilds and economic regulation, the disparities of wealth remained, or had become again, very marked. The picture seen at Toulouse is similar to that discernible almost everywhere in the more developed centers of western European life in the late middle ages and early modern times. Everywhere, just as at Toulouse, the role of the kings and princes was not revolutionary, but instead one that sought to keep every social element in its place to the monarchy's profit. In a negative sense, this almost late Roman division of society into social orders each with its function and due remuneration was an expression of the opportunism characteristic of monarchy and its method of "divide et impera." In a positive sense, it was evidence of the ability of

monarchy, by coercion, to harmonize the whole of society and still internal
war by protecting each social class and group, high or low, in its station.

D. RADICAL HOPE

Although the angers directed against religious minorities seen in the previous chapter may have helped to block radical change, one nevertheless
wonders why the leaders and members of this society made no more of the
rise of the people to a measure of participation in the political and social
structure during the thirteenth century. Ancient empires and some modern
progressive despotes have shown the capacity of rulers to cement their
authority for a time by means of a kind of continuing revolution. In this
system, the ambitions, angers and even the ineptitudes of the plebs are
drawn on in order to render powerless and occasionally replace those who
plan and direct society or the state. And, in fact, some pieces of this system
are to be seen in the late medieval and early modern principates and monarchies when princes called on lesser social elements to replenish their
officers from below and thereby weaken the shackling power of their nobili-
ties and burgher patriciates. But this kind of continuing revolution played
only a modest role in most late medieval European states, and one is therefore driven to ask why the princes and the people allied to them were unable to carry out this curious miracle of repetitive democratization.

Their incapacity to do so cannot have had much to do with the resistance of the privileged orders sheltering themselves behind the walls of an
ingrained localism derived from a once decentralized and feudal political
order. This familiar interpretation may seduce historians of France, but has
no appeal to those of the Italian city republics whose history is in several
ways similar to that of Toulouse. There was, however, a power to be reckoned with in the thirteenth century, one whose origins and functions had
made it into an agency fitted to combat, or to moderate the excesses of, late
Rome's popular tyranny and those of its conquering and barbarian successors at the dawn of the middle ages. This was the church. Although already
weakening in the face of nascent secular authority, the exemptions and privileges of the church and its still popular appeal to a purportedly divine
court whose judgments were beyond the reach of human reason made the
church what Montesquieu (d. 1755) thought the nobility and the privileged
orders of the eighteenth century to have been, a natural, if inadvertent,
defender of freedom.

More than a merely obscurantist defence of privilege was visible here.
When Waldes (d. 1216) sought to establish in poverty an ideal apostolic
communitarianism and when Robert of Curzon (d. 1218) preached the same

in order to purify Latin Europe and revive the flagging crusade, one sees the potentiality for social change and even revolution in the teaching of the ecclesiastics. Mighty though this propaganda for brotherhood and apostolic communism was in the first age of the growth of the gild and corporate system, it seems to have been defeated in the thirteenth century by two institutional manifestations. The first of these was the practical ideology of the gilds, one founded on the technological possibility of efficient production of useful and beautiful objects within the system of the family ownership of individual workshops. Once protected against entrepreneurial exploitation and established in society, the gildsman's idea was that of the leveller within the group and not that of the brother seeking brethren among all mankind. The gilds therefore pushed the quasi-religious communitarian groups out of the main stream of industry during the thirteenth century.

The second reason accords with the first but has to do with the institutional church. Medieval man had inherited from Rome a way of dividing society into clearly demarcated social orders whose members had styles of life and social behaviour differing one from the other. In this system, it had long been traditional to consider the orders of the church, monastic and eremitical, as the places where the utopian urges of the ideal sharing or communism of the brethren could best be acted out, away from the world but subvented by those remaining in the world and reflecting their longing to share what they could not afford to live. In the context of the widespread utopianism of the early thirteenth century, the subordination of their movements to the church by such leaders as the reconciled Waldensians and Francis of Assisi (d. 1226) was surely traditionalist and perhaps even reactionary because they removed dangerous utopian urges from the world to enclose them in the cloister, hermitage or in petty sects of lay-women and men.

All the same, the advantage (if such it was) of this separation of functions or roles was that it enabled people in the world to divorce the excesses of ideological adventurism from practical living and thereby to justify the latter in its own worldly terms. Admittedly, to some such as Giles of Rome (d. 1316), the ability of the church to live according to a divinely recommended community of goods free from the cares of the world while secular folk were left wallowing in the agonies or filth of private property was merely another proof of the superiority of the clergy over the laity and a reminder of the duty of the latter to support, and be ruled by, the former. To John Quidort of Paris (d. 1308), however, the private ownership of property characteristic of lay society was not only justified in terms of the natural or human order of things, but was itself a divinely inspired and positive good, to be defended against any claim or ideology, even that of

the church and its pontiffs. And what may be noted here about these clerical doctrines on private right is not only that they suited gildsmen once
they had risen from their earlier utopianism to respectability or participation in the thirteenth century, but also that they were largely in harmony
with the social pluralism characteristic of the middle and upper ranges of
the population.

Perhaps, in fine, the orthodox religion helped shatter the Cathar minority, expropriate the Jewish community, deflect the political aim of Toulouse's quasi-republican leadership and even dash society's hopes for a
more radical solution. But, if so, the church also helped limit the poten-
tial totalitarianism of both secular monarchy and popular extremism. Until
severely impaired in modern times, the "via regia" of employing a continuing revolution or forced democratization by recruiting from the lower
levels of the population to break the resistance of the educated elites and
propertied classes was not available to late medieval and early modern
princes or despots.

Speculation aside, all that can surely be said is that, by 1250 or not
long therafter, all classes in Toulouse, high and low, were unable or unwilling to advance and protect the measure of religious diversity and political republicanism that had characterized town society around 1200.

⊻

Appendix One

Family Histories

1. ARNALDUS

The capacity of Toulousans around 1200 to use a very common Christian name to serve as a family identification is both illustrated and qualified by the history of a family named Arnaldus, four of whose five members bore this name as a second name or surname. The one who did not bore the distinctive name of Deusaiuda (Deide).[1]

Son of a Bernard Arnaldus, a widower named Peter Arnaldus drew his testament in 1194, naming as his executors a relative called Bernard Arnaldus who was absent at the time, his brother Gerald Arnaldus, his brother-in-law Bernard Bonushomo and William Pons de Prignaco. The testator allocated a hundred shillings for charity, specifically assigning sixty-seven shillings six pence to ecclesiastical and charitable institutions, to his own parish the Daurade and especially to Saint-Étienne (twenty-five shillings and a bed) for final care and burial as a "frater." Fifteen shillings were allocated to godchildren and various recipients, including two shillings "cum premio" to the "nutrissa" of his son Pons, a bequest telling us that his wife had died in childbirth or soon thereafter. The remaining seventeen shillings six pence were left to his executors to distribute as they saw fit.

Peter's children and equal heirs were his sons Deusaiuda and Pons. These children were entrusted to his sister Bruna and his brother-in-law Bernard Bonushomo to be raised until their fourteenth year. Starting on the coming November first, the guardians were to be given thirty shillings for each child yearly, for Deusaiuda for six years and for Pons for eleven years.[2] Deusaiuda was therefore about eight years old and his brother Pons about three when their father died.

Seventeen years later in 1211, the two brothers, described as the sons of the deceased Peter de Bernardo Arnaldo [son of their deceased grandfather], divided their inheritance. Deusaiuda took the town houses, one of which abutted

---

1   [1]See another and unrelated Deide, Deusaiuda Sutor, a cobbler, who witnessed the act of 1211 cited in note 3 below.
   [2]Appendix 8, No. 13 below (September 1194).

on the "carraria maior pontis [veteris]" (possibly the modern rue de la Daurade). Deusaiuda's brother, now called Pons Arnaldus, was given two arpents of new vineyard the brothers had planted at Motte-Saint-Hilaire (just southeast of Saint-Cyprien), two and a half arpents of arable there and a rent of four shillings on a vineyard.[3] Later that year, Deusaiuda rented one of his two adjoining houses to Bernard Garnerius "junior," an action that shows how landlords made out in Toulouse at that time. Deusaiuda's property consisted of a "stabulum" (probably a one-story house because Deide usually refers only to his two houses), a "domus" or house and an "aula lapidea." This was a substantial property because the house and hall were on the "carraria maior pontis" four "brassa" two palms wide (ca. 7.6 meters or 25 feet) and ran from an adjoining alley to another property fourteen "brassa" and five palms (ca. 26.4 meters or nearly 85.5 feet) in depth. For one of these buildings, he paid a fixed rent ("oblie") of nine pennies yearly and the one he rented for a term of two years in a contract called a "conductio" gave him a yearly "premium" of forty shillings.[4]

Nothing more in known about Pons Arnaldus, though a person of this undistinguished name who lived "ad furnum Bastardi" is seen in a charter of 1238 surrounded by the usual crafts- and tradesmen who appear in his brother's documents.[5]

TABLE 1   ARNALDUS

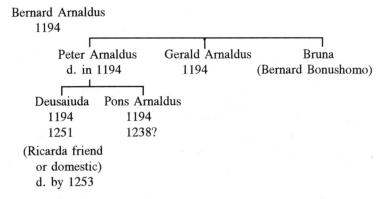

[3]Malta 1 19 (July 1211).

[4]Malta 1 18 (November 1211). The description of the house and hall and of Deusaiuda's relationship with his landlord who was a Noerio according to Malta 1 33 (June 1253) and ibid. 1 54 (July 1253). The "stabulum" was leased from the Gaitapodium family for an unknown sum.

[5]E 501 ii (August 1238, copied in 1255). The Four Bastard was a block in the City not far from Deusaiuda's place.

Deusaiuda, however, appears again. In 1251 when about sixty-five years old and "infirmitate detentus," Deusaiuda bought a corrody from the Hospitalers. He gave that institution his houses and stone hall, reserving these properties in usufruct. Until his death, he was to receive a pension of four "cartones" of grain and two "modii" of unwatered wine annually and, at the end, three hundred shillings to pay his debts, charities and restitutions to those from whom he had taken usury. After his death, Ricarda, a woman "qui tunc manebat cum eo," was to live on one of these houses and have a half of the pension described above until her demise. Were the Hospital not to wish to give her the stated pension, she was to collect "totum premium aliarum predictarum domorum," a return which could hardly have been less than the forty shillings collected by Deusadiuva in 1211.[6] Deusaiuda was dead by 1253 when we hear of an action taken by two of his executors, the notary Bernard de Samatano and Stephen Facit Sanguinem "parator."[7] What the nature of the relationship between Deusaiuda and Ricarda was is not discernible, but it was evidently very close.

2. BARBAORDEUS

Variously given as Barba de Ordeo, Barbaordei and Barbadors (barley silk or wool), this modest family of the Daurade parish is first seen in the person of an Arnold Barbaordei in 1145. Although property he owned can be traced to 1232 through an individual named Barbaordeus, then to another Arnold and his wife Petrona (who was dead by 1209), and subsequently to yet another person named Barbaordeus, it is not known how this line relates to the family described below about which more detail is available in the charters.[1] It nevertheless seems likely that the three loose Barbaordei, one a Bernard seen in 1202, a cousin named Arnold in 1223 and an Arnold Raymond Barbaordei who helped the relatively well documented family seen below in 1260, were from this line or were related to it.

[6]Appendix 8, No. 80 (December 1251). This document was not a testament, but note that the notary and finisher mentioned in the subsequent act of 1253 attended its rendition.

[7]Malta 1 33 (June 1253). The executors detailed the size and ownership of Deusaiuda's properties, the latter being described as the son of the onetime Peter Arnaldus. In ibid. 1 34 (July 1253), the Noerio sold the "oblie" paid by the deceased to the Hospital as well as the rent on the "domus" and "aula lapidea."

2 [1]Malta 1 129 i (May 1145, copied in 1223) with property of Arnold; iv (June 1192), the same now of Barbaordeus; vi (June 1209), the same now of Petrona Barbaordei; viii (August 1232), now of Barbaordeus. In the meantime in Saint-Étienne 227 (26 DA 2 57) (January 1200), Arnold Barnaordei and his wife Petrona appear. When the name Barbaordeus is the only appellation of an individual, the nominative case was used; when it was a last name, it was in the genitive.

That family begins with two brothers Raymond and William, first seen in 1181, the latter of whom shared property with an otherwise unknown Bernard Barbaordei in 1202.[2] Bernard and William disappear at these dates, leaving only Raymond who was surely dead by 1232.[3] Raymond's heirs are then heard of, the brothers Arnold, Raymond and Peter, who split their modest inheritance in 1240, dividing a house and the rest of the property in three parts.[4]

In the meantime, Arnold had married a woman named Stephania with the consent of his brothers and of a cousin also named Arnold Barbaordei in 1223. This marriage settlement was very modest and involved only a half arpent of land and a "dotalicium" of twenty shillings.[5] Although Peter disappeared after 1240, the brothers Arnold and Raymond are seen in 1254 and 1260.[6] By the latter date, Stephania had vanished and Arnold is revealed as married to a second wife, Jordana. In that year, furthermore, Arnold bought himself care and a pension by giving property to the Temple, arranging, with the consent of his wife, to hold it in usufruct until he wished to enter the order.[7] It seems that Arnold was absent from Toulouse, ill or otherwise *hors de combat* in that year, because, shortly after his arrangement with the Temple, his wife Jordana and her brother-in-law Raymond sold some property to a relative named Arnold Raymond Barbaordei "ad persolvendum sua [Arnold's] debita."[8]

Ten years later all was changed. Whereas his brother Raymond had disappeared, Arnold had recovered and served both as the executor ("spondarius") and heir of his uncle Arnold Petrus "coquinarius," a cook who chose a miller as his other executor.[9] He is again seen in 1293 when he finally entered the Temple, giving it the long-since promised property with an increment. All told, he disposed of two small houses on the streets of the Carmelites and Saint-Rémézy and other properties, vineyards and arable, most of them already seen

---

[2]E 506 i (February 1181, copied in 1260) (also in Malta 2 155 and Saige, *Juifs du Languedoc*, No. 6) and E 506 8 i (April 1202, copied in 1229) (Malta 3 155 i and Saige, *Juifs du Languedoc*, No. 11). The family name is here given as Barba de Ordeo, but later charters on the same membranes contain the standard version. Barbadorz/-s becomes more common in the later thirteenth century charters cited below.

[3]Raymond in E 506 iii (March 1229) and a reference to property once owned by him in ibid. i and iii (both dated April 1232) (also in Malta 3 161 i and iii and Saige, *Juifs du Languedoc*, Nos. 28 and 30), charters witnessed by his son Arnold, for whom see below.

[4]Malta 2 155 and E 506 (October 1240, both copied in 1260).

[5]E 509 (January 1223) where, other than the Barbaordei, a witness was a dice maker or "dazerius," presumably a relative of the bride.

[6]Malta 17 74 ii (August 1254) and see note 8 below.

[7]E 506 iii (January 1260), where Arnold with the consent of Jordana, gives the Temple an "inter vivos" gift reserving usufruct. The charter mentions his brother Raymond.

[8]Malta 17 90 (March 1260), a half "medellata" of vineyard.

[9]Malta 2 163 (March 1270), in which Jordana also appears.

in the earlier charters of the family. The property went partly to the Temple, partly to his widow Jordana to repay her marriage settlement with increment and partly to his long since emancipated daughter, Geralda.[10]

The reader will note the commitment of this family to the name Barbaordeus and also that the family was in the crafts and trades. The Arnold Barbaordei of the line that can be traced must have been at least eighty-five years old when he finally entered the Temple. He had also assured himself of a pension and final care some thirty-three years before he took up the option. Members of this humble clan are not to be found in any extant political document nor in any concerning heresy.

TABLE 2 BARBAORDEUS

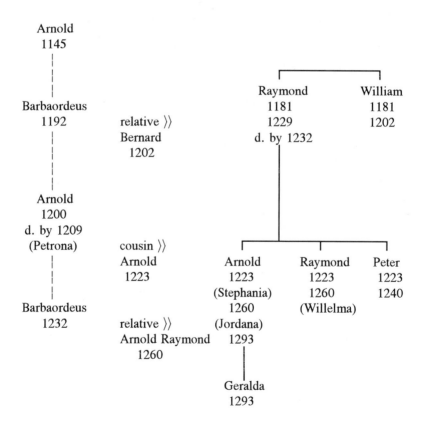

[10]Malta 2 178 (May 1293).

3. CARBONELLUS AND PRINACO

In 1130 or 1131 a Carbonellus "Coquinarum," that is, of Saint-Pierre-des-Cuisines, owed Saint-Sernin a halfpenny rent for a meadow next to the Garonne, a location that was later to be called the Pré Carbonnel.[1] This meadow was just outside the Bazacle near Combe Salomon and was the place where the consuls were often to hold general assemblies.[2] Carbonellus' successor was a Vital Carbonellus who was seen as early as 1141, when he bought a property for 100 shillings "ad Canalem" and likewise acquired the rent on this property as a "pignus" for ten shillings, a profit of five percent annually.[3] Seen as one of the "bonihomines" of the town council in 1148, Vital was dead by 1158 or 1159, leaving his name to be carried not only by the line described below, but also by the Prinaco family.[4]

Vital's most successful successor was a miller or mill owner at the Bazacle who made a fortune. A man whose only known name was Raymond Galterius (Walter), Raymond was a chapterman in 1184, and a consul for no less than four terms in the eleven-nineties.[5] In 1193 he lost two significant lawsuits before the consuls to the mill owners of the Daurade-Bazacle and those of the Château Narbonnais. The testimony shows that the gate of the Bourg leading to the Bazacle was then called the gate of Vital Carbonellus, and that Raymond Galterius owned most of the waterfront at or near the Bazacle.[6]

3   [1]Douais, *Cartulaire de Saint-Sernin*, No. 128 (March 1130 or 1131).
    [2]It lay in the tithing of Saint-Sernin and is seen on maps in the departmental archives, Plans anciens No. 214, and Saint-Bernard 25. A meeting of a town general assembly there is recorded in AA 2 83 (August 1226).
    [3]Daurade 7 (April 1141, copied in 1198), the place being near the Hers river in the region of the Pont des Clèdes.
    [4]Saint-Bernard 36, ii (March 1158 or 1159, copied in 1205), a lot once his at Combe Salomon, a property that, as seen below in the next note, remained in his family's hands. The Prinaco are described later in this family history.
    [5]Other than the name of Raymond's son who was called Vital Carbonellus, the act that proves filiation is Saint-Bernard 36 i (September 1202, copied in 1205) where land at Combe Salomon mentioned above in note 4 is described as being owned by Raymond. Consul in 1192-1193, 1195, 1196-1197 and 1198-1199.
    [6]AA 1 20 and 21 (respectively dated March and February 1193). The latter contained the charges of the Château's millers that Raymond seized whatever lumber and wrecks drifted down from their mills to land on his property. The former suit was levied by the prior of the Daurade and a Bazacle miller named Raymond Besantus, the prior speaking for the "upper" (the later Daurade mills) and Raymond for the "lower" (the later Bazacle) mills. The complaint of the Bazacle millers was that they had to ask permission to enter their mills because Raymond Galterius claimed he owned all the banks of the Garonne "a porta que dicitur Vitalis Carbonelli" up to a juncture, the "puncta que est subtus pratum ubi Brassolum se coniungit cum Garonna." The gate in question was surely the Bazacle Gate because there were then no outlying fortifications around the

Pitifully little is known about the career of this obviously enterprising and pugnacious man. He was assuredly deceased by 1202, if not shortly before, leaving his widow Costancia and three minor sons, Vital Carbonellus, later usually called Vital Galterius, Walter and Raymond Galterius.[7] Around 1200 his wife renegotiated a "pignus" owed her husband by the lord of Isle-Jourdain and the charter describes her as holding the "castrum" of Lavalette near Verfeil in pledge for 4000 shillings.[8] Later information records that Costantia was from the line of the lords of Bessières, northeast of Toulouse on the Tarn river, one of whose lords also held property at Grisolles on the Garonne river just north of Toulouse.[9] Her husband's death left Costantia a rich widow. In 1202 she married William Peter de Caramanno, a landed gentleman presumably from Caraman in the Lauragais, a man related to one of the Villanova clans of the region. So valuable was she that William Peter paid as her prime dowry 2000 shillings and, after twelve years of marriage, added a further 500 shillings.[10] The other women in the family were Costantia's daughters, Estigborg and Ramunda, the latter of whom married a man whose name is not known, by whom she had a son named Pons Berengar who became Costantia's own oldest son's principal heir.[11]

Because forenames are hard to track, Raymond Galterius' children are followed with difficulty. Vital Galterius or Carbonellus was so rarely active in his town that he never served as consul and is seen only among the consuls' councilors in 1221 and 1222.[12] Perhaps he was a merchant or a landed gentleman who preferred to live out of town during the war. He is seen again in 1236 when he reported that his mother Costantia, having been widowed again and having entered a convent, had sold him her dowry.[13] Vital took oath to maintain the Peace of Paris in February 1243, drew his last will in March and was certainly deceased by October of the same year.[14]

Bazacle except the "castrum," a fort then owned by the Guilaberti family. See also the property of Vital Galterius in his will of 1243 recorded in Appendix 8, No. 72.

[7]See note 5 above, and E 509 (July 1205) where he is described as deceased, and his sons, not named, are mentioned. See also the note below.

[8]MADTG, A 297, fols. 89v-90v (probably dated August 1200) where Costantia's sons were minors, the eldest being called Vital Carbonellus.

[9]Douais, *Cartulaire de Saint-Sernin*, No. 106 (dated 1155), referring to the building of the "castrum" of Grisolles. PAN, J 322 66 (March 1243) contains the will of her son Vital Galterius, in which he refers to his "avus" Walter de Vesceriis. This will is calendared as Appendix 8, No. 72 (March 1243).

[10]PAN, J 322 52 i (July 1202) and ii (November 1216).

[11]The sisters are mentioned in Vital's will of 1243, and it is apparent that Estigborg was not married.

[12]TAM, AA 1 90 and 75 (respectively dated August 1221 and March 1222).

[13]PAN, J 322 52 iii (March 1236).

[14]For the Peace in February, see Appendix 3, No. 21 below; March Appendix 8, No. 72; and October in note 18 below.

TABLE 3 GALTERIUS LINE ASSOCIATED WITH THE CARBONELLUS-PRIGNACO FAMILY

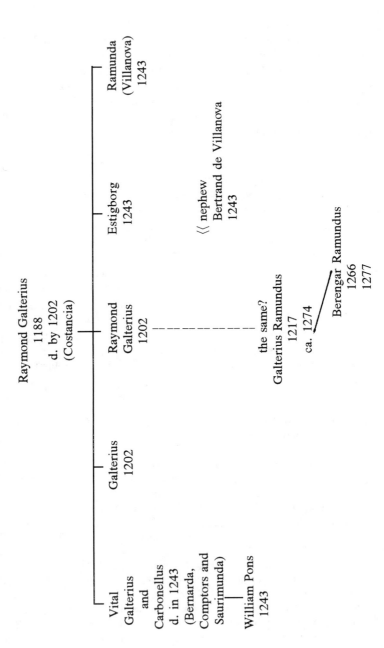

Raymond Galterius
1188
d. by 1202
(Costancia)

Galterius
1202

Raymond
Galterius
1202

Estigborg
1243

Ramunda
(Villanova)
1243

Vital
Galterius
and
Carbonellus
d. in 1243
(Bernarda,
Comptors and
Saurimunda)

William Pons
1243

the same?
Galterius Ramundus
1217
ca. 1274

Berengar Ramundus
1266
1277

《 nephew
Bertrand de Villanova
1243

Vital's testament is an eye-opener because his properties were extensive and illuminate the history of his family. In town, his "domus maior" with its portico was just on the square facing Saint-Pierre-des-Cuisines, his parish church which he gratified with ample donations. A group of five houses and the rents from eighteen rented houses adjoining the "domus maior" were assigned by this testator to create a residential college for the university of Toulouse, a college to be under the auspices of the bishop and the Dominicans and Franciscans. Vital therefore owned or dominated the whole corner of the Bourg between Saint-Pierre and the Bazacle Gate, once called that of Vital Carbonnellus. His rural holdings were quite as impressive. He owned much just outside of the Bazacle in the area of the Pré Carbonnel and Combe Salomon. To the north along the frontier of the vicarage of Toulouse, his lands extended from Fontanas eastward through Pechbonnieu to Labastide-Saint-Sernin on the Giron river. He had lands and houses and occasional servile tenants both at Bessières on the Tarn river and, as a result of his mother's second marriage, far to the southeast of Toulouse at Saint-Germier and Caraman. In the latter place, he possessed a large stone house and had close relations with the parish priest. His holdings at Fontanas derived from his maternal grandfather of Bessières and from the lordly lines of Verfeil and Isle-Jourdain.

Vital was clearly a gentleman: when called for military service, he served as a knight. He willed his destrier and palfrey to Bernier de Montebertio (Montbartier near Montech well to the north of Toulouse). His holdings and dependents at Bessières went to Bertrand of Vesceriis, one of the lords of Bessières, a personage sometimes in the retinue of Count Raymond VII and one called on for a personal oath of allegiance to Alphonse of Poitiers in 1249.[15] One of his nephews and heirs was a Bertrand de Villanova of the Lauragais Villanovas, issue perhaps of his mother's second husband.[16] His was also a receptive mind. Although one suspects that Vital's foundation of a house for twenty scholars was probably the brain child of an ecclesiastic, of the bishop or of Raymond de Fuxo (Foix), the Dominican prior who witnessed his testament, the idea was right for the times. Still, there was disappointment here. Although Vital gave much to charity and provided for the restitution of his ill-gotten gains (and for those of his mother and father), it was only in his own will that he gave force to the charitable provisions of his parents' and first wife's testaments. God, he may have thought, could well afford to wait, and that for upwards of forty years. And, although the provision in his will founding a residential house for students at the university would surely have immortalized his

---

[15]See *HGL* 8: Nos. 345, 415 and 482 (respectively dated December 1241, December 1249 and February 1260).

[16]The Lauragais Villanovas are not to be confused with the Villanovas of Toulouse, whose history is in my *Repression of Catharism*, pp. 292-303.

APPENDIX ONE

name, nothing ever came of it. Following Vital's own model prudence regarding his elders, perhaps, his heirs may have scotched this expensive donation.

Vital had been twice married, first to a Bernarda and then to Comptors. The latter was left a widow and was given various gifts of silver, jewelry, clothing, etc. and her marriage settlement of 1200 shillings was returned to her. Given the testator's wealth, there was nothing especially generous here. From these legal marriages, Vital had no surviving children and, as a consequence, his principal heirs were his nephews, a cousin, his two sisters and friends. Given the manners of the time, a modest but not niggardly bequest was left to William Pons, his son by a woman name Saurimonda, a person who was not Vital's wife, by whom he may have had two sons.

Little or nothing can be done about the history of Vital's brothers, Walter and Raymond Galterius, but Vital's testament enables one to do somewhat better with the next generation. His cousin Raymond Arnold escapes sure identification, but his nephew Bertrand de Villanova will be treated below and his nephew Pons Berengarius, the son of his sister Ramunda, who inherited his great house, may have been the frequent consul of that name and one of Simon de Montfort's "curiales viri."[17] There remain the two other nephews, Walter Berengarius and Arnold Berengarius who inherited Vital's properties at Fontanas and nearby places, to whom this history will return in a moment.

Another descendant of the family was a Walter Ramundus. One divines this not only because of the similarity of his name to those used in the family (one would normally guess, indeed, that he was the son of Vital's brother Raymond Galterius), but also because, as shall be seen, he held lands at Fontanas. Vital's testament, it has been noted, gave his lands there, lands acquired partly, as the document says, from the lord of Isle-Jourdain, to two nephews, the Arnold and Walter Berengarius mentioned in the paragraph above. These good people are seen in October 1243 listed among the creditors of the lords of Isle-Jourdain by the consuls of Toulouse, there being called Walter Raymond and Arnold Berengar de Villanova.[18]

Because Toulousans played about with the Christian names quite as much as they did with their surnames, it is possible that Walter Berengarius is the same person as Walter Ramundus. Whatever the case, as noted above, Walter Ramundus held substantial property at Fontanas. It was he who appealed to Innocent IV levying a charge of usury against the monastery of Saint-Sernin and Bernard de Baregiis in 1250, a case settled in or around 1256.[19] This indivi-

---

[17]Nothing can be done with the name or names Raymond Arnaldus or Arnold Ramundus; they abound in the sources. A Pons Berengarius was a consul in February 1212 and 1215-1216 and "curialis vir" in 1217, but few things are less convincing than this evidence.

[18]MADTG, A 297, fol. 385 (October 1243), a debt of thirty pounds eight shillings owed by Jordan de Insula to the deceased Vital Galterius to be paid to Walter Raymond and Arnold Berengar de Villanova.

[19]For this document and history, see my "Farm of Fontanas at Toulouse," pp. 29-40.

dual is known to have been quite a personage. He had a son named Berengar Ramundus, and lived to a ripe old age.[20] Around 1274 he was one of the crown's witnesses at the inquiry into the rights of the prince in town government.[21] The old gentleman accurately remembered much of what had happened in Toulouse during the crusader occupation, but was clearly a minor at that time because he got his information from report. By the time Count Amaury had succeeded his father Simon de Montfort, however, he knew about it first hand, because he was serving in harness himself. At King Louis VIII's passage by Toulouse in 1226 he was wounded by a quarrel from a crossbow. Unlike his grandfather who bore the same name and who served as a consul in 1192-1193, he was the count's, not the republic's, man. He was appointed consul, he reports, by Raymond VII at the time of the Peace of Paris, and he later served the count as a consul during the twelve-forties. He was deceased by 1277 when his son Berengar Ramundus is again seen.[22]

Other than its meteoric rise from the smithy and milling to rural lordship, the family Carbonellus-Galterius is fascinating for yet another reason. It was closely related to another patrician line, one that probably also derived from the original progenitor Carbonellus and that also used the name Carbonellus, but that usually bore the surname [de] Prinaco. Variously spelled Prinag, Prinhaco, Prignaco, etc., the name may have derived from Preignac on the Garonne river not far south of Bordeaux.[23] It therefore seems likely that the surname Prinaco records the origin of both Carbonellus families. It is also certain, as shall be seen, that the branch that bore this surname busied itself in the wine trade down river to Bordeaux.

The first Prinaco to appear in the charter is a Raymond de Prinaco. Seen from 1157, he was a mill owner at the Bazacle and acquired property to the east of the town around the Hers river on the way to Verfeil.[24] The facts that someone in every generation of Raymond's heirs was called Carbonellus and that some of his heirs attended several of the most serious and ceremonious occasions in the life of the Carbonellus-Galterius line shows that the two families were closely related.[25] The further fact that Raymond de Prinaco owed a mill at the Ba-

---

[20]Grandselve 5 i (October 1266, copied in 1298).
[21]PAN, J 305 32, fols. 2v-3, the dating being supplied by Molinier.
[22]Grandselve 15 ii (January 1277, copied in 1298).
[23]There are two other Prignacs near Bordeaux, one near Blaye and the other near Bourg, but who can say?
[24]Douais, *Cartulaire de Saint-Sernin*, No. 492 (April 1157); ibid., No. 50 (March 1171); Sicard, *Moulins de Toulouse*, pp. 363, 377-378 (April 1177 and June 1184), as a mill owner; Malta 119 379 (June 1184), where he held the lordship of land near the "Pons Cledarum" or Pont des Clèdes.
[25]PAN, J 322 52 i (July 1202), the marriage of Costancia to Caramanno mentioned above was witnessed by Vital, William Pons Carbonellus and Raymond de Prinhaco.

zacle just as did Raymond Galterius shows that they were both heirs of Vital Carbonellus, and therefore that they were probably brothers or half-brothers.

Raymond was last seen in 1184, was probably dead by 1187 and certainly gone by 1194.[26] A son, brother or cousin of the above was a William Pons de Prinaco who was associated with Raymond's heirs and was perhaps active in town government until 1214.[27] Apart from him, however, Raymond had at least three sons and one daughter: Vital, the heir to his interest in the mills, Pons, Carbonellus and Prima.[28]

To trace first the second son Pons, who appears in the charters from 1187 until 1225, nothing is known about his succession, but it may be conjectured that either he or the William Pons mentioned above had a son named Walter de Prinaco, unless, of course, this Walter was the brother of the Vital Carbonellus Galterius who died in 1243.[29] At any rate, the mill owner Vital de Prinaco lived at least until 1214 and had a son named Peter Raymond who was briefly seen in 1206 or 1207.[30] Three brothers, a Raymond, William and Oldric de Prinaco, are also seen. These brothers, of whom the first appears as early as 1202, may also have been Vital's sons. They were assuredly his heirs as is reported by a charter of 1219, a document permitting the guess that Peter Ray-

---

Ibid. iii (March 1236), the record of the sale of her dowry to her son Vital Galterius was witnessed by the brothers Peter and Raymond de Prinaco.

[26]A chapterman in 1164, and also see the references in notes 25 above and 32 below.

[27]Other than as a consul in 1213-1214, William Pons is seen in E 2 (September 1194) where he was the executor of Peter Arnold, and again with other Prinaco in the charter of 1202 concerning the second marriage of Costancia in note 25 above, hence he was clearly a member of the family.

[28]Malta 116 10 (February 1187), a charter mentioning, other than the boys, Prima's husband Fort de Devesa, witnessed by Raymond Galterius, the husband of Costancia. There is no mention of their father in this charter, but that these were his children is urged by the facts that Vital was heir to his mill at the Bazacle in Sicard, *Moulins de Toulouse*, pp. 367-368 (June 1194) and that, as seen in notes 32 and 34 below, these brothers owned his property near the Pont des Clèdes in 1227 and 1234.

[29]Other than 1187 given immediately above, Pons is seen as a consul and councilor in 1192-1193, 1222, and 1225. Unlike numerous families, the name Prinaco is sufficiently infrequent to allow such guesses. Walter de Prinaco is seen as a councilor in TAM, AA 1 75 (April 1222).

[30]E 538 i (December 1207) contains a reference to the executors appointed by a Lucia, Bernard Peter Carbonellus and Oldric de Guamevilla, who sold a property given Lucia by Peter Raymond, son of Vital de Prinaco, who confirmed this sale. Peter Raymond's surrender of the property to the executors is in E 571 (September 1207). It will be noted that Vital is not described as deceased in these documents and, indeed, he is seen as a consul in 1214-1215.

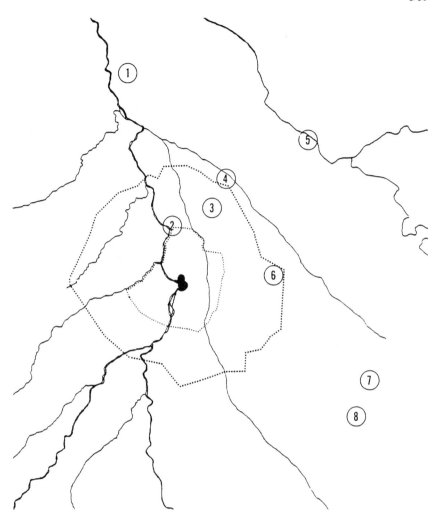

MAP 3 CARBONELLUS AND PRIGNACO PROPERTIES

1 = Grisolles   5 = Bessières
2 = "Fontanas"   6 = Lavalette
3 = Pechbonnieu   7 = Caraman
4 = Labastide-Saint-Sernin   8 = Saint-Germier

TABLE 4 PRIGNACO LINE OF THE CARBONELLUS-PRIGNACO FAMILY

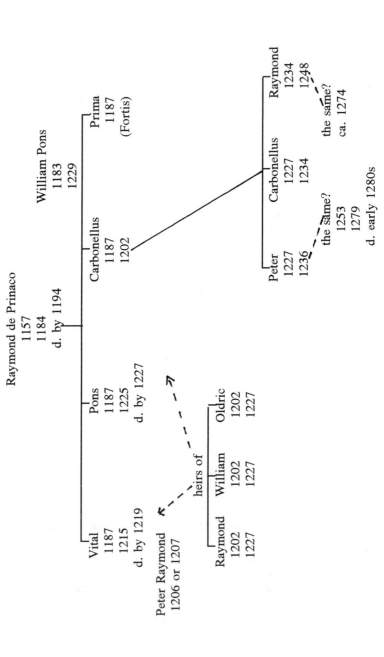

mond had died or vanished by this time.[31] Seen acting together until 1227, the three brothers thereafter disappear.[32]

In the meantime, Raymond's son Carbonellus, who was alive in 1202 but deceased by 1227, had had two sons named Peter and Carbonellus, who shared property with the William, Raymond and Oldric mentioned above, property clearly deriving from their grandfather Raymond.[33] In 1234 Peter and Carbonellus are discovered to be the oldest of five or more brothers, the name of the third brother being Raymond.[34] Peter and Raymond are heard of again in 1236, but afterwards all is conjecture, except that it is surely Raymond who appears in a document of 1248.[35] It may in fact have been this Raymond who was later termed a "jurisperitus," and who, around 1274, served as a witness about the government of the town. His testimony shows that he was a minor during the war, but a major in the twelve-thirties and forties, a man, then, if it is the same Raymond, in his late sixties in 1274.[36] As to his older brother Peter, it is either he or a successor of the same name who was still active in the wine trade on the Garonne river in the early twelve-eighties and who was called a merchant in 1283.[37] No evidence shows that this was the original Peter who would have been somewhere in his mid-seventies or early eighties in 1283.

Other than some Prinaco and Carbonelli with whom nothing can be done, there remain three others, a Pons de Prinaco active in the midcentury as a consul and a Peter Raymond and Oldric de Prinaco who served as petitioners for the amnesty of heretical inheritances in 1279.[38] One cannot tell for whose in-

[31]Seen as early as 1202 (note 25 above), Raymond was consul in 1212, 1215-1216, 1222-1223 and 1225-1226. Grandselve 5 (February 1219) mentions all three brothers, heirs to property of Vital de Prinaco deceased.

[32]Malta 116 23 (January 1227) property near the Pont des Clèdes owned by Peter Carbonellus and his brother Carbonellus, sons of the deceased Carbonellus, and by the brothers Raymond, William and Aldric de Prinaco.

[33]For 1202, see note 25 above, and for 1227, the previous note. Meantime Carbonellus was a consul in 1200-1201 and a councilor in 1222.

[34]Saint-Bernard 36 (April 1234), a half "arpent" of land on the Hers river next to the road to Verfeil owned by Peter Carbonellus and Raymond de Prinaco and other brothers not named in the charter and obviously minors.

[35]Anent Peter and Raymond who were witnesses of the charter in which Vital Galterius recorded the purchase of his mother's dowry in note 25 above, thus again showing filiation. MADTG, A 297, fol. 385 (December 1248) where Raymond witnessed an act about the debts of the lords of Isle-Jourdain.

[36]PBN, Collection Doat 73: 47v (December 1268) as a "jurisperitus"; TAM, II 9 (March 1270), as the same and a consul; and PAN, J 305 32 3v for his testimony of ca. 1274.

[37]TAM, II 63 (undated, but clearly in the early twelve-eighties), MADTG, A 297, fols. 782 and 788 (respectively dated August and October 1283), the first reporting that Berengar Caraborda had owed him seventeen pounds ten shillings, and the second that he was a "mercator."

[38]On Pons, see the consular lists of 1246 and 1251-1252, and, for 1279, see my

heritance Peter Raymond was petitioning in 1279 (there were no Carbonelli or
Prinaco listed there) nor who he was, except that he could hardly have been the
the son of Vital who bore the same name in 1207. Although there is an outside
chance that Oldric, who was petitioning as an tutor of the children of a "dominus" William de Tolosa, is the one of the same name who was the son of Vital
de Prinhaco, it is more likely that he was one of the unnamed sons of Carbonellus in the twelve-thirties.[39] Whatever the case, this Oldric was a mill owner
and a lord of property along the waterfront from 1253 to 1276 and was even
then associated with the William de Tolosa whose executor he was to be.[40]
He was also prominently mentioned as a wine merchant by the witnesses to the
inquiry of the early twelve-eighties, but was there described as deceased.[41]

Apart from the fact that both branches, the Carbonelli-Gauterii and the Car-
bonelli-Prinaco were among the patrician lines that led Toulouse toward political
liberty in the eleven-nineties, what intrigues one about this family is that it never
settled on one family name. Its members were obviously not ashamed of being
called Carbonellus, a name redolent of the smithy, one probably having the ca-
chet of working with one's hands, of generative strength. Prinaco probably
showed where the family had originated or suggested the wine business they
were engaged in, so that it too became a name to be reckoned with. The problem is to explain why the issue of the original Vital Carbonellus were called
Raymond Galterius and Raymond de Prinaco. Although this question cannot be
answered, one certainly knows what reinforced the separation of the clans. It
will be recalled that Raymond Galterius' wife Costancia was the daughter of the
rural knight and magnate Walter de Vesceriis. It may therefore be guessed that
her son, Vital Carbonellus, he with the destrier, palfrey and gallant wounded
nephew Walter Raimundus, preferred to style himself Vital Galterius.

The Prinaco flourished into the fourteenth century and were still patricians
and mill owners. In 1343 Alfred Jeanroy records, Pons de Prinaco, a knight and
consul of Toulouse, won the violet at the "Joies du Gai Savoir."[42]

Repression of Catharism, p. 124. The most significant of the unidentified persons bearing
these names were the Bernard Carbonellus in E 506 i (April 1202, copied in 1229) and
II 75 ii (November 1224) and iii (March 1226, copied in 1234); the Bernard Peter Carbonellus of 1207 in note 30 above. A William Aton and Pons de Prinaco are seen taking
oath to maintain the Peace of Paris in February 1243. Pons may also be seen below.
The brothers Raymond and Bertrand Carbonellus who appear in E 286 (May 1251) were
burghers of Montauban and not of Toulouse as Grandselve 9 (June 1257), ibid. 11 i
(May 1261) and the correspondence and registers of Alphonse of Poitiers show.

[39]To be the former, he would have had to be nearly eighty years old.

[40]His property at the mills of the Daurade and Château are seen in TAM, DD 1 1
4 iv (June 1264); DD 1 1 4 i and ii (December 1253 and January 1255); and DD 1 16
6 (February 1276). He was also a consul in 1268-1269.

[41]TAM, II 63 (undated).

[42]Wolff, *"Estimes" Tolousaines*, p. 80; Jeanroy, *La poésie lyrique des troubadours* 1:415.

4. Caturcio

Originally from the town of Cahors or possibly the nearby community of Cadours to the northwest of Toulouse, this family appears first in the person of a Gausbert de Caturcio. Heard of from the eleven-forties or fifties, Gausbert founded the leperhouse outside the Villanova Gate in his testament of 1175. This small installation was named after its founder and all its successive "patroni" derived from his small family.[1]

Gausbert's successor as patron of the leperhouse was Gerald. Seen as early as 1176, Gerald was an active man, serving as chapterman in 1180, as consul in 1193 or 1194 and as a witness to the treaty of peace with Verfeil in 1203.[2] Gerald's successor as "patronus" to the lepers was a Bernard de Caturcio. In 1240 Bernard and his brother Gerald divided their not very large inheritance, a document stating that their principal properties lay in and near the Bourg near the Villanova and Matabiau gates. Although Gerald was active in the twelve-thirties and had a married daughter in 1240, he disappears from the charters after that date, but his brother Bernard, who served as a consul in 1247-1248, was still alive in 1253.[3]

Bernard's successor as patron of the lepers was Raymond. First seen during the constitutional crisis of 1268 and 1269, Raymond was a consul in 1279-1280

---

4 [1]Douais, *Cartulaire de Saint-Sernin*, No. 350 (ca. 1150); Grandselve 1 i (April 1155) concerning property at Gratalauze; TAM, AA 1 3 (November 1164); Malta, *Inventaire* 1: 27v-28r, a reference to the patron in 1303, namely Bernard de Caturcio, and to the founder's testament in 1175.

[2]Ourliac and Magnou, *Cartulaire de Lézat*, No. 1457 (May 1176); Saint-Bernard 138 61r (January 1186) concerning the lepers' property at Montvincent; Grandselve 2 1 (May 1187, copied in 1195); Saint-Bernard 138 116v (January 1203); TAM, AA1 64 (January 1203); and Malta 17 19 (August 1203, copied in 1254) concerning a wood owned by Gerald.

[3]Ourliac and Magnou, *Cartulaire de Lézat*, No. 1383 (December 1234) with Gerald; Saint-Sernin 599 (10 35 17) fifth of nine tied acts (January 1235) recording a debt owed Gerald of 32 s 6 d; Malta 116 28 (December 1240) mentioning Bernard; Malta 27 65 (January 1240) where Bernard, with the advice of his wife Arnalda, and Gerald divide their parental inheritance, giving Gerald a house next to a property once belonging to Gausbert de Caturcio "qui modo est dirrutus" and all property "inter portas Villanove et Matabovis," and to Bernard in return land "in condamina apud Matabove," and the "casales" between the above gates; E 502 and TAM, II 71 i (September 1242 copied in 1258) for the lepers by Bernard; Grandselve 8 (October 1242) where Bernard buys a lot for a house bearing a rent of twelve pence; and Grandselve 9 (October 1253) referring to Bernard. In J 305 29 (February 1243) Durand and Gausbert de Caturcio swear to uphold the Peace of Paris.

and served the lepers until 1296.[4] Raymond's successor as patron of the lepers was Bernard de Caturcio, who is seen in 1303.[5]

TABLE 5 CATURCIO

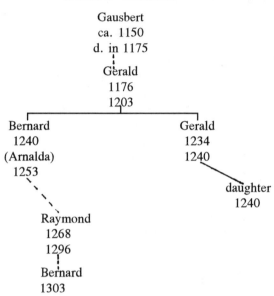

```
              Gausbert
               ca. 1150
              d. in 1175
                  ¦
                Gerald
                 1176
                 1203
        ┌──────────┴──────────┐
    Bernard                 Gerald
     1240                    1234
   (Arnalda)                 1240
     1253                        ╲
        ╲                         ╲
         ╲                      daughter
          ╲                       1240
        Raymond
         1268
         1296
           ¦
        Bernard
         1303
```

5. CERDANUS

An example of modest social mobility, largely lateral, is seen in this history. A baker at the Matabiau Gate, Peter Cerdanus "furnarius" is seen acquiring a "malol" or vineyard at Gratelauze (on a hillock just northeast of town) in 1166 and eventually, together with his son John, selling it in 1201.[1] Peter is seen for

[4]PBN, Collection Doat 73 64r-65v recording a general assembly of the town dated April 1269 attended by Raymond de Caturcio and William de Caturcio "campsor"; PAN J 306 88 (January 1275) where Raymond was a "sponderius" of Raymond de Ponte; Malta 7 64 (March 1286) with Raymond and the lepers; and E 569 (March 1296) where Raymond was the lepers' "patronus."

[5]See note 1 above.

5 [1]Grandselve 4 1 (September 1201, copied in 1209) in which Peter and his son John sell the vine at Gratelauze to a Bernard "furnarius"; in ibid. ii (June 1171) a Raymond Petrus enfeoffed the same to Peter; in iii (November 1166) a Peter Sicfredus enfeoffed the same to Peter Cerdanus "furnerius"; in iv (April 1157) the same Sicfredus sold two parts of the tithe of this vineyard to the baker; in v and vi (respectively April 1157 and September 1170) where the baker cleared other charges from this property.

the last time in an instrument of 1205 in which he served as an executor for the widow of a cutler and in which his son John was a witness.[2] It is probable that John Cerdanus was a public scribe who instrumented at least until 1214.[3] In 1202 John served as an executor for the modest will of Peter Karolus. The deceased left a "malol" to the son of a friend or relative, various movables and some grain to a Petrona "qui manet mecum" and his house with its equipment to his nephews, Raymond and Peter Cerdanus, in return for burial, payment of debts and an "emina" of grain for charity. It is likely that Peter Karolus' deceased wife was John Cerdanus' sister and that John was the father of Raymond and Peter.[4] In 1208 the brothers Raymond and Peter sold the house they inherited; it bore a rent of six pence.[5] Raymond is not seen thereafter, but Peter Cerdanus, titled "macellarius" or butcher, appears as a witness to a charter drawn by his presumed father John, the public notary, in 1214.[6]

TABLE 6 CERDANUS

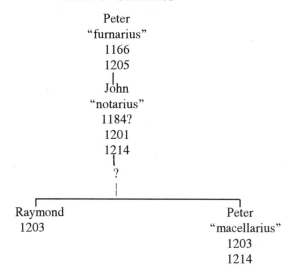

Peter
"furnarius"
1166
1205
|
John
"notarius"
1184?
1201
1214
?
|

Raymond   Peter
1203   "macellarius"
         1203
         1214

[2]Grandselve 2 (August 1175) where Peter was a witness; E 538 iii (December 13181, copied in 1202): "Petrus Cerdanus furnarius de furno et de furnile et de domo in quod est apud portam de Matabove," being later referred to simply as Peter "furnerius"; E 575 (November 1183) as a witness; and Grandselve 4 (February 1205) where Peter Cerdanus "furnarius" was the "spondarius," and the witnesses were John Cerdanus and Bernard Scriba de Ulmeto.

[3]John's first extant act is E 538 (October 1201) and his last is seen below in note 6.

[4]See Appendix 8, No. 25 below.

[5]E 510 i (May and June 1208).

[6]Malta 1 21 (June 1214).

This modest family is worth noting because of its devotion to the name Cerdanus and because of its diversification into the alimentary trades of baker and butcher and the literate profession of notary.

Another family bearing the name Cerdanus is seen at Castanet just south of Toulouse, but is not known to have any relationship to the above Cerdani. Called Cerdanus de Castaneto, it appears in the documents of the monastery of Lézat from 1154 to 1195 and is represented by an innkeeper named John Cerdanus de Castaneto "albergator," his wife Ricsenda and a Raymond of the same name.[7]

6. DAVINUS

The origin of the name Davinus may have been "de Avignone" (from Avignonet, south of Toulouse), hence Davinho and Davinus.[1] Whatever the origin of this surname, a charter of 1229 records that two brothers named Bernard and William Davinus held property near the Arnaud-Bernard Gate in the Bourg acquired thirty-five or more years earlier by their deceased grandfather William and transmitted to them by their deceased father Bernard.[2]

The original William Davinus was therefore alive ca. 1194. His son Bernard turns out to have been a public notary whose extant instruments date from 1211 until 1215 and who died sometime in that year or the next.[3] In the documents of 1229 cited in the previous paragraph, Bernard's sons Bernard and William are reported to have divided an arpent of land bordered by lots owned by the Mainaderie, the baker of the Arnaud-Bernard Gate and their own vineyards. William is perhaps the Davinus with this Christian name seen

[7]Ourliac and Magnou, *Cartulaire de Lézat*, Nos. 1386, 1388, 1389, 1391, 1464, 1468, 1470 and 1489.

6 [1]Although these persons have no known relationship to those being described here, note in Grandselve 4 i and ii (respectively dated March 1156 or 1157 and January 1176, copied in 1203) the acquisition and sale of a vineyard at Montvincent by Pons de Avignho, later called Pons Davino (and his wife Garsenda). Note also the Guilhe Davinho in Saint-Bernard 32 (dated September 1212) published in my *Liberty and Political Power*, No. 12, who acted for the consuls in confiscating goods from the Hospice of Grandselve in the Bourg. He was probably a consular "nuncius" or constable. See also the William Davinus mentioned below.

[2]E 81 i and ii (respectively dated September and October 1229 and copied in 1235) first recording a division of the lot between the brothers and, second, an attestation by three notables that the property was owned as stated in the text above.

[3]Grandselve 6 ii (January 1174 copied in April 1211) where Bernard was a cosigner of the copy, and E 501 i (February 1215), an act witnessed by Raymond Davinus and received by Bernard. The latter having died, the consuls assigned his notes to Isarn Grillus in August 1216 in an appended act copied in 1230.

swearing to uphold the Peace of Paris in 1243, and was probably either the William Davinus called "pellicerius" (furrier) or, more likely, the one called "fivelerius" (buckle or claspmaker) in 1257.[4]

More is known about William's brother Bernard. He was seen alienating a property together with his two sons sometime in the forties or fifties and was there described as a "fibularius" (the same as "fivelarius").[5] The sons were Peter Raymond Davinus and a minor named Bernard who is not thereafter heard of again. Like his grandfather, Peter Raymond was a notary who is first seen instrumenting in 1242 and continued until 1271.[6]

TABLE 7 DAVINUS

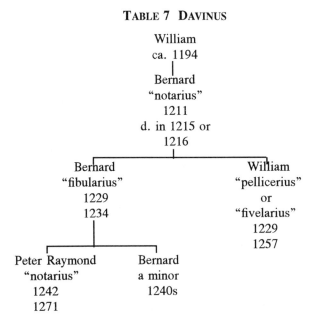

William
ca. 1194

Bernard
"notarius"
1211
d. in 1215 or
1216

Bernard
"fibularius"
1229
1234

William
"pellicerius"
or
"fivelarius"
1229
1257

Peter Raymond
"notarius"
1242
1271

Bernard
a minor
1240s

[4]PAN, J305 29 (February 1243) the two bearing this name are a Davinus and William Davinus; Grandselve 9 (June 1257), the "pellicerius"; and Grandselve 9 (October 1257) the "fivelerius" and his wife Ramunda.

[5]TAM, II 93, the date on this document having been lost. The notary who recorded it was Peter Raymond Pelissonus who is seen in Grandselve 6 (August 1239) and in TAM, II 96 (June 1257). Curiously, given the practice of Toulousan notaries at this time, the craft and professional titles of both the father and son are given in the act.

[6]Grandselve 7 (April 1234 copied in March 1213 with another copy in May 1242 made by Peter Raymond); Grandselve 9 (February 1254) where Raymond Davinus sells property in the Bourg with the consent of his wife Ramunda in an act notarized by Peter Raymond; Grandselve 9 (September 1257) and ibid. 11 (March 1271) both of these acts by Peter Raymond deal with the region of the Portaria.

In the meantime, other than another possibly related line, there were one or more Raymond Davini who appear related to this family.[7] One of these Raymonds served as a witness to a family act; the other was a "fivelerius" who had an act drawn by the notary Peter Raymond.[8]

Like the Cerdanus family described above, the Davini not only bore a surname that lasted for at least four generations, but also illustrate the marriage between the modest crafts and the humble side of the liberal arts or professions in this period. One wonders if the "fibularius" named Bernard could read the Latin of the charter his father and son, both public notaries, were able to write. It seems reasonable to assume that he did.

7. FALGARIO

There were one or more families in Toulouse whose names derived from Le Fauga to the south of Muret on the Garonne river. The name appears not infrequently in the twelfth century, but nothing can be done with occasional references.[1] One of these isolated persons was a Bernard de Felgar or Falgario who was perhaps seen swearing to uphold the Peace of Paris in 1243 and was a consul in 1276-1277.[2] Sometime around 1279 and 1283, Bernard was sixty years old, lived in the Bazacle region (of the Bourg) and was a merchant in the wine trade on the Garonne.[3] This or another Bernard with the same name was consul in 1280-1281.

More interesting are the brothers Arnold and William. These knights were the brothers of Raymond de Falgario or de Miramonte (south of Toulouse in the valley of the Ariège river) who was an early companion of the founder Dominic and the first member of the Dominican order ever to be elected bishop. His see was Toulouse, where he served from 1232 to 1270. His tenure ended in disaster or threatened disaster. Among other crimes, the bishop was charged

---

[7]The other possibly related line is seen in Daurade 145 (January 1221) where William Davinus with the consent of his wife Aladaicia and that of his brothers Bartholomew and Peter Raymond sold a share of a Bazacle mill to Martin Chivus. The similarity with the Davini described above is perhaps reflected in the name Peter Raymond.

[8]See the act of 1215 in note 3 above; Grandselve 6 (April 1225) with a Raymond Davinus "mercerius"; ibid. (March 1230) referring to Raymond's property "ad Gravarias"; and, relating possibly to a different Raymond, the act of 1254 cited in note 6 above where Raymond is called a "fivelerius." Note also the house of Peter and Raymond Davinus in Grandselve 13 (February 1282).

[7] ¹E 2 (September 1194) records a Dominic de Felgare, brother-in-law of a Bernard Bonushomo, for example.

[2]PAN, J 305 23 (February 1243), "de Felgar."

[3]TAM, II 64 (dated between 1279 and 1283).

with nepotism, dissipation of church property, simony, infamy and even fratricide, charges so serious that he fled Toulouse. The initial stages of the investigation under the archbishop of Narbonne took place during 1264, and letters about the case were written by that prelate, by Urban IV and by the count of Toulouse and his officers.[4] The bishop was defended by his vicar general, but the cathedral provost, Bertrand de Insula (son of Bernard Jordan II, lord of Isle-Jourdain), who was to succeed Raymond as bishop after his death in 1270, although initially charged by the archbishop of Narbonne with impeding the investigation, seems eventually to have aided it on the orders of Urban IV.[5] The Benedictines who compiled the Gallia Christiana noted that, in July 1265, Clement IV released the bishop "ad cautelam" from the archiepiscopal excommunication and, in October and December of the same year, urged him to prepare his case against about a hundred witnesses who had testified against him. They concluded that, since he seemed in control of his office in October 1267, Bishop Raymond had been cleared of the charges.[6] Whatever the truth of the astonishing charges described above, the testimony of the hundred or so witnesses (the bishop impugned the veracity of forty-eight) shows that the end of Raymond's pontificate was very unhappy indeed. The loss of the evidence for and against the bishop was also very costly for Toulousan social history.

Raymond was elected bishop in 1232, and it looks as if his brothers came to town not long after.[7] Arnold is seen in Toulouse in 1237 and William in 1245.[8] It seems more than probable that they were not yet citizens in 1243 when 1028 of the leading inhabitants of the town of Toulouse took oath to uphold the Peace of Paris.[9] As late as 1249, in fact, both brothers were considered rural notables and, as such, individually swore allegiance to the new count, Alphonse of Poitiers.[10] There was probably an overlap here, however. William de Falgario was already a citizen when he served as one of Count Raymond VII's hand-picked consuls in 1249, the consulate that was to be thrown

[4]This history is recorded in HGL 6: 877-879, Gallia Christiana 13: 28-29, and in the material cited in the notes immediately below.

[5]HGL 8: No. 509 and the cameral register of Urban IV, Nos. 412, 415, 417, 419-421, 429, 437, and 445-446. The evidence for the provost's action against the bishop is in Clement IV's register, No. 757 (October 1265).

[6]The Benedictines used the letters of Clement IV published in Martène and Durand, Thesaurus novus anecdotorum 2 (Paris 1717): Nos. 108, 378, 418 and 543.

[7]PAN, J 308 71 (December 1249): "Arnaldus de Felgari et Willelmus de Felgari fratres domini episcopi Tholosani".

[8]Ibid. 328 14 (December 1237), as a witness for an act of the count, and there called the brother of the bishop, and ibid. 307 8 (September 1245), with both brothers as witnesses in town.

[9]Ibid. 305 23 (February 1243).

[10]Ibid. 308 71 (December 1249).

out of office by a popular rising in town shortly after this prince's death in September of that year.

Owing to their situation or character, if the two can ever be distinguished, the brothers were very combative persons. In the twelve-sixties, William sought to reduce to servitude, or reclaim the service of, the inhabitants of his community of Venerque in the Ariège valley. A witness and his "consortes" complained that this knight was trying to tax them at will as serfs, and that he, taking advantage of the absence of the vicar's judge Berengar Peutrici, had employed the notary of that court to take testimony against them.[11] Venerque was one of the three communities in the Ariège and Garonne valleys attacked by the consuls (the others being Sabonnères and Verdun) during Raymond VII's absence in Provence from 1246 to 1248 in order to advance the town's doctrine of free trade for its merchants.[12] The brothers subsequently asserted in the courts their right to tax Toulousan traffic at Venerque. That lawsuit may have begun earlier when the two knights, Arnold and William, took issue with the consuls and appealed to the vicar about a matter not described in the document. Whatever the truth, the vicar's judge had refused to sit the case and in 1267 the count ordered his vicar to have him adjudicate it or appeal it.[13] In 1268 and 1269 it is reported that the courts had failed to handle the matter of Venerque to the litigants' satisfaction. What had happened, it appears, was that the seneschal Peter de Landreville had assigned the case to his judge of appeals William de Furno whose commission expired because of the seneschal's death before litigation began. The count had then assigned it to Master William Ruffi. Since this judge had not acted by 1268, William de Falgario, knight, asked that Sicard Alaman or someone else be assigned to settle the case.[14] The litigation was ventilated before April 1274 and decided by the seneschal in that month. The document touching on this event also refers to a decision of the judge of the Lauragais according Toulousan citizens exemption from the toll initially granted to William de Falgario by Raymond VII.[15] On this evidence, it is impossible to say what exactly happened about the toll at Venerque.

This expression of the conflict between rural notables, their communities and the town of Toulouse was exacerbated by another protracted legal battle between the Falgario and the consulate. Enjoying the rights of citizenship and

[11]Molinier, *Correspondance administrative*, Nos. 786 and 788 (June 1268), the village leader being Peter Raymond Ripparia.
[12]*HGL* 8: No. 455 (dated 1255).
[13]Ibid., No. 522 iii (September 1267): the vicar's judge "voluntate propria destitit a cognicione dicte cause."
[14]Molinier, *Correspondance administrative*, No. 794 (June 1268) and No. 1284 (July 1269). The first entry is also in *HGL* 8: No. 512 ix.
[15]TAM, II 15 (August 1274).

even serving as consuls as William did in 1249 and Arnold in 1259-1260, the brothers claimed that they were not obligated to pay tax in town on their rural properties. Sometime before mid-July 1272, a substantial body of testimony was collected in the City on this point and, not surprisingly, the bulk of the consuls' witnesses agreed that citizens with rural properties had traditionally paid tax on them. Ranging all the way from the knightly Bernard Raymond de Tholosa and Bernard Aimericus, a notary who long served the counts, to simple craftsmen, the witnesses were never quite sure how long the brothers had resided in town, anywhere from eighteen to about thirty years being mentioned.[16] The wide range of variation was partly because, like many rural folk, they first rented houses there. A witness remarked that, although he knew "ex certa scientia" that both brothers were citizens for at least eighteen years, their "lares" in Toulouse were "non tamen continuo."[17] By the time the testimony was taken everyone agreed that the brothers owned houses in town and that Arnold lived in the "partita" of the Daurade and William in that of the Old Bridge.[18] It was noted that they had always been difficult and recalcitrant, William having once been fined a palfrey for non-payment of taxes and Arnold a mule and some wheat. The especially reliable Bernard Aimericus, the notary who, like the brothers, had long been enrolled in the prince's as against the "republican" or consuls' party, recorded that, when he was himself a consul in the term of 1266-1267, William had protested his tax. The consuls summoned before them the "comunalerii" of his "partita," one of whom read them the record of the tax paid by William sometime earlier.[19]

Like that of the tolls of Venerque, one cannot be sure of the outcome of this case, but the brothers enjoyed occasional serious victories over the community in which they lived. In 1273 the vicar's court adjudged them the sum of 4130 shillings to be paid by the town. Until this substantial sum was paid, the vicars gave the brothers the (income from the) weights of the mills of the Château Narbonnais and the Daurade and the house containing them.[20]

---

[16]Ibid. 10 (March 1271 to July 1272), the witnesses most informative about the Falgario being Arnold de Blanhaco, Peter Laurencii, "dominus" Bernard Raymond de Tholosa, Raymond de Vaqueriis "pelherius," William Amelii "cervunarius," Bertrand de Morlas and the notary Bernard Aimericus.

[17]Ibid., testimony of Bernard Raymond de Tolosa concerning the "domus conductoria" (rented house) lived in by William and his wife, stating that he did not know when they bought houses; other similar testimony came from Raymond de Vaqueriis "pelherius."

[18]Ibid. and also Grandselve 11 (March 1271) where Arnold bought a house on the rue des Couteliers from John de Castronovo (Curtasolea), a domicile once owned by William Raymond Baranhonus.

[19]Ibid.

[20]Ibid. 39 (March 1273).

The Falgarios' way of life is shown by the evidence adduced above. They were both knights, serving as such on campaign in Gascony. Their wealth, furthermore, is shown by testimony of the reliable Bernard Aimericus who reported that, at the time before 1271, when William paid his tallage in town, his fortune was estimated at 60,000 shillings of Toulouse (120,000 of Tours). Interesting evidence of tax rates at Toulouse, his tax was a mere thirty shillings, a halfpence on each 1,000 shillings or one percent.[21] Their wealth was therefore substantial, but not equal to that of great families, knightly or commoner, such as the Castronovo (Castelnau-d'Estretefons), Maurandi, Roaxio, Turribus and Villanova or exceptionally wealthy individuals like Pons de Capitedenario and Bernard de Miramonte.[22] In fact, one conjectures that the estate of a self-made merchant active in the Garonne wine trade named Arnold Unde in 1276 would have equalled 80,000 shillings.[23] Still, if not among the richest citizens, the Falgario did well enough. The house Arnold bought on the "carraria cultelleriorum" in 1271 measured about forty-three by twenty-seven meters (over 141 feet by eighty-eight) and had a garden attached to it.[24]

When the two original brothers died is not known, but it is evident that their sons not only inherited their property but also something of their litigiousness. Seen as early as 1268, Arnold "iuvenis," son of William, was in the service of his uncle the bishop. In 1268 the count complained that Arnold de Falgario "junior" and Magister Peter de Altarippa, acting "vices" the bishop, had failed to assign a pension to one of his clerks.[25] He was also close to his uncle Arnold, because he was a witness when that knight bought the house described above in 1271.[26] No longer called junior, it was probably this knight and not his uncle who served as a proctor for the recuperation of heretical inheritances in 1279.[27] He may there have been acting for the bishop or even for the abbot of Saint-Sernin both of whose institutions had acquired

[21]Ibid. 10 cited in note 16 above, the specific phrase of the testimony saying that William paid "ad extimacionem .lx. milium sol. tol., scilicet .xxx. sol. tol., pro miliario .vi. d. tol." Another witness, Raymond de Vaqueriis, said that William had paid a tax (when?) of twenty shillings.

[22]The histories of these families and individuals is in my *Repression of Catharism*, pp. 155-167, 178-190, 251-283 and 292-304. For the Turribus, see No. 15 below; for Bernard de Miramonte, Appendix 8, No. 68 (August 1237) and my *Men and Women*, Marriage No. 132.

[23]TAM, II 63 (August 1276), a record of his petition to the consuls against the tax. This analogy may be inaccurate. Unde was being taxed forty shillings sometime after William and one cannot be sure that the rate of tax per unit of wealth was the same.

[24]See the document cited in note 18 above.

[25]Molinier, *Correspondance administrative*, No. 821 (January 1268).

[26]See the document cited in note 18 above.

[27]PAN, J 313 95 (March 1279), but it cannot be surely asserted that this is not the uncle.

property from onetime Cathars or their families.[28] In the same year, an Arnold de Falgario, presumably the onetime junior, although not called so, balked at serving as consul of Toulouse. A judgment of no less a court than the "parlement" of Paris ordered him to serve and, in fact, he is listed among the consuls of 1278-1279 and again in 1280-1281.[29]

The older Arnold had two sons. The first reference to these brothers is curious. Among the witnesses deposing against Peter de Dalbs, abbot of Lézat, in 1253 and 1254 were several who stated that that prelate had had carnal relations with the wife either of Thomas de Falgario or his brother.[30] Whatever the truth of this allegation, we know that there were two brothers and that one was named Thomas. William "juvenis" is seen in 1269 charged with damaging the property of another knight, Sicard de Sanna (Sana near Cazères, far south of town).[31] Thomas is seen in town from 1267 to 1270 and at the latter date sold properties near Castres to the viscount of Lautrec.[32] In the meantime, there had been mayhem in the family. By 1267 Thomas had married either as his first or second wife Esclarmonda, niece of the notable Sicard de Montealto, lord of Montaut.[33] From this remove, this seems a satisfactory marriage, but Thomas' father Arnold thought otherwise. In 1268 we hear that Arnold senior not only refused to fulfill the marriage convention, but also that the seneschal of Toulouse ordered him to provide his son and the latter's wife victuals and maintenance sufficient for their "noble" station.[34] Perhaps peace eventually descended on this tumultuous family. Some years later, a witness recalled that Thomas' wife died in her father-in-law Arnold's house in 1270.[35]

[28]See my *Repression of Catharism*, p, 38, where acts settling questions about their holdings between these prelates and the crown are settled.

[29]TAM, AA 3 118 (May 1279) for the Paris decision.

[30]MADTG, G 722 bis (October 1253 to May 1254). The monk Augerius, witness No. 2, mentioned Thomas or his brother at Muret, but not the name of the woman. Witness No. 6, the prior of Saint-Béat, mentioned a Sibilia de Falgar at Muret compromised by the abbot, but does not advert to Thomas or his brother.

[31]Molinier, *Correspondance administrative*, No. 1306 (July 1269).

[32]Fournier and Guébin, *Enquêtes administratives*, p. 348b (dated 1270), the place called Verdale.

[33]Ibid., p. 249b (June 1267) where one sees Thomas and Sicard together at an important act of the prince.

[34]Molinier, *Correspondance administrative*, Nos. 818 and 884 (respectively June and October 1268): "in victualibus pro modo facultatum dicti Arnaldi et secundum condicionem nobilitatis Thome et Esclarmonde predictorum."

[35]In the document of 1271-1272 cited in note 16 above, a Peter Ainardi, the "extimator" for the "focagium" of 1270 in the "partita" of Saint-Romain, remarked that in that year the young wife "jacuit prope parentes in domo dicto domini Arnaldi."

The Falgario reflect a change in institutional climate. Like other rural magnates of the past and especially younger sons, the brothers had come to town to make their fortunes. Because they were helped by their brother the bishop and also sided with the count against the traditional liberties of the consulate, they did well. All the same, they represented the newer spirit of the rural leaders and of what was coming to be the nobility. They wanted to live in town and exploit its advantages, but did not want to join the community.

8. MARCILLO

A Peter de Marcillo is seen in 1196, but what his relationship to the line seen below cannot be ascertained.[1]

A Marcillo line that can be traced somewhat exiguously appears a few years later. First seen in 1199 and last in 1221, a Marcillus (Marcellus) served in the consulate of 1202-1203, the time of the victory of the popular party.[2] In 1220 William de Marcillo, his son, makes his appearance serving as a witness of the testament of a patrician named Stephen Astro.[3] William served as a councilor for the consuls in 1222 along with a Bernard Peter de Marcillo, of whom nothing more is known.[4] In 1233 a William de Marcillo "de Suburbio" witnessed a charter.[5] This poses a problem because, although the William being discussed here both above and below clearly lived in the Bourg ("suburbium"), notaries often distinguished persons with the same names who lived in the Bourg or the City with an appended phrase such as the above. It is therefore possible that there was a William de Marcillo "de Civitate." Sometime between 1243 and 1245 and again in 1251-1252, William was a consul for the count's party and is thereafter seen in charters into the twelve-sixties.[6]He was deceased by 1266 when his son Arnold, a Franciscan friar, was an adviser to his mother Paris, who had been made an executor of her husband's will. Other than by Friar Arnold, William was survived by his sons William and Marcillus.[7] William's son William was last seen in 1270.[8]

---

8 [1]Grandselve 3 (December 1196).
[2]E 538 (March 1199); E 509 (October 1215, copied in 1218); E 510 (June 1221).
[3]Grandselve 5 (March 1220, copied in 1228).
[4]TAM, AA 1 75 (March 1222).
[5]Malta 5 299 (June 1233).
[6]Grandselve 8 (August 1244, copied in 1247); ibid. 9 (June 1257); and Saint-Sernin 68 (20 72 nn) (March 1262).
[7]Grandselve 15 i (October 1266, copied in 1298) recording a sale of property to the north of the Bourg at Lalande by Paris.
[8]E 257 (November 1270).

TABLE 8 MARCILLUS

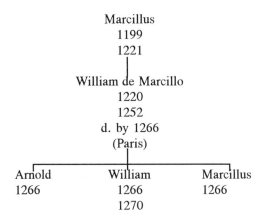

Marcillus
1199
1221

William de Marcillo
1220
1252
d. by 1266
(Paris)

Arnold   William   Marcillus
1266   1266   1266
                1270

The aged witness William de Setes of around 1274 recalled both William de Marcillo and a William "del Marciol," the vernacular version of the name.[9] That this clan had achieved some stature is shown by the three persons who took oath to maintain the Peace of Paris in 1243. These were a Bernard, Gerald and Raymond de Marcillo who have not surfaced elsewhere in my notes.[10]

9. NAJACO

Two parchments, one containing eight acts and the other three, record four generations of a family of craftsfolk. In 1167 or 1168 a "casal" near the Pousonville Gate was rented to a Bernard Magister, a name or term that often refers to a craftsman, and his brother Peter.[1] This Peter was probably the Peter Gasco who, in a much destroyed testament of 1185, left two sons named Peter and Raymond, one a minor.[2] An heir, either of the original Peter Gasco or of one of his sons (about whom nothing more is known), was a woman named Pictavina.[3] In 1197 Pictavina married a Bernard de Najaco bringing with her a dowry of 300 shillings, a quite substantial sum for a woman of her background.[4] In

[9]J 305 32 (ca. 1274).
[10]Appendix 3, No. 2.

9 [1]Grandselve 41 iv (March 1167 or 1168, copied in 1258 and 1264).
[2]Ibid. i (February 1185, copied as above in note 1). The document is all but unreadable.
[3]All eight acts on the Grandselve 41 parchment concern Pictavina and her properties.
[4]Grandselve 41 ii (April 1197), for which see my *Men and Women*, No. 23. Bernard's name presumably derived from the Najac near Villefranche-en-Rouergue or another in the Hérault near Siran.

1206 Bernard bought a house near the Pousonville Gate.[5] Other than bearing the name Najaco, Bernard was also called Amalvinus. This appellation derived from his father's Christian name, and, although the form "Bernardus Amalvinus" was used, Bernard was sometimes called "Bernardus de Amalvino" and "Bernardus Amalvini."[6]

The marriage of this pair lasted about thirty-four or thirty-five years, Bernard dying somewhere between March 1231 and March 1232.[7] After a widowhood of about seventeen years, Pictavina herself died sometime between the drawing up of her testament in November 1247 and the quittances recorded for the charities therein contained in an act dated January 1248. She was therefore a woman not younger than sixty-two at the time of her death. Her testament and subsequent documents clearly show Pictavina and her husband's social status. Other than the "subcapellanus" of her parish of Saint-Sernin, one of her executors was a "pelherius" (a furrier or skin artisan), and among the witnesses to her various acts were another "pelherius" and a weaver. Her total charities to Saint-Sernin and to the recluses, lepers and bridges of the town were under six shillings, although she also gave her pillows, linens and a blanket to the Hospital of Saint-Raymond where she presumably had had final care. Her grandchildren were gratified with thirty shillings and a chest and her daughter Willelma was her heir.[8]

Pictavina and Bernard de Najaco had had two daughters. The one named Sybilia was not mentioned in her mother's will, probably because she had been married and apportioned before her father's death, and hence his wife and other daughter Willelma had been joint heirs to the estate. Sybilia was alive and well in 1252, when, described as the widow of a Bernard Lumbardus and the sister of Willelma, she together with her son Bernard Lumbardus surrendered all rights on the house and "casal" mentioned above to her sister, who was characterized as Bernard's aunt.[9] Willelma was also a widow and had three children, two daughters and a son, about whom nothing more is known.[10]

[5]Grandselve 41 iii (January 1206). That this property was near that gate is shown by the fact that two witnesses in acts listed in notes 8 and 10 below lived "apud portam de Posamilano."

[6]E 503 contains three acts about a property adjacent to that of Bernard de Najaco: ii (November 1214) where Bernard's property is described as that of Bernard Amalvini; i (March 1231) as that of Bernard de Amalvino; and iii (March 1232) as that of Pictavina.

[7]See the sequence of time in the acts cited in the previous note.

[8]Appendix 8, No. 78 (November 1247) wherein her husband was called Bernard Amalvinus; and vii (January 1248) wherein the quittances were listed.

[9]Grandselve 41 vii (April 1252) where Willelma is Bernard Lumbardus junior's "matertera." Perhaps Sybilia was a child of an earlier marriage by Bernard de Najaco, but, given the sequence of time, that seems unlikely.

[10]In the will mentioned in note 8 above, their grandmother gave Bruna twenty shillings, Raymond Aimeric five shillings and Petrona another five shillings plus an "archa."

TABLE 9 NAJACO

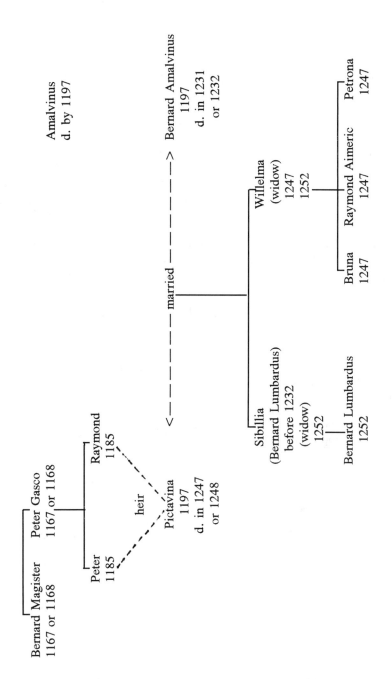

10. NOERIO

Sarracena was a daughter or near descendant of the notable Raymond Sarracenus, son-in-law of a Toulousan service magnate named Toset de Tolosa.[1] Sarracena married Walter (Gauterius) de Noerio, lord of the castle and village of Noé not far from Muret to the south of Toulouse. Husband and wife were seen acting together in 1157 but Sarracena was widowed by 1187.[2] Thereafter she seems to have spent much time in her native town. Acting with the consent of her sons Walter and Pons Arnold de Noerio and with that of her nephew Bernard de Montealto, she alienated to the knight Aimeric de Castronovo her "curia" and rights in Launac (Launaguet) and all property between the Bourg, Montmazalguer (near modern Saint-Caprais), Saint-Loup-Cammas, the essart of Villèle (?), Castelginest, Matepezoul (near Saint-Caprais?), Saint-Martin and Fontanas.[3] Later, sometime in 1204, she granted the monastery of Longages and its Toulousan hospital of Sainte-Catherine's all she had in the tithings of Saint-Jory, Novital, and Lespinasse to the north of town, those of "Rosers" (Rosiès, modern La Roseraie?), "feudum regis" (?), the essart of Villèle (?), Baussan/Baissan immediately east of town and at Lantourville and Ramonville to the south.[4] Seemingly inactive because her son Pons Arnold often acted for

---

10 [1]This is argued from the transmission of a piece of property at Ysola Rando, the modern Redon near Belsoleil (for this see Caster, "Le vignoble suburbaine," p. 216) by Raymond Sarracenus and his wife Sibilia to Sarracena in E 510 i and ii (respectively dated December 1152 and June 1184, copied in 1192 and 1206), and in E 538 (December 1197).

[2]Malta 3 178 (March 1156 or 1157) recording property at Le Férétra (Felétra, etc.), a Roman necropolis near Saint-Roch just south of town (see Caster, op. cit, p. 215), adjacent to that of Toset de Tolosa, whose lords were Walter and Sarracena; ibid. 3 12 (November 1181), property of the same; ibid. 1 11 (January 1182), again at Férétra; ibid. 3 14 i and ii (respectively May 1183 and January 1193), the first recording a property of Walter and Sarracena and the second the same property now of the widow Sarracena; E 510 iii (June 1184, copied in 1207), Walter and Sarracena at Ysola Rando; Malta 3 147 i (February 1188, copied in 1224), Sarracena as widow; Malta 3 14 ii (January 1194, copied in 1221), Sarracena lord of the property of May 1183 mentioned above in this note in a charter witnessed by her son Vital; PAN, J 330 6 (February 1194), Sarracena as lord of a bakery next to the Dalbade; PAN, JJ 19 119r (February 1194), the butchers of the City on the tables of a Bernard Arnold de Tolosa and Sarracena; and Saint-Bernard 138, fols. 79ff. (December 1197), Saracena and others as lords.

[3]Saint-Sernin 599 (10 35 16) 5th of a group of acts tied together iii (January 1200, copied in 1219 and 1220).

[4]E 973 (February 1211, copied in 1212): the actual donation was seven years before the "conscriptio" of the document, and the donor was still alive. In Saint-Sernin 689 (21 73 1) (October 1206), a definition of the tithing of Saint-Sernin places Baussan/Baissan in the general region of the Pouzonville Cross, Mont (Motte)-Saint-Hilaire, Mont Vincent (or Montvincent), the Hers river, etc.

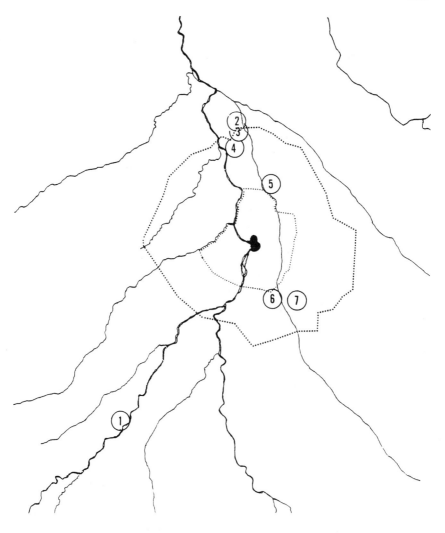

MAP 4 **PROPERTIES OF SARRACENA DE NOERIO**

1 = Noé   5 = Launaguet
2 = Saint-Jory   6 = Lantourville
3 = Novital   7 = Ramonville-Saint-Agne
4 = Lespinasse

her, it is known that she had economic difficulties during the Albigensian war.[5] A much destroyed charter of 1216 or 1217 records that Peter de Tolosa, presumably a "fideiussor" of a debt owed by Sarracena and her son Pons Arnold, was condemned to pay at least 800 shillings of Toulouse to the creditor by the "viri de curia" or Simon de Montfort, then count of Toulouse, in Lantourville south of Toulouse.[6] However hard this decision was upon the pair, Pons Arnold acted for his mother Sarracena in 1224.[7] Still alive when her son became a canon of the cathedral of Saint-Étienne sometime between 1225 and 1233, this aged woman (surely in her eighties) died shortly thereafter.[8]

Presumably the oldest of her three sons, Walter succeeded to the lordship of Noé. We see him in 1197 when the bishop and chapter of Saint-Étienne granted him lifetime patronage of, and revenues from, the church at Noé.[9] His station is shown in 1201 or 1202 when he served with the count of Comminges, ten other rural notables, including the lords of Lanta, Montaut, and Verfeil, and four consuls of Toulouse including Aimeric de Castronovo, settling a dispute between the counts of Toulouse and Foix over Saverdun.[10] Walter predeceased his mother, and, as he lay dying in 1205, returned the church of Noé to Saint-Étienne.[11] Although it is not the business of this history to trace rural families, it may be noted that Walter left three sons, Arnold Pons, Roger, and Walter. Winning fame and a mention in the great war poem called the *Canso* as one of the active defenders of Toulouse during the crusader siege of 1218, Roger later joined two local lords, Bernard de Seysses and Bernard de Orbessano, in fortifying Le Fousseret and Sénarens well to the southwest of

---

[5]Malta 5 291 May 1215, copied in 1218 and 1221, Sarracena and her son Pons Arnold; ibid. 58 9 (May 1216), property at Rosers with Pons Arnold acting for self and his mother Sarracena.

[6]E 573 (1216 or 1217, copied in [month illegible] 1230, and again in November 1234).

[7]Malta 3 147 v (February 1224).

[8]In Saint-Étienne 242 (32 B 1) (May 1233, copied in 1254), the chapter gave Pons Arnold permission to do what he wanted with the property given him by his mother when he became a canon. As shall be seen below, Pons Arnold was a layman as late as 1225.

[9]*Gallia Christiana* 13: Instrument No 40 (February 1197). In order to pay a debt burdening their tithe, the bishop, provost, and chapter granted Walter "nomine bajulationis ecclesiam de Noer" three parts of the tithe and the "primicie" for life. Further, Walter "ibi eligat idoneum capellanum et presentet eum episcopo et preposito qui capellanus accipiat ab episcopo curam animarum." This parish priest "reddat archipresbytero sinodales nummos et preposito et celerario annuatim in quadragesima intrante decem solidos" in the cloister of Saint-Étienne.

[10]*HGL* 8: No. 3, possibly to be dated to 1200 or 1201 because the consular lists for the preceding and following annual terms exist. See Appendix 4.

[11]*Gallia Christiana* 13: Instrument No 41 (July 1205), together with some other properties with the consent of his wife Saura. The act was written in Toulouse.

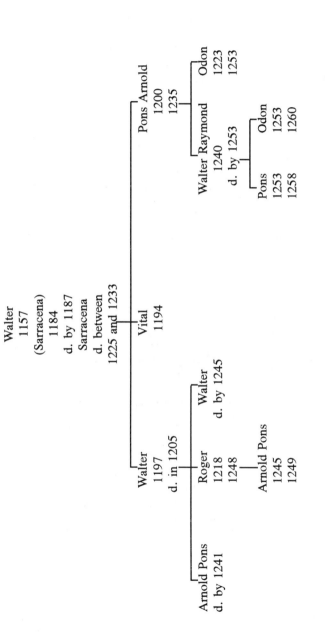

TABLE 10 NOERIO

Walter
1157
(Sarracena)
1184
d. by 1187
Sarracena
d. between
1225 and 1233

Vital
1194

Walter
1197
d. in 1205

Arnold Pons
d. by 1241

Roger
1218
1248

Walter
d. by 1245

Arnold Pons
1245
1249

Pons Arnold
1200
1235

Walter Raymond
1240
d. by 1253

Odon
1223
1253

Pons
1253
1258

Odon
1253
1260

Muret.[12] Arnold Pons was dead by 1241, when Roger met with his brother Walter in his house in Toulouse and settled the problem of the inheritance deriving from his father (in "fratrisca") and from their childless brother.[13] His brother Walter having died, Roger, squeezed by economic need, sold Le Fousseret, Sénarens, etc. to the count in 1245.[14] In the same year, he emancipated his son Arnold Pons who swore homage for the castle and town of Noé to Raymond VII, count of Toulouse, and did the same to his successor Alphonse of Poitiers in 1249.[15]

To return to Sarracena and Walter's other sons, Vital was seen only briefly in 1194, but Pons Arnold had a long career in the town of Toulouse.[16] First seen with his brother, the lord of Noé, in 1200, he served as a judge in consular "curie jurate" in 1215 and 1225, and was a consul in 1224.[17] Later on in 1231, he became a canon of Saint-Étienne and sold in 1233 his "curia" at Lantourville, property at Rosers (modern La Roseraie?) and in the City to Peter de Tolosa, a scion of the family from which his mother derived. He last appears in 1235.[18]

Before entering the clergy, Pons Arnold had two sons, a William Raymond de Noerio and Odon. William Raymond is seen only in 1240 and was mentioned as deceased in 1253.[19] Odon appeared earlier in 1233, served as a consul in

[12]Martin-Chabot, ed., *Canso* 3: 313, where the editor notes that Roger was in town later on in 1222. Also PAN, J 327 2 i (January 1226), witnessed by his brother Walter.

[13]PAN, J 327 2 ii (November 1241) at which time neither the deceased brother nor Walter had male children, but Roger's sons Walter and Arnold Pons were mentioned. In J 330 20 (July 1241) Roger had increased his share of Le Fousseret by lending money to Bernard de Seysses.

[14]PAN, JJ 19 68r-70v (April 1245), mentioning his wife Nempsos, his son Arnold Pons, and the latter's wife India.

[15]PAN, J 314 32 (July 1245), the emancipation of Arnold Pons making him "paterfamilias" and giving him the "castrum" of Noé for which he gave liege homage to Raymond VII. J 308 71 (December 1249), oath to Alphonse for Noé.

[16]For Vital, see the charter of January 1194 in note 2 above.

[17]For the brothers Walter and Pons Arnold in January 1200, see note 3 above; E 501 i (March 1214, copied in 1233), Pons Arnold as a consular judge; May 1215 and May 1216, see note 5 above; Grandselve 5 (December 1218); Malta 15 117 (August 1223) with a mention of Odon, son of Pons Arnold; for February 1224 see note 7 above; and E 573 (March 1225, copied in 1233), as a consular judge.

[18]Malta 3 160 (October 1231), as a canon of Saint-Étienne; May 1233, see note 8 above; Malta 5 294 (June 1233), a sale to Peter, son of Toset, to pay the debts he and his mother had contracted; and PAN, J 322 56 (July 1235), as a canon.

[19]Malta 2 155 ii and E 506 ii (both dated October 1240, copied in 1268), with property of William Raymond; ibid. 1 33 (June 1253) referring to the stone hall, house, and stable, partly held of Odon and his nephews, sons of the deceased William Raymond; and ibid. 1 34 and also 4 218 (both dated July 1253) where Odon and the execu-

1239-1240 and is last seen when sick in 1253.[20] At that time, he was working together with his brother's two sons, Pons and Odon. These two, in turn, are seen throughout the fifties.[21]
These two not very prominent burghers were cousins of the lord of Noé. The urban line of the Noerio seems to have petered out.

11. PETRICOLA

An individual named Petricola served as consul of Toulouse in 1220, in wartime. Toward the end of the war in 1228, he acted as a consular judge delegate along with Aimeric de Sancto Romano.[1] Petricola was still alive in 1237 or 1238 when he rented property at a place called Terra Blanca just to the east of the City.[2] After this, neither the individual nor the name is heard of again until 1243 when a Peter Petricola was among the Toulousans who swore to uphold the Peace of Paris.[3] Peter reappeared again in 1262 when two charters record that he and his brother Arnold Peter Petricola, described as the sons of a Petricola "macellarius," sold properties to members of the Unde family of the Croix Baragnon region in the City.[4] In all probability, given the rarity of the name, the butcher Petricola was the consul of 1220.

12. PODIOBUSCANO

An oddity about the history of the Podiobuscano (Puybusque, Pechbusque, a locality immediately south of the town) is that males who were demonstrably members of the family do not appear until after the females. A male line bears the name but goes nowhere. In 1177, Stephana and her sister Willelma acted

---

tors of William Raymond's estate sold the Hospital nine pence of rent on the above property, located on the "carraria maior pontis [veteris]."
[20]For August 1223, see note 17 above; PAN, JJ 19 40v (October 1236); J 305 29 (February 1243), swearing to uphold the Peace of Paris; and for June 1253, see the note above.
[21]Malta 1 35 (February 1258), where the two brothers confirmed the sale of June 1253 made by their uncle and the executors of their father's estate. Malta 2 155 iii (January 1260, copied in 1260), where property of Odon inherited from William Raymond de Noerio is mentioned.

11 [1]In both TAM, AA 6 131 and Saint-Sernin 599 (10 35 4) (February 1228).
[2]Daurade 189 iv (the month in 1237 is missing; copied in July 1240). For the location of Terre Blanche, see Wolff, *Commerce et marchands*, map no. 3.
[3]PAN, J 305 29 (February 1243).
[4]E 504 (February 1262) and E 510 (March 1262); for the Unde, see my *Repression of Catharism*, pp. 290-291.

with their husbands in a charter witnessed by a Peter de Podiobuscano to surrender all they had acquired from their father William de Podiobuscano to a
William de Pinsagello.[1]

The line that can be followed, however, begins with the progenitor of a
Puybusque wife. To follow a monograph published by a descendant of the family in 1912, two women who held a half arpent of land in fief of Arnold Signarius are heard of in 1196. These are Pagesia, the daughter of a Cortesia, who
gave the use right of the land in question to her daughter Cortesia, a woman
obviously named after her grandmother. The first or earlier Cortesia probably
had been the wife of a Raymond Arsinus, who had acquired the half arpent
from a William de Lantario in 1158.[2] In 1205 John Signarius enfeoffed the
same property to Cortesia, recording the death of her mother Pagesia.[3] In the
same year or thereabouts, Cortesia is found to have had a brother named Raymond Arsivus who sold property at that time to his sister and her sons, whose
names are Raymond, William, and Bernard de Podiobuscano.[4] In 1219 Cortesia, who had died by that time, is disclosed to have been the wife of Bernard
de Podiobuscano, and that the relief for the property described above was paid
by her son William to a P[eregrin] Signarius.[5]

After 1219 the only son appearing in the charters is Raymond. He was a
consul in 1222-1223 and possibly again in 1230 or 1231. In 1238 he was a share-
holder in one of the mills of the Château Narbonnais, an investment he retained
in 1250.[6] In 1244 Raymond and Arnold de Falgario were litigating about the
inheritance of a Stephen Casals at Saint-Martin-de-Mauremont. Stephen had
been hanged for having slain a pilgrim, a crusader, that is, "murdered" him
during a truce: "quan le coms de Montfort era en treva ab le conte de Tolosa
... et dis hom que Carcasona fo desamparada per franceses ... ."[7] By the time
Raymond composed his testament in 1258, he was reasonably well-off. Living
in the parish of Saint-Étienne, he gave about 500 shillings for charity, of
which eighty-three went to his parish, fifty to have him buried as a "frater et
donatus," and some smaller sums to the other parishes of the town and to the
town's mendicants. The testator's sons were minors, but were not placed in the
charge of their mother, Saptalina, who was merely given her marriage portion.

12 [1]E 510 (November 1177).

[2]Puybusque, *Généalogie Puybusque*, No. 8 (January 1158) and No. 10 (December 1196).

[3]Ibid., No. 13 (May 1205).

[4]Ibid., No. 14 (the "conscriptio" is dated August 1208 and recorded an "actio" taken
three years previously). Ibid., No. 15 records an action of August 1208 in which another
relative of this mother, named William Arsivus, sold the family other holdings.

[5]Ibid., Nos. 16-17 (September 1219).

[6]PAN, J 330 5 ii (May 1238) speaks of a mill "inter furnam molindini" of Raymond
and his "parierii" and other mills, and JJ 330 28 i refers to it again.

[7]Puybusque, *Généalogie Puybusque*, No. 18, and especially No. 26.

TABLE 11 PODIOBUSCANO

Raymond Arsivus
1158
(Cortesia d. in 1196)

Pagesia
1196
d. by 1205

Cortesia   — — married — —   William
1205   1205
d. by 1218   1219

Bernard
1204

Bernard
1205
1208

《 nephew
William
1258
1268 or 1269

Raymond Arsivus
1205

Raymond
1205
1250

(Saptalina d. by 1290)

Bordolesia
(William de Neutze)
1258

Bernard Raymond
minor
1258
1290

Raymond
minor
1258
1290
d. by 1297
(Pagesia)

The testament of 1297

Daughters   *Sons*
Bordalesia   Peter Raymond
Mascarosa   Bernard Raymond
Ramunda   Bernard

He instead entrusted them to his daughter Bordalesia, called Petrona, the wife of William de Neutze (Nempze), who was further gratified with substantial gifts in property and the full payment of her dowry. Lastly, the will gives one to understand that one of Raymond's brothers had left issue, his nephew William. One of the executors of this will was an "affactator."[8]

These heirs are seen again. A William de Podiobuscano was a popular leader in a crisis over tolls of 1268 and 1269.[9] Under twenty-five years of age in 1258, Raymond's sons, Bernard Raymond and Raymond, are surely the old men who are seen in 1290 when they divided the inheritance of their deceased mother, Saptalina. Dated 1297 Raymond's testament gives evidence that the family was in the lower ranks of the town patriciate. Raymond described himself as Raymond, son of the quondam Raymond de Podiobuscano, and stated that he derived "de carraria affactatorum Tholose" (modern rue Merlan). The fact that he lived near the Place Mage does not prove that Raymond was in the leather business, but he probably was because the witnesses to his testament were "affactatores."[10] If so, the family was in the entrepreneurial end of the profession and were not registered masters either in 1239 nor in 1280 when many are listed.[11]

The will is an interesting one, involving domestics, collateral family members and charities to the church especially to the parish of Saint-Étienne and the Carmelites in whose robe the testator was to be buried.[12] His wife Englesia was left in charge of the minor children and the heirs were his sons named Peter Raymond and Peter Bernard who received much real property in town and out. Two favored daughters, Bordalesia and Mascarosa whose legitimacy was stressed, were given 1000 shillings for marriage and suitable equipment or "harness." A third son named William and another daughter named Ramunda were given only 500 shillings each and the latter was to enter religion.

13. RAISSACO

In the vicarage to the south of Toulouse along the Hers river near Castanet and south of that village in the tithing of Péchabou lay the community of Raissac.[1] A farming family called the "Raisacs" in the vernacular took its name from

---

[8]Appendix 8, No. 90 (November 1258).
[9]*HGL* 8: No. 526, ii, cols. 1651-1653 (July 1268).
[10]Puybusque, *Généalogie Puybusque*, No. 60 (February 1290).
[11]TAM, II 44 (February 1239) and the "affachayres" in NAP J 328 47 (April 1280).
[12]Appendix 8, No. 103 (June 1297).

13 [1]Raissac, Raixsag, Raisag, etc. cannot be found on available maps, including Cassini's, nor is it mentioned in Léon Dutil's *La Haute Garonne et sa région*.

this small place.[2] The family appears only in documents recorded in the mid-thirteenth century cartulary of Lézat, a Benedictine monastery located south of Muret on the Lèze river.

Heard of when dead in 1192 or 1193, an Arnold of Revigano (Rebigue, a place in the canton of Castanet) had presumably died or disappeared before 1154 when his three sons, Peter, Arnold and Bernard Arnold, all called "de Raissaco," acted independently.[3] Clearly the eldest sibling, Peter appears in charters until 1181 and is not declared deceased until a document of 1200.[4] The instrument of 1200 also stated that he had had children, but, since they never appear in these charters, they may have been gone elsewhere or died.[5] Peter was anyway an exceptional member of the family because, in 1179, he was described as a "clericus," but what that title means in terms of ecclesiastical orders is not specified.[6] The parchment of 1200 also describes a second brother, Arnold, who is referred to as dead in 1191.[7] A third brother, Bernard Arnold, acted in 1198, gave testimony in a charter of 1200 and, in another of the same date, is referred to as having male and female issue.[8] In the meantime, Stephen, a son of the second brother Arnold, appeared as adult (hence at least fifteen years of age) in a document dated 1171 or 1172 and is last seen in 1192 when he witnessed two documents together with his uncle Bernard Arnold.[9]

What makes this brief history worth recording is the relationship of the Raissaco family to the priory of Saint-Antoine. This priory was located immediately south of Toulouse and was a dependency of the monastery of Lézat, in whose cartulary the priory's acts are recorded. The Raissacos were serfs, "men" of, or "men peculiar" to, the prior, their "carnal" or "natural lord."[10]

Apart from Saint-Antoine, this family had relations with others both superior and inferior in economic status in the region. The first document in the family dossier records a lease to a man and wife in 1154 by the brothers Peter, Arnold and Bernard Arnold de Raissaco of land to be cleared in return for a share of the crop and other customary charges.[11] In 1171 or 1172, Peter and

[2]A marginal note in Magnou and Ourliac, *Cartulaire de Lézat*, No. 1487 (August 1191) reads: "donum dels Raisacs."
[3]Ibid., No. 1496 (March 1192 or 1193), and for the other information the forthcoming notes in this family history.
[4]Ibid., No. 1498 (January 1181).
[5]Ibid., No. 1079 (March 1200).
[6]Ibid., No. 1080 (July 1179).
[7]Ibid., Nos. 1468 and 1487 (both dated August 1191).
[8]Ibid., Nos. 1079 and 1497 (March 1200).
[9]Ibid., No. 1490 (March 1171 or 1172) and Nos. 1462 and 1464 (both July 1192).
[10]Ibid., No. 1495 (December 1179) and No. 1497 (March 1200): "homines" or "homines proprii" of their "dominus carnalis" or "naturalis."
[11]Ibid., No. 1489 (January 1154): "unum trossiculum de barta ad trahendum" and pay an unspecified "agrarium de labore terre ... in area ubi blatum tenetur."

Arnold, together with Arnold's son Stephen, pledged for an unknown sum the income and two parts of the harvest they owned on two lots of land, one at the base of the meadow of Castanet.[12] Three individuals in 1178 leased to Bernard Raymond de Raissaco a piece of land and a grove (of trees or brush) near the bank of the Hers river and next to the "casal de Raisag" for a share of the fruits.[13] As late as 1191, an otherwise unknown Raymond Bernardus surrendered to Bernard Arnold de Raissaco a property adjacent to his.[14] A late document of 1200 also shows that others in addition to Lézat and Saint-Antoine had rights over the farm of Raissac and the brothers.[15]

The first reference to Saint-Antoine and this family appears in July 1179 when, specified as serfs, Peter and his brothers admitted that they owed to Saint-Antoine an annual "albergum" (hospitality service) for two monks and one servant ("serviens").[16] In December of the same year, the prior brought the brothers before William of Castronovo, abbot of Lézat and prior of the Daurade in Toulouse, who had "in suo consilio" the well-known notables Toset de Tolosa, Pons de Villanova, Peter Brunus, Bernard Seillanus and others not named. For thirty or more years, the prior of Saint-Antoine testified, save for lands held of other persons, all the brothers' property in the tithing of Péchabou had been held of their carnal lord, the abbot of Lézat and the prior of Saint-Antoine. This dignitary proved his case by adducing the document of July 1179 described above and by the testimony of witnesses. A decisive witness was Pons Villanove (or de Villanova), who reported that, when he was vicar of Toulouse in the midcentury, perhaps around 1164, he had arrested the brothers for an offense about which nothing is known.[17] They and all their goods were, he said, in his power, but through the intervention of his friend, Amelius de Bordis, then prior of Saint-Antoine, he had let them go, although he had badly wanted their money.[18]

According to the prior, the "albergum" owed by the Raissacos was "secundum voluntatem" of the lord. It consisted of money, grain, bread, meat, wine, wood, straw, hay, lambs, trout, hens and eggs and was to be delivered to three

---

[12]Ibid., No. 1490 (March 1171 or 1172): "ad fundum prati de Castaned."

[13]Ibid., No. 1485 (May 1178): a piece of land and a "barta" for the "agrarium de fructibus."

[14]Ibid., No. 1494 (May 1191).

[15]Ibid., No. 1079 (March 1200) records a cession of rights over both to Saint-Antoine by persons bearing the surname Caraman.

[16]Ibid., No. 1080 (July 1179): the specific holdings are not described, but what they owe is called the "esquazechas" (debts) and the hospitality charge to be paid "in domo illorum [Saint-Antoine]."

[17]Pons was vicar and chapterman of Toulouse in November 1164 and served as chapterman in 1152 and again in 1181-1182, for which see my *Repression of Catharism*, p. 293.

[18]Ibid., No. 1495 (December 1179): "in potestate mea per incursos et volebam et peciebam illis ut darent mihi totum suum posse ... ."

monks and a "serviens" either at Raissac "in their houses" or at the priory just outside the walls of Toulouse.[19] Another Amelius de Bordis, a homonym of the past prior, reported the arrival of the Raissacos at Saint-Antoine's with four or five pack animals bearing loads of firewood, cakes, meat, chicken and eggs.[20]

Two years later in 1181, the prior brought the brothers before the abbot of Lézat, who, as arbiter, arranged a "transactio" between the parties. It was there stated that all the property owned by the three brothers in the tithing of Péchabou, save for a vineyard and three plots of land held of others, were held of Saint-Antoine as a fief and "pro hominio." Replacing the old "albergum," a new rent of four quarters of grain and three shillings of Toulouse was established, and, as long as the grove remained, the priory was allowed to send an agent or "nuncius"" to cut wood for the use of the priory but not to be sold. Quaintly, the collector of the "albergum" with his animal was to be housed if the weather was bad.[21]

In 1183 or 1184, Peter having disappeared, his brother Arnold and the latter's son Stephen confessed that they held from the prior four arable properties near Castanet, adjacent to Frenchman's Road. The charter failed to mention the rent owed the lord and the word "hominium" seen above in 1181 is also no longer included. It is therefore possible that some or all of the Raissacos had been freed.[22] All the same, it seems sure that the family was still required not only to pay part of its rent in kind but also deliver it to Castanet and Toulouse.[23] This modernization (if the term is permitted) whereby rents in money and kind replaced an "albergum" may have been too expensive for the family. A document probably dated to 1183 or 1184 contained a deposition before eight named "probihomines" and others not named, in short, before the community,

---

[19]Ibid.: "in hac villa, scilicet in domo ecclesie Sancti Antonii vel extra, scilicet ad Raissacum in eorum domibus ... debebant eis servire de denariis et de blato et de pane et de carne et de vino et de ligneis et de paleis et de feno et de agnis et de tessonibus et de gallinis et de porcis et de omni alio servicio quod aliquis homo debet facere domino suo naturali, secundum voluntatem domini abbatis ... et prioris ... ."

[20]Ibid.: "cum .iiii^{or}. vel .v. saumatis de lignis et cum placentis et carne et gallinis et porcis et fecerunt ei albergum ... ."

[21]Ibid, No. 1498 (January 1181): "et quamdiu boscus vel barta fuerit in toto illo honore supradicti feudi retinuit prior ... ut posset ibi nuncius suus cedere ligna quantum necessaria fuerint ei ad ardendum in domo Sancti Antonii Tholose non ad vendendum neque ad dandum, exceptis azinis casalis de Raissaco quod in azinis predicti casalis neque in azinis domorum neque predictus prior ... neque aliquis pro eo debet cedere ligna; et si magna pluvia vel aliqua necessitate superveniente nuncius prioris predicti ibi remanserit, debent ei et bestie sue Petrus de Raisaco et fratres ejus predicti ... prout opus fuerit necessaria ministrare bona fide ... ."

[22]Ibid., No. 1467 (March 1183 or 1184).

[23]Ibid., No. 1483 (February 1201) where a Raymond Cerdanus was obligated to perform this service for lands acquired of Stephen de Raissaco.

alleging that Arnold, his son Stephen and brother Bernard Arnold had been unable to "serve" the fief and consequently owed the prior fifty and more shillings. With the consent of the fiefholders, the prior pledged a part of this property between the "caminum Francigenum" and the bank of the Hers river to a Pons Scriptor for fifty shillings, retaining for the priory the rent owed by the Raissacos.[24] By 1189 the economic condition of the fiefholders had worsened: during five years, one learns, they had not been able to pay the fifty shillings owed to Pons Scriptor from the rent they owed of four "cartones" of grain and three shillings. The prior therefore freed the fief from the pledge by paying off Pons Scriptor and established the fifty shillings as a debt owed by the fiefholders, making the contract into something like a later "census" contract.[25] Early in 1192 or 1193 the brother named Bernard Arnold swore before the same notary that the properties mentioned above had come to him from his father Arnold de Revigano and his brothers, stating that the family had held them for forty or more years. His nephew Stephen and several other local persons attested the same for thirty-odd years.[26] By 1193 things had gone from bad to worse. Bernard Arnold and his nephew Stephen, the son of the deceased Arnold, admitted that they owed the prior nearly 85 shillings for the farm. The settlement required the loss of two thirds of the property at Péchabou to Saint-Antoine, one third being that once held by Stephen and his quondam father and the other third the pledged property redeemed by the prior from Pons Scriptor.[27]

A possible explanation for the deterioration of the Raissaco fortunes is seen earlier. In 1191 Arnold and his son Stephen gave themselves to the priory in an act of voluntary servitude.[28] In the same act and in another one of the same date written by the same notary, they surrendered to the same all property derived from Arnold's brothers and held by themselves.[29] What this means is difficult to say. Perhaps, as stated above, the modernization of the family's rents had ruined it. Alternately, perhaps, because he is seen here for the last time, Arnold had retired into Lézat or the priory to serve there or as an oblate for final care.[30]

[24]Ibid., No. 1500 (March 1183 or 1184).

[25]Ibid., No. 1501 (November 1189). The act seems to show that a "cartonus frumenti" was valued at 1 s 9 d.

[26]Ibid., No. 1496 (March 1192 or 1193).

[27]Ibid., No. 1499 (January 1193): the debt amounted to 32 "cartoni frumenti" and 24 shillings, hence, at 1 s 9 d per "cartonus," 60.8 s plus 24 s = 84.8.

[28]Ibid., No. 1487 (August 1191): "... pro Dei amore et pro redemptione animarum nostrarum, donamus nosmetipsos domino Deo et beate Marie et sancto Antonio et tibi Bernardo, priori ... ."

[29]Ibid., No. 1468 (August 1191), the notary being Arnold Ferrucius.

[30]See the passages on pensioners, oblates, etc. in my "Charity and Social Work," pp. 258ff. and especially 268-269 where the contracts of serving oblates are mentioned.

This history illustrates a kind of modernization by means of a gradual change from a rent in service and kind to a rent in money and kind. It also shows how a family moved from dependency to personal freedom and back again, and that, even when serfs, its members were enfeoffed or rented property by other landlords than their primary lord and themselves enfeoffed property to other fiefholders or tenants. Unfortunately, what the Raissaco debt of fifty shillings described in the charters dated 1183 or 1184 and 1189 reviewed above means in terms of real wealth or poverty cannot be discerned. The family also seemed to have disintegrated or split up. Peter and his heirs vanished and perhaps settled elsewhere. Another of the remaining brothers, namely Bernard Arnold, did not share the fate, good or bad, of Arnold and his son. Lastly the resumption of dependency to the priory by Arnold and his son, shortly before the father's death or disappearance, does not tell the observer what the pair's motive was. Whatever it was, this family history exemplifies the limited economic and social mobility of dependent farmers in regions close to Toulouse.

Readers are urged to remember that these documents do not tell everything about the economic means of this family, on whom they depended or who depended on them. All they talk about is what was owed Saint-Antoine at one time or another. Happy or unhappy, the memory of this family was recorded in two documents about the quondam Raissaco farm dated 1200 and 1201.[31]

14. SEILLANUS

Variously spelled Seilhanus, Seillanus, Sillanus, Cellanus, etc., the name may well reflect the place of origin of this family. There is a Pyrenean Seilhan near Barbazon in the region of Saint-Gaudens, and also a nearer Seilh near Grenade to the north of Toulouse on the west bank of the Garonne river.[1] The most common form of the name in the charters is Seillanus.

The earliest member of this family seen in the documents is a William who served as a witness to acts by the count of Toulouse in 1168, thus showing that, from the family's earliest moments in the town, the Seillani were comital servants or ministers. William is seen again, this time with his son also named William, dealing with property south of Toulouse to the north of Gardouch in the Lauragais in 1174.[2] One or both of these Williams served as the count's vicar of the town in 1175 and as an untitled agent or bailiff for the count from 1184 to 1186.[3] One of these Williams was deceased by 1188 when a Raymond

---

[31]Ibid., Nos. 1079 (March 1200) and 1483 (February 1201).

14 [1]A river with much the same name flows near Carcassonne.

[2]Saint Bernard 14 (November 1168), and PAN, J 321 24 (December 1174), property at "Vallum Motae" (?).

[3]Malta 6 57 (October 1175, copied in 1223) where the count represented by William, his vicar, and Ispanolus, his subvicar, granted the Hospital the right to have a bakery. In Ourliac

de Montelauro (Montlaur near Montgiscard, not far from Gardouch) was serving as the guardian for the heirs of a William Seilanus. The fact that a Bernard Seillanus witnessed this action leads one to that closely related group bearing the same family name.[4]

Presumably the same as the above, a Bernard Seillanus first appears in the charters in 1170. In 1174 he is seen acquiring a large property near the old "salvetat" of Matapezoul and the community of Saint-Jory north of the town.[5] Along with other notables, he served in 1179 as a judge in a case involving the priory of Saint-Antoine.[6] Sometime before 1180, Bernard was appointed vicar. He was an active officer and is seen judging a case between private persons and the chaptermen of the town at that date and appeared thereafter as vicar from 1181 through 1186.[7] In 1182 he also acquired more property in Saint-Jory and, two years later, he and an otherwise unknown priest named John who lived with him witnessed an act.[8] In the meantime, the picture is made more complex by the fact that Bernard appears to have had a brother named Arnold. The two brothers are seen together in 1183 and 1184, but Arnold died in February 1186.[9] His brother Bernard was at the death and one notes that, on his deathbed, Arnold willed a person named William Mancipius a property just west of the Château Narbonnais, adjacent to, or part of, what shall be seen to have been the family home that was later to become the headquarters of the Inquisition.[10] A Bernard is seen as a witness in 1186, 1188 and 1189.[11]

---

and Magnou, *Cartulaire de Lézat*, No. 1344 (February 1184), Douais, *Conférence de Paléographie*, No. 9 containing two acts (both dated February 1186), and again in *Cartulaire de Lézat*, No. 1346 (May 1186) where a William Seilanus enfeoffed property for the count.

[4]Malta 3 100 (April 1188).

[5]PAN, J 321 20 (November 1170) as a witness, and J 303 44 (March 1174). Bernard bought property worth 200 shillings Morlaas between the Garonne and Hers rivers near the "salvetat" and the bridge of Cordoneras ("Cordonariis" in Latin) "aput Sanctum Georgium qui vocatur vulgariter Sent Iori."

[6]Ourliac and Magnou, *Cartulaire de Lézat*, No. 1495 (December 1179).

[7]TAM, AA 1 19 (before November 1180); Ourliac and Magnou, *Cartulaire de Lézat*, No. 1498 (January 1181); Léonard, *Catalogue des actes de Raymond V*), No. 122 (September 1185); and Ourliac and Magnou, *Cartulaire de Lézat*, No. 1373 (December 1186).

[8]PAN, J 321 29 (June 1181) about Saint-Jory, and Ourliac and Magnou, *Cartulaire de Lézat*, Nos. 1397-1398 (both dated November 1184) reading: "Johannes sacerdos qui tunc manebat cum Bernardo Seillano."

[9]Ourliac and Magnou, *Cartulaire de Lézat*, No. 1393 (November 1183) not mentioning the relationship, and, as brothers, ibid., No. 1500 (March 1183 or 1184).

[10]Douais, *Conférence de Paléographie*, No. 9 (February 1186). Composed of two acts, the second involved William Seilanus acting for the count because the dying Arnold Seillanus gave property held of the count to William Mancipius. The property is described as being bounded by an honor of Peter William Pilistortus, the "terrarium quod est in plano ante Castrum Narbonenesem et tenet usque ad murum de quo clauditur civitas Tolose."

[11]Ourliac and Magnou, *Cartulaire de Lézat*, Nos. 1373, 1476, 1501, 1358 and 1357

As noted above, a Bernard witnessed an act of the count's officers in 1188 and, in 1191, a person of this name had a son also called Bernard (who may well have been one of those called Bernard seen above). In 1193 one learns that the William Mancipius mentioned above in 1186 was his son-in-law.[12] After this, a Bernard Seillanus was active to 1203, but which of the two, father or son, is not known.[13] In all cases save the charters of April 1199 and 1203, Bernard was seen only as a witness. The other acts dealt with his property and, in that of 1203, Bernard acquired property at Saint-Ybars. This acquisition may indicate the family's origins. Saint-Ybars was to the south of Toulouse near Lézat.

In 1207 a charter records that the brothers Bernard and Peter Sillanus, sons of the deceased Bernard, were given the lordship of property held by the Jew Provincialis and his brothers at Lespinet (just south of town near Pourvourville) because their father had guaranteed the debts that the said Jew, together with his brothers and nephews, owed "erga Poncium David."[14] Peter appears to have been in the count's service as early as 1188. In that year, Roger of Hoveden, the English chronicler, mentions that a "serviens" of the count of Toulouse named Peter "Seillun" was captured by the Angevins.[15] A few years later in 1214, it appears that the brothers were in debt, but, in the same year, were among the heirs of a wealthy rural gentleman from the region of Lanta named Raymond de Montelauro.[16] Raymond, it may be remembered, was seen above in 1188 when he served as a guardian for the heirs of William Seillanus in a charter witnessed by Bernard Seillanus, the presumed father of the brothers Bernard and Peter, thus reinforcing the conjectural linkage between the two groups of Seillani earlier proposed in this family history.[17]

(respectively dated December 1186, August 1188 and November 1189 [twice] and December 1189).

[12]See Malta 3 100 (April 1181); Ourliac and Magnou, *Cartulaire de Lézat*, No. 1496 (May 1191); ibid., No. 1469 (September 1191) the two Bernards, father and son; ibid., No. 1401 (January 1192); and ibid., No. 1499 (January 1193) with his "gener" William Mancipius. For whom, see February 1186 in note 10 above.

[13]E 973 (February 1193); Ourliac and Magnou, *Cartulaire de Lézat*, No. 1484 (May 1195); ibid., No. 1486 (February 1199); E 505 (April 1199); Ourliac and Magnou, *Cartulaire de Lézat*, No. 1079 (March 1200); ibid., No. 1479 (March 1200); ibid., No. 1483 (February 1201); ibid., No. 1385 (February 1202); ibid., No. 1352 and 1353 (both dated December 1202); and PAN, J 322 44 (May 1203).

[14]PAN, J 318 Nos. 13 and 14 (respectively December 1207 and December 1208). Although the word "nepotes" found in the charter can mean grandchildren, it seems more probable that it means nephews here.

[15]Rolls Series 51 part 2: 339.

[16]PAN, J 317 13 (April 1214), a modest debt of 150 shillings to a Peter de Anhas.

[17]Appendix 8, No. 34 (September 1214) records Raymond's testament. He was related to Mascaron, the provost of Saint-Étienne, was a creditor of Raymond Unaldus,

In 1215 the two brothers, Bernard and Peter, divided their inheritance. The instrument of division states that Peter was associated with Dominic who, as "dominus" of the brethren of the Dominican order then being founded, himself received Peter's share. This included that part of the family home facing the Château Narbonnais which later became the house of the Inquisition. Bernard received the rest of the property, a half of the house near the Château, shares in a mill, vineyards, rents in town and a "curia" or farm at Saint-Jory. It will be remembered that their father Bernard had been acquiring property in that place in 1174 and 1182 and that the property near the Château has been seen in the testamentary bequest of Arnold Seillanus in February 1186 above.[18]

After this act, Bernard Seillanus is never seen again in available documents, but he may have had an heir. In 1230 and again in 1235, a Raymond Seillanus is seen with a property at Lespinet, presumably the same piece mentioned above in 1207 concerning the property of the Jew Provincialis.[19]

The last Seillanus recorded at Toulouse is the brother Peter, the early apostle of Dominic. Prominent in the contemporary account of the Dominican William Pelisson, the count's chaplain William of Puylaurens and the later Dominican historian and inquisitor Bernard Guy, Peter's history is well known. He joined the Dominican group around 1214, and remained in Toulouse debating the Cathars until Dominic ordered his followers out just before Simon de Montfort's crusaders were driven from town in 1217.[20] On returning from a visit to Paris in 1219, he founded the Dominican house at Limoges and served as prior there until 1233. He then worked as an inquisitor at Toulouse, one so thrusting as to be described as an enemy by Count Raymond VII who prevailed

---

one of the lords of Lanta, and a debtor of Peter Grivus de Roaxio, against whom he believed he had a claim for usury. Bernard Sillanus was given a rent of 4 s 11 d presumably on property in Toulouse. Most of Raymond's property was at Vieillevigne, Coumbel, Gardouch and involved servile persons. Raymond considered himself to be a parishioner of Saint-Étienne in Toulouse as well as of the church of Lanta.

[18]PAN, J 321 60 (April 1215), partially published in *Layettes du Trésor*, No. 1118, records that the brothers, Bernard and Peter, divided the inheritance of their deceased father Bernard Seillanus. Peter's share, namely half of the house "iuxta castrum Narbonenssem et portalem," was given to the Dominicans or rather to "domino fratri Dominico qui hoc accepit pro eodem Petro Seilano et pro se et pro omnibus suis successoribus et habitatoribus domus quam idem dominus Dominicus constituerat." Bernard received the other half of the house "ante castrum Narbonenssem infra vallatum," shares in mills at the Château Narbonnais, vineyards, lands and rents, and finally the "curia" or farm at Saint-Jory.

[19]Malta 3 170 ii (August 1230) and vi (June 1235). See note 14 above, and Appendix 2, No. 2.

[20]TBM, MS 609, fol. 58v, testimony of 1245 about thirty-odd years before where Peter "disputavit cum dictis hereticis" in a house in the Bourg.

on the papal legate to transfer him to Quercy.[21] When already elderly, he held the post of prior at the mother house in Toulouse from 1235 to 1237, was a busy inquisitor in 1241 and 1242 in Quercy, and died, according to Bernard Guy, in February 1258.[22]

15. TURRIBUS

A peculiarity of the surname Turribus seen from the latter years of the eleventh century was that the family name, or that attached to individual members of the family, was sometimes recorded as Turrensis and sometimes as Turre.[1] Curiously, as if having more than one tower was especially aristocratic, the Latin "de Turribus" (Lastours) seems to have been thought more chic than the simple "de Turre" (Latour).

The earliest Turribus to appear was a Bernard Peter de Turribus seen about 1080.[2] There are references to other persons called Turribus or Turrensis in the first half of the twelfth century, one of whom is named Fulk, a Christian name to be seen again in the family history.[3] A traceable family, however, begins to emerge only in two charters dated 1151 and 1154 about property at "Flaubas" (alternately "Flaugas").[4] These instruments record the brothers Curvus de Turribus, Bellotus (Turrensis), and Arnold de Sancto Dionisio acting together with their uncle Royscius.[5] These persons were knights, clearly above the level of the ordinary "cabalarius." Bellotus Turrensis is seen in a comital privilege of about 1120 and he and his son William donated to the Templars

---

[21]Appropriate text is found in Chapter Three, pp. 57-58 above.

[22]For Peter, see the references listed in the indices of Dossat, *Les crises de l'Inquisition toulousaine*, Kolmer, *Ad capiendas vulpes*, Vicaire, *Dominique et ses prêcheurs*, Bernard Guy's *De fundatione*, ed. Amargier, especially pp. 11, 15, 43, 50, and 58-59, and also Pelisson's *Chronique*, ed. Duvernoy, pp. 17, 26, 68-70 and 90, the latter page calling him "grandevus" when prior at Toulouse.

15 [1]On the various families named Turre, see *Repression of Catharism*, pp. 285-289.

[2]Douais, *Cartulaire de Saint-Sernin*, No. 133 (dated about 1080).

[3]For the earlier and unidentified people, see ibid., No. 75 (undated), Calvet de Turribus. The Christian name Fulk is seen in TAM, AA 1 28 (December 1148), Fulcharius Turrensis and his sister Ricarda; Malta 1 96 (April 1145), Fulcarius Turrensis; and Douais, *Cartulaire de Saint-Sernin*, No. 84 (August 1160), surrender of a tithe by Folcherius de Turribus.

[4]Malta 1 100 (April 1180) has a Flaubas near Saint-Agne just south of town.

[5]E 575 i and ii (dated respectively December 1141 and June 1154) mentioning the uncle, the three brothers and another person who was surely a relative called Bernard Peter Dagasag. Some of the property at Flaugas was in pledge to Montarsinus and Peter Tronus, to be seen below. These were either brothers, or, more likely, sons of one of the above persons who had been assigned rents on the properties in the form of "pignora" for family reasons.

about 1130. In the latter act, Curvus also appears promising at death his armor and horse (or, lacking the horse, 100 shillings) pledged on his "bovaria" (farm) at Pouvourville.[6] These, especially Curvus, were clearly weighty persons in the community. Thereafter, in a charter of 1161 concerning their properties at Pouvourville, the brothers Montarsinus, Curvus de Turribus, Arnold de Sancto Dionisio and Peter Tronus Bestiacius appeared together.[7] What their exact relationship to the Turribus mentioned above cannot presently be determined.

Other than these four brothers from whom emerged the line that can best be traced, a few unidentified Turribus appear in the documents, some of whom may well have been the issue of two of the brothers whose history is to be sketched below. They are three. A Pons, variously called Turre and Turribus, is seen from 1149 to 1164 and a Bernard held property in the Close of Saint-Sernin in 1156.[8] A weightier person was a William Hugh de Turribus who appears together with his wife NaFassa dealing with his and his mother Ermengarda's lands at Campferrand near Montaudran in the early 1180s.[9] William Hugh was dead by 1202, leaving sons named Bertrand de Sancto Lo and Bernard Hugh in 1187 or 1188. Nothing can be done with these sparse references, but one wonders if Bertrand was not the lord of Saint-Loup-Cammas just northeast of Toulouse.[10] Furthermore, the rare name Royscius carried by the uncle of the first set of brothers in the previous paragraph persisted. A Royscius de Turribus was serving as a councilor of the consuls in 1222. He was probably deceased by 1235 when the vicar of Toulouse informed the canons of the cathedral that they were wrong to detain property at Castanet given them by a Royscius.[11]

<hr />

[6]TAM, AA 1 14 (about 1120) with Bellotus Turrensis, and Malta 1 45 published in d'Albon, *Cartulaire général de l'Ordre du Temple*, No. 20 (dated from 1128 to 1132). Bellotus promised sixpence annually to the Temple but his gift "ad obitum" was left blank. His son William offered his "equm et arma ad suum obitum." Curvus' obit is recorded in Chapter Five, note 6 above. He was also a witness in Douais, *Cartulaire de Saint-Sernin*, No. 371 (August 1145).

[7]Malta 3 54 (August 1161).

[8]Douais, *Cartulaire de Saint-Sernin*, No. 93 (October 1149), Pons de Turribus, and E 501 i and ii (respectively dated December 1152 and June 1184, copied in 1190 and 1206), the first recording a sale by Pons de Turre, son of Laura, and his brother-in-law, Stephen de Carcassona, and the second a property of Pons and Stephen held in pledge. Bernard de Turribus and his wife Barrava's property in Douais, *Cartulaire de Saint-Sernin*, No. 78 (October 1156).

[9]Saint-Bernard 36 (December 1180), Malta 3 186 (March 1182 or 1183), and ibid. 1 72 i (August 1183).

[10]Malta 3 189 (October 1202), and the sons in ibid. 4 191 i (March 1187 or 1188, copied in 1203).

[11]TAM, AA 1 75 (March 1222) and PAN, J 322 56 (July 1235).

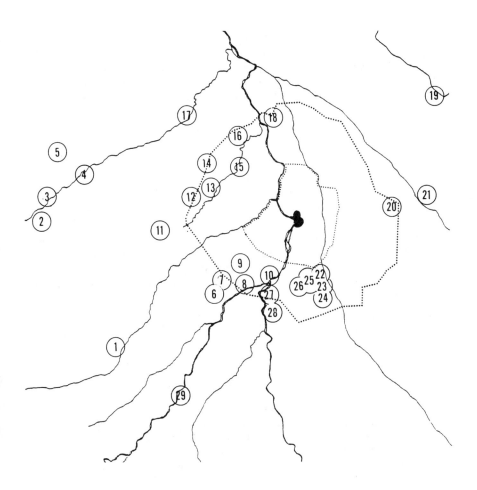

MAP 5 PROPERTIES OF THE TURRIBUS FAMILY

1 = Poucharramet	11 = Fontenilles	21 = Verfeil
2 = Endoufielle	12 = Léguevin	22 = Ramonville-Saint-Agne
3 = Marestaing	13 = Pibrac	23 = Auzeville
4 = Isle-Jourdain	14 = Mondonville	24 = Castanet
5 = Beaupuy	15 = Cornebarrieu	25 = Pechbusque
6 = Seysses	16 = Aussonne	26 = Vielle-Toulouse
7 = Frouzins	17 = Saint-Paul	27 = Lacroix-Falgarde
8 = Roques	18 = Lespinasse	28 = Goyrans
9 = Cugnaux	19 = Buzet	29 = Mauzac
10 = Portet	20 = Lavalette	

Returning to the four brothers mentioned above, Montarsinus who was seen in the act of 1154 cannot be followed. All that can be said is that a person bearing his name appears again in family charters dated 1221 and 1243. The reader may note, however, that various persons with this rare name are mentioned in the family history of the Descalquencs printed elsewhere, and that one of them had property on the Montardy Square ("Planum Montarsini") in the City which is where, as shall be seen, the later Turribus had a house or houses also.[12]

Curvus de Turribus is a kettle of very different fish. He appears in connection with town government and the count. In 1180 one hears of his tile or brick works to the south of the town, and he is last seen in 1185.[13] The brother called Arnold de Sancto Dionisio (named after the close of that name in Pouvourville), however, was dead by 1196, when he left two sons, a Bestiacius de Sancto Dionisio and a Galembrunus, one of whom was alienating serfs at Pouvourville and the other a third portion of a "fratrisca" in the close mentioned above.[14] One knows nothing more about these sons save that persons named Sancto Dionisio and Galembrunus continue to appear in the documents, including those of interest to the Turribus family, into the thirteenth century.[15] It is perhaps significant that the name Galembrunus smacks of the knightly lines domiciled at Verfeil to the east of Toulouse, a daughter of whose premier lord, as shall be seen, was to marry the most successful son of the Peter Tronus Bestiacius who shall now be considered.[16]

[12]For June 1154, see note 5 above; for August 1221 and May 1243, note 15 below. The history of the Descalquencs is sketched in my *Repression of Catharism*, p. 209.

[13]PAN, J 328 1 i and viii (respectively August 1173 and February 1175), as witnesses; Malta 1 100 (April 1180), the "tegularium Curvi"; for August 1185, see note 17 below.

[14]Malta 12 23 first and second of a group of ten acts tied together (respectively dated October and December 1196), sales by Bestiacius and Galembrunus. Ibid. 50 not numbered has a copy of the act of October 1196.

[15]A Sicard Galembrunus in March 1237 in note 19 below; Malta 27 52 fourth of a group of acts tied together about property of the Temple near Lespinet (dated March 1185 or 1186) with Arnold de Sancto Dionisio; ibid., first document of the same group (August 1221) with Montarsinus; ibid., seventh of the same group (January 1243), Adalbert de Sancto Dionisio together with Curvus, Guy, and Bertrand de Turribus; PAN, J 324 13 (May 1243), recording the sale of a property at Ramonville to Bertrand and Guy de Turribus, witnessed by Curvus de Turribus, Montarsinus and Adalbert de Sancto Dionisio; lastly in PAN, J 305 29 (February 1243), the family witnesses at the oath to uphold the Peace of Paris were Azalbert de Sancto Dionisio, and Arnold, Bertrand, Curvus, Fulk and Guy de Turribus.

[16]TAM, AA 1 64 (June 1203) has Isarn de Viridifolio, Bertrand Galembrunus, and simple Galembrunus among the sixteen "domini," "milites" and "homines" of Verfeil making peace with Toulouse. An Arnold Bestiacius was a witness to this transaction.

TABLE 12 SOME TURRIBUS LINES

«uncle
Royscius
1151
1154

Curvus de Turribus
ca. 1130
1154

Bellotus Turrensis
ca. 1120
1154
William
ca. 1130

Arnold de Sancto Dionisio
1151
1154

Peter Tronus Bestiacius
1161
d. by 1185

brothers

Montarsinus
1161

Curvus de Turribus
1161
1185

Arnold de Sancto Dionisio
1161
d. by 1196

Galembrunus
1196

Bestiacius de Sancto Dionisio
1196

Arnold Bestiacius
1185
1201
see Table 13 below

William
1185

Peter Tronus Bestiacius
1185
1196

Pilistortus
1185

Peter "iudex"
1185

Arnold Bestiacius
1196
1203

heirs

Arnold Bestiacius
1237
1244

Bertrand Bestiacius
1237
1248

The brother named Peter Tronus, sometimes called Bestiacius, was first seen in 1154 and was deceased by 1185, at which time he had five sons. These were William Bestiacius de Turribus (also Turre), Arnold, Peter Tronus, Pilistortus, and Peter "iudex" who in the latter year referred to one of the "pignora" at Pouvourville inherited from their father, Peter Tronus Bestiacius, an action witnessed by their uncle Curvus de Turribus.[17] Nothing is known about Pilistortus and the "iudex" Peter, surely a comital officer, but Peter Tronus Bestiacius had died by 1196, leaving a son named Arnold, who, since both were busy with the Galembruni of Verfeil, was probably the Arnold Bestiacius who appears until 1203.[18] Later, from 1237 until the late twelve-forties, the brothers Arnold and Bertrand de Turribus appear. Their relationship to the above persons is not known. At any rate, a Bertrand de Turribus was consul in 1247-1248, and it is to be noted that the brothers Arnold and Bertrand sometimes carried the name Bestiacius and shared in business dealings with William Bestiacius de Turribus' children, who were surely their cousins. That they were wealthy persons is also shown by the facts that they surrendered their claim on what the notable Aimeric de Castronovo "probushomo" had bequeathed the Hospitalers at Estaquebiou and Bolencs near Saint-Génies and, in 1237, sold a third part of Buzet on the Tarn river to the count.[19]

The brother whose descent may best be tracked is William Bestiacius de Turribus. He divided the properties derived from his father Peter Tronus in 1185 with his brothers, and thereafter appears in documents concerning Pouvourville and Saint-Denis, an area where he was acquiring "pignora," property and contracts for service with his dependent farmers.[20] Sometime around or

[17]Malta 12 23, one of ten charters tied together (August 1185): "Sciendum est quod tunc quando Willelmus Bestiacius de Turribus partivit cum fratribus suis, cum Arnaldo et cum Petro Trono et cum Curvo et cum Pelistorto et cum Petro iudicio, advenit tunc Willelmo Bestiacio de Turribus illa pignora de .iii. solidis Tol. quam Petrus de Altaripa, filius Raimundi de Altaripa, misit eorum patri Petro Trono Bestiacio qui fuit, que pignora est in Stephanum de Guotza de Espasa et in eius uxorem et in filios et in filias illorum et in eorum tenenciam; et istam pignoram totam solverunt cabalem et servicium quod debet dare inde Willelmo Bestiacio de Turribus et eius ordinio sui supradicti fratres absque ulla retinencia quam ibi non retinuerunt."

[18]For October and December 1196, see note 14 above. An Arnold Bestiacius in Malta 15 69 (September 1200), an act of William Bestiacius de Turribus. Arnold, the son of the deceased Peter Trunnus Bestiacius, served as guardian for the children of the dead Ademar Galembrunus of Verfeil when they sold Cépet, Bolencs, etc. to Arnold Bestiacius in Malta 123 8 and 9 (March 1196). For June 1203, see note 16 above.

[19]Malta 123 11 (March 1237), the Hospital, witnessed by Fulk and Curvus de Turribus and Sicard Galembrunus; PAN, J 328 14 (December 1237), Buzet, witnessed by Folquoissius and Curvus de Turribus; see note 15 above for January and February 1243, and note 40 below for Bertrand in April 1244 and June 1245.

[20]For the acts of October and December 1196, see note 14 above, and, included in

before 1200, William married Sicarda, daughter of Isarn Jordan, a premier lord of Verfeil.[21] Previously married to Odon de Montealto, a baron of Montaut, this rich bride brought William 620 shillings worth of annuities ("pignora") and unspecified properties extending from Verfeil to the east of town to Isle-Jourdain in the west, and around Pechbusque and Castanet to the south.[22]

William profited from this marriage. In 1200 he sold to Aimeric de Castronovo what he had acquired from his wife, her father and previous husband Odon de Montealto at Vieille-Toulouse, Pechbusque, Auzeville and Ramonville just south of Toulouse.[23] The money thus acquired was soon invested because, in 1209, William acquired from his father-in-law Isarn Jordan de Viridifolio what appear to have been vast properties at Bouzigues, Poucharramet, Portet, Fontenilles, Léguevin, Mondonville, Carterpuech, Isle-Jourdain and Beaumont and Saint-Paul on the Save river, all to the west of Toulouse.[24]

In 1215 William was either at war, otherwise absent or inactive because, in that year, his two oldest sons alienated some property at Roziès (Rosers or La Roseraie ?) just east of town with the consent of their mother Sicarda.[25] Four years later, William and his wife appear to have prepared to retire into

---

the group of ten acts tied together in Malta 12 23 are some ranging from April 1197 to January 1207 containing servile homage offered by four men, a woman and a married couple. William is here variously called de Turribus, de Turre, and Bestiacius, and various combinations of the three.

[21]The actual date is unknown partly because, at this time, Toulousan notaries were only beginning to distinguish between the "actio" and the "conscriptio" of their documents. The marriage charter with Odon de Montealto is dated 1197.

[22]Although the fifteenth century copier of the Saume de l'Isle often erred and may have done so in recording the date of April 1211 for the marriage of Sicarda and William in MADTG, A 297, fols. 840ff., the marriage could scarcely have been before 1206 because Fulk who became bishop in 1206 was called so in the date elements. The dowry given William in 1211 mentions that he was to have the property "de dote Poncii Oldrici et Sicarde quondam uxoris sue," a mysterious reference to family members not otherwise known. At any rate, the provisions of the contract of 1211 and that of September 1197 in Malta 165 4 with Odon de Montealto have similarities because both contracts describe the dower as Sicarda's father's property in Toulouse and between the Hers river and the Garonne to the east, and toward the west between the Save and Garonne rivers and beyond the Save near Isle-Jourdain. The grants to the south of Toulouse are also similar, being in Pechbusque, "Salviolas" (?), Castanet, Vieille-Toulouse, Grezac near Flaugas, "Podium Ardinegium"(?), Lézat and Castagnac.

[23]Malta 15 69 (September 1200) wherein William is named both Turribus and Turre. In addition to the places listed above, there was a community called Bonavalle which I have not located.

[24]MADTG, A 297, fols. 866ff. (June 1209).

[25]Malta 5 291 (May 1215, copied in 1218 and 1221), Folcuissius and Curvus for their father who was called "dominus" William de Turre Bestiacius.

the convent of Lespinasse as oblates. With the consent of their children, Fulk, Curvus, Guy and Alcaya (Alcaida, Algaya, etc.), they sold and donated all property received from Isarn Jordan de Viridifolio and Odon de Montealto at Aussonne, Mondonville, Lespinasse and Cornebarrieu to effect this end.[26] These were very considerable properties because it is known that Isarn de Viridifolio and William Assalitus had shared Mondonville half and half, and that the former's share had gone to William and Sicarda.[27] This action did not mean that the pair had entered the house, but was probably insurance for the future. William continued active in business in 1219 and served as a councilor for the consuls in 1222.[28] Thereafter he disappeared and was, it appears, dead by 1224 when his children, spoken for by Fulk and his widow, confirmed the arrangement with Lespinasse.[29]

William and Sicarda's sons Fulk and Curvus may have been majors in 1215, but were also still under their mother's tutelage or were being represented by her during an absence. Their two younger children Guy and Algaya only reached majority in 1219. The sister is heard of only once again, probably sometime in the midcentury, when she and her brother Guy gave a relative a family house on the Montardy Square.[30]

The oldest brother Fulk was a knight, served one term as a consul and was last seen at the division of the family property with his brothers in 1255.[31] In 1231 a document states that he had married Longa, the daughter of a Raymond de Insula, who was clearly a relative of the lordly family of Isle-Jourdain, in which town, indeed, the young couple shared a "castellum" with the baronial line.[32] Longa is seen again. As Fulk's widow, she issued in 1261 the

[26]MADTG, A 297, fols. 111ff. and also 846vff. (May 1219, wrongly dated in the Saume as 1200, Fulk being the bishop in the date elements), the donation and their claim to be "participes" in the order, followed on 112vff. and 848ff. by a sale of the same goods to Lespinasse.

[27]Ibid., fols. 844vff. (February 1229).

[28]Ibid., fols. 839v and 829 (respectively dated August 1219 and October 1222) where William, his wife Sicarda and her father Isarn acted together. TAM, AA 1 75 (March 1222) records as councilors William Bestiacius de Turribus, his son Folcoycius and a Roycius.

[29]MADTG, A 297, fol. 831v (July 1224).

[30]See the discussion on p. 355 below. One wonders if Alcaya had married.

[31]Consul in 1239, but, as seen in note 28 above, he had been a councilor in March 1222. MADTG, A 297, fol. 831v (July 1224) records an agreement between Lespinasse and William's issue. Here the mother Sicarda was still alive and the children were spoken for by Fulk, indicating that he was the eldest. The division of the brothers' inheritance in November 1255 is examined on p. 356 below.

[32]Malta 165 11 (November 1231) where Folquois and Longa sold the Temple their half of the "castellum de Patras in burgo ville Insule inter clausuras eiusdem burgi." Ibid. 12 (August 1231) shows that the other half of this "castellum" was owned by

customs for the community of Endoufielle near Isle-Jourdain, acting for her minor son Curvus.[33]

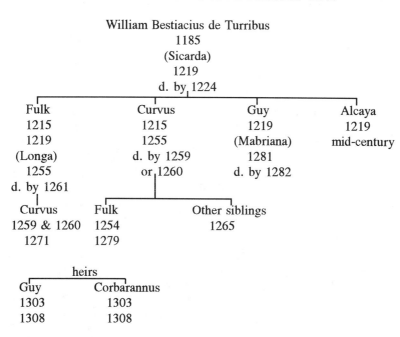

TABLE 13 WILLIAM BESTIACIUS DE TURRIBUS' LINE

William Bestiacius de Turribus
1185
(Sicarda)
1219
d. by 1224

Fulk	Curvus	Guy	Alcaya
1215	1215	1219	1219
1219	1255	(Mabriana)	mid-century
(Longa)	d. by 1259	1281	
1255	or 1260	d. by 1282	
d. by 1261			

Curvus	Fulk	Other siblings
1259 & 1260	1254	1265
1271	1279	

heirs

Guy	Corbarannus
1303	1303
1308	1308

Although clearly younger than twenty-five, Fulk's son Curvus must have been over fifteen years of age in 1259 and 1260, when he offered to do battle for Isarn Jordan de Insula in the litigation against his cousin, the premier lord of Isle-Jourdain.[34] Thereafter he appears as one of the lords of Endoufielle and as a noble busy in Armagnac and Gascony.[35] His successors are seen at

---

Bernard Jordan de Insula, son of the deceased Bernard Jordan. This was Bernard Jordan III, lord of Isle-Jourdain, who died in 1240, son of Bernard Jordan II, likewise lord, who died in 1228. Fulk was among those taking oath to uphold the Peace of Paris in February 1243, as above in note 15.

[33]Dossat, *Saisimentum comitatus Tholosani*, No. 17, p. 105.

[34]PBN, MS nouv. acq. lat. 2046 (December 1259–April 1260).

[35]Fournier and Guébin, *Enquêtes administratives*, No. 39, p. 135 (January 1263) where, along with other barons, Curvus guaranteed Gerald, count of Armagnac. Ibid.,

the turn of the fourteenth century. The campaigns of Navarre and Aquitaine in the twelve-nineties involved the two lords and brothers of Endoufielle, the "domicelli" Guy and Corbarannus de Turribus. These worthies were at the siege of Bordeaux to stifle the rebellion of 1303, and were still busy negotiating payment for their service in 1308.[36] From the name of Corbarannus, it is evident that the family had not surrendered its penchant for curious monikers.

To turn back to the William Bestiacius who was dead by 1185, his second son was named Curvus. This knight was several times a consul, and last appeared in 1255 when he and his brothers divided their inheritance.[37] He was deceased by 1259 or 1260 when his son, the squire Fulk, guaranteed the side of Isarn Jordan de Insula in the judicial proceedings about Isle-Jourdain.[38] This Fulk is seen again at Verfeil, dealing with the properties of the other issue of his father at Verfeil in 1265 and again at Cugnaux in 1279, one of the family lordships.[39] The charter of 1265 mentioned that Fulk had siblings, but who they were is not known.

The last of the William of 1185's sons was named Guy who outlived his brothers and was probably in his seventies when he died. First seen in 1219, he was a creditor (a usurious one at that) of the Jew Belitus and owned property to the south of Toulouse.[40] He married Mabriana, the daughter of William de

No. 40, p. 136 where he is called Curvus de Andosvilia or Endoufielle. Lastly Dossat's *Saisimentum comitatus Tholosani*, No. 15, pp. 107a and 379a (October 1271) lists him among the nobles of the bailiwick of Gascony.

[36]Dossat "Quelques documents inédites sur les Juifs," pp. 785-786.

[37]For May 1215, see note 25 above; as a consul in the count's party in 1235-1238 or 1239 and again in 1246; for March and December 1237, see note 19 above; for February and May 1243, see note 15 above; for November 1255, see p. 356 below; anent his death before 1261 and an action of his widow, see note 33 above.

[38]PBN, MS nouv. acq. lat. 2046 (December 1259–April 1260) where his father is described as a quondam knight.

[39]See E 493 (April 1265, copied in 1271) concerning Verfeil, and Malta 138 2 (August 1279) recording arbitration between the Hospital and the "domicellus" Fulcois-shius de Turribus over Cugnaux.

[40]For May 1219, see note 26 above; for his acquisition of rents at Roziès from the Castronovo family in January 1243 and his duty as a citizen in February, see note 15 above; PAN, J 324 13 and 16 (May 1243), where he together with Bertrand de Turribus acquired the "curia" of the deceased Bertrand de Gavarerio on Frenchman's road near Lespinet and Ramonville; PAN, J 324 18, published in Saige, *Les Juifs de Languedoc*, No. 35 (April 1244) containing the avowal of a debt of ninety shillings owed by Belitus to Guy with a stipulated penalty interest payment of two pennies "per diem," an annual rate, that is, of just over sixty-six percent, guaranteed on lands held by the debtor in the "curia" of the above Bertrand de Gavarerio and some lands at "Celata." The brothers Arnold and Bertrand de Turribus were witnesses; PAN, J 324 22 (June 1245) where Guy gave the count the debt of ninety shillings owed him by Belitus and another debt of 480

Gamevilla, one of the several lords of Bessières on the Tarn river.[41] Perhaps without issue, he and his wife retired into the Hospital of Saint John in 1262, giving property at Cugnaux, Léguevin, Pibrac, Pouvourville and Verfeil worth about 10,000 shillings.[42] They were accompanied into the order by two of their dependent servants and their families.[43] The elegant "dominus frater Guido de Turribus donatus" lived as an Hospitaler until his death in 1282.[44]

Earlier on, in 1278, Guy's house on the Montardy Square had gone to a relative of his wife, the squire Oldric de Gamevilla.[45] A later document of 1290, however, states that the lord of this property was a squire named William de Turre who had been given it by Guy and his sister Alcaida, and that, retaining rent, he had sold or leased it to Bastard de Gamevilla, also a squire, from whom it had come to Oldric. The property was evidently charged with quite a number of rents.[46]

In 1297 a reference to the brothers Curvus and Bertrand de Turribus appears, but what their relationship is to the family to which they were obviously related is not known.[47]

---

shillings owed him and Bertrand de Turribus; PAN, JJ 19 58v (June 1245) where Bertrand and Guy de Turribus sold the "curia" of Bertrand de Gavarerio to the count; and both Curvus and Guy were witnesses in PAN, J 330 26 ii (January 1248).

[41]The Gameville family history is to be seen in *Repression of Heresy*, pp. 221-225.

[42]Malta 2 157 (January 1262, copied in 1265). Guy is there described as a knight and Mabriana as the daughter of the deceased William de Gamevilla and some of her property came from her brothers, Pons and Bertrand de Gamevilla. A copy of this act is also found in the register Malta 139 1r.

[43]Malta 27 69 (January 1262). One of the dependents was from Pouvourville and the other from Cugnaux and they gave themselves and their families to the Hospitalers, presumably to serve as domestics for Guy and Mabriana.

[44]PAN, KK 1228 5r (January 1273) where the "hospitalerius" gave evidence; Malta Caignac 2 56 (February 1281) as simple "frater"; ibid., Caignac 1 6 (December 1281) as "dominus frater"; and Malta 8 31 (April 1282) about the house on the "Planum Montarsini" of the dead knight, "frater" and "donatus" of the Hospital. Argument over the price paid for this costly retirement is seen in Molinier, *Correspondance administrative*, No. 359 (December 1267) where the ban on transferring Guy's property to the Hospital was lifted and in Malta Caignac 2 4 (dated 1268) where the value of 10,000 shillings is put on them.

[45]Malta 8 66 (June 1278) when the Hospital rented Guy's quondam house to this squire for ten pounds of Tours annually.

[46]E 510 (the "actio" is dated April 1290, but the "conscriptio" October 1303) records the renting of this house by its lord William de Turre, and E 502 (January 1286) records from whom William had gotten it. The property was immediately adjacent to a house owned by a Bernard de Turribus.

[47]Grandselve 15 (June 1297).

The main document left by this family during the thirteenth century is the division of the inheritance of the three brothers, Fulk, Curvus and Guy, in 1255. They determined to continue to share but subdivided their "curia" or great house in Toulouse (probably on Montardy Square) and their castle of Cugnaux near Portet, together with their holdings at Verfeil, Frouzins and Roques near Muret, and at Maurens near Cazères. The properties divided between the three were at Pouvourville, Ramonville, Roziès, Beaupuy near Isle-Jourdain, Marestaing to the west, and Mauzac near Noé and Seysses near Muret to the south. The Turribus, in short, were nearly baronial landed nobles.[48] The family had apparently split, one part essentially remaining around town and reaching into Gascony only at Cugnaux, the other being largely based at the Gascon community of Endoufielle to the west near Lombers.

A family of Toulousan "cabalerii" in the service of the counts from its earliest days, this family of mixed rural and urban origins subsequently served as citizens and consuls of the town and, at the same time, were almost baronial. An especially remarkable quality about the clan is that, although related by marriage or business to the lords of Verfeil, the Castronovo family and those of Descalquencs and Gamevilla, all of which were deeply involved in Catharism, no person with the surname Turribus is to be seen in any document concerning that religion. Anent this, it was noted above that Sicarda, wife of William de Turribus Bestiacius, was the daughter of Isarn Jordan or Isarn de Viridifolio, the "maior dominus" of Verfeil. The historian William of Puylaurens called Isarn "nebulatus," adding in his chronicle that he, when a child, saw this baron, "said to be surely a hundred years old at Toulouse, living very modestly and content with a rouncy."[49] "Nebulatus" was clearly an epithet because words like "nebulator" and "nebulatrix" mean anything from a fool to a harlot. William probably wanted to show that Bernard of Clairvaux' famous curse had worked its magic on Verfeil, as indeed it had to some degree because Simon de Montfort had confiscated that community and given it to the bishop of Toulouse. But, to judge by his grandchildren, Isarn could not have been reduced quite as much as William thought. Besides, at about a hundred years of age, who needs more than a rouncy? It would be enough to be able to ride at all.

[48]Malta 138 1 (November 1255) and ibid., fols 1v-2v.

[49]*Chronica*, ed. Duvernoy 28: "qui bene dicebatur esse etate centenarius, Tholose contentum uno roncino pauperrrime commorantem."

16. YSPANIA

What follows is not a family history, but instead the record of a man and wife in their late life. Peter de Yspania first appears as a serf being enfranchised in 1191.[1] Thereafter he is seen as a witness to charters dated 1194 and 1201, the latter an emancipation of another person by a lord of Montesquieu in the Lauragais, perhaps the region from which he derived.[2] The first evidence that Peter had acquired property in town is dated 1202.[3]

After this threadbare prologue, Peter and his wife Garsenda (seen here for the first time), surely worried by the tumult occasioned by the Albigensian Crusade, entered the monastery of Saint-Sernin in 1215 as "brethren and oblates." They gave the abbot their property in and just outside the Bourg reserving 200 shillings for deathbed gifts, in return for which they were made participants in the spiritual and temporal benefits of the house. The abbot promised to receive them as canons when they wished, in short, when old or sick to death for burial in the robe.[4] The property this pair surrendered (to receive back in "commenda" for life) was several small houses and shops just on the "carraria maior" in the Bourg (the present rue du Taur), a vineyard near the Villanova leprosery just outside the town walls, and an adjacent plot of land.[5] That these properties constituted an accumulation typical of modest businessfolk or substantial artisans is shown by Peter and Garsenda's vineyard. It lay adjacent to a large plot of land that paid Pons de Capitedenario no less than twenty-five shillings in

---

16 [1]Saint-Sernin 502 (1 1 57) (March 1191, copied in August 1208 and August 1224), the emancipators being a Peter de Malsamont and seven others including a brother Gerald de Sancto Johanne. Neither of these persons can be identified.
[2]Saint-Sernin 678 (5 20 69) (December 1195, copied in January 1216, and in 1225 and 1228) and again in ibid. 502 (1 1 57) ii (September 1201). William Peter de Lux was the emancipator, and was later called in about 1237 a lord of Montesquieu. On him, see MS 609, fol. 102v (June 1246).
[3]Saint-Bernard 138, fols. 118v-122 (January 1202).
[4]Saint-Sernin 502 (1 1 38) i (March 1215, copied in September 1223): Peter and wife "concedimus nos ipsos deo et Beate Marie" etc. "per fratres et donatos," thereby becoming "participes," and the abbot, speaking in the first person, promised that, when they wanted, "recipiam vos per canonicos." Martin-Chabot, "Mésaventures d'un donat," *Mélanges d'histoire du moyen-âge dédiés à la mémoire de Louis Halphen*, p. 505: "per fraires e parsoners de la maiso els bes temporals e els espiritals."
[5]Saint-Sernin 502 (1 1 38) ii (March 1215, copied in September 1223): the houses and "operatoria" lay between those of another property holder and the "carraria balneorum" (of the public baths), and that of another property holder and the rue du Taur of the Bourg. The other properties were near the lepers and the "clausu Vasarum," according to Caster, "Le vignoble suburbain," p. 217, the "Clos des Vases," is perhaps the present rue des Vases outside the Saint-Étienne Gate.

annual rent, a property subdivided between fifty-six tenants whose average rent was just under fivepence.[6]

Sometime after the contract with Saint-Sernin was made, presumably between the date when the town rose against the crusaders and was defeated by Montfort in September 1216 (an event mentioned in Peter's letter) and possibly before the victorious rising of the Toulousans a year later, Peter described what had happened to him. The troubles were apparently bad enough to make him wish to switch his oblature to the Hospitalers of Saint John if Saint-Sernin would permit it.[7] For whatever reason, he did not do so because, in 1226, the landlord of his vineyard confirmed Peter's initial grant to Saint-Sernin and the monastery's "commanda" of the same to Peter.[8] In 1234 the abbot of Saint-Sernin confirmed the old arrangement in terms identical to the charter of 1215.[9] To close Peter's story, it is possible that, in spite of the charter of 1234, he had died by 1232 because a document refers to one of his bits of property as being of the "deceased Peter de Yspania."[10]

The petition to the abbot of Saint-Sernin mentioned above conveys an idea of Peter's wealth and age. Either too old or unwilling to fight, when the crusaders ran through the town spreading fire and destruction, he rushed to Saint-Sernin whose abbot received him in his chambers but then sent him to the adjacent Hospital of Saint Raymond. He left his armor and a good bow and arrows and linens, etc. with the abbot who, however, had to buy back his houses occupied by Montfort's tax collectors for a half year or so for 200 shillings.[11] When Peter re-entered his home, he found it robbed of all "grain and wood."[12]

Peter's letter illustrates what a good oblate was supposed to do: gratify the canons with gifts. He had donated thirty shillings worth of linen cloth and also a large cloth for covering the altars. When the abbot had gone to Rome, presumably for the Lateran Council of 1215, he had lent the house 200 shillings and, for other needs of the house, including the repair of a gate, festivities for the reception of canons etc., nearly 100 more.[13] Just as important was the fact

---

[6]Saint-Bernard 138, fols. 118-122v (January 1203).

[7]Oblate contracts usually contained a clause forbidding such changes, for which, see my "Charity and Social Work," pp. 264-265.

[8]Saint-Sernin 502 (1 1 43) (March 1226): John de Perticis and his mother were the lords.

[9]Saint-Sernin 502 (1 1 41) (September 1234).

[10]E 575 (February 1232): Peter de Yspania "qui fuit."

[11]Martin-Chabot. "Mésaventures d'un donat," p. 505: "E can lo coms de Montfort mes la trebala del fog e la vila ... ." For the armor, see below. For the 200 shillings, the abbot "don avian li comunaler de comte de Montfort tengudas las claus be meg an."

[12]Ibid.: "trobé la maiso rabauda tota esters del blad et de la fusta."

[13]Ibid.: "E can aisa fo fit, compregi .xxx. soldadas de draps de li e unas bonas to-

that he reported that, among the things lost at the time of the crusader irruption, were "the documents of the debts owed him": in short, when active in business, he had lent money.[14] Peter was also a typical footman in the militia. During the tumult of these years among other things including bedding, he lost his leather coat, helmet, and iron hat and his good bow was destroyed.

---

alas de .iii. alnas que foro dadas e messas a vos altres de la maiso; et can vos, senher n'abas, anes a Roma prestè vos .cc. sol. tol. a vos e al covent de la maiso; e can mosen-her l'abas fo destrigaz per W. Arnaldo e fo tornaz, dè .l. xx. sol. tol. per estrena; et a la bestorreta de la porta far degui .x. sol.; e am W. At, can sos fraires [s] fé canonjes, degui .v. sol., qu'en Ramons Espertz me dis cófes; et per companagge [e] obs dels ca-nonjes ad .i. dimenje dé lor .vi. sol. e .vj. galinas, per dit d'en Peire de Castelgenest."

[14]Ibid.: "et amarvi lor las cartas de mos deudes, don les ago, que eu esters no'ls avia."

Appendix Two

Jewish Family Histories

As Gustave Saige long ago remarked, it is difficult to trace the family lines of Jewish clans. The major reason is the lack of a family surname in Latin charters. Another is that those of this faith did not donate to the church whose archives contain most of the information about real property in this period. A final explanation is that circumstances did not allow its members to hold real property for a long time. This said, a few families can be traced for two or three generations.

1. ALACER AND HIS SONS

In 1181 Alacer "judeus" is seen renting land to Raymond Barba de Ordeo and in 1194 renting a house adjacent to another property owned jointly by him and his partners ("parierii"), one of whom was a Christian named Garsio Carbonus.[1] In 1217 he showed his leadership of the Jewish community by appearing as the "bailiff for the whole body of the synagogue" handling another rental contract.[2] Alacer was deceased by 1228 according to a charter that names his sons, Abraham and Belitus.[3]

A Jew named Belitus and his brothers are referred to as property owners as early as a charter of 1183, but there is no way of knowing if this is Alacer's son.[4] What is sure is that Alacer had died sometime before 1228 and that sons named Abraham and Belitus who are certainly his are seen in charters from 1202. The two brothers worked together until 1228, when the count granted them the right to alienate what they and their father had acquired.[5]

[1]E 506 i (February 1181, copied in 1260) published in Saige, *Juifs du Languedoc*, No. 6 from Malta 2 155, and E 579 i (October 1194).
[2]Barrière-Flavy, *L'Abbaye de Calers*, No. 18 (June 1217): "qui inde erat baiulus pro omni conventu schole iudeorum."
[3]Malta 3 156 (February 1228) in Saige, *Juifs du Languedoc*, No. 23.
[4]E 896 (November 1183).
[5]E 506 (January 1202) in Saige, *Juifs du Languedoc*, No. 10 from Malta 14 11: at Prat Lobatum (?) as fiefholders; ibid., No. 12 from PAN, J 324 5 (February 1207, copied in 1243): acquisition by the brothers of part of a "curia" once of Bertrand de Gavarrerrio near Frenchman's Road; Malta 1 17 (January 1208, copied in 1214, 1221,

Among other things, the brothers were moneylenders. The large farm or "curia" which bore the name of a Bertrand de Gavarrerio who had accumulated it came into their hands in 1207 because the monks of the house of Roncesvalles in Navarre had fallen into debt.[6] Located on Frenchman's Road north of Castanet, this farm was an ample property because its recognitive rents added up to over four shillings. Again, in 1227, the count gave Durand de Sancto Barcio who was both his vicar and creditor to the tune of 5000 shillings the right to collect debts owed to Abraham and his brother Belitus.[7] This does not mean that the brothers were out of business, merely that Durand could re-coup his salary as vicar from the share of their profits that normally went to the count.

Abraham may have died in 1228, sometime between February and March, because, at the latter date, his brother Belitus sold a rent they had once held jointly to the Temple and the sale document does not mention him.[8] In 1244 Bernard Aimericus, the notary in comital service, acting for the vicar Berengar de Promilhaco, placed Astrugus, son of the deceased Abraham, Alacer's son, in possession of his half of the farm of Bertrand de Gavarrerio and its attachments to enable him to pay off the dowry of his mother, the widow Gauzios, amounting to 1550 shillings of Toulouse.[9]

1227 and 1239) mentions a property of Belitus. This is the only document showing a Belitus acting alone (perhaps the one with this name mentioned at the beginning of the paragraph?); Malta 27 64 (January 1212) with property of the brothers in the close called Champ Ferrand in Montaudran; Saige, *Juifs du Languedoc*, No. 21 from Malta 4 141 (November 1218): "et postquam Abra habuerit laudatum dominationum, Belitus non tenetur de guirencia nisi de medietate"; Malta 5 192 (May 1221): property of the brothers "ad quercum apud Rosarios" (Rosers south of town near Lespinet); E 506 (May 1222) in Saige, *Juifs du Languedoc*, No. 22 from Malta 17 32: property of the brothers, and Abraham called son of Alacer; E 506 (March 1222): brothers sell rent to Temple; Saige, *Juifs du Languedoc*, No. 23 from Malta 3 156 (February 1228): the count gave the brothers described as sons of deceased Alacer right to alienate all property and "licentiam et liberum posse ... concordandi, recuperandi, solvendi ac componendi cum debitoribus de omnibus illis debitis et baratis eisdem ... [Belitus and Abraham] ... et Alacri judeo patri eorum qui fuit ullo modo debebantur."

[6]Saige, *Juifs du Languedoc*, No. 12 from PAN, J 324 5 (February 1207, copied in 1243): the "frater ... preceptor et constitutus dominus" and two "fratres hospitalarii ... per illas impeditiones et per illa debita que in multis modis debebant per predictam domum Tolose hospitalis Roscide Vallis et ad persolvenda illa debita vendiderunt ... curiam" and its dependencies.

[7]PAN, J 317 16 and J 320 42 (both dated November 1227): in the first of which the count confesses that he owes Durand 4000 shillings and in the second an additional 1000.

[8]Malta 3 153 (March 1228) in Saige, *Juifs du Languedoc*, No. 24. In fact, Abraham never again appears in the charters, except as deceased.

[9]PAN, J 324 19 (July 1244) in Saige, *Juifs du Languedoc*, No. 36 v: "illius curtis que vocatur denGavar."

In the meantime, Abraham's brother Belitus continued his business activity
around the end of the great war. In 1228 the count granted Arnold William de
Sancto Barcio the right to sell all property and rents owned by the two brothers.[10]
What that meant is not clear because in 1231 the count granted Belitus all the
property he and his brother Abraham had acquired at the "curia" of Bertrand
de Gavarerio and attachments at "Roserios" and "Alguerias" and Arnold William returned to him all he had obtained from him.[11] Belitus seems to have
been selling out, but something may have been going wrong. With the consent
of his wife Montaneira, he sold a property to the Temple in 1232 and in 1243
the main family property, namely all he had acquired from Bertrand de Gavarrerio at Le Buguet in Montaudran and all he held there from Arnold and Pons
de Pinu, to the very rich notables Bertrand and Guy de Turribus.[12] In 1244
Belitus and his wife confessed that they owed Guy de Turribus ninety shillings
of Toulouse.[13] It is also known that they borrowed more money from these
brothers because in 1245 Guy and Bertrand gave the count's vicar Berengar de
Promilhaco their claims for the debts of ninety and 480 shillings owed them by
Belitus as well as the "curia" described so frequently above.[14] That Belitus
was either suffering confiscation, selling out or was otherwise in difficulties is
shown by the terms of the loan of ninety shillings mentioned above. Interest
in the form of a penalty payment was supposed to start on August 15th and
amounted to two pennies daily. If the terms of the loan were not fictional, the
loan would have accumulated interest for about three hundred days until the
Turribus surrendered it to the count's vicar, which means an interest rate of
approximately fifty-five and a half percent. Penalty payment aside, this loan
seems usurious. On this possibly sad but actually inconclusive note, the history
of Alacer and his sons ends.

2. PROVINCIALIS AND HIS SONS

Provincialis was associated with the administration of the count of Toulouse
and one of his sons, Bonuspuer or Bonusmancipius, was in the same service or
business. Provincialis is first seen in 1191 assisting a vicar in selling a piece of

[10]Malta 3 155 ii (June 1228, copied in the same year).
[11]PAN, J 324 7 (June 1231) and ibid. 12 (September 1231, copied in 1244): the
transaction involved all that Belitus, his brother and father had acquired.
[12]Malta 3 164 i-iii (April 1232) in Saige, *Juifs du Languedoc*, Nos. 28-30, and PAN,
J 324 13, 14 and 16 (May 1243) in ibid., No. 26 i-iii.
[13]PAN, J 324 18 (April 1244) in Saige, *Juifs du Languedoc*, No. 36 iv.
[14]PAN, J 324 22 and 23 (June 1245) in JJ 19, fol. 60v and Saige, *Juifs du Languedoc*, No. 36 vi.

the count's property and thereafter appears again in 1192 and 1194.[15] However prosperous he may have been, he was also in debt because the sons of a
onetime vicar named Bernard Seillanus, deceased by this time, noted that their
father had guaranteed a debt of 450 shillings of Toulouse owed by him, his
brothers and his nephews, to the noted minter and usurer Pons David.[16] Provincialis borrowed thirty-five shillings from Peter de Roaxio and put in pledge
to the creditor a property held of the Hospital in 1208. One cannot tell what
the interest on this loan was to be because the profit was clearly the unknown
income from the pledged property.[17] More or less following the terms of this
contract, two years later in 1210, the Hospital took over the pledged property and recorded Peter de Roaxio's satisfaction for his "sors et lucrum."[18]
Around the time of these events, Provincialis disappears from the charters.

The son named Bonuspuer or Bonusmancipius (Bonmacip) picks up the
story, not only of the family but also of its service to the count. A mass of
acts record his participation in government from 1219 to 1247, along with
occasional bits of private business.[19] In 1240 these cryptic official records

[15]Saint-Étienne 239 (30 3 nn) (May 1191) in Saige, *Juifs du Languedoc*, No. 7: the
vicar of Toulouse, Raymond "qui vocatur Monacus," acted "consilio et voluntate
Provincialis judei"; E 506 (March 1192) Provincialis dealing with his rents, and, in
PAN, J 330 6 and 40 (February 1194, one copied in 1223 and other in 1275) as a
witness to a charter.

[16]PAN, J 318 13 (December 1207) in Saige, *Juifs du Languedoc*, No. 14: two brothers "laudaverunt et concesserunt" to the two Seillani, Bernard and Peter, 400 shillings
"per pignus" on vineyards held by Provincialis and his brothers at Lespinet, "scilicet
pro omnibus illis baratis et debitis que Bernardus Silanus pater eorum, qui fuit, firma-
verat pro predicto Provinciale judeo, vel pro fratribus suis, vel pro nepotibus suis, aut
pro aliquo eorum erga Poncium David," as in the debt documents. PAN, J 318 14 (December 1207) in Saige, *Juifs du Languedoc*, No. 15: the additional debt of 50 shillings.

[17]E 506 (December 1208) in Saige, *Juifs du Languedoc*, No. 17 from Malta 18 13:
after a year, the debtor owes "lucrum penale deinde" and land held of the Hospital at
"Podium" (where ?) was put in pledge. The lord, namely the preceptor of the Hospital,
confirms the arrangement, reserving a reversionary right for his institution. This is
probably the field held from the Hospital at "Podium" paying a quarter of its fruits and
a penny of rent seen in Malta 27 68 (December 1208) in ibid., No. 16. It could also be
related to another field in "Valle Gairaldo" (where ?) paying two pennies in rent in
Malta 15 114 i (March 1209, copied in 1222, 1229 and 1242).

[18]Malta 58 7 (February 1210).

[19]Almost invariably called the son of the deceased Provincialis, he is seen in the following official records: TAM, AA 2 76 (September 1219); PAN, J 330 9 (July 1222) concerning
the town's butchers; JJ 19, fol. 120 (July 1222); J 317 14 (August 1224); ibid. 16 (November
1227); Malta 3 156 (February 1228) in Saige, *Juifs du Languedoc*, No. 23; PAN, J 330 12
(July 1228); JJ 19, fol. 38v and J 314 12 (July 1234) concerning the mills; JJ 19, fol. 121
and J 322 58 and J 323 77 (February 1237); JJ 19, fol. 70v; J 317 32 and 33 (April 1245);

364   APPENDIX TWO

break off to mention that Bonuspuer had a daughter named Massilia and that
she had married a Clarionus who is undoubtedly the one bearing that name
seen earlier in 1237.[20] It is possible that this government servant left a somewhat durable memory. In 1306 an inexpensive house (72 pounds of Tours or
720 shillings of Toulouse) was described as being once owned by "Bonusmancipius jugerius judeus."[21]

It will be remembered that in 1207 Bonmacip's father was reported to have
had brothers and nephews. One knows nothing about these relatives, but it can
be shown that Provincialis had more than one son. Bonuspuer's brother Solomon (Salomon) is seen briefly in 1222 and then disappears from the record.[22]
What is more, the charter about Massilia and her husband Clarionus was witnessed by an Astrugus "judeus," described as the brother of Bonuspuer. Although it cannot be proved, Astruc may have been the "judaeus de Tolosa"
who was a merchant and moneylender at Llobregat near the Catalan town of
Lérida in 1249 and 1251.[23]

Fragmentary though this family's record is in the documents, it also left a
memory in town. Provincialis had once owned or collected rent from a bakery.
In 1257 a William "furnerius" served as a witness to a public document and
was there identified as he "who lives in the bakery once of the Jew Provincialis."[24] It is likely that the bakery and perhaps Provincialis' own residence was
on the street bounding the block occupied by the Carmelites to the south called
the "carraria Provincialis [Provensal] judei" in 1288 and 1290.[25] Another in-
triguing reference is to two houses, one adjacent to the synagogue and the
other next to its very gate which "once" were of "Salomonis Alacris," possibly
the Solomon, son of Alacer, seen very briefly above. One of these homes was
valued at 330 pounds of Tours, that is, about 3300 shillings of Toulouse, and

JJ 19, fol. 59 (June 1245); ibid., fol. 155v (September 1245); and ibid., fol. 60v and J 324
25 (April 1247). The private charters where he was a witness or property holder are TAM,
II 75 i (August 1224, copied in 1226 and 1236); ibid. iii (March 1226, copied in 1236);
Malta 3 169 (March 1236) in Saige, *Juifs du Languedoc*, No. 31; and Saint-Étienne 3 30 nn
i and ii (January 1247) in ibid., No. 37 i and ii.

[20]Malta 4 205 ii (September 1240, copied in 1240 and 1242) in Saige, *Juifs du
Languedoc*, No. 33, and Malta 4 205 i (March 1237) and No. 32 in Saige.

[21]Ibid., No. 47 vi (November 1306).

[22]E 506 (May 1222) in Saige, *Juifs du Languedoc*, No. 22, from Malta 17 32: described as a son of Provincialis.

[23]Lldonosa Pujol, "Marchands Toulousains a Lérida," p. 229.

[24]Malta 4 223 (February 1257): William "furnerius qui manet in furno que fuit
Provincialis judei."

[25]Chalande, *Histoire des rues de Toulouse*, Section 138, pp. 290-291.

the other at 150 pounds of Tours, or 1500 Toulousan shillings.[26] Good and substantial housing.

3. ISPANIOLUS AND HIS SON SOLOMON

A fragmentary history is that of Ispaniolus (Yspanolus, etc.) and his son Solo-man (Salomon and Salamon). In 1178 Ispaniolus first appears when he acquired a "casal" near a "furnile" once owned by Vidianus Frenarius and Raymond Carabordas and his brothers' property and shortly afterward a "solarium" (presumably an apartment) on the alley that led to the house of the Carabordas, the Portaria ["castellum portarie"] and partly fronting on the "carraria maior de Freneriis" (the present rue du Taur).[27] This property was rounded out in 1183 by a purchase from the executors of Oldric Carabordas' will, one of whom was a Gerald Saquetus who had married Bruna, Raymond Carabordas' daughter.[28] Ispaniolus, indeed, seems to have been acquiring a substantial residence, buying up rents on the property and lending money to achieve his objective.[29]

Ispaniolus died or disappeared sometime between 1192 and 1202, the latter date being when his son Solomon acquired more property adjacent to his father's house near the town hall.[30] Although presumably raised in Toulouse, Solomon lived in Verdun-sur-Garonne, a place on the left bank of the Garonne river well north of Toulouse.[31] He settled a pledge of 300 shillings his father had financed for the notable William Pons Astro for the very modest annual increment of just under three percent (an annual rent of eleven shillings three-pence), and in 1207 acquired an additional small rent.[32]

---

[26]Saige, *Juifs de Languedoc*, No. 47, v and x (dated respectively November 1306 and March 1307).

[27]E 506 (August 1178) in Saige, *Juifs du Languedoc*, No. 5, and Grandselve 2 (September 1178).

[28]E 506 (November 1183): selling a "capud cornu de eorum casale" next to Ispaniolus' property and the alley.

[29]E 506 (March 1192): sixpence rent; Grandselve 4 (April 1201): where Raymond Rotbertus "de Tauro" and William de Pozano sold to "Yspanioli iudeo de Verduno" a smaller rent on property next to the bakery of the sellers and an "honor" of Raymond William Atadilis; TAM, AA 1 36 (November 1202): Atadilis and his wife sold to the consuls their house next to the City wall and Yspanolus' property. For the loan, see the next footnote.

[30]Grandselve 4 (December 1202): an aquisition from Atadillis and also a charter of the "gadanni quod Ispanholis qui fuit a Geraldo Saqueto fecit."

[31]Malta 1 24 xvi (February 1206): the count acted about property "in Castroverduni in salvetate de foris" next to Solomon's house.

[32]E 506 (June 1206): Solomon "iudeus de Verduno" was specifically called son of the deceased Ispaniolus. The pledge was half of a "pignus" William Pons held of some-

It appears, however, that Solomon wanted to go north again to Verdun. In 1212 this "judeus de Verduno" acquired from the count the right to dispose of his house "ad Frenerias" near the town hall and the rent rolls his father had acquired.[33] In that year and the next, he together with his wife Bona disposed of the lot to Pons de Capitedenario and his partner Arnold Asicius and the count confirmed the action.[34] During the great war, Verdun was certainly further from the front than was Toulouse.

4. THE BROTHERS ISAAC AND MOSES

In 1188 Isaac acquired property at Fontanas, just north of Toulouse. The charter shows that he held other property there, and among its witnesses was a Jew named Maurellus.[35] In 1192 he acted together with his brother Moses (Mosse).[36] In a charter dated 1200 and witnessed by Bonafos, a Jew of Verdun, Abraham, a Jew of Carcassonne, and the Maurellus seen above in 1188, the transfer of a house and its emplacement once owned by Moses was confirmed by the cellarers of Saint-Étienne to "domina" Aster, widow of Pirlonis "judeus," and her sister Galda for 1200 shillings of Toulouse.[37] Aster appears to have sold this property by 1223 when the cellarers of Saint-Étienne recorded her cession of it to Raymond Arnold de Villanova. In this charter, the house is described as having been owned by Moses "de Lacaustra."[38] Evidence of the circles Aster was moving in here is that Raymond Arnold de Villanova and his brother Bernard were among the notable patricians of the town condemned for Catharism later on.[39]

It may well be the same Moses to whom, in 1213, the count rented a property in Champ-Ferrand in Montaudran just east of town, but the charter reads "Mosse de Castello."[40] In 1222 a Moses who is surely the one seen above or a son bearing his name obtained a vineyard in another charter remarkable for

---

body else for 1200 Melgueil shillings. The rents acquired were in shillings of Toulouse. The threepence rent is in E 506 (March 1207) in Saige, *Juifs du Languedoc*, No. 13.

[33]E 506 (April 1212) in Saige, *Juifs du Languedoc*, No. 18.

[34]E 506 i-iii (May 1212) in Saige, *Juifs du Languedoc*, No. 19, and Saint-Bernard 138, fols. 152v-53v (May 1213).

[35]Malta 58 nn (November 1188).

[36]TAM, II 71 i (May 1192, copied in 1249 and 1280).

[37]Saint-Étienne 239 (30 3 nn) (June 1200, copied in 1247) in Saige, *Juifs du Languedoc*, No. 12.

[38]Saint-Étienne 242 (32 4 5) (December 1223, copied in 1247).

[39]The Villanova material is in my *Repression of Catharism*, pp. 301-302.

[40]Malta 1 109 (May 1213).

its witnesses. These include members of two of the families recorded above, Abraham son of Alacer and Solomon son of Provincialis.[41] Nothing more is seen of Moses, but his son Durand appears in 1269 as one of the owners of the tolls collected in the markets of Toulouse.[42] After a lengthy investigation, Durand, described as the son of the deceased Moses "de Curia" and acting with the consent of his mother, the widowed Regina, sold his share to the government for 4000 shillings.[43] "Castellum," "caustra," "claustrum" and "curia" – why not?

[41]E 506 (May 1222) in Saige, *Juifs de Languedoc*, No. 22.

[42]Molinier, *Correspondance administrative*, No. 1314 (July 1269).

[43]PAN, J 324 26 ix (July 1274). The forced sale is discussed in Chapter Four, p. 79 above.

Appendix Three

Oath To Maintain the Peace of Meaux-Paris
February 1243

Excluding the consuls, 1028 names are recorded in PAN, J 305 29. The document containing the list is here transcribed, and the list of the jurors is arranged by line. The advantage of this way of presenting the document is that it shows who stood next to whom during the oathtaking. All the names of the jurors in this Appendix are to be found in the general index under their surname or second name, and the page number of the Appendix on which each name occurs is italicized there. For reasons of space, the lists published in this appendix are printed in parallel columns, hence the reader moves from the bottom of the column on the left to the top of that on the right. The reader is also to note the marks attached to the entries, namely:

a "/" placed at the end of each of the lines of the manuscript except in the lines containing only names. The lines are identified by numbers, starting at 7, meaning line number seven of the document.

a "⟩" placed at the end of a name means that the name is split between one line and the next.

a "⟩⟩" means that the name is the last in a given line.

For those interested in orthography and nomenclature, I have identified the different spellings of the name William (Willelmus and Guillelmus), Willelmus being overwhelmingly the most frequent. In response to earlier and possibly justified criticism of the document published in my *Repression of Catharism*, this list is the only one in this book in which the names are kept in the form they are seen in the document. This means that many craftsmen or professional persons I know to be such do not have their title distinguished from their name. The punctuation of the document is retained, but capitalization has been partially modernized.

Noverint universi presentes litteras inspecturi quod nos consules urbis et suburbii Tolose

Villanova, Bernardus de	Castronovo, Ramundus de
Ramundus maior, Petrus	Ponte, Ramundus de
Septenis, Willelmus de	Portallo, Berengarius de
Bonushomo, Vitalis	Jordanus, Arnaldus
Salvitate, Petrus Bernardus de	Bosqueti, Bruno
Marcillo, Willelmus de	

voluntate et mandato speciali expresso domini nostri Ramundi dei gratia comitis Tolose filius domine regine Johanne et in presencia eiusdem promisimus et tactis sanctis dei evangeliis juravimus illustri domino Lodovico regi Fran-/corum quod si dominus comes Tolose vel alius nobiscum habuit consilium de pace facta Parisius consulemus eis quod eam servent et servabimus eam quantum ad nos pertinet posse nostro, et dabimus operam efficacem quod dominus comes Tolose servet eam, et si dominus comes Tolose veniret contra adherebi-/mus ecclesie et domino rege Francorum contra ipsum nisi infra .xl. dies monitus fuit hoc emendaverit vel iuri steterit coram ecclesia de his que ad ecclesiam pertinent et iuri coram domino rege Francorum de his que ad dominum regem Francorum pertinentur. Juravimus etiam quod nos juva-/bimus ecclesiam contra hereticos credentes et receptatores hereticorum et omnes alios qui ecclesie contrarii existerent occasione heresis vel contemptus excommunicati ... in terra ista, et dominum regem Francorum iuvabimus contra omnes et quod eis faciemus vivam guerram donec ad mandatum / ecclesie et domini regis Francorum reverterantur. Et si dictus comes Tolose moveret guerram domino regi Francorum vel heredibus ejusdem quod absit adhereremus domino regi Francorum et heredibus eius contra eundem dominum comitem Tolosanum. Juramento autem predicto sic a nobis corporaliter prestito in palacio / comuni, nos dicti consules de voluntate et mandato speciali eiusdem domini nostri comitis supradicti in presentia nostra promittere fecimus et jurare domino regi Francorum sub predictis verbis et forma predicta concives nostros quorum nomina sunt inferius adnotata. videlicet

7.

Castrumnovum   Montibus, Petrum de ⟩

8.

Turribus, Curvum de	Castronovo, Geraldum de
Sancto Luppo, Bertrandum de	Turribus, Bertrandum de
Gamevilla, Guillelmum de	Montibus, Bertrandum de
Raynaldum, Bernardum	Baranhonum, Bernardum Ramundum
Borrellum, Brunonem	Garinum, Hyspanum
Turribus, Folcoys de	Palatio, Ugonem de ⟩

9.

Artus, Bernardum
Sancto Paulo, Petrum de
Atadil, Ramundum Willelmum
Notarium de Portaria, Arnaldum
Porterium, Petrum
Lissaco, Ramundum de
Vendinis, Willelmum de

Borrellum, Bernardum Ramundum
Garinum, Ramundum
Galhaco, Poncium de
Vendinis, Bernardum de
God, Ramundum
Robertum, Willelmum ⟩

10.

Insula, Ramundum de
Amereo, Ramundum de
Olerium, Willelmum
Cruce, Ramundum de
Fivelerium, Willelmum Petrum
Magistrum, Poncium
Stephanum, Poncium

Atadil, Bernardum
Progetum, Willelmum
Galhaco, Johannem de
Vendinis, Ramundum de
Samatano, Geraldum de
Maynatam, Poncium
Sancium, Arnaldum ⟩

11.

Turribus, Guidonem de
Garinum, Bernardum
Atadils, Ramundum Willelmum
Catalanum, Ramundum
Pictavinum, Guillelmum
Azam, Bernardum den

Raynevilla, Arnaldum de
Macellarium, Petrum Johannem
Pictenerium, Gausbertum
Villanova, Poncium de
Altarippa, Bertrandum de
Turribus, Arnaldum de ⟩

12.

Montarzinum, Bernardum
Vasconem, Guillelmum
Rostannum, Arnaldum
Estanherium, Bernardum
Olerium, Willelmum Vasconem
Bastardum, Petrum
Magister, Petrum
Belis, Bernardum

Bitortum, Stephanum
Belis maiorem, Bernardum
Tarcherium, Willelmum
Albiaco, Petrum de
Vendinis, Bartholomeum de
Guotum, Bertrandum
Quimillo, Petrum de
Audoynum, Ramundum ⟩

13.

Ade, Geraldum de
Raditorem, Arnaldum
Tornerium (?), Ramundum
Sancto Dionisio, Azalbertum de
Maynatam, Jacobum
Guod, Petrum Ramundum
Sancto Paulo, Bernardum de
Embrardum

Willemotam, Petrum
Vicecomitem, Bernardum
Fivelerium, Willelmum Petrum
Bovilla, Bertrandum de
Briccio or Baccio, Bernardum de
Briccio or Baccio, Vitalem de
Gausbertum, Petrum
Magistrum, Poncium ⟩⟩

14.

Agenno, Petrum de
Villanova, Ramundum Arnaldum de
Villanova, Arnaldum de
Montarzinum
Pelliparium, Bertrandum
Ulmo, Arnaldum de
Ulmo, Petrum de

Fabrum, Petrum Willelmum
Casanova, Bernardum de
Sancto Paulo, Willelmum de
Faia, Ramundum
Montealbano, Ramundum de
Marquesium, Petrum
Pelissonem, Durandum
Fontana, Ramundum ⟩

15.

Avinione, Benedictum de
Martinum, Tolosanum
Rotbertum, Petrum
Bonetum, Vitalem
Furnerium, Poncium
Baucio, Ramundum de
Boninum, Ramundum
Johanne, Arnaldum de

Ulmo, Petrum Willelmum de
Maranum, Bernardum
Tolozinum, Willelmum
Varenis, Petrum Arnaldum de
Atone, Arnaldum de
Sancto Saturnino, Poncium de
Vauro, Guillelmum Johannem de ⟩⟩

16.

Amelium, Petrum
Furcadam, Ramundum
Vauro, Arnaldum de
Fabrum de Monte Caprario, Petrum
Ferriolum, Ramundum
Brunetum, Guillelmum
Calvetum
Monteesquivo, Petrum de
Forcadam, Guillelmum

Borrellum, Ramundum
Quinto, Petrum de
Podio, Bernardum de
Palheriis, Willelmum de
Cerveriam, Stephanum
Pinu, Arnaldum de
Bonetum, Willelmum
Fabrum, Petrum Ramundum ⟩

17.

Cossaco, Jauffredum de
Jornal, Bernardum
Monteacuto, Bernardum de
Johanne, Arnaldum de
Ulmo, Poncium de
Poncium, Bernardum
Carrigiam, Petrum
Villanova, Ramundum de

Petri, Willelmum
Sancto Stephano, Thomam de
Fabrum, Bernardum
Gardam, Guillelmum
Sancta Natoli, Willelmum de
Ucatorem, Willelmum
Darat, Petrum Ramundum
Fabrum, Poncium Ugonem ⟩

18.

Martinum, Ramundum
Magistrum, Ramundum
Rubeum, Bernardum

Bonetum, Petrum
Galvannum, Bernardum
Mercerium, Johannem

Ganterium, Ramundum Petrum
Textorem, Petrum Arnaldum
Ortolanum, Petrum Ramundum
Estanherium, Ramundum
Olerium, Petrum

Samatano, Arnaldum de
Sequerium, Petrum
Villa, Stephanum de
Suavum, Ramundum
Ferre, Poncium de 〉〉

19.
Prato, Stephanum de
Olierium, Arnaldum
Cavanaco, Ramundum de
Rotbertum, Ramundum
Sutorem, Petrum
Barravum, Petrum
Barravum, Aimericum
Barravum, Rogerium
Barravum, Bernardum

Barravum, Guillelmum
Barravum, Stephanum
Barravum, Bertrandum
Barravum, Arnaldum fratrem
   Petri Arnaldi Barravi
Palatio, Willelmum Petrum de
Varens, Sancium de
Primam, Thomam 〉

20.
Gaitapodium, Willelmum Johannem
Galterium, Arnaldum
Pullerium, Arnaldum
Morlis, Poncium de
Pozano, Ramundum Bernardum de
Pozano, Willelmum de
Bequinum, Willelmum
Guidonem, Ramundum

Sancium, Willelmum
Pozano, Ugonem de
Guilabertum, Bernardum
Palatio, Rogerium de
Cauzitum, Bernardum
Morlis, Johannem de
Baranonum, Berengarium
Tolosa, Petrum Ramundum de 〉

21.
Baranonum, Arnaldum Ramundum
Batalhono, Geraldum de
Mercerium, Guillelmum Bernardum
Barreriam, Petrum
Quimbaillo, Bernardum de
Iudicem, Willelmum Ramundum
Paganum, Arnaldum
Quimbaillo, Arnaldum de

Iudicem, Petrum
Primam, Bernardum
Porta, Stephanum de
Piperum
Barbam, Ramundum
Rubeum, Petrum Ramundum
Segaraina, Arnaldum
Fusterium, Bernardum Ramundum
Siollio, Poncium de 〉

22.
Podio, Vitalem de
Donatum, Ramundum
Cervunerium, Willelmum Poncium
Sancto Stephano, Ramundum de
Benedictum, Willelmum

Gordalencz, Petrum Ramundum de
Olierium, Garsionem
Pictavinum
Pairolerium, Bernardum
Grimam Tozorerium, Johannem

Calvomonte, Petrum de
Becenquis, Willelmum de
Auriolum, Poncium

Sancto Amancio, Bernardum de
Calvetum, Willelmum ⟩

23.

Montetotino, Willelmum de
Sartorem, Philippus
Navarco, Willelmum de
Carias, Bernardum den
Johannem, Poncium
Johannem, Willelmum
Corderium, Vitalem
Claromonte Corderium, Willelmum de

Poncio, Ramundum de
Amelium, Arnaldum Guillelmum
Senterium, Willelmum
Autardum, Vitalem
Vitalem, Arnaldum
Anglada, Vitalem de
Anelerium, Petrum Arnaldum ⟩

24.

Paratico, Ramundum Petrum de
Cruce, Ramundum de
Picapairol, Bernardum
Picapairol, Arnaldum fratrem eius
Fivelerium, Ramundum Bernardum
Guenho or Guinho, Guillelmum
Ovelerium, Petrum Ramundum

Picapairol, Willelmum
Pairolerium, Johannem
Samatano, Bernardum de
Acromonte, Gauterium de
Arnaldum, Geraldum
Deusaiuda
Sancto Romano, Poncium de
Arnaldum, Bertrandum ⟩⟩

25.

Sancto Romano, Petrum Ramundum de
Lerato, Poncium de
Nemore, Bartholomeum de
Samara, Guillelmum de
Talhaferrum, Petrum
Arnaldum, Estultum
Sancto Romano, Petrum Willelmum de
Talhafer, Guillelmum

Barravum, Durandum
Jacobum, Petrum
Agenno, Vitalem de
Barravum, Willelmum
Geraldi Petri, Bernardum
  Ramundum
Signaronum, Petrum Willel-
  mum ⟩⟩

26.

Durandum, Eleazarum
Rayna maiorem, Willelmum de
Figareda, Bernardum de
Arsivum, Vitalem
Pelliparium, Vitalem
Gaitapodium, Philippum
Ponte, Bernardum Petrum de
Laurentium, Ramundum

Engoleune, Ramundum de
Fabrum, Petrum Johannem
Rotberti, Willelmum
Garaudum, Willelmum
Lerato, Vitalem de
Dalbs, Ramundum de
Manso, Vitalem de ⟩

27.

Sancto Barcio, Petrum de
Mescalqum, Johannem
Andura, Ugonem de
Petricola, Petrum
Altaraco, Willelmum de
Danoilh, Willelmum
Fulhadam, Ugonem
Barravum, Vitalem

Rayna iuvenem, Willelmum de
Pairas, Arnaldum de
Malhorguis, Ramundum de
Manso, Willelmum de
Sauzeto, Ramundum de
Causaubico, Ramundum de
Sancto Romano, Bernardum Ramun-
　dum de 〉

28.

Acromonte, Arnaldum de
Ponte, Petrum de
Lerato, Bernardum de
Sancto Martino, Bernardum de
Bladerium, Willelmum
Trunnum, Ramundum
Asitanum, Petrum
Feltrerium, Petrum

Grandis, Willelmum
Bonuspuer, Willelmum
Paitesio, Ademarum de
Romerium, Bernardum
Vaqueriis, Ramundum de
Azam, Guillelmum den
Gaudia, Petrum de
Manso, Sancium de 〉

29.

Carcassona, Bartolomeum de
Ponte, Petrum Geraldum de
Fabrum Burgensem, Willelmum
Lambertum, Bertrandum
Leonem, Geraldum
Progetum, Willelmum Ramundum
Guidonem, Arnaldum

Facit Sanguinem, Stephanum
Ponte, Arnaldum de
Mescalqum, Poncium
Caramanno, Willelmum de
Nepotem, Bernardum
Castronovo, Willelmum de 〉〉

30.

Furnerium Mercerium, Petrum
Ferrandum, Petrum
Grandis, Bernardum
Figareda, Petrum de
Mercerium, Geraldum
Mercerium, Ademarum
Verneto, Willelmum de
Castronovo, Ramundum de

Castronovo, Peter de
Villanova, Jordanum de
Villanova, Bertrandum de
Quinto, Guillelmum de
Roaxio, Ugonem de
Roaxio, Willelmum de
Roaxio, Grivum de 〉

31.

Roaxio, Ugonem de
Roaxio, Rogerium de
Roaxio, Bertrandum de
Roaxio, Stephanum de
Roaxio, Petrum de

Barravum, Helyas
Gamevilla, Poncium de
Vasconem, Willelmum
Notarium, Petrum Ramundum
Melle Verneta, Bernardum de

Montebruno, Petrum de
Leus, Willelmum de

32.

Escafrenum, Ugonem
Macellarium, Petrum Vitalem
Nemore Mediano, Arnaldum de
Monte Aygone, Bernardum de
Gazarniam, Bernardum
Gazarniam, Arnaldum
Hyspanollum Monetarium
Golmarium, Arnaldum

33.

Brantalono, Petrum de
Albegesio, Bernardum de
Paratorem, Bernardum
Cedacerium, Petrum
Anhelerium Turnerium, Willelmum
Paratorem, Petrum
Socorrium, Bernardum
Afiaco, Petrum de
Ganterium, Isarnum

34.

Altarippa, Bernardum Vitalem de
Rostannum, Ramundum
Rogerium, Odonem
Vitalem, Willelmum
Furnerium, Willelmum
Berengarium, Willelmum
Cruce, Arnaldum de
Sutorem, Willelmum Poncium

35.

Curia, Ramundum de
Arcmanno, Bartholomeum de
Pancosserium, Ramundum
Arcmannum, Geraldum
Stephanum, Petrum
Magistrum, Vitalem
Augerium, Willelmum
Turnerium, Willelmum
Sartorem, Petrum Ramundum
Pelliparium, Adam

Savarto, Petrum Willelmum de
Almoravium, Poncium ⟩⟩

Raditorem, Sancium
Trunnum, Arnaldum Willelmum
Figueriam, Bernardum
Gauterium, Petrum
Franciscum, Bernardum
Talhaferrum
Bonumhominem, Petrum
Castellano, Petrum de ⟩

Paratorem, Guillelmum
Salvitate, Petrum de
Onda, Arnaldum
Castris, Bernardum de
Pradella, Guillelmum de
Fabrum, Ramundum
Sancto Amancio, Petrum de
Geraldum, Poncium
Serra, Vitalem de ⟩

Bladerium, Bertrandum
Gaudium Hereis, Arnaldum
Penchererium, Willelmum
Balsanum, Bertrandum
Vesceriis, Geraldum de
Carbonellum, Bernardum
Pleissaco, Arnaldum de
Germanum, Arnaldum
Olerium, Thomam ⟩⟩

Romanum, Willelmum
Sancium, Jordanum
Leone, Arnaldum de
Turribus, Arnaldum de
Pebrellum, Arnaldum
Avinione, Petrum de
Deyde, Petrum
Bonetum, Ramundum
Sancto Barcio, Durandum de⟩

36.

Podiosiurano, Bernardum de
Sancto Barcio, Arnaldum Willel-
mum de
Molinum, Arnaldum
Laurentium, Willelmum
Castella, Willelmum de
Castaneto, Bernardum de
Serra, Willelmum de

Fabrum de Altarippa, Willelmum
Mercatorem, Willelmum Petrum
Trageto, Arnaldum de
Planis, Arnaldum de Ortolanum,
Petrum Ramundum
Paganum de Albata, Arnaldum
Junquerium, Willelmum
Cambiatorem, Petrum Arnaldum ⟩

37.

Agulherium, Bartholomeum
Bozigas, Petrum de
Samata, Bernardum de
Cortesium, Willelmum
Gauderiis, Ramundum de
Trageto, Bernardum de
Iustarete, Willelmum de
Totencis, Ramundum de

Fabrum de Altarippa, Petrum
Montelauro, Willelmum Petrum de
Planha, Willelmum de
Montelauro, Petrum Ramundum de
Noerio, Odonem de
Garsionem, Bernardum den
Paratorem, Jacobum ⟩

38.

Moltonem, Arnaldum
Trageto iuvenem, Bernardum de
Macellarium, Gitbertum
Sutorem, Poncium Stephanum
Grandis Paratorem, Bernardum
Sancto Romano, Aimericum de
Capelerium, Petrum Vitalem

Cunnofaverio, Petrum Arnaldum de
Floissum, Bernardum
Tozorerium, Bernardum Ramundum
Vasconem, Willelmum
Tolosa, Bernardum Ramundum de
Devezia, Vitalem de
Auriaco, Petrum Bernardum de ⟩

39.

Caulerium, Bernardum
Sartorem, Philippum
Pairanis, Poncium de
Oliverium, Willelmum
Borrello, Petrum de
Appamiarum, Martinum
Durandum, Willelmum
Britonum, Arnaldum

Hospitali, Dominicum de
Sausinum, Willelmum
Garaud, Ramundum
Pelliparium, Arnaldum
Raynaldum, Ramundum
Canavesio, Johannem de
Castaneta, Petrum de
Fuxo, Willelmum de ⟩

40.

Sancto Remedio, Willelmum Pet-
rum de
Fabrum de Altarippa, Ramundum
Sancto Paulo, Ramundum de
Morlencs, Petrum de

Moltonem, Petrum
Maxellam, Bernardum
Trobatum Agulerium, Petrum
Massonerium, Poncium
Paganum, Petrum

Cosinerium, Ramundum
Paratorem, Arnaldum Amelium
Vilaudran, Bernardum de

41.

Vasconem, Willelmum Petrum
Arquerium, Ramundum
Bartelam, Vitalem
Sutorem, Petrum Bernardum
Rotbertum, Estultum
Rainerium, Ramundum
Pictorem, Ugonem
Jordanum, Petrum Stephanum
Bonetum, Willelmum

42.

Montelanderio, Johannem de
Podiolaurentio, Ramundum de
Villafranca, Poncium de
Garrigiis, Ramundum de
Salomonem, Bernardum
Loricarium, Ramundum
Aurevez, Ramundum de
Astre, Aimericum
Gausbertum, Ramundum

43.

Pegulano, Arnaldum Petrum de
Clavelerium, Poncium Stephanum
Amelio, Petrum de
Serris, Arnaldum de
Berengarium, Willelmum
Tornerium, Durandum
Equum, Ramundum
Pinu, Arnaldum de
Pelherium, Petrum
Celerium, Aimericum

44.

Johannem, Arnaldum
Costantium, Stephanum
Pegulano, Petrum de
Mancium *or* Vinacium, Ramundum
Mirapisce, Stephanum de
Sartorem, Thomam

Agulerium, Ramundum
Garaud, Vitalem
Sutorem, Jacobum ⟩⟩

Vitalem, Bernardum
Devezia, Petrum de
Rotbertum, Petrum
Mercerium, Arnaldum
Estampis, Petrum de
Gastonem, Willelmum
Pictorem, Willelmum Ato
Aimericum, Willelmum Poncium
Rupibus, Willelmum de ⟩⟩

Raynerium
Ulmo, Petrum de
Cascavelerium, Bernardum
Valle, Arnaldum de
Stephanum, Petrum
Basterium, Poncium
Rivis, Ramundum de
Monjoire, Poncium de ⟩⟩

Avinione, Petrum Ramundum de
Castilhono, Arnaldum de
Dominicum, Bernardum
Urit canem, Willelmum
Serris, Willelmum de
Rupibus, Bernardum de
Furgonem, Ramundum
Goironis, Ramundum de
Umbertum, Petrum ⟩

Paratorem, Bernardum
Ioculatorem, Bernardum
Magistrum, Ramundum
Bosquetum, Petrum Ramundum
Calvetum, Ugonem
Berardum, Ramundum

Serris, Bernardum de
Sartorem, Ramundum Bernardum
Fogacerium, Willelmum

Bosquetum, Willelmum
Sancto Anhano, Geraldum de
Aurevez, Poncium de 〉

45.

Avinione, Bernardum de
Guidonem, Bernardum
Pelegrinum
Godafre, Rotbertum
Esquivum, Petrum
Serralher, Ramundum
Rivis Asterium, Ramundum de
Logai, Petrum de
Viridario, Petrum de

Vaqueriis, Geraldum de
Delbosc, Ramundum
Mirabello, Petrum de
Dalbi, Willelmum
Andream, Ramundum
Clavelerium, Ramundum
Vasconem, Ramundum
Ruppe, Poncium de
Signarium, Peregrinum 〉

46.

Escalquencs, Bertrandum de
Garrigiis, Bertrandum de
Carabordam, Stephanum
Turre, Willelmum de
Carabordam, Bernardum
Orto, Willelmum de
Astronem, Willelmum Poncium
Pilistortum, Willelmum Petrum
Sutorem, Petrum

Pascal, Willelmum
Montealbano, Willelmum de
Martinum, Poncium
Vasconem, Willelmum Petrum
Rogerium, Ramundum
Portallo, Petrum de
Ruffum, Ermengavum
Portallo, Tholomeum de 〉

47.

Montealbano, Bernardum de
Boumero, Arnaldum Ramundum
Fromatgerium, Willelmum
Carabordam, Berengarium
Carrugerium, Willelmum
Basterium, Ramundum
Brisenerium, Petrum
Ramundum, Vitalem
Gausbertum, Bernardum

Barbam, Willelmum
Fortonem, Dominicum
Furnerium, Willelmum
Basterium iuvenem, Ramundum
Carrariam, Ramundum
Busquetum, Ramundum
Willemota
Tolosa
Nava, Ramundum de 〉〉

48.

Gotvesio, Poncium de
Berrianum, Petrum Bernardum
Avinione, Willelmum de
Martinum, Petrum
Celerium, Johannem
Brisonerium, Ramundum
Esquivatum, Petrum

Montealba, Ramundum de
Orto, Petrum Willelmum de
Basterium, Poncium
Sutorem, Geraldum
Jaquam, Petrum
Adam, Arnaldum
Calvetum, Petrum

Vitalem, Ramundum Geraldum
Sobaccum, Ramundum

49.

Carrugerium, Bernardum
Vernol, Dominicum de
Raditorem, Bernardum
Goderiam, Willelmum
Faiam, Cerninum de
Roquis, Bernardum de
Poncium, Willelmum
Sutorem, Geraldum
Faiam, Willelmum de
Terrenum, Bernardum

50.

Furnerium, Ramundum
Fabrum, Geraldum
Arquerium, Bernardum
Belcastel, Bernardum de
Textorem, Bernardum
Claromonte, Arnaldum de
Magistrum, Arnaldum
Geraldum, Arnaldum
Aldoynum, Bernardum

51.

Bertrandum, Petrum
Prulheco, Petrum de
Gausbertum, Petrum
Johannem, Willelmum
Villalonga, Poncium de
Miramonte, Ramundum de
Carabordam, Mattheum
Guilabertum, Petrum
Sancto Martino, Willelmum de

52.

Maurandum iuvenem
Escalquencs, Petrum Ramundum de
Montanhagol, Willelmum de
Turre, Bertrandum de
Maurandum, Aldricum
Caturcio, Gausbertum de
Sancto Cezerto, Ramundum de

Sancto Felicio, Ramundum de
Carrugerium, Poncium 〉〉

Deide, Stephanum
Vauro, Willelmum de
Godvesio, Arnaldum de
Porta, Petrum de
Celerium, Poncium
Arcambaldum, Petrum
Agulerii, Bernardum
Bosquetum, Nicholas
Brugueria, Ramundum de
Bosquetum, Willelmum 〉

Marquennio, Bernardum de
Roais, Petrum de
Vilana, Petrum de
Curtasolam, Stephanum
Escalquencis, Arnaldum de
Ruffum, Ramundum
Astronem, Poncium
Maurandum, Bonumpuerum
Turre, Vasconem de 〉〉

Guiscardum, Johannem
Embrinum, Petrum
Turre, Johannem de
Maurandum, Petrum
Sancto Genesio, Ramundum de
Castronovo, Johannem de
Arnaldum, Poncium
Curtasoleam, Johannem 〉

Caturcio, Bernardum de
Gras, Arnaldum Poncium
Poncium, Bernardum
Gavalde, Poncium
Galhaco, Arnaldum de
Marcillo, Ramundum de
Cadullo, Stephanum de
Sancto Cezerto, Arnaldum de 〉〉

53.

Inter Ambabus Aquis, Arnaldum de
Gasca, Arnaldum de
Baretges, Willelmum de
Calcaterram, Terrenum
Terrasona, Petrum de
Anceanis, Brunonem de
Ecclesia, Johannem de
Vicarium, Bernardum
Vicarium, Johannem

Poncium, Petrum
Filiis, Bernardum de
Campis, Willelmum
Galhaco, Bernardum de
Benedictum, Poncium
Sutorem, Ramundum
Benedictum maiorem, Poncium
Bigorram, Petrum
Villalonga, Ugonem de ⟩

54.

Montecitario, Willelmum de
Vasconem, Willelmum
Sancto Cezerto, Poncium de
Fabrum, Bernardum
Tolosa de Blanhaco, Poncium de
Mercerium, Bonumpuerum
Sancto Lionis, Petrum Ramundum
    de
Textorem, Petrum Willelmum

Bertinium *or* Beravium, Bernardum
Raditorem, Petrum Willelmum
Moscana, Arnaldum de
Adam, Willelmum
Agulerium, Johannem
Brunum, Bernardum
Petrum, Arnaldum
Gitbertum, Bernardum ⟩⟩

55.

Bernardum, Dominicum
Furnerium, Petrum
Bernardum, Poncium
Cate, Petrum
Maurandum, Bertrandum
Montanhagol, Geraldum de
Geraldum, Bernardum
Chivum, Martinum
Inter Ambabus Aquis, Bernardum
    de

Villalonga, Poncium de
Montaboleto, Bernardum de
Penchererium, Ramundum
Ferran, Ramundum
Maurandum, Bonumpuerum
Claustro, Petrum Willelmum de
Astronem, Johannem
Sobaccum, Petrum
Magistrum, Poncium ⟩

56.

Bitortum, Jacobum Petrum
Gras, Vitalem
Capelerium, Willelmum
Lause, Willelmum de
Magistrum, Jacobum
Gauffredum, Bernardum
Notarium, Willelmum
Fabrum, Tos
Maurinum, Willelmum
Pellicerium, Johannem

Fabrum, Bonetum
Tolosa, Petrum Ramundum de
Albigesio, Petrum de
Trencateule, Ramundum
Porta, Ramundum de
Martinum, Willelmum
Recorde, Petrum
Ribas, Willelmum de
Caviola, Arnaldum ⟩

57.
Gausbertum, Ramundum
Nicol, Petrum
Caturcio, Durandum de
Ursetum, Willelmum
Mascaronum, Petrum
Colerium, Stephanum
Baines, Vitalem de
Ortolanum, Petrum
Frontonnio, Bernardum de

Matfre, Petrum
Villanova, Bernardum de
Saugueda, Bernardum de
Calsada, Arnaldum de
Pigassam, Geraldum
Fabrum, Vitalem
Fontanis, Bernardum de
Bertrandum, Johannem
Geraldum, Willelmum ⟩

58.
Daguz, Bernardum
Villamuro, Bernardum de
Vasconem, Willelmum
Navarrum, Petrum
Tolosanum, Petrum
Stephanum, Willelmum
Porta, Petrum de
Cristianum, Petrum
Espelitum, Petrum
Johannem, Ramundum

Fabrum de Castro Maurono,
    Ramundum
Espelitum, Bernardum
Centullum, Sancium
Arnaldum, Johannem
Graricum *or* Grarericum, Arnaldum
Fabrum, Vitalem
Castronovo, Stephanum de
Borrellum, Ramundum ⟩

59.
Garsiam, Petrum
Fabrum, Arnaldum
Aventurerium, Arnaldum
Peiro, Willelmum del
Vidiatum, Nicholas
Ulmis, Stephanum de
Fabrum, Johannem
Bladerium, Poncium
Borrellum, Willelmum
Fabrum, Bernardum

Gleisolis, Bertrandum de
Judicem, Bernardum
Gasquetum, Ramundum
Stephanum, Petrum
Seguinum, Arnaldum
Rotles, Ramundum
Ramundum, Arnaldum
Porta, Bertrandum de
Sutorem, Johannem
Sayssum, Willelmum ⟩

60.
Teulerium, Petrum Ramundum
Sutorem, Johannem
Sutorem, Arnaldum
Benas, Bernardum de
Capelerium, Magistrum Ramundum
Grillum, Isarnum
Arnaldum, Petrum
Leuzino, Willelmum Ramundum de
Fabrum, Poncium

Iordanum, Johannem
Julianum
Arnaldum, Poncium
Montealbano, Geraldum de
Ramundum, Galterium
Bertrandum, Ramundum
Garrigia, Willelmum Ramundum de
Berengarium, Arnaldum ⟩

61.

Cossas, Ramundum de
Cambiatorem, Jacobum
Martellum, Arnaldum
Carabordam, Bernardum
Turre, Arnaldum de
Berengarium, Ramundum
Cossas, Petrum de
Novilla, Bertrandum de
Avinione, Bernardum de

Cossas, Bernardum de
Iulianum, Arnaldum
Senheriam, Stephanum
Iulianum, Stephanum
Martellum, Ramundum Petrum
Cambiatorem, Ramundum Willelmum
Marchum
Bernardum, Arnaldum
Rotondum, Willelmum ⟩

62.

Bequinum, Petrum
Sutorem, Cerninum
Sutorem, Bernardum
Pelliparium, Willelmum Ugonem
Sancto Bertrando, Ramundum de
Pictavinum, Petrum
Sutorem, Cerninum

Bequinum, Willelmum
Aissada, Cerninum
Laurentium, Petrum
Capitedenario, Ramundum de
Carabordas
Vadigia, Bertrandum de
Maurandum de Pulchropodio
Carabordam, Aldricum ⟩

63.

Bonetum, Arnaldum
Cauzitum
Marcillo, Bernardum de
Fabrum, Bernardum
Rossellum, Willelmum
Nemore, Petrum de
Ruffum, Arnaldum
Willelmum, Petrum
Sancto Juliano, Bernardum de
Geraldum, Petrum

Pinolibus, Petrum de
Davinum
Gaianis, Petrum de
Corna, Ramundum
Vestitum, Ramundum
Ferratum, Petrum
Seralherium, Willelmum
Sancto Juliano, Petrum Ramundum de
Poncium, Ramundum
Bertrandum, Ramundum ⟩

64.

Orto, Vitalem de
Amalvinum, Willelmum
Vitalem, Petrum
Lerato, Sancium de
Frontonnio, Ramundum de
Nepotem, Bernardum
Fabrum, Petrum
Rotundum, Vitalem
Maurellum, Willelmum
Sairaco, Ramundum de

Furnerium, Ramundum
Pesair, Ramundum
Isambardum, Arnaldum
Faciem Fabris, Ramundum
   Bernardum
Mancipium, Arnaldum
Sancium, Arnaldum
Fumello, Vitalem de
Catainelator, Bernardum ⟩

65.

Capellum, Poncium	God, Arnaldum
Medicum, Bernardum	Gasc, Willelmum
Durando, Willelmum de	Proaud, Petrum de
Garsionem, Ramundum	Vinarola, Bernardum
Ebraudum, Bernardum	Calvetum
Fumello, Arnaldum de	Buzeto, Johannem de
Lerato, Willelmum de	Gasc, Arnaldum
Baronum, Willelmum	Vasconem, Julianum
Capellum, Poncium	Floribus, Willelmum de ⟩
Fabrum, Bernardum	

66.

Magistrum, Bernardum	Fumello, Arnaldum de
Furnerium, Willelmum	Petrum, Willelmum
Buzeto, Bernardum de	Fontibus, Bernardum de
Vasconem, Poncium	Codonherium, Ramundum
Barbadellum, Willelmum	Caucidiis, Arnaldum de
Sancto Subrano, Stephanum de	Galterium, Vitalem
Ruffum, Bernardum	Fenolheto, Phylippum de
Marcafava, Willelmum de	Blazinum, Petrum Vitalem ⟩
Hyspania, Phylippum de	

67.

Vasconem, Willelmum	Surdum, Willelmum
Dardum, Willelmum	Palmata, Willelmum
Engilbertum, Willelmum	Clericum, Petrum
Brunum, Egydium	Puer, Petrum
Escafrenum	Marcillo, Geraldum de
Sancium, Willelmum	Sutorem, Symonem
Fumello, Ramundum de	Canaterium, Ramundum
Chivum, Ramundum	Pabia, Bernardum de
Prinhaco, Poncium de	Miramonte, Arnaldum de ⟩⟩

68.

Engilbertum	Roquis, Andream de
Felgar, Bernardum de	Loba, Willelmum
Furno, Willelmum de	Fontanas, Bernardum
Terreno, Arnaldum de	Prinhaco, Willelmum Ato de
Blazinum, Thomam	Caradefaure, Arnaldum Ramundum
Montebruno, Petrum de	Sancto Subrano, Poncium de
Sederium, Arnaldum	Caradefaure, Bernardum
Bigard, Thomam de	Laurens, Willelmum de ⟩⟩
Dartigas, Bernardum	

69.

Massos, Poncium de
Olerium, Petrum Vitalem
Vitalem, Willelmum
Garaud, Bernardum
Ferrerium, Petrum

Notarium, Poncium Stephanum
Davinum, Willelmum
Cansas, Arnaldum Ramundum de
Marsano, Ramundum de ⟩

Post isto autem de voluntate et mandato speciali domini nostri Ramundi comitis Tolosani in presentia nostra promittere fecimus et jurare / domino regi Francorum universitatem et singulos de universitate civitatis et suburbii Tolose a .xv. annis et supra sub predictis verbis et forma predicta. Hec autem omnia supradicta facta fuerunt posita et concessa in presentia Johannis clerici et Oddardi de Vileriis qui a domino rege Francorum fue-/runt ad capienda predicta juramenta a predictis consulibus et aliis universis et singulis specialiter deputati. In quorum omnium testimonio presentem paginam nos consules urbis Tolose et suburbii sigillo nostri munimine fecimus roborari. Actum est in vigilia beati Mathie. regnante eodem / Lodovico Francorum rege. eodem domino Ramundo comite Tolose. Ramundo episcopo. anno domini .m. cc. xl. secundo.

Matthias' day being February 24, the date is 23 February 1243.

Appendix Four

Chaptermen and Consuls

Most of the lists up to 1229 printed here have been previously published either by Limouzin-Lamothe, *La commune de Toulouse et les sources de son histoire*, pp. 243-256, or in my *Liberty and Political Power*, pp. 173-188, I have nevertheless thought it useful to publish the lists of "bonihomines," "capitularii" (including the "iudices" and "advocati" of the count of Toulouse's old court) and "consules" from the earliest date ca. 1120 because it is advantageous to have them all in one place and because there are occasional additions to old lists. Largely new lists from 1229 to 1280 inclusive are also included and cease at that date because Germain de la Faille's *Annales de la ville de Toulouse depuis la réunion de la comté de Toulouse à la couronne* of 1687-1701 begins its lists then. Although imperfect, La Faille's are useful bases for further research. Readers may note that, in general, the first half of the group listed usually sat for the City and the second half for the Bourg. On the other hand, because partial and disordered lists cause many exceptions, no sure reliance can be placed on the order of the names unless further evidence is adduced. Lastly, many lists are incomplete. Each list is preceded by the archival source or sources. TAM, AA 1 and AA 2 have been published in Limouzin-Lamothe in *La commune de Toulouse*. Similar official collections are found at Paris, PAN, JJ 21 and Vienna, MS lat. 2210* and both are here listed (by folios). In addition, occasional other documents are listed. Lastly, a few acts contained in AA 1 and Vienna lack consular lists, for example, AA 1 37 and Vienna, fols. 49-50 (March 1205).

The books publishing lists of consuls prior to his *La commune de Toulouse* were listed by Limouzin-Lamothe on pp. 241-42. A useful concordance of the documents in TAM, AA 1 and AA 2, as published in Limouzin-Lamothe and PAN, JJ 21, was published by Lifshitz, "Le serment de fidélité de la ville de Toulouse (1203): Quelques notes sur un texte et sa transmission," *Annales du Midi* 97 (1985) 433.

For the purpose of brevity some of the repetitious archival references are omitted and some are abbreviated.

References to TAM, AA 2, for which there are copies in TAM, AA 1, have been omitted, but are signaled in Limouzin-Lamothe's edition of the cartularies of the City and Bourg in *La commune de Toulouse*.

The abbreviations are

TAM, AA 1 = AA 1
Vienna, MS lat. 2210* = Vienna

Somewhere in the eleven-nineties the annual renewal of the consulate was systematized and, with variations during the early twelve-thirties, continued throughout the long period treated in this book. Exceptions apart, the date of the installation of the new chapter or consulate followed the beginning of the year which was, in this region, the Annunciation of the Virgin on March 25 or, starting in the eleven-nineties or perhaps a trifle before, the first of April, a date adopted or introduced by the public notariate of Toulouse. This rigidity has advantages. If, for example, a date of December 1256 is given in an extant consular list, this refers to the consular term of 1256-1257, a term for which, in reality, a list has not yet been found.

CA. 1120: the "probihomines de Tolosa et burgo" in AA 1 14 and Vienna, fols. 33-34v.

William Petrus	Bellotus Turrensis
Vital Andraldus	Bernard Arnaldus
Bruno Signarius	Bruno Gali
Pons de Garrigi[i]s	Calvetus
Raymond Alcotonarius	Stephanus
Pons de Villanova	Bruno de Tabula
Hugh de Perticis	Calvetus, Bruno's brother

1121-1130: Daurade 145, Catel, *Mémoires de l'histoire du Languedoc*, p. 156, and *Gallia Christiana* 13: Instr. No. 19, listing witnesses to an act of Count Alphonse of Toulouse.

Odon (Dodon) de Caumonte	Peter, his son
Stephen Caraborda	Augerius
Belengarius	Arnold Geraldus
Bonmacip Maurannus	Bernard de Sancto Martino
Bernard Raymond Baptizatus	Pilistortus and his brothers
Arnold William de Claustro	Bernard Raimundus
Radulfus "vicarius"	Peter Guillelmus
Arnold Guilabertus	

MAY 1130: Toulousan members of the count's court in *HGL* 5: No. 513, from a lost cartulary of Moissac.

Stephen Carabolla (Caraborda)	Senioretus
Raymond Baptizati	Ademar Carabolla (Caraborda)
Arnold Guilaberti	Peter Vitalis

NOVEMBER 1141: "bonihomines" in AA 1 1, JJ 21, fols. 1-3 and Vienna, fols. 1-2.

Arnold Gilaberti
Arnold Geraldi
Bernard Segnerelli
Peter Alcotonarii
Augerius Botlerius
Bastard Descalquensis
Pilistortus
Adalbertus
Peter Willelmi
William de Brugariis

Stephen Caraborda
Ademar Caraborda
Bonmacip Mauranni
Peter Vitalis
Hugh Comtorius
Pons de Soreda
Bernard Raymond Baptizatus
Bernard Raymond Maleti
Bertrand de Tauro

JULY 1147: "bonihomines" in AA 1 2, JJ 21, fols. 3-4 and Vienna, fols. 2-2v.

Stephen Caraborda
G-William Raimundi
Bonmacip Mauranni
Peter Guido
Tosetus

Pons de Soreda
Pons de Villanova
Peter de Roais
G-William de Brugariis
Curvus de Turribus

DECEMBER 1148: "bonihomines" in AA 1 28 and Vienna, fols. 44v-45v.

Peter Caraborda
Vital Carbonelli

Adalbert de Villanova
Raymond Durandi
Stephen de Perticis

OCTOBER 1150: "bonihomines" in AA 1 34, JJ 21, fols. 64-65 and Vienna, fols. 7-7v

Hugh Comtorus
Arnold Signarius
Bernard Sancti Romani

Brus de Tabula
Peter Arnaldi
Vizianus Frenarius

1152: "capitularii" in AA 1 4 and 5, JJ 21, fols. 7-10 and Vienna, fols. 2v-6

Pons de Villanova
G-William de Brugariis
Senoretus de Ponte
Peter Gui
Raymond Guilelmi
Bernard Mandadarius

Peter de Roais "judex"
Maurinus "judex"
Pons de Soreda "iudex"
Arnold Petri "judex"
William Rainaldi "advocatus"
Arnold Signarius "advocatus"

APRIL 1158: "capitularii" in JJ 19, fols. 40v-41v.

Peter Willelmus
Peter de Roais

Bernard Adalbertus

1163 OR 1164: "capitularii" in Francisque Duchesne, *Historiae Francorum Scriptores* 4: 714, No. 415, dated by Jacques Flach, *Les origines de l'ancienne France* 4: 617, note 1.

Raymond Capiscolis   Stephen minister of Saint-Pierre-
G-William de Sancto Johanne   des-Cuisines
John Signarius

The "capiscolis" mentioned here is not the head of the cathedral school. As remarked in Saint-Étienne 227 (36 DA 1 5) (March 1144 or 1145) and ibid. (36 DA 1 1), one of a group of acts tied together (January 1153), the canon and "capiscolis" of the time at the cathedral was named William. On the other hand, there was a Raymond bearing this title at the basilica of Saint-Sernin who, according to documents contained in Douais, *Cartulaire de Saint-Sernin*, p. xlix, was heard of until around 1150 and who is not known to have been replaced until 1164 by a William. The minister or prior of Saint-Pierre-des-Cuisines was Stephen de Montevaldrano as is seen in Grandselve 58, Roll I verso ii (January 1169). Although I do not wish here to go into the history of the council of the "capitularii" which is discussed in my *Liberty and Political Power*, pp. 39-40 and 56-58, it is worth noting that among the ambassadors to the king of France mentioned in the letter published by Duchesne were two councilors, Peter de Roais and William Raimundi. A subsequent letter from Toulouse to the king published by the same editor, 720, no. 432, mentions another embassy, this one composed of

CITY	BOURG
Peter de Roais	William Raimundi, and his
Bernard Arnold de Ponte	brother Peter Raimundi
----------	Bernard Mandatarius

The letter does not describe them as "capitularii."

NOVEMBER 1164: "capitularii" in AA 1 3, JJ 21, fols. 10-11v and Vienna, fols. 6-7.

Pons de Villanova "et vicarius"   Peter de Libraco
Raymond Arnold de Bovilla   Raymond de Prignaco
William Duranni   Bernard Adalberti "advocatus"
Segneronus de Ponte   William Rodberti "advocatus"

MARCH 1164 OR 1165: "capitularii" in Saint-Sernin 688 (21 79 6), third act of tied bundle published in my *Liberty and Political Power*, p. 196.

Bernard Adalbertus   William Rotberti
Martin Girmundi   Stephanus
Amelius Engilvini

Girmundi was called Germon in Grandselve 58, Roll I recto viii, and Stephanus was the "scriba" de Populivilla in Malta 4 191.

MARCH 1172 OR 1173: "baiuli de confratria" of the Bourg – an unknown but possibly political organization in Douais, *Cartulaire de Saint-Sernin*, No. 58.

Bernard Adalbertus	William Rufi
Bertrand de Saona	Pons Rufi

MARCH 1175 OR 1176: "capitularii" and "consules" in AA 1 33, JJ 21, fols. 61v-64 and Vienna, fols. 45v-47.

CITY	BOURG
Raymond de Roaxio	Olric Carabordas
Raymond Galinus	Stephen de Montevaldrano
G-William Raymond de Portaria	Peter Rufus
Bernard de Sancto Romano	Arnold Raimundus, son of
Raymond Gaitapodium	Raymond Frenarii
Stephen de Populivilla	Bertrand Raimundus
-----------	Peter Guitardus

BEFORE NOVEMBER 1180: "capitularii" in AA 1 19, JJ 21, fols. 36-39v and Vienna, fols. 24-26.

Raymond Capiscolis	Arnold Raimundus
Bertrand de Roais	G-William Raimundus
Raymond de Faiaco	G-William Pons Astro
Pons de Gamevilla	Peter de Sancto Martino
Raymond de Castronovo	G-William Decanus
Berengar Karolus	"et eorum socii"
Artaldus	

NOVEMBER 1180: "capitularii" in AA 1 19, JJ 21, fols. 36-39v and Vienna, fols. 24-26.

CITY	BOURG
Tosetus de Tolosa	G-William Raimundus
Bernard de Sancto Romano	Pons Guillelmus
Ademar de Ponte	Peter Rufus
Peter de Roais	Bernard Peter de Cossa
David de Roais	Bernard Rufus
G-William de Castronovo	Stephen Carabordas
Raymond Ato de Montibus	Bernard Carabordas
Arnold de Villanova	Peter Raymond Descalquencs
Bertrand de Montibus	Bertrand Raimundus

Heliazar

Bertrand Ato [de Tolosa]

Peter Guitardus

Peter Bertrand de Tauro

Gerald de Caturcio

AFTER NOVEMBER 1180: "capitularii" in ibid.

Peter de Sancto Romano

Arnaldus Oto

Bernard Arnaldus

Raymond Guilabertus

Berengar de Sancto Roman

Gerald Petrus

Peter Bernard de Rivis

Peter, son of Bernard de Sancto
    Barcio

Pons William de Sancto Romano

William de Gardogio

Raymond Arnold de Morlis

Raymond Bonetus

Peter de Blanag

William Hugh Rainaldus

Stephen Barbarossa

William de Poza

William Arnold "macellarius"

Hugh Macellarius

Raymond William Boaterius

Peter Faber

Raymond Arnold Mainada

MAY–AUGUST 1181: "capitularii" in Vienna, fols. 7v-8v (May 1181), published in my *Liberty and Poltical Power*, pp. 196-197, and AA 1 6, JJ 21, fols. 11v-14v and Vienna, fols. 22-23v (August 1181).

CITY

Raymond Capiscolis

Arnold de Roais

Hugh de Roais

Peter de Sancto Romano

Raymond de Castronovo

Pons de Villanova

Bernard Arnaldus

Pons de Gamevilla

Vital Barravus

BOURG

Olric Carabordas

Peter Raimundus

Stephen de Montevalrano

Arnold Rufus

Arnold Raimundus "frenerius"

John Signarius

Raymond Bezantus

Pons Umbertus

Raymond Garsias

Raymond Rotbertus,

and the act also mentions two members "de concilio":

Toset de Tolosa

William Raimundi

JANUARY–MAY 1184: "capitularii" in AA 1 71, JJ 21, fols. 71-72v and Vienna, fols. 92-93 (January) and AA 1 15, JJ 21, fols. 24v-36 and Vienna, fols. 73v-74.

CITY

Toset de Tolosa

Bernard de Sancto Barcio

BOURG

Peter Raimundi

Bernard Peter de Cossa

Peter de Sancto Romano
Bernard Petrus
Bernard Raymond Barravus
Arnold William Rainaldus
Pons de Gamevilla
Jordan de Villanova
Raymond de Faiaco
Raymond Galinus

Raymond Willelmi
Pons Umbertus
Peter Maurandus
Abrinus
Arnold Rufus
Bertrand Raimundi
Peter Bertrand de Tauro
Peter Bertrand de Villanova
Raymond Gauterius
William Pons de Prinag

SEPTEMBER 1186: "capitularii" in Emile Léonard, *Catalogue des actes de Raimond V*, No. 122.

Bernard Peter de Cossano
Bernard Raymond Barravus
Peter de Sancto Romano
Ademar de Ponte

Peter Raymond de Surburbio
Bernard Arnold de Ponte
William Caraborda
Bernard de Sancto Barcio
Aimeric de Castronovo

JANUARY–NOVEMBER 1189: "consules" in AA 1 8, JJ 21, fols. 16-18 and Vienna, fols. 8v-9v and AA 1 9, JJ 21, fols. 18-19v and Vienna, fols. 10-11 (both in January), and the vicar's court in Saint-Étienne 227 (26 DA 1 17) (November).

Bertrand de Montibus
Arnold de Villanova
Arnold William Rainaldus
Peter de Marcafaba "judex"
Peter Rogerius "advocatus"
Raymond Galinus

Arnold Rufus
Bernard Peter de Cossa "judex"
Pons Umbertus
G-William Pons Astro
Peter Raymond Descalquencs
Raymond Gerald Vitalis
Raymond Rotbertus "advocatus"

To these may be added the two notables who, together with Bishop Fulcrand, arbitrated the conflict of town and count:

Toset de Tolosa

Aimeric de Castronovo

OCTOBER 1190: "consules" (always called so from now on) in AA 1 31 and Vienna, fols. 34v-35.

Bernard Peter de Cossa
Arnold Rufus
Raymond Geraldus
Peter Raymond Descalquencs
Bernard Rufus

Stephen Caraborda
Arnold William Rainaldus
David de Roais
Bernard de Sancto Barcio

MARCH 1192 OR 1193 – FEBRUARY 1193: AA 1 16, JJ 21, fols. 24-25, Vienna, fols. 15-16, AA 1 20, JJ 21, fols. 39v-42 and Vienna, fols. 13-15 (all in March 1192 or 1913), and AA 1 21, JJ 21, fols. 43-46v and Vienna, fol. 17r (February 1192 or 1193), and Saint-Étienne 227 (26 DA 1 19) (March 1192 or 1193).

Bertrand de Villanova
William de Turre
Peter de Roaxio, called Grivus
Peter Rogerius
Pons William de Sancto Romano
Gerald Arnaldus
Bernard Peter de Ponte, son of
    Peter Arnaldus
Arnold Barravus
William Ato de Sancto Barcio
Arnold William Rainaldus
Raymond Galinus
Hugh de Palacio

Arnold Rufus
Stephen Carabordas
William Bertrandus
Peter Raymond Descalquencs
Raymond Gerald Vitalis
Belengar Raimundus
Raymond Pilificatus
Peter Maurandus
Pons de Prinaco
Arnold Johannes "espazerius"
Raymond Gauterius
Bernard Peter de Cossano

MARCH 1193 OR 1194: consuls of the Bourg in AA 1 32 and Vienna, fols. 35-36v.

Peter de Sancto Martino
William Raimundus de Burgo
Raymond Rotbertus
William Raimundus, son of Peter
    Raimundus
Gerald Esquivatus
Vital de Prinaco

William Raymond Descalquencs
Arnold Raymond, his brother
William Pons Astro
Stephen Carabordas
Gerald de Caturcio
Aimengavus Rufus

JANUARY 1195: AA 1 10, JJ 21, fols. 19v-21v, and Vienna, fols. 30-31, AA 1 11, JJ 21, fols. 21v-23v and Vienna, fols. 31-32, and E 501 (all dated January 1195), the latter act published in my *Liberty and Political Power*, p. 199.

Peter de Roaxio, called Grivus
Peter Rogerius
William de Turre
William de Gamevilla
Raymond Galinus
William Hugh Rainaldus
Peter Raymond de Montetotino
Bernard Raymond Barravus
William Ato de Sancto Barcio
Peter de Sancto Romano
Gerald Arnaldus
Bernard Barravus

Stephen Carabordas
Bernard Peter de Cossano
William Carabordas
William Isarnus
Peter Surdus
Belengar Raimundus
Peter Raymond Descalquencs
Peter Ibrinus
Raymond Gauterius
John Signarius
Raymond Gerald Vitalis

NOVEMBER 1196 – APRIL 1197: AA 1 12, JJ 21, fols. 29v-31v and Vienna, fols. 18-19, and Saint-Sernin 680 (20 72 nn) (all dated November 1196), the latter act published in my *Liberty and Political Power*, pp. 199-202, and AA 1 17, JJ 21, fols. 25-27 and Vienna, fols. 17-18 (April 3 1197).

Raymond de Castronovo	Bernard Carabordas
Jordan de Villanova	G-William Carabordas
Hugh de Roaxio	Stephen Carabordas
Ademar de Ponte	Peter Raymond Descalquencs
William de Gardogio	Arnold Raymond, his brother
Bernard Barravus	Raymond Willelmus
Raymond Ato de Tolosa	Raymond Gauterius
Bernard Raymond Barravus	Raymond Gerald Vitalis
Hugh de Palacio	Gerald Esquivatus
Raymond Gallinus	Belengar Raimundus
Peter de Tolosa	John Signarius
Peter Raimundus "maior"	Aimengavus Rufus

NOVEMBER 1197 – APRIL 1198: AA 1 18, JJ 21, fols. 27-28v and a fragment in Vienna, fol. 16v (November 1197), and Douais, *Cartulaire de Saint-Sernin*, Ap. No. 33 (April 1198).

Arnold de Villanova	Peter de Sancto Martino
Bertrand de Villanova	Raymond Rotbertus
Peter William Pilistortus	William Raymond Descalquencs
Aimeric de Castronovo, his nephew	Vital de Prinhaco
Peter de Roaxio, called Grivus	William Bertrandus
Bernard Raymond de Tolosa	Peter Embrinus
Gerald Arnaldus	William Raimundus, son of
Raymond Bernard Barravus	Peter Raimundus
Pilistortus	Raymond Maurandus
Arnold Guilabertus	Arnold Rufus
William Durannus	William Isarnus
	Oalric Maurandus

DECEMBER 1198 – APRIL 1199: Saint-Étienne 227 (36 DA 1 10) (December 1198), published in my *Liberty and Political Power*, pp. 202-03, and AA 1 22, JJ 21, fols. 46v-51 and Vienna, fols. 37v-39 (all dated 12 April 1199).

Raymond de Castronovo	Peter Raymond Descalquencs
Bernard Raymond Barravus	Gerald Esquivatus
Peter de Tolosa	Pons Caraborda
Arnold de Roaxio	William Caraborda
Peter Sancti Romani	Peter Lambertus
Ato de Montibus	William de Turre

Peter Rogerius "causidicus"
Raymond Durandus
Pons de Villanova
Hugh de Palacio
Bernard Peter de Cossano
Raymond Gerald Vitalis

Peter Maurandus
John Signarius
Raymond Gauterius
Raymond Willelmus, son of
William Raimundus
Berengar Raimundus

MARCH 1200 – MARCH 1201: AA 1 13. JJ 21, fols. 31v-34v and Vienna, fols. 21-22 (all dated March 1200) and AA 1 23, JJ 21, fols. 51-52v and Vienna, fols. 21-22 (all dated March 1201).

Bertrand de Montibus
Raymond de Castronovo
Raymond Arnold de Bovilla *or*
Villanova
Hugh de Roaxio
Bernard Raymond de Tolosa
Raymond Guilabertus
Arnold Odo
John de Sancto Romano
William Ato de Sancto Barcio
Arnold Barravus
Bertrand Ato
Hugh de Palacio

William Raymond de Burgo
Stephen Caraborda
Bernard Caraborda
Carbonellus
William Raimundus son of
Peter Raimundus
Peter Embrinus
"Magister" Bernardus
Arnold Raymond Descalquencs
Raymond Willelmus
Raymond Maurandus
Aimengavus Rufus

If the members of the count's court listed below were consuls, the dating is either 1200 or 1201, but if they were not members of that board, the editor's dating in *HGL* 8: No. 3 of ca. 1202, copied in August 1226, is to be adopted.

Aimeric de Castronovo
Bernard Peter de Cossa

Peter Rogerius "causidicus"
Raymond Centullus

AUGUST 1201: AA 1 27, JJ 21, fols. 59v-61v and Vienna, fols. 39-40. AA 1 25, JJ 21, fols. 55-56v and Vienna, fols. 26-27, with original in E 501 (April 1202) contains the consuls given below, describing them as "qui cum eorum sociis in alio anno fuerunt de capitulo."

Peter William Pilistortus
Jordan de Villanova
Arnold de Villanova
Ato de Montibus
Arnold Bestiacius
Arnold Guilabertus
Peter de Tolosa
Bernard Peter de Ponte

William Bertrandus
Gerald Esquivatus
Vital de Prinhaco
Gerald de Caturcio
Peter de Roaxio, called Grivus
Peter de Sancto Barcio
Peter de Sancto Romano
William Isarnus

Raymond Bernard Barravus	Stephen Karaborda "iuvenis"
Peter Raymond Descalquencs	Oldric Maurandus
Raymond Gerald Vitalis	Belengar Raimundus
John Signarius	Peter Maurandus

APRIL 1202 – APRIL 1203: AA 1 35 and Vienna, fols. 47-49 (dated April or November 1202), and AA 1 25, JJ 21, fols. 55-56v and Vienna, fols. 26-27, with original in E 501 (April 1202). AA 1 59, Vienna, fols. 75v-76 (June 1202), AA 1 29 and Vienna, fols. 40-41v (June 1202), AA 1 60 and Vienna, fols. 76v-77 (June 1202), AA 1 38 and Vienna, fols. 37-38 (June 1202), AA 1 39 and Vienna, fols. 38-39 (June 1202), AA 1 40 and Vienna, fols. 52-53 (June 1202), AA 1 41 and Vienna, fols. 53-54 (June 1202), AA 1 56 and Vienna, fols. 72v-73 (July 1202), AA 1 30 and Vienna, fols. 27-29v (August 1202), AA 1 42 and Vienna, fols. 54-55 (September 1202), AA 1 24, JJ 21, fols. 52v-55 and Vienna, fols. 41v-43 (February 1203), AA 1 50 and Vienna, fols. 63-64 (March 3 1203), AA 1 57 and Vienna, fols. 73-74 (March 19 1203), AA 1 58 and Vienna, fols. 74v-75v (March 19 1203), AA 2 84 (April 23 1203), AA 1 36 and Vienna, fols. 55v-56 (November 1204).

Arnold William Piletus	Raymond Centulus
Peter Raimundus "maior"	Pons de Capitedenario
Bernard Karaborda	Raymond Pilificatus
Raymond Pullarius *or* Polerius	Marcellus
Raymond Guido	Peter de Ponte
"Magister" William Lambertus	Odo Gausbertus
William Raymond de Insula	Raymond Crassus
Martin de Lambes	Raymond Bernard Vitalis
Bernard Ortolanus "mercator"	Raymond de Cassanello
William Johannes	Raymond de Saissonibus
Raymond Carpinus	Pons de Pegulano
Arnold Figaria	Pons Mancipius *or* Puer

APRIL 1203 – JUNE 1204: AA 1 48 and Vienna, fols. 60v-61v (April 23 1203), AA 1 43 and Vienna, fols. 54-57v (May 1203), AA 1 45 and Vienna, fols. 58-59 (May 1203), AA 1 47 and Vienna, fols. 60-60v (May 1203), AA 1 44 and Vienna, fols. 57v-58 (May 1203), AA 1 46 and Vienna, fols. 59-59v, AA 1 49 and Vienna, fols. 61v-62v (May 1203), AA 1 62 and Vienna, fols. 78v-80v (May 1203), AA 1 64 and Vienna, fols. 81v-83 (June 1203), AA 1 67 and Vienna, fols. 86-87 (September 1203), AA 1 51 and Vienna, fols. 64-64v (October 1203), AA 1 65 and Vienna, fols. 83-84 (October 1203), AA 1 61 and Vienna, fols. 77v-78v, AA 1 68 and Vienna, fols. 87v-88v (February 1204), AA 1 66 and Vienna, fols. 84-85v (February 1204), AA 1 63 and Vienna, fols. 80v-81v (March 1204), Catel, *Histoire des comtes de Toulouse*,

p. 236 (March 1204), PAN, JJ 21, fols. 77-79v (March 1204) published in
Lifshitz, "Le serment de fidélité (1203)," pp. 430-435, AA 1 70 and Vienna,
fols. 88v-89v (April 1204), AA 1 69 and Vienna, fols. 90-91 (April 1204) and
AA 1 26, JJ 21, fols. 56v-59v and Vienna, fols. 43-44v (June 1204).

William de Pozano	"Magister" Bernardus
Pons Belegarius	Raymond Gamiscius
William de Vendinis	Toset Aribertus
Peter de Miramonte	Bernard Raterius
Terrenus de Serris	Bernard de Cadoil or Cadullo
Arnold Bernardus	Peter Vitalis
Martin Ruffatus	William Paganus
Talafferus "mercator"	Hugh Johannes
William Pons Maschalcus	Bernard Gausbertus
Bernard Molinus	Arnold Mancipius or Puer
Bernard Bonushomo	Arnold de Pegulano
Vital Niger	Bernard de Leuzino

JUNE 1204 – JULY 1205: AA 1 53 and Vienna, fols. 67-68v (June 1204), AA
1 52, JJ 21, fols. 65-69 and Vienna, fols. 64v-67v (March 1205), AA 1 54, JJ
21, fols. 69-71 and Vienna, fols. 68v-69v (March 1205) and AA 1 55, JJ 21,
fols. 72v-77 and Vienna, fols. 69v-72 (act recording testimony of March, dated
May 1205).

Pons William de Sancto Romano	Pons Guitardus
Tolosan de Lesato	Oliver de Pruleco
Bernard William de Palacio	Oldric de Portale
Arnold Maynada "iuvenis"	Arnold Rufus
Bertrand de Pozano	Bonet Borsella
Bernard de Turre	Peter Brunus
Peter Constantinus	Vital Geraldus
Bernard Rogerius	Arnold Aiscius "iuvenis"
Arnold Guido	William Cascavelerius
Constantinus	Raymond de Ulmo
Pons de Quinto	William de Leuzino
Bernard Faber	Pons Palmata

JULY 1205 – MARCH 1206: AA 1 72 and Vienna, fols. 92-93 (July 1205) and
Malta 15 107 (March 1206).

William Arnold de Montetotino	Aimengavus Ruffus
Ademar de Turre	Adalbertus
Peter Gerald de Rocacirera	Bernard Raymond Astro
William Pons de Morlis	John de Turre

Raymond Arnold de Pozano
Stephen de Deveza
Raymond Rainaldus
Tolosan Talafferum
Tolosan de Suoil
Raymond Pilificatus *or* Pilusfixus
Peter Lumbardus

William Gallaco
William Aiscius
Raymond Guitardus
Raymond Peter de Sancto
Martino
Raymond de Fanis
Pons de Pruleco
Peter Gasco

DECEMBER 1207 – MARCH 1208: Vienna, fols. 93r-94r (December 1207), published in my *Liberty and Political Power*, pp. 204-206, AA 1 88, Vienna, fols. 96-96v (March 1208) and AA 1 89 and Vienna, fols. 94-96 (AA 1 89 is misdated as October 1207, but Vienna has the correct date of March 1208).

Arnold Bernardus
William Ademarius
Peter Bernard de Colommio
Bernard Bonushomo
Peter Amelius
Raymond de Ulmo
Arnold de Miramonte
William Arnold Talaferrum
Raymond Molinus
Arnold Petrus
Bernard de Sancto Romano
Arnold Galterius

"Magister" Bernardus
Raymond Pelliparius
William Raymond de Leuzino
Pons Astro
Raymond Adalbertus
Raymond William de Laura
Peter William de Orto
Raymond de Pegulano
Pons Barbadellus
William Peter Rainardus
Pons Palmata "iunior"
William de Sarramezana

FEBRUARY 1212: E 973 (February 1212) and undated Saint-Bernard 32 in an eighteenth century copy of Livre Noir, fol. 4.

Raymond de Castronovo
Aimeric de Castronovo "iuvenis"
Hugh de Roaxio, son of
    Arnold de Roaxio deceased
Peter de Montibus
Pons Arnaldus
Raymond Guilabertus
Pons Berengarius
Galterius de Acrimonte
Arnold de Septenis

William Raymond de Suburbio
Geraldus Esquivatus
Raymond Aimeric de Coceanis,
    son of Bernard Peter de Cossano
Bernard Raymond Astro
Raymond Gerald Vitalis
Arnold William Pilistortus
Arnold Raymond de Escalquencis
Raymond de Prinhaco

JANUARY – SEPTEMBER 1212: Catel, *Histoire des comtes de Toulouse*, pp. 275-276 (January 1212), and Saint-Bernard 32 in an eighteenth century copy of the Livre Noir, fol. 4 (September 1212).

Bertrand de Sancto Luppo
Arnold de Castronovo
Bernard Peter Trytius
Arnold Gilabertus
Peter de Sancto Romano
G-William de Posano
Arnold de Roaxio, son of Arnold de
    Roaxio deceased
Raymond de Roaxio
G-William de Montetotino
Bernard Arnold Rainaldus
Stephen Vitalis

Raymond Vital de Dalbata
Bernard Peter de Cossano
G-William Isarnus
Raymond Robertus de Tauro
Vital de Prinhaco
Peter Embrinus
G-William Pons Astro
Berengar Raimundus
Raymond de Scalquencibus
Hugh Surdus
Bernard Geraldus
Stephen Signarius

The Saint-Bernard act is in the vernacular and lists only the consuls of the
Bourg. The reader may note that the names in the Latin charter published by
Catel misplaced one of the Bourg's consuls:

B. P. de Cossas
Guilhe Issarns
R. Rocbert
Vital de Pinhas
P. Embris
Guilhe Pons Astre

Berenguers Ramons
R. Descalquens
Ug Sords
B. Guyrald
Esteve Seners
A. de Roais

FEBRUARY 1213 – MARCH 1214: E 501 ii and E 579 ii (both February 1214,
respectively copied in 1214 and 1270), TAM, II 45 and 75 (both dated March
1214) and Douais, *Conférences de Paléographie*, No. 16, p. 25 (March 3
1214). See also Limouzin-Lamothe, *La commune de Toulouse*, p. 250, note 3.

Bernard William de Palacio
Bernard Caraborda de Portaria
Arnold Maynata
Arnold William Piletus
William Pons Mascalcus
Peter Vitalis "macellarius"
Peter Raimundus "maior"
Raymond Pullarius
Bernard Ortolanus
Arnold Figueria *or* Ficaria
Constantine de Ponte
Pons de Capitedenario

Arnold Aiscius
"Magister" Bernardus
Arnold Rufus
William Pons de Prinhaco
Peter William Gausbertus
Stephen de Cassanello
Adalbertus
Martin de Lambes
Peter de Ponte
Pons Mancipium *or* Puer
Vital Willelmus
Pons Guitardus

FEBRUARY 1214 – APRIL 1215: Catel, *Histoire des comtes de Toulouse*, pp.
302-303 (February 1214), *HGL* 8: No. 174, from PAN, J 304 (April 1214),

TAM, II 70 (April 1214, copied in November 1226), Malta 1 21 (June 1214) published and misdated in my *Liberty and Political Power*, pp. 207-208 and PAN, J 305 51 (April 1215).

Jordan de Villanova
Aimeric de Castronovo
Arnold Bernard de Andusia *or*
Dendura
Arnold Barravus
Vital de Prinhaco
Peregrin Signarius
G-William Bertrandus
Bertrand de Montibus
Peter Rogerius
Hugh de Palatio

Bernard Raymond Baranonus
William de Brugariis
Raymond Rotbertus
Peter Maurandus
William Ramundus, son of Peter
  Ramundus deceased
William Bertrandus
Bernard Raymond Astro
John Curtasolea
Arnold Raymond Descalquencs

OCTOBER 1215 – FEBRUARY 1216: TAM, II 46 and 53 (dated respectively October 1215 and February 1216), and E 501 (February 1216).

Arnold Guilabertus
Pons Berengarius
Bernard Caraborda
Stephen Vitalis
Peter Bernard de Columbariis
Montarsinus
Bernard Ortolanus
Peter Raymond de Sancto Romano
Pons ....
Galterius de Acromonte
Raymond de Malorquis
Arnold Galterius

Raymond de Prinhaco
Berengar Aldra
Benedict Arnaldus
Bertrand Rainardus
Bruno Pennavaria
Stephen de Cassanello
William Aimeric de Pegulano
Pons de Villafrancha
Bernard Medicus
Peter de Montelauderio
William de Montelauderio

APRIL – SEPTEMBER 1217: Simon de Montfort's "curiales viri" in E 573 (ca. 1217, copied in 1234), Malta 15 112 (April 1217), E 501 (September 1217, copied in December 1243) and Douais, *Conférences de paléographie*, No. 17 (September 1217). *HGL* 10: Note 38, No. 1, from PAN, J 305 32, fols. 3v, 6, 7v and 8v (ca. 1274).

Bernard Raymond de Tolosa
Pons Berengarius
Bernard Caraborda
Bernard Arnold de Portaria

Raymond Rotbertus de Tauro
Peregrin Signarius
Pons de Capitedenario
Pons Guitardus

Bernard Arnaldus, Pons Berengarius, Bernard Caraborda, Pons Guitardus and
Raymond Rotbertus were given by Peter Mauran on fol. 6 and Arnold de Vasco
on fol. 7v, witnesses of ca. 1274. One witness, however, Bernard Hugh de Ses-
quieras on fol. 8v, remarked that he had seen others exercising the consular
"merum et mixtum imperium" in the Château Narbonnais for Simon de Montfort, naming them as

Arnold Bernard de Andusia   Bernard Peter de Cossa
Hugh de Palatio

It is therefore possible that these were among the persons who served as Montfort's consuls or "curiales viri" during the period from April 1216 when he
really took over the government of the town until the first and unsuccessful revolt of the town against the crusaders in August and September of the same
year. Thereafter, as may be seen from the dates of the documents given above,
the "curiales viri" headed by Bernard Raymond de Tolosa were put in office.
It is perhaps worth noting that, although, as in the Malta document cited above,
the "curiales viri" judged important cases themselves, even criminal ones, they
also followed older consular practice of appointing judge-delegates to settle
some of the litigation. The difference between the old deputizing and that of
Montfort's time was that the French seneschal, Gervais de Chamigny, presumably supervised these appointments. The only known board of such delegates is
seen in the documents cited above from series E and the charter published by
Douais where they are named

William Pons Maschalchus   Bernard Peter son of Bernard
Pons Astro   Ortolanus
Raymond de Fumello   William Aimeric de Pegulano
------------   Arnold de Samatano

SEPTEMBER 1218: Limouzin-Lamothe, *La commune de Toulouse*, p. 251, note
3, Malta 1 116, ibid. 4 206, and ibid. 7 76 i (all dated September 1218).

Peter de Castronovo   "Magister" Bernardus de Burgo
Oldric de Gamevilla   Bernard Aimeric de Cossano
Arnold de Villanova, son of Jordan   Bernard Raymond Astro
Arnold Gerald de Montelauro   Bernard Berengarius
Peter de Roaxio   Arnold Mancipium *or* Puer
Ugolenus de Ponte   Hugh Johannes
Bernard Raymond Barravus   Embrinus
Arnold William Piletus   Raymond Descalquensis
Pons de Morlis *or* Morlanis   Bernard Signarius
Stephen de Devesa   Raymond Tapierius
Arnold Guido "iuvenis"   Peter William de Orto

NOVEMBER 1218 – OCTOBER 1219: AA 1 92 (November 1218), AA 2 77 (August 1219), ibid. 76 (September 1219) and Malta 1 117 (October 1219).

Raymond Molendinus
William Pons Maschalcus
Vital Bonushomo
Arnold Guido "maior"
Raymond Baranonus
Peter Amelius "mercator"
Arnold de Varanhano
Bernard Arnaldus "mercator"
Bartholomew Salnerius
Raymond de Calhavo
Arnold Onda
Peter William Faber

Raymond Pilificatus
Gerald Pictavinus
Arnold de Sancto Felicio
Arnold de Fanis
Pons Palmata
William Bosquetus
Peter William Gausbertus
Bernard Gairaldus
Aimeric Ausberguerius
William Peter de Casalibus
John de Montelanderio

SEPTEMBER–NOVEMBER 1220: AA 1 94 (September 1220), E 579 in *HGL* 8: No. 210 (October 1220) and AA 1 95 (November 1220).

CITY
Bernard Raymond Baranonus
Pons Gasco
Tolosan de Siolio
Raymond de Montetotino *or* de Fide
Arnold Molinus
Petricola
Peter de Altarippa
Bernard Faber
William Peter Rainardus
Vital Willelmus (Bourg?)
Peter Rogaterius
Raymond Guifredus

BOURG
Azalbertus
Peter de Ponte
Raymond Gamiscius
Hugh Ausberguerius
Stephen de Cadullo
William Barbadellus
Peter Sobaccus
Bernard de Murello
Bernard de Miramonte
Arnold Pons de Lesato
Arnold Ademarius
Arnold de Ulmo

JANUARY–AUGUST 1221: AA 1 90 and 93 (both dated August 1221), Saint-Bernard 138, fols. 171r-72r (January 1221), Grandselve 5 iv (January 1221).

Peter Constantinus
William de Sancto Petro
Raymond Arnold de Pozano
Pons de Sioil
Bertrand Garinus
Tolosan Talliaferrum
Bernard Ficcaria *or* Figueria
Peter Arnold de Cunnofaverio

Pons Astro
Martin Chivus
Peter de Ponte "iuvenis"
Bernard Pilificatus
Pons Arnaldus "notarius"
Arnold Julianus
William de Cadullo
Arnold Equus

William de Equodorso *or* Cavaldoss
Raymond de Ulmo
Arnold Rapa
Vasco de Turre

Peter Bernard de Castro
Sarraceno
John Arnaldus
Aimeric de Sancto Romano
Martin Miles

APRIL 1222 – APRIL 1223: AA 1 75, 76 and 77 (all dated April 1222), ibid. 78 (May 1222), ibid. 80 (September 1222), ibid. 79 (September 1222), ibid. 81 (beginning here to the last act in this paragraph, all acts are dated December 1222), ibid. 82, 83, 84, 85, 86, 99 and 74, and ibid. 87 (April 1223).

Bertrand de Montibus
Peter Bernard de Cervuneriis *or*
"cervunerius"
Bertrand de Roaxio
Raymond de Podiobuscano
William de Leus *or* Leuzino
Bernard Bonushomo
Arnold William de Sancto Barcio
Arnold Barravus
Martin de Lambes
Bernard de Sancto Romano
Raymond Bernard de Sancto Barcio

Bernard Faber "espetierius"
Raymond de Prinaco
Peter de Fulonibus
Arnold Rogerius
Peter de Prulheco
Arnold de Escalquenquis
Raymond Signarius
Arnold John Caballus
John Barravus
William Raymond de Claustro
Isarn Grillus "notarius"
Arnold Puer *or* Mancipius
William Peter de Casalibus

Perhaps in error, AA 1 99 added an Arnold Raymond de Claustro to the above list.

JANUARY – MARCH 1224: MADTG, A 294, fol. 807 (January 1224) and PBN, Collection Doat 103: fol. 11 in *HGL* 8: No. 235 (March 1224).

Pons Arnold de Noerio
Bernard Raymond Baranonus
William de Pozano
Pons Ortolanus
Raymond Molinus
Peter Raimundus "maior"
Arnold Pullerius
William Pons Mascalcus
Gerald de Samatano
Bernard Arnaldus "mercator"
Bernard William Gaitapodium
Bernard Martinus

"Magister" Bernardus
Azalbertus
Bernard Curtasoleria
Bernard Arnold Pelegrinus
Bernard Gastonus
William Peter Rainardus
Vital Rotbertus
Pons Palmata
William Barbadellus
Laurentius de Coquinis
John de Montelanderio
Raymond de Rivis

JANUARY – MARCH 1225: TAM, AA 6 129 and 130 (respectively January and February 1225), E 573 (consular attestation dated March 1225 of an act drawn by a public notary of Isle-Jourdain in January 1225).

Hugh de Roaxio
Grivus de Roaxio
Bernard Raymond Barravus
Walter de Acrimonte
Bernard de Miramonte
G-William John Gaitapodium
Peter Constantinus
Peter Sancius
William de Pinu
Bernard Faber
William de Planea
Peter Arnold de Cunnofaverio

John Curtasolea
Arnold Raymond Descalquenciis
Bruno de Garrigiis
Raymond Berenguerius
Peter Trunnus
Pons de Prinaco
Raymond Gamiscius
Hugh de Murello
Raymond Tapierius
Arnold de Sancto Felicio
Vital Willelmus
Raymond Arnold de Saxonibus

APRIL 1225 – APRIL 1226: Malta 3 149 (April 1225), AA 1 97 (March 1226) and ibid. 96 (April 1226).

Raymond de Castronovo
Bertrand de Montibus
Arnold Barravus
Arnold de Roaxio
Ugolenus
Arnold William de Sancto Barcio
Raymond William Atadillus
Arnold Guido "iuvenis"
Peter Bernard de Columbariis
Berengar Baranonus
William Raymond Ursdetus *or*
    Ursetus
William de Ulmo

William Ramundus, son of
    Peter Ramundus
Raymond Isarnus
Pons de Capitedenario
William de Turre
John de Garrigiis
Stephen Curtasolea
Raymond de Prinaco
Arnold de Escalquencs
Calvet de Anceanis
Vital Rotbertus
Peter de Ponte "iuvenis"
Raymond Peter Martellus

APRIL–AUGUST 1226: Malta 1, 122 (April 1226), PBN, Collection Doat 169: fol. 169 in *HGL* 8: No. 250 (May 1226), AA 1 102 (June 1226) and AA 2 83 (August 1226).

Raymond Garinus
Peter Aonda
Raymond Catalanus
Durand de Levis
Arnold de Pairanis
William Gitbertus "iuvenis"

Raymond Borrellus
Raymond Rainerius
John Selerius
Vital Faverius
Stephen de Camarada
Arnold Andreas

Peter Aimericus
Peter de Vindemiis *or* Vendinis
Raymond Peter Moysetus
Arnold de Nemoremediano
Tolosan de Siolio "iuvenis"
Hugh de Sancto Amancio
Pons Gairaldus

Raymond Guido
Peter Vital Blazinus
William Ugo
Raymond de Aurevez
William Bequinus *or* de
  Montebequino

MAY–DECEMBER 1227: AA 1 73 (May 1227), TAM, II 63 (November 1227), Gardouch 2 and PBN, Collection Doat 87: fol. 7ff. (both dated December 1227).

Arnold Raymond Baranonus *or*
  Baranhe
Gerald de Vendinis
Pons de Siollio
Raymond Auriollus
Vital de Manso
John Mascalqus
Bertrand Pelliparius *or*
  Pellicerius
Bernard Pelliparius *or*
  Pellicerius
Arnold de Trageto
Bernard William de Samatano
Peter Vitalis "capellerius"
Bernard de Rocovilla

Terrenus Oddo *or* Hodo
William Raymond Proietus *or*
  Proget
Bertrand de Novilla
Raymond de Sancto Cezerto
Raymond de Terrassona
Terrenus Martin de Cassanello
Arnold de Godvesio
William de Sancto Cipriano
Fort de Devezia *or* de Villanova
Peter de Gano *or* Guano
Peter John de Ulmo *or*
  "mercator"
Pons Capellerius

AUGUST 1230: Saint-Sernin 680 (20 72 nn) i (August 1230, copied in 1235 and 1252).

Bernard Barravus
Durand de Sancto Barcio "iuvenis"
Bernard Faber de Sancto Stephano
Arnold de Payranis

Arnold de Nemoremediano
Bonmacip Maurandus
Vasco de Turre
Oldric de Prinhaco
Arnold Andreas

Either 1230 or 1231: E 573 (a copy of an original dated ca. 1216 or 1217 attested by the consuls in [the month was obliterated 1230 and copied in November 1234).

... Gerald ...
Bernard Raymond Baranonus
"Magister" Poncius
Peter Raimundus "maior"
Raymond Bernard de Sancto Barcio

... Raymond de Podiobuscano
Arnold Rufus
Peter Caraborda
Bernard Caraborda
Arnold de Aulaviridi

AUGUST 1231 – JANUARY 1232: J 322 54 in *HGL* 8: No. 294 (August 1231) and Malta 1, 112 (January 1232). JJ 19, fols. 92v-94 (August 1231) has William Rotbertus in place of Vital Rotbertus.

Arnold G-William de Sancto Barcio	Peter G-William de Orto
Bernard Faber	Karabordas
Bertrand Petrarius	Bernard Signarius
Raymond Baranhonis	Raymond Maurandus
Peter de Turre	Vital Rotbertus

The first three and last three of these consuls also served as judges in a comital court.

JUNE 1235 TO 1238: Saint-Étienne 230 (27 1 nn) v (June 1235, copied in 1244), PAN, J 328 1 x (consular attestation in June 1235 of an act dated December 1234), and MADTG, A 294, fol. 870 (June 1235). Pelisson's *Chronique*, ed. Duvernoy, p. 102 and PBN, Collection Doat 21: fol. 159vff., published (with the aid of other copies) by Dossat, *Les crises de l'Inquisition*, pp. 343-344, recorded the excommunication of these consuls in November 1235, which ban was lifted early in 1236 according to ibid. p. 135, and the renewed excommunication of the same board of consuls together with the vicar Peter de Tolosa in July 1237 in PBN, Collection Doat 21: fol. 145vff., a ban lifted in its turn in late 1238 as described in Dossat, op. cit., pp. 141-143. The order of the names derives from Bernard Guy's *De fundatione*, ed. Amargier, p. 49 (November 1235). Pelisson's partial list follows a different order, one marked below by appended Arabic numbers.

Bernard de Miramonte *or* Miramundo – 4	Bernard Signarius – 7
Arnold Barravus – 2	Raymond Rogerius – 9
Grivus de Roaxio – 1	Raymond Borrellus – 8
Arnold William de Sancto Barcio – 5	Oldric (or Bonmacip?) Maurandus
Curvus de Turre *or* Turribus -3	Maurandus de Bellopodio *or*
Pons de Siolh *or* Suollio – 6	"iuvenis"
	Peter Embrinus

This list is especially interesting because two of its members disappeared during the consulate's extended term of office. Peter Embrinus was mentioned only in the first charter cited above, curiously, because the second charter listed above is dated on exactly the same day, June 25. Peter, then, had disappeared early on. Raymond Rogerius, on the other hand, was mentioned in all of the earlier acts, including the excommunication of November 1235, but was omitted in that of July 1237. All of this fits with other information. According to Pelisson's *Chronique*, ed. Duvernoy, p. 96, Peter Embrinus' body was disinterred and burned as that of a Cathar in 1237. He had, in short, died in office. The same source, ed. Molinier, pp. 30-31 and 39, and Douais, pp. 101-102 and 106, reports that Raymond Rogerius was condemned as an heretic in the same year, a fact confirmed by the inquisitorial record in PBN, Collection Doat 21: fols. 145v-149v, where much of his history is related, stating that he was condemned as relapsed in March 1238. The aged witness Raymond de Gordonio "sartre" of ca. 1274 in PAN, J 305 32, fol. 3v, reports that Count Raymond had installed the consuls of this period and went on to name four of them, two of whom are listed above, Grivus de Roaxio and Pons de Siollio. He also added two other names that seem to derive from the next consular list, for which see below.

MARCH 1239: Daurade 117; PAN, J 305 32, fol. 3v(dated ca. 1274) where Raymond de Gordonio "sartre" named Bertrand de Garrigiis and Bonmacip Maurandus.

Stephen Barravus	Bernard Raymond Baranhonus
William de Roaxio	Peter Maurandus
Hugh de Andusia	Bertrand de Garrigiis
Macip de Tolosa	Arnold Johannis
Folcoys de Turribus	Bonmacip Maurandus

OCTOBER 1239 – AUGUST 1240: TAM, II 61 (October 1239) and AA 1 100 (August 1240).

Ispanus Garinus *or* Guarinus	Bertrand de Villanova
Peter Vitalis	Bernard de Marcillo "notarius"
G-William Gitbertus called "Piper"	Raymond Bernard Faciemfaber
Oddo de Noerio	Arnold de Guotvesio
Raymond de Sancto Cezerto	Raymond Guido
"notarius"	Philip [Gaitapodium]

Dated 1240, a garbled list published by Rozoi, *Annales* 4: Note 3, pp. 37-38, is probably the same consulate.

Philip de Marvilla – ?
Bernard de Marvilles – surely Marcillo
Pons Dastarac – see the next consular list
Raymond de Sancto Ceser – surely Sancto Cezerto

FEBRUARY 1243 – SEPTEMBER 1245 (?): TAM, AA 6 123 (February 1243), PAN, J 305 29 (February 1243), J 322 64 (copied February 1247) in *HGL* 8: No. 361 (September 1243), MADTG, A 294, fol. 384 (October 1243), TAM,

AA 6 134 (February 1244), Hôtel-Dieu IB/1 (September 1245). PAN, J 305 32, fols. 2, 3, 5v, 6v and 7v (ca. 1274).

Bernard de Villanova "miles"
Peter Raimundus "maior"
William de Septinis, Serris or Seres
Vital Bonushomo
Peter Bernardus de Salvitate,
  Boaterius, or Servinerius and de
  Servineriis

William de Marcillo or Marciol
Raymond de Castronovo, son of
  Stephen Curtasolea
Raymond de Ponte
Berengar de Portallo
Bruno Bosquetus
Arnold Jordanus
Arnold Destarac or de Astaraco

A witness in ca. 1274, William de Seres on fol. 2, not only stated that he had served as consul for three years, but also named all the above consuls. He was alone in recording Arnold de Astaraco.

Another witness Walter (Galterius) Raimundus on fol. 3 remarked that he himself had served for two years.

Peter Bernard Boaterius on fol. 6v observed that he had served for four years and that he had wanted to quit at the end of three, but that the count prevailed on him to stay in office because of his projected visit to Provence.

Two other witnesses Bernard Vaquerii and Arnold Vasco on fols. 5 and 7v mention William de Seres and Peter Bernard "cervener."

Note also that the knightly title accorded Bernard de Villanova is not found in any official list, but only in the testimony of William de Seres who carefully called him "dominus" as well as "miles." Lastly, the count's consuls must have been overthrown after September 18, 1245, the exact date of the Hôtel-Dieu document cited above.

JANUARY–NOVEMBER 1246: TAM, II 61 (January 1246), Douais, *Documents pour servir à l'inquisition dans le Languedoc* 2: 1-36 (March to July 1246), TAM, AA 6 94 (April 1246) and PAN, JJ 21, fol. 79v (November 1246). Referred to also in AA 1 101 (July 101).

Hugh de Roaxio
Bertrand de Villanova
Curvus de Turribus
Bernard Raymond de Tolosa
Roger Barravus
Gerald Arnaldus
William de Pozano
Bernard de Quinbalho
Vital de Ageno
Bernard Saurellus

Raymond Berengarius
Pons Astro
Pons de Prinhaco
Bertrand de Escalquencis
Vital Faber Oddo
Raymond de Sancto Cezerto
Raymond Raynerius
Arnold Caballus or Cavallus
Peter Vital Blazinus
Stephen Magister "pelliparius"

Bernard de Trageto
Peter Raymond Godus
Bonmacip Maurandus

William Hugh "pelliparius" *and*
"pellicerius"

Douais' lists include others among the "capitularii," who were presumably members of the consuls' council:

Bernard Descalquencs
Grivus de Roaxio

Jordan de Villanova
Pons Magister

JULY 1247 – JANUARY 1248: AA 1 101 (July 1247), Douais, *Documents pour servir à l'histoire de l'inquisition* 2: 66ff. (November 1247) and AA 1 103 (January 1248).

Isarn de Villanova
Bertrand de Turribus
Bertrand Barravus
Vital Guilabertus
Montarsynus
Peter Raymond de Tholosa
Peter William de Sancto Romano
Roger de Roaxio
Bernard de Sancto Paulo
Peter Rotbertus
Peter de Borello
Arnold Amelius

Raymond de Castronovo, son of
    Stephen Curtasolea
Oldric Caraborda
Raymond Ruffus
Stephen Signarius "juvenis"
Aimeric Astro
Bernard de Caturcio
Raymond Ausberguerius
William Pons Astro
William Barbadellus
Julian Gasco
Peter Garsias "cambiator"
Raymond Brizonerius

JUNE 1248 – MARCH 1249: PAN, KK 1228, fols. 8v-9 (June 1248) and TAM, AA 6 133 (March 1249).

Arnold Guido
Pons de Siollio
Raymond Baranonus (?)
Bernard Parator
Arnold Onda
William Junquerius "cambiator"
"Magister" Bernard de Burguetonovo
Arnold Bruno
Arnold Boninus
William de Mossenquis
William de Vendemiis
Berengar de Portallo *or* Portale

Arnold de Godvesio
Pons Arnaldus "cambiator"
Bruno Busquetus
Pons de Villafranca
Raymond Garcionus *or* de
    Garsioni
Peter Umbertus
Aimeric Selerius (Celerius)
Terrenus Calcaterra
Arnold Julianus
Raymond de Miramonte

JULY 1249: MADTG, A 294, fol. 393.

Bernard Gaitapodium	Bernard Johannes
Peter de Ulmo	Raymond Gerald Vitalis
Peter Guitardus	Philip de Fenolheto
Raymond Guido	Stephen de Camarada
Peter de Avinone	G-William de Falgario
Peter Faber de Altaripa	Raymond Johannes "legista"

PAN, J 305 32, fol. 4 (ca. 1274), testimony of Arnold de Fumello as to who the consuls were. Bernard den Garsio says (3r) that "tempore mortis dicti domini Raimundi comitis [September 27, 1249], illi qui erant consules pro ipso et ab ipso positi fuerunt expulsi viliter de consulatu, videlicet Raimundus Johannes legista et Raimundus Gui et eorum socii."

DECEMBER 1249 – APRIL 1250: PAN, J 192 5 (December 1249), ibid., JJ 21, fol. 79v in *HGL* 8: No. 416 iv (April 1250) and ibid., JJ 19, fol. 39v (April 1250) which mentions Raymond de Dalbs and Stephen Carabordas.

Raymond de Dalbs	Vital Guilabertus
Stephen Carabordas	Pons Berengarius
	Gauterius Raimundus

EARLY 1250S: The dating is a guess based on a record of testimony collected in Toulouse for three suits against Toulousan usurers sent to the archiepiscopal tribunal in Narbonne in May 1255 and published in Alphonse Blanc, *Le livre de comptes de Jacme Olivier* 2: 333-344. Witnesses nos. 4 and 19 remarked that they were among the consuls ("consul Tholose seu unus de capitulariis") who decided a case against a debtor. Other witnesses dated the duration of the creditors' reputation as usurers as being from three to fifteen years, with most favoring five years. Hugh d'en Dura (Dendura), witness no. 12, a principal and one of the two "fideiussores" of the debt, said that the debt occurred about five years prior to 1255, but no witness, even those involved in the transactions either as principals or notaries, actually dated the consular trial itself. One therefore guesses that the debt was dated around 1250 and the consular case in any one of the three missing terms, 1250-1251, 1252-1253 and 1253-1254, presuming, of course, that the terms were limited to one calendar year. The consuls were

Raymond Carabordas	Vital Durandus

MAY 1251 – JANUARY 1252: TAM, II 61 and 62 (both dated May 1251), Malta 17 67 ii (January 1252, copied in 1252, 1273 and 1277), ibid. 123 15 (January 1252) and ibid. (an act of April 1245 assigned by the consuls to another notary in January 1252).

Peter de Tholosa
William de Gamevilla
Raymond Arnold de Villanova
Peter de Leus
William de Roaxio
Stephen Barravus
Stephen Arnold de Ponte
William de Pozano *or* Pozanis
Arnold Molinus
Arnold de Vauro
William de Astaraco
Arnold Scriptor *or* Escrivarius

Peter de Cossano
Maurand de Bellopodio
Raymond de Ponte
Oldric Maurandus
Pons de Prinhaco
William de Marcillo
Raymond de Garrigiis
Vital Willelmus "legista"
Raymond Sobaccus
Stephen Magister
Peter de Prato
Peter de Sancto Subrano *or*
    Cypriano

FEBRUARY 1255: Malta 17 76.

Bertrand de Tolosa
William Rotberti
Arnold Peter de Devesia
Philip de Cornelhano
Bernard de Trageto
Raymond Rotberti de Affactatoribus
Vital Boneti "notarius"
Peter Feltrerius "notarius"

William de Gano
Peter de Terrasona
John de Turre
Peter Raymond de Varanhano
Arnold Belengarius
William de Mozenquis
    "notarius"
Hugh Pelliparius
Arnold Mancipius

DECEMBER 1255 – JUNE 1256: PAN, J 896 31 (December 1255 – "supplicatio consulum Tholose"), Dominicans 11 (December 1255, copied in May 1257) and Malta 12 8 (June 1256).

Peter Guitardus
Peter Niger de Portaria
Bernard Gaitapodium
Arnold Johannes
Arnold Boninus
Peter de Avinhone

Raymond Johannes "legista"
Raymond de Aurevez
William Johannes "mercator"
Vital de Fumello
Sernin Ayssada
Thomas *or* Tos Faber

J 896 81 also contains a list of the "consiliarii" of the consuls, who are:

G-William de Nemore "notarius"
Peter de Castronovo "miles"
Roger Barravus
Peter Raimundus "maior"
Arnold Guido
Aimeric Celerius

G-William Servunerius
Raymond Bolenq
Bertrand de Garrigiis
Vital Guillelmus
Peter Raymond de Avinone
Pons Capellus

JANUARY 1258 – MARCH 1259: TAM, II 49 (January 1258, copied in 1268); DD1 1 3 i (August 1258, copied in 1261 and 1270); TAM, II 61 (March 1259).

Peter de Castronovo	Bernard Vicecomes
William Rotbertus "legista"	Bernard Aimericus
Peter Rotbertus de Afactatoribus	Vital de Anglata
"Magister" Raymond Capellerius	Bertrand de Montibus
"legista"	Pons de Villafranca
	William Bequinus

JULY 1259 – OCTOBER 1260: Sainte-Claire 24 iv (July 1259), Malta 4 224 and ibid. 10 27 i, ibid. 21 51, and ibid. 24 20 (all four Malta acts are dated August 1259), MADTG, A 294, fol. 86v (August 1259) and fol. 110v (October 1260) and Saint-Étienne 231 (26 6 nn) (October 1260).

Macip de Tholosa	Bernard Raynaldus de Portaria
Arnold de Castronovo	Arnold de Scalquencis
Peter Amelius "mercator de Plano	Vital Faber Oto, Odo or Oddo
Sancti Stephani"	Arnold Johannes
Arnold de Falgario or Felgar	Hugh Pelliparius
Peter Feltrerius "notarius"	William Vasco "mercator"

DECEMBER 1261: TAM, DD 1 1 3 ii (act of January 1261 with consular attestation of December 1261, copied in 1268 or 1270).

Jordan de Villanova	G-William Descalquencs
Peter Iudex	G-William Peter Pagesia
Bernard Jornal	Arnold Raimundus "cambiator"
Arnold Johannes "cambiator"	Bernard Fabri "carrugerius"

OCTOBER 1262 – OCTOBER 1263: *Gallia Christiana* 13: Instr. No. 52 (October 1262), TAM, II 75 (January 1263, copied in 1276 and 1306), E 573 (February 1263), PBN, Collection Doat 73: fol. 202v (February 1263), TAM, DD 1 1 4 (August 1263, copied in 1268 and 1270) and Malta 10 8 v (October 1263, copied in 1264).

William de Roaxio	Bernard Pons de Galhaco
Bertrand de Palacio	"notarius"
William de Septenis	Pons Basterius "notarius"
William Saurinus	Vital de Fumello
Bernard Raymond Baranonus	Bertrand Pictavinus
Adam Cerninus	Bertrand de Garrigiis
Berengar de Portallo	

FEBRUARY 1264 – APRIL 1265: TAM, HH 5 Appendix 1 (February 1264), II
79 (April 1264), II 32 (September 1264, copied in 1265, 1271 and 1333),
Malta 135 46 (dated 1239 with consular attestation dated April 1265) and
MADTG, A 294, fols. 387v-388 (April 1265). The last two references contain
consular transferences of notarial materials and the dates may be late because
the notaries wrote the acts up after the consuls' term had expired.

CITY	BOURG
Bernard de Roaxio	Bernard Karabordas
Raymond Buxus "mercator"	G-William de Mosenquis
Peter Laurencius de Pena "notarius"	Arnold de Gotvesio
Bernard de Serris "notarius"	Arnold de Fumello "notarius"
Peter Raymond de Launaco	Tolosanus Barravus "mercator"
Arnold Boninus	Stephen Bequinus

JUNE 1265: Grandselve 10 (June 1265) and PBN, MS lat. 10918, fol. 34r, in HGL
8: No. 515: "Articuli civium Tholosanorum," dated by the editors ca. 1265, containing two of the consuls named below, namely Escalquencs and Sancto Barcio.

Arnold de Escalquencs	Raymond Furnerius
Humbert Laurencii	G-William Amelii
Hugh Pelhicerius	William Tolosinus
G-William de Ga	G-William Vasco
Durand de Sancto Barcio	

JULY 1266 – AUGUST 1267: TAM, BB 189, fol. 10v (July 1266) and ibid., fols.
2, 3v-4 (respectively dated July 1266 and August 1267).

CITY	BOURG
"Magister" Benedict [de Insula]	Bertrand de Garrigiis
"jurisperitus"	Vital Faber Oddo
Pons Vasco "mercator"	Pons de Villafranca
Raymond Pelliparius "mercator"	G-William Vasco
Bernard Bombellus "mercator"	Raymond Johannes de Veteri-
Bernard Aimericus "notarius"	villa "legista"
--------------	Peter Gamardus "mercator"

By this time, as may easily be seen in the matricule of the notaries (BB 189
above), many scribes preferred the recent reintroduction of the genitive for all
second names, as, for example, Bernard Bombelli and Peter Gamardi. Others
still stuck to late twelfth and early thirteenth century practice with the names in
the nominative. When I remember, I will do the same, but warn the reader
that, by the time these lists finish, almost all second names are in the genitive,
as Bernard Fabri "carrugerius" in 1261 above.

JUNE 1268 – FEBRUARY 1269: Saint-Sernin 680 (no Cresty reference) (June 1268), ibid. 599 (10 35 19) (July 1268), TAM, II 31 two acts (July and August 1268) and PBN, Collection Doat 73: fols. 43-53 (July 1268 to February 1269).

Raymond de Castronovo "miles"   Arnold de Fumello "notarius"
Raymond Caraborda   John de Paolhaco
Berengar de Portali   Stephen Galterius "notarius"
Stephen Constantinus   Arnold Caregia *or* Carregia
Oldric de Prinhaco   Arnold Onda

APRIL 1269 – MARCH 1270 ?: PAN, J 192b, a roll partly published in *Layettes du Trésor* 4: 320ff. (April 1269), PBN, Collection Doat 73: fols. 62-65 (April 1269), TAM, BB 189, fols. 2v and 5 (respectively October and December 1269), ibid., AA 3 129, col. 197-200 (December 1269) and ibid., II 9 (March 1269 or 1270).

CITY   BOURG
G-William de Vendinis   Pons de Avinione
G-William Vitalis "parator"   Arnold Ramundus "campsor"
Peter Niger   John Bequinus
Bernard de Trageto, son of Bernard   Pons Vasco de Coquinis
  de Trageto deceased   G-William Vasco "mercator"
Arnold Guido   G-William Rotbertus
Arnold Boninus

There is a mystery here. A riot occurred on February 20 1269, and testimony concerning it was presented in the vicar's court in sessions starting on March 5 of the same year. The defendant, Garnerius Fabri "campsor," several times refers to persons who were consuls in the term of 1269 before this one as being consuls at the time of the riot. The other consular lists and especially the information contained in PBN, Collection Doat 73, mentioned above, contradict this. I therefore feel that the testimony presented in the vicar's court called these men consuls because it was written up during the period when they were consuls (the testimony, it may be noted, is incomplete, the last segments being added late in April 1269) and because it was in the interest of the defendant to show that members of the present town administration had themselves been involved in the riot. The list in TAM, AA 3 129, col. 197 (December 1269) states that William Rotbertus of the Bourg had died in office.

SEPTEMBER 1270 – MARCH 1271: TAM, BB 189, fols. 5v and 6r-v (April, September, November, and December 1270), AA 3 128 (June 1270), BB 204, fol. 6v (November 1270) which lists in the nominative under nos. 58 and 59 all the consuls, and II 9 (March 1271).

"Dominus" Aimeric de Roaxio
Bernard Raymond Baranhonus
Bernard Jornallus
Bernard de Serris
Matthew Bequinus
Raymond de Prinhaco

Peter Raymond Descalquenchis
William Peter Pagesia
Vital Willelmus
William de Mosenquis
Raymond Ausberguerius
William de Rippis or Ripis

APRIL 1271 – JULY 1272: TAM, BB 189, fols. 7v-8 (April and September 1271), Saint-Étienne 239 (30 1 nn) (June 1271), MADTG, A 294, fol. 38v (June 1271), La Faille, *Annales de la ville de Toulouse* 1: abregé 2 (September 1271), TAM, BB 204, fol. 7v, No. 84 and fol. 8, No. 95 (both dated September 1271), the latter having all names in the nominative, TAM, II 61 (October 1271) with division between City and Bourg, Dossat, *Saisimentum comitatus Tholosani*, p. 78 (September 1271) and p. 204 (December 1271), Malta Garidech 1 (1 4) assignment of notary's materials in July 1272, MADTG, A 294, fols. 220, 292v and 391v (all dated July 1272), Malta 2 158 and 165 (from here to the end of the list, all are dated July 1272), ibid. 4 198 and 227, ibid. 10 93, ibid. 15 169, ibid. 17 67 i (copied 1277) and ibid. 180 17.

Raymond Ato de Tholosa
    "domicellus"
Raymond de Roaxio, son of
    G-William de Roaxio deceased
Azemar de Acromonte or Agromonte
Peter Raymond (sometimes P) Godus
    or Got
Bernard Bombellus

John de Grosso "textor"
Maurand de Bellopodio or
    Pulchropodio
Berengar Raimundus
Vital Faber (Faure) Odo
G-William Pictor "notarius"
Raymond Basterius
Peter (or Raymond) de Sancto
    Cipriano or Sancto Subrano

Note the comment above under the consular list of 1264, and also that all acts here dated 1272 were assignments by the consuls of notarial materials.

SEPTEMBER 1272 – JUNE 1273: TAM, II 9 and 70 (both September 1272), ibid. 46 (two acts of February and March 1273) and ibid. BB 189, fol. 8 (June 1273). Rozoi, *Annales* 2: 49, replaced both Castellumnovum or Bernard de Solerio with a Peter de Castronovo.

Castellumnovum
Doat de Roaxio
Peter Secorioni
Vital Bonetus
Aimeric Fortanerius
Arnold Raimundus "cambiator"
Jordan de Castronovo

Bertrand de Garrigiis
Raymond Maurandus
Pons de Villafranca
Bernard Medicus de Sancto Paulo
Bernard de Solerio

JANUARY 1274 – SEPTEMBER 1275: TAM, II 9 (January 1274), MADTG, A 294, fol. 107v (August 1274), TAM, BB 189, fol. 9v (August 1274) and ibid. II 15 (September 1274).

"Dominus" Arnold de Castronovo
"miles"
Arnold Barravus
Raymond Buxus "mercator"
Bernard Hugh de Albata
Arnold de Vauro de Sancto Stephano
Pons de Gaure "mercator"

Raymond de Castronovo
Berengar de Portali or Portallo
Pons de Avignone "pictor"
G-William Vasco "mercator"
G-William Vital Vasco
"affactator"
Arnold Columbus "affactator"

JANUARY – OCTOBER 1275: TAM, II 9 (January and March 1275); ibid., II 61 (April 1275); ibid., BB 189, fols. 3, 4r and 7 (June, August and September 1275), repeated in La Faille, *Annales de la ville de Toulouse* 1: abregé 2, and Grandselve 13 (October 1275, copied in 1280).

"Dominus" Peter de Castronovo
"miles"
Durand de Sancto Barcio
Bernard de Acromonte
G-William Poncius "fusterius"
Bernard Raymond Baranhonus

John de Castronovo
Peter Guilabertus
G-William Peter Pagesia
Raymond Carabordas
Raymond Ausberguerius
Pons Furnerius de Ponte
Bernard Saurellus

AUGUST 1276 – FEBRUARY 1277: TAM, II 61 and 63 (both August 1276) and ibid., DD 1 1 1 (February 1277).

Raymond Johannes "maior"
Stephen Galterius of Saint-Pierre-Saint-Géraud
Peter Botelherius
Peter de Pozanis
Bernard Jornalus "mercator"

G-William de Galhaco
G-William de Mozenquis
Arnold Clavellus
John Bequinus
Bernard de Felgario

APRIL 1277 – SEPTEMBER 1278: TAM, BB 189, fols. 10 and 13 (April and July 1277), ibid. II 63 and 87 (acts dated April and December 1277) and Malta 1 68 (September 1277, copied in 1289).

Arnold Barravus
Hugh de Palacio
Raymond de Dalbs or Dalbis
Bernard de Samatano
Vital Bonetus "notarius"
Peter Feltrerius "notarius" and "monetarius"

Berengar Raimundus
Raymond Maurandus
Peter de Prinhaco
Vital Faber Oddo
William Pictor "notarius"
G-William Vasco "mercator"

JUNE 1278 – APRIL 1279: TAM, II 61 (June 1278), ibid., BB 189, fol. 15 (June 1278), ibid., II 77 (December 1278, copied in 1306); ibid., AA 1 104 (April 1279) and Mulholland, *Early Gild Records of Toulouse*, p. 14 (April 1279).

Arnold de Falgario *or* Felgario "miles"
Bernard Raymond Barravus
Bernard (*or*, in BB 189, Doat) de Roaxio
"Magister" Raymond Azemarius "legista"
Bernard de Trageto

Bertrand de Garigiis "domicellus"
Arnold Raimundus "campsor"
Pons de Prulheco
G-William de Fulhonibus *or* Fulhos
G-William de Gano
Arnold Columbus

AUGUST 1279 – MARCH 1280: Malta 17 134 (August 1279), TAM, BB 189, fol. 15v (February 1280) and ibid., II 63 (March 1280)

"Dominus" Matthew Bequini
Raymond Buxus
Raymond Molinus
Peter Raymond Godi *or* Got
Bernard Bombelli
Peter de Portalli "iuvenis"

Tholosanus Barravus "mercator"
Peter Raymond de Garrigia
Raymond de Caturcio
Berengar de Portalli
G-William Vital Vasco "affachator"

AUGUST 1280 – MARCH 1281: PBN, MS lat. 9993, fol. 28va (August 1280) and TAM, HH 1 5 11-12 (March 1281).

Arnold de Castronovo "miles"
Arnold de Falgario "miles"
Peter de Tholosa
Durand Adhemarius
Raymond de Caramanno

John Bequinus
Peter de Montelanderio
Bernard de Falgario
Arnold de Galhaco
Bertrand de Garrigiis

Appendix Five

Consuls and Heretics

1. Heretics in Family Histories

This list is built by using the family sketches published in earlier works and this one. Of the total of forty-eight families or family names whose histories I have written up, Barbaordeus, Raissaco and Yspania in the present volume have been withheld, the first and last because they were about one generation and the Raissaco because they were rural. The histories of the Claustro and the Tolosa of the Bourg were published in my "Farm of Fontanas," pp. 29-40 and "Urban Society and Culture," pp. 229-247. Those with the names Arnaldus, Carbonellus-de Prignaco, Caturcio, Cerdanus, Davinus, Falgario, Marcillo, Najaco, Noerio, Petricola, Podiobuscano, Seillanus and Turribus are to be found in the present study in Appendix One, the Astro, Raina, Sobaccus and Tonenquis families in my *Men and Women*, pp. 173-194, and all the rest in my *Repression of Catharism*, pp. 129-303. The families together with their town locations in the Bourg and City are the following:

With known Cathar or Waldensian members

1. Baranonus (City)	13. Guido (Bourg)
2. Barravus (Bourg)	14. Maurandus (Bourg)
3. Barravus (City)	15. Montibus (City)
4. Capitedenario (Bourg)	16. Ponte (City)
5. Caraborda (Bourg)	17. Roaxio (City)
6. Castronovo (City)	18. Sobaccus (Bourg)
7. Corregerius (Bourg)	19. Tolosa (City)
8. Curtasolea (Bourg)	20. Trageto (City)
9. David (City)	21. Turre (Bourg)
10. Descalquencs (City)	22. Turre (City)
11. Embrinus (Bourg)	23. Unde (City)
12. Gameville (City)	24. Villanova (City)

Without known Cathar or Waldensian members

25. Arnaldus (City)	36. Marcillo (Bourg)
26. Astro (Bourg)	37. Najaco (Bourg)
27. Barbaordeus (City)	38. Noerio (City)
28. Caraborda (City)	39. Petricola (City)
29. Carbonnellus (Bourg)	40. Podiobuscano (City)
30. Caturcio (Bourg)	41. Raina (City)
31. Cerdanus (Bourg)	42. Seillanus (City)
32. Claustro (Bourg)	43. Tolosa (Bourg)
33. Cossano (Bourg)	44. Tonenquis (City)
34. Davinus (Bourg)	45. Turribus (City)
35. Falgario (City)	

2. CONSULATES CONTAINING THE NAMES OF CONDEMNED HERETICS

Because partial lists hide much, only complete or all but complete consular lists from 1202 to 1249 are counted here. When consulates consisted of twenty-four officers, only those with twenty-two known members and up are listed and in those with twelve members only those with ten and up. The table will give the date of, and number of consuls in, each consular list followed by the names of those condemned for heresy and later listed in the royal diploma of 1279. Each name is accompanied by the number assigned it in my publication of that amnesty of the inheritances of dead heretics (*Repression of Catharism*, pp. 77-115).

1. 1202-1203: 24 CONSULS
Peter de Ponte 57
Pons Mancipius *or* Puer 40

2. 1203-1204: 24 CONSULS
Raymond Gamiscius 54

3. 1204-1205: 24 CONSULS
Bernard de Turre 96
Arnold Guido 16
Bernard Faber 19 & 94
Pons Palmata 15
Raymond de Ulmo 18

4. 1205-1206: 22 CONSULS
Ademar de Turre 95

5. 1207-1208: 24 CONSULS
Peter de Ponte 57
Pons Mancipius *or* Puer 40
Peter William de Orto 86
Pons Palmata 15

6. 1212: 23 CONSULS
Arnold de Roaxio 14
William Isarnus 193

7. 1213-1214: 24 CONSULS
Peter de Ponte 57
Pons Mancipium *or* Puer 40

8. 1215-1216: 23 CONSULS
Peter de Ponte 57
Pons Mancipius *or* Puer 40

Benedict Arnaldus 273
Bernard Medicus 61

9. 1218: 22 CONSULS
Oldric de Gamevilla 111
Peter de Roaxio 214
Arnold de Villanova 23
Arnold Guido 16
Embrinus 112
Peter William de Orto 86
Bernard Signarius 6
Raymond Tapierius 109

10. 1218-1219: 23 CONSULS
Raymond Baranonus 114
Arnold Guido 16
Arnold de Sancto Felicio 87
Arnold Onda 8
Pons Palmata 15
William Bosquetus 103

11. 1220: 24 CONSULS
Arnold Molinus 268
Raymond de Montetotino 191
Bernard Faber 19 & 94
Raymond Gamiscius 54
Peter de Ponte 57
Peter Sobaccus 107
Peter Rogaterius 46

12. 1221: 24 CONSULS
Pons de Saoil 148
William de Cavaldos 120
Vasco de Turre 56
Raymond de Ulmo 18

13. 1222-1223: 24 CONSULS
Bertrand de Montibus 133
Bertrand de Roaxio 158
Bernard Faber "espetierius" 94
Arnold Barravus 145
William Peter de Casalibus 101
Isarn Grillus 267
Arnold Rogerius 11
Raymond Signarius 7

14. 1224: 24 CONSULS
Bernard Martinus 82
Bernard Curtasolea 132
Pons Palmata 15

15. 1225: 24 CONSULS
John Curtasolea 12
Bernard Faber 19 & 94
Raymond Gamiscius 54
Hugh de Murello 80
Arnold de Sancto Felicio 87
Raymond Tapierius 109

16. 1225-1226: 24 CONSULS
Raymond William Atadillis
116 & 157
Arnold Barravus 145
Bertrand de Montibus 133
Arnold de Roaxio 14
William de Turre 100
Peter de Ponte 57
Raymond Ysarnus 77 & 192

17. 1226: 24 CONSULS
Peter Aonde (or Unde etc.) 9
Peter de Vendinis 37

18. 1227: 24 CONSULS
Bernard Pellicerius 64
Bernard de Rocovilla 121
Arnold de Trageto 33
Raymond de Terrasona 73
Terrenus Cassanellus 29

19. 1235-1238: 12 CONSULS
Arnold Barravus 145
Pons de Suollio 148
Bernard Signarius 6
Raymond Rogerius 17 & 81
Raymond Borrellus 55
Oldric Maurandus 128
Bonmacip Maurandus 153
Peter Embrinus 59

20. 1239: 10 CONSULS
Bonmacip Maurandus 153

21. 1239-1240: 11 CONSULS
    none reported

22. 1243-1245 ?: 12 CONSULS
    Vital Bonushomo 127
    Raymond de Ponte 58

23. 1246: 24 CONSULS
    Bertrand Descalquencs 66

24. 1247-1248: 24 CONSULS
    Peter Garsias 252

25. 1249: 12 CONSULS
    none reported

Appendix Six

Documents of the Tolosa Family

1. Dating a Family Cartulary

Saint-Étienne 227 (xxvi DA 2 79) titled "Breve de pignori[bu]s" was copied from a charter described as that of a Raymond Stephanus ("Regimundus Stephanus"), a person several times mentioned as acquiring rights. The list of the witnesses at the end of the document is preceded by "Hec carta est tracta de illa carta que fuit Raimundi Stephani." It contained notes on twenty-six transactions:

1 gift
1 sale
1 lease
3 installations of persons in a property
3 naming personal guarantors of debts or loans
8 "pignora"
9 cancellations of "pignora"

After the first action, the next ten were taken by a Raymond (Regimundus), who may be the Raymond Stephanus mentioned above and are written in the first person, showing that Raymond was either literate or had a scribe at his elbow as he compiled his checklist. After the eleventh act, Raymond disappears but his brothers are thereafter seen speaking in the third person. In short, the "Breve" was a family record that ended up in the archives of the chapter of Toulouse when it was given the property. The actors in the charter were all members of the Tolosa family, for which, see my *Repression of Catharism*, pp. 269-270.

Since the past transactions were not recorded in authenticated copies as they would have been once the secular notariate was established, the document must have been composed late in the eleventh or early in the twelfth century. This is proved by several facts: one of the abstracts mentions Gilbert ("Girbertus"), prior of the Daurade monastery, and another refers to Isarn, bishop of Toulouse. The prior assisted at the founding of the Hospital of Saint-Raymond in Douais, *Cartulaire de Saint-Sernin*, Nos. 546 and 457. Although the documents about this founding are undated, Count William IV of Toulouse, his wife Matilda and Bishop Isarn are mentioned in them. The count ruled from 1061 to 1093 and Isarn was installed as bishop in ca. 1072, hence that passage in the "Breve" derived from sometime between 1072 and 1093.

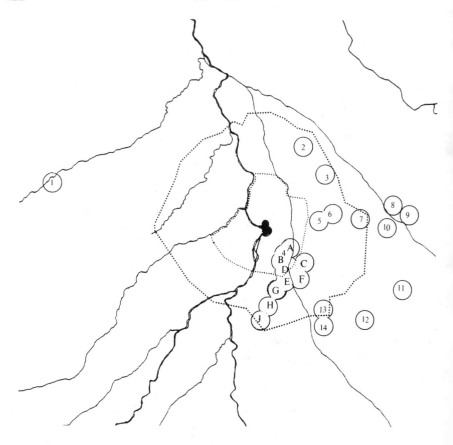

MAP 6 PROPERTIES OF THE TOLOSA SISTERS

LANDED PROPERTIES AT
A = Montaudran
B = Lespinet
C = Lantourville
D = Le Palais
E = Ramonville and Saint-Agne
    as two separate communities
F = Labège
G = Auzeville
H = Mervilla
J = Aureville
....
....
....

INVESTMENTS AT
1 = Isle-Jourdain
2 = Saint-Loup-Cammas
3 = Castelmaurou
4 = Saint-Denis in Montaudran
5 = Busquet
6 = Pin-Balma
7 = Lavalette
8 = Verfeil
9 = Gaillaguet
10 = Saint-Martin (Cassini)
11 = Lanta
12 = Fourquevaux
13 = Escalquencs
14 = Belberaud

2. A DIVISION OF AN INHERITANCE

In Malta 4 191 i (March 1187 or 1188, copied in 1203), Titburgis and Guillelma, daughters of Peter de Tolosa and granddaughters of William de Tolosa, along with their spouses, divided their inheritance. For the history of these women, their family and husbands, see my *Repression of Catharism*, pp. 277-280. William, their grandfather, was first seen in 1150 and had died by November 1177; their father Peter was deceased sometime before the confection of the charter of 1187 or 1188. An entry, No. 18, contains an undated record of a loan made by William and Peter's widows on properties to Isarn Jordan de Saissaco, and No. 19 reports that, sometime afterwards, the two sisters Titburga and Willelma, aided by a third party, presumably a relative or executor of their parents' estate, lent money to a Bertrand de Saisag. Both loans were on property in Pin-Balma.

The young heiresses were obviously single at the time of that loan, but were both married by the time of the charter of 1187 or 1188. Titburga had married a rural lord named Peter de Montebruno (Montbrun-Lauragais near Montgiscard southeast of Toulouse). This couple are seen in 1203 and again in 1214 when the husband was one of the heirs of a rural notable named Raymond de Montelauro (Montlaur near Montbrun and Montgiscard), seen here in Appendix 8, No. 34. Peter had died by 1227 when his widow and son, also named Peter, sold property near the Château Narbonnais. Willelma had married Raymond de Recalto, a notable who became the first vicar general or seneschal of Toulouse. Raymond was still alive in 1221, but his spouse was widowed when last seen in 1233. In 1203 their daughter Mathelda married William Saisset, a lord of Laurac (well south of Toulouse near Castelnaudary), in a sumptuous ceremony attended by the count of Toulouse. This lord of Laurac had died by 1211, leaving a son named Raymond. To conclude, the two sisters who divided their inheritances in 1187 or 1188 were very rich young women.

In the account given below of this division of inheritance, all sums listed are either shillings of Morlaas or Toulousan "solidi deceni," save a late contract which used Toulousan "moneta septena" (No. 27). Only Morlaas will be signaled consistently along with the one "septena." Entries where an annual rate of return on the investment can be established will close with a percentage figure. The values of the Toulousan shilling and that of Morlaas were roughly equivalent at this time.

Notum sit omnibus hominibus presentibus atque futuris ... quod filie dicte Petri de Tolosa, scilicet Titburgis et Guillelma et mariti eorum Petrus de Monbru et Raimundus de Recalt venerunt ad divisionem de hereditate quam habeant predicte domine, et venit

1. ad porcionem Titburgis et Petri de Montbru" all at Auzeville, Ramonville, the tithing of Saint-Martin, all "subtus hospitali Poncii Aimardi," all in the

tithing of Saint-Agne (reads "Anha"), and Mervilla ("Marvillar"), everything "scilicet curia cum omni pertinenti hedificio et aptamenta que est intus et homines et femine et terre culte et inculte et vinee et prata et pascua et decime et oblie et dominationes et census et usus et queste et ademprivi et introiti et exiti" and, in addition, "pignora" to value of 1553 shillings as listed below.

2. Toset de Tolosa and unnamed brothers owed "pignus" of 130 shillings and 370 shillings Morlaas on property at Labège owing an annual service charge ("servicium") of forty shillings Morlaas on November 29 (Saint Sernin). (8% annually)

3. Raymond Unaldus de Lanta pledged half his "honor" of Fourquevaux to William de Tolosa for 150 shillings "per explectare."

4. Sicard de Gavarred pledged to William de Tolosa for ninety shillings Pons Vital de Scalusa, his brothers, their wives, issue and tenements, one "quartonus frumenti in estate et due saumate vini in martrore vel usque in Martrore" (November 1), rent of five shillings less a penny, a "barralis" of wine and four loaves of bread each large enough for three men.

5. "Item in alio pignore" Peter Raymond Gausbertus of Verfeil, his brother Bernard de Cuc, Pons Hugh de Vassaros and his brother William Sicardus "miserunt in pignore Willelmo de Tolosa .x. sol. obliarum [rent] ... pro .lx. sol. tol. decenos, et debentur reddi predicti .x. sol. tol. singulis annis in festo sancte Marie augusti" deriving from Lavalette, Saint-Marcel-Paulel ("de Valeta, de Paulello") and Verfeil for sixty shillings with annual "servicium" of ten shillings of Toulouse on Saint Mary of August (August 15). (16.6% annually)

6. Raymond de Ysla pledged to William de Tolosa for fifty shillings Isarn de Gauro, his brother, etc. with yearly return of ten shillings on Saint Michael (September 29). (20% annually)

7. Pons Hugh de Vassaros of Verfeil and William Sicardus his brother pledged to Peter de Tolosa the "villa" of Marceil (in Cassini, now Saint-Marcel-Paulel) for 250 shillings with payment of thirty shillings yearly in "Martrore" (November 1). (12% annually)

8. Peter Raymond Gausbertus de Verfeil and Bernard de Cuc his brother and William Raymond their nephew pledged to William de Tolosa for 100 shillings Durand Textor de Aquisvivis, Peter Azalbert, Peter Bonet and Pons Daurinus, their wives, etc. for ten shillings "servicium" on Saint Thomas (December 21). (10% annually)

9. Raymond William de Viridifolio and sons Berengar and Peter pledged to William de Tolosa all they have at Saint-Martin for seventy shillings, paying ten shillings "servicium" on Saint Thomas (December 21). (14.2% annually)

10. Raymond de Ysla and William his brother pledged to William de Tolosa Bertrand de Samol, his brother, etc. for seventy shillings with "servicium" of ten shillings and "quartum de avene" on "Natalis Domini" (25 December).

11. William Peter de Castello Maurono pledged to Peter de Tolosa for 100 shillings Forto Barta, Pons Rossellus, Peter Rosellus and their wives and Peter Amalvinus, Peter de Baregas and Raymond de Baregas and their children, etc. for "servicium" of three shillings in Martrore (November 1). (3% annually)

12. Arnold de Sancto Dionisio pleged to William de Tolosa for 100 shillings Morlaas two parts of the "condamina de Campo Ebrino" and "terram del Gres" for "servicium" of fifteen shillings "in quadragesima intrante" (Shrove Tuesday). (15% annually)

13. Raymond Isarn de Viridifolio pledged to William de Tolosa for thirteen shillings Peter Benedictus and Raymond Benedictus, their wives, etc. for "servicium" of three shillings on Saint Thomas (December 21). (23% annually)

14. Guillelma and husband Raymond de Recalt acquire all "honores" from father Peter de Tolosa and grandfather William de Tolosa "ad Abrevila" (modern Aureville southwest of Castanet or Auzielle near Saint-Orens?), Lantosvilla (Lantourville next Saint-Orens-de-Gameville), Labège, the tithing of "Petrosa inter curiam de Hugonis de Palatio" (modern Palais near Ramonville), the bridge over the Hers river near Montaudran, "ad Roserios" (near Lespinet) and the "terra de la Paissera et dels Cairos" (?), as well as 2000 less thirty-three shillings "cum eseg" ("eisec" in Levy means share or division) which Titburga and her husband gave them for having first pick of the above properties.

15. The brothers Isarn Jordan and Jordan de Saissag and their nephew Hugh de Saissaco pledged William de Tolosa all properties at "Pinum" (Pin-Balma) and nearby Busquet for 620 shillings for "servicium" of thirty-nine shillings, seven "saumata vini" and one "barralis" from Saint Michael (September 29) to Martrore (November 1) and twelve "quartones frumenti" and one of "avene" on Saint Mary of August (August 15).

16. Raymond Unaldus de Lanta, Willelma his wife and their son Raymond Unaldus pledged to William de Tolosa all they have at Pin-Balma for 100 shillings Morlaas with "servicium" of fifteen shillings. (15% annually)

17. William de Tolosa "prestavit" sixty-seven shillings Morlaas to Isarn Jordan de Saissaco and Bertrand his nephew and was given lands and meadows "prope Anorum [with labial over the n] ad explectandum."

18. "Domina Titburga qui fuit uxor Willelmi de Tolosa et Austorga qui fuit uxor Petri de Tolosa prestaverunt" 100 shillings to Isarn Jordan de Saissaco on the properties at Pin-Balma "ultra omnia alia pignora."

19. "Item" Bertrand de Saisag pledged for 500 shillings Melgueil (250 shillings of Toulouse) "et per lucrum panalium Willelmo Seillano et filiabus Petri de Tolosa totum honorem de Pinu ultra alia pignora que ibi habebant."

20. Isarn de Viridifolio son of Bertrand Jordanus pledged to William de Tolosa for 115 shillings the "villa" of Gaillaguet near Verfeil with "servicium" of fifteen shillings. (13% annually)

21. William Hugh de Turribus pledged to William de Tolosa for fifty shillings Morlaas all at Saint-Loup-Cammas with "servicium" of ten shillings in Martrore (November 1). (20% annually)

22. Deceased Isarn Jordan de Viridifolio, brother of William Asalid, pledged William de Tolosa Peter Martin de Taulaz, Benedict son of Peter Calveti, Stephen de Roiolibus, Arnold de Fonte Petra, Bernard de Fontepetra, Bernard de Rivale, Arnold de Taulaz, Bernard de Campo Marsa, and their wives for sixty shillings "decenos," for yearly "quadragesima intrante" (Shrove Tuesday) payment of twelve shillings "servicium." (20% annually)

23. Bernard Jordan de Isla (surely Bernard Jordan I, lord of Isle-Jourdain) and Jordan his son pledged to William de Tolosa for 100 shillings all they have "ad Mainadas" (?) for annual "servicium" of twenty shillings. (20% annually)

24. Isarn de Riol pledged to William de Tolosa for sixty shillings Morlaas William Gausbert de Sancto Proiecto, his brother, Bernard Bonafos and Raymond Benedict and their wives and "tenentias" for ten shillings on Easter. (16.6% annually)

25. Raymond de Ysla and brothers William and Vital pledged to William de Tolosa and to his son Peter de Tolosa all they have "ad Yslam" (?) for 130 shillings Morlaas for "servicium" of nineteen shillings Morlaas and one "quartum de avene" on Saint Thomas (December 21).

26. Bernard Isarn de Viridifolio and Fiandina his wife pledged to William de Tolosa for fifteen shillings "decenos" three (twelve or seven?) shillings of "obliarum" and six "sextarios de avena."

27. Bertrand de Montibus pledged to Willelma and Raymond de Recalt for 300 shillings "monete septene" all he has at Escalquens and Belberaud with "servicium" of thirty shillings in Martrore (November 1), All Saints and Christmas. (10% annually)

28. Finally, to Titburga and husband "venit turris et camera et casalis qui fuit Raimundi de Paulel et fratrum eius et palarga (palatga?) que est foris" and her sister Willelma got the "turris et alia domus et casalis qui fuit Willelmi de Tolose."

The witnesses included Bernard Sellanus, Peter Burdus de Tolosa, Bertrand de Montibus, Pons de Gamevilla and William de Gamevilla. The scribe was Arnold Ferrucius and the charter was copied in November 1203,

TO THIS ACT WAS APPENDED AS NUMBER II

Titburga, the daughter of Peter de Tolosa "qui fuit" and her husband Peter de Montebruno sell William Raymond prior of the Hospital "duas partes totius illius decime quem prior et" Hospital ought to pay on all those "honores" which were of Bernard David and his son Pons David "pro aliquo lucrativo titulo vel aliqua adquisitione vel aliqua emptione quam habuissent [Hospitalers] factam ab eodem Poncio David," namely all "honores" "inter rivum de Flamolriu et honores" of Bernard de Miramonte and "tenet de honore" of Aimeric de Castronovo "usque ad flumen Garonne" and the other part of the same "honores inter honorem" of Aimeric de Castronovo and "honores" of the Hospital, totaling two parts of the said tithing. Peter de Montbru agreed to this contract. Witnesses were Pons de Villanova, his brother Jordan, Bernard Raymond and his brother Peter de Tolosa, sons of the deceased Toset de Tolosa, and Arnold their brother, etc. Written on a Saturday in November and confirmed on November 18 or 19, 1203.

AND ANOTHER AS NUMBER III

For the sale made by Domina Titburga and Peter de Montebru, these two render to the Hospital four "carte":

1. One contains two charters, one written by William Portarius and the other by Stephanus (very probably the Stephen de Populivilla seen below). William Portarius recorded that the two brothers Crispin and Arnold "venerunt ad finem et ad concordiam de toto illo honore qui fuit de patrimonio eorum," etc. Stephen recorded that Arnold Sancti Genesii gave at fief half of the church of "Sancti Aniani" (Saint-Agne) to Crispin and his brother Arnold.

2. In the second charter Stephen de Populivilla states that Arnold Sancti Genesii pledged to William de Tolosa and his wife twelve pennies "oblie" and "omne servicium quod per ecclesiam Sancti Aniani et per ecclesiasticum et per illum honorem ecclesie pertinentem debent fieri et reddi."

3. "et est ibi in illis quatuor instrumentis alia carta" which Stephen de Populivilla wrote saying that Bonusmancipius, son of Raymond Massurri, and his brothers Toset and Sicard pledged to William de Tolosa their part of the church of Saint-Agne, "scilicet de decimis, de primiciis, et de cimiterio, et de precantu," etc.

4. A charter written by the scribe named Magnes wherein Bernard Rufus, brother of Arnold Rufus, "cognovit et concessit per bonas et per veras in placito omnes has cartas predictas sicut continetur in eadem carta quam Magnes scripsit. Tali pacto reddiderunt eis has cartas ut fratres predicti hospitalis debent eas tenere bene et fideliter, et si Petrus et Titburga placitum habebant huius predicte decime ipsi aut eorum ordinium fratres predicti hospitalis debent eis trahere et monstrare has predictas cartas ad bonam fidem ad deffendendum seipsos de guirentia ... ."

The four charters were copied by the scribe William on November "feria quarta, tresdecima die in exitu," 1203.

To this large parchment were attached several original charters, but, since the sewing has partially disintegrated, it is hard to say what in the "liasse" was originally attached. Here are two:

1. Arnold de Sancto Genesio and his "nepos" William Peter pledged William de Tolosa and wife those twelve pence "obliarum quos ipse eis debebat fieri vel reddi per .x. sol. de tol. decenos," and "terminus redimendi" this "pignus" is yearly "in quadragesima intrante" (Shrove Tuesday). Raymond de Capitedenario guaranteed the pledge. Written by Stephen on May "feria tertia" 1157. (10% annually)

2. "Arnoldus et Crespinus fratre suo venerunt ad finem et concordiam de totam illam honorem qui fuit patrimonio eorum. Et debent inter eos illam honorem partire qui fuit Bernardo Augerio qui est in claustra Sancti Saturnini per medietatem sine enganno. Et aliam totam honorem qui fuit Bernardus Augerio, teneat pater eorum in vita sua. Post mortem pater eorum debent partire Arnaldus et Crespinus totam et ab integram illam honorem qui fuit Bernardo Augerio inter eos per medietatem per bene et per fide sine enganno. Et totam alteram honorem que ad eos adveniet ex parte patris eorum debent partire per fraternitatem ... ." This final phrase states that the brothers will hold their useful domain of the church of Saint-Agne in "fratrisca." Done "in carreira maiore devant turre Ramundo Baptizato" by William Porterius who did not date the act save as "feria quinta" June, Louis king of France.

Appendix Seven

The Early "Gasalha" Contract

Mireille Castaing-Sicard's study of contract forms in medieval Toulouse published in 1959 has preempted that field of research for sometime to come.[1] The author's treatment is especially rich regarding the "societas" or partnership, whether of persons or of capital. The rarer of the two, the "societas" involving capital, was particularly well exemplified at Toulouse by the mills of the Bazacle, a forerunner of the modern joint stock company with limited liability about which Castaing-Sicard's husband, Germain Sicard, published a fine study in 1953.[2] The kind of partnership of persons called the "gasalha" is even rarer in the documents. This brief note re-examines the available evidence to push forward the date at which documentation for this contract is found near Toulouse.

The verb "gazanar" meant to gain or to invest in order to gain. A charter dated 1163 records two persons dividing property but retaining in partnership "pignora" held at Saint-Geniès just north of Toulouse. The contract provided that if any of these were terminated by the debtors, the profit was to be divided in half. A futher provision required that, if either invested or further profited ("gazagnare"), the other partner was to be consulted and the gains mutually divided.[3] The term "gazanha" was employed both about investments and the acquisition of land. An emancipation dated 1174 rendered in the church of Saint-Sernin stated that a father gave his son, a major, all "profits" he and his son had made in the past and likewise all property they had acquired. The verb used to describe both profit and acquisition is "gadanare," and the terms of the emancipation show that father and son had worked together before emancipation and planned to do so afterward.[4] In credit contracts, "gazan" meant "lucrum" and

---

[1]*Les contrats dans le très ancien droit Toulousain.*

[2]*Aux origines des sociétés anonymes: Les moulins de Toulouse au moyen-âge.*

[3]Malta 123 1 v (December 1163, copied in 1225 and 1239): "si in istis predictis pignoribus ullus [either Peter Rufetus or Bernard Azalbertus] prestabat plus vel gazagnabat ullo modo faciat consilio alterius, et si revertebatur in partizo sicut suprascriptum est, alter redderet medietatem precii."

[4]Appendix 9, No. 8, with forms of the verb "gadanare," the use of "habere" as an auxiliary verb, etc.

was therefore contrasted with "cabal" or, in the Latin of Toulousan charters, with "cabale" (from "capitale") which meant invested capital.[5]

Although the meaning of "gazan" as "lucrum" persisted, "gazan," like its Latin equivalent, suffered from the taint of usury and, as the clerical prohibition of that practice began to take hold, became rare in ordinary commercial contracts.[6] This reason, perhaps, and the maturing economy gradually fostered a specialized use of the term "gasalha" to describe a specific contract whereby an investor capitalized, and a working partner labored at, stock raising or animal husbandry. This is what the *Custom* of Toulouse referred to when it stated that a tenant could do a variety of things, including "gasalha," even against his lord's will.[7]

Basing her opinion on the *Custom* of Toulouse promulgated in 1286, Castaing-Sicard alleged that the institution was widespread, indeed, known to everybody. She also conjectures that few "gazalha" contracts can be found until the fourteenth century, because they were then so simple that they were not composed by public notaries.[8] The notion that much business was not recorded in notarized form is true and this author proved it by citing a testament dated 1206 in which a Bernard Raymond Garnerius, a friend of the decedent, was supposed to contribute the sum of 500 shillings to an unborn child of the dying William Raymond de Insula. In spite of its size, this debt was enshrined in a minute, not a notarized document.[9] Again, a document of 1326 states that a number of debts owed a businessman named William Prima were recorded "on a certain paper," a phrase clearly meaning that they were not in notarial instruments.[10]

Notarized charters nevertheless exist. Most of Prima's contracts were actually notarized. And there are early examples. In 1201 a partnership constituted by a harness-maker, his son and a third party for the exploitation of property at Saint-Geniès was dissolved and the father and son promised to destroy all public acts concerning this "societas" or "gasalha."[11]

---

[5]For the word "cabal," see E 573 (March 1225) where the consuls confirmed "omne illud ius et rationem quam habebat ipse Petrus Rainaldus et habere debebat in illis .dc. sol. Tol. quos ipse Petrus Rainaldus et Guillelmus de Quinto miserant in capitale Bernardi de Sancta Columba sicut continebatur in carta illa quam Arnaldus de Brantalono [a public notary] inde scripserat."

[6]Castaing-Sicard, *Contrats dans le très ancien droit Toulousain*, especially pp. 263-264.

[7]Gilles, *Coutumes de Toulouse*, Article No. 149: "quod homines qui habent dominos possunt bona sua mobilia vendere et alienare et tenere gassallias et recipere nomine gasallie animalia que prius habebant propria et etiam alia, sine consensu dominorum suorum."

[8]*Contrats dans le très ancien droit Toulousain*, pp. 131-132 and 452.

[9]See Appendix 8, No. 26.

[10]Clares 26 (November 1325 and May 1326): a small debt recorded "in quodam papiru" and another debt "in dicto papiru."

[11]Saint-Étienne 366, (February 1201): "Concordia talis fuit quod Arnaldus Raimundus et Poncius Raimundus eius filius solverunt ac reliquerunt Arnaldo Mancipio et suo ordinio totum hoc quod ei petebant vel petere [poterant] vel putabant pro illa societate

Contracts about animal husbandry involved two kinds of enterprise: 1) raising animals for meat, hides, wool or milk or 2) using them for ploughing or transportation. Both kinds are referred to in the passage of the *Custom* cited above and are amply evidenced in the charters. The word "laborantia" meant the working of a farm: the farms of the convent of Lespinasse north of Toulouse, for example, were worked by hired laborers, ploughmen and herdsmen called "nuncii" in Latin. In 1224 the consuls relieved the debt-ridden sisters and lay brethren by prohibiting their creditors from confiscating draft animals and other beasts, namely the sisters' ten pairs of oxen and five other beasts in Lespinasse and five pairs and two pack animals at Mondonville (opposite the house on the left bank of the Garonne).[12] In 1230 an individual named Fort Boerius conceded that the prioress, the lady cellarer, three attached brothers, the male "capellanus" and a cowherd or cattleman for the Fontevrault nunnery of Lespinasse had paid him the third part of those twenty "vacce vitularie" (calves or milchcows) which he and a Peter Buxus had in "gasalha" for 340 shillings of Toulouse, as well as his third part of the 400 shillings the prioress and her convent owed him for the "income of the said cows" to be paid in three installments. Because Lespinasse was in financial trouble at this time, Fort had perhaps settled for the modest sum of 120 shillings, but it is also possible that profit was disguised.[13] A little over a year later, the convent, headed by the

---

sive pro illa gasala vel pro illa laborantia quam simul fecerant vel habuerant apud Sanctum Genesium et de omnibus convenientiis quas pro predicta laborantia eius predictus Arnaldus Mancipium fecerat sine aliquo retentu quem ibi ei ullo modo non fecerunt, et convenerunt predicto Arnaldo Mancipio quod si aliquas cartas habebant quod de predicta societate vel de gasala vel de laborantia essent vel pertinerent quod omnes illas frangerent, et quod inde crederentur eorum plano verbo sine sacramento et testibus nam ita convenerunt ei et suo ordinio in pace et sine omni placito." The partner promised the same.

[12]MADTG, A 297, fols. 807-808 (January 1224): the convent informed the consuls "quod conventus eiusdem domus debebat multa debita et baratas et quod pro illis debitis et baratis creditores pignorabant continue eos et non poterant ... laborare in honoribus Spinassie neque in honoribus de Mondoville et quod etiam amici eis nolebant succurrere in aliquo timore ipsorum creditorum." The consuls granted them a stay until Christmas and then a further year for payment of their debts to protect their ability to farm: "quod dictus conventus Spinassie et eorum amici teneant usque ad decem paria bovum in domo Spinassie et cum ipsis ibi laborent secure et v [an illegible number] de aliis bestis scilicet ad eorum carrugam et ad res alias defferenda quas necesse fuerint ipsi conventui, et apud Mondovilla similiter teneant quinque paria bovum et duos saumerios ... . Et de laboratu quod cum istis bobus fiet habeat conventus sua necessaria et nuncios qui necessarii fuerint huic laborancie, et tractis inde missionibus et seminibus et de mercedibus nunciorum et de ferro et ligno, et residuum quod de illa laborancia superaverit persolvatur creditoribus domus ... ."

[13]Lespinasse 28 ii (June 1230): "... quod Forto Boerius sua sponte habuit et tenuit se pro bene paccato de domina Margarita priorissa domus Spinachie et de domina

same prioress, acting together with four sisters and the male prior and four brothers, settled what they owed to a William Magister "pellerius" (an artisan or merchant in leather) for the "gazalha" and "laborantia" in Mondonville, computing the value of his investment at 680 shillings and pledging him the crops of the "house and grange of Mondonville" until repaid.[14]

Written "gasalha" contracts were therefore well known. That they are not frequently found in private or institutional archives is because, like other temporary contracts or partnerships, copies were retained after their terms expired only by accident. This specialized use of the term "gasalha" did not mean that other ways of expressing contracts of this kind were ruled out. Some of these show that, just as with loans in money, one way of effecting the same economic objective was a deposit contract. In 1230 a Toulousan citizen recognized that the sisters of Lespinasse had paid him 400 of the 700 shillings of Toulouse worth of lambs he had "placed in deposit" at the said house.[15] A later undated example from the end of the thirteenth century records that a jurist

---

Bernarda de Roquis cellararia eiusdem domus et de fratre Raimundo de Claromonte and de Raimundo Boerio et de Petro Raimundo capellano domus eiusdem et de fratre Willelmo clerico et de fratre Petro clerico de sua tercia parte de illis .xx. vaccis vitulariis quas ab eodem Fortone et a Petro Buxo tenebant in gasalem, que vacce constaverant .ccc.xl. sol. Tol. sicut in cartis illius gasale continetur divisis per alphabetum quas Petrus Raimundus [a public notary] scripserat. Similiter dictus Forto ... tenuit se pro bene paccato de sua tercia parte illorum .cccc. sol. Tol. quos predicta domina priorissa et domina Bernarda de Roquis et alii debitores predicti debebant eidem Fortoni et Petro Buxo persolvere in quatuor temporibus pro explecta predictarum vaccarum sicut in carta continetur persolutionis quam predictus Petrus Raimundus scripserat." The receipt is then repeated and followed by the following phrase: "et recognovit et concessit quod inde habuerat ipse Forto Boerius .c.xx. sol. Tol." "Boerius" may well be a surname, but note also that "boer," "bovarius" etc. meant cowherd or cattleman.

[14]MADTG, A 297, fols. 805v-07 (December 1231): The sisters, etc. "venerunt ad computum et ad concordiam cum Guillelmo Magistro ... de omnibus illis debitis et baratis que domus de Spinassie et domus de Mondonvilla ... eidem Guillelmo Magistro debebant et ad faciendum habebant pro gazalha et laborantia de Mondonvilla et de omnibus illis missionibus et accomodationibus sicut melius in carta ipsius gazalhe ... continetur ... ." With the expenses paid by the convent, the creditor was to receive in payment "totum illud blatum et omnia illa blata que sunt seminata et fuerunt seminata usque in festo natalis domini." Note that Mondonville is called "domus et grangia."

[15]Lespinasse 28 i (November 1230): "... Raimundus Medicus ... concessit quod ex illis .dcc. sol. Tol. quos domus Spinachie eidem Raimundo [Medico promiserat pro il]lis fedis quas predicte domui in depositum miserat, habuerat ... ex illis predictis .dcc. sol. Tol... . idem Raimundus Medicus .cccc. sol. Tol. de quibus se habebat [et tenebat pro bene] paccato ... ." The vernacular word "feda" means lamb but also any wool-producing beast, such as a goat.

joined with the house of Lespinasse in a lifetime partnership involving the grange of Pradel near Saint-Jory north of Toulouse. Both partners shared expenses half and half together with the goods involved, namely riding horses, plough oxen, a cow and calf and forty-three wool-bearing animals, the latter being in "gasalha" from a Toulousan citizen.[16]

If contracts are few, references to the enterprise are more frequent. A town notable, for example, willed a brother his half of all they had in "gasalha" in his testament of 1235.[17] The *Custom* of Le Castéra in Gascony northwest of Toulouse in 1240 mentioned "gasalhani et porciarii (swineherds)" among the inhabitants of the "castella," and the later custom of Sainte-Marie-du-Désert in 1273 spoke of the place's "gasalliani."[18] In 1249 the monks and others of the Cistercian house of Calers were allowed to construct "cabana" and have pasture for all their animals, whether personal or in "gasalha," by Peter de Mahornaco on his property at Mahornac.[19] "Cabana" were larger than the word sounds in English. A testament of 1235 notes that at least three mares and eight milch cows were housed in one.[20]

Although overlaps remained, the Latin derivative of the word "gasalha" became increasingly associated with animal husbandry. When Pons de Capitedenario drew his will in 1229, he mentioned the sheep he and his family owned or in which they invested, some as far away as at Gimont (about forty-five kilometers west of Toulouse), but did not say that they were in "gasalha."[21]

---

[16]ADML, Lespinasse Register (XVIIth century), No. 7, fols. 4-4v: the convent, its syndic and prior with the consent of the "grangerius grangie de Pradello ... accepit et acculhuit dominum Magistrum Johannem de Sancto Forti jurisperitum in comuni societate dicte grangie de Pradello et in omnibus bonis et rebus et iuribus que sunt et erant in dicta grangia ... quamdiu vixerit, et specialiter in duobus roscinis et duobus bobus arantibus et in una vacca cum suo vitulo et in quadraginta tribus bestiis omnibus cum lana cum suo ovili quas tenet a Guillelmo Soquerio cive Tholose ad gasalham," and generally half of the property and fruits.

[17]Appendix 8, No. 63.

[18]Cabié, *Coutumes de la Gascogne Toulousaine*, p. 48 (November 1240), and p. 66 (April 1273). Near Cadoux, Sainte-Marie is now called Bellegarde-Sainte-Marie.

[19]Barrière-Flavy, *L'Abbaye de Calers (1147-1790)*, p. 68 (March 1249): "... quod monachi et fratres et donati vel eorum nuncii sive familie possint libere et sine ulla contradictione construere seu facere cabanas vel caulas ad opus animalium suorum ... sive animalia illa sint propria sive de gasaliis ... ."

[20]See my "Village, Town and City," p. 189: "... quod totum predictum pecus erat in cabana Petri Stephani de Fenolheto et Guillelmi Militis ... ."

[21]PBN, Collection Doat 40: fols. 216v-231 and, in a transcription of 1764 in Saint-Bernard 21 (March 1229): the testator mentions "oves" owned by himself, his wife and daughter, and also gave an individual, Vasco, the son of Dominica, "omnem meam partem de illis ovibus quas habeo ad Gimontem ... ." For Capitedenario, see my *Repression of Catharism*, pp. 136-154, and Appendix 8, No. 51 below.

When a smith or iron-monger had his will written in 1257, he or his notary specifically took care to do so.[22] By that time, the contract was so common that when two notables asked the convent of Lespinasse to guarantee a debt owed them in 1269, the religious pledged all their credit including that from "gasalha."[23]

A reader may have noted that most references in this early period derived from Gascony. This region was becoming a center of transhumance for wool-bearing animals, especially sheep. By early modern times, in 1485, a Béarnais rented pasture at Pardmillan twenty kilometers north of Marmande on the Garonne, a distance of about 150 to 160 kilometers from his native province.[24] Around Toulouse in this earlier period, things were not yet quite so specialized, but were already pretty well developed. In 1325 the benefactor of the Clares named William Prima seen above in this appendix drew his testament leaving all his wealth to the sisters on the death of his wife. In the next year, the proctor and syndic of the Clares came before the court of the vicar of Toulouse, stating that the donor had died bankrupt and presented an account of his recoverable assets.[25] Prima had been involved in four "societates" with other merchants, two from Toulouse and two from Castres and its region in the Albigeois far to the east of Toulouse, involving nearly 300 pounds of Toulouse. There were documents to show that he was owed a trifle over 460 shillings of Toulouse, mostly from the region immediately north and west of town, at Saint-Jory, Blagnac and Cornebarrieu, but almost a quarter from Castres. Instruments proved that rent was owed him on twenty-four pieces of property at Leyrac near Blagnac.[26] In the "bovaria" of the same village, he had 114 "animalia ad lana," and, at nearby Blagnac, a person "held in gasalha" from him forty-nine animals whose wool was valued at over twenty-three pounds of Toulouse.[27]

[22]Appendix 8, No. 89.

[23]ADML, Lespinasse Register, No. 17, fol. 10r-v (May 1269): "pro debitis videlicet vel barratis aut pro gazaillis vel s[ocieta]tibus seu computis vel comandis aut pro obliis vel redditibus seu fructibus proventibus vel expletis vel alio modo ... ."

[24]This history is described in Luc, *Vie rurale et pratique juridique en Béarn aux XIVe et Xve siècles, passim,* and, for the story of 1485, pp. 180-181.

[25]Clares 26 (November 1325 and May 1326).

[26]Ibid.: in Clares 24 i (November 1285) Leyrac is called Saint-Martin-de-Alayraco, a place located near Cornebarrieu, Blagnac and Colomiers marked on Cassini's XVIIIth century map.

[27]Ibid.: the farmer at Blagnac "tenet in gazalha a dicto Guillelmo Prima .xlviiii. animalia cum lana in precio" of £ 47 4 s of Tours (sums in pounds were counted in those of Tours, valued at half a Toulousan pound; those in shillings in that of Toulouse). In the "bovaria" were "animalia ad lana."

Appendix Eight

A Calendar of Testaments

INTRODUCTION

Wills are limited documents. They frequently do not distribute all the property of a decedent. Property was disposed by codicil as well as by gift prior to a final will, a matter of significance when it is remembered that many Toulousans bought corrodies or other care from the church. Furthermore, the final arrangement of a marital jointure was often taken care of in a separate act, one often rendered more or less at the same time as a testament. On the whole, however, the testaments give a fair idea of the means possessed by an individual, especially if the testator was a modest person lacking large amounts of real property. Unhappily, the rich disposed of such quantities of that commodity and were so succinct about it that it is nearly impossible to evaluate their worth.

Social historians who compare charitable donations and the assignment of inheritances know that the 103 documents calendared here will not give them as complete a reading of the comparative social standing of decedents and families as do dowries and marriage gifts. Readers are therefore urged to compare these aspects of the testaments by examining other materials. Approximately three-quarters of the charters described in this calendar have had their records of marital portions omitted or abbreviated, but these are to be found in an appendix called "Charters dealing with Women" published in my *Men and Women*, pp. 131-162. Other materials are to be found in that study also, especially in the statistics comparing charitable donations with marriage settlements assembled in Appendix Two, pp. 164-172, and the general discussion of economic means in the text on pp. 105-108. For ease of consultation, the entries in Appendix One of *Men and Women* will be signaled here in abbreviated form (*M&W* followed by the number).

In listing these documents, attention will be paid to the parish of the town or the locality from which the testator came. The appointment of executors will be mentioned and the usual term for these is "spondarii" or "sponderii," later replaced by words and phrases such as "sponderii et executores." Sometimes, persons, often ones of considerable prestige, were appointed "consiliatores" or advisers and others were even simply called "testes." Testators leaving minors usually appointed "tutores," who were much like "sponderii." Although sometimes not appointed, especially in the earlier testaments, "spondarii" appear to have been pressingly recommended, although not imposed, by law or custom sometime in the late twelfth century. The history of the Toulousan "sponderagium" is to be found in Boyer's "La nature juridique de l'exécution testamentaire dans le très ancien droit toulousain (X-XIIIe siècles)," first published in 1951 and reissued again in his *Mélanges*, pp. 159-188.

The amount given in charity to the church, eleemosynary institutions, bridges and other public works, private persons, especially relatives and godchildren, and restitution for usury will be noted, although rarely in detail. Some documents assign a simple or unspecified sum of money to charity. Testators with issue usually bequeathed more to relatives and friends than to the church. The beneficiaries and the survivors or relicts shall also be cataloged.

1. AUGUST 1150: Saint-Étienne 227 (26 DA 2 91). "Hec est carta testamenti et adornationis quod fecit domina Prima mater Iohannis Raterii in ultima voluntate et in ultimo suo testamento" at Braqueville near Toulouse. Widow of Raterius, she appointed no "spondarii" and, as charity, proposed that her son John "semper omni tempore vite sue in unaquaque hebdom[ad]a faceret ei unam missam dicere pro dei amore et pro sua anima." Mistakenly (?) called a sister by the scribe, a daughter named Rica was dowered (*M&W* 2). Rica and her four brothers, John, Arnold, Peter Bernard and Robert Raterius, were to share certain properties "communiter per frairescam." John was especially advantaged among the children, being granted "omnia illa lucra que ipse fecerat cum ea ad Bracavillam post mortem Raterii patris sui dicti," etc. because Prima "misit et laxavit Rotbertum filium suum et suum honorem predictum et omnia alia sua iura in potestate et in baiulatione de Johanne filio suo fratre Rotberti et in dei mercede et sua de decem annis." The honor mentioned in that passage was his "medietas pignoris de Castaned" valued at 141 shillings threepence. The rest of the property was to be divided among the male heirs, even the "honores" which the testator "adquisivit cum Johanne filio suo post mortem Raterii."

2. JANUARY 1164: Douais, *Cartulaire de Saint-Sernin*, Appendix No. 47 and Saint-Sernin 600 (10 36 8). Gerald de Castilone (Castillon, just north of town) created a will without any "spondarii." His childless widow, Arsenda, was given her dotal settlement and additional property (*M&W* 3). He gave Saint-Sernin a mill on the Giron river that had been pledged to him by Peter Belis, reserving the gains, namely the "expletas illius molendini ... sub nomine pignoris per .l. solidos et per lucrum," on the condition that the fifty shillings and gains are returned to Peter, "et lucro paccato sit molendinus de opera et de Petro Munione [Sancti Saturnini]." A mare was divided between Peter Belis (three shares) and Raymond de Capitedenario (one share), etc. The testator "fecit suum testamentum et suam dispositionem" in the presence of Peter "capellanus" Saint-Sernin "feria .iiii. mane ante lucem mense ianuarii; et in

eadem ebdomada in feria .vi. mortuus fuit atque sepultus secundum dicta testium; auctoritate illorum testium Stephanus scripsit."

3. MAY, SEPTEMBER AND DECEMBER 1166: Grandselve 58 Roll 1 recto vi, vii and viii. Bruno Trenca of Saint-Pierre-des-Cuisines appointed three advisers, including a monk of Grandselve, to which monastery he gave a two arpent vineyard. His widow Lumbarda was to have 500 shillings and a new vineyard, if she allowed the bequest to Grandselve. Later in the charter, the testator added that she was to have "tercia pars de .c. morbetis" of a "pignus" on a piece of property (100 "maravedi" would be about 125 shillings of Toulouse). His daughters Esclarmunda, Petrona and Bernarda were treated differently. Probably married, Bernarda got 100 shillings, the other two siblings were to go to religion with 150 shillings endowment each, although one could be married instead with 200 shillings. His sons Peter Robert and Bernard were the heirs, having much of the property given them "in frairescam," and Peter Robert "debet tenere companiam Bernardo suo fratri pro bono et fide .x. annos post mortem Bruni sui patris." The testator's debts of thirty shillings were to be paid, and 195 shillings was set aside for his "conquerentes," that is, for restitution of usury.

After this "computus," there followed what are, in effect, two codicils rounding out the will. The first one dated September states "quod ego ... disposui in testamento meo ut omnes esquazeite mee darentur pro salute anime mee secundum dispositionem spondariorum meorum. Nunc autem in mea plena memoria statuo ut absque alicuius dispositione omnes esquazeite mee darentur" to Grandselve save for thirty shillings that are to pay his debts to four persons. The vernacular word "escazensa" means debts, things owed to or by the testator. In December Bruno drew up a second codicil or testament, reading: "Hec est carta testamenti et dispositionis quam fecit Bruno Trenca in infirmitate de qua obiit in ultima voluntate in domo Grandissilve." Here he confirmed his donations to the monks, added that the 195 shillings his son Peter Robert had acquired was first to be spent "paccari suos conquerentes," and after that was completed, given to Grandselve. He also gave his widow a further 100 shillings "qui venerant per successionem per filiam suam que iam mortua erat quando carta ista facta fuit." This sum had been assigned in the first will to Grandselve, were the child to die, but is here given instead to his wife to add to the sum already given her (M&W 5) so that she will not contest the disposition of her husband's property to Grandselve. If she refused her husband's right to dispose of his property freely, she is to have only the sum for life, after which it is to go to Grandselve. The witnesses were three monks, and, on their avowal, the instrument was made by a public scribe of Toulouse named Stephen de Pobolvilla who was also a "capellanus."

4. OCTOBER 1168: Saint-Étienne 114. Arsenda, widow of John Taliati, testamented in the presence of Bertrand Feirolus. Her present husband Arsivus

was to have half a "casal" (probably a small house or lot), half of its equipment, and a half arpent vineyard in or near Braqueville. The "capellanus" of Saint-Étienne witnessed the charter.

5. 1171 WITHOUT MONTH: Grandselve 58 Roll 2 recto ii. Having already entered the monastery as an oblate and manager of the monks' hospice in Toulouse in ibid. i (September 1147), Bernard de Manso "apud Grandem Silvam talem debitorum suorum supputationem et rerum suarum disposicionem fecit." Leaving the monks all his property, the testator required them to pay his debts of 274 shillings and collect the debts owed him of 232 shillings. In ibid. Roll 1 recto iv (December 1178), Bernard's widow Petrona gave over all her property to the monks of Grandselve. The "arenga" of her donation reads: "Quoniam humana fragilitas labilis est ad peccandum et dies hominis breves, propheta testante, 'homo sicut fenum et dies ut flos agri' [Isaiah 40 6-8], et Jacobus apostolus, 'que est vita nostra nisi pavor ad modicum parens [James 4 14: "Que est enim vita vestra ? Vapor ad modicum parens, et deinceps exterminabitur"],' et dominus in evangelio nos hortatur, dicens, 'vendite et date que possidetis et facite thesauros in celo non deficientes [Luke 12 33],' idcirco ego Petrona ... dono," etc. In ibid. v of the same date, she entered the monastery and was assured of retaining her property for life and guaranteed maintenance in case the income was insufficient.

6. OCTOBER 1176: Grandselve 2 ii (copied in 1201). Bernard de Bruniqueld had bought a "casal" "foris portam de Crosis" in the Bourg in February 1156, and now "in sua infirmitate unde obiit fecit suam dispositionem" bequeathed it to his daughter Ramunda with no "spondarii" and no charities. Although a testament, this instrument may not have contained all of Bernard's dispositions.

7. OCTOBER 1186: Ourliac and Magnou, *Cartulaire de Lézat*, No. 1475. Geralda de Labigia "in sua ultima infirmitate de qua obiit ad suum extremum computum quod fecit in suo ultimo testamento, sua propria voluntate dedit" to her son Stephen a small piece of arable. There were no "spondarii" or charities.

8. FEBRUARY 1187: Malta 1 80. "In sua ultima infirmitate de qua grave infirmabatur," Arnold de Pissavacca drew his testament and reaffirmed his gift of self and property to the Hospitalers. His son William Arnold and grandson Gerald, together with his two daughters (one married), confirmed this gift. Arnold's other son Bernard was to receive 285 shillings, but, were he to attack the donation to the Hospital, only fifty shillings. Were he to do so, also, he was to know that he acted "cum maleditione sui patris Arnaldi et domini nostri Ihesu Christi, et deus omnipotens deducat eum in profundum inferni cum Datan et Abiron."

9. MARCH 1189: Malta 58 3 (copied in 1241). Bernard Ortolanus (probably not a gardener) of the Daurade and Saint-Cyprien regions appointed his wife Riqua

and three men "spondarii." He gave twenty-five shillings, a "lorica" and some clothes to his executors and a nephew. His property was to be sold with a fourth going to charity, a fourth to his wife and a half to his two daughters, both minors, in equal division (*M&W* 13). His "spondarii" were also termed "tutores," obviously for his daughters.

10. MAY 1189: Malta 3 147 iii, copied in 1204. Married in February 1188 (ibid. ii), Raymond Faber "coltellarius" (cutler) guaranteed his widow Maria 200 shillings etc., and left the rest of his property to his brother William Coltellarius. A parishioner of the Dalbade, Raymond left no charities and had no "spondarii."

11. APRIL 1191: E 973 xi, copied in 1204. Unmarried and childless, William de Paratge left much of his property to William Arnold "medicus," the founder of the Hospital of Sainte-Catherine, for whom he worked and with whom he was going on pilgrimage overseas. The document was rendered because the testator "voluit pergere in illo viatico cum domino suo Willelmo Arnaldo, scilicet ultra mare." Rendering the will in the first person, William proposed to help finance a leper in the leprosery outside the Narbonne Gate. He ordered that from ".x. cartones blati sint persoluti debita mea, scilicet .xii. sol. tol. et .ii. d. in unoquoque mense de lucro Bernardo Bego .... et lucrum quod habui de Willelmi Bosquet de .vi. sol. tol. quos tenuit a me de quibus sum persolutus, et lucrum quod habui Stephani Boneti de Carraz de frumento quod ei accomodavi et omnia querimonia .... homo faceret de eo ut fuissent persoluti de supradicta pecunia, et de supradictis .x. cartonibus blati dispo[no] dari .i. carto fabe nepote mee Endie, et .i. carto dispono dari capellano Sancti Salvatoris .... .i. trentanium missis" [thirty requiem masses to Saint-Sauveur]. Another niece named Alazais was given an "archa plana." William had two brothers, Bernard and William, who were to be his heirs if they did not contest the will. He had one "spondarius" and the "capellanus" of Saint-Quentin witnessed the will.

12. JANUARY 1193: Malta 1 87. Peter de Murello of the Dalbade parish, without "spondarii," willed half his small estate that included a house to his widow Petrona (*M&W* 19) and the other half to the Hospitalers.

13. SEPTEMBER 1194: E 2. Peter Arnaldus of the Daurade, a widower, whose "spondarii" were his brother, another citizen and Bernard Bonushomo his brother-in-law. His 100 shillings in charity and gifts included twenty-five and a bed to the canons of Saint-Étienne so as to be buried there in the robe and a gift to a "nutrissa," obviously the wetnurse of his second child. His children, Deusadiuva and Pons, were minors and were placed "in posse" to be raised by Bernard Bonushomo and his wife Bruna, Deusadiuva for six years and Pons for eleven, being paid thirty shillings yearly for each child "pro illo nutrimento et

pro illis missionibus ... in victu et vestitu et per eorum tenere ad custodiendum et regendum ... ." A "sutor" and a "faber" were witnesses. For details of this testament and for this family, see Appendix 1, No. 1 above. Deusadiuva's later testament is No. 80 dated December 1251 below.

14. JUNE 1195: Malta 1 92 (copied in 1227). Unmarried and childless, Pons Vitalis' "avunculus" and "spondarius" was Peter Rogerius. His charities and gifts involved a total of 610 shillings cash and some property of which 500 went to his mother Aladaicia and his three married sisters Saptalina, Philippa and Brunissenda, and twenty shillings each to the Daurade and Dalbade. The Temple received a small property and his uncle inherited the rest.

15. OCTOBER 1195: Saint-Sernin 678 (20 49 7) iv (copied in 1225 and 1228). A childless man, Jacob donated modest sums equally to the Daurade, Saint-Pierre-des-Cuisines and Saint-Sernin. Two of his four "spondarii" were "lavandarii" (washers of leather or cloth, laundrymen?), and it is worth noting that the street named after this profession ran across the frontier of the Bourg and the City between Saint-Pierre and the Daurade. Jacob was survived by his wife and his father-in-law, William Peter de Claromonte, who still owed him seventy shillings on his wife's dowry, but to whom the testator gave his "lorica." His modest economic status is shown by his close relationship to Ricsenda, his "matrina" (godmother or stepmother); he was described as her "nepos." In iii October 1190 on the same parchment, Ricsenda had given him her modest property in return for keep and twenty shillings for charity, a gift implemented in this will (M&W 20). In the above cited act, she had been called Rixenda "conversa saveneria" (veil or lace maker) and No. i, dated January 1163 on the same parchment, tells that her deceased husband's name was John Textor, an individual also remembered in Jacob's will. Jacob's charities and gifts totaled twenty-three shillings to the church, including two outlying monasteries, and 190 shillings to friends and to his sister. He also left some clothing and linens to an "ancilla" named Bernarda as well as forty shillings "quos ei debebat."

16. DECEMBER 1195: E 510 v (copied in 1197). Peter Raimundus drew his testament "in manu" of Pons de Capitedenario and three other "spondarii." Other than forty shillings for unspecified charities, gifts and burial to be distributed by his mother and Pons de Capitedenario, all property went to his mother Stephana.

17. JUNE 1196: Daurade 118 ii (copied in 1197 and 1204). Terrenus Martinus delivered his testament "in manu" William Arnold de Saugeda (also Saugueda) and Raymond Escobonerius and his brother Arnold Escobonerius making them "testes et sponderii" in the presence of Raymond Maurinus, Gausbert Doza, Raymond Arnold "notarius." A nephew Peter de Frontoliho was given two houses and "casales," and his heirs were his two sons Terriquus (also Terricus) Martinus and Pons (later called Pons Stephen) in equal portions. Although the testator left a widow Ricsenda who was given an unspecified portion, the two

children were placed "in tutela et in bailia" of the three "sponderii" mentioned above (*M&W* 22). These were instructed "quod ipsi prebeant eis omnia necessaria de explectis honorum ac aliarum rerum tam mobilium quam inmobilium donec sint perfecte etatis." Two charters of March 1197 (ibid. i and iii) record that the "sponderii" enfeoffed several houses. They were empowered by that "posse" which Terrenus Martinus "dedit suis sponderiis ... quod illa vendicio et totum hoc quod ipsi fecerunt de suis honoribus ac rebus cognitione [the three witnesses listed above are named here] [is to be] sicut ita bonum et firmum ac semper stabile" as if the decedent had done it himself. The sons were to confirm this act at majority and in ibid., dated May 1203, Pons Stephen, son of Terrenus Martin, "postea ... fuit cognitus perfecte etatis a consulibus Tolose sicut in carta quam Poncius Arnaldus scripsit continetur," confirmed it, retaining his sixpence annual rent.

18. APRIL 1199: E 505. In a will without charities or "spondarii," Raymond de Villata bequeathed his small properties to his widow Johanna, daughter Martina, and a nephew Raymond (*M&W* 28). Were the latter beneficiary to die, his share was to go to the testator's mother Raimunda.

19. SEPTEMBER 1199: E 501 (copied in 1203). An inhabitant of the parish of Saint-Sernin, Maria (described in the charter as the mother of sons named Vital Arnaldus and William Durandus) appointed three executors, including Raymond Sederius (silk dealer?). She gave sixty shillings and a "linteola," a "culcitra" and a "fleciata" in charity and for burial. Her two sons, named above, were heirs in equal portions, each getting a house and two arpents "malolum veterum" (genitive plural) and two arpents "vetera de terra." William was a minor "in posse et in baiulatione" of his brother Vital Arnaldus "donec sit perfecte etatis."

20. JUNE 1200: Saint-Bernard 36 ii (copied in 1231). Of the parish of Saint-Sernin, William de Caneto appointed four executors, including Peter Savenerius (textiles?). He bequeathed half a house and "solarium," a third of another house, and a third of a piece of arable to his widow Aldiarda (*M&W* 30). On payment of debts and burial expenses, the rest was to go to his children Peter, Arnold, Guillelma, Bernarda and his wife in equal portions. A "tegularius" (tile or brick maker) and a "faber" were among the witnesses. For the testament of William's son Peter de Caneto, see No. 48 dated August 1227 below.

21. AUGUST 1200: MADTG, A 297, fols. 21v and 158r and *HGL* 8: No. 102 iv (recorded in August, rendered into a charter in September 1200 and copied in April 1231). The testament of Jordan III, lord of Isle-Jourdain, commences with gifts of real property, tithes and money to monasteries, churches and persons in the region of Isle-Jourdain. In addition, houses and hospitals in Gimont and Sabaillan, the military orders and churches in Toulouse were gratified. His widow Esclarmunda's 2000 shillings Morlaas was assigned on the community of Thil, and she also received an additional gift and some silver (*M&W* 31).

He owed his daughter Escarona and her husband 9000 shillings Melgueil (4500 Toulouse) based on their "pignus" on Le Castéra and to his daughter Obica and her husband 6000 shillings Melgueil (3000 Toulouse) on Mérenvielle and Moufielle. The lord's heirs were his sons Bernard Jordan, Jordan and Odo Bernard. The principal heir was Bernard Jordan who received Isle-Jourdain and Le Castéra. Bernard Jordan was also given the lord's daughter Philippa in order to find a husband for her "secundum consilium aliorum fratrum et amicorum suorum" with a dowry of 5000 shillings Melgueil (2500 Toulouse) or a mark of silver. The second son Jordan was given Lavalette and Verfeil east of Toulouse, and, to the west of the Garonne, Bretx, Caubiac, Launac and Thil. The son named Odo received Le Grès, Pelleport, Colomiers near Toulouse, and other places. He was also given half of the "conquesta Gimoës," of which the other half went to his brothers mentioned above.

There then followed two sentences concerning the transmission of the rights and properties of the lords of Isle-Jourdain on future occasions: "Preterea volo et statuo et dispono imperpetuum cum autoritate et voluntate domini mei Raimundi comitis Tolosani, quod numquam de cetero aliqua mulier et filia habeat aliquam portionem in omni prescripta hereditate, sed filie cum pecunia maritentur. Item dico et statuo et dispono cum auctoritate et voluntate domini predicti quod nunquam villa de Insula cum suis tenenciis et dominationibus nec alii honores prescripti dividantur sed semper primogenitus habeat hereditatem ut superius dictum est, scilicet legitimus." The last sentence is not in the transcription published in the *HGL*.

A final son named Bertrand was given a serf and all the taxes the lord raised from the church of Saint-Martin of Isle-Jourdain, just as long as Bertrand governed that church. The decedent's last provision was that his debts were to be paid, including 4000 shillings on Lavalette near Verfeil. This will was received by a public notary of Isle-Jourdain, in the presence of the counts of Toulouse and Foix, the bishop of Agen, the lords of Montaut and Verfeil, and other notables.

22. MARCH 1202: Malta 15 104 ii (copied in May 1202). Raymond Furnarius, a baker in the Dalbade parish, bequeathed his wife Willelma 100 shillings, etc. (*M&W* 32 and 34). On paying his debts, Raymond assigned 130 shillings to charity, of which thirteen pence went to the Dalbade, nine shillings "ad suum fornimentum," five shillings each to a goddaughter and his sister Willelma who also received an "archa," and the rest, over 100 shillings, to be distributed in "pro panem pauperibus." Raymond's brother Peter received fifty shillings and was in charge of selling the bakery May 1202. According to ibid. iii (January 1200, copied May 1202) Raymond had bought the bakery from his brother Peter and his wife Rixenda in 1200, and in ibid. i (May 1202) Peter sold it to Raymond Bascol, another baker.

23. JULY 1201: E 501 v (copied in 1207). In a will without charities or executors, Peter de Rocovilla left his widow Alamanda (previously married to John de Villanova, as is seen in ibid. ii dated May 1164) and his son Peter a house and a half arpent of vineyard at Bonagazanha. Peter was given another half arpent "malol" in addition, and Alamanda a bed, linens and clothing. Peter was also to look after his mother "secundum suum locum et posse ... quamdiu Alamanda vixerit." She was also promised 100 shillings if she wished to leave the house and 100 to dispose of at the end if she remained there. Peter's other son Bernard Peter de Rocovilla was given twenty shillings "sine plure." In vi and vii of the same parchment August and September 1206, Peter cut out, giving his mother his half of the "malol" they shared and his brother Bernard Peter half of the house shared with her.

24. APRIL 1202: Malta 118 180. Among the witnesses to the testament of Pons Bernard de Magantruno was the "capellanus" of Saint-Sernin and his two executors, William de Trenis (the founder of the hospital bearing his name for which see my "Charity and Social Work," p. 220) and Gerald Mercerius (a mercer?). Among the 1000 shillings assigned to charity and gifts, fifty went to Saint-Sernin "pro canonico" (a gift presumably purchasing burial in a canon's robe), thirty to the testator's "famula" Ricsenda, and all remaining property was to be equally divided between William de Trenis and Gerald and Pons, the sons of Gerald Mercerius.

25. JUNE 1202: E 510 ii (copied in 1203). Peter Karolus rendered his testament before four witnesses, including William de Faniavo and John Cerdanus "notarius." He gave a "malol" to Peter Bruno, son of William de Faniavo, and household effects and grain to Petrona "qui manet mecum" (M&W 35), and his "domus" and its remaining equipment to his nephews, the brothers Raymond and Peter Cerdanus. In Grandselve 2 i-v (September 1183 to February 1203, copied in 1205), Karolus' house was next to that of Willelma Trevinhana near or outside the Pouzonville Gate. His heirs and nephews were to pay his debts and also to give "una emina frumenti" to charity.

26. NOVEMBER 1206: Malta 1 14 and also 1 105. William Raymond de Insula of the Dalbade parish appointed four "spondarii," two of whom were Raymond Rotbertus and Bernard Raymond Garnerius, a business associate who owed the testator 500 shillings. Of the sum of over 300 shillings set aside for charity, 200 200 along with his bed went to the Hospital for burial as a brother, forty-eight to the nunnery of Lespinasse and much to churches in Toulouse. After the death of his son, alive at the time this will was rendered, his houses and their lots were to go to the Hospital to endow a priest to sing daily masses. His wife Bernarda received her undescribed marriage portion (M&W 46) and his son Bernard the usufruct of the estate. A thousand shillings were placed in a partnership or "societas" with William Hugh de Algario and his brother Raymond

for seven years until the young Bernard reached his majority, the son to receive half the profits. If Bernard was "stultus et male sit verssatus infra predictos .vii. annos," he is to be given 100 shillings for charity and burial, the rest of the 1000 being divided by the Hospital and the "sponderii" after the child's death. The child with whom his wife was pregnant was allotted 600 shillings and nothing more, and 500 of that sum was to come from the Bernard Raymond Garnerius mentioned above "de baratis minudas de quibus non est carta." In a provision that makes one wonder who the testator thought was the child's father, Bernard Raymond was to raise this child. The vernacular word "minuda" means a note or minute, not a legal document. Finally, this curious person proposed that, if anything remained over, it was to be invested "in faciendo illo muro qui est inter honores meos et honores de filiis de na Albia donec murus sit supra tectum domorum."

27. JANUARY 1208: Malta 1 17 (copied in 1214, 1221, 1227 and 1239). Hospitalers and four laymen, including two Tolosa relatives of his first wife Bruna, were the "spondarii" of the childless minter Pons David. The Hospital was the principal heir, but others, including domestics and his brother Bertrand David, were assigned lifetime pensions in this institution and were further gratified by gifts of money and property. Note Audiarda, his "pedisseca," who received either 100 shillings and a bed "vel sua necessaria victus et vestitus infra domum Hospitalis Iherusalem ... ad electionem ipsius Audiarde," whose son Raymond was given 100 shillings. His brother Bertrand was promised either "necessaria victus et vestitus" in the Hospital "sicut uni [de] dominis" or annually "pro stipendia .ii. cartones frumenti et .i. modium vini et .xx. sol. Tol. pro indumenta." Two of his executors were given the same necessaries just as "domini et fratres" of the order and a woman was given 100 shillings "si ipsa Petrona fecerit se monacham." Pons disposed of nearly 6200 shillings in cash, 2000 to "conquerentibus suis de usura," 2000 in specific gifts to the Hospital, 870 to friends and servants, 1900 to his widow Pagesia (M&W 48) and about seventy shillings to the churches, hospitals, bridges (Old and New), etc. of the town. A beneficiary was given 100 shillings and "omnia aptamenta ... ferri et coire [leather] et metalli excepta lorica et goniones et enses et alia munimenta hominis." One of the gifts to the Hospitalers was of 1000 shillings to support an additional priest to sing a daily mass. Other than that of the Hospitalers, the only specific church mentioned was Saint Mary "de Palacio," the later Saint-Barthélemy, perhaps Pons' parish center, the mint being close at hand. At the close of the instrument, the testator stated that, unless, by chance, his wife should bear a legitimate child, "si aliquid aliud testamentum nec dispositionem faciebam nec aliquis homo cum carta vel scripto aut testibus venire temptaverit, mando ... quod totum illud destruatur et cum isto illud rumpatur et in irritum deducatur et quod non habeat aliquid robur nec stabilitatem nec firmitatem ... ."
See the David history in my *Repression of Catharism*, pp. 203-208.

28. APRIL 1209: E 507. Pons Martinus founded his testament "in manibus et in presentia proborum hominium," namely Pons de Villafranca, Raymond de Corunsaco, and Raymond Peter his brother. Seventy-six shillings were set aside for unspecified charity and his "furnimentum." All other property and money were to go to his widow Sibilia, son Peter Martinus and daughter Ermesendis "in equalibus portionibus," the daughter being given forty shillings "ancabada" before the wife and son (M&W 52). The children were to be in the "custodia et tutela" of their mother for six years, disputes to be settled by the "spondarii."

29. MAY 1209: Malta 9 96 ii (copied in 1230 and 1232). On paying his debts, William Vasco instructed his executors, including the "capellanus" of Saint-Étienne, to give all his property to his wife Poncia except for about thirty shillings (M&W 53), of which a little over a third went to private persons, including a nephew, and the rest to the church and charity, five shillings being specifically allocated for burial. If the widow remarried, however, half the estate was to be assigned to charities named by his "sponderii."

30. JUNE 1212: E 501 i (copied in 1228). The three "spondarii" of Raymond Peter Regerannus, among whom was numbered his wife Guillelma, were to give the said Guillelma her nuptial portion and a gift (M&W 58). The rest of his property was to go to charity, a "convivium" or feast to the sisters of Lespinasse, ten shillings to the house of Pinel, about forty to private persons and the remainder of these seventy-five shillings to churches, hospitals, bridges (Old and New), etc. Raymond Peter appears to have been from the parish of Saint-Pierre-des-Cuisines but also to have been fond of the Daurade. To pay his charities an arpent of arable was sold in ibid. ii February 1213 to a Stephen Lavanderius and one therefore guesses that his house was on the "rue des Blanchers."

31. JULY 1212: Saint-Sernin Canonesses 6 iii, copied in 1240. A parishioner of the Taur, Arnold Furnerius "de Aguleriis" (modern Romiguières) appoints as his executors his wife Marita and son Arnold (obviously emancipated) together with Peter Martinus "asterius" (spit or lance maker), Stephen Textor, William Furnerius, Arnold de Vaqueriis, William Olierius (oil dealer), and William Bernardus "notarius" who are to assign 200 shillings for charities including trousseaux for two of his goddaughters. The testator's sister Bernarda was to receive fifty shillings promised her in her mother Garsenda's testament, and she, her husband Arnold de Vaqueriis and the testator's son Arnold are each given fifty shillings if they uphold the will. The baker's wife is to look after the remaining minor children, the heirs of the estate, at home for three years, and is then to receive 300 shillings. If she remarries, however, Arnold de Vaqueriis and his wife are to take the kids (M&W 59). One child may wish to become a monk at the Daurade and is assigned 100 shillings, money for "vestes monachales" and a "convivium omni conventu." The other two children will divide the estate equally.

32. SEPTEMBER 1213: Malta 3 152 i (copied in 1225). Bernard Ganterius "volens ire ad exercitum apud Murellum" appointed three executors, Pons Vitalis "ganterius," Peter Aimeric de Dealbata and Peter Raymond de Samatano "notarius," who, together with his widow Bernarda, were to give unspecified charities and gifts of 100 shillings. Bernarda was also charged with raising their two minor daughters, Anglica and Bona, until majority and was stuck with maintaining the testator's mother Rica (M&W 60) for life. In ibid. ii (April 1225), Peter Aimeric de Dealbata, acting as "spondarius" before the consuls, sold the testator's house, thus showing that Bernard's parish was the Dalbade. In this latter act, it is noted that the executor named Pons Vitalis "ganterius" was dead and we see why in the next act calendared here.

33. NOVEMBER 1213: Malta 9 42 ii (copied in 1258Z). Stephen de Montesquivo, Pons Pausatus and Raymond Gasco report that Pons Vitalis, "vulneratus in captione in qua erat apud Murellum," had declared that he owed Peter Furnerius nineteen shillings, William de Trenis two shillings sixpence, and a certain woman three obols. These debts being paid, the deceased willed three "medellata" of "malol" (a vineyard elsewhere described as being a half arpent and half of another half arpent) to Peter Furnerius de Condomio (vernacular Condom in other acts on the same parchment) in order that Peter "faceret aliquid bonum sue nepti Aladaicie."

34. SEPTEMBER 1214: Saint-Étienne 221 (22 3 7bis) (copied in 1259). The rural gentleman Raymond de Montelauro (Montlaur near Montgiscard in the Lauragais) rendered his will in Toulouse. He first "disposuit reddi .c. sol. tol. suis conquerentibus de usuris." His nephew Peter de Montebruno (Montbrun near the same) was given the "forcia" at Vieillevigne (near Villefranche-de-Lauragais) with all its dependent inhabitants and their holdings and also his uncle's property at Coumbel (near La Capelle just south of Vieillevigne) and Baziège save for a dependent family and its "casalis ... cum omnibus tenenciis" which was given to Mascaronus, provost of Saint-Étienne. Fabrissa (M&W 63), a daughter of this family, was to be "franca de omnibus amparatoribus ex parte dominationis si ipsa Fabrissa accipiet Arnaldum de Fronte, tamen si ipsa Fabrissa non accipiet Arnaldum de Fronte per virum uti predictum est, ipsa Fabrissa sit et remaneat domino proposito predicto ..." A goddaughter Titburgis received a debt ("barata") of 100 shillings owed Raymond by Raymond Unaldus and his wife Marquesia. Bernard Sillanus was given four shillings eleven pence land rent ("oblie") presumably in Toulouse, and he and William Arnold and Pons Vitalis, sons of Arnold William Pullinus, were to have all Montlaur's property in the "villa" of Gardouch. In return, the beneficiaries of this will were to bury the decedent, pay 100 shillings to his sister and a niece and 150 shillings to the churches and bridges of the town of Toulouse at the discretion of Bishop Fulk and the provost Mascaronus. Lastly, his cousin Titburgis was given a claim for the restitution of usury the deceased had paid to Peter Grivus

de Roaxio on a "barata" of 200 shillings on which Montlaur had paid thirty shillings of usury annually for twelve years. The entry reads: "Item ipse Ramundus de Montelauro recognovit ... super sacrosancta evangelia juravit quod quandam baratam de .cc. sol. tol. debuerat Petro Grivo de Roaxio et illam quod tenuerat .xii. annos et amplius et quod persolverat inde eidem Petro de Roaxio .xxx. sol. tol. de lucro quoque anno de istis predictis .xii. annis, et totum illud jus et totam rationem illam et totam illam petitionem quam ipse Ramundus ... poterat facere Petro Grivo de Roaxio ... pro ista predicta barrata totum hoc dedit, disposuit et reliquit ipse Ramundus ... domine Titburgi cognate sue ... pro omni sua voluntate inde facienda."

35. FEBRUARY 1215: Malta 1 110 ii (copied in 1225). Daughter of the deceased Pons de Venerca, also called Pons Seger (Seguer) de Caniaco in his testament in ibid. i (August 1214), Aladaicia gave twenty-two shillings sixpence to charity (of which fourteen percent went to lay friends). This sum was to be raised by selling her "domus," "tamen si ipsi [Arnold Bernard and William, sons of Arnold William de Tudela, one of her executors] aut aliquis amicus eorum voluerint cito post decessum ipsius Alazacie persolvere" the said sum "de elimosina," they could have the house themselves. Although the "capellanus" of Saint-Étienne was one of her executors, her masses were to be sung at Saint-Romain and she gave fifteen shillings to the Hospital for her burial.

36. MAY 1216: Ourliac and Magnou, Cartulaire de Lézat, No. 1452, and PBN, Collection Doat 40: fol. 161v. William Pons Astro, in a will jammed with executors including the abbot of Saint-Sernin, but really directed by his wife Ermengarda (M&W 71) and William de Turre, set aside 1000 shillings for charity. 150 shillings was to go to Saint-Sernin, largely, it appears, for a lavish funeral, 250 to close relatives and friends, ninety to pay back what he held from the hospital called the Mainaderie and the rest to his "conquerentes" for usury. His heir was his son Pons William (later called William Pons) who was in the charge ("bailia") of his mother and William de Turre for the next three years. Were he to die before majority, half of the estate was to go to the children of the deceased Stephen Caraborda and William Pons' daughter Dias and half to the issue of the same Dias with her present husband Vasco de Turre. The heirs were burdened with maintaining a lamp in the Mary Chapel of Saint-Sernin and an annual "convivium" for a hundred poor persons. The testator ordered his widow and William de Turre "quod interim reddant computum dictis probis hominibus [the other "sponderii"] semel in anno de predicta bailia." See the family in my Men and Women, pp. 173-183.

37. OCTOBER 1216: PAN, J 330 12 ii. Bernard Stephanus called Bernard Balderia, an inhabitant of the parish of Saint-Étienne, gave twenty shillings in charity, small properties to his wife Sibilia and his daughters, Guillelma and Sibilia (M&W 73). His heirs were his sons William and Peter, both minors, to

APPENDIX EIGHT

448

whom he gave his "domus." The dying man feared that his heirs and partner Stephen Medicus would have to sell their rights in the mills of the Château Narbonnais as well as the grain, wine and equipment of his house in order to pay his and his partner's debts and therefore authorized the sale of this property. If, on the other hand, the debts could be paid, he ordered them to retain their shares in the mill and the house, half for Stephen Medicus and half for his two sons. He added that Stephen Medicus "maneat cum suis filiis predictis et faciat captinium [a partnership] cum eis donec omnia ista predicta debita persolvantur, et quod faciat Sibilie uxori Bernardi Stephani suum opus victus et vestitus tantum quantum sine viro manere voluerit, et quod ipsa mitat in captinio explectam sui malolis predicti. Item hoc totum uti superius dictum est fuit factum consilio et voluntate Stephani Medici predicti qui hoc totum voluit et concessit ita fieri. Preterea ipse Bernardus Stephanus dedit Stephano Medico mansionem in ista domo predicta cum omnibus suis rebus in sua vita ... ." The debts were in fact paid and the rather happy result is to be seen in Appendix 9, No. 36.

38. OCTOBER 1216: J 330 12 ii. In a will rendered at Toulouse, Arnold Raymond de Pibraco (Pibrac to the west of the town) gave the Hospital four shillings of rent and half of a "casal" at Pibrac, but the rest of his property there and at Cornebarrieu, etc. was to go to his wife Paris and minor daughter Ramunda in equal parts (M&W 74). Ramunda was to be "in tutela" of his wife, for which the latter had "antecabada" or first claim on property at Cornebarrieu.

39. JULY 1217: J 328 6. A rural gentleman, William de Busqueto (Le Bousquet) of Lanta in the Lauragais, gave fifteen shillings to the cathedral of Toulouse and ten to churches at Lanta. Survived by his mother Aladaicia, his brother Bernard Unaldus, a sister Titberga and his wife Salamandra, William's principal heirs were Bernard de Rocovilla (Roqueville near Bélesta), son of Bertrand de Rocovilla, and his sister, although some Unaldi, members of the lordly line of Lanta, Alaman de Roaxio and his wife Lumbarda, a "scutifer" from Lanta and others shared substantial gifts of real property in and around Lanta. The testator gave his widow her nuptial portion and an added gift (M&W 75). The will also mentions payments in cash of 830 shillings, of which fifty were owed to the testator by other Unaldi. The estate was also burdened by a debt ("barata") of 100 shillings.

40. SEPTEMBER 1217: Malta 4 206 (copied in 1243). Appointing the "capellanus" of the Dalbade, Terrenus Boerius (ploughman or herder?) and another layman as executors, William Niger requested that the marriage portion first be returned to his wife Esclarmunda, and then that forty shillings be dispensed to charity. The rest of the estate was to be given to the child with whom his wife was then then pregnant. Were the child to die, twenty-five shillings were to go to his widow Esclarmunda and a like sum to his sisters Willelma and Aimengarda, the latter of whom, being a minor, was to be in his widow's "bailia" (M&W 76).

41. AUGUST 1218: E 501 (copied in 1223). Pons Furnerius of the parish of the Taur appointed three lay executors, including Peter Faber de Noerio, to sell property in order to give 100 shillings for charity, part to the church, part to secular monuments, especially the "pons sancti Petri de Bazagle," and part to nieces, godchildren, two women and finally (and curiously) his son Vital. Vital was to receive five shillings "pro hereditate quos mei predicti sponderii ei donent de meis bonis sine plure." His wife Sibilia got his house on the "carraria de Agulheriis" and some vineyards (*M&W* 77).

42. SEPTEMBER 1218: Malta 1 117 (copied in 1219). Among the three "probihomines" serving as the executors of Stephen Regannus was William de Serra "sutor" (cobbler). The Hospital was given the testator's part of a piece of arable at Nogaret shared with his brother Peter Regannus. After paying his debts, the decedent's daughter Fabrissa (*M&W* 78) was to collect all the debts owed her father, and his son Peter was the general heir for unspecified properties including houses.

43. AUGUST 1219: Malta 17 14 ii (copied in 1244) and ibid. 21 89 ii (copied in 1244). Grimaldus Capellarius (although the word also means "hatter," he was probably a maker of helmets or of crucibles or vats) of the Dalbade parish gave twenty shillings to charity. He was survived by his wife Geralda (*M&W* 86) and children Peter Vitalis, Bartholomew, Ramunda and Gracia. The boys were heirs in equal portions and the daughters were to be dowered and married. For the unions, see ibid. iii (January 1224) and Malta 17 18 iii (August 1235, copied in 1242) and also *M&W* 98 and 126. His widow and son Peter Vital, who also served in lieu of "sponderii," were instructed that "starent insimul cum omnibus eorum infantibus .v. annos post suum decessum," for which service Peter was to receive fifty shillings and "maioria et antecabada pre cunctis aliis suis filiis, tamen si aliquis illorum infantium erat stultus et voluerit se cabdelare [look after himself], cognitione domine Geralde matris sue aut aliorum eorum amicorum, talis qui ita fuerit stultus et follus exeat inde cum .v. sol. tol. per aparciamentum ... et non plus." The testament of one of Grimald's sons-in-law, William Castanherius "faber," is No. 64 dated August 1235 below.

44. NOVEMBER 1219: Malta 9 92 ii (copied in 1230). Having among his four executors an "olerius" (oil dealer), a childless Aimeric "qui stabat in carraria de scola Iudeorum" (modern Joutz-Aigues in the Dalbade parish) willed twelve shillings to unspecified charity. His wife Guillelma (*M&W* 88) was given his house and a half arpent "malol."

45. MARCH 1220: Grandselve 5 (copied in 1228). Three of the six "spondarii" of Stephen Astro were from his own family. "In primis ego [Stephen Astro] ... accipio de meis bonis .c. sol. tol. quas Valeria uxor mea ... reddat meis conquerentibus quorum lucrum acceperam ... ." Next he assigned 1000 shillings "de meis melioribus baratis ad capiendum virum cognitione sue matris" to his

daughter Bernarda. His daughter Ticburga (*M&W* 89) was given five arpents of arable to enter religion at Lespinasse. His two sons Raymond Arnold and William Pons were heirs to his estate, but, were they to die, all went to the above Bernarda. The children and their property were put "in custodia et in balia" of their mother who was to be the "domina et prepotens" until the boys were of age, Bernarda married and Ticburga safely in the monastery. Valeria agreed to remand recuperating her widow's portion until after the payment of Bernarda's dowry and the executors were to give advice "pie et prudenter ... sine omni dolo." See the Astro history in my *Men and Women*, pp. 173-183.

46. AUGUST 1222: E 509 (copied in 1225). "Qui terrenis testatur heredibus Christum successorem instituere nichilominus et heredum, idcirco ego" Raymond Martinus instituted his wife Stephana and his father-in-law Stephen de Garrigia "tutores et spondarii." They were to assign twenty shillings for charity and were to see that his daughters Bermunda and Stephana were married. These young women were his heirs, but, were they to die, his wife succeeded (*M&W* 94).

47. NOVEMBER 1222: PAN, J 323 70. The testament of William Unald, lord of Lanta, mentioned his mother, two sisters, his widow Gauda and a child yet unborn who turned out to be a daughter named Marquesia. William's son Raymond is not mentioned in this instrument, probably because he was emancipated and already installed in the lordship of Lanta. Raymond was a celebrated person, being one of the heroes of the southern side in the Albigensian Crusade and was described by the Dominican inquisitor William Pelisson (*Chronique*, ed. Duvernoy, p. 108) as condemned for heresy after his death. Although the testator was either inclined toward, or tolerant about, divergent religion, he left 200 shillings to the Premonstratensians of La Capelle for charity and burial as well as eighty-odd shillings to bridges and churches at Toulouse, Lanta, Fourquevaux and Montesquieu. He also returned his wife Gauda's dowry, and, in addition, gave her a gift and belatedly paid the dowries of two of his sisters and a niece, a total of 3500 shillings. Gauda was placed "in posse et custodia et protectione" of Sicard de Montealto, the testator's brother-in-law and executor, who was requested to marry her off. Montaut was also placed in charge of the child with whom Gauda was pregnant "donec sit etatis" (*M&W* 95). A baron of grade equal to that of the dying William, Montaut was also informed that two young squires, William de Vilela and Alaman de Roaxio, the latter Unald's godson, were to be in his "posse et custodia" in order that "ipse faceret eos milites." Rural clergy were present at the instrumenting.

48. AUGUST 1227: Saint-Bernard 36 i (copied in 1231). Of the parish of Saint-Sernin, Peter de Canedo (see above No. 20 dated June 1200 for his father William's testament) appointed his mother Aldiarda and brother Arnold as executors. Peter assigned forty shillings to charity, twenty to a goddaughter

"quando virum acceperit" and 150 shillings or a "domus" to his niece Proba. Lastly, his mother and brother were to raise his nephew Adam for ten years, after which they were to share the estate in equal portions (*M&W* 105).

49. MARCH 1228: MADTG, A 297, fol. 12v, and *HGL* 8: No. 215 iii, that in A 297 being copied in Toulouse in July 1230. In the presence of his wife, "domina" Endia, one lay notable and the "capellanus" of Saint-Martin of Isle-Jourdain, Bernard Jordan II, lord of Isle and son of the deceased Jordan, rendered his testament. Gifts, including a stallion, a mule, armor, silver utensils and property went to neighboring monasteries, Roncesvalles in Navarre, the Temple of Toulouse and churches in and around Isle-Jourdain. His widow Endia then received 10,000 shillings Morlaas or Toulouse as her nuptial portion (*M&W* 106). His son Bernard Jordan was principal heir, receiving the lordship of Isle-Jourdain, Mérenvielle, Le Castéra, Lévignac, Pradère, Le Cluzel and other places, as well as rights over "milites et milicias" and dependent men and women. His son Jordan received Montaigut-sur-Save, Léguevin and all rights in Gimoës. The baron proposed that, if the child his wife was carrying was male, he was to become a canon at Saint-Étienne in Toulouse, and, if female, to be sent to the convent of Lespinasse with an endowment of 300 shillings Toulouse. The children were all to be "in posse et bailia et sub tutela et procuratione domine Endie uxoris mee et in ejus spondaratico" unless she remarried. The final provision was a confirmation of all the "libertates et mores et consuetudines" given by his grandfather and great grandfather to the town of Isle-Jourdain to repair "injurie, violencie et crudelitates" he had visited on that community.

50. NOVEMBER 1228: Grandselve 6. "In manu" of the "capellanus" of Saint-Pierre-des-Cuisines and in the presence of an officer of the hospital called the Mainaderie and two laymen, one a mercer, Dohaz put everything in his wife's hands. For charity, he allocated half a "malol" and fifty shillings part for his burial at Grandselve whose various infirmaries he also gratified. He also mentioned the church of Saint-Julien in the Bourg. His wife Petrona was his general heir for a house and a little property (*M&W* 107).

51. MARCH 1229: Saint-Bernard 21 and PBN, Collection Doat 40: fol. 216v. Pons de Capitedenario's huge testament cannot be summarized. He left a widow, Aurimunda and a daughter Stephana, wife of Roger Barravus, and his four "spondarii," who included Roger, were really subordinate to those women, who were to be aided by "consulatores" of much weight, the abbots of Grandselve and Saint-Sernin. Although Aurimunda's widow's portion was modest, the testator gave her a legacy from her father's estate, 250 shillings "quos ego habui ex illis animalibus que Bruno de Garrigiis ei relinquerat" and a fourth part of the sheep owned by his daughter, wife and self (*M&W* 108). His relicts were to live in his recently acquired "domus et albergum" with its "aula lapidea et

honor tam de petra quam de lignis" at the estate's expense together with the requisite "ancille" and a "scutifer" for Roger Barravus. The testator's heir was his soon-to-die daughter Stephana. He also left the enormous sum of 10,000 shillings, which his wife and daughter "donent et divident meis conquerentibus ... et pro animabus illorum quorum ego nec meus pater nec mei fratres aliquid iniuste habueramus et pro satisfactione illius injurie ... ." From this sum were also gratified some fourteen monastic houses and the "boni homines qui vocantur Menudelli," the Franciscans, that is. See my *Repression of Catharism*, pp. 157-158.

52. APRIL 1229: E 509. Juliana de Vauro appointed three executors, including her daughter Bernarda, wife of Peter de Lantare, and died in the presence of several friends, among whom were a Bernard Domengui "textor" and Raymond Escafrenus "notarius." A sum of fifteen shillings was left for unspecified charities, and all other property went to her daughter.

53. APRIL 1230: Malta 3 158 (copied in 1230). The "capellanus" of the Dalbade and two "pelliparii," one being his nephew Vital, were the executors of Raymond Peter Pelliparius. Raymond Peter gave his house to the nephew and a total of sixty-nine shillings to friends. His remaining property, which, as we learn from ibid. iii (July 1230), consisted of a half arpent "malol," was given to the poor.

54. OCTOBER 1230: Malta 15 153 (copied in 1243). Executed by John de Vadegia and Raymond de Albeiesio, Pons Rufatus' will assigned thirty shillings to charity largely to churches in the parish of Saint-Étienne and to the Trinitarians and Saint-Martin of Portet. The testator's own clothes were given to an individual, and the children of a Marinerius were assigned a "tunica de pannis huius ville Tolose." His children, Peter and Arnalda, were heirs in equal portions and his widow Willelma received a small gift to add to her dowry (*M&W* 110). Were the children to die, the latter was to receive ten shillings more for deathbed distribution. Over a decade later in ibid. iv (January 1243), Peter Martinus was declared to be a major of fourteen years by his mother and by her brother Peter Martinus, showing that her son had taken her brother's surname.

55. DECEMBER 1230: TAM, II 71 ii (copied in 1280). The "computus" of William Probus (Pros) of the Dalbade parish, among whose witnesses were "pelliparii," assigned twenty-one shillings to charity including the hospital "de Ronsavals," a house etc. to his wife Ramunda and three "tonelli" to his daughters Willelma and Septa (*M&W* 111).

56. MARCH 1232: Malta 9 150 (copied in 1257). Willelma, wife of Adam de Villa, placed her testament "in manibus proborum hominum" Bernard Setorini and Raymond Salvitatis. She gave a total of fifty shillings for her soul, of which three shillings fivepence were to be rendered to the fabric, "capellanus,"

"subcapellani," deacon and subdeacon of the Dalbade, fifteen shillings to layfolk, etc. The bulk went elsewhere: "Item Willelma predicta iussit et disposuit reddi suis conquerentibus de usuris .xx. sol. tol. de istis predictis .l. sol. cognitione Ade de Villa mariti sui ... ." Her husband inherited the bed and furnishings and a "medalata" of "malol."

57. MAY 1232: Archdiocese 838. Aimengarda Vaqueria of the parish of Saint-Étienne left her house to Arnold de Mazeraguello, her nephew, distributed 120 shillings and objects including new clothing to her nieces and nephews, friends and domestics, twenty shillings worth of bread and wine for the poor on the day of her death and thirteen shillings sixpence to churches and hospitals.

58. DECEMBER 1233: E 125. Adhemar Ganterius (glover), whose executors were Raymond de Devesia, the "capellanus" of the Daurade, and the son of a butcher, ordered 100 shillings "de denariis qui sunt in archa ipsius Ademarii" to be spent for charity. His wife Constancia received a house and a small vineyard, and to Dulcia and Bernard Amelius, respectively children of his deceased brothers Pons Vital and Peter Amelius, a "casal" and a house were given (M&W 117).

59. JANUARY 1234: E 579. Arnold Nona appointed four "spondarii," one of whom was a "capellerius" and another his son-in-law. The 100 shillings assigned to charity went to his own parish of the Daurade, five other churches in Toulouse, three hospitals and two leperhouses, the Dominicans and the Franciscans, and four outlying monasteries. Arnold's sister and niece were each given forty shillings. His daughter Arnalda received a "domus," and all the rest of his property went to her and her husband Bernard de Sancto Martino de Ponte (M&W 118).

60. SEPTEMBER 1234: E 501 i (copied in 1241). In the presence of the "capellanus" of Saint-Sernin, two Dominicans, two Franciscans, his wife Maria and three laymen, later called "probihomines," Hugh Willelmus "pelliparius" assigned 300 shillings to charity, especially to Saint-Sernin, and to the convents, churches, hospitals and bridges of the town. The executors were to see to it that his wife Maria received all she had been promised "pro matrimonio" and also half of whatever she and her husband had acquired together (M&W 120). His two sons Peter Aton and Hugh Willelmus were to divide the inheritance in half which they did in ibid. ii (April 1236) as in Appendix 9, No. 40.

61. APRIL 1235: Grandselve 7. Appointing William Ugo "pelliparius," Raymond de Podio "sutor," and Peter de Proald to be his "sponderii," Peter de Estanco "sutor" of the Taur parish donated about 245 shillings to charity, the largest single beneficiary being the monastery of Grandselve, followed by the Dominicans and Franciscans. Seventy shillings were given his niece, daughter of Bernard Parator, "cum quibus maritetur vel mittatur in ordine." The

cobbler's principal heirs were Peter de Proald, the son of his sister Ramunda, and his partner Raymond de Podio. The property owned by these partners, both cobblers, consisted of a house and "operatorium" (workshop), a piece of arable and a "malol," shared equally. Obviously, the partnership was dissolved by death and the cobbler Raymond de Podio retained his half and received Peter's half of their house and shop. It may be noted that the size of the gift to Grandselve clearly indicated that the testator was to receive, or was receiving, final care there and burial in the robe.

62. MAY 1235: PAN, J 330 25. A very different parishioner of the Taur, the widower Hugh Johannes, onetime vicar of Toulouse, friend of Count Raymond VI, etc., placed his testament in the hands of his sons, but gave a role of counsel to Bernard, Francis and Peter de Montibus and to Raymond Tapierius (carpet dealer or maker?). Hugh gave 500 shillings for charities of which something under 100 went to specific institutions, especially the Taur, and the rest, at the discretion of his sons and heirs, was assigned to "mei conquerentes a quibus aliquid iniuriose habui." A son named Hugh was to become a canon at Saint-Sernin and a daughter Aimengarda a "monacha," but, if the counselors wanted it, she could be married (M&W 123). A presumably married daughter Gensers was given a gift, and two sons, Arnold Johannes and Raymond Johannes, were heirs in equal shares of all property, "bovarie" or large farms being mentioned but not identified, as well as dependent tenants. The brothers were to remain together for ten years, keeping the property undivided for that time. Arnold was given "antecabada et maioria ante" his brother, who was probably still a minor, and also was granted the sole inheritance of Hugh's "aula lapidea" and attached houses and "honor," in short, the big town house. In September 1221 (J 330 24 i and ii, copied in 1248), calendared in M&W 93, Hugh's daughter Ramunda had married Bernard de Miramonte, dowered with the "bovaria" of Cépet, and her mother Francischa and brother Arnold Johannes were mentioned as applauding this action.

63. JUNE 1235: Malta Garidech 1 (1 2) (copied in 1238). In a testament written by his nephew Peter Rotbertus "notarius," the well-to-do Vital Rotbertus appointed his brother Stultus and two others "sponderii." A thousand shillings were assigned for charity, of which only about 250 went to churches, hospitals and bridges, especially his parish church of the Taur. Small bequests were given to his nephew the notary, a cousin Ramunda and the "nutrix" of his son. Flos, the daughter of his wife Willelma by a earlier marriage, was forgiven a debt of 200 shillings owed to the testator (M&W 63). Vital's brother William Rotbertus was to get "omnem lauratem [Latin: laboratum] et bestiarium quod habemus in gasaliam." His widow Willelma was to raise the children and remain in his property and "quod sit inde domina et potens dum ipsa remanserit sine viro." Were she to marry and leave the domicile, she was to recuperate her "dos" and "dotalicium." The testator's son William was to be given "tota aula lapidea cum

duabus domibus"; all other houses and property were to be divided equally with his brother, if the child with which Willelma was pregnant should be male. If the child was female, she was to receive a 1500 shilling dowry.

64. JUNE 1235: Saint-Sernin 145 (copied in 1286). A testament implying earlier settlements is that of the heirless patrician Peter de Turre de Portaria "qui manebat [in the hospital] quod habitatores domus Fulhensis habebant in Tholosa" either as a pensioner or for final care. His four "sponderii" were to render his wife Bernarda her "dos" and "dotalicium" of 2400 shillings and gifts or property, jewelry and money (M&W 125). The monks of Feuillans, whose abbot came to see the testator before he died, were given two beds, about 180 shillings went to other churches, hospitals etc., and about 150 shillings to private persons. In what may be restitution for usury, Pons Adalbertus received a house at Montaygon that the testator had acquired from the deceased William Adalbertus. Peter's parish was the Daurade.

65. AUGUST 1235: Malta 17 18 iv (copied in 1242). Childless, William Castanherius "faber" of the Dalbade parish appointed his wife Gracia, Peter Vitalis "capellerius" and William Johannes as "sponderii." Two hundred shillings were given in charity, half going to institutions, including thirty shillings to the Temple for burial and two rural monasteries, and half to various relatives, the children of his deceased brother Peter de Alsona, the three children of his sister Bernarda, and another sister Willelma. To raise the cash for the charities listed above, he instructed his executors to sell a "malol" and one arpent of arable land. In ibid. iii of the same date, William had given his wife her widow's portion of 400 shillings, a house and other property (M&W 126).

66. DECEMBER 1235: E 501, published in "Village, Town and City," pp. 188-190. The executors of the testament of William Peter de Bolhaco (Bouillac near Grandselve) "vaquerius" (dairyman?) include a minter and a merchant. Twelve shillings were given to ecclesiastical institutions, especially to Grandselve, where he intended to be buried, Saint-Étienne, his parish in Toulouse, and the Daurade. Seventy shillings were given to godchildren and relatives, especially to his sister Geralda and her three daughters. "Suus filius" Arnold "filius Guillelme de Vesceriis [Bessières]" received a mere ten shillings, a sum equaled by the testator's gifts to several of his godchildren. A feature of this will is that the testator gave three mares, eight milchcows, and one calf to institutions and persons, including one cow to a nephew who was an "heremita" in Grandselve and three to his wife Ramunda. His heir was the child with whom his widow was pregnant (M&W 128). For the names of the cows, see my Men and Women, p. 40.

67. FEBRUARY 1237: MADTG, A 297, fols. 19v and 23v, copied in December 1268. The testament of Bernard Jordan III, lord of Isle-Jourdain, promised payment of his debts and restitution of 200 shillings Morlaas to individuals for losses incurred while in his prison. Damages and gifts were to be given to local

monasteries, Roncesvalles in Navarre and local churches at Isle-Jourdain and Ségoufielle. The widow Englesia's portion was assigned on income from Le Castéra. The general heir of this lord was his brother Jordan who was responsible for making the bequests mentioned above, and was also held to give the testator's daughter Nalpais 100 marks of silver "iure institutionis et hereditatis et apparciamenti" on the town of Isle-Jourdain (M&W 129).

68. AUGUST 1237: PAN, J 328 24 (copied in 1248). Bernard de Miramonte de Portaria arranged that his executors, his cousin Peter Niger and his nephew Pons de Galhaco, were first to pay his debts and "concordent cum suis conquerentibus de usuris." A thousand shillings were then allocated for unspecified charities to be distributed by the counselor of his will, his brother-in-law Bernard Raymond Baranonus with whose "consilio et assensu" almost everything had to be done. As in M&W 132, this worthy made settlements for his mother, wife and daughter Francisqua. Truly baronial in scale, the dowries ranged from three to five thousand shillings. Without a son, he hoped for a grandson by his daughter whose marriage to Stephen de Castronovo (a Curtasolea) he arranged and dowered in his will. The hope was vain because Francisqua died without issue, for which see Appendix 9, Nos. 41 and 50 below and the Curtasolea-Castronovo history in my Repression of Catharism, pp. 197-202. Further benefactions totaling 16,000 shillings were given to near relatives, cousins and nephews, named Peter Niger and his two brothers, Pons de Galhaco and his two brothers, and to the two sons of Bernard Raymond Baranonus. Bernard also created something like an extended family with rights of habitation in his big house. Were Francisqua to have male issue, these children were to inherit the estate, but, until their majority, Peter Niger and Pons de Galhaco could live together with the married couple and the testator's mother in his house, all "measured and moderate" expenses paid, until the boy or boys had reached majority. They were also to manage Francisqua's estate until that time. Were the issue of the marriage with Castronovo a girl, she was to receive a dowry of 5000 shillings, and the property was to pass to the aforesaid relatives. Individuals who appear to have been servants or business associates, to one of whom Bernard owed money, and one godson were to be gratified with from five to 500 shillings. The amount of money distributed in this will totaled at least 25,000 shillings, and there was a much real property as well, including a farm at Cépet.

69. MARCH 1238: Daurade 117 (copied in 1238). Arnold Guido, son of William Guido, "volens ire in partibus transmarinis ratione penitentie sibi iniuncte a domino Romano apostolice sedis legato" gave six shillings to the Dalbade and twenty-five to his "ancilla" Brayda. His nephew Bernard, son of the testator's cousin Arnold and grandson of the deceased Raymond Guido, was given his house, located next door to that of Bernard's father. The testator's cousin Bruna, wife of Bernard Raymond de Ponte, was bequeathed his "pars ... in loco

illorum molendinorum qui quondam constructi fuerint in flumine Garonne inter
carraria Sancti Cipriani et Fontem Augerii et albardillum [albarède]," adjoining
pastures, etc. The rest of Arnold's property went to his cousin Arnold mentioned
above. See the Guido history in my *Repression of Catharism*, pp. 225-228.

70. AUGUST 1240: Malta 17 64 iv (copied in 1253). Bernard Garinus "austaderius" (poultryman, after the local field-duck?) gave twenty shillings for charity,
especially to the Dalbade, whose "capellanus" headed the three who were to
distribute this sum. Fifteen shillings went to his daughter Willelma and her son
William. Bernard's son Bernard had "ancabada" with sixty shillings before his
other sons Arnold and Raymond, who were all jointly heirs in equal portions.
Their inheritance was to be transmitted after their mother's dowry was paid.
She was also to be "domina et potens" over the estate until her sons' majority
(*M&W* 136).

71. DECEMBER 1242: Malta 17 65. Arnold Austaderius appointed his brother
Raymond Austaderius and his sister's husband Arnold de Serris "sponderii."
These were to supervise the distribution of fifty shillings, about half going to
godchildren, cousins, etc. and half to charity, especially to his parish of the
Dalbade. His widow Bruna was to receive her widow's portion and his mother
thirty shillings (*M&W* 139). His daughter Willelma was to be raised until majority by her aunt and uncle, at which time she and they were to divide the
estate equally.

72. MARCH 1243: PAN, J 305 29. Probably about as wealthy as Bernard de
Miramonte or Pons de Capitedenario (see Nos. 51 and 68 above), Vital Galterius (Gauterius – Walter in English) of the parish of Saint-Pierre-des-Cuisines
left cash bequests amounting to just under 1500 shillings. The bulk of this went
to Comptors, his second wife (the first, Bertranda, was deceased) (*M&W* 141).
Vital's gifts were principally real property, heavily concentrated in and around
the town, but extending from Bessières far to the north to Caraman far to the
south. Although the will is somewhat confused, it seems that Vital had had no
legitimate children, although he had one or two natural sons. His heirs were
nephews, a male cousin and his two sisters. Sign of the testator's station, both
his "equus et meus palafredus" were bequeathed to a relative from Montbartier
near Montech to the north. The will is famous and partly published because it
gave eighteen houses near the Bazacle to found a residential college for at least
twenty scholars at the University of Toulouse, an institution that was never
created. Other than to the town's churches, Vital gave grants to the Franciscans
and the Dominicans of Toulouse, the Premonstratensians of La Capelle, the
"capellanus" of Caraman and not a few clergy in Toulouse. Supervised by the
bishop of Toulouse. his heirs "satisfaciant omnibus meis conquerentibus tam
super usuris quam aliis iniuriis, si forte aliqui de me conquerentes apparuerint
ultra loca et personas quibus superius satisfeci ... ." See the Carbonellus-
Prinaco history in Appendix 1, No. 3.

73. APRIL 1243: Malta 133 49. Without child or wife, William de Altarippa died in the Daurade parish. Although he left a house in town to relatives, his inheritance largely went to the Temple, whose chaplain was one of his executors and whose commandery of Larramet was given his "bestiarium" (herd or stable of cattle). The Templars' churches at Lavilledieu (near Castelsarrasin), Laramet and Toulouse (Holy Mary of Bethlehem) also received more than half of the 112 shillings devoted to churches and charity, although this testator not only gave to the house of Calers near Muret, but also to one of the San Salvadors in Asturias ("ecclesia Sancti Salvatoris de Esturiis"). Although one of William's executors was a "textor," TAM, II 4 (February 1239) records that persons bearing the family name were among the leaders of the leather industries, one being Raymond William de Altarippa. It therefore seems that William was a leather dealer and investor in livestock in the valleys of the Ariège and Garonne rivers. For information on this clan, see my *Repression of Catharism*, p. 59.

74. DECEMBER 1243: Malta 1 28. Childless widow of John Macellarius, Tolosana gave fifteen shillings of charity especially to her parish of the Dalbade and also distributed the fifty shillings her husband had earlier left to charity. The rest of the estate went to the Hospitalers, and consisted of her widow's portion based on a house in town worth fifty shillings and a vineyard (*M&W* 145).

75. APRIL 1245: Malta 118 346 ii (copied in 1246). A parishioner of the Taur, Peter Ovelherius de Villanova gave ten shillings to charity, dividing the rest of his undisclosed property, half to his two sons, Peter and Arnold, and half to his wife Grauzida (*M&W* 149). The three executors and witnesses were the "capellanus," a "subcapellanus" of the Taur and Stephen Clavelerius (nail maker). Peter's house was on the rue du Taur, the "carraria maior" of the Bourg.

76. FEBRUARY 1247: Malta 17 98 ii (copied in 1247). Peter Nepos of the Daurade parish, whose executors included a butcher, weaver, "teulerius" (brick or tile maker), "olierius" (oil dealer) and a deacon, gave ten shillings in charity. His son German was heir if he attained majority, otherwise his wife Aladaycia. The testator had had a daughter by his first wife Ramunda (*M&W* 152). She, also named Ramunda, is seen in ibid. iii (March 1264) with her half-brother German and his mother, when she, as heir of "Ramunde alie uxoris" of Peter Nepos, approved the sale of a property to pay debts owed to a "pelliparius." Ramunda and Peter were married when Peter and his brother Arnold Nepos divided their property in ibid. i (October 1231) (for which see Appendix 9, No. 38). Arnold is not seen in this testament.

77. NOVEMBER 1247: Malta 17 60. Bernarda Guisona gave an undetermined sum for thirty masses and other benefactions to the parish of Saint-Étienne and to the church of Saint-André in Pompertuzat deep in the Lauragais, a bed to the Sainte-Trinité Hospital, five shillings "in camisiis" to the poor, two "cartones"

of millet to nephews of the Guido family and a little vineyard to Estevena (Stephana), her daughter and the wife of Peter Vitalis "ganterius" (M&W 154).

78. November 1247: Grandselve 41 v (copied in 1258 and 1264). Calling her witnesses and "sponderii" "probihomines" and including among them a Raymond Borrellus "pelherius," the "subcapellanus" of Saint-Sernin and Peter Sobaccus "notarius," Pictavina, widow of Bernard Amalvinus de Najaco, residing near the Pouzonville Gate, gave a little over six shillings in charity and some bedclothes to the Hospital of Saint-Raymond, thirty shillings and an "archa" to the son and two daughters of her heir, her own daughter Willelma. Ibid. vi (January 1248) tells us that these bequests had been honored, and vii (April 1252) that Willelma's sister Sibilia had married the deceased Bernard Lumbardus whose son, bearing the same name, gave a portion of a "domus" to his aunt. Ibid. ii (April 1197) records the marriage of Picatavina and Bernard de Najaco so the widow could not have been less than sixty-two years of age in 1247. See the Najaco history in Appendix 1, No. 9 and M&W 23 and 155.

79. FEBRUARY 1251: E 501 iii (copied in 1251). Among Peter de Galhaco's "sponderii" was his wife Lumbarda. Twenty shillings went for charity, especially to his parish and its churches of Saint-Étienne, Saint-Sauveur and Montaygon. Peter's heir was his daughter Ramunda, wife of Martin de Sancto Caprario. We learn from other acts on the same membrane that Peter had two brothers, John and Deodatus (sometimes William Deide) de Galhaco. The brothers divided their holdings in 1239, giving John a house "ad furnum Bastardi" (in the City) and Peter a "malol," and both brothers survived Peter. In October 1251 Lumbarda and Ramunda divided the property, the "malol" going to the former and the house near the "motta veteri civitatis" to the latter. See M&W 157 and Appendix 9, No. 48.

80. DECEMBER 1251: Malta 1 131. Deusajuda "infirmitate detentus tamen cum suo bono sensu et memoria perfecta fecit suum ultimum testamentum et suam supremam dispositionem." First, Deide left his houses to the Hospitalers on the condition that he "teneat et explectet omnes predictas domos omnibus diebus vite sue," the Hospitalers being obligated to pay him a yearly pension of four quarters ("cartones") of grain, two measures ("modii") of unwatered wine and, in his final days, 300 shillings to pay his debts "et ad faciendum restitutiones omnibus illis personis a quibus usuram acceperat." After his death, furthermore, Ricarda "qui tunc manebat cum eo" should live in the house where he lived among the ones he rented ("collocare") and receive from the Hospital half of the allotment mentioned above. Were the Hospital not to wish this, Ricarda could collect "totum premium aliarum predictarum domorum" for her support (M&W 159). The Hospital then accepted Deide as a "particeps" in all spiritual and material benefits and promised him the habit on the deathbed. As we learn from Malta 1 33 (June 1253) Deide's "sponderii" were Bernard de Samatano

"notarius" and Stephen Facit Sanguinem "parator" who remarked that the testator was the son of Peter Arnaldus who, as is seen above in No. 13 (September 1194), died at that date, leaving Deide, a child of eight or nine years of age, to be raised by relatives. In short, Deide was either sixty-eight or sixty-nine at the time this testament was rendered and had died within two years after the arrangement was made with the Hospital. His complex of houses also included an "aula lapidea" and a "stabulum." See the Arnaldus family history in Appendix 1, No. 1.

81. AUGUST 1252: Malta 17 68 i (copied in 1264). Witnesses informed the notary that Raymond Sancius had left his wife Bernarda sixty shillings for her widow's portion, allowing her to sell vineyards for her needs and to pay an outstanding debt of sixteen shillings nine pence (M&W 160).

82. AUGUST 1252: MADTG, A 297, fol. 880. The will of the rich Bertrand Descalquenquis of the parish of Saint-Sernin was rendered in the presence of his three "sponderii." He allocated 200 shillings to charity, and his widow Aymengarda received an unspecified marriage portion and maintenance for life (M&W 161). The testator's sister Alfavia was accorded five years of revenue from his holdings at Pibrac and his son Arnold a property at Cornebarrieu. His son Peter Raymond was to inherit his "aula lapidea et albergum et honor" and this child and his three brothers, Durand de Sancto Barcio, Arnold Raymond Descalquenquis and Raymond Descalquenquis were constituted general heirs in equal shares. Much of the testament is taken up with transmitting the "albergum" seen above: there was to be no joint ownership. Were each successive heir among the brothers to die without leaving legitimate male issue, it was to go to the next sibling and so on down the line. They were also permitted to sell the "domus" or "albergum" in which William Peter Pilistortus (a "sponderius") was living, William Peter having the first option on it. For Peter Raymond Descalquenquis' testament, see below No. 98 (May 1277).

83. JULY 1253: TAM, II 45 ii, copied in 1281. Appointing two "sponderii," Guillelma, widow of William Bosquerius of the parish of Saint-Sernin, allocated eighty shillings for charity, of which about twenty were assigned to churches, etc. and the rest was to be put toward her burial or given to her son Bertrand. Above this, her three sons, John, Bruno and Bertrand, and a niece were to receive a total of 300 shillings in cash and real property consisting of two "maloles" and a piece of land.

84. AUGUST 1253: Malta 123 16. The complicated testament of William Usclacanus, a smith in the Taur parish, who, reports the document, "sanus et ylaris et cum suo bono sensu et perfecta memoria testamentum suum condidit." The decedent appointed three executors, one of whom was a "cambiator" and another William's own "discipulus" Peter Vitalis, who he obviously hoped would succeed him in his business. Childless, William left his wife Johanna her

unspecified widow's portion, and also lifetime usufruct of his town property as long as she did not remarry (*M&W* 162). Although some went to godchildren and friends, the principal benefactions went to ecclesiastical institutions, especially Grandselve, which house received his half share of the "bovaria" at Estacabiau near Saint-Génies, a farm worth 20,000 shillings in 1226. William's beneficiaries were given in both property and kind and his cash donations were above 1400 shillings. Besides granting twelvepence to each hospital and leper house, he gratified two of the town's mendicant orders, the Clares and upwards of seventeen outlying monasteries. He also donated fifty shillings to the "operi pontis de Badacleo" and ten shillings each to the Old and New Bridges, and further added ".xv. miliaria de tegula plana bene cocta ponti de Badacleo et jubeo largiri ibi dictam tegulam a predictis meis spondariis de bonis mei in primo pilario quod ibi inceptum fuerit ad faciendum."

85. FEBRUARY 1256: MADTG, G 712 iii (copied in 1269). Arnold de Petro Johanne, Arnold Raymond "sabaterius" (shoemaker) and Bernard Vicecomes were left with the confusing duty of fulfilling the incoherent will of Arnold Willelmus "macellarius," brother of Peter Johannes "macellarius." Arnold assigned 400 shillings to charity of which small sums went to his parish of the Daurade, five shillings to Saint-Étienne and fifty to Grandselve, a total of about 120 shillings. Thereafter the money for charity was given to friends and family: no less than seven godchildren, two of whose names the testator could not remember ("illo de Rabastenquis"), two closely related religious, one at Goujon and the other at Lespinasse, as well as a gaggle of relatives. After the charities, there were two further lists of benefactions, thus causing the distribution of money to equal 1150 shillings. Arnold's wife Bernarda was to receive her marriage portion and either fifty shillings or the right to live in his house for two years, expenses paid (*M&W* 165). His daughter Guillelma was to have 300 shillings, a bed and "vestes nuptiales" and to share the rest of the inheritance equally with her sister Riqua. Riqua, wife of the "sponderius" Arnold Raymond "sabaterius," and her daughter Johanna were gratified with cash gifts of 150 shillings. The three sons of Arnold's brother Peter Johannis, the "sponderius" Arnold, the latter's brothers Raymond and Bernard and his sisters Pros and Ramunda were given 210 shillings. Lastly, the good butcher's natural son William ("filius meus naturalis") was dropped with seventy-five shillings. Arnold's god was a family man.

86. AUGUST 1256: MADTG, A 297, fols. 202-204v and *HGL*: No. 464 i. The testament of the rural notable Raymond Jordan de Insula, son of the quondam Odo de Terrida, had two "sponderii" and two "conciliatores," the abbot of Grandselve and a Dominican. Money, a horse, a mare and foal, a rouncy, the complete equipment a "miles debet habere," a bed and silver cups were given to Grandselve and the churches of Bretx and Thil. After assigning seventeen "porci pingues" to his creditor Ptolemy de Portale of Toulouse, the testator

ordered the sale of all his pigs and half his sheep and goats. The money realized by this sale was to pay a squire 100 shillings Morlaas to go on pilgrimage to Saint James of Compostella as promised by the dying man. It also endowed other pilgrimage centers, monasteries, and the Dominicans and Franciscans and the churches of the Dalbade, Daurade and Saint-Étienne in Toulouse. The other half of the total sum realized went to his widow Guillelma. Other donations given in this disorganized (deathbed?) will include another rouncy and mare with foal, a bed with coverlets, one of squirrel fur, two hauberks, two pourpoints, greaves ("calige") and armored coats ("cooperte ferree"), part to the Temple of Toulouse and part to the Hospital of Roncesvalles. A hundred shillings were bequeathed to individuals in order to replace pigs and cattle "devastati" by the testator, along with crops and real property. These persons included a woman and Raymond Jordan's brothers Arnold Bernard and William Arnold. The testator's brothers Garsia and Bernard were accorded the "dominium" of Garac and Lévignac, and his son Bertrand received houses in Saint-Cyprien in Toulouse, other goods and regained from his dying father the honors his mother Helia had given him. Apparently beside himself, the testator then remarked that he owed the celebrated Raymond d'Alfario 3000 shillings Morlaas or Toulouse. His creditor had died and he therefore expressed the hope that the Toulousan notary who recorded the debt had not rendered it into public form. This hopeless claim he left to his widow, who also was to receive the 1000 shillings he had from her "ratione matrimonii" (M&W 167). His nephew Odo de Terrida, the son of his sister "domina" Alpays and Bernard de Astafort her husband, was given the castle of Thil and the town of Bretx. Lastly, he placed his heirs under the protection of the counts of Toulouse, Foix and Armagnac. The abbot of Grandselve attested the testament along with not a few important Toulousans, including the moneylender Ptolemy mentioned above.

87. OCTOBER 1256: MADTG, A 297, fol. 240v. The second testament of Raymond Jordan de Insula repeated all the charities found in "suum primum testamentum," but radically changed the basic distribution of property. The testator's cousin, Isarn Jordan, son of the deceased Bertrand Jordan de Insula, was here given a half of the castle of Thil and the town of Bretx, the other half remaining in the hands of the nephew mentioned in Testament No. 86 above. The latter is the senior heir, however, having "maioria et antecabada," and the grant to Isarn Jordan is limited by the fact that he may build a "domus plana" in Thil but not a "fortitudo" which may harm Odo. This testament was rendered at Saint-Cyprien in Toulouse.

88. MARCH 1257: Malta 10 8 ii (copied in 1264) A cobbler, two "ortolani" (truckgardeners?) and a "braserius" (a laborer or a brewer) testified that Bernard Radulfus left ten shillings in charity to Saint-Étienne, Saint-Barthélemy "de Palatio," Saint-Jacques, the Clares, etc., and to his goddaughter Flos, daughter of Bernard de Petragore of Puybusque. His wife, also named Flos, was made

"domina et potens" to look after their children, Sancius and Bruna, both minors (*M&W* 168). If, however, Flos "dictos infantes volebat dimittere et volebat ducere virum," she is to be given half of the estate and the children the other half. For Flos' testament, see No. 193 (August 1261) below. Note also that the marriage contract between Bernard and Flos was ibid. iii (April 1245) in *M&W* 150.

89. MAY 1257: Malta 10 21 ii (copied in 1257). Arnold Guilabertus "ferraterius" (farrier or blacksmith) appointed as "sponderii" another blacksmith, a "raditor" (a shaver or barber?) and a nephew named John Guilabertus, brother of Pons, who happened to owe the testator seven shillings sixpence. He gave 180 shillings in charity. Benefactions went to his parish of Saint-Étienne, the Templars and five rural monasteries. His widow Ramunda (*M&W* 169) received her marriage portion, and John Guilabertus was given the testator's share "de illis ovibus quas Willelmus de Ponte de Odarcio ab eodem Arnaldo tenebat in gazalha," obviously at Odars near Montgiscard to whose church of Saint-Papoul the testator also left a small gift. Finally his "sponderii" were gratified with sixty shillings and were ordered to devote the remainder of his small estate (ibid. iii shows that it was a fragment of a "malol") to be given "in pannis lane et lini de quibus pauperes et leprosi induantur" in Toulouse.

90. NOVEMBER 1258: Puybusque, *Généalogie Puybusque*, pp. 48-53. Of the parish of Saint-Étienne, Raymond de Podiobuscano appointed two "sponderii," one living on the "carraria de affactatoribus" (near the Place Mage), and disposed of charities of 500 shillings to be distributed by the executors and his daughter Bordolesia. Other than to his parish in which he was to be buried and where he became a "donatus" and a "frater" (presumably of the canons regular of the cathedral), his principal benefactions were to the mendicants, both Dominicans and Franciscans, and to the Clares, along with a sister who was a nun at Grâce-Dieu. Raymond's widow Saptalina was given an unspecified marital settlement and a nephew received ten arpents at Bovilla near Lardenne and at other places including Pechaimeric. The decedent's major heirs were his sons Bernard Raymond and Raymond who were given his properties at Péchabou and elsewhere. His daughter Bordolesia, called Petrona, wife of William de Neutze (for Nempze ?), was given a claim for her dowry and, in addition, some real property at Le Travers (*M&W* 170). This daughter was put in charge of his sons and their estates until they attained majority. Although not as favored as his brother in this will, the son named Raymond outlived his sibling as we see in Testament No. 103 below. See the family in Appendix 1, No. 12.

91. MAY 1259: Malta 10 26 ii (copied in 1259). In a much destroyed document, John de Campanha allocated ten shillings to charity. His wife served as his "sponderius" but was instructed to seek the advice of the "maior capellanus," two "subcapellani" and of Arnold de Brassaco, a scholar in his parish of Saint-Étienne. Small benefactions went to the Carmelites, Clares and the Friars of the

Sack, as well as the town's three bridges, Old, New and Bazacle. His widow Johanna inherited half the remaining estate and his three sons Bernard Johannis, Raymond Johannis and William Johannis the rest (*M&W* 171).

92. APRIL 1260: Malta 13 24 ii. Stephen de Goza "ortolanus" made his wife, who was one of his three "sponderii," his heir (*M&W* 172). He also gave forty shillings to charity, especially to his parish of Saint-Étienne and the monastery of Eaunes. The pair was already married in ibid. i (March 1229).

93. AUGUST 1261: Malta 10 8 iv (copied in 1264). Widow of Bernard Radulfus to whom she was married in April 1245 (*M&W* 150 and No. 88 (March 1257) for her husband's testament), "domina" Flos appointed as her "sponderii" her godfather Vasco de Lambes and her son-in-law Bernard Columbus "ortolanus." She gave just under thirty-two shillings to charity, including godchildren and Saint-Étienne, and appears to have been something of a mendicant buff, mentioning six orders and the Clares. Her son appears to have died or disappeared since 1257 and, consequently, her daughter was heir. Though still a minor (under age twenty-five?), this person was married to the executor named Columbus mentioned above (*M&W* 173).

94. NOVEMBER 1263: Malta 17 68 iii (copied in 1264). William John Mota "de carraria Asinorum" appointed his son William Mota and his son-in-law Bernard de Podio "sponderii" to distribute twenty shillings, especially to Saint-Étienne and Saint-Barthélemy and to five mendicant orders. He also assigned an unspecified marital portion to his wife Maria (*M&W* 174). Both apparently majors, his daughters Petrona and Englesia were given a house. The rest of his estate was to go to his sons William, Arnold and Bartholomew, several of whom were minors, and to a child as yet unborn.

95. MAY 1265: Malta 17 69 ii. Of Saint-Étienne parish, Arnold de Podio appointed four executors, two bearing his surname, one of them a "frenerius" (metalware for saddles, etc.). He left thirty-five shillings to charity of which no less than twenty-eight went to layfolk, including his brother William de Podio. Childless, his widow Bruna was to receive eighty shillings "in digna helemosina" (*M&W* 180) The decedent listed debts equaling twenty-three shillings sixpence, one to a "mercator" and two to "frenerii," and what was left was to go to the poor and leprous in the form of shirts, breeches and shoes, and to pay restitution for usury to his "conquerentes."

96. MARCH 1270: Malta 2 163. Arnold Petrus "coquinarius" (cook) in the Dalbade parish gave twenty shillings to charity and an eighth of an arpent of "malol" to the Temple for burial. A gift of fifty shillings was made to a Martina de Goza and fifty more were assigned "in vestibus tam lane quam lini quas vestes predictas dent ipsi spondarii ... pauperibus et hegenis orphanis." The rest went "jure hereditario" to his nephew Arnold Barbaordeus whose wife Jordana also received ten shillings.

97. APRIL 1272: Malta 2 166. Peter Paganus "nauta" (boatman) left sixty shillings for charity, especially to his parish of the Dalbade. All remaining property went to his wife (*M&W* 184). After her death, however, his house was to go to the Hospital where he had been looked after in his last days.

98. MAY 1277: MADTG, A 297, fol. 877v. The son of Bertrand Descalquenquis whose testament is No. 90 (August 1242) above, Peter Raymond Descalquenquis appointed as executor his son Bertrand, giving him as counselors his two uncles and another member of the family. A parishioner of Saint-Sernin, Peter Raymond set aside 300 shillings for charity. The larger portion went to institutions in town, but some to the church in Pibrac, of which community the testator was a lord. Some of money also went to an "ancilla" and to Arnalda "nutrix et mater" of his son Bertrand, the latter's real mother having presumably died in childbirth. Peter Raymond ordered that "de bonis suis restituantur et darentur .cc. sol. tol. tam per restitutionem quam amore Dei et quod de illis restituantur Guillelmo Arnaldo de Franco et heredibus Guillelmi Johannis Casanhe qui fuit et Martino de la Terrada et Vitali Casanhe totum hoc quod ab eis vel ab aliquo illorum idem testator habuerat vel receperat per usuram vel aliter minus iuste et quod predicte persone inde credantur de toto cum sacramento quod inde prestent, … ," adding that his executor "concordet se cum suis aliis conquerentibus si apparuerint," and that what remained of the modest sum of 200 shillings should then be given to hospitals and the poor. Peter Raymond's only child Bertrand received the whole inheritance together with a cash gift of 1000 shillings. After Bertrand's death, all was to go to his children "de legitimo matrimonio procreatis si apparuerint pro omni voluntate eorum infantium vel infantis equis portibus facienda postquam etatis quatuordecim annorum fuerint."

99. OCTOBER 1278: Malta 2 171. His son Paul having predeceased him, Paulus "notarius" of the parish of Saint-Étienne first promised "quod fiat restitutio de bonis meis conquerentibus de me a quibus apareret me aliquid indebite extorsisse si qui aparuerint tres annos post obitum mei testatoris predicti, et hoc de plano sine strepitu iudiciario," at the discretion of his six "sponderii et executores" who included a notary, a butcher and two merchants (one from Cahors). He then left the very large sum of 3400 shillings for charity as well as a rent roll of two shillings threepence yearly on some houses near Saint-Barthélemy and some "maloles" described in ibid. 172 i and ii (January 1281). The larger part of these benefactions went to the Hospital, the rents and 200 shillings to individual officers and 900 each to the work of the Hospital in Toulouse and "ad subsidium Terre Sancte." Other interesting bequests were 500 shillings for the marriage of poor young women, 150 shillings to pay the charity promised in the wills of his deceased mother Petrona and his step-father Raymond Estultus, and fifty shillings to the "nutrix" of his dead son Paul. The

notary's wife Ramunda was to get her marriage portion, 100 shillings her father Bernard Fogascerius had given her and usufruct of his remaining properties, themselves eventually to go to the Hospital (*M&W* 187).

100. JULY 1282: Grandselve 13. Sister of Matheva Sobacca, Marcibilia's much destroyed will gave "restitutio integra omnibus conquerentibus" and distributed 800 shillings especially to Grandselve and its hospice and chapel in Toulouse, to "pauperes puelle" and also to friends and grandnephews, sons of William Rossellus. Her real heirs were her [grand]niece Esquiva and grandnephews, sons of the deceased Raymond Ruffus "legista," who received a house in the "barrio porte Matabovis" and the usual vineyard. The Sobaccus family history is in my *Men and Women*, pp. 185-190.

101. JANUARY 1283: Saint-Sernin 699 (22 74 2). "Factis restitutionibus omnibus conquerentibus," Ademar Maurandus turned to the church, dividing 300 shillings and annual rents between his parish of Saint-Sernin, the Franciscans, whose "gardianus" was at his bedside, churches and bridges in town, outlying monasteries such as Prouille, and the churches and bridges of his villages of Flourens, Mons and Quint to the south of town. About 1950 shillings were given close relatives and godchildren. The sum is minimal because Ademar tired of listing them all and simply gave ten shillings a head to all the rest. Petrona, his "filia naturalis," wife of Peter Agassa, received 1000 shillings. His widow Bosencontres received her unspecified nuptial portion, a gift, and lifetime residence in his "hospitium" (*M&W* 188). Childless but rich in relatives, he designated nephews and grandnephews his heirs. See the Maurandi family in my *Repression of Catharism*, pp. 229-241.

102. FEBRUARY 1285: Malta 2 175. Parishioner of the Dalbade, Franca de Sancto Gaudentia entrusted her modest means to her executors who included a cutler and a "rasorerius" (razor or knife maker). They were to forgive her nephews a debt they owed her, and to give a total of about sixty shillings to charity. The larger part of this sum went to the Hospitalers, thirty shillings for masses, seven shillings sixpence "pro pitancia" and burial and an equal sum "ad opus passagii ultramarini seu subsidium Terre Sancte."

103. JUNE 1297: Puybusque, *Généalogie Puybusque*, pp. 61-69. Raymond de Podiobuscano, son of the quondam Raymond de Podiobuscano "de carraria affactatorum Tholose" (modern rue Merlan), appointed as witnesses to his will "affactatores," leather workers or merchants who, like the deceased, lived near the Place Mage. His charities to churches and orders totaled about 100 shillings and were especially devoted to the parish of Saint-Étienne and the Carmelites in whose robe he wished to be buried. An approximately equal sum was given to individuals. Among these were his own "nutrix" and the two "nutrices" of his sons. A son of his brother Bernard Raymond, a Dominican named Bernard, was modestly gratified and a William de Podiobuscano "mercator" served as a

witness. The settlement with his wife Englesia about her marital portion must have been made before the will, but she was here given housing and keep, being made "domina et potens dum tamen sine marito permanserit" over the children, only some of whom, it appears, were hers (*M&W* 190). The heirs were his two sons Peter Raymond (who received all property in Toulouse, on the banks of the Hers river, and at Bayssa) and Peter Bernard (all property at Mauremont, whose village church received a bequest of ten shillings, and Puybusque). The heirs naturally had to pay the legacies and debts of the estate, but were given three years before the former were due. A third son named William was to receive 500 shillings but could remain at home until he collected that sum. Raymond also had three daughters. Two of these, his daughters Bordalesia and Mascarosa, "filie ejusdem testatoris legitime et naturales," were favored and assigned dowries of 1000 shillings, etc. following the "jus hereditorie institutionis et apparciamenti." Both William and his sisters could have 100 shillings for charity were they to die before marriage or adulthood. The final sibling, named Ramunda, was assigned 500 shillings deriving from the estate of the testator's deceased mother Saptalina "pro dei servicio religio seu ordo." The testator's mother had lived until about February 1290 when Raymond and his brother Bernard Raymond submitted their dispute about her succession to arbitration (ibid. 59-60). Raymond's father's testament is No. 90 above, and the family history is in Appendix 1, No. 12.

Appendix Nine

A Calendar of Estates

INTRODUCTION

The documents calendared below are collected to examine the way in which family property and inheritances were treated in Toulouse. About twenty-three charters contain divisions of estates among heirs, and nineteen joint actions by groups of heirs. Three charters describe the apportionment of an heir before the demise of his father, and one establishes a lineage right among three heirs. The rest of the documents illustrate actions of the consuls to protect widows and children, private "sponderii" or "tutores" and lawsuits. Many other similar acts have been noted in the archives, but most, save for family histories, are too uninstructive to be recorded in this calendar.

1. UNDATED EARLY XIITH CENTURY, for which see above Appendix Six, p. 428. Two brothers divide their inheritance but hold the church of Saint-Agne in "fratrisca."

2. NOVEMBER 1135: Saint-Sernin 600 (10 36 5). A division between Raymond de Castilione and his brothers Bernard and Gerald beginning: "Hec est carta rememorationis de participatione quam fecerunt inter se de toto illo honore quem pater eorum tenuit scilicet Arnold Mascalcus in alodio de Castilione [Castillon] et usque ad Yrcium. Raymond de Castilione cepit ad suam partem ... ."

3. DECEMBER 1157: E 501. An action taken by Peter, Raymond, William and Pagana, children of the deceased Paganus Porcellus, with the consent of their mother Ricardia.

4. APRIL 1160: Saint-Étienne 227 (26 DA 2 7 and 90). "Hec carta est rememorationis de divisione quam fecerunt inter se gratis et sine inganno Johannes Raterii et fratres eius, Arnaldus scilicet atque Petrus Bernardi, ex paterna sive materna eorum hereditate, sive ex adquisicionibus honorum per se factis ... ." The division followed the instructions in their mother's will to erect and maintain a "fratrisca" for ten years, for which, see Appendix 8, No. 1 (August 1150).

5. AUGUST 1162: Malta 12 4. An action taken by Toset Tolose, Raymond Aton, William Tolose and Guillelma, children of Bruna and the deceased Gerald

A CALENDAR OF ESTATES 469

Engilbertus, with the consent of their mother. See the Tolosa history in my *Repression of Catharism*, pp. 268-283.

6. NOVEMBER 1169: E 501 iii (copied in 1207). After the death of Tolosanus de Bochariis, his sons Raymond Tolosanus, Pons Tolosanus and Raymond Carpinus, together with their mother Ramunda sold some property.

7. OCTOBER 1170: Saint-Étienne 227 (26 DA 2 102), copied in 1198. "Hec est carta partitionis et divisionis bonorum quam fecit Bernardus Raimundus Pilistortus" with his brothers Peter William and Raymond Garsias on the death of their father Bernard Raymond.

8. APRIL 1174: Grandselve 3 iii (copied in 1196). "Per computum atque per ordinationem" Bernard Grillus "hereditavit suum filium Petrum Bernardum Grillum et dedit ei maiori omnes illos gadannos quos factos habebat et quos in antea faciet, scilicet totam illam pecuniam quod habet gadanatam et que inantea gadanabit, et totum illum honorem quod habet gadanatum mecum et emptum, et que inantea gadanaverit neque emerit ubicumque sit, sive sint terre vel vinee vel oblie vel queque gadanatum sit ullo modo, totum dedit ei ... suus pater dictus ad faciendam omnem suam voluntatem." He also assigned him by "istud computum neque ereditatio ista" specific properties in which neither his brother William Raymond Grillus "neque sue sorores non habeat ibi aliquid." The sisters were not named.

9. APRIL 1180: Malta 1 100. With the consent of his wife Rica, his son Bertrand, Bertrand's wife Brus Martina, and his daughter Bonafos with her husband Raymond Ispaniolus, Bernard David "venit ad finem et concordiam" with his son Pons David, giving him the region around Pechdavid and the Garonne waterfront as well as the "terciam partem in illis iuribus monete que Bernardus David habebat in moneta" and also a third part of the mint itself ("domus que est monete"). With the consent of his wife Bruna, Pons David surrendered all claims on his father's and sibling's' property. The David history is in my *Repression of Catharism*, pp. 203-208.

10. JANUARY 1181: Saint-Étienne 227 (26 DA 2 50) (copied in 1183). "Hec est carta comemoracionis et divisionis et particionis" of the sons of Raymond Guilabertus, namely Arnold, Raymond, Bernard and Peter; "et divisiones et particiones suorum facte de eorum curia de Saulonare [in Saint-Cyprien] ... , et tres partes predicte curie ... remanserunt insimul," namely the three parts attributed to Arnold, Bernard and Peter Guilabertus. The fourth part went to Raymond. "Set predicti fratres ... retinuerunt insimul pro indiviso omnia pascua et aquas," etc.

11. AUGUST 1185: A charter recording that when William Bestiacius de Turribus "partivit cum fratribus suis," namely Arnold, Peter Tronus, Curvus, Pilistortus and Peter Judex, he received a particular "pignus." Details are found in the Turribus history in Appendix 1, No. 15, note 17 above.

12. SEPTEMBER 1186: Malta 182 29. The onetime vicar of Toulouse and minter Ispaniolus entered the Hospitalers with the consent of his sons Galhard, Sicard, Raymond, Gerald and Ispanus, the latter still a minor.

13. FEBRUARY 1187: Grandselve 2 iv. William Poncius "ortolanus" and his son Arnold gave another son named William Pons specific properties, stating that "hoc donum dederunt ei pro hereditate, et Willelmus Poncius accepit illud donum pro hereditate patris suis et matris ... , et tunc ibidem Willelmus Poncius solvit ac reliquit ... patri suo et ... fratri suo et eorum ordinio totum suum alium honorem et omnia sua bona tam mobilia quam imobilia que inde habent vel inantea habuerint ad totam eorum voluntatem faciendam." This was done with the consent of the donors' wives.

14. MARCH 1187 OR 1188, a division of a Tolosa inheritance. See above Appendix 6, No. 2.

15. NOVEMBER 1189: Saint-Sernin 599 (10 35 16) 5th of a group of membranes tied together i, copied in 1220. The division of the "curia" of Valségur and its appendices by Stephen and Arnold Maurandus, the heirs of Maurandus. The division had taken place four or more years before it was recorded in an instrument. The Maurandi history is in my *Repression of Catharism*, pp. 229-241.

16. JANUARY 1191: Saint-Bernard 138, fol. 24. One of several charters of the same date referring to the brothers Pons and Peter Raymond Grillus and their sister Englesia who obviously hold property in "fratrisca," although the term does not appear.

17. JUNE 1192: E 503 i (copied in 1203). An instrument "de una partidone" between Jordan de Villanova and his brothers Pons and Stephen of a portion of their properties, especially the town house and lands on the left bank of the Garonne river. The Villanova history is in my *Repression of Catharism*, pp. 292-304.

18. NOVEMBER 1193: Grandselve 3. Raymond Bertrandus, Hugh Bertrandus, Bertrandus and Arnold Petrus sell to Isarn Bertrandus "quatuor partes de quinque partibus" of seventeen shillings less threepence "oblie," "nam ipsi recognoverunt et concesserunt quod quinta pars predictarum obliarum ... erat ipsius Isarni Bertrandi pro sua fratrisca."

19. APRIL 1196: Grandselve 7 v (copied in 1236). A "carta divisionum" between the brothers Peter Brugaterius, William Arnaldus and Raymond Petrus of a house, some vineyards and land. Not called "fratrisca," this community had lasted at least nine years because in ibid. ii (March 1187) the brothers acquired property together.

20. JANUARY 1197: Daurade 118 i (copied in 1204). The "sponderii" of Terrenus Martinus (see Appendix 8, No. 17 dated June 1196) acted for the minor

children Terricus, Martin and Pons Stephanus with the consent of their mother Ricsenda. The third of these children attained majority in ibid. iv July 1203.

21. OCTOBER 1197: Malta 145 (copied in 1281). Peter de Orbessano gave at fief to Bernard de Sancto Barcio and his sons, Peter, Durand, Aimeric, Arnold, William de Sancto Barcio and Raymond Durandus the castle and "villa" of Pibrac which they are to share with the lord of Isle-Jourdain.

22. MAY 1198: Grandselve 3 iv. The sons of Raymond Baranonus (alive in ibid. iii September 1187), Bruno Baranonus, Raymond Bernard, Bernard Raymond, Berengar, William Bernard and Arnold Raymond Baranonus acted for themselves and their two married sisters as a "fratrisca." See the Baranoni in my *Repression of Catharism*, pp. 131-135.

23. JANUARY 1200: Saint-Étienne 227 (26 DA 2 57) (copied in 1258). With the assent of their mother Esclarmunda, widow of Arnold de Roaxio, Raymond, Arnold and their minor brothers Hugh, Gerald and Alaman took action about property. The Roaxio family is in my *Repression of Catharism*, pp. 251-267.

24. JUNE 1204: Grandselve 4 i and ii (copied in 1204). John Curtasolea and his brothers Stephen, Peter Raymond and their minor sibling Bernard Curtasolea sold a rent to Grandselve. The Curtasolea family is in my *Repression of Catharism*, pp. 197-202.

25. NOVEMBER 1208: E 501 (copied in 1214). "Domina Ramunda quondam uxor Petri qui vocabatur Monsacutus Astro" gave her sons Bernard de Monteacuto and Aimeric Astro money and property, part deriving from her deceased father's will and part from her marriage portion. The Astro history is in my *Men and Women*, pp. 173-183.

26. JULY 1211: Malta 1 19. Deusaiuda and his brother Pons Arnold, sons of Peter de Bernardo Arnaldo, divided their inherited property. Details are in the Arnaldus history in Appendix 1, No. 1.

27. MARCH 1214: E 501 published in Fons "Chartes inédites relatives au jugement des affaires concernant la succession des Toulousains tués à la bataille de Muret," *Recueil de l'Académie de Législation de Toulouse* 20 (1871) 18-22. A court appointed by the consuls heard claims on the estate of the baker Raymond Bascol who had died intestate in the battle of Muret. The claimants were three: 1) his wife Willelma for her dowry and share of their joint acquisitions, 2) Ermesendis, the daughter of Bascol's deceased sister and hence his "consanguinea germana," and 3) Dominic and Raymond Lerida "per parentelam consanguinitatis germani ex parte matris" of Raymond Bascol. The court decided that Ermesendis was heir "ratione cognationis et parentele," but asserted that the award was "salvo jure et ratione dotis et adquisitionis dicte Willelme, et salvo jure" of the counsins-german Dominic and Raymond, and also any claim on the estate

by creditors. In E 509 May 1214, having received eighty shillings from Wil-lelma, the "consanguineus" Dominic confessed himself satisfied.

28. APRIL 1215: Grandselve 6 iv (copied in 1211 and 1227). With the consent of his wife and son, Arnold de Tolosa and his nephew Peter Raymond de Tolo-sa, acting with the agreement of the latter's sister Arnalda, ended a "fratrisca" and divided what they shared. The "fratrisca" presumably began after the death of Peter Raymond's father Raymond de Tolosa whose testament is recorded in ibid. iii (November 1201) and an action by Peter Raymond in ibid. v (December 1201). The "fratrisca" had lasted just over thirteen years. See the family in my "Urban Society and Culture," p. 244.

29. APRIL 1215: The division by Bernard and Peter, sons of Bernard Seillanus, of their inheritance: a house in town near the Château Narbonnais, a farm at Saint-Jory and other pieces of property. The document's contents are listed in Appendix 1, No. 14, note 18.

30. AUGUST 1216: Grandselve 5. With the approval of her daughters Ermesen-dis, Mabriana and Blancha, Domina, widow of Peter Corregerius, gave her sons Arnold Corregerius, Peter and Raymond all property but retained residence rights in the family house, etc. The brothers then "fecerunt convenientiam inter eos unusquisque alteri quod si de aliquo eorum descedebat, scilicet quod desce-deret absque infante uxoris, quod tota sua pars de predictis rebus remaneret aliis pro omni eorum voluntate inde facienda, et si de duobus descedebant, scilicet quod descederent sine infante uxoris, quod tota eorum pars de predictis rebus remanerent tercio pro omni sua voluntate inde facienda." The family history is in my *Repression of Catharism*, pp. 191-192.

31. SEPTEMBER 1218: E 575 (copied in 1281). With the consent of the widow Bona, the "sponderii" of Bernard de Tabula sold property for his children, Ri-carda, wife of Bernard Bastonus, and Ramunda, wife of Peter de Devesia, and for their absent brother William de Tabula.

32. SEPTEMBER 1219: E 472. At the time of the marriage of Peter Sobaccus and Matheva, Matheva's coheirs "ratione fratrische" were her brother William Rosellus and her sister Marissibilia. See the Sobaccus history in my *Men and Women*, pp. 185-190.

33. DECEMBER 1222: MAT AA 1 74. Arnold Guilabertus, his wife Gentilis and his sons William de Brugueriis, Arnold Guilabertus and Bernard William de Brugueriis sold the place "in quo pons Basaclei est constructus."

34. MARCH 1223: PAN, J 318 26. The "sponderii" of Raymond Durandus acted for the latter's sons Bernard, Vital, Bertrand, Heleazar, Raymond and Pons Durandus, the latter three being minors. In MAT II 97 (January 1230),

the Durandi siblings divided the "castrum" of Colomiers. Bernard had already entered the Temple in Malta 1 122 (April 1226) with his brothers' consent.

35. MARCH 1223: Douais, *Conférence de paléographie*, No. 18. A division of their inheritance by William, Bernard and Aldric de Roaxio, sons of the deceased David de Roaxio. The Roaix family is in my *Repression of Catharism*, pp. 251-267.

36. APRIL 1225: PAN, J 330 12 iii (copied in 1250 and 1277). Referring to the property left them in their father's will (Appendix 8, No. 37 dated October 1216), Peter Bernard Balderia gave his brother William Balderia all claim on property held together "per fratriscam," confessing that he did so because his brother "pro hac solucione dederat ei de sua pecunia."

37. AUGUST 1230: Saint-Sernin 680 (20 72 nn) (copied in 1252). A court case before the consuls involves Petrona, widow of Bernard Benedictus, and her two children, Arnalda and Bona, the latter a minor.

38. OCTOBER 1231: Malta 17 98 (copied in 1247). The brothers Peter and Arnold Nepos divided their humble estate of a house and vinyeards in Saint-Cyprien. Other small properties, including a house "in qua manebant" were retained in common. Peter Nepos's testament is calendared in Appendix 8, No. 76.

39. APRIL 1234: Saint-Sernin 599 (10 33 15). Raymond Aimeric, Peter and Gerald de Cossano fulfilled a testamentary disposition made by their father Bernard Peter de Cossano. The Cossano family history is in my *Repression of Catharism*, pp.193-196.

40. APRIL 1236: E 501 ii (copied in 1241). A charter written for Peter Aton and Hugh Willelmus, sons of the quondam Hugh Willelmus, divided their modest property, including two adjacent houses, household equipment and various bits of real property. The sons were obeying their father's will in Appendix 8, No. 60 (September 1234).

41. JUNE 1238: PAN, J 330 14. The children of Hugh Johannes, namely Ramunda, widow of Bernard de Miramonte, and her brothers Arnold and Raymond Johannes, pay Ramunda her dowry and recuperate the farm at Cépet for the family.

42. AUGUST 1239: E 501 ii (copied in 1251). The brothers Peter de Gaillaco, William Deide (Deodatus) and John de Gaillaco with spousal consent divided a house and some vineyards. Ibid. i (month lost 1224) tells us that the brothers had jointly acquired property together at that time. Peter's testament is Appendix 8, No. 79 (February 1251) and see entry no. 48 below.

43. JANUARY 1240: Malta 27 65. A division of what they hold "ratione fratrisce" between the brothers Bernard and Gerald de Caturcio. See Appendix 1, No. 4, for the Caturcio.

44. OCTOBER 1240: Advised by their widowed mother Jordana, Arnold and his wife Stephania, Raymond and wife Willelma and Peter Barbaordeus, sons of the deceased Raymond Barbaordeus, divided their property into three parts. See Appendix 1, No. 2, for this family.

45. MARCH 1241: Malta 17 55 ii (copied in 1244). A division of the estate left by Bernard Vitalis assigned his son Bernard Vitalis "bursellarius" some vineyards but gave his widow, Ramunda, the family "domus."

46. MARCH 1243: Grandselve 8 i and ii. Advised by their mother Ricardia, widow of Peter William de Orto, and their "procuratores," William de Orto, his brothers Peter William and Gerald de Orto and their sister Alamanda, wife of Arnold Puer, sold a large urban property to Arnold Johannes "cellerius."

47. OCTOBER 1251: Malta 2 147 ii and ibid. 4 215 (February 1253). A property was held jointly by the brothers Peter, William, Bertrand and Arnold Barravus for at least two years. See the Barravus family in my *Repression of Catharism*, pp. 136-154.

48. OCTOBER 1251: E 501 iv. A division of a house and vineyard left by Peter de Galhaco (Gaillaco) made by Peter's widow Lumbarda and her daughter Ramunda, wife of Martin de Montecaprario. See Appendix 8, No. 79 (February 1251) and entry No. 42 (August 1239) above.

49. JANUARY 1252: Malta 17 67 ii (copied in 1273). Petitioned by the widow Vitalia, the consuls assigned tutors to Johanna and Navarra, daughters of the notary Bernard de Podiosiurano who had died intestate.

50. MARCH 1254: MAT II 39 (copied in 1286). A division of the extensive properties of the deceased Francisca, daughter of Bernard de Miramonte. The widower Stephen de Castronovo received two of ten parts, one of which he had acquired from Bernard Raymond Baranonus. Three parts went to the three Niger brothers, one of whom was deceased, and the last five parts to the Galhaco brothers, one share to one brother and two to two others. For Bernard de Miramonte's will of December 1237, see Appendix 8, No. 68.

51. DECEMBER 1255: a "divisio et partita" of the castles, houses, dependents, rents and real property of the sons of William de Turre or Turribus, Curvus, Fulk and Guy. Some properties were kept in community, but some were divided. For this act, see above, p. 356.

52. FEBRUARY 1258: Lespinasse 24. Aimeric de Castronovo and Castellus-novus, sons of the deceased Castellusnovus, paid a bequest made by their father. The Castronovo history is in my *Repression of Catharism*, p. 187.

53. FEBRUARY 1263: E 573. Sibilia, widow of Bernard Adevus, burdened by her husband's debts, her unfunded widow's portion and two sons to raise, tells the consuls that her husband "ipsam dominam et potentem in suo testamento constituit ... nulla mentione facta de sponderiis vel consiliatoribus." The consuls acceded to her request for two "tutores vel consiliatores" to help her out.

54. FEBRUARY 1265: E 502. Bernarda, wife of John de Torrindo, daughter of Bernard Boerius of Bastide-Saint-Sernin, gave her share of the parental inheritance to her sisters Dyas and Gracia, surrendering all she had "jure institutionis vel hereditatis vel pro fratrisca, dono legato, mandamentis vel convenienciis vel ullo quolibet alio modo."

55. MARCH 1272: E 65. The "sponderii" of the deceased Martin Brunus acted for the widow Petrona and her children William, Peter and Milhers.

56. NOVEMBER 1284: Malta 123 19, fourth of several membranes tied together. A sale by Arnold Bernard de Sancto Genesio (Saint-Génies) executed with the consent of five persons: his wife Rixendis, Ramunda, widow of the quondam Bernard de Turre, Bertrand de Turre, (another) Bernard de Turre and Mauranda de Turre, "fratres ipsius venditoris." These persons surrendered their rights "nomine dotis," "pro fratrisca successionis," etc. The three last named "fratres" stated that they were "minores .xxv. annis, majores tamen .xiv." and promised to confirm the sale when they had reached majority. See the Turre history in my *Repression of Catharism*, pp. 285-289.

Documents, Texts and Bibliography

1. ARCHIVAL DOCUMENTS AND MANUSCRIPT TEXTS

Most of the documents used in this book derive from Montauban, Paris and Toulouse but a few are found in Cambridge, Oxford and Vienna. The collections have been described in almost identical terms both in my *Repression of Catharism*, pp. 305-310, and *Men and Women*, pp. 213-218. A comment in the latter on p. 217 corrected the earlier publication's reference to Jean de Doat by noting, as stated by Walter Wakefield in a review, that Doat was the president of the Chambre de Comptes of Navarre (1665-1670) and not a mere notary. It also added on p. 218 that the manuscript cartulary of the monastery of Lézat had been published after the earlier study had appeared. Although the first of my two monographs is already out of print and the second soon to be, scholars with access to major libraries and the appropriate French archives will be able to consult either of these works.

In principle, registers and cartularies are cited by foliation and date, boxes ("boites") or folders ("liasses") by document number and date. All references will begin with a conventional abbreviation directing readers to the appropriate archive. No abbreviation for the Departmental Archives of the Haute-Garonne is used, however, because so many cited documents are from this repository. The collections cited are the following:

PAN: Paris, Archives Nationales.

J – These charters are calendared and sometimes published in the five volumes of the *Layettes du Trésor des Chartes*.

JJ – registers of the Trésor.

KK – a register of lawsuits in the early twelve-seventies.

AADML: Angers, Archives départmentales de Maine-et-Loire.

Lespinasse (in Series H) – a register of the Toulousan house of the order of Fontevrault.

MADTG: Montauban, Archives départementales de Tarn-et-Garonne.

A 297 – the cartulary of the Armagnac Collection.

G – the charters of the Benedictines of Moissac and its dependencies, namely the Daurade in Toulouse and Lézat south of Toulouse with its appendage of Saint-Antoine just outside the town's walls.

Toulouse, Archives départmentales de la Haute-Garonne.
The series divisions of this archive are not employed because they are unnecessary. When consulting the archives they are useful, however, and are:

7 D (educational establishments, see Saint-Bernard below); 1 E (family history. The letter (without the number) will be retained here because other identification is lacking). 1 and 4 G (respectively the archdiocese and the cathedral chapter of Saint-Étienne). H (all regular clergy – Saint-Sernin is 101 H, for example, the Daurade is 102 H, the Dominicans 112 H, etc.). Lastly, the Bazacle archives lack an identifying letter because they have been integrated into the archives only recently.

The archival collections used here are:

Archdiocese

Bazacle – the mills of that name

Clares

Daurade – the Benedictine priory of Moissac

Dominicans

E

Grandselve – a Cistercian house

Lespinasse – a Fontevrault female house

Malta and Malta Garidech – two commanderies of the Ordre de Malte

Saint-Bernard – charters cited as above save the Capdenier cartulary, No. 138, which is foliated.

Saint-Étienne – a typical reference is Saint-Étienne 227 (26 DA 2 47) (November 1230). The number "229" refers to the modern "liasse," and the material in the first set of parentheses refers to the archival identifications derived from Claude Cresty, *Répertoire des titres et documents concernants les biens et droits du chapitre de Saint-Étienne*, 2 vols. and another of tables (1734-1737) which are useful for identification.

Saint-Sernin – a typical reference is: Saint-Sernin 132 (20 70 12) (July 1222). The number "229" refers to the modern "liasse," and the material in the first set of parentheses refers to Cresty's *Répertoire des titres et documents concernants les donations . . . et divers autres droits appartenants à l'auguste chapitre de Saint-Sernin*, 2 vols. and another of tables (1728-1730).

478 DOCUMENTS, TEXTS AND BIBLIOGRAPHY

TAM: Toulouse, Archives Municipales

AA 1 and AA 2 – Catalogued by Ernest Roschach, *Inventaire-sommaire des archives communales de la ville de Toulouse antérieures à 1790*, vol. 1 (Toulouse, 1891). Both registers are published and numbered by Limouzin-Lamothe, *La commune de Toulouse*, for which see the Bibliography below.

BB 204 – The matricule or register of the notaries of Toulouse.

DD – The charters of the mills of the Château Narbonnais.

II – The charters in the onetime "Layettes," catalogued by Odon de Saint-Blanquat in his *Inventaire des archives de la ville de Toulouse antérieures à 1790*, vol. 2 in 2 parts (Toulouse, 1976-1977).

PBN: Paris, Bibliothèque nationale

Doat. registers referred to here as "Collection Doat," followed by volume number, foliation and date.

MS lat. 6009 – a cartulary of Grandselve.

MS lat. 9189 – the cartulary of Lézat, now published by Ourliac and Magnou, for which see the list of "Published Documents and Texts" below.

MS lat. 9994 – a cartulary of Grandselve.

MS nouv. acq. lat. 2406 – testimony before the vicar of Toulouse dated December 1259 and January-April 1260.

TBM: Toulouse, Bibliothèque municipale

MS 609 – register of depositions copied under William Bernard and Reginald de Chartres, inquisitors at Toulouse, sometime between 1258 and 1263. Mostly dated to 1245-1246, the last deposition is of October 1258. Now housed in the Institut de Recherche des Textes at Paris.

Other Libraries

Cambridge, Gonville and Caius College, MS Add. B. 65, fol. 1ff. *Regula mercatorum Tholosanorum*.

Oxford, Lincoln College, MS Latin 81, fol. 34ff. *Regula mercatorum Tholosanorum*.

Vienna Staatsbibliothek MS Palatinus 2210*, fols. 1-96v. A copy of the cartulary of the town of Toulouse described in my *Liberty and Political Power*, pp. 335-336, note 42, with a concordance with TAM, AA 1 and AA 2 on pp. 217-219.

A word about Toulousan surnames, such as that of the family called "Tolosa" or "de Tolosa": the Latin (or charter) form for all surnames is retained; when possible, all first or Christian names are in English equivalents.

2. PUBLISHED DOCUMENTS AND TEXTS

d'Abadal i Vinyals, Ramón and Ferrán Valls Taberner, eds. *Usatges de Barcelona.* Barcelona, 1913.

Albe, Edmond. *Inventaire raisonné des archives municipales de Cahors.* 1er. partie: XIIIe siècle. Cahors, 1915.

Albon, Guiges Alexis Sainte-Marie Joseph André, Marquis d', ed. *Cartulaire général de l'Ordre du Temple 1119-1150.* Paris, 1913.

Bastardas, Joan, ed. *Usatges de Barcelona: El codi a mitjan segle XII.* 2nd ed. Barcelona, 1991.

Beaumanoir, Philippe de. *Coutumes de Beauvaisis,* Am. Salmon, ed. 2 vols. Paris, 1899-1900.

Benedictus XII, pope. Le registre d'inquisition de Jacques Fournier, évêque de Pamiers (1318-1325). Jean Duvernoy, ed. 3 vols. Toulouse, 1965. *Corrections.* Toulouse, 1972.

Bênoit, Fernand, ed. *Recueil des actes des comtes de Provence appartenant à la maison de Barcelone.* 2 vols. Monaco and Paris, 1925.

Brunel, Clovis, ed. *Les plus ancienne chartes en langue provençale. Recueil des pièces originales antérièures au XIIIe siècle publiées avec une étude morphologique.* Paris, 1926.

Cabié, Edmond. *Chartes de coutumes inédites de la Gascogne Toulousaine.* Paris and Auch, 1884.

Chanson de la croisade albigeoise. Eugène Martin-Chabot, ed. Les classiques de l'histoire de France au moyen-âge. 3 vols. Paris, 1931-1973.

———. Paul Meyer, ed. 2 vols. Paris, 1875-1879.

Chevalier, Ulysse, ed. *Cartulaire de l'abbaye de Saint-Chaffre du Monastier suivi de la Chronique de Saint-Pierre du Puy.* Paris, 1884.

Christine de Pisan. *Le livre du corps de policie.* Robert H. Lucas, ed. Geneva and Paris, 1967.

Dossat, Yves, ed. *Saisimentum comitatus Tholosani.* Paris, 1966.

Douais, Célestin, ed. *Mémoire suivi du texte ... de Guilhem Pelisso.* Paris, 1881.

———. *Cartulaire de l'abbaye de Saint-Sernin de Toulouse.* Paris and Toulouse, 1887.

———. *Documents pour servir à l'histoire de l'inquisition dans le Languedoc.* 2 vols. Paris, 1900.

———. *Travaux pratiques d'une conférence de paléographie.* Toulouse, 1900.

Duchesne, Francisque, ed. *Historiae Francorum Scriptores.* Vol. 4. Paris, 1641.

Fournier, Jacques. *See* Benedictus XII
Fournier, Pierre-François and Pascal Guébin, eds. *Enquêtes administratives d'Alphonse de Poitiers. Arrêts de son parlement tenu à Toulouse et textes annexes.* Paris, 1959.
Friedberg, Emil, ed. *Corpus iuris canonici.* 2 vols. Leipzig, 1879-1881.
Galabert, François. *Album de paléographie et de diplomatique.* Toulouse, 1912.
Gallia Christiana in provincias ecclesiasticas distributa in qua series et historia archiepiscoporum, episcoporum et abbatum regionum omnium quas vetus Gallia complectebatur, ab origine ecclesiarum ad nostra tempora deducitur. 16 vols. Paris, 1715-1865. Volume XIII (Provinciae Tolosana et Trevirensis), Jean Thiroux, ed.
Gilles, Henri, ed. *Coutumes de Toulouse (1286) et leur premier commentaire (1296).* Toulouse, 1969.
Giry, Arthur, ed. *Documents sur les relations de la royauté avec les villes de France.* Paris, 1885.
———. *Les etablissements de Rouen.* 2 vols. Paris, 1883-1885.
Gregorius VII, Roman pontiff. *Gregorii VII registri VI.* Philipp Jaffé, ed. *Bibliotheca rerum Germanicarum: Monumenta Gregoriana 2.* Berlin, 1865.
Gui, Bernard. *Bernardus Guidonis de fundatione et prioribus conventuum provinciarum Tolosanae et Provinciae ordinis praedicatorum.* P. A. Amargier, ed. *Monumenta ordinis fratrum praedicatorum historica,* vol. 24. Rome, 1961.
Heisterbach, Caesarius of. *Dialogus miraculorum.* J. Strange, ed. 2 vols. Cologne, 1851.
Hoveden, Roger of. *Chronica.* William Stubbs, ed. *Rerum Britannicarum medii aevi scriptores* 51. 4 vols. London, 1868-1871.
La Faille, Germain. *Annales de la ville de Toulouse depuis la réunion de la comté de Toulouse à la couronne.* 2 vols. Toulouse 1687-1701.
Laurent, Marie-Hyacinthus, ed. *Monumenta historica sancti patris nostri Dominici, fasc. 1: Historia diplomatica S. Dominici. Monumenta Ordinis fratrum praedicatorum historica,* vol. 15, fasc. 1. Paris, 1933.
Layettes du Trésor des Chartes. 5 vols. Paris, 1863-1909.
Léonard, Emile. *Catalogue des actes de Raimond V.* Nîmes, 1932.
Liber instrumentorum memorialium. Cartulaire des Guillems de Montpellier. Alexandre Germain, ed. Montpellier, 1881-1886.
Lifshitz, Felice. "Le serment de fidelité de la ville de Toulouse (1203): Quelques notes sur un texte et sa transmission." *Annales du Midi* 97 (1985) 427-433.
Limouzin-Lamothe, Roger. *La commune de Toulouse et les sources de son histoire 1120-1249.* Paris and Toulouse, 1932.

Llull, Ramon. *Libro de la orden de caballeria* in *Obras literarias*. Miguel Batllori S.I. and Miguel Caldentey T.O.R. Madrid, 1948.
——. *Libro de caballeria* in *Obres essentiels*, vol. 1. Barcelona, 1957.
——. *Livre de l'ordre de chevalerie*. Vincenzo Minervini, ed. Bari, 1972.
Lombard, Peter. *Sententiae in IV libris distinctae*. 2 vols in 3, Rome, 1971-1981.

Mansi, Giovanni Domenico, ed. *Sacrorum conciliorum nova et amplissima collectio* ... . Vol. 23, Paris, 1799.
Martène, Edmond and Ursin Durand. *Thesaurus novus anecdotorum*. Vol. 2. Paris 1717.
Maulde-la-Clavière, René de, ed. *Coutumes et règlements de la république d'Avignon au treizième siècle*. Paris, 1879.
Meijers, Eduard M., ed. *Responsa doctorum Tholosanorum*. Haarlem, 1938.
Molinier, Auguste, ed. *Correspondance administrative d'Alphonse de Poitiers*. 2 vols. Paris, 1894-1900.

Ourliac, Paul and Anne-Marie Magnou, eds. *Cartulaire de l'abbaye de Lézat*. 2 vols. Paris, 1984-1987.

Pales-Gobilliard, Annette, ed. *L'inquisiteur Geoffroy d'Ablis et les Cathares du Comté de Foix (1308-1309)*. Paris, 1984.
Paris, Matthew. *Vita sancti Stephani archiepiscopi Cantuariensis*. Felix Liebermann, ed. In *Ungedruckte Anglo-Normannische Geschichtsquellen*, pp. 323-329. Strasbourg, 1879.
Pelisson, Guillaume. *Chronicon*. The Duvernoy edition (cited below) is used in this book.
——. Molinier, Charles, ed. *De Fratre Guillelmo Pelisso veterrimo inquisitionis historico Thesim* of William Pelisson. Aniché, 1880.
——. Douais, Célestin, ed. *Mémoire suivi du texte ... de la chronique de Guilhem Pelisso et d'un fragment d'un registre de l'Inquisition*. Paris, 1881.
——. Duvernoy, Jean, ed. and transl. *Guillaume Pelhisson Chronique (1229-1244) suivie de récit des troubles d'Albi (1234)*. Paris, 1994.
Peñafort, Raymond of. *Summa de poenitentia et matrimonio cum glossis Joannis de Friburgo*. Rome 1603, reprint 1967.
Percin, Jean Jacob. *Monumenta conventus Tolosani ordinis fratrum praedicatorum primi ex vetustissimis manuscriptis originalibus transcripta et sanctorum ecclesiae patrum placitis illustrata*. Toulouse, 1693.
Peter Cantor (Grand Chanter of Notre-Dame). *Summa de sacramentis et animae consiliis*. J.A. Dugauquier, ed. Louvain and Lille, 1962.
Peter Lombard. *Sententiae in IV libris distinctae*. 2 vols. Rome, 1971-1981.
Puylaurens, William of. *Chronica Magistri Guillelmi de Podio Laurentii*. Jean Duvernoy, ed. Paris, 1976.

Ramière de Fortanier, Jean, ed. *Chartres de franchises de Lauragais*. Paris, 1939.
Registre d'inquisition de Jacques Fournier. See Benedictus XII
Robert de Curzon. "Le traité 'de usura' de Robert de Courçon." G. Lefèvre, ed. *Travaux et mémoires de l'Université de Lille* 10 (1902), No. 30.
Rosell, Francisco Miquel, ed. *Liber feudorum maior. Cartulario real que se conserva en el Archivo de la Corona de Aragón*. 2 vols. Barcelona, 1945.
Rouquette, Jean-Baptiste, ed. *Cartulaire de Béziers (Livre Noir)*. Vol 1 (all published). Paris and Montpellier, 1918.

Tilander, Gunnar, ed. *Los fueros de Aragón. Acta regiae societatis humaniorum litterarum Lundensis* 35. Lund, 1937.

Usatges de Barcelona. See Abadal i Vinyals and Valls Taberner, *and* Bastardas above

Vaux de Cernay, Pierre de. *Historia Albigensis*. Pascal Guébin and Ernest Lyon, eds. 3 vols. Paris, 1926-1939.
Vigeois, Geoffrey de. *Chronicon. Recueil des historiens des Gaules et de la France*. Vol. 12. Paris, 1877.

3. BIBLIOGRAPHY OF SECONDARY WORKS

Arbois de Joubainville, Henry de. *Histoire des ducs et de comtes de Champagne*. 7 vols. Paris, 1859-1866.

Baldwin, John W. *Masters, Princes and Merchants: The Social Views of Peter the Chanter and his Circle*. Princeton, 1970.
Barrière-Flavy, Casimir. *L'Abbaye de Calers (1147-1790)*. Toulouse, 1887.
Barthélemy, Dominique and Stephen D. White. "Debate: The 'Feudal Revolution.'" *Past and Present* 152 (1996) 196-223.
Benjamin, Richard, "A Forty Years War: Toulouse and the Platagenets, 1156-1196." *Historical Research. The Bulletin of the Institute of Historical Research* 61 (1988) 270-285.
Biraben, Jean-Noël. "La population de Toulouse au xive et xve siècles." *Journal des Savants* (1964) 285-300.
Bisson, Thomas N. *Medieval France and her Pyrenean Neighbours — Studies in Early Institutional History*. London, 1989.
———. "The 'Feudal Revolution.'" *Past and Present* 142 (1994) 6-42.
Blanc, Alphonse. *Le livre de comptes de Jacme Olivier, marchand narbonnais du XVe siècle*. II, part 2 (all published). Paris, 1899.
Bois, Guy. *La mutation de l'an mil*. Paris, 1989.
Bonnassie, Pierre. *La Catalogne du milieu du Xe à la fin du XI siècle: Croissance et mutations d'une société*. 2 vols. Toulouse, 1975-1976.
———. *From Slavery to Feudalism in Southwestern Europe*. Chicago, 1991.

Borst, Arno. *Die Katharer*. Stuttgart, 1953.

Boutaric, Edgard. "Organisation judiciaire du Languedoc au moyen-âge." *Bibliothèque de l'Ecole des Chartes* XVI (1855) 200-230 and 532-560, and XVII (1856) 97-122.

Boyer, Georges. *Mélanges I: Mélanges d'histoire du droit occidental*. Paris, 1962.

Bressolles, Gustave and Ad. Jouglar. "Etude sur une charte inédite de 1270 contenant les statuts de la réformation du comté de Toulouse." *Recueil de l'Académie de Législation de Toulouse* IX (1860) 309-380.

Castaing Sicard, Mireille. *Les contrats dans le très ancien droit Toulousain — Xe-XIIIe siècle*. Toulouse, 1959.

Caster, Giles. "Le vignoble suburbaine de Toulouse au XIIeme siècle." *Annales du Midi* 78 (1966) 201-217.

Catel, Guillaume. *Histoire des comtes de Tolose, avec quelques traitez et chroniques anciennes, concernans la mesme histoire*. Toulouse, 1623.

———. *Mémoires de l'histoire du Languedoc, curieusement et fidèlment recueillis de divers autheurs grecs, latins, français et espagnols, et de plusieurs titres et chartes tirés des archivs des villes et communautez de la mesme province et autres circonvoisines*. Toulouse, 1633.

Cau-Durban, Abbé D. *L'abbaye de Mas d'Azil*. Foix, 1896.

Chalande, Jules. *Histoire des Rues de Toulouse — Monuments, Institutions, Habitants*. Toulouse in three separately paginated parts 1919, 1927 and 1929. Reprint Marseille, 1982.

———. Cau, Christian. *Histoire des Rues de Toulouse*. Index and tables. Marseille, 1981.

Christiani, Emilio. "Note sulla legislazione antiusuraria Pisana (secolo XII-XV)." *Bollettino storico pisano* 22 (1953) 3-53.

Contrasty, Jean. *Histoire de Saint Jory, ancienne seigneurie féodale erigée en baronnie par Henri IV*. Toulouse, 1922.

Coulanges, N.-D. Fustel de. *L'alleu et la domaine rural*. Paris, 1889.

Dahm, Georg. *Untersuchungen zur Verfassung und Strafrechtsgeschichte der italienischen Stadt im Mittelalter*. Hamburg, 1941.

Delpech, Henri. *La bataille de Muret et la tactique au XIIIme siècle*. Paris, 1878.

Denholm-Young, Noël "The Merchants of Cahors." *Medievalia et Humanistica* 4 (1946) 37-44.

Devic, Claude and Jean Vaissete. *Histoire générale de Languedoc*. (Private edition) 15 vols. Toulouse, 1872-1893.

Dickson, Marcel and Christiane. "Le cardinal Robert de Courson." *Archives d'histoire doctrinale et litteraire du moyen-âge* 9 (1934) 54-142.

Dilcher, Gerhard. *Entstehung des lombardischen Stadtkommune*. Aalen, 1967.

Dockès, Pierre. *La libération médiévale*. Paris, 1979.

Dossat, Yves. *Les crises de l'Inquisition toulousaine au XIII siècle 1233-1273.* Bordeaux, 1959.

——. "Les vaudois méridionaux d'après les documents de l'Inquisition." *Cahiers de Fanjeaux* 2 (1967) 207-226.

——. "Les Juifs à Toulouse. Un demi-siècle d'histoire communautaire." *Cahiers de Fanjeaux* 12 (1977) 117-139.

——. *Eglise et hérésie en France au XIIIe siècle.* London, 1982.

Duby, Georges. "La diffusion de la titre chevaleresque sur le versant méditerranéen de la Chrétienté latine." In *La noblesse au moyen-âge: XI-XV siècles. Essais à la mémoire de Robert Boutruche,* Philippe Contamine, ed., pp. 45-69. Paris, n.d.

Duffaut, H. "Recherches historiques sur les prénoms en Languedoc." *Annales du Midi* 12 (1900) 180-193 and 329-354.

Du Mège, Alexandre. *Histoire des institutions de la ville de Toulouse.* 4 vols. Toulouse, 1844-1846.

Dupont, André. *Les cités de la Narbonnaise Première depuis l'invasions germaniques jusqu'à l'apparition du consulat.* Nîmes, 1942.

——. "L'Evolution social du Consulat nîmois du milieu du XIIIe au milieu du XIV siècle." *Annales du Midi* 72 (1960) 287-308.

——. "L'Evolution des institutions municipales de Beaucaire du début du XIIIe à fin du XVe siècle." 77 (1965) 257-274.

Durozoy. *See* Rozoi

Ekwall, Eilert. *Early London Personal Names.* Lund, 1947.

Emery, Richard Wilder. *The Jews of Perpignan in the Thirteenth Century.* New York, 1959.

Evans, Austin Patterson. *Essays in Medieval Life and Thought presented in honor of A.P. Evans,* eds. J.H. Mundy, R.W. Emery and B.N. Nelson. New York, 1955, reprint 1965.

Fitting, Hermann. *Das castrense peculium in seiner geschichtlichen Entwicklung und heutige gemeinrechtlichen Geltung.* Halle, 1871.

Fiumi, Enrico. "L'imposta diretta nel comuni medioevali della Toscana." *Studi in onore di Armando Sapori* (2 vols., Milan, 1957) 1: 329-353.

Flach, Jacques. *Les origines de l'ancienne France.* 4 volumes. Paris, 1886-1917.

Fons, Victor. "Conditions des débiteurs à Toulouse, selon deux chartes du XIIe sièvle." *Recueil de l'Académie de Législation de Toulouse* 6 (1857) 156-193.

——. "Chartes inédites relatives au jugement des affaires concernant la succession des Toulousains tués à la bataille de Muret." ibid. 20 (1871) 13-27.

Fossier, Robert. *L'enfance de l'Europe (XIe-XIIe siècles): Aspects économique et sociaux.* Paris, 1982.

Galabert, Firmin. "Le nombre des hommes libres dans le pays de Tarn et Garonne aux XIe et XIIe siècles." *Bulletin archéologique et historique de la société archéologique de Tarn et Garonne* 29 (1901) 29-50.

——. "Le rôle des bons hommes dans le pays du Tarn et Garonne." Ibid. 237-248.

Gaudenzi, Augusto. *Sulla storia del cognome a Bologna nel secolo XIII* in *Bollettino dell'Istituto storico Italiano* 19 (1898) 1-161.

Généstal, Robert. *Le rôle des monastères comme établissements de crédit étudié en Normandie*. Paris, 1901.

Gilles, Henri. "Commentaires méridionaux des prescriptions canoniques sur les Juifs." *Cahiers de Fanjeaux* 12 (1977) 24-50.

Gramain, Monique, "*Castrum*, Structures féodales et peuplement en Biterrois au xie siècle." In *Structures féodales et féodalism dans l'occident méditerranéen*, Pierre Toubert, ed., pp. 119-134.

Grayzel, Solomon. *The Church and the Jews in the Thirteenth Century*. Philadelphia, 1933.

Griffe, Elie. *Les débuts de l'aventure cathare en Languedoc 1140-1190*. Paris, 1969.

Guilhermoz, Paul Emilien. *Essai sur l'origine de la noblesse en France au moyen-âge*. Paris, 1902, recently reprinted.

Head, Thomas and Richard Landes, eds. *The Peace of God: Social Violence and Religious Response in France around the Year 1000*, Ithaca, 1992.

Huberti, Ludwig. *Studien zur Rechtsgeschichte der Gottesfrieden und Landfrieden*. Vol. 1: *Die Friedensordnungen in Frankreich*. Ansbach, 1892.

Jeanroy, Alfred. *La poésie lyrique des troubadours*. 2 vols. Toulouse and Paris, 1934.

Julien, R.C. *Histoire de la paroisse de Nôtre-Dame la Dalbade*. Toulouse, 1891.

Keller, Hagen. *Adelsherrschaft und städtische Gesellschaft in Oberitalien — 9. bis 12. Jahrhundert*. Tübingen, 1979.

Kiener, Fritz. *Verfassungsgeschichte der Provence seit der Ostgothenherrschaft bis zur Errichtung der Konsulate — 510-1200*. Leipzig, 1900.

Kolmer, Lothar. *Ad capiendas vulpes: Die Ketzerbekämpfung in Südfrankreich in der ersten Hälfte des 13. Jahrhunderts und die Ausbildung des Inquisitionsverfahrens*. Bonn, 1982.

La Faille, Germain. *Annales de la ville de Toulouse depuis la réunion de la comté de Toulouse à la couronne*. 2 vols. Toulouse 1687-1701.

Langlois, Charles-Victor. "Les doléances des communautés du Toulousain contra Pierre de Latilli et Raoul de Breuilly (1297-1298)." *Revue historique* 95 (1907) 23-53.

Lejeune, Rita. "L'évêque de Toulouse Folquet de Marseille et la principauté de Liège." *Mélanges Félix Rousseau. Etudes sur l'histoire de pays mosan au moyen-âge.* Brussels, 1968, pp. 433-448.

Lestocquoy, Jean. "Les usuriers du début du moyen-âge." *Studi in onore di Gino Luzzato* (3 vols. Milan, 1949-1950) 1: 67-77.

Limouzin-Lamothe, Roger. *La commune de Toulouse et les sources de son histoire.* Toulouse and Paris, 1932.

——. *Bibliographie critique de l'histoire municipale de Toulouse des origines à 1789.* Toulouse and Paris, 1932.

——. "La chronologie du cartulaire du consulat de Toulouse, 1120-79." *Annales du Midi* 65 (1933) 310-316.

Lldonosa Pujol, José. "Marchands Toulousains à Lérida aux XIIe et XIIIe siècles." *Annales du Midi* 70 (1958) 223-230.

Luc, Pierre. *Vie rurale et pratique juridique en Béarn aux XIVe et XVe siècles.* Toulouse, 1943.

Lynch, Joseph H. *Simoniacal Entry into Religious Life from 1000 to 1260: A Social, Economic and Legal Study.* Columbus, 1976.

Magnou, Elisabeth. *Reforme Grégorienne à Toulouse — fin XIe-début XIIe siécle.* Toulouse, 1958.

Magnou-Noirtier, Elisabeth. *La société laïque et l'église dans la province ecclé-siastique de Narbonne [zone cyspyrénéenne] de la fin du Xe à la fin du XIe siécle.* Toulouse, 1974.

Martin-Chabot, Eugène. "Mésaventures d'un donat." *Mélanges d'histoire du moyen-âge dédiés à la mémoire de Louis Halphen* (Paris, 1951) 501-506.

Mayer, Ernst. *Deutsch und französische Verfassungsgeschichte von 9. bis zum 14. Jahrhundert.* Leipzig, 1899.

McDonnell, Ernst W. *The Beguines and Beghards in Medieval Culture.* New Brunswick, 1954.

McLaughlin, Terence P. "The Teaching of the Canonists on Usury (XII, XIII and XIV Centuries)." *Mediaeval Studies* 1 (1939) 81-147 & 2 (1940) 1-22.

Michaelsson, Karl. *Etudes sur les noms de personne français d'après les rôles de taille parisiens.* Uppsala, 1927.

Michaud-Quantin, Pierre. *Sommes de casuistique et manuels de confession au moyen-âge.* Louvain, 1962.

——. "Textes penitentiels Languedociens au XIIIe siècle." *Cahiers de Fanjeaux* 6 (1971) 151-172.

Michel, Robert. *L'administration royale dans la Sénéchaussée de Beaucaire au temps de Saint Louis.* Paris, 1910.

Molinier, Victor. "Condition des debiteurs à Toulouse selon deux chartes du XIIe siècle." *Recueil de l'Académie de Législation de Toulouse* 6 (1857) 156-193.

Mulholland (Sister Mary Ambrose BVM). *Early Gild Records of Toulouse.* New York, 1941.

———. "Statutes on Clothmaking: Toulouse 1227." In *Essays in Medieval Life and Thought*, pp. 167-180.

Mundy, John Hine. *Liberty and Political Power in Toulouse, 1100-1230.* New York, 1952.

———. "Un usurier malheureux" In *Hommage à M. François Galabert* (Toulouse 1956) 117-125.

———. "Charity and Social Work in Toulouse 1100-1250." *Traditio* 22 (1966) 203-288.

———. "Noblesse et hérésie. Une famille Cathare: Les Maurand." *Annales: ESC* (1974) 1211-1223.

———. "The Origins of the College of Saint-Raymond at the University of Toulouse." In *Philosophy and Humanism*. Edward P. Mahoney, ed., pp. 454-461. Leiden, 1976.

———. "The Farm of Fontanas at Toulouse: Two Families, a Monastery, and a Pope." *Bulletin of Medieval Canon Law* (n.s.) 11 (1981) 29-40.

———. "Village, Town, and City in the Region of Toulouse." In *Pathways to Medieval Peasants*, J.A. Raftis, ed., pp. 142-190. Toronto, 1981.

———. "Urban Society and Culture: Toulouse and Its Region." In *Renaissance and Renewal in the Twelfth Century*. Robert L. Benson and Giles Constable eds. with Carol D. Lanham, pp. 229-247. Cambridge, MA, 1982.

———. *The Repression of Catharism at Toulouse — The Royal Diploma of 1279.* Toronto, 1985.

———. *Men and Women at Toulouse in the Age of the Cathars.* Toronto, 1990.

———. "The Parishes of Toulouse from 1150 to 1250." *Traditio* 46 (1991) 171-204.

———. "Medieval Urban Liberty." In *The Origins of Modern Freedom in the West*, Richard W. Davis, ed., pp. 101-134. Stanford, California, 1995.

Nahon, Gérard. "Les juifs dans les domaines d'Alfonse de Poitiers, 1241-1271." *Revue des études juives* 124 (1966), 157-211.

Nelli, René. *L'érotique des troubadours.* Toulouse, 1963.

Nelson, Benjamin. *The Idea of Usury: From Tribal Brotherhood to Universal Otherhood.* 2nd edition. Chicago, 1969.

Noonan Jr., John T. *The Scholastic Analysis of Usury.* Cambridge, MA, 1957.

Ourliac, Paul. *Etudes d'histoire du droit médiévale.* Paris, n.d.

Ourliac, Paul and Jehan de Malafosse. *Histoire du droit privé.* 3 vols. Paris, 1957-1968.

Paterson, Linda M. *The World of the Troubadours. Medieval Occitan Society, c. 1100—c. 1300.* Cambridge 1993.

Petit-Dutaillis. Charles. "La prétendue commune de Toulouse." *Comptes rendus des séances de l'Académie des Inscriptions et Belles-Lettres de Paris* (1941) 57.

Poly, Jean-Pierre and Eric Bournazel. *La mutation féodale: Xe et XIe siècle.* Paris, 2nd ed. 1991.

Post, Gaines. *Studies in Medieval Legal Thought: Public Law and the State, 1100-1322.* Princeton, 1964.

Puybusque, Guillaume Albert de. *Contribution à l'histoire du vieux Toulouse. Généalogie de la famille de Puybusque.* Toulouse, 1902.

Reichert, Hermann. *Die deutschen Familiennamen, nach Breslauer Quellen des 13. und 14. Jahrhunderts.* Breslau, 1908.

Reynolds, Susan. *Fiefs and Vassals: The Medieval Evidence Reinterpreted.* Oxford, 1994.

Richardot, Hubert. "Le fief roturier à Toulouse." *Revue historique de droit français et étranger* 4th series XIV (1935) 307-358 and 495-569.

Rosenstock-Huessy, Eugen. *Die Europäischen Revolutionen, Volkscharaktere und Staatenbildung.* Jena, 1931.

——. *The Driving Power of Western Civilization: The Christian Revolution of the Middle Ages.* Boston, MA, 1950.

——. *Out of Revolution: Autobiography of Western Man.* Providence and Oxford, 1993.

Rozoi, Barnabé Farmian du. *Annales de la ville de Toulouse.* 4 vols. Paris, 1771-1776.

Saige, Gustave. *Les Juifs du Languedoc antérieurement au XIVe siècle.* Paris, 1881.

——. "Une alliance défensive entre propriétaires allodiaux aux xiie siècle." *Bibliothèque de l'Ecole des Chartes* 2 (1861) 374-440.

Saint-Blanquat, Odon. "Comment se sont crées les bastides du sud-ouest de la France." *Annales: ESC* 3 (1949) 278-289.

——. "Sur l'Etablissment de deux Bastides aux portes de Toulouse, en 1303." *Receuil de l'Académie de Législation de Toulouse* n.s. 1 (1951) 164-172.

Schaub, Franz. *Der Kampf gegen den Zinswucher, ungerechten Preis und unlautern Handel im Mittelalter von Karl des Grossen bis Papst Alexander III.* Freiburg in Breisgau, 1905.

Shatzmiller, Joseph. *Shylock Reconsidered: Jews, Moneylending, and Medieval Society.* Berkeley and Los Angeles, 1990.

Sicard, Germain. *Aux origines des sociétés anonymes: Les moulins de Toulouse au moyen-âge.* Paris, 1953.

Stronski, Stanislaw. *Le troubadour Folquet de Marseille.* Cracow, 1910.

Thouzellier, Christine. "Polémiques autour de la notion de pauvreté spirituelle." In *Etudes sur l'histoire de la pauvreté*, Michel Mollat, ed., 1: 371-387.

Toubert, Pierre. *Les structures du Latium médiéval: Le Latium meridional et la Sabine du IXe siècle à la fin di XIIe siècle.* Rome, 1974.

———, ed. *Structures féodales et féodalism dans l'occident méditerranéen (Xe-XIIIe siècles).* Rome, 1980.

Vicaire, Marie-Humbert, OP. *Dominique et ses prêcheurs.* Paris-Fribourg, 1977.

Vitry, M.U. "Recherches sur l'ancienne mesure Toulousaine appelée brassa." *Mémoires de l'Académie royale des sciences, inscriptions et belles-lettres de Toulouse*, 3 sér., III (1847) 336-345.

Wakefield, Walter. *Heresy, Crusade and Inquisition in Southern France 1200-1230.* London, 1974.

Weber, Hildburg. *Die Personennamen in Rodez um die Mitte des 14. Jahrhunderts.* Jena and Leipzig, 1934.

Werveke, Hans van. *"Burgus:" Versteking of Nederzetting?* Brussels, 1965.

White, Stephen D. *See above under* Barthélemy, Dominique

Wolff, Philippe. *Commerce et marchands de Toulouse vers 1350–vers 1450.* Paris, 1954.

———. *Les "estimes" Toulousaines des XIVe et XVe siècles.* Paris and Toulouse, 1956.

——— et al. *Nouvelle Histoire de Toulouse.* Toulouse, 1974.

———. *Regards sur le Midi médiéval.* Toulouse, 1978.

———. "La noblesse Toulousaine: Essai sur son histoire médiévale." In *La noblesse au moyen-âge: XIV siècles. Essais à la mémoire de Robert Boutruche*, Philippe Contamine, ed., pp. 153-174. Paris, n.d.

Index

Listed here are the names of medieval and modern persons, texts, terms, institutions, rivers and place names. In the latter are coded identifications, namely 1) directions and a rough kilometer count, if near Toulouse, eg. "Aussonne 13 km NW of T," 2) by province if elsewhere, eg. "Arles in Provence," and 3) an order name if a monastery was located in the place. Italicized page numbers indicate that the person cited on that particular page is one of those listed in Appendix Three who swore to maintain the Peace of Meaux-Paris in 1243.

Abbate de Rivis, *see* Amigo de Rivis
Abraham "judeus" 59; of Carcassonne 366
Abrinus 391
"acaptum" 216
Acromonte (Acrimonte): Arnold de *374*; Azemar de 414; Bernard de 415; Walter de *373*, 399, 403
"actor sequitur forum rei" 52
Acts of the Apostles 206, 209, 287
Adalbertus 387, 396, 398, 401-402; Bernard 387-388; Raymond 397
Adam, Arnold *378*; William *380*
Ade, Gerald de *370*
Ademarius (Adhemarius): Arnold 401; Durand 416; Raymond 416; William 397
"adoratio" 83
Afiaco, Peter de *375*
Agen 95 km NW of T 91, 95, 239
Agenno (Ageno): Peter de *371*; Vital de *373*, 407
Agromonte, *see* Acromonte
Agulerii, Bernard *379*
Agulerius (Agulherius): Bartholomew *376*; John *380*; Raymond *377*
Aiguesmortes in maritime Languedoc 262

Aimeric "qui stabat in carraria de scola Iudeorum" 449
Aimericus, Arnold 11; Bernard 236, 321, 361, 411-412; Peter 404; William Pons *377*
Aiscius – family 130; Arnold 396, 398; William 397
Aissada, Cerninus *382*
Alacer "judeus" and his sons 58, 282-283, 360-362
Aladaicia, daughter of Pons de Venerca 447
Alais in maritime Languedoc 233
Alaman, Sicard 244-248, 263, 266-267, 288
Albata, Bernard Hugh de 415
Albegesio, Bernard de *375*
"albergum" 42, 150, 337, 339, 451, 460
Albi 69 km E of T 248
Albiaco, Peter de *370*
Albigensian Crusade 2, 9-10, 67, 87, 90, 102, 105, 119, 121, 186, 204, 218, 226, 234-235, 237-238, 244, 250, 262, 267, 269, 272-273, 279
Albigeois, the region of Albi 6 (Map1)
Albigesio, Peter de *380*
Alcotonarii, Peter 387

Clavelerius, Pons Stephen *377*;
    Raymond *378*
Clavellus, Arnold 415
Clement IV, Roman pontiff 245,
    269, 319
Clericus, Peter *383*
"cliens" 92
closes, *see* Daurade, Saint-Étienne,
    Saint-Pierre-des-Cuisines and
    Saint-Sernin
Coceanis, *see* Cossano
Codonherius, Raymond *383*
Colerius, Stephen *381*
"collega" 192
College of Saint-Bernard 151
"collocare" 149 (note 25), 459
Colomiers 10 km W of T 32, 442,
    473
Colommio, *see* Columbariis
Coltellarius, William 439
Columbariis, Peter Bernard de 397,
    399, 403
"columbarium" 117
Columbus, Arnold 415-416
Commentary on *Custom* of Tou-
    louse, see *Custom* of Toulouse
Comminges, county 6(Map1), 33,
    90, 95, 119, 234; Comminges
    Bridge 11-12, 16
commonalty, *see* "cuminaltatz"
"communitas" and "communitas
    popullarium" 263
Companha, Willelma, daughter of
    Aymengarda 162
"companhia" 92
"computus" 437, 438, 447, 469
Comtorius, Hugh 387
"comunarius" or "comunalerius"
    63, 261
"concio" 266
Condom in Lomagne 119
Condors, wife of William Vital
    Parator 170

"conductio" 149, 299
confraternity, *see* Black Confra-
    ternity and White Confraternity;
    Confraternity of Saint-Sernin 169
"conquerens" 183, 199, 437, 456,
    457, 464, 465, 466
"consiliator" 436, 475
Constantinus 396; Peter 396, 401,
    403; Stephen 413
"constitutio" 224
"consul" 61, 235; "consules cabale-
    riorum" 51-52
"contado" 49, 253
"contradictores" 267
"conveniencia" 472
"convivium" 445, 445, 447
Copha, *see* Castronovo, Aimeric de
Corderius, Vital *373*
Corna, Raymond *382*
Cornebarrieu 9 km NW of T 125,
    173, 347(Map5), 352, 434, 448,
    460
Cornelhano, Philip de 410
Corregerius – Bourghal family 417
Cortesius, William *376*
Cosinerius, Raymond *377*
Cossa, *see* Cossano
Cossaco, Jauffredus de *371*
Cossano (Cossas) – Bourghal fami-
    ly 418; Bernard de *382*; Bernard
    Peter de, 389-391, 394, 398,
    400, 473; Peter de *382*, 410;
    Raymond de *382*; Raymond
    Aimeric de 397
Costantius, Stephen *377*
Coumbel 28 km S of T 446
Council, II Lateran 1139 180; IV
    Lateran 60, 209, 363; Council of
    Toulouse 1229 192, 276; Coun-
    cil of Vienne 1311-1312 180,
    202, 204
Crassus, Raymond 395
"credens" 4, 287

Fusterius, Bernard Raymond 15-16, *372*
Fuxo, Raymond de 305; William de *376*

Ga, William de 412
"gadanare," *see* "gazanare"
"gadannum" 469
Gaianis, Peter de *382*
Gaillac on Tarn, *see* Montagut
Gaillaco, *see* Galhaco
Gaillaguet 20 km E of T 422(Map6)
Gairaldus, *see* Geraldus
Gaitapodium, Bernard 260, 409-410; Bernard William 402; Philip *373*, 406; Raymond 389; William John *372*, 403
Galda "judea" 150, 366
Galembrunus, *see* Turribus family
Galhaco, Arnold de *379*, 416; Bernard de *380*; Bernard Pons de 411; John de *370*; Peter de 459, 473-474; Pons de *370*; William de 415
Gali, Bruno 386
Galinus, Raymond 389, 391-393
Gallaco, William 397
Gallia Christiana 319
Gallinus, *see* Galinus
Galterius, Arnold *372*, 397, 399; Raymond 222; Stephen 261, 413, 415; Vital 25, 126, *381*, 457; family, *see* Carbonallus and Prignaco
Galvannus, Bernard *371*
Gamardus, Peter 412
Gamevilla – City family 151, 255, 417; Bastard de 355; Oldric de 400, 419; Pons de 115, *374*, 389-391; William de *369*, 354-366, 392, 410
Gamiscius, Raymond 396, 401, 403, 418-419

Gano, Peter de 404; William de 410, 416
Ganterius, Ademar 453; Bernard 446; Isarn *375*; Raymond 166; Raymond Peter *372*
Garac 30 km NW of T, W of Le Castéra 462
Garaud, Bernard *384*; Raymond *376*; Vital *377*
Garaudus, William *373*
Garcias de Aurievalle, William 98
Garcias de Borgueto Novo, Peter 275
Garcionus or de Garsioni, Raymond 408
Garda, Bernard de 113; William *371*
"gardiage" of Toulouse 6(Map1), 71, 93, 103, 226
"gardianus" 466
Gardogio, William de 390, 393
Gardouch 16 km SW of T 118, 342, 446
Garigiis, Bertrand de 416
Garinus, Bernard *370*, 457; Bertrand 401; Hyspanus or Ispanus *369*, 406; Raymond *370*, 403
Garnerius, Bernard 298; Bernard Raymond 131, 430
Garonne river 6
Garrhac, *see* Garac
Garrigia, Peter Raymond de 416; William Raymond de *381*
Garrigiis, Bertrand de *378*, 406, 410-411, 414, 416; Bruno de 403; John de 403; Pons 139, 386; Raymond de *377*, 410
Garsenda, wife of Peter de Yspania 85, 357-358
Garsia, Peter *381*, 420; *see also* Faber, Garsia
Garsias, Peter 408; Raymond 390
Garsio, Bernard den 161, *376*

Gregory IX, Roman pontiff 11,
191, 201, 239
Grillus – family 132; Bernard 469;
Isarn, *381*, 402, 419; Peter
Raymond 470; Pons 470
Grima, John *372*
Grisolles 27 km N of T 309(Map3)
Grosso, John de 414
Guano, *see* Gano
Guarinus, *see* Garinus
Guarnerius 62, 283
Guelph party 237
Guenho or Guinho, William *373*
Gui, Bernard, Dominican 146-147,
207, 344-345; Peter 387
Guido – Bourghal family 160, 417;
Arnold *374*, 396, 400, 403, 408,
410, 413, 418-419, 456; Bernard
378; Peter 387; Raymond *372*,
395, 404, 406, 409
Guifredus, Raymond 401
Guilabertus – family 173; Arnold
386, 393-394, 399, 463, 472;
Bernard *372*; Bertrand 173; Peter
379, 415; Raymond 390, 394,
397, 469; Vital 408-409
Guilalmonus Dalart 242
Guilelmi, Raymond 387
Guillelma, daughter of Peter de
Tolosa 217, 423; widow of
William Bosquerius 460; wife of
Raymond Guillelmus 140
Guillelmus, Peter 386; Pons 389;
Raymond 140; Vital 410
Guillem Figuera 11, 113, 206, 275
Guiscardus, John *379*
Guitardus, Peter 389-390, 409-410;
Pons 396, 398-399; Raymond
397
Guod, Peter Raymond *370*
Guotus, Bertrand *370*
Guotvesio, Arnold de 406
Guy, Dominican 113, 192

Heliazar, *see* Eliazar
"hereditas" 470
"heremita" 455
"hereticus" and "heretica" 4, 78
Hermann, Rachel xiii
Hispan-, *see* Yspan-
Hodo, *see* Oddo
homage 43, 69, 75, 86, 339
"hominium," *see* homage
"homo" 82; "homo [or] femina de
corpore" 68-69; "homo [or]
femina de corpore sine casalagio" 69; "homo feodalis, nobilis
sive ignobilis" 102, 110; "homo
proprius [or] femina propria [et]
ligius [or] ligia" 69
"honor" 40-43, 46, 69, 149-150;
"h. casalis" 145; "h. liber" 72
Hospital, Novellus 14; H. of La
Grave 14; H. of Saint-Jacques
271, 285; H. of Saint-Raymond
358, 421, 459; H. of Saint John
of Jerusalem 8, 7, 116, 186,
207, 216, 270, 358, 363, 438,
459, 462, 465; hospitals 270-271
Hospitali, Dominic de *376*
"hospitium" 150, 152
Hostiensis, Henry of Susa, cardinal
182 (note 9), 210
Hoveden (Howden): Roger of 56,
89, 343
Huesca in Aragon 108
Huguenots 206
Humiliati, religious order 213
Hungary 93
Hyspania, Philip de *383*; *see also*
Yspania
Hyspanollus, *see* Ispaniolus

Ibrinus, Peter 392
Ile-de-Tounis, *see* Tounis
Innocent III, Roman pontiff 60,
182, 184, 203, 276-277; IV,
Roman pontiff 239, 306

380, *381*, *383*, 411-413, 415, 445; William Peter *377-378*; William Vital 415-416
Vasco de Coquinis, Pons 413
Vassaros, Pons Hugh de 424
"vasvassor," *see* "vavassor"
Vauro, Juliana de 452; William de *379*; William John de *371*
Vauro de Sancto Stephano, Arnold de *371*, 410, 414
Vaux-de-Cernay, Peter de 204-206
"vavassor," "valvassor," and "vasvasssor" 32-33, 46, 150
"venator" 92
Vendinis (Vendemiis): Bartholomew de *370*; Bernard de *370*; Gerald de 404; Peter de 404, 419; Raymond de *370*; William de *370*, 396, 408, 413
Venerca, Pons de 171
Venerque 17 km S of T 103, 251, 320
Venice, Italy 204, 242
Verdun-sur-Garonne 33 km N of T 6(Map1), 58, 251, 320, 366
Verfeil 17 km E of Toulouse 6 (Map1) 52, 73, 90, 118, 217-218, 305, 307, 347(Map5), 350, 352-353, 356, 422(Map6)
Verneto, William de *374*
Vernol, Dominic de *379*
Vesceriis, Gerald de *375*
Vestitus, Raymond *382*
Veterivilla, Raymond Johannes de 412
vicar ("vicarius") and vicarage of Toulouse xii, 6(Map1), 7, 15, 51, 55-58, 61, 71, 86, 92-93, 99, 114, 118, 132, 138, 140, 223-228, 237, 239-243, 245-248, 249, 253-254, 257-261, 267, 281-282
Vicarius, Bernard *380*; John *380*

Vicecomes, Bernard *370*, 411
Vidal Mayor of Canyellas 108
Vidiatus, Nicholas *381*
Vieille-Toulouse 7 km S of Toulouse 347(Map5)
Vieillevigne 27 km SE of T 446
Vilana, Peter de *379*
Vilaudran, Bernard de *377*
"villa" 20-21, 38, 43, 48, 82, 446
Villa, Stephen de *372*
Villafranca (Villafrancha): Pons de 135, *377*, 51, 399, 408, 411-412, 414
Villalonga, Hugh de *380*; Pons de *379*, *380*
Villamuro, Bernard de *381*
Villanova – City family 56, 97, 117, 129, 151, 156, 171, 247, 417; Adalbert de 387; Arnold de *371*, 389, 391, 393-394, 400, 419; Bernard de *381*, 366, *369*, 407; Bertrand de *374*, 305, 392-393, 406-407; Fort de, *see* Devezia, Fort de; Isarn de 408; Jordan de 116, *374*, 391, 393-394, 399, 408, 411, 427, 470; Peter Bertrand de 391; Pons de 56, 101, 245, 247, *370*, 206, 338, 341, 386-388, 390, 394, 427, 470; Raymond Arnold de 97, *371*, 203, 366, 388, 394, 410; Raymond de, also de Rabastenquis 174, *371*; Salamandra de 139; Stephen 470
Villanova leprosery 85
"villanus" 38, 82
Villata, Raymond de 441
Villemur-sur-Tarn 30 km NE of T 6(Map1)
Villeneuve-la-Comtale 52 km SE of T 137, 140, 247
Villeneuve Gate 8, 21
Vinacius, *see* Mancius